W9-APK-087

THE LOEB CLASSICAL LIBRARY

FOUNDED BY JAMES LOEB, LL.D.

EDITED BY

G. P. GOOLD, PH.D.

FORMER EDITORS

†T. E. PAGE, C.H., LITT.D.   †E. CAPPS, PH.D., LL.D.
†W. H. D. ROUSE, LITT.D.   †L. A. POST, L.H.D.
E. H. WARMINGTON, M.A., F.R.HIST.SOC.

VIRGIL

IN TWO VOLUMES

I
ECLOGUES
GEORGICS
AENEID I–VI

American ISBN 0–674–99070–6

British ISBN 0 434 99063 9

First Printed 1916
Reprinted 1920, 1922, 1925, 1926, 1927, 1929
1930 (3 times), 1932
New and revised edition 1935
Reprinted 1938, 1940, 1942, 1946, 1950
1953, 1956, 1960, 1965, 1967, 1974, 1978, 1986

Printed in Great Britain
by Richard Clay Ltd, Bungay, Suffolk

VIRGIL AND THE MUSES OF HISTORY AND TRAGEDY

From a mosaic (*c.* A.D. 100) found at Hadrumetum in Africa, now in the Bardo Museum.

The poet holds in his left hand a half open roll on which may be read the letters:—

MUSAMIHICAV
SASMEMORA
QUONUMINE
LAESOQUIDVE
(Aen. l. 8.)

Reproduced from Mr. G. F. Hills' *Illustrations to School Classics*, Macmillan and Co., by kind permission of the author and publisher.

VIRGIL

WITH AN ENGLISH TRANSLATION BY
H. RUSHTON FAIRCLOUGH

PROFESSOR OF CLASSICAL LITERATURE IN
STANFORD UNIVERSITY, CALIFORNIA

IN TWO VOLUMES

I
ECLOGUES
GEORGICS
AENEID I–VI

REVISED EDITION

CAMBRIDGE, MASSACHUSETTS
HARVARD UNIVERSITY PRESS
LONDON
WILLIAM HEINEMANN LTD
MCMLXXXVI

CONTENTS

BIBLIOGRAPHICAL NOTE

VARIOUS editions and translations, in whole or in part, bear witness to the continued esteem in which Virgil is held by the modern world, not least in Britain where the Virgil Society has made significant contributions to knowledge and appreciation of his poetry and spirit. We select the following editions for special mention.

R. A. B. Mynors, Oxford Text. 1969

R. Sabbadini, Rome. 1930

H. Goelzer, *Bucolics* (*Eclogues*). Budé, Paris. 1925

H. Goelzer, *Georgics*. Budé, Paris. 1926

H. Goelzer (ed.) and A. Bellesort (French translation), *Aeneid* books 1–6. Budé, Paris. 1925

R. Durand (ed.) and A. Bellesort (trans.), *Aeneid* books 7–12, 6th edition, Budé, Paris. 1957

R. D. Williams, edition of *Aeneid* books 1–6. Basingstoke and London. 1972

H. H. Huxley, edition of *Georgics* books 1 and 4. London. 1963

E. V. Clausen, F. R. D. Goodyear, E. J. Kenney, J. A. Richmond, *Appendix Vergiliana*. Oxford Text. 1966

LIFE OF VIRGIL

Publius Vergilius Maro was born October 15, 70 b.c., at Andes, a district near Mantua. He was "of rustic parentage, and brought up in the bush and forest,"[1] but his father gave him a careful education, first at Cremona, then at Milan, and lastly at Rome. In the capital he studied especially under Epidius the rhetorician, and Siro, a distinguished Epicurean.

To his student-days belong the short poems known as *Catalepton* (κατὰ λεπτόν, *i.e.* "small"), some of which are probably genuine. To the same period would belong the rest of the minor poems—the *Culex, Ciris, Copa, Dirae,* and *Moretum*—though it is very doubtful whether any of these are authentic.

Virgil's second period begins with 43 b.c., when, after Caesar's assassination, we find the poet again in Mantua. In that year the second triumvirate was formed, and in the year following Brutus and Cassius were defeated at Philippi. In the subsequent allotment of lands to the victorious veterans Cremona and Mantua suffered severely. The poet was dispossessed of his farm and, attempting resistance, barely escaped with his life. However, he found a friend in C. Asinius Pollio, governor of

---

[1] Macrobius, *Saturnalia*, V. ii. 1.

LIFE OF VIRGIL

Cisalpine Gaul, and in Pollio's successor (41 B.C.),
L. Alfenus Varus. Through Pollio he was intro-
duced to Octavius, and either recovered his farm or
received in compensation an estate in Campania.

The poems in which Virgil records his experience
at this time are the ten *Eclogues,* or *Bucolics,* which
were published in their present order in 37 B.C.
The two that are mainly concerned with the poet's
expulsion from his farm are the first and ninth, but
at least three, viz. the second, third, and fifth (with
probably the seventh as well), preceded the first in
point of time and, like it, were written in the poet's
native district. The sixth and ninth were composed
at Siro's villa; the remainder, viz. the fourth,
eighth, and tenth, were written in Rome. The
first doubtless won its place in the series because of
the tribute it pays to Octavius, who before 37 B.C.
had become sole ruler in Italy.

Seven years were devoted to the *Georgics,* the four
books of which were published in 29 B.C., two years
after the battle of Actium. The work was under-
taken at the request of Maecenas, to whom it is
dedicated. Though a didactic poem, being a treatise
on agriculture, the *Georgics* are perhaps the most
carefully finished production of Roman literature.

The rest of Virgil's life was devoted to the *Aeneid,*
the greatest of Roman epics. Before it was ready
for publication Virgil set out in 19 B.C. for Greece
and Asia, where he intended to spend the next
three years in revising his work. At Athens, how-
ever, meeting Augustus on his homeward journey
from the East, he was induced to return with the
Emperor to Italy. A fever, contracted at Megara,
grew worse during the voyage, and ended in his
death at Brundisium, a few days after landing, in the

x

LIFE OF VIRGIL

fifty-first year of his age, September 22, 19 B.C. He was buried at Naples, and on his tomb was inscribed the epitaph:

MANTUA ME GENUIT, CALABRI RAPUERE, TENET NUNC
PARTHENOPE ; CECINI PASCUA, RURA, DUCES.

Conscious of many imperfections in the *Aeneid*, Virgil had begged Varius (who along with Tucca was Virgil's literary executor), in the event of his death, to burn the epic. It was published, however, by order of Augustus, who directed the executors to edit it, removing all superfluities, but making no additions. Examples of passages removed are furnished by the prooemium of four lines at the beginning of the *Aeneid*, and by the Helen episode in the second book (ll. 567–588). In both cases Virgil's dissatisfaction with the passages may have been known to his literary friends.

MANUSCRIPTS

THE text of Virgil has been remarkably well preserved. In the large number of Virgilian manuscripts there are as many as eight that can safely be assigned to an age as early as the fourth or fifth century. These are the following, all written in capital letters, square or rustic:

A. *Fragmentum Augusteum,* or *Schedae Berolinenses,* partly in Rome and partly in Berlin; containing portions of *Georg.* I and III, with *Aen.* IV, 302-305.

B. *Codex Mediolanensis,* in the Ambrosian Library at Milan. A palimpsest, comprising four passages from *Aen.* I (81 verses in all), accompanied by a Greek rendering.

F. *Schedae Vaticanae,* in Rome; containing portions of *Georg.* III, IV, and *Aen.* I–XI, and preserving some interesting miniatures.

G. *Schedae Sangallenses,* at St. Gall, Switzerland. Eleven leaves of a palimpsest, including portions of *Georg.* IV and *Aen.* I, III, IV, VI.

M. *Codex Mediceus,* in the Laurentian Library at Florence. Written before A.D. 494. Contains *Ecl.* from VI, 48, *Georg.* and *Aen.*

MANUSCRIPTS

P. *Codex Palatinus,* in the Vatican Library, Rome, but up to 1622 in the Palatine Library at Heidelberg. Out of 280 leaves, 32 here and there are wanting.

R. *Codex Romanus,* in the Vatican Library. Out of 309 leaves, 77 here and there are lost. Illustrated.

V. *Schedae Veronenses,* a palimpsest at Verona. The 51 leaves include fragments from *Ecl., Georg.,* and *Aen.*

Of the many cursive manuscripts, the most important are the *Codex Gudianus* (γ) of the ninth century, and three *codices Bernenses* (a, b, c) of the same century.

For a full account of the MSS., see Henry, *Aeneidea,* vol. i; Ribbeck, *Prolegomena ad Vergilium,* vol. iv; and Sabbadini's edition, vol. i, pp. 19–29.[1]

[1] How far the capital MSS. are available is indicated at the side of the text by the several capital letters employed. The cursive MSS. are referred to only in the registry of variant readings at the foot of the page. When a MS. reading has been corrected by a later hand, the original and the correction are indicated respectively by the Arabic numerals [1] and [2]. Still later corrections are noted simply as *late.* For further details see Appendix.

Inasmuch as in the *apparatus criticus* numerous references must be made to Ribbeck and Sabbadini, the abbreviations *Rib.* and *Sabb.* are commonly employed.

EDITIONS AND COMMENTARIES

THE *editio princeps* appeared in Rome (probably 1469).
Of subsequent editions the most important are those
of Heinsius (1664–88), Heyne (1767–75, 4th ed. by
Wagner, 1830–41), Ribbeck (1859–68), Forbiger
(1872–75), Benoist (1876), Thilo (1886), Hirtzel
(Clarendon Press, 1900), Walter Janell (Leipzig,
1920), Henri Goelzer (Paris, 1925), R. Sabbadini
(Rome, 1930). Complete annotated editions in
English are by Kennedy (1879), Papillon (1882),
Sidgwick (1890), Conington (completed and revised
by Nettleship, 1st vol. re-edited by Haverfield,
1898), and Page (1900–2). Partial editions in
various languages are very numerous, the most
conspicuous of recent years being E. Norden's *Aeneid*,
Book VI, with German commentary and translation
(1903),[1] H. E. Butler's *Aeneid*, Book VI (Oxford, 1920),
and J. W. Mackail's complete *Aeneid* (Oxford, 1930).

The ancient commentary of Servius (fourth cen-
tury) was printed as early as 1471, and is given in
several editions of Virgil.[2] It is edited separately by

[1] Certain disputed passages are discussed by the translator
in the Fairclough-Brown edition of the *Aeneid*, Books I–VI
(Sanborn and Co., Boston : latest reprint 1930), and in the
*Transactions and Proceedings of the American Philological
Association* for 1907, vol. 38, pp. xxxvi ff.

[2] Additions to the original text are known as Daniel-
Servius or D. Servius. Besides Servius, occasional references
are made in the notes to the grammarians, Nonius, Charisius,
Donatus, and Philargyrius.

EDITIONS AND COMMENTARIES

Lion (1826) and by Thilo and Hagen (1878 *sqq.*).
The Berne *Scholia* are edited by Hagen (1867). An
account of all the ancient Virgilian commentators is
given by Ribbeck in his *Prolegomena*, and by Coning-
ton, vol. i. The latest Index to Virgil's works is
Wetmore's *Index Verborum Vergilianus* (1911).

Henry's *Aeneidea* (1873–92) is a valuable work on
the interpretation of the *Aeneid*; so is Heinze's
Virgils Epische Technik (1903). Glover's *Studies in
Virgil* (1904)[1] illuminates all of the poet's work.
Other important books on Virgil are Sainte-Beuve's
Étude sur Virgile (1859); Comparetti's *Vergil in the
Middle Ages* (translated by Benecke, 1895); Nettle-
ship's *Virgil* (1879); and Boissier's *Nouvelles Pro-
menades Archéologiques* (1886), translated as *The
Country of Horace and Virgil*, by Fisher (1895).

Noteworthy essays on Virgil are in Green's *Stray
Studies* (1876); Sellar's *Roman Poets of the Augustan
Age: Virgil* (2nd ed. 1883); F. W. H. Myers,
Classical Essays (1883); Patin, *Essais sur la Poésie
latine* (4th ed. 1900); Tyrrell, *Latin Poetry* (1898);
Mackail, *Latin Literature* (3rd ed. 1899); Woodberry's
Great Writers (New York, 1907). See also Appendix,
pp. 573 ff.

[1] Fifth edition, 1923.

ECLOGUES

ECLOGAE

I

MELIBOEUS

Tityre, tu patulae recubans sub tegmine fagi   PR
silvestrem tenui musam meditaris avena:
nos patriae finis et dulcia linquimus arva;
nos patriam fugimus: tu, Tityre, lentus in umbra
formosam resonare doces Amaryllida silvas.   5

TITYRUS

O Meliboee, deus nobis haec otia fecit.
namque erit ille mihi semper deus, illius aram
saepe tener nostris ab ovilibus imbuet agnus.
ille meas errare boves, ut cernis, et ipsum
ludere quae vellem calamo permisit agresti.   10

MELIBOEUS

Non equidem invideo; miror magis: undique totis
usque adeo turbatur agris.   en, ipse capellas
protinus aeger ago; hanc etiam vix, Tityre, duco.
hic inter densas corylos modo namque gemellos,
spem gregis, a! silice in nuda conixa reliquit.   15

---

¹² turbamur *PRγ* : turbatur *read by Quintilian*, I. ɪᴠ 28,
and preferred by Servius.

2

ECLOGUES

I

MELIBOEUS

You, Tityrus, lie under your spreading beech's covert, wooing the woodland Muse on slender reed, but we are leaving our country's bounds and sweet fields. We are outcasts from our country; you, Tityrus, at ease beneath the shade, teach the woods to re-echo "fair Amaryllis."

TITYRUS

O Meliboeus, it is a god who wrought for us this peace—for a god he shall ever be to me; often shall a tender lamb from our folds stain his altar. Of his grace my kine roam, as you see, and I, their master, play what I will on my rustic pipe.[1]

MELIBOEUS

Well, I grudge you not—rather I marvel; such unrest is there on all sides in the land. See, heart-sick, I myself am driving my goats along, and here, Tityrus, is one I scarce can lead. For here just now amid the thick hazels, after hard travail, she dropped twins, the hope of the flock, alas! on the naked flint.

---

[1] In this allegory Tityrus may represent Virgil, who went to Rome and appealed successfully to Octavian (afterwards Augustus) against the confiscation of his farm. But see Appendix, p. 575.

3

VIRGIL

saepe malum hoc nobis, si mens non laeva fuisset,
de caelo tactas memini praedicere quercus.
sed tamen, iste deus qui sit, da, Tityre, nobis.

TITYRUS

Urbem, quam dicunt Romam, Meliboee, putavi
stultus ego huic nostrae similem, quo saepe solemus
pastores ovium teneros depellere fetus.   21
sic canibus catulos similis, sic matribus haedos
noram, sic parvis componere magna solebam.
verum haec tantum alias inter caput extulit urbes,
quantum lenta solent inter viburna cupressi.   25

MELIBOEUS

Et quae tanta fuit Romam tibi causa videndi?

TITYRUS

Libertas, quae sera tamen respexit inertem,
candidior postquam tondenti barba cadebat,
respexit tamen et longo post tempore venit,
postquam nos Amaryllis habet, Galatea reliquit.   30
namque, fatebor enim, dum me Galatea tenebat,
nec spes libertatis erat, nec cura peculi.
quamvis multa meis exiret victima saeptis,
pinguis et ingratae premeretur caseus urbi,
non umquam gravis aere domum mihi dextra redibat

MELIBOEUS

Mirabar, quid maesta deos, Amarylli, vocares,   36
cui pendere sua patereris in arbore poma:
Tityrus hinc aberat.   ipsae te, Tityre, pinus,
ipsi te fontes, ipsa haec arbusta vocabant.

[37] *R originally had* mala *for* poma.

4   [1] pinus] nobis *P¹*.

ECLOGUE I

Often, I mind, this mishap was foretold me, had not my wits been dull, by the oaks struck from heaven. But still tell me, Tityrus, who is this god of yours?

TITYRUS

The city which they call Rome, Meliboeus, I, foolish one! thought was like this of ours, whither we shepherds are wont to drive the tender younglings of our flocks. Thus I knew puppies were like dogs, and kids like their dams; thus I used to compare great things with small. But this one has reared her head as high among all other cities as cypresses oft do among the bending osiers.

MELIBOEUS

And what was the great occasion of your seeing Rome?

TITYRUS

Freedom, who, though late, yet cast her eyes upon me in my sloth, when my beard began to whiten as it fell beneath the scissors. Yet she did cast her eyes on me, and came after a long time—after Amaryllis began her sway and Galatea left me. For—yes, I must confess—while Galatea ruled me, I had neither hope of freedom nor thought of savings. Though many a victim left my stalls, and many a rich cheese was pressed for the thankless town, never would my hand come home money-laden.

MELIBOEUS

I used to wonder, Amaryllis, why so sadly you called on the gods, and for whom you let the apples hang on their native trees. Tityrus was gone from home. The very pines, Tityrus, the very springs, the very orchards here were calling for you!

VIRGIL

Quid facerem? neque servitio me exire licebat   40
nec tam praesentis alibi cognoscere divos.
hic illum vidi iuvenem, Meliboee, quotannis
bis senos cui nostra dies altaria fumant.
hic mihi responsum primus dedit ille petenti:
" pascite, ut ante, boves, pueri ; submittite tauros."

MELIBOEUS

Fortunate senex, ergo tua rura manebunt.   46
et tibi magna satis, quamvis lapis omnia nudus
limosoque palus obducat pascua iunco.
non insueta gravis temptabunt pabula fetas,
nec mala vicini pecoris contagia laedent.   50
fortunate senex, hic inter flumina nota
et fontis sacros frigus captabis opacum.
hinc tibi, quae semper, vicino ab limite saepes
Hyblaeis apibus florem depasta salicti
saepe levi somnum suadebit inire susurro ;   55
hinc alta sub rupe canet frondator ad auras :
nec tamen interea raucae, tua cura, palumbes,
nec gemere aëria cessabit turtur ab ulmo.

TITYRUS

Ante leves ergo pascentur in aethere cervi,
et freta destituent nudos in litore piscis,   60
ante pererratis amborum finibus exsul
aut Ararim Parthus bibet aut Germania Tigrim,
quam nostro illius labatur pectore voltus.

---

[59] pascuntur *P.*
[63] labatur *P*[1] : labantur *P*[2].

6

ECLOGUE I

TITYRUS

What was I to do? I could not quit my slavery nor elsewhere find gods so ready to aid. Here, Meliboeus, I saw that youth for whom our altars smoke twice six days a year. Here he was the first to give my plea an answer: "Feed, swains, your oxen as of old; rear your bulls."

MELIBOEUS

Happy old man! So these lands will still be yours, and large enough for you, though bare stones cover all, and the marsh chokes your pastures with slimy rushes. Still, no strange herbage shall try your breeding ewes, no baneful infection from a neighbour's flock shall harm them. Happy old man! Here, amid familiar streams and sacred springs, you shall court the cooling shade. On this side, as aforetime, on your neighbour's border, the hedge whose willow blossoms are sipped by Hybla's bees shall often with its gentle hum soothe you to slumber; on that, under the towering rock, the woodman's song shall fill the air; while still the cooing wood-pigeons, your pets, and the turtle-dove shall cease not their moaning from the skyey elm.

TITYRUS

Sooner, then, shall the nimble stag graze in air, and the seas leave their fish bare on the strand— sooner, each wandering over the other's frontiers, shall the Parthian in exile drink the Arar, and Germany the Tigris, than that look of his shall fade from my heart.

VIRGIL

MELIBOEUS

At nos hinc alii sitientis ibimus Afros,
pars Scythiam et rapidum Cretae veniemus Oaxen
et penitus toto divisos orbe Britannos.   66
en umquam patrios longo post tempore finis,
pauperis et tuguri congestum caespite culmen
post aliquot, mea regna videns, mirabor aristas ?
impius haec tam culta novalia miles habebit,   70
barbarus has segetes.   en quo discordia civis
produxit miseros : his nos consevimus agros.
insere nunc, Meliboee, piros, pone ordine vitis.
ite meae, quondam felix pecus, ite capellae.
non ego vos posthac viridi proiectus in antro   75
dumosa pendere procul de rupe videbo ;
carmina nulla canam ; non me pascente, capellae,
florentem cytisum et salices carpetis amaras.

TITYRUS

Hic tamen hanc mecum poteras requiescere noctem
fronde super viridi : sunt nobis mitia poma,   80
castaneae molles et pressi copia lactis ;
et iam summa procul villarum culmina fumant
maioresque cadunt altis de montibus umbrae.

[66] *Servius read* cretae, *governed by* rapidum, " *ialk-rolling.*"
[74] felix quondam *R.*
[79] hac . . . nocte *P².*
[83] de *P²* : a *P¹.*

ECLOGUE I

MELIBOEUS

But we must go hence — some to the thirsty Africans, some to reach Scythia and Crete's swift Oaxes, and the Britons, wholly sundered from all the world. Ah, shall I ever, long years hence, look again on my country's bounds, on my humble cottage with its turf-clad roof—shall I, long years hence, look amazed on a few ears of corn, once my kingdom? Is a godless soldier to hold these well-tilled fallows? a barbarian these crops? See to what strife has brought our unhappy citizens! For these have we sown our fields! Now, Meliboeus, graft your pears, plant your vines in rows! Away, my goats! Away, once happy flock! No more, stretched in some mossy grot, shall I watch you in the distance hanging from a bushy crag; no more songs shall I sing; no more, my goats, under my tending, shall you crop flowering lucerne and bitter willows!

TITYRUS

Yet this night you might have rested here with me on the green leafage. We have ripe apples, mealy chestnuts, and a wealth of pressed cheeses. Even now the house-tops yonder are smoking and longer shadows fall from the mountain-heights.

VIRGIL

II

FORMOSUM pastor Corydon ardebat Alexim,
delicias domini, nec, quid speraret, habebat.
tantum inter densas, umbrosa cacumina, fagos
adsidue veniebat.   ibi haec incondita solus
montibus et silvis studio iactabat inani.   5

   " O crudelis Alexi, nihil mea carmina curas ?
nil nostri miserere ? mori me denique coges.
nunc etiam pecudes umbras et frigora captant,
nunc viridis etiam occultant spineta lacertos,
Thestylis et rapido fessis messoribus aestu   10
alia serpullumque herbas contundit olentis.
at mecum raucis, tua dum vestigia lustro,
sole sub ardenti resonant arbusta cicadis.
nonne fuit satius, tristis Amaryllidis iras
atque superba pati fastidia ? nonne Menalcan,   15
quamvis ille niger, quamvis tu candidus esses ?
o formose puer, nimium ne crede colori :
alba ligustra cadunt, vaccinia nigra leguntur.
despectus tibi sum nec, qui sim, quaeris, Alexi,
quam dives pecoris, nivei quam lactis abundans :   20
mille meae Siculis errant in montibus agnae ;
lac mihi non aestate novum, non frigore defit.
canto, quae solitus, si quando armenta vocabat,
Amphion Dircaeus in Actaeo Aracyntho.
nec sum adeo informis : nuper me in litore vidi,   25
cum placidum ventis staret mare ; non ego Daphnim
iudice te metuam, si numquam fallit imago.

    [1] Corydon pastor *Rγ*.   [7] cogis *Pγ*.   [9] lacertas *P¹*.
    [11] ac *R*.   [22] lact *P*.   [27] fallat *PᵃRγ*.

ECLOGUE II

II[1]

CORYDON, the shepherd, was aflame for the fair Alexis, his master's pet, nor knew he what to hope. As his one solace, he would day by day come among the thick beeches with their shady summits, and there alone in fruitless passion fling these artless strains to the hills and woods :

6 " O cruel Alexis, care you naught for my songs ? Have you no pity for me ? You will drive me at last to death. Now even the cattle court the cool shade ; now even the green lizards hide in the brakes, and Thestylis pounds for the reapers, spent with the scorching heat, her savoury herbs of garlic and thyme. But as I scan your footprints, the copses under the burning sun ring with the shrill cicala's voice along with mine. Was it not better to brook Amaryllis' sullen rage and scornful disdain ? or Menalcas, though he was swart and you are fair ? Ah, lovely boy, trust not too much to your bloom ! The white privets fall, the dark hyacinths are culled !

19 " You scorn me, Alexis, and ask not what I am— how rich in cattle, how wealthy in snow-white milk ! A thousand lambs of mine roam over the Sicilian hills ; new milk fails me not, summer or winter. I sing as Amphion of Dirce used to sing, when calling home the herds on Attic Aracynthus. Nor am I so unsightly ; on the shore the other day I looked at myself, when, by grace of the winds, the sea was at peace and still. With you for judge, I should fear not Daphnis, if the mirror never lies !

[1] This Eclogue, probably the earliest in the collection, is largely an imitation of two Idylls of Theocritus, viz. the third, in which a slighted lover pours forth his complaint, and the eleventh, in which the Cyclops Polyphemus bewails the cruelty of Galatea.

VIRGIL

o tantum libeat mecum tibi sordida rura
atque humilis habitare casas et figere cervos
haedorumque gregem viridi compellere hibisco !   30
mecum una in silvis imitabere Pana canendo.
Pan primum calamos cera coniungere pluris
instituit, Pan curat ovis oviumque magistros
nec te paeniteat calamo trivisse labellum :
haec eadem ut sciret, quid non faciebat Amyntas ? 36
est mihi disparibus septem compacta cicutis
fistula, Damoetas dono mihi quam dedit olim
et dixit moriens ' te nunc habet ista secundum.'
dixit Damoetas, invidit stultus Amyntas.
praeterea duo, nec tuta mihi valle reperti,   40
capreoli, sparsis etiam nunc pellibus albo ;
bina die siccant ovis ubera ; quos tibi servo.
iam pridem a me illos abducere Thestylis orat ;
et faciet, quoniam sordent tibi munera nostra.
huc ades, o formose puer : tibi lilia plenis   45
ecce ferunt Nymphae calathis, tibi candida Nais,
pallentis violas et summa papavera carpens,
narcissum et florem iungit bene olentis anethi ;
tum, casia atque aliis intexens suavibus herbis,
mollia luteola pingit vaccinia caltha.   50
ipse ego cana legam tenera lanugine mala
castaneasque nuces, mea quas Amaryllis amabat ;
addam cerea pruna : honos erit huic quoque pomo ;

[33] primus *bc*, *Servius* (at *Ecl.* III. 25).   [41] albo] ambo *R.*

12

²⁸ " O if you would but live with me in our rude
fields and lowly cots, shooting the deer and driving
the flock of kids to the green mallows !¹ With me
in the woods you shall rival Pan in song. Pan it was
who first taught man to make many reeds one with
wax ; Pan cares for the sheep and the shepherds of
the sheep. Nor would you be sorry to have chafed
your lip with a reed ; to learn this same art, what
did not Amyntas do ? I have a pipe formed of
seven uneven hemlock-stalks, a gift Damoetas once
gave me, and said on his death-bed, ' Now it claims
thee as second master.' So said Damoetas ; Amyntas,
foolish one, felt envious. Nay more, two roes—I
found them in a dangerous valley—their hides still
sprinkled with white, drain a ewe's udders twice a
day. These I keep for you. Thestylis has long been
begging to get them from me—and so she shall, as
in your eyes my gifts are mean.

⁴⁵ " Come hither, lovely boy ! See, for you the
Nymphs bring lilies in heaped-up baskets ; for you
the fair Naiad, plucking pale violets and poppy-heads,
blends narcissus and sweet scented fennel-flower ;
then, twining them with cassia and other sweet herbs,
sets off the delicate hyacinth with the golden mari-
gold. My own hands will gather quinces, pale with
tender down, and chestnuts, which my Amaryllis
loved. Waxen plums I will add—this fruit, too,
shall have its honour. You too, O laurels, I will

¹ Perhaps, "with a green hibiscus switch" (Page). What
the *hibiscus* was is uncertain. Dioscorides and Palladius
identify it with the marsh-mallow, but Pliny says it is like a
parsnip. In x. 71 it is used for making baskets. Keightley
is therefore inclined to suspect that it was some kind of
willow. The common interpretation is that of Servius, who
takes *hibisco* for *ad hibiscum*, comparing *it clamor caelo* (*Aen.*
v. 451).

13

et vos, o lauri, carpam et te, proxima myrte,
sic positae quoniam suavis miscetis odores.   **55**
rusticus es, Corydon ; nec munera curat Alexis,
nec, si muneribus certes, concedat Iollas.
heu heu, quid volui misero mihi ? floribus Austrum
perditus et liquidis immisi fontibus apros.
quem fugis, a ! demens ? habitarunt di quoque silvas
Dardaniusque Paris. Pallas, quas condidit arces, 61
ipsa colat: nobis placeant ante omnia silvae.
torva leaena lupum sequitur, lupus ipse capellam,
florentem cytisum sequitur lasciva capella,
te Corydon, o Alexi : trahit sua quemque voluptas.
aspice, aratra iugo referunt suspensa iuvenci,   66
et sol crescentis decedens duplicat umbras :
me tamen urit amor ; quis enim modus adsit amori ?
ah, Corydon, Corydon, quae te dementia cepit ?
semiputata tibi frondosa vitis in ulmo est.   70
quin tu aliquid saltem potius, quorum indiget usus,
viminibus mollique paras detexere iunco ?
invenies alium, si te hic fastidit, Alexim."

III

MENALCAS

Dic mihi, Damoeta, cuium pecus ? an Meliboei ? PR

DAMOETAS

Non, verum Aegonis ; nuper mihi tradidit Aegon.

---

⁵⁶ es] est *P¹R.*   **⁵⁷** certet *R.*   **⁶¹** quae *R.*
      ⁷⁰ est *om. P.*   **⁷³** Alexis *P²γ.*

pluck, and you, their neighbour myrtle, for so placed you blend sweet fragrance.

[56] " Corydon, you are a clown! Alexis cares naught for gifts, nor if with gifts you were to vie, would Iollas yield. Alas, alas! what wish, poor wretch, has been mine? Madman, I have let in the south wind to my flowers, and boars to my crystal springs! Ah, fool, whom do you flee? Even the gods have dwelt in the woods, and Dardan Paris. Let Pallas dwell by herself in the cities she has built; but let my chief delight be the woods! The grim lioness follows the wolf, the wolf himself the goat, the wanton goat the flowering clover, and Corydon follows you, Alexis. Each is led by his liking. See, the bullocks drag home by the yoke the hanging plough, and the retiring sun doubles the lengthening shadows. Yet me love still burns; for what bound can be set to love? Ah, Corydon, Corydon, what madness has gripped you? Your vine is but half-pruned on the leafy elm. Nay, why not at least set about plaiting some thing your need calls for, with twigs and pliant rushes? You will find another Alexis, if this one scorns you?"

III[1]

MENALCAS

TELL me, Damoetas, who owns the flock? Is it Meliboeus?

DAMOETAS

No, but Aegon. Aegon the other day turned it over to me.

---

[1] This *amoebaean* pastoral, in which two swains contend in alternate song (see l. 59), is largely imitative of the fourth and fifth Idylls of Theocritus.

VIRGIL

Infelix o semper, ovis, pecus ! ipse Neaeram
dum fovet ac, ne me sibi praeferat illa, veretur,
hic alienus ovis custos bis mulget in hora,   5
et sucus pecori et lac subducitur agnis.

DAMOETAS

Parcius ista viris tamen obicienda memento.
novimus et qui te, transversa tuentibus hircis,
et quo (sed faciles Nymphae risere) sacello.

MENALCAS

Tum, credo, cum me arbustum videre Miconis   10
atque mala vitis incidere falce novellas.

DAMOETAS

Aut hic ad veteres fagos cum Daphnidis arcum
fregisti et calamos : quae tu, perverse Menalca,
et cum vidisti puero donata, dolebas,
et si non aliqua nocuisses, mortuus esses.   15

MENALCAS

Quid domini faciant, audent cum talia fures ?
non ego te vidi Damonis, pessime, caprum
excipere insidiis, multum latrante Lycisca ?
et cum clamarem "quo nunc se proripit ille ?
Tityre, coge pecus," tu post carecta latebas.   20

16

ECLOGUE III

Poor sheep, ever luckless flock! While your master courts Neaera, and fears lest she prefer me to him, this hireling keeper milks his ewes twice an hour, and the flock are robbed of strength and the lambs of milk.

DAMOETAS

Yet have a care to fling these taunts more sparingly at men. We know who was with you while the goats looked askance, and in what chapel—but the easy Nymphs laughed.

MENALCAS

The day, of course, when they saw me hacking Micon's plantation and his young vines with malicious knife.

DAMOETAS

Or it was here, by the old beeches, when you broke Daphnis' bow and arrows; for you were sore, you spiteful Menalcas, when you saw them given to the boy, and could you not have harmed him in some way, you would have died.

MENALCAS

What are masters like to do, if their knaves[1] are so bold? Did I not see you, rascal, snaring Damon's goat, while his mongrel barked madly? And when I cried: "Where is yon fellow running? Tityrus, round up the flock!" you were skulking beyond the sedge.

[1] Servius says: "*pro servo furem posuit.*" An alternative rendering is: "What can owners do when thieves are so daring?" So Page and Waltz.

VIRGIL

DAMOETAS

An mihi cantando victus non redderet ille,
quem mea carminibus meruisset fistula caprum ?
si nescis, meus ille caper fuit ; et mihi Damon
ipse fatebatur ; sed reddere posse negabat.

MENALCAS

Cantando tu illum ? aut umquam tibi fistula cera   25
iuncta fuit ? non tu in triviis, indocte, solebas
stridenti miserum stipula disperdere carmen ?   PRV

DAMOETAS

Vis ergo inter nos, quid possit uterque, vicissim
experiamur ? ego hanc vitulam (ne forte recuses,
bis venit ad mulctram, binos alit ubere fetus)   30
depono : tu dic, mecum quo pignore certes.

MENALCAS

De grege non ausim quicquam deponere tecum :
est mihi namque domi pater, est iniusta noverca,
bisque die numerant ambo pecus, alter et haedos.
verum, id quod multo tute ipse fatebere maius,   35
(insanire libet quoniam tibi) pocula ponam
fagina, caelatum divini opus Alcimedontis ;
lenta quibus torno facili superaddita vitis
diffusos hedera vestit pallente corymbos.
in medio duo signa, Conon et—quis fuit alter,   40
descripsit radio totum qui gentibus orbem,
tempora quae messor, quae curvus arator haberet ?
necdum illis labra admovi sed condita servo.

---

²⁶ vincta *PR*γ.   ²⁷ stipula miserum *V*.
³⁸ facili γ, *known to Servius:* faclis *P*¹ : factis *P*² : facilis
V, Donatus, Berne Scholia: fragilis *R.*

18

ECLOGUE III

DAMOETAS

Did I not beat him in singing, and was he not to
pay me the goat my pipe had won by its songs? If
you must know, that goat was mine; Damon himself
owned to it, but said he could not pay.

MENALCAS

You beat him in singing? Why, did you ever own
a wax-jointed pipe? Was it not you, Master Dunce,
who at the cross-roads used to murder a sorry tune
on a scrannel straw?

DAMOETAS

Well, would you have us try together, turn about,
what each can do? I'll stake this cow. Now, don't
draw back! She comes twice a day to the milking-
pail, and suckles two calves. Now tell me, for what
stake you will match me.

MENALCAS

From the herd I'd dare not stake anything with
you. I have at home a harsh father and stepmother;
and twice a day both count the flock, and one of them
the kids as well. But—and you will yourself own it for
a far greater wager—since you are on folly bent, I will
stake two beechen cups, the embossed work of divine
Alcimedon. On these a pliant vine, laid on by the
graver's skill, is entwined with spreading clusters of
pale ivy. In the midst are two figures, Conon and—
who was the other,[1] who marked out with his rod
the whole heavens for man, what seasons the reaper
should claim, what the stooping ploughman? Nor have
I yet put my lips to them, but keep them in store.

[1] The other astronomer was probably Eudoxus of Cnidus
whose *Phaenomena* was versified by Aratus.

19

VIRGIL

DAMOETAS

Et nobis idem Alcimedon duo pocula fecit,
et molli circum est ansas amplexus acantho,   45
Orpheaque in medio posuit silvasque sequentis;
necdum illis labra admovi, sed condita servo:
si ad vitulam spectas, nihil est, quod pocula laudes.

MENALCAS

Numquam hodie effugies; veniam, quocumque vocaris.
audiat haec tantum--vel qui venit ecce Palaemon. 50
efficiam, posthac ne quemquam voce lacessas.

DAMOETAS

Quin age, si quid habes ; in me mora non erit ulla,
nec quemquam fugio : tantum, vicine Palaemon,   PR
sensibus haec imis (res est non parva) reponas.

PALAEMON

Dicite, quandoquidem in molli consedimus herba. 55
et nunc omnis ager, nunc omnis parturit arbos,
nunc frondent silvae, nunc formosissimus annus.
incipe, Damoeta ; tu deinde sequere, Menalca:
alternis dicetis; amant alterna Camenae.

DAMOETAS

Ab Iove principium, Musae : Iovis omnia plena;   60
ille colit terras, illi mea carmina curae.

60 musae (*genitive*), *known to Servius.   So Sabb.*
20

ECLOGUE III

DAMOETAS

I also have two cups, made for me by the same
Alcimedon, and he has clasped their handles with
twining acanthus, and in the centre placed Orpheus
with the woods that follow him.   Nor have I yet put
my lips to them, but keep them in store.   If you but
look at the cow, you will have no praise for the cups.

MENALCAS

You shall never, never get off!   Wherever you call
me, I will meet you.   Only let the one to hear us be
—or take the man coming yonder, Palaemon.   I will
see that hereafter you challenge nobody to sing.

DAMOETAS

Nay come, if you have any song; with me there
shall be no delay.   No umpire do I shun.   Only,
neighbour Palaemon, give this your closest heed; it
is no trifling matter.

PALAEMON

Sing on, now that we are seated on the soft grass.
Even now every field, every tree is budding; now
the woods are green, and the year is at its fairest.
Begin, Damoetas; then you, Menalcas, must follow.
Turn about you shall sing; singing by turns the Muses
love.

DAMOETAS

With Jove I begin, ye Muses; of Jove all things
are full.   He makes the earth fruitful; he pays heed
to my songs,

VIRGIL

MENALCAS

Et me Phoebus amat; Phoebo sua semper apud me
munera sunt, lauri et suave rubens hyacinthus.

DAMOETAS

Malo me Galatea petit, lasciva puella,
et fugit ad salices, et se cupit ante videri.　　　　　　65

MENALCAS

At mihi sese offert ultro, meus ignis, Amyntas,
notior ut iam sit canibus non Delia nostris.

DAMOETAS

Parta meae Veneri sunt munera: namque notavi
ipse locum, aëriae quo congessere palumbes.

MENALCAS

Quod potui, puero silvestri ex arbore lecta　　　　　70
aurea mala decem misi : cras altera mittam.

DAMOETAS

O quotiens et quae nobis Galatea locuta est!　　　R
partem aliquam, venti, divom referatis ad auris.

MENALCAS

Quid prodest, quod me ipse animo non spernis,
　　　　Amynta,
si, dum tu sectaris apros, ego retia servo?　　　　75

DAMOETAS

Phyllida mitte mihi : meus est natalis, Iolla ;
cum faciam vitula pro frugibus, ipse venito.

---

⁷⁷ vitula *Servius, Macrobius:* vitulam *most MSS.*

22

ECLOGUE III

MENALCAS

And me Phoebus loves; Phoebus ever finds with me the offerings he loves, laurels and sweet-blushing hyacinths.

DAMOETAS

Galatea, saucy girl, pelts me with an apple, then runs off to the willows—and hopes to be seen first.

MENALCAS

But my flame Amyntas comes to me unsought, so that now Delia is not better known to my dogs.

DAMOETAS

Gifts I have found for my love; for I have myself marked where the wood-pigeons have been building high in the air.

MENALCAS

I have sent my boy—'twas all I could do—ten golden apples, culled from a tree in the wood. To-morrow I will send a second ten.

DAMOETAS

O the times and the things Galatea has spoken to me! Waft some part, ye winds, to the ears of the gods.

MENALCAS

What boots it, Amyntas, that you yourself scorn me not in heart, if, while you follow the boars, I watch the nets?

DAMOETAS

Send Phyllis to me; it is my birthday, Iollas. When I sacrifice a heifer for the harvest, come yourself.

23

VIRGIL

Phyllida amo ante alias : nam me discedere flevit,
et longum "formose, vale, vale" inquit, "Iolla."

DAMOETAS

Triste lupus stabulis, maturis frugibus imbres,   80
arboribus venti, nobis Amaryllidis irae.

MENALCAS

Dulce satis umor, depulsis arbutus haedis,
lenta salix feto pecori, mihi solus Amyntas.

DAMOETAS

Pollio amat nostram, quamvis est rustica, Musam :
Pierides, vitulam lectori pascite vestro.   85

MENALCAS

Pollio et ipse facit nova carmina : pascite taurum,
iam cornu petat et pedibus qui spargat harenam.

DAMOETAS

Qui te, Pollio, amat, veniat, quo te quoque gaudet;
mella fluant illi, ferat et rubus asper amomum.

MENALCAS

Qui Bavium non odit, amet tua carmina, Maevi,   90
atque idem iungat vulpes et mulgeat hircos,

24

ECLOGUE III

MENALCAS

Phyllis I love beyond all ; for she wept at my leaving, and in lingering tones cried: "Farewell, farewell, my lovely Iollas!"

DAMOETAS

Baneful to the folds is the wolf, to the ripe crop the rains, to trees the gales, and to me the anger of Amaryllis !

MENALCAS

Sweet to the corn is a shower, to the new-weaned kids the arbute, to the breeding flock the bending willow, and to me Amyntas alone !

DAMOETAS

Pollio loves my Muse, homely though she be ; Pierian sisters, feed a calf for your reader !

MENALCAS

Pollio himself, too, makes new songs. Feed ye a bull, able even now to butt with the horn and to spurn the sand with his hoofs.

DAMOETAS

May he who loves you, Pollio, come [1] where he joys that you, too, have come ! For him may honey flow, and the rough bramble bear spices !

MENALCAS

Let him who hates not Bavius love your songs, Maevius ; and let him also yoke foxes and milk he-goats !

[1] *i.e.* into a state of happiness, such as was enjoyed in the golden age.

25

VIRGIL

Qui legitis flores et humi nascentia fraga,
frigidus, o pueri, fugite hinc, latet anguis in herba.

MENALCAS

Parcite, oves, nimium procedere : non bene ripae
creditur ; ipse aries etiam nunc vellera siccat.   95

DAMOETAS

Tityre, pascentis a flumine reice capellas :
ipse, ubi tempus erit, omnis in fonte lavabo.

MENALCAS

Cogite ovis, pueri : si lac praeceperit aestus,
ut nuper, frustra pressabimus ubera palmis.

DAMOETAS

Heu heu ! quam pingui macer est mihi taurus in ervo!
idem amor exitium pecori pecorisque magistro.   101

MENALCAS

His certe—neque amor causa est—vix ossibus haerent.
nescio quis teneros oculus mihi fascinat agnos.

DAMOETAS

Dic, quibus in terris (et eris mihi magnus Apollo)
tris pateat Caeli spatium non amplius ulnas.   105

---

[100] arvo *R*.
[101] exitium pecori *c:* exitium est pecori *Ilγ²a:* exitium
pecori est *γ¹b*.

26

ECLOGUE III

DAMOETAS

Ye who cull flowers and low-growing strawberries,
away from here, lads; a chill snake lurks in the
grass.

MENALCAS

Forbear, my sheep, to go too far; 'tis ill to trust
the bank. The ram himself is even now drying his
fleece.

DAMOETAS

Tityrus, turn back from the stream the grazing
goats; when the time comes, I'll wash them all in
the spring myself.

MENALCAS

Round up the sheep, my lads; if the heat fore-
stalls the milk, as it did of late, in vain shall our
palms press the teats.

DAMOETAS

Alas, alas! how lean is my bull amid the fattening
tares! The same love is the bane of the herd and
the herd's master.

MENALCAS

As to mine at least—and love is not to blame—
their skin scarce clings to the bones. Some evil eye
bewitches my tender lambs.

DAMOETAS

Tell me in what land—and you shall be my great
Apollo—Heaven's space is but three ells broad.[1]

[1] The solution of this riddle is uncertain. One explanation
refers it to a spendthrift Mantuan named Caelius, who was
left with only enough ground to be buried in. More probably
it refers to one looking up at the sky from the bottom of a
well or cavern.

27

VIRGIL

MENALCAS

Dic, quibus in terris inscripti nomina regum
nascantur flores, et Phyllida solus habeto.

PALAEMON

Non nostrum inter vos tantas componere lites :
et vitula tu dignus et hic—et quisquis amores
aut metuet dulcis aut experietur amaros.   110
claudite iam rivos, pueri : sat prata biberunt.

IV

SICELIDES Musae, paulo maiora canamus.   R
non omnis arbusta iuvant humilesque myricae ;
si canimus silvas, silvae sint consule dignae.
    Ultima Cumaei venit iam carminis aetas ;
magnus ab integro saeclorum nascitur ordo.   5
iam redit et Virgo, redeunt Saturnia regna ;
iam nova progenies caelo demittitur alto.
tu modo nascenti puero, quo ferrea primum
desinet ac toto surget gens aurea mundo,
casta fave Lucina : tuus iam regnat Apollo.   10

        ⁷ dimittitur *R*.

---

¹ The flower referred to is the hyacinth, marked with AI,
the first letters of Αἴας, or with Y, the initial letter of ῾Υάκινθος.
Ajax and Hyacinthus, favourite of Apollo, were both sons of
kings.
    ² This poem is "a vision of the new golden age under
Augustus," which Virgil connects with the birth of a certain
child (ll. 8–10). Who this child was is unknown, but most
scholars incline to the view that it was the infant son of

28

ECLOGUE IV

MENALCAS

Tell me in what land spring up flowers with royal names written thereon[1]—and have Phyllis to yourself!

PALAEMON

It is not for me to settle so high a contest between you. You deserve the heifer, and he also—and whoever shall fear the sweets or taste the bitters of love. Shut off the rills now, my lads; the meadows have drunk enough.

IV [2]

SICILIAN [3] Muses, let us sing a somewhat loftier strain. Not all do the orchards please and the lowly tamarisks. If our song is of the woodland, let the woodland be worthy of a consul.

[4] Now is come the last age of the song of Cumae; the great line of the centuries begins anew.[4] Now the Virgin [5] returns, the reign of Saturn returns; now a new generation descends from heaven on high. Only do thou, pure Lucina, smile on the birth of the child, under whom the iron brood shall first cease, and a golden race spring up throughout the world! Thine own Apollo now is king!

C. Asinius Pollio, in whose consulship, 40 B.C., the poem was written (l. 11). See Appendix.
[3] Called Sicilian because Virgil's model in pastoral poetry, Theocritus, was a Sicilian.
[4] The Sibylline books, supposed to record the utterances of the famous Sibyl of Cumae, contained the prophecy of a new circuit of the ages after the Age of Iron had passed.
[5] i.e. Astraea or Justice, last of the immortals to leave the earth.

teque adeo decus hoc aevi, te consule, inibit,
Pollio, et incipient magni procedere menses ;
te duce, si qua manent sceleris vestigia nostri,
inrita perpetua solvent formidine terras.
ille deum vitam accipiet divisque videbit   15
permixtos heroas et ipse videbitur illis,
pacatumque reget patriis virtutibus orbem.

  At tibi prima, puer, nullo munuscula cultu
errantis hederas passim cum baccare tellus
mixtaque ridenti colocasia fundet acantho.   20
ipsae lacte domum referent distenta capellae
ubera, nec magnos metuent armenta leones ;
ipsa tibi blandos fundent cunabula flores.
occidet et serpens, et fallax herba veneni
occidet ; Assyrium volgo nascetur amomum.   25
at simul heroum laudes et facta parentis
iam legere et quae sit poteris cognoscere virtus.
molli paulatim flavescet campus arista,
incultisque rubens pendebit sentibus uva
et durae quercus sudabunt roscida mella.   30
pauca tamen suberunt priscae vestigia fraudis,
quae temptare Thetim ratibus, quae cingere muris
oppida, quae iubeant telluri infindere sulcos.
alter erit tum Tiphys, et altera quae vehat Argo
delectos heroas ; erunt etiam altera bella   35
atque iterum ad Troiam magnus mittetur Achilles.
hinc ubi iam firmata virum te fecerit aetas,
cedet et ipse mari vector, nec nautica pinus
mutabit merces ; omnis feret omnia tellus.
non rastros patietur humus, non vinea falcem ;   40

   [26] ac *R.*   parentis γ^1bc, *Servius, Nonius:* parentum $R\gamma^2$.
   [28] flavescit $R\gamma^1$.   [33] tellurem infindere sulco *R.*

[11] And in thy consulship, Pollio, yea in thine, shall this glorious age begin, and the mighty months commence their march; under thy sway, any lingering traces of our guilt shall become void, and release the earth from its continual dread. He shall have the gift of divine life, shall see heroes mingled with gods, and shall himself be seen of them, and shall sway a world to which his father's virtues have brought peace.

[18] But for thee, child, shall the earth untilled pour forth, as her first pretty gifts, straggling ivy with foxglove everywhere, and the Egyptian bean blended with the smiling acanthus. Uncalled, the goats shall bring home their udders swollen with milk, and the herds shall fear not huge lions; unasked, thy cradle shall pour forth flowers for thy delight. The serpent, too, shall perish, and the false poison-plant shall perish; Assyrian spice shall spring up on every soil.

[26] But soon as thou canst read of the glories of heroes and thy father's deeds, and canst know what valour is, slowly shall the plain yellow with the waving corn, on wild brambles shall hang the purple grape, and the stubborn oak shall distil dewy honey. Yet shall some few traces of olden sin lurk behind, to call men to essay the sea in ships, to gird towns with walls, and to cleave the earth with furrows. A second Tiphys shall then arise, and a second Argo to carry chosen heroes; a second warfare, too, shall there be, and again shall a great Achilles be sent to Troy.

[37] Next, when now the strength of years has made thee man, even the trader shall quit the sea, nor shall the ship of pine exchange wares; every land shall bear all fruits. The earth shall not feel the harrow, nor the vine the pruning-hook; the sturdy ploughman, too,

robustus quoque iam tauris iuga solvet arator;
nec varios discet mentiri lana colores,
ipse sed in pratis aries iam suave rubenti
murice, iam croceo mutabit vellera luto;
sponte sua sandyx pascentis vestiet agnos.   **45**

    " Talia saecla " suis dixerunt " currite " fusis
concordes stabili fatorum numine Parcae.

    Adgredere o magnos (aderit iam tempus) honores,
˙ara deum suboles, magnum Iovis incrementum !
aspice convexo nutantem pondere mundum   **50**
terrasque tractusque maris caelumque profundum ;
aspice venturo laetentur ut omnia saeclo !   PR
o mihi tum longae maneat pars ultima vitae,
spiritus et, quantum sat erit tua dicere facta :
non me carminibus vincet nec Thracius Orpheus,   **55**
nec Linus, huic mater quamvis atque huic pater adsit,
Orphei Calliopea, Lino formosus Apollo.
Pan etiam, Arcadia mecum si iudice certet,
Pan etiam Arcadia dicat se iudice victum.
incipe, parve puer, risu cognoscere matrem :   **60**
matri longa decem tulerunt fastidia menses.
incipe, parve puer : cui non risere parentes,
nec deus hunc mensa, dea nec dignata cubili est.

---

[52] laetentur $P\gamma$: laetantur R.
[53] longe $P\gamma$.
[55] vincat $P^1\gamma^2$.
[62] cui $PR\gamma$, *Servius:* qui, *Quintilian:* quoi, *Sabl.* *See Appendix.*

32

shall now loose his oxen from the yoke. Wool shall
no more learn to counterfeit varied hues, but of himself
the ram in the meadows shall change his fleece, now
to sweetly blushing purple, now to a saffron yellow;
of its own will shall scarlet clothe the grazing lambs.

⁴⁶ " Ages such as these, glide on ! " cried to their
spindles the Fates, voicing in unison the fixed will of
Destiny !

⁴⁸ Enter on thy high honours—the hour will soon be
here—O thou dear offspring of the gods, mighty seed
of a Jupiter to be ![1] Behold the world bowing with
its massive dome—earth and expanse of sea and
heaven's depth ! Behold, how all things exult in the
age that is at hand ! O that then the last days of a long
life may still linger for me, with inspiration enough
to tell of thy deeds ! Not Thracian Orpheus, not
Linus shall vanquish me in song, though his mother
be helpful to the one, and his father to the other,
Calliope to Orpheus, and fair Apollo to Linus. Even
Pan, were he to contend with me and Arcady be
judge, even Pan, with Arcady for judge, would own
himself defeated.

⁶⁰ Begin, baby boy, to know thy mother with a smile
—to thy mother ten months have brought the weari-
ness of travail. Begin, baby boy ! Him on whom
his parents have not smiled, no god honours with his
table, no goddess with her bed ![2]

---

[1] Some take the phrase to mean "that from which a
Jupiter, or lord of the world, shall grow." As Jupiter rules
in heaven, so the child is to rule on earth. But see Appendix.

[2] *i.e.* such a child can never win the rewards bestowed on
a hero, such as Hercules (*cf.* Homer, *Odyssey*, XI. 601).

VIRGIL

V

MENALCAS

Cur non, Mopse, boni quoniam convenimus ambo, pr
tu calamos inflare levis, ego dicere versus,
hic corylis mixtas inter consedimus ulmos?

MOPSUS

Tu maior; tibi me est aequum parere, Menalca,
sive sub incertas Zephyris motantibus umbras,   5
sive antro potius succedimus. aspice, ut antrum
silvestris raris sparsit labrusca racemis.

MENALCAS

Montibus in nostris solus tibi certat Amyntas.

MOPSUS

Quid, si idem certet Phoebum superare canendo?

MENALCAS

Incipe, Mopse, prior, si quos aut Phyllidis ignis   10
aut Alconis habes laudes aut iurgia Codri.
incipe; pascentis servabit Tityrus haedos.

MOPSUS

Immo haec, in viridi nuper quae cortice fagi
carmina descripsi et modulans alterna notavi,
experiar: tu deinde iubeto ut certet Amyntas.   15

⁸ certet *Pγ*.   ¹⁵ iubeto ut certet *Ra*.

---

1 In this poem two shepherds engage in a friendly song
contest, the one relating the death of Daphnis, the other his

ECLOGUE V

V[1]

MENALCAS

Mopsus, now that we have met, good men both, you at breathing in slender reeds, I at singing verses —why not seat us among these elms, with hazels interspersed?

MOPSUS

You are the elder, Menalcas: it is fitting that I obey you, whether we pass beneath the shades that shift at the Zephyrs' stirring, or rather into the cave. See, how the wild vine with its stray clusters has overrun the cave.

MENALCAS

Among our hills your only rival is Amyntas.

MOPSUS

What if he should rival Phoebus, too, for the prize of song?

MENALCAS

Begin first, Mopsus, if you have any strains on your flame Phyllis, or in praise of Alcon, or in raillery at Codrus. Begin. Tityrus will tend the grazing kids.

MOPSUS

Nay, I will try these verses, which the other day I carved on the green beech-bark, and set to music, marking words and tune in turn. Then do you bid Amyntas rival me!

deification. The death of Daphnis is also bewailed in the first Idyll of Theocritus; his deification, which is original with Virgil, probably has an allegorical reference to Julius Caesar.

MENALCAS

Lenta salix quantum pallenti cedit olivae,
puniceis humilis quantum saliunca rosetis,
iudicio nostro tantum tibi cedit Amyntas.
sed tu desine plura, puer: successimus antro.

MOPSUS

" Exstinctum Nymphae crudeli funere Daphnim   20
flebant (vos coryli testes et flumina Nymphis),
cum complexa sui corpus miserabile nati
atque deos atque astra vocat crudelia mater.
non ulli pastos illis egere diebus
frigida, Daphni, boves ad flumina; nulla neque amnem   25
libavit quadrupes nec graminis attigit herbam.
Daphni, tuum Poenos etiam ingemuisse leones
interitum montesque feri silvaeque loquuntur.
Daphnis et Armenias curru subiungere tigris
instituit, Daphnis thiasos inducere Bacchi   30
et foliis lentas intexere mollibus hastas.
vitis ut arboribus decori est, ut vitibus uvae,
ut gregibus tauri. segetes ut pinguibus arvis,
tu decus omne tuis.   postquam te Fata tulerunt,
ipsa Pales agros atque ipse reliquit Apollo.   35
grandia saepe quibus mandavimus hordea sulcis,
infelix lolium et steriles nascuntur avenae;
pro molli viola, pro purpureo narcisso
carduus et spinis surgit paliurus acutis.
spargite humum foliis, inducite fontibus umbras,   40
pastores (mandat fieri sibi talia Daphnis),
et tumulum facite et tumulo superaddite carmen :
' Daphnis ego in silvis, hinc usque ad sidera notus,
formosi pecoris custos, formosior ipse.' "

27 gemuisse *R.*   **38** violae *P*[1] : viola et *R.*   **40** umbras] aras *R.*

ECLOGUE V

MENALCAS

As far as the lithe willow yields to the pale olive, as far as the lowly Celtic reed yields to crimson rose-beds, so far, to my mind, does Amyntas yield to you. Nay, say no more, lad; we have passed into the cave.

MOPSUS

"For Daphnis, cut off by a cruel death, the Nymphs wept—ye hazels and rivers bear witness to the Nymphs—when, clasping her son's piteous corpse, his mother cried out on the cruelty of both gods and stars. On those days, Daphnis, none drove the pastured kine to the cool streams; no four-footed beast tasted the brook or touched a blade of grass. Daphnis, the wild mountains and woods tell us that even African lions moaned over thy death.

[29] "Daphnis it was that taught men to yoke Armenian tigers beneath the car, to lead on the dances of Bacchus and entwine in soft leaves the tough spears. As the vine gives glory to its trees, as the grape to the vines, as the bull to the herd, as the corn to rich fields, thou alone givest glory to thy people. Since the Fates bore thee off, even Pales has left our fields, and even Apollo. Often in the furrows, to which we entrusted the big barley-grains, luckless darnel springs up and barren oat-straws. Instead of the soft violet, instead of the gleaming narcissus, the thistle rises up and the sharp-spiked thorn. Strew the turf with leaves, ye shepherds, curtain the springs with shade—such honours Daphnis charges you to pay him. And build a tomb, and on the tomb place, too, this verse: 'Daphnis was I amid the woods, known from here even to the stars. Fair was the flock I guarded, but fairer was I, the master.'"

VIRGIL

Tale tuum carmen nobis, divine poeta,   45
quale sopor fessis in gramine, quale per aestum
dulcis aquae saliente sitim restinguere rivo.
nec calamis solum aequiperas, sed voce magistrum.
fortunate puer, tu nunc eris alter ab illo.
nos tamen haec quocumque modo tibi nostra vicissim
dicemus, Daphnimque tuum tollemus ad astra;   51
Daphnim ad astra feremus: amavit nos quoque
      Daphnis.

MOPSUS

An quicquam nobis tali sit munere maius?
et puer ipse fuit cantari dignus, et ista
iam pridem Stimichon laudavit carmina nobis.   55

MENALCAS

"Candidus insuetum miratur limen Olympi
sub pedibusque videt nubes et sidera Daphnis.
ergo alacris silvas et cetera rura voluptas
Panaque pastoresque tenet Dryadasque puellas.
nec lupus insidias pecori nec retia cervis   60
ulla dolum meditantur; amat bonus otia Daphnis.
ipsi laetitia voces ad sidera iactant
intonsi montes; ipsae iam carmina rupes,
ipsa sonant arbusta: 'deus, deus ille, Menalca!'
sis bonus o felixque tuis! en quattuor aras: 65
ecce duas tibi, Daphni, duas altaria Phoebo.
pocula bina novo spumantia lacte quotannis
craterasque duo statuam tibi pinguis olivi,

---

[46] lassis *R.*   [49] ab illo] Apollo *R.*
[51] Daphnin *R.*   [52] Daphnin *R.*

ECLOGUE V

Your lay, heavenly bard, is to me even as sleep on
the grass to the weary, as in summer-heat the slaking
of thirst in a dancing rill of sweet water. Not with
the pipe alone, but in voice do you match your
master. Happy lad ! now you will be next after
him. Still I will sing you in turn, poorly it may
be, this strain of mine, and exalt your Daphnis to
the stars. Daphnis I will exalt to the stars ; me, too,
Daphnis loved.

MOPSUS

Could any boon be greater in my eyes than this ?
Not only was the boy himself worthy to be sung,
but long ago Stimichon praised to me those strains
of yours.

MENALCAS

" Daphnis, in radiant beauty, marvels at Heaven's
unfamiliar threshold, and beneath his feet beholds
the clouds and the stars. Therefore frolic glee seizes
the woods and all the countryside, and Pan, and the
shepherds, and the Dryad maids. The wolf plans no
ambush for the flock, and nets no snare for the stag;
kindly Daphnis loves peace. The very mountains,
with woods unshorn, joyously fling their voices star-
ward ; the very rocks, the very groves ring out the
song : ' A god is he, a god, Menalcas !' Be kind and
gracious to thine own ! Lo here are four altars [1]—
two, see, for thee, Daphnis ; two for Phoebus ! Two
cups, foaming with fresh milk, will I year by year set
up for thee, and two bowls of rich olive oil ; and, for

[1] The *ludi Apollinares* were celebrated on July 6 ; the birth-
day of Caesar on July 4.

et multo in primis hilarans convivia Baccho,
ante focum, si frigus erit, si messis, in umbra   70
vina novum fundam calathis Ariusia nectar.
cantabunt mihi Damoetas et Lyctius Aegon,
saltantis Satyros imitabitur Alphesiboeus.
haec tibi semper erunt, et cum sollemnia vota
reddemus Nymphis, et cum lustrabimus agros.   75
dum iuga montis aper, fluvios dum piscis amabit,
dumque thymo pascentur apes, dum rore cicadae,
semper honos nomenque tuum laudesque manebunt.
ut Baccho Cererique, tibi sic vota quotannis
agricolae facient; damnabis tu quoque votis."   80

MOPSUS

Quae tibi, quae tali reddam pro carmine dona?
nam neque me tantum venientis sibilus Austri
nec percussa iuvant fluctu tam litora, nec quae
saxosas inter decurrunt flumina vallis.

MENALCAS

Hac te nos fragili donabimus ante cicuta.   85
haec nos "formosum Corydon ardebat Alexim,"   PRV
haec eadem docuit "cuium pecus? an Meliboei?"

MOPSUS

At tu sume pedum, quod, me cum saepe rogaret,
non tulit Antigenes (et erat tum dignus amari),
formosum paribus nodis atque aere, Menalca.   90

---

my chief care, making the feast merry with wine—
in winter, before the hearth ; in harvest-time, in the
shade—I will pour from goblets the fresh nectar of
Chian wine. Damoetas and Lyctian Aegon shall sing
for me, and Alphesiboeus mimic the dancing Satyrs.

[74] " These rites shall be thine for ever, both when
we pay our yearly vows to the Nymphs, and when we
purify our fields.   Long as the boar loves the moun-
tain ridges, as the fish the streams ; long as the bees
feed on thyme and the cicalas on dew, so long shall
thy honour and name and glories abide.   As to
Bacchus and Ceres, so to thee, year by year, shall
the husbandmen pay their vows ; thou. too, shalt
bind them to their vows."

MOPSUS

What gifts, pray, can I give you for such a song ?
For no such charm for me has the rustle of the rising
South, nor the beach lashed by surge, nor streams
tumbling down amid rocky glens.

MENALCAS

This frail reed I will give you first.   This taught
me " Corydon was aflame for the fair Alexis"; this
too : " Who owns the flock ?   Is it Meliboeus ? "

MOPSUS

But do you, Menalcas, take this crook, which
Antigenes won not, often as he begged it of
me—and in those days he was worthy of my
love—a goodly crook, with even knots and ring of
bronze.

41

VIRGIL

VI

PRIMA Syracosio dignata est ludere versu

nostra nec erubuit silvas habitare Thalia.

cum canerem reges et proelia, Cynthius aurem

vellit et admonuit : " pastorem, Tityre, pinguis

pascere oportet ovis, deductum dicere carmen."   5

nunc ego (namque super tibi erunt, qui dicere laudes,

Vare, tuas cupiant et tristia condere bella)

agrestem tenui meditabor harundine Musam.

non iniussa cano. si quis tamen haec quoque, si quis

captus amore leget, te nostrae, Vare, myricae,   10

te nemus omne canet ; nec Phoebo gratior ulla est,

quam sibi quae Vari praescripsit pagina nomen.

   Pergite, Pierides.   Chromis et Mnasyllos in antro

Silenum pueri somno videre iacentem,

inflatum hesterno venas, ut semper, Iaccho ;   15

serta procul, tantum capiti delapsa, iacebant

et gravis attrita pendebat cantharus ansa.

adgressi (nam saepe senex spe carminis ambo

luserat) iniciunt ipsis ex vincula sertis.

addit se sociam timidisque supervenit Aegle,   20

Aegle, Naiadum pulcherrima, iamque videnti

sanguineis frontem moris et tempora pingit.

ille dolum ridens " quo vincula nectitis ? " inquit.

"solvite me, pueri : satis est potu sse videri.

carmina, quae voltis, cognoscite ; carmina vobis,   25

huic aliud mercedis erit."   simul incipit ipse.

tum vero in numerum Faunosque ferasque videres

---

   ² silvis *R*.   ⁵ diductum *PV*.   ²² inridens *P²*.

VI

My Muse first deigned to sport in Sicilian strains, and blushed not to dwell in the woods. When I was fain to sing of kings and battles,[1] the Cynthian plucked my ear and warned me: "A shepherd, Tityrus, should feed sheep that are fat, but sing a lay fine-spun." And now—for enough, and more, wilt thou find eager to sing thy praises, Varus, and build the story of grim war—now will I woo the rustic [2] Muse on slender reed. Unbidden strains I sing not; still if any there be to read even these my lays—any whom love of the theme has won, 'tis of thee, Varus, our tamarisks shall sing, of thee all our groves. To Phoebus no page is more welcome than that which bears on its front the name of Varus.

[13] Proceed, Pierian maids! The lads Chromis and Mnasyllos saw Silenus lying asleep in a cave, his veins swollen, as ever, with the wine of yesterday. Hard by lay the garlands, just fallen from his head, and his heavy tankard was hanging by its well-worn handle. Falling on him—for oft the aged one had cheated both of a promised song—they cast him into fetters made from his own garlands. Aegle joins their company and seconds the timid pair—Aegle, fairest of the Naiads—and, as now his eyes open, paints his face and brows with crimson mulberries. Smiling at the trick, he cries: "Why fetter me? Loose me, lads; enough that you have shown your power. Hear the songs you crave; you shall have your songs, she another kind of reward." Therewith the sage begins. Then indeed you might see Fauns

---

[1] Referring to epic poetry.

[2] The present poem, though called *agrestis*, is rather mythological and philosophic (in the ancient sense of the word).

VIRGIL

ludere, tum rigidas motare cacumina quercus;
nec tantum Phoebo gaudet Parnasia rupes,
nec tantum Rhodope miratur et Ismarus Orphea.   30
   Namque canebat, uti magnum per inane coacta
semina terrarumque animaeque marisque fuissent
et liquidi simul ignis; ut his exordia primis,
omnia et ipse tener mundi concreverit orbis;
tum durare solum et discludere Nerea ponto   35
coeperit et rerum paulatim sumere formas;
iamque novum terrae stupeant lucescere solem,
altius atque cadant submotis nubibus imbres;
incipiant silvae cum primum surgere, cumque
rara per ignaros errent animalia montis.   40
   Hinc lapides Pyrrhae iactos, Saturnia regna,
Caucasiasque refert volucres furtumque Promethei.
his adiungit, Hylan nautae quo fonte relictum
clamassent, ut litus "Hyla, Hyla" omne sonaret.
et fortunatam, si numquam armenta fuissent,   45
Pasiphaen nivei solatur amore iuvenci.
a! virgo infelix, quae te dementia cepit!
Proetides implerunt falsis mugitibus agros: MPR
at non tam turpis pecudum tamen ulla secuta
concubitus, quamvis collo timuisset aratrum   50
et saepe in levi quaesisset cornua fronte.
a! virgo infelix, tu nunc in montibus erras:
ille, latus niveum molli fultus hyacintho,
ilice sub nigra pallentis ruminat herbas,
aut aliquam in magno sequitur grege. "claudite,
      Nymphae,   55
Dictaeae Nymphae, nemorum iam claudite saltus,
si qua forte ferant oculis sese obvia nostris
errabunda bovis vestigia; forsitan illum

---

³⁰ mirantur *R*.   ³³ exordia] ex omnia *P*.   *So Sabb.*
³⁴ omnisa *corr. into* omnia *P*¹.   *Sabb. reads* omnis.
⁴⁰ ignotos *Pγ*. ⁴¹ Hic *Pγ*. ⁴⁹ secuta est *Rγ*. ⁵¹ quaesissent *P*.

and fierce beasts sport in measured time, then stiff
oaks nod their tops. No such joy has the rock of
Parnassus in Phoebus ; no such a marvel to Rhodope
and Ismarus is Orpheus.

[31] For he sang how, through the great void, were
brought together the seeds of earth, and air, and sea,
and streaming fire withal ; how from these elements
came all beginnings and even the young globe of the
world grew into a mass ; how then it began to harden
the ground, to shut Nereus apart in the deep, and,
little by little, to assume the forms of things; how
next the earth is awed at the new sun shining and
from the uplifted clouds fall showers ; when first
woods begin to arise, and living things roam here and
there over mountains that know them not.

[41] Then he tells of the stones that Pyrrha threw,
of Saturn's reign, of the birds of Caucasus, and the
theft of Prometheus. To these he adds the tale of the
spring where Hylas was left, and how the seamen
called on him, till all the shore rang "Hylas! Hylas!"
Now he solaces Pasiphaë—happy one, if herds had
never been !—with her passion for the snowy bull.
Ah, unhappy girl, what madness seized thee ? The
daughters of Proetus filled the fields with unreal
lowings, yet not one was led by so foul a love for
beasts, albeit each had feared the yoke for her neck,
and often looked for horns on her smooth brow. Ah!
unhappy girl, thou art now roaming on the hills : he,
pillowing his snowy side on soft hyacinths, under a
dark ilex chews the pale grass, or courts some
heifer in the great herd. "Close, Nymphs, Nymphs
of Dicte, close ye now the forest glades, if so, per-
chance, the bull's truant footsteps may meet my
eyes; it may be that, tempted by a green meadow

45

VIRGIL

aut herba captum viridi aut armenta secutum
perducant aliquae stabula ad Gortynia vaccae."   60
tum canit Hesperidum miratam mala puellam ;
tum Phaethontiadas musco circumdat amarae
corticis atque solo proceras erigit alnos.
tum canit, errantem Permessi ad flumina Gallum
Aonas in montis ut duxerit una sororum,   65
utque viro Phoebi chorus adsurrexerit omnis ;
ut Linus haec illi divino carmine pastor,
floribus atque apio crinis ornatus amaro,
dixerit: "hos tibi dant calamos, en accipe, Musae,
Ascraeo quos ante seni, quibus ille solebat   70
cantando rigidas deducere montibus ornos.
his tibi Grynei nemoris dicatur origo,
ne quis sit lucus, quo se plus iactet Apollo."

Quid loquar, aut Scyllam Nisi, quam fama secuta est
candida succinctam latrantibus inguina monstris   75
Dulichias vexasse rates et gurgite in alto
a ! timidos nautas canibus lacerasse marinis ;
aut ut mutatos Terei narraverit artus,
quas illi Philomela dapes, quae dona pararit,
quo cursu deserta petiverit et quibus ante   80
infelix sua tecta super volitaverit alis ?
omnia quae Phoebo quondam meditante beatus
audiit Eurotas iussitque ediscere laurus,
ille canit (pulsae referunt ad sidera valles),
cogere donec ovis stabulis numerumque referre   85
iussit et invito processit Vesper Olympo.

    ⁶¹ capit *M*¹.   **⁷⁴** ut *R.*   **⁸⁵** referri *M²P²γ.*

46

or following the herd, he will be led home by some
cows to our Cretan stalls."

⁶¹ Then he sings of the maid who marvelled at the
apples of the Hesperides; then he encircles Phaë-
thon's sisters in moss of bitter bark, and raises them
from the ground as lofty alders. Then he sings of
Gallus, wandering by the streams of Permessus—how
one of the sisterhood led him to the Aonian hills, and
how all the choir of Phoebus rose to do him honour;
how Linus, a shepherd of immortal song, his locks
crowned with flowers and bitter parsley, cried to him
thus: "These reeds—see, take them—the Muses give
thee—even those they once gave the old Ascraean,[1]
wherewith, as he sang, he would draw the unyielding
ash-trees down the mountain-sides. With these do
thou tell of the birth of the Grynean wood, that there
may be no grove wherein Apollo glories more."

⁷⁴ Why tell how he sang of Scylla, daughter of
Nisus, of whom is still told the story that, with howling
monsters girt about her white waist, she harried the
Ithacan barques, and in the swirling depths, alas!
tore asunder the trembling sailors with her sea-dogs?
Or how he told of Tereus' changed form, what
feast, what gifts Philomela made ready for him, on
what wise she sped to the desert, and with what
wings, luckless one! she first[2] hovered above her
home?

⁸² All the songs that of old Phoebus rehearsed,
while happy Eurotas listened and bade his laurels learn
by heart—these Silenus sings. The re-echoing valleys
fling them again to the stars, till Vesper gave the
word to fold the flocks and tell their tale, as he set
forth over an unwilling sky.

---

[1] *i.e.* Hesiod, poet of the *Works and Days*, born at Ascra, in
Boeotia.
[2] *i.e.* before she sped to the desert.

VIRGIL

VII

Forte sub arguta consederat ilice Daphnis,   MP
compulerantque greges Corydon et Thyrsis in unum,
Thyrsis ovis, Corydon distentas lacte capellas,
ambo florentes aetatibus, Arcades ambo,
et cantare pares et respondere parati.   5
huc mihi, dum teneras defendo a frigore myrtos,
vir gregis ipse caper deerraverat, atque ego Daphnim
aspicio.   ille ubi me contra videt, "ocius" inquit
"huc ades, o Meliboee: caper tibi salvus et haedi:
et si quid cessare potes, requiesce sub umbra.   10
huc ipsi potum venient per prata iuvenci,
hic viridis tenera praetexit harundine ripas   MPV
Mincius, eque sacra resonant examina quercu."
quid facerem? neque ego Alcippen nec Phyllida
     habebam,
depulsos a lacte domi quae clauderet agnos;   15
et certamen erat, Corydon cum Thyrside magnum.
posthabui tamen illorum mea seria ludo.
alternis igitur contendere versibus ambo
coepere, alternos Musae meminisse volebant.
hos Corydon, illos referebat in ordine Thyrsis.   20

CORYDON

Nymphae, noster amor, Libethrides, aut mihi carmen,
quale meo Codro, concedite (proxima Phoebi
versibus ille facit); aut, si non possumus omne
hic arguta sacra pendebit fistula pinu.

⁶ hic *P*.
¹⁹ volebam *known to Servius*.
²³ possimus *M¹P¹γ¹*.   *So Sabb*.

ECLOGUE VII

VII[1]

MELIBOEUS

DAPHNIS, it chanced, had made his seat beneath a whispering ilex, while Corydon and Thyrsis had driven their flocks together — Thyrsis his sheep, Corydon his goats swollen with milk—both in the bloom of life, Arcadians both, ready in a match to sing, as well as to make reply. To this place, while I sheltered my tender myrtles from the cold, my he-goat, the lord of the flock himself, had strayed ; and lo ! I catch sight of Daphnis. As he in turn saw me, "Quick," he cries, "come hither, Meliboeus ; your goat and kids are safe, and if you can idle awhile, pray rest beneath the shade. Hither your steers will of themselves come over the meadows to drink ; here Mincius fringes his green banks with waving reeds, and from the hallowed oak swarm humming bees."

[14] What could I do ? I had no Alcippe or Phyllis to pen my new-weaned lambs at home ; and the match—Corydon against Thyrsis—was a mighty one. Still, I counted their sport above my work. So in alternate verses the pair began to compete ; alternate verses the Muses were fain to recall.[2] These Corydon, those Thyrsis repeated in turn.

CORYDON

Ye Nymphs of Libethra, my delight, either grant me such a strain as ye gave my Codrus—the lays he makes come nearest to Apollo's—or, if such power is not for us all, here on the hallowed pine shall hang my tuneful pipe.

[1] This is a purely pastoral, amoebaean poem, imitative of Theocritus.

[2] The Muses are the daughters of Mnemosyne, "Memory."

VIRGIL

Pastores, hedera nascentem ornate poetam, 25
Arcades, invidia rumpantur ut ilia Codro ;
aut, si ultra placitum laudarit, baccare frontem
cingite, ne vati noceat mala lingua futuro.

CORYDON

Saetosi caput hoc apri tibi, Delia, parvus
et ramosa Micon vivacis cornua cervi. 30
si proprium hoc fuerit, levi de marmore tota
puniceo stabis suras evincta coturno.

THYRSIS

Sinum lactis et haec te liba, Priape, quotannis
exspectare sat est : custos es pauperis horti.
nunc te marmoreum pro tempore fecimus ; at tu, 35
si fetura gregem suppleverit, aureus esto.

CORYDON

Nerine Galatea, thymo mihi dulcior Hyblae,
candidior cycnis, hedera formosior alba, MP
cum primum pasti repetent praesepia tauri,
si qua tui Corydonis habet te cura, venito. 40

THYRSIS

Immo ego Sardoniis videar tibi amarior herbis,
horridior rusco, proiecta vilior alga,
si mihi non haec lux toto iam longior anno est.
ite domum pasti, si quis pudor, ite iuvenci.

---

²⁵ nascente *M*¹ : nascentem *Servius :* crescentem *PM²γ,*
Servius (*at* IV. 19) : -ntem *V.*

---

¹ It was thought that an evil tongue could, by extravagant
50

ECLOGUE VII

Shepherds of Arcady, crown with ivy your rising bard, that Codrus' sides may burst with envy; or, should he praise me unduly, wreathe my brow with foxglove, lest his evil tongue harm the bard that is to be.[1]

CORYDON

To thee, Delia, young Micon offers this head of a bristling boar and the branching antlers of a long-lived stag. If this fortune still abides, thou shalt stand full length in polished marble, thy ankles bound high with purple buskins.

THYRSIS

A bowl of milk, Priapus, and these cakes, are all thou canst expect year by year; the garden thou watchest is poor. Now we have made thee of marble for the time; but if births make full the flock, then be thou of gold.

CORYDON

Galatea, child of Nereus, sweeter to me than Hybla's thyme, whiter than swans, lovelier than pale ivy, soon as the bulls come back from pasture to the stalls, if thou hast any love for thy Corydon, come hither!

THYRSIS

Nay, let me seem to thee more bitter than Sardinian herbs, more rough than gorse, more worthless than upcast seaweed, if even now I find not this day longer than a whole year. Go home, my well-fed steers, if ye have any shame, go home!

praise, provoke the jealousy of the gods. Foxglove was a charm against such bewitchment.

51

VIRGIL

CORYDON

Muscosi fontes et somno mollior herba,   **45**
et quae vos rara viridis tegit arbutus umbra,
solstitium pecori defendite: iam venit aestas
torrida, iam laeto turgent in palmite gemmae.

THYRSIS

Hic focus et taedae pingues, hic plurimus ignis
semper et adsidua postes fuligine nigri: **50**
hic tantum Boreae curamus frigora, quantum
aut numerum lupus aut torrentia flumina ripas.

CORYDON

Stant et iuniperi et castaneae hirsutae,
strata iacent passim sua quaeque sub arbore poma,
omnia nunc rident: at si formosus Alexis   **55**
montibus his abeat, videas et flumina sicca.

THYRSIS

Aret ager, vitio moriens sitit aëris herba,
Liber pampineas invidit collibus umbras:
Phyllidis adventu nostrae nemus omne virebit,
Iuppiter et laeto descendet plurimus imbri.   **60**

CORYDON

Populus Alcidae gratissima, vitis Iaccho,
formosae myrtus Veneri, sua laurea Phoebo:
Phyllis amat corylos; illas dum Phyllis amabit,
nec myrtus vincet corylos nec laurea Phoebi.

[48] lento *PM*² ; *cf.* III. 38.   [54] quaque *bc*².   [56] aberit *P*.

52

ECLOGUE VII

CORYDON

Ye mossy springs, and grass softer than sleep, and the green arbutus that shields you with its scant shade, ward the noontide heat from my flock. Now comes the summer's parching, now the buds swell on the gladsome tendril.

THYRSIS

Here we have a hearth and pitchy brands; here, a good fire ever blazing and door-posts black with never-failing soot. Here we reck as much of the chill blasts of Boreas as the wolf of the number of sheep, or rushing torrents of their banks.

CORYDON

Here stand junipers and shaggy chestnuts; strewn about under the trees lie their own divers fruits; now all nature smiles; but if fair Alexis should quit these hills you would see the very rivers dry.

THYRSIS

The field is parched; the grass is athirst, dying in the tainted air; Bacchus has grudged the hills the shade of his vines: but at the coming of my Phyllis all the woodland will be green, and Jupiter, in his fullness, shall descend in gladsome showers.

CORYDON

The poplar is most dear to Alcides, the vine to Bacchus, the myrtle to lovely Venus, and his own laurel to Phoebus. Phyllis loves hazels, and while Phyllis loves them, neither the myrtle nor laurel of Phoebus shall outvie the hazels.

VIRGIL

THYRSIS

Fraxinus in silvis pulcherrima, pinus in hortis, 65
populus in fluviis, abies in montibus altis :
saep us at si me, Lycida formose, revisas,
fraxinus in silvis cedat tibi, pinus in hortis.

MELIBOEUS

Ha c memini, et victum frustra contendere Thyrsim.
ex illo Corydon Corydon est tempore nobis. 70

VIII

Pastorum Musam Damonis et Alphesiboei, MP
immemor herbarum quos est mirata iuvenca
certantis, quorum stupefactae carmine lynces,
et mutata suos requierunt flumina cursus,
Damonis Musam dicemus et Alphesiboei. 5
    Tu mihi, seu magni superas iam saxa Timavi,
sive oram Illyrici legis aequoris,—en erit umquam
ille dies, mihi cum liceat tua dicere facta ?
en erit, ut liceat totum mihi ferre per orbem
sola Sophocleo tua carmina digna coturno ? 10
a te principium, tibi desinam.   accipe iussis
carmina coepta tuis atque hanc sine tempora circum
inter victrices hederam tibi serpere laurus.

   ⁶⁸ cedet *Pγ*.
   ¹¹ desinet *Mγ²*, *Berne Scholia*: desinit *b*.

---

  ¹ Others take it thus : " Corydon is Corydon to us." *i.e.*
Corydon, in our judgment, is the best of poets.
  ² This is an amoebaean poem, in which one shepherd sings
of the despair of a jilted lover, and the other of the charms

54

ECLOGUE VIII

THYRSIS

Fairest is the ash in the woods, the pine in the gardens, the poplar by rivers, the fir on mountain-tops ; but, if thou, lovely Lycidas, shouldst often visit me, the ash in the woods and the pine in the gardens would yield to thee.

MELIBOEUS

This I remember, and how Thyrsis, vanquished, strove in vain. From that day it is Corydon, Corydon with us.[1]

VIII[2]

THE pastoral Muse of Damon and Alphesiboeus, at whose rivalry the heifer marvelled and forgot to graze, at whose song lynxes stood spell-bound, and rivers were changed and stayed their course—the Muse of Damon and Alphesiboeus I will sing.

[6] But thou, my friend,[3] whether even now thou art passing the crags of great Timavus, or skirting the coast of the Illyrian main—O will that day ever come when I shall be free to tell thy deeds ? O shall I ever be free to spread through all the world those songs of thine, alone worthy of the buskin of Sophocles ? From thee is my beginning ; in thy honour shall I end. Accept the songs essayed at thy bidding, and grant that about thy brows this ivy may creep among the victor's laurels.

used by a deserted maiden to bring back her fickle Daphnis. The latter song is copied from the second Idyll of Theocritus.

[3] This Eclogue is dedicated to Pollio, now returning from his successful campaign against the Parthini in Illyricum. The date is 39 B.C.

VIRGIL

Frigida vix caelo noctis decesserat umbra,
cum ros in tenera pecori gratissimus herba,   15
incumbens tereti Damon sic coepit olivae.

DAMON

" Nascere, praeque diem veniens age, Lucifer,
   almum,
coniugis indigno Nysae deceptus amore
dum queror et divos, quamquam nil testibus illis MPV
profeci, extrema moriens tamen adloquor hora.   20

   incipe Maenalios mecum, mea tibia, versus.

Maenalus argutumque nemus pinosque loquentis
semper habet, semper pastorum ille audit amores
Panaque, qui primus calamos non passus inertis.

   incipe Maenalios mecum, mea tibia, versus.   25

Mopso Nysa datur : quid non speremus amantes ?
iungentur iam grypes equis, aevoque sequenti
cum canibus timidi venient ad pocula dammae.

   incipe Maenalios mecum, mea tibia, versus.   28ᵃ

Mopse, novas incide faces : tibi ducitur uxor ;
sparge, marite, nuces : tibi deserit Hesperus Oetam.

   incipe Maenalios mecum, mea tibia, versus.   31

o digno coniuncta viro, dum despicis omnis
dumque tibi est odio mea fistula, dumque capellae
hirsutumque supercilium promissaque barba
nec curare deum credis mortalia quemquam.   35

   incipe Maenalios mecum, mea tibia, versus.

---

²⁰ adloquar M^1P^2V.   ²⁴ primum M.
²⁸ timidae M: timide P^1: timidi $P^2V\gamma$, *Servius, Bern-Scholia.* ²⁸ᵃ *This verse is given only by* γ. ²⁴ demissaque *'*

56

ECLOGUE VIII

Scarce had night's cool shade left the sky, what time the dew on the tender grass is sweetest to the flock, when, leaning on his shapely olive-staff, Damon thus began :

DAMON

" Rise, O morning star, heralding genial day, while I, cheated in the love which my promised Nysa spurned, make lament, and, though their witnessing has availed me naught, yet, as I die, I call on the gods in this my latest hour.

Begin with me, my flute, a song of Maenalus !

Maenalus hath ever tuneful groves and speaking pines ; ever does he listen to shepherds' loves and to Pan, who first awoke the idle reeds.

Begin with me, my flute, a song of Maenalus !

To Mopsus is Nysa given ! For what may we lovers not look ? Griffins now shall mate with mares, and, in the age to come, the timid deer shall come with hounds to drink.

Begin with me, my flute, a song of Maenalus !

Mopsus, cut new torches ! For thee they bring the bride ! Scatter, bridegroom, the nuts ! For thee the Evening-star quits Oeta !

Begin with me, my flute, a song of Maenalus !

O wedded to a worthy lord ! even while thou scornest all men, and while thou hatest my pipe and my goats, my shaggy eyebrows and unkempt beard, and thinkest that no god recks aught of the deeds of men !

Begin with me, my flute, a song of Maenalus !

saepibus in nostris parvam te roscida mala
(dux ego vester eram) vidi cum matre legentem.
alter ab undecimo tum me iam acceperat annus,
iam fragilis poteram ab terra contingere ramos.   40
ut vidi, ut perii ! ut me malus abstulit error !

   incipe Maenalios mecum, mea tibia, versus.

nunc scio, quid sit Amor.   duris in cotibus illum
aut Tmaros aut Rhodope aut extremi Garamantes
nec generis nostri puerum nec sanguinis edunt.   MF

   incipe Maenalios mecum, mea tibia, versus.   46

saevus Amor docuit natorum sanguine matrem
commaculare manus : crudelis tu quoque, mater.
crudelis mater magis, an puer improbus ille ?
improbus ille puer : crudelis tu quoque, mater.   50

   incipe Maenalios mecum, mea tibia, versus.

nunc et ovis ultro fugiat lupus, aurea durae
mala ferant quercus, narcisso floreat alnus,
pinguia corticibus sudent electra myricae,
certent et cycnis ululae, sit Tityrus Orpheus,   55
Orpheus in silvis, inter delphinas Arion.

   incipe Maenalios mecum, mea tibia, versus.

omnia vel medium fiat mare.   vivite silvae;
praeceps aërii specula de montis in undas
deferar ; extremum hoc munus morientis habeto.   60

   desine Maenalios, iam desine, tibia, versus.''

     [43] duris] nudis P^1.   *So Sabb.*
     [54] fiant γab^2c.

ECLOGUE VIII

Within our garden-close I saw thee—I was guide for both—a little child, along with my mother, plucking dewy apples. My eleventh year finished, the next had just greeted me ; from the ground I could now reach the frail boughs. As I saw, how was I lost! How a fatal frenzy swept me away !

Begin with me, my flute, a song of Maenalus !

Now know I what Love is; on flinty crags Tmarus bare him—or Rhodope, or the farthest Garamantes, a child not of our race or blood !

Begin with me, my flute, a song of Maenalus !

Ruthless Love taught a mother[1] to stain her hands in her children's blood ; cruel, too, wast thou, O mother. Was the mother more cruel, or that boy more heartless ?   Heartless was he ; cruel, too, wast thou, O mother !

Begin with me, my flute, a song of Maenalus !

Now let the wolf even flee before the sheep, let rugged oaks bear golden apples, let the alder bloom with narcissus, let tamarisks distil rich amber from their bark, let owls, too, vie with swans, let Tityrus be an Orpheus—an Orpheus in the woods, an Arion among the dolphins !

Begin with me, my flute, a son of Maenalus !

Nay, let all become mid-ocean !   Farewell, ye woods !   Headlong from some towering mountain-crag I will plunge into the waves ; this take thou as my last dying gift !

> *Cease, my flute, now cease the song of Maenalus !"*

[1] *i.e.* Medea.

VIRGIL

Haec Damon : vos, quae responderit Alphesiboeus,
dicite, Pierides ; non omnia possumus omnes.

ALPHESIBOEUS

" Effer aquam et molli cinge haec altaria vitta
verbenasque adole pinguis et mascula tura,   65
coniugis ut magicis sanos avertere sacris
experiar sensus ; nihil hic nisi carmina desunt.

    ducite ab urbe domum, mea carmina, ducite
       Daphnim.

carmina vel caelo possunt deducere lunam,
carminibus Circe socios mutavit Ulixi,   70
frigidus in pratis cantando rumpitur anguis.

    ducite ab urbe domum, mea carmina, ducite
       Daphnim.

terna tibi haec primum triplici diversa colore
licia circumdo, terque haec altaria circum
effigiem duco ; numero deus impare gaudet.   75

    ducite ab urbe domum, mea carmina, ducite
       Daphnim.

necte tribus nodis ternos, Amarylli, colores ;
necte, Amarylli, modo et ' Veneris ' dic ' vincula
       necto.'

    ducite ab urbe domum, mea carmina, ducite
       Daphnim.

limus ut hic durescit et haec ut cera liquescit   80
uno eodemque igni, sic nostro Daphnis amore.
sparge molam et fragilis incende bitumine laurus,

60   **82** lauros *Py.*

ECLOGUE VIII

Thus Damon.   Tell ye, Pierian maids, the answer of Alphesiboeus.   Not all things can we all do.

ALPHESIBOEUS

" Bring out water, and wreathe these shrines with soft wool; and burn rich herbs and male frankincense, that I may try with magic rites to turn to fire my lover's coldness of mood.   Naught is lacking here save songs.

Bring Daphnis home from town, bring him, my songs!

Songs can even draw the moon down from heaven; by songs Circe changed the comrades of Ulysses; with song the cold snake in the meadows is burst asunder.

Bring Daphnis home from town, bring him, my songs!

Three threads here I first tie round thee, marked with three different hues, and three times round these shrines I draw thy image.   In an uneven number heaven delights.

Bring Daphnis home from town, bring him, my songs!

Weave, Amaryllis, three hues in three knots; weave them, Amaryllis, I beg, and say, ' Chains of love I weave!'

Bring Daphnis home from town, bring him, my songs!

As this clay hardens, and as this wax melts in one and the same flame, so may Daphnis melt with love for me!   Sprinkle meal, and kindle the crackling

61

VIRGIL

Daphnis me malus urit, ego hanc in Daphnide
    laurum.

    ducite ab urbe domum, mea carmina, ducite
    Daphnim.

talis amor Daphnim, qualis cum fessa iuvencum   85
per nemora atque altos quaerendo bucula lucos
propter aquae rivum viridi procumbit in ulva,
perdita, nec serae meminit decedere nocti,
talis amor teneat, nec sit mihi cura mederi.

    ducite ab urbe domum, mea carmina, ducite
    Daphnim   90

has olim exuvias mihi perfidus ille reliquit,
pignora cara sui : quae nunc ego limine in ipso,
terra, tibi mando ; debent haec pignora Daphnim.

    ducite ab urbe domum, mea carmina, ducite
    Daphnim.

has herbas atque haec Ponto mihi lecta venena   95
ipse dedit Moeris (nascuntur plurima Ponto),
his ego saepe lupum fieri et se condere silvis
Moerim, saepe animas imis excire sepulchris
atque satas alio vidi traducere messis.

    ducite ab urbe domum, mea carmina, ducite
    Daphnim.   100

fer cineres, Amarylli, foras rivoque fluenti
transque caput iace, nec respexeris. his ego
    Daphnim
adgrediar ; nihil ille deos, nil carmina curat.

    ducite ab urbe domum, mea carmina, ducite
    Daphnim.

[87] concumbit <i>P</i>[1]γ[1].

bays with pitch. Me cruel Daphnis burns; for
Daphnis burn I this laurel.

> *Bring Daphnis home from town, bring him, my
> songs!*

May such longing seize Daphnis as when a heifer,
jaded with the search for her mate amid woods and
deep groves, sinks down by a water-brook in the
green sedge, all forlorn, nor thinks to withdraw
before night's late hour—may such longing seize
him, and may I care not to heal it!

> *Bring Daphnis home from town, bring him, my
> songs!*

These relics that traitor once left me, dear pledges
for himself. Now, on my very threshold, I commit
them, O Earth, to thee. These pledges make
Daphnis my due.

> *Bring Daphnis home from town, bring him, my
> songs!*

These herbs and these poisons, culled in Pontus,
Moeris himself gave me—they grow plenteously in
Pontus. By their aid I have oft seen Moeris turn
wolf and hide in the woods, oft call spirits from the
depth of the grave, and charm sown corn away to
other fields.

> *Bring Daphnis home from town, bring him, my
> songs!*

Carry forth the embers, Amaryllis, and toss them over
your head into a running brook; and look not back.
With these I will assail Daphnis; he recks naught
of gods or songs.

> *Bring Daphnis home from town, bring him, my
> songs!*

63

aspice, corripuit tremulis altaria flammis   105
sponte sua, dum ferre moror, cinis ipse.   bonum s;t!
nescio quid certe est, et Hylax in limine latrat.
credimus? an qui amant, ipsi sibi somnia fingunt?

   parcite, ab urbe venit, iam parcite carmina,
     Daphnis."

IX

LYCIDAS

Quo te, Moeri, pedes? an, quo via ducit, in urbem? MP

MOERIS

O Lycida, vivi pervenimus, advena nostri
(quod numquam veriti sumus) ut possessor agelli
diceret: "haec mea sunt; veteres migrate coloni."
nunc victi, tristes, quoniam fors omnia versat,   5
hos illi (quod nec vertat bene) mittimus haedos.

LYCIDAS

Certe equidem audieram, qua se subducere colles
incipiunt mollique iugum demittere clivo,
usque ad aquam et veteres, iam fracta cacumina,
   fagos
omnia carminibus vestrum servasse Menalcan.   10

---

[107] Hylas *MSS.*
[109] carmina parcite *M.*
[9] vetoris *Pγ, Berne Scholia:* fagi *Pγ.*

Look! the ash itself, while I delay to carry it forth,
has of its own accord caught the shrines with quiver-
ing flames. Be the omen good! 'Tis something surely,
and Hylax is barking at the gate. Can I trust my
eyes? Or do lovers fashion their own dreams?

> Cease! Daphnis comes home from town;
> cease now, my songs!"

IX[1]

LYCIDAS

WHITHER afoot, Moeris? Is it, as the path leads, to
town?

MOERIS

O Lycidas, we have lived to see the day—an evil
never dreamed—when a stranger, holder of our little
farm, could say: "This is mine; begone, ye old
tenants!" Now, beaten and cowed, since chance
rules all, we send him these kids—our curse go with
them!

LYCIDAS

Yet surely I had heard that, from where the hills
begin to rise, then sink their ridge in a gentle slope,
down to the water and the old beeches with their
now shattered tops, your Menalcas had with his songs
saved all.

[1] The ninth Eclogue is purely personal, and has to do with
the same subject as the first. Perhaps it is a poetical appeal
to Varus for assistance. Under the person of Menalcas Virgil
himself is concealed. Moeris is the poet's *vilicus* or bailiff.

VIRGIL

MOERIS

Audieras, et fama fuit; sed carmina tantum
nostra valent, Lycida, tela inter Martia, quantum
Chaonias dicunt aquila veniente columbas.
quod nisi me quacumque novas incidere lites
ante sinistra cava monuisset ab ilice cornix,   15
nec tuus hic Moeris, nec viveret ipse Menalcas.

LYCIDAS

Heu, cadit in quemquam tantum scelus? heu, tua
    nobis
paene simul tecum solacia rapta, Menalca?
quis caneret Nymphas? quis humum florentibus
    herbis
spargeret aut viridi fontis induceret umbra?·   20
vel quae sublegi tacitus tibi carmina nuper,
cum te ad delicias ferres, Amaryllida, nostras?
" Tityre, dum redeo (brevis est via) pasce capellas,
et potum pastas age, Tityre, et inter agendum
occursare capro (cornu ferit ille) caveto."   25

MOERIS

Immo haec, quae Varo necdum perfecta canebat:
" Vare, tuum nomen, superet modo Mantua nobis,
Mantua vae miserae nimium vicina Cremonae,
cantantes sublime ferent ad sidera cycni."

LYCIDAS

Sic tua Cyrneas fugiant examina taxos,   30
sic cytiso pastae distendant ubera vaccae:
incipe, si quid habes. et me fecere poetam
Pierides, sunt et mihi carmina, me quoque dicunt

---

¹⁷ cadet *P*.   ²⁹ ferant *P²γ*.
³⁰ Cyrneas *M¹*: cry- *M (late)*: Grynaeas *P, Berne Scholia.*

ECLOGUE IX

You had heard, and so the story ran. But amid the weapons of war, Lycidas, our songs avail as much as, they say, the doves of Chaonia when the eagle comes. So, had not a raven on the left first warned me from the hollow oak to cut short, as best I might, this new dispute, neither your Moeris here nor Menalcas himself would be alive.

Alas! can any man be guilty of such a crime? Alas! was the solace of thy songs, Menalcas, almost torn from us, along with thyself? Who would sing the Nymphs? Who would strew the turf with flowery herbage, or curtain the springs with green shade? Or those songs I slyly caught from thee the other day, when thou wert faring to our darling Amaryllis? "Tityrus, till I return—the way is short—feed my goats; and when fed, drive them, Tityrus, to water, and in driving, have a care not to get in the he-goat's way—he butts with his horn."

Nay, these lines, not yet finished, which he sang to Varus: "Varus, thy name, let but Mantua be spared us—Mantua, alas! too near ill-fated Cremona —singing swans shall bear aloft to the stars."

As you would have your swarms shun the yews of Corsica, and your heifers browse on clover and swell their udders, begin, if you have aught to sing. Me, too, the Pierian maids have made a poet; I, too, have songs; me also the shepherds call a bard, but I

67

vatem pastores ; sed non ego credulus illis.
nam neque adhuc Vario videor nec dicere Cinna   35
digna, sed argutos inter strepere anser olores.

MOERIS

Id quidem ago et tacitus, Lycida, mecum ipse voluto,
si valeam meminisse ; neque est ignobile carmen.
" huc ades, o Galatea ; quis est nam ludus in undis ?
hic ver purpureum, varios hic flumina circum   40
fundit humus flores, hic candida populus antro
imminet et lentae texunt umbracula vites :
huc ades ; insani feriant sine litora fluctus."

LYCIDAS

Quid, quae te pura solum sub nocte canentem
audieram ? numeros memini, si verba tenerem.   45
" Daphni, quid antiquos signorum suspicis ortus ?
ecce Dionaei processit Caesaris astrum,
astrum, quo segetes gauderent frugibus et quo
duceret apricis in collibus uva colorem.   49
insere, Daphni, piros ; carpent tua poma nepotes."

MOERIS

Omnia fert aetas, animum quoque ; saepe ego longos
cantando puerum memini me condere soles :
nunc oblita mihi tot carmina : vox quoque Moerim
iam fugit ipsa ; lupi Moerim videre priores.
sed tamen ista satis referet tibi saepe Menalcas.   55

---

[35] Varo *MP, Berne Scholia, known to Servius.*
[46-50] *assigned to* Moeris *by MSS., except* Mγ. *So Sabb.*

trust them not. For as yet, methinks, I sing nothing worthy of a Varius or a Cinna, but cackle as a goose among melodious swans.

MOERIS

That's what I am about, Lycidas, silently turning it over in my mind, in case I can recall it. And no mean song it is.

[39] "Come to me, Galatea! What sport can there be in the waves? Here is rosy spring; here, by the streams, Earth scatters her varied flowers; here the white poplar bends over the cave, and the clinging vines weave shady bowers. Come to me; let the wild waves lash the shore."

LYCIDAS

What of the lines I heard you singing alone beneath the cloudless night? The measure I remember, could I but keep the words.

[46] "Daphnis, why art thou gazing at the old constellations rising? See! the star[1] of Caesar, seed of Dione, has gone forth—the star to make the fields glad with corn, and the grape deepen its hue on the sunny hills. Graft thy pears, Daphnis; thy children's children shall gather fruits of thine."

MOERIS

Time robs us of all, even of memory; oft as a boy I recall that with song I would lay the long summer days to rest. Now I have forgotten all my songs. Even voice itself now fails Moeris; wolves have seen Moeris first. Still Menalcas will repeat you your songs, often as you will.

[1] This is Horace's *Iulium sidus* (*Carm.* I. XII. 47), the comet which appeared just after the death of Julius Caesar, and was commonly supposed to be Caesar's deified soul.

VIRGIL

Causando nostros in longum ducis amores.
et nunc omne tibi stratum silet aequor, et omnes,
aspice, ventosi ceciderunt murmuris aurae.
hinc adeo media est nobis via; namque sepulchrum
incipit apparere Bianoris: hic, ubi densas   60
agricolae stringunt frondes, hic, Moeri, canamus;
hic haedos depone, tamen veniemus in urbem.
aut si, nox pluviam ne colligat ante, veremur,
cantantes licet usque (minus via laedit) eamus;
cantantes ut eamus, ego hoc te fasce levabo.   65

MOERIS

Desine plura, puer, et quod nunc instat agamus;
carmina tum melius, cum venerit ipse, canemus.

X

Extremum hunc, Arethusa, mihi concede laborem: MP
pauca meo Gallo, sed quae legat ipsa Lycoris,
carmina sunt dicenda: neget quis carmina Gallo?
sic tibi, cum fluctus subterlabere Sicanos,
Doris amara suam non intermisceat undam,   5
incipe; sollicitos Galli dicamus amores,
dum tenera attondent simae virgulta capellae.
non canimus surdis, respondent omnia silvae.

---

⁵⁹ hic *P*.   ¹ laborum *P*¹.

70

ECLOGUE X

LYCIDAS

By your pleas you put off my longing. Now the whole sea-plain lies still and silent, and lo! every breath of the murmuring breeze is dead. Just from here lies half our journey, for Bianor's tomb is coming into view. Here, where husbandmen are lopping the thick leaves—here, Moeris, let us sing. Here put down the kids—we shall reach the town all the same. Or if we fear that night may first bring on rain, we may yet go singing on our way—it makes the road less irksome. That we may go singing on our way, I will relieve you of this burden.

MOERIS

Say no more, lad; let us to the task in hand. Our songs we shall sing the better, when the master himself is come.

X [1]

My last task this—vouchsafe me it, Arethusa [2]! A few verses I must sing for my Gallus, yet such as Lycoris herself may read! Who would refuse verses to Gallus? If, when thou glidest beneath Sicilian waves, thou wouldst not have briny Doris blend her stream with thine, begin! Let us tell of Gallus' anxious loves, while the blunt-nosed goats crop the tender brakes. We sing to no deaf ears; the woods echo every note.

[1] In this tenth Eclogue the poet sings the love of his friend C. Cornelius Gallus for a mistress who had deserted him. The scene is laid in Arcadia.
[2] Invoked as a Sicilian Muse and inspirer of Theocritus.

71

VIRGIL

Quae nemora aut qui vos saltus habuere, puellae
Naïdes, indigno cum Gallus amore peribat?   MPR
nam neque Parnasi vobis iuga, nam neque Pindi   11
ulla moram fecere, neque Aonie Aganippe.
illum etiam lauri, etiam flevere myricae,
pinifer illum etiam sola sub rupe iacentem
Maenalus, et gelidi fleverunt saxa Lycaei.   15
stant et oves circum (nostri nec paenitet illas,
nec te paeniteat pecoris, divine poeta:
et formosus ovis ad flumina pavit Adonis);
venit et upilio, tardi venere subulci,
uvidus hiberna venit de glande Menalcas.   20
omnes "unde amor iste" rogant "tibi?" venit Apollo:
"Galle, quid insanis?" inquit. "tua cura Lycoris
perque nives alium perque horrida castra secuta est."
venit et agresti capitis Silvanus honore,
florentis ferulas et grandia lilia quassans.   25
Pan deus Arcadiae venit, quem vidimus ipsi
sanguineis ebuli bacis minioque rubentem:
"ecquis erit modus?" inquit. "Amor non talia curat:
nec lacrimis crudelis Amor nec gramina rivis
nec cytiso saturantur apes nec fronde capellae."   30
tristis at ille "tamen cantabitis, Arcades" inquit,
"montibus haec vestris, soli cantare periti
Arcades. o mihi tum quam molliter ossa quiescant,
vestra meos olim si fistula dicat amores
atque utinam ex vobis unus vestrique fuissem   35
aut custos gregis aut maturae vinitor uvae.
certe sive mihi Phyllis sive esset Amyntas
seu quicumque furor (quid tum, si fuscus Amyntas?
et nigrae violae sunt et vaccinia nigra),

10 periret $M^1\gamma^2$.   12 Aoniae $MR\gamma$: Aoinie P.
19 opilio *Berne Scholia*.   20 umidus R.
23 castra] saxa P^1.   26 et quis P^1R.
29 ripis M^1.   32 nostris P^1.

ECLOGUE X

[9] What groves, what glades were your abode, ye virgin Naiads, when Gallus was pining with a love unrequited? For no heights of Parnassus or of Pindus, no Aonian Aganippe made you tarry. For him even the laurels, even the tamarisks wept. For him, as he lay beneath a lonely rock, even pine-crowned Maenalus wept, and the crags of cold Lycaeus. The sheep, too, are standing around—they think no shame of us, and think thou no shame of the flock, heavenly poet; even fair Adonis fed sheep beside the streams.

[19] The shepherd came, too; slowly the swineherds came; Menalcas came, dripping, from the winter's mast.[1] All ask: "Whence this love of thine?" Apollo came. "Gallus," he said, "what madness this? Thy sweetheart Lycoris hath followed another amid snows and amid rugged camps." Silvanus came, with rustic glories on his brow, waving his fennel flowers and tall lilies. Pan came, Arcady's god, and we ourselves saw him, crimsoned with vermilion and blood-red elderberries. "Will there be no end?" he cried. "Love recks naught of this: neither is cruel Love sated with tears, nor the grass with the rills, nor bees with the clover, nor goats with leaves."

[31] But sadly Gallus replied: "Yet ye, O Arcadians, will sing this tale to your mountains; Arcadians only know how to sing. O how softly then would my bones repose, if in other days your pipes should tell my love! And O that I had been one of you, the shepherd of a flock of yours, or the dresser of your ripened grapes! Surely, my darling, whether it were Phyllis or Amyntas, or whoever it were—and what if Amyntas be dark? violets, too, are black and black are hyacinths—my darling would be lying at

---

[1] Acorns, steeped in water, were food for cattle in winter.

mecum inter salices lenta sub vite iaceret;   40
serta mihi Phyliis legeret, cantaret Amyntas.
hic gelidi fontes, hic mollia prata, Lycori,
hic nemus; hic ipso tecum consumerer aevo.
nunc insanus amor duri me Martis in armis
tela inter media atque adversos detinet hostis :   45
tu procul a patria (nec sit mihi credere tantum)
Alpinas a! dura, nives et frigora Rheni
me sine sola vides. a! te ne frigora laedant!
a! tibi ne teneras glacies secet aspera plantas!
ibo et Chalcidico quae sunt mihi condita versu   50
carmina pastoris Siculi modulabor avena.
certum est in silvis, inter spelaea ferarum
malle pati tenerisque meos incidere amores
arboribus : crescent illae, crescetis, amores.
interea mixtis lustrabo Maenala Nymphis,   55
aut acris venabor apros. non me ulla vetabunt
frigora Parthenios canibus circumdare saltus.
iam mihi per rupes videor lucosque sonantis
ire ; libet Partho torquere Cydonia cornu
spicula—tamquam haec sit nostri medicina furoris, 60
aut deus ille malis hominum mitescere discat.
iam neque Hamadryades rursus neque carmina nobis
ipsa placent; ipsae rursus concedite silvae.
non illum nostri possunt mutare labores,
nec si frigoribus mediis Hebrumque bibamus   65
Sithoniasque nives hiemis subeamus aquosae,
nec si, cum moriens alta liber aret in ulmo,
Aethiopum versemus ovis sub sidere Cancri.
omnia vincit Amor: et nos cedamus Amori."

my side among the willows, under the creeping vine—
Phyllis culling me garlands, Amyntas singing songs.
Here are cold springs, Lycoris, here soft meadows,
here woodland; here, with thee, time alone would
wear me away. But now a mad passion for the stern
god of war keeps me in arms, in the midst of weapons
and opposing foes; while thou, far from thy native soil
—O that it were not for me to believe such a tale !—
art gazing, ah, heartless one ! on Alpine snows and
the frost-bound Rhine, apart from me, all alone. Ah,
may the frosts not harm thee ! Ah, may not the
jagged ice cut thy tender feet !

⁵⁰ "I will be gone, and the strains I composed in
Chalcidian verse [1] I will play on a Sicilian shepherd's
pipe. Well I know that in the woods, amid wild beasts'
dens, it is better to suffer and carve my love on the
young trees. They will grow; thou, too, my love,
wilt grow. Meanwhile, with the Nymphs I will roam
o'er Maenalus, or hunt fierce boars. No frosts will
stay me from girdling with my hounds the glades of
Parthenius. Even now, methinks, I pass over rocks
and echoing groves; 'tis a joy to wing Cydonian
shafts from my Parthian bow ! As if this could heal
my frenzy, or as if that god could learn pity for
human sorrows ! Now once more, nor Hamadryads
nor even songs have charms for me; once more
adieu, even ye woods ! No toils of ours can change
that god, not though in the heart of winter we
drink the Hebrus and brave the Thracian snows and
their wintry sleet, not though, when the bark dies
and withers on the lofty elm, we drive to and fro
the Aethiopians' sheep beneath the star of Cancer !
Love conquers all; let us, too, yield to Love !'"

[1] *i.e.* Gallus' imitations of Euphorion of Chalcis.

Haec sat erit, divae, vestrum cecinisse poetam,   70
dum sedet et gracili fiscellam texit hibisco,
Pierides; vos haec facietis maxima Gallo,
Gallo, cuius amor tantum mihi crescit in horas,
quantum vere novo viridis se subicit alnus.
surgamus: solet esse gravis cantantibus umbra,   75
iuniperi gravis umbra, nocent et frugibus umbrae.
ite domum saturae, venit Hesperus, ite capellae.

[74] subducit *R*: subrigit π (*a Prague MS. of ninth century*).

ECLOGUE X

70 These strains, Muses divine, it will be enough for your poet to have sung, while he sits idle and twines a basket of slender hibiscus. These ye shall make of highest worth in Gallus' eyes—Gallus, for whom my love grows hour by hour as fast as in the dawn of spring shoots up the green alder. Let us rise ; the shade oft brings peril to singers. The juniper's shade brings peril ; hurtful to the corn, too, is the shade. Get ye home, my full-fed goats—the Evening-star comes—get ye home !

GEORGICS

GEORGICON

LIBER I

Quid faciat laetas segetes, quo sidere terram   MPR
vertere, Maecenas, ulmisque adiungere vites
conveniat, quae cura boum, qui cultus habendo
sit pecori, apibus quanta experientia parcis,
hinc canere incipiam.   vos, o clarissima mundi   5
lumina, labentem caelo quae ducitis annum,
Liber et alma Ceres, vestro si munere tellus
Chaoniam pingui glandem mutavit arista,
poculaque inventis Acheloia miscuit uvis ;
et vos, agrestum praesentia numina, Fauni,   10
(ferte simul Faunique pedem Dryadesque puellae !)
munera vestra cano.   tuque o, cui prima frementem
fudit equum magno tellus percussa tridenti,
Neptune ; et cultor nemorum, cui pinguia Ceae
ter centum nivei tondent dumeta iuvenci ;   15
ipse, nemus linquens patrium saltusque Lycaei,
Pan, ovium custos, tua si tibi Maenala curae,
adsis, o Tegeaee, favens, oleaeque Minerva

       ⁷ numine *M* (*late*).   ¹³ fundit *P*₍

GEORGICS

BOOK I

WHAT makes the crops joyous, beneath what star,
Maecenas, it is well to turn the soil, and wed vines
to elms, what tending the kine need, what care the
herd in breeding, what skill the thrifty bees—
hence shall I begin my song.[1] O ye most radiant
lights of the firmament, that guide through heaven
the gliding year, O Liber and bounteous Ceres, if by
your grace Earth changed Chaonia's acorn for the
rich corn-ear, and blended draughts of Achelous
with the new-found grapes, and ye, O Fauns the
rustics' ever-present gods (come trip it, Fauns, and
Dryad maids withal!), 'tis of your bounties I sing.
And thou, O Neptune, for whom Earth, smitten by thy
mighty trident, first sent forth the neighing steed;
thou, too, O spirit of the groves,[2] for whom thrice
an hundred snowy steers crop Cea's rich thickets;
thyself, too, O Pan, guardian of the sheep, leaving thy
native woods and glades of Lycaeus, as thou lovest
thine own Maenalus, come of thy grace, O Tegean

[1] The subjects of the four books are here given, viz. tillage,
planting, the rearing of cattle, and the keeping of bees. Then
follows the invocation of the rural powers, beginning with the
sun and moon, and closing with Caesar Augustus, who has yet
to choose his divine sphere.
[2] *i.e.* Aristaeus.

81

inventrix, uncique puer monstrator aratri,
et teneram ab radice ferens, Silvane, cupressum ;   20
dique deaeque omnes, studium quibus arva tueri,
quique novas alitis non ullo semine fruges,
quique satis largum caelo demittitis imbrem ;
tuque adeo, quem mox quae sint habitura deorum
concilia, incertum est, urbisne invisere, Caesar,   25
terrarumque velis curam et te maximus orbis
auctorem frugum tempestatumque potentem
accipiat, cingens materna tempora myrto,
an deus immensi venias maris ac tua nautae
numina sola colant, tibi serviat ultima Thule,   30
teque sibi generum Tethys emat omnibus undis,
anne novum tardis sidus te mensibus addas,
qua locus Erigonen inter Chelasque sequentis
panditur (ipse tibi iam bracchia contrahit ardens
Scorpios et caeli iusta plus parte reliquit) :   35
quidquid eris (nam te nec sperant Tartara regem
nec tibi regnandi veniat tam dira cupido,
quamvis Elysios miretur Graecia campos
nec repetita sequi curet Proserpina matrem),
da facilem cursum, atque audacibus adnue coeptis,   40
ignarosque viae mecum miseratus agrestis   AMPR
ingredere et votis iam nunc adsuesce vocari.

[25] urbesne *M :* urbisne (v. *A. Gellius,* XIII. xxi. 4).
[35] relinquit *P.*
[36] sperent *M²P² γ, Servius.*

lord ! Come thou, O Minerva, inventress of the olive ;
thou, too, O youth,[1] who didst disclose the crooked
plough ; and thou, O Silvanus, with a young uprooted
cypress in thy hand ; and ye, O gods and goddesses all,
whose love guards our fields—both ye who nurse the
young fruits, springing up unsown, and ye who on
the seedlings send down from heaven plenteous rain !

[24] Yea, and thou, O Caesar, whom we know not what
company of the gods shall claim ere long ; whether
thou choose to watch over cities and care for our
lands, that so the mighty world may receive thee
as the giver of increase and lord of the seasons,
wreathing thy brows with thy mother's myrtle ;
whether thou come as god of the boundless sea and
sailors worship thy deity alone, while farthest Thule
owns thy lordship and Tethys with the dower of
all her waves buys thee to wed her daughter ; or
whether thou add thyself as a new star to the
lingering months, where, between the Virgin [2] and the
grasping Claws, a space is opening (lo ! for thee even
now the blazing Scorpion draws in his arms, and has
left more than a due share of the heaven !)—whate'er
thou art to be (for Tartarus hopes not for thee as
king, and may such monstrous lust of empire ne'er
seize thee, albeit Greece is enchanted by the Elysian
fields, and Proserpine reclaimed cares not to follow
her mother), do thou grant me a smooth course, give
assent to my bold emprise, and pitying with me the
rustics who know not their way, enter on thy worship,
and learn even now to hearken to our prayers !

---

[1] *i.e.* Triptolemus, son of Celeus of Eleusis, and favourite of
Demeter.
[2] One of the signs of the Zodiac, called in Greek Erigone.
The " Claws " are the Scorpion. Libra was later introduced
between Scorpios and Virgo.

Vere novo, gelidus canis cum montibus umor
liquitur et Zephyro putris se glaeba resolvit,
depresso incipiat iam tum mihi taurus aratro   45
ingemere, et sulco attritus splendescere vomer.
illa seges demum votis respondet avari
agricolae, bis quae solem, bis frigora sensit ;
illius immensae ruperunt horrea messes.
at prius ignotum ferro quam scindimus aequor,   50
ventos et varium caeli praediscere morem
cura sit ac patrios cultusque habitusque locorum,
et quid quaeque ferat regio et quid quaeque recuset.
hic segetes, illic veniunt felicius uvae,
arborei fetus alibi, atque iniussa virescunt   55
gramina.   nonne vides, croceos ut Tmolus odores,
India mittit ebur, molles sua tura Sabaei,
at Chalybes nudi ferrum, virosaque Pontus
castorea, Eliadum palmas Epiros equarum ?
continuo has leges aeternaque foedera certis   60
imposuit natura locis, quo tempore primum
Deucalion vacuum lapides iactavit in orbem,
unde homines nati, durum genus.   ergo age, terrae
pingue solum primis extemplo a mensibus anni
fortes invertant tauri, glaebasque iacentis   65
pulverulenta coquat maturis solibus aestas ;
at si non fuerit tellus fecunda, sub ipsum
Arcturum tenui sat erit suspendere sulco :
illic, officiant laetis ne frugibus herbae,
hic, sterilem exiguus ne deserat umor harenam.   70
    Alternis idem tonsas cessare novalis
et segnem patiere situ durescere campum ;
aut ibi flava seres mutato sidere farra,

---

⁵⁰ ac *MPR ; so Sabb.* . at γ.   ⁵⁷ mittet *P*¹ : mittat *M*ˣ.
⁶⁰ alterna *P.*   ⁶⁶ frugibus *R.*
⁷³ semine *R.*

[43] In the dawning spring, when icy streams trickle
from snowy mountains, and the crumbling clod breaks
at the Zephyr's touch, even then would I have my
bull groan over the deep-driven plough, and the share
glisten when rubbed by the furrow. That field only
answers the covetous farmer's prayer, which twice
has felt the sun and twice the frost; from it
boundless harvests burst the granaries. Yet ere
our iron cleaves an unknown plain, be it first our
care to learn the winds and the wavering moods of the
sky, the wonted tillage and nature of the ground,
what each clime yields and what each disowns.
Here corn, there grapes spring more luxuriantly;
elsewhere young trees shoot up, and grasses un-
bidden. See you not, how Tmolus sends us saffron
fragrance, India her ivory, the soft Sabaeans their
frankincense; but the naked Chalybes give us iron,
Pontus the strong-smelling beaver's oil, and Epirus
the Olympian victories of her mares? From the
first, Nature laid these laws and eternal covenants
on certain lands, even from the day when Deucalion
threw stones into the empty world, whence sprang
men, a stony race. Come then, and where the earth's
soil is rich, let your stout oxen upturn it straight-
way, in the year's first months, and let the clods
lie for dusty summer to bake with her ripening
suns; but should the land not be fruitful, it will
suffice, on the eve of Arcturus' rising, to raise it lightly
with shallow furrow—in the one case, that weeds
may not choke the gladsome corn; in the other,
that the scant moisture may not desert the barren
sand.

[71] In alternate seasons you will also let your fields
lie fallow after reaping, and the plain idly stiffen
with scurf; or, beneath another star, sow yellow

unde prius laetum siliqua quassante legumen
aut tenuis fetus viciae tristisque lupini   75
sustuleris fragilis calamos silvamque sonantem.
urit enim lini campum seges, urit avenae,
urunt Lethaeo perfusa papavera somno :
sed tamen alternis facilis labor, arida tantum
ne saturare fimo pingui pudeat sola neve   80
effetos cinerem immundum iactare per agros.
sic quoque mutatis requiescunt fetibus arva,
nec nulla interea est inaratae gratia terrae.
saepe etiam steriles incendere profuit agros
atque levem stipulam crepitantibus urere flammis; 85
sive inde occultas vires et pabula terrae
pinguia concipiunt, sive illis omne per ignem
excoquitur vitium atque exsudat inutilis umor,
seu pluris calor ille vias et caeca relaxat
spiramenta, novas veniat qua sucus in herbas,   90
seu durat magis et venas adstringit hiantis,
ne tenues pluviae rapidive potentia solis
acrior aut Boreae penetrabile frigus adurat.

    Multum adeo, rastris glaebas qui frangit inertis
vimineasque trahit crates, iuvat arva, neque illum 95
flava Ceres alto nequiquam spectat Olympo ;
et qui, proscisso quae suscitat aequore terga,
rursus in obliquum verso perrumpit aratro,
exercetque frequens tellurem atque imperat arvis.

    Umida solstitia atque hiemes orate serenas,   100
agricolae : hiberno laetissima pulvere farra,
laetus ager ; nullo tantum se Mysia cultu
iactat et ipsa suas mirantur Gargara messes.

    [82] requiescent *R.*   [102] Moesia *AP².*   [103] miratur *P².*

corn in lands whence you have first carried off the
pulse that rejoices in its quivering pods, or the fruits
of the slender vetch, or the brittle stalks and rattling
tangle of the bitter lupine. For a crop of flax
parches the ground; oats parch it, and poppies,
steeped in Lethe's slumber. Yet by changing crops
the toil is light : only be not ashamed to feed fat the
dried-out soil with rich dung, and to scatter grimy
ashes over the exhausted fields. Thus also, with
change of crop, the land finds rest, and meanwhile
not thankless is the unploughed earth. Often, too,
it has been useful to fire barren fields, and burn the
light stubble in crackling flames; whether it be that
the earth derives thence hidden strength and rich
nutriment, or that in the flame every taint is baked
out and the useless moisture sweats from it, or that
that heat opens fresh paths and loosens hidden
pores, by which the sap may reach the tender
blades, or that it rather hardens the soil and narrows
the gaping veins, that so the searching showers mǎy
not harm, or the blazing sun's fierce tyranny wither
it, or the North-wind's piercing cold.

⁹⁴ Yea, and much service does he do the land who
with the mattock breaks up the sluggish clods, and
drags over it wicker hurdles; nor is it for naught
that golden Ceres views him from high Olympus.[1]
Much service, too, does he who turns his plough and
again breaks crosswise through the ridges which he
raised when first he cut the plain, ever at his post to
discipline the ground, and give his orders to the fields.

¹⁰⁰ For moist summers and sunny winters, pray,
ye farmers! With winter's dust most gladsome is
the corn, gladsome is the field : under no tillage does
Mysia so glory, and then even Gargarus marvels

[1] *i.e.* she rewards him richly.

quid dicam, iacto qui semine comminus arva
insequitur cumulosque ruit male pinguis harenae, 105
deinde satis fluvium inducit rivosque sequentis
et, cum exustus ager morientibus aestuat herbis,
ecce supercilio clivosi tramitis undam
elicit ? illa cadens raucum per levia murmur
saxa ciet scatebrisque arentia temperat arva.   110
quid qui, ne gravidis procumbat culmus aristis,
luxuriem segetum tenera depascit in herba,
cum primum sulcos aequant sata ? quique paludis
collectum umorem bibula deducit harena ?
praesertim incertis si mensibus amnis abundans 115
exit et obducto late tenet omnia limo,
unde cavae tepido sudant umore lacunae.
     Nec tamen, haec cum sint hominumque boumque
          labores
versando terram experti, nihil improbus anser
Strymoniaeque grues et amaris intiba fibris   120
officiunt aut umbra nocet.   pater ipse colendi
haud facilem esse viam voluit, primusque per artem
movit agros, curis acuens mortalia corda,
nec torpere gravi passus sua regna veterno.
ante Iovem nulli subigebant arva coloni ;   125
ne signare quidem aut partiri limite campum
fas erat : in medium quaerebant, ipsaque tellus
omnia liberius, nullo poscente, ferebat.
ille malum virus serpentibus addidit atris,
praedarique lupos iussit pontumque moveri,   130

[106] fluentes *R*.   [114] diducit *A*.

---

[1] *i.e.* no tillage can do so much for Mysia as wet summers,
followed by dry winters.   These produce extraordinary crops
on the rich slopes of Gargarus.
   [2] The water, which runs in a banked-up channel on a

GEORGICS BOOK I

at his own harvests.[1] Need I tell of him who
flings the seed, then, hoe in hand, closes with the
soil, and lays low the hillocks of barren sand? next
brings to his crops the rills of the stream he guides,
and when the scorched land swelters, the green
blades dying, lo! from the brow of the hill-side
channel decoys the water?[2] This, as it falls, wakes
a hoarse murmur amid the smooth stones, and with
its gushing streams slakes the thirsty fields. Need
I tell of him who, lest the stalk droop with heavy ears,
grazes down his luxuriant crop in the young blade,
soon as the growing corn is even with the furrow's
top? or of him who draws off a marsh's gathered
moisture with soaking sand[3]—chiefly when, in
changeful months, a river at the full o'erflows, and
far and wide covers all with muddy coat, making the
hollow ditches steam with warm vapour?

[118] Nor yet, though toiling men and oxen have
thus wrought in oft turning the land, does the
rascally goose do no mischief, or the Strymonian
cranes, or the bitter-fibred succory, nor is the shade
of trees harmless. The great Father himself has willed
that the path of husbandry should not be smooth, and
he first made art awake the fields, sharpening men's
wits by care, nor letting his realm slumber in heavy
lethargy. Before Jove's day[4] no tillers subdued the
land. Even to mark the field or divide it with bounds
was unlawful. Men made gain for the common store,
and Earth yielded all, of herself, more freely, when
none begged for her gifts. 'Twas he that in black
serpents put their deadly venom, bade the wolves

hill-side or other high ground, is tapped by the farmer for
the fields below.
  [3] *i.e.* by filling in the marshy place with sand.
  [4] *i.e.* in the Golden Age, when Saturn reigned.

mellaque decussit foliis, ignemque removit,
et passim rivis currentia vina repressit,
ut varias usus meditando extunderet artis
paulatim et sulcis frumenti quaereret herbam,
et silicis venis abstrusum excuderet ignem.   135
tunc alnos primum fluvii sensere cavatas ;
navita tum stellis numeros et nomina fecit,
Pleïadas, Hyadas, claramque Lycaonis Arcton ;
tum laqueis captare feras et fallere visco
inventum et magnos canibus circumdare saltus ; 140
atque alius latum funda iam verberat amnem
alta petens, pelagoque alius trahit umida lina ;
tum ferri rigor atque argutae lammina serrae
(nam primi cuneis scindebant fissile lignum),
tum variae venere artes.   labor omnia vicit   145
improbus et duris urgens in rebus egestas.
prima Ceres ferro mortalis vertere terram
instituit, cum iam glandes atque arbuta sacrae
deficerent silvae et victum Dodona negaret.
mox et frumentis labor additus, ut mala culmos   150
esset robigo segnisque horreret in arvis
carduus ; intereunt segetes, subit aspera silva,
lappaeque tribolique, interque nitentia culta
infelix lolium et steriles dominantur avenae.
quod nisi et adsiduis herbam insectabere rastris 155
et sonitu terrebis aves et ruris opaci
falce premes umbram votisque vocaveris imbrem,
heu magnum alterius frustra spectabis acervum
concussaque famem in silvis solabere quercu.

　　Dicendum et quae sint duris agrestibus arma, 160
quis sine nec potuere seri nec surgere messes :

---

[135] et *A :* ut *other MSS.   So Sabb.*　　　[139] tunc M^1.
[146] surgens $A M^1 P^1$.　　　[155] terram *APR.*
[157] umbram *MRγ, Nonius, Servius :* umbras *AP.*

plunder and the ocean swell; shook honey from the
leaves, hid fire from view, and stopped the wine that
ran everywhere in streams, so that practice, by taking
thought, might little by little hammer out divers
arts, might seek the corn-blade in furrows, and strike
forth from veins of flint the hidden fire. Then first
did rivers feel the hollowed alder; then the sailor
numbered the stars and called them by name,
Pleiades, Hyades, and Arctos, Lycaon's gleaming off-
spring. Then men found how to snare game in toils,
to cheat with bird-lime, and to circle great glades
with hounds. And now one lashes a broad stream
with casting-net, seeking the depths, and another
through the sea trails his dripping drag-net. Then
came iron's stiffness and the shrill saw-blade—for
early man cleft the splitting wood with wedges;
then came divers arts. Toil conquered the world,
unrelenting toil, and want that pinches when life is
hard.

[147] Ceres was the first to teach men to turn the
earth with iron, when the acorns and arbutes of the
sacred wood began to fail, and Dodona denied men
food. Soon, too, on the corn fell trouble, the baneful
mildew feeding on the stems, and the lazy thistle
bristling in the fields; the crops die, and instead
springs up a prickly growth, burs and caltrops, and
amid the smiling corn the luckless darnel and barren
oats hold sway. Therefore, unless your hoe, time and
again, assail the weeds, your voice affright the birds,
your knife check the shade of the darkened land,
and your vows invoke the rain, vainly, alas! will you
eye your neighbour's big store, and in the woods
shake the oak to solace hunger.

[160] I must tell, too, of the hardy rustics' weapons,
without which the crops could neither be sown nor

vomis et inflexi primum grave robur aratri,
tardaque Eleusinae matris volventia plaustra,
tribulaque traheaeque et iniquo pondere rastri;
virgea praeterea Celei vilisque supellex,   165
arbuteae crates et mystica vannus Iacchi.
omnia quae multo ante memor provisa repones,
si te digna manet divini gloria ruris.
continuo in silvis magna vi flexa domatur
in burim et curvi formam accipit ulmus aratri.   170
huic a stirpe pedes temo protentus in octo,
binae aures, duplici aptantur dentalia dorso.
caeditur et tilia ante iugo levis altaque fagus
stivaque, quae currus a tergo torqueat imos,
et suspensa focis explorat robora fumus.   175

  Possum multa tibi veterum praecepta referre,
ni refugis tenuisque piget cognoscere curas.
area cum primis ingenti aequanda cylindro
et vertenda manu et creta solidanda tenaci,
ne subeant herbae neu pulvere victa fatiscat,   180
tum variae inludant pestes: saepe exiguus mus
sub terris posuitque domos atque horrea fecit,
aut oculis capti fodere cubilia talpae,
inventusque cavis bufo et quae plurima terrae
monstra ferunt, populatque ingentem farris acervum
curculio atque inopi metuens formica senectae.   186
contemplator item, cum se nux plurima silvis
induet in florem et ramos curvabit olentis:

[166] vallus *R* (*and known to Varro, according to Servius*): *so Sabb.*
[175] exploret *AM* (*late*).
[181] inludunt *M²P²*: ludunt *A.*
[187] nux se *A.*

raised. First the share and the curved plough's heavy frame, the slow-rolling wains of the Mother [1] of Eleusis, sledges and drags, and hoes of cruel weight; further, the common wicker ware of Celeus, arbute hurdles and the mystic fan of Iacchus. All of these you will remember to provide and store away long beforehand, if the glory the divine country gives is to be yours in worthy measure. From the first, even in the woods, an elm, bent by main force, is trained for the stock, and receives the form of the crooked plough. To the stem of this is fitted a pole, eight feet in length, with two mould-boards, and a share-beam with double back. A light linden, too, is felled beforehand for the yoke, and a tall beech for the handle,[2] to turn the car below from the rear; and the wood is hung above the hearth for the smoke to season.

[176] I can repeat for you many olden maxims, unless you shrink back and are loath to learn such trivial cares. And chiefly, the threshing-floor must be levelled with a heavy roller, kneaded with the hand, and made solid with binding clay, lest weeds spring up, or, crumbling into dust, it gape open, and then divers plagues make mock of you. Often under the ground the tiny mouse sets up a home and builds his storehouses, or sightless moles dig out chambers; in holes may be found the toad, and all the countless pests born of the earth; or the weevil ravages a huge heap of grain, or the ant, anxious for a destitute old age.

[187] Mark, too, when in the woods the almond clothes herself richly [3] in blossom and bends her

---

[1] *i.e.* Demeter, identified with Ceres.
[2] Taking *stivaque* as explanatory of *fagus*, a sort of hendiadys.
[3] Or *nux plurima*, "many an almond."

si superant fetus, pariter frumenta sequentur,
magnaque cum magno veniet tritura calore ;   190
at si luxuria foliorum exuberat umbra,
nequiquam pinguis palea teret area culmos.
semina vidi equidem multos medicare serentis
et nitro prius et nigra perfundere amurca,
grandior ut fetus siliquis fallacibus esset,   195
et, quamvis igni exiguo, properata maderent.
vidi lecta diu et multo spectata labore
degenerare tamen, ni vis humana quotannis
maxima quaeque manu legeret.   sic omnia fatis
in peius ruere ac retro sublapsa referri,   200
non aliter, quam qui adverso vix flumine lembum
remigiis subigit, si bracchia forte remisit,
atque illum in praeceps prono rapit alveus amni.

Praeterea tam sunt Arcturi sidera nobis
Haedorumque dies servandi et lucidus Anguis,   205
quam quibus in patriam ventosa per aequora vectis
Pontus et ostriferi fauces temptantur Abydi.
Libra die somnique pares ubi fecerit horas
et medium luci atque umbris iam dividit orbem,
exercete, viri, tauros, serite hordea campis   210
usque sub extremum brumae intractabilis imbrem ;
nec non et lini segetem et Cereale papaver
tempus humo tegere et iamdudum incumbere aratris,
dum sicca tellure licet, dum nubila pendent.

[192] terit *R.*   [200] et *P.*
[203] illum praeceps prono *P :* illum prono in ceps (pre *added
above by late hand*) trahit *R.*
[208] die *AM¹Pγ* : diei *M(late)R :* dies (v. *A. Gellius,* IX.
14) ; *so Sabb.*   [209] dividet *Rγ.*   [213] rastris *AM²P (late)R.*

94

fragrant boughs: if the fruit prevails, the corn crops
will keep pace with it, and a great threshing come
with a great heat; but if the shade is abundant in the
fullness of leafage, in vain shall your floor thresh
stalks, rich only in chaff. Many a sower have I seen
treat his seeds, drenching them first with nitre and
black oil-lees, that the deceitful pods might yield
larger produce, and the grains be sodden quickly, how-
ever small the fire. I have seen seeds, though picked
long and tested with much pains, yet degenerate,
if human toil, year after year, culled not the largest
by hand. Thus by law of fate all things speed
towards the worst, and slipping away fall back; even
as if one, whose oars can scarce force his skiff against
the stream, should by chance slacken his arms, and
lo! headlong down the current the channel sweeps
it away.

[204] Furthermore, we must watch the star of
Arcturus, the days of the Kids,[1] and the gleaming
Snake,[2] even as they do who, sailing homeward over
windswept seas, brave the Pontus and the jaws of
oyster-breeding Abydus.   When the Balance makes
the hours of daytime and sleep equal,[3] and now parts
the world in twain, half in light and half in shade,
then, my men, work your oxen, sow barley in your
fields, as late as the eve of winter's rains, when work
must cease. Then, too, is the time to hide in the ground
your crop of flax and the poppy of Ceres; and high
time is it to bend to the plough, while the dry soil
will let you and the clouds are still aloft.   Spring is
the sowing-time for beans; then, too, the crumbling

---

[1] The Kids are two stars in Auriga, which rises April 25
and September 27 and brings storms.

[2] The Anguis is between the two Bears near the north pole.

[3] *i.e.* at the autumnal equinox.

vere fabis satio; tum te quoque, Medica, putres 215
accipiunt sulci et milio venit annua cura,
candidus auratis aperit cum cornibus annum
Taurus et adverso cedens Canis occidit astro.
at si triticeam in messem robustaque farra
exercebis humum solisque instabis aristis, 220
ante tibi Eoae Atlantides abscondantur
Gnosiaque ardentis decedat stella Coronae,
debita quam sulcis committas semina quamque
invitae properes anni spem credere terrae.
multi ante occasum Maiae coepere; sed illos 225
exspectata seges vanis elusit aristis.
si vero viciamque seres vilemque phaselum,
nec Pelusiacae curam aspernabere lentis,
haud obscura cadens mittet tibi signa Bootes;
incipe et ad medias sementem extende pruinas. 230
   Idcirco certis dimensum partibus orbem
per duodena regit mundi sol aureus astra.
quinque tenent caelum zonae: quarum una corusco
semper sole rubens et torrida semper ab igni;
quam circum extremae dextra laevaque trahuntur
caeruleae, glacie concretae atque imbribus atris; 236
has inter mediamque duae mortalibus aegris
munere concessae divom, et via secta per ambas,
obliquus qua se signorum verteret ordo.
mundus ut ad Scythiam Riphaeasque arduus arces
consurgit, premitur Libyae devexus in Austros. 241
hic vertex nobis semper sublimis; at illum

²¹⁸ adverso *M : averso *most *MSS*. *Both known to Servius.*
²²⁶ avenis *Pγ*.   ²²⁹ mittit *AM*.

---

¹ *adverso astro*, viz. *Tauro*. The sun enters Taurus on
April 17 ("month of opening," *quia ver aperit tunc omnia:* Ovid,
Fasti, IV. 87). Sirius (the *Canis* of l. 218) appears to set at the
end of April, when it draws nearer to the sun. There is also a
reference here to the milk-white oxen with gilded horns, which
figured in Roman triumphs.

furrows welcome thee, Median clover, and the millet
claims our yearly care, when the snow-white Bull
with gilded horns ushers in the year, and the Dog
sets, retiring before his confronting star.[1] But for
harvest of wheat and for hardy spelt you ply the
ground, and if grain alone is your aim, first let the
daughters of Atlas [2] pass from your sight in the morn,
and let the Cretan star of the blazing Crown [3] with-
draw ere you commit to the furrows the seeds due,
or hasten to trust the year's hope to a reluctant soil.
Many have begun ere Maia's setting, but the looked-
for crop has mocked them with empty ears.   Yet if
you choose to sow the vetch or homely kidney-bean,
and scorn not the care of Egyptian lentil, setting
Boötes will send you no doubtful signs.   Begin, and
carry on your sowing to midwinter's frosts.

[231] To this end the golden Sun rules his circuit,
portioned out in fixed divisions, through the world's
twelve constellations.[4]   Five zones comprise the
heavens; whereof one is ever glowing with the
flashing sun, ever scorched by his flames.   Round
this, at the world's ends, two stretch darkling to
right and left, set fast in ice and black storms.
Between these and the middle zone, two by grace of
the gods have been vouchsafed to feeble mortals ; and
a path [5] is cut between the two, wherein the slanting
array of the Signs may turn.   As our globe rises steep
to Scythia and the Riphaean crags, so it slopes down-
ward to Libya's southland.   One pole is ever high
above us, while the other, beneath our feet, is seen

[1] The Pleiades set in the morning of November 11, accord-
ing to Pliny.   Cf. *Geor.* iv. 232, and note.
[3] The apparent evening setting of the *Corona borealis* is
November 9.
[4] *i.e.* the twelve signs of the Zodiac.
[5] *i.e.* the ecliptic or sun's path through the heavens.

sub pedibus Styx atra videt Manesque profundi.
maxumus hic flexu sinuoso elabitur Anguis
circum perque duas in morem fluminis Arctos,   245
Arctos Oceani metuentes aequore tingui.
illic, ut perhibent, aut intempesta silet nox,
semper et obtenta densantur nocte tenebrae ;
aut redit a nobis Aurora diemque reducit,
nosque ubi primus equis Oriens adflavit anhelis,   250
illic sera rubens accendit lumina Vesper.
hinc tempestates dubio praediscere caelo
possumus, hinc messisque diem tempusque serendi,
et quando infidum remis impellere marmor
conveniat, quando armatas deducere classis,   255
aut tempestivam silvis evertere pinum.
nec frustra signorum obitus speculamur et ortus,
temporibusque parem diversis quattuor annum.
  Frigidus agricolam si quando continet imber,
multa, forent quae mox caelo properanda sereno,   260
maturare datur : durum procudit arator
vomeris obtunsi dentem, cavat arbore lintres,
aut pecori signum aut numeros impressit acervis.
exacuunt alii vallos furcasque bicornis
atque Amerina parant lentae retinacula viti.   265
nunc facilis rubea texatur fiscina virga,
nunc torrete igni fruges, nunc frangite saxo.
quippe etiam festis quaedam exercere diebus
fas et iura sinunt : rivos deducere nulla
relligio vetuit, segeti praetendere saepem,   270
insidias avibus moliri, incendere vepres,
balantumque gregem fluvio mersare salubri.

[248] densentur *PR*.   [252] praedicere *AR*.   [260] post *M*.
[266] facili *P*.   Rubea *Scholia on Horace*, Serm. I. v. 96 ; *known
to Servius*.   [269] diducere *M*.

of black Styx and the shades infernal. Here, with
his tortuous coils, the mighty Snake glides forth,
river-like, about and between the two Bears—the
Bears that shrink from the plunge 'neath Ocean's
plain. There, men say, is either the silence of lifeless
night, and gloom ever thickening beneath night's
pall; or else Dawn returns from us and brings them
back the day, and when on us the rising Sun first
breathes with panting steeds, there glowing Vesper
is kindling his evening rays. Hence, though the sky
be fitful, we can foretell the weather's changes, hence
the harvest-tide and sowing-time; when it is meet to
lash with oars the sea's faithless calm, when to launch
our well-rigged fleet, or in the woods to fell the pine
in season. Not in vain do we watch the signs, as
they rise and set, and the year, uniform in its four
several seasons.

259 Whenever a cold shower keeps the farmer
indoors, he can prepare at leisure much that ere long
in clear weather must needs be hurried. The plough-
man hammers out the hard tooth of the blunted share,
scoops troughs from trees, or sets a brand upon his
flocks and labels upon his corn-heaps.[1] Others sharpen
stakes and two-pronged forks, or make bands of Ame-
rian willows for the limber vine. Now let the pliant
basket be woven of red twigs, now roast corn by the
fire, now grind it on the stone. Nay, even on holy days,
the laws of God and man permit you to do certain
tasks. No scruples ever forbade us to guide down[2] the
water-rills, to defend a crop with a hedge, to set snares
for birds, to fire brambles, or to plunge bleating flocks
into the health-giving stream. Oft, too, the driver

---

[1] *numeros* = *tesseras*, *i.e.* labels or tickets, designating
quantity, &c.
[2] *i.e.* in irrigation; *cf.* l. 108.

saepe oleo tardi costas agitator aselli
vilibus aut onerat pomis, lapidemque revertens
incusum aut atrae massam picis urbe reportat.   275
   Ipsa dies alios alio dedit ordine Luna
felicis operum. quintam fuge : pallidus Orcus
Eumenidesque satae ; tum partu Terra nefando
Coeumque Iapetumque creat saevumque Typhoea
et coniuratos caelum rescindere fratres.   280
ter sunt conati imponere Pelio Ossam   MPR
scilicet, atque Ossae frondosum involvere Olympum ;
ter pater exstructos disiecit fulmine montis.
septima post decimam felix et ponere vitem
et prensos domitare boves et licia telae   285
addere. nona fugae melior, contraria furtis.
   Multa adeo gelida melius se nocte dedere,
aut cum sole novo terras inrorat Eous.
nocte leves melius stipulae, nocte arida prata
tondentur, noctes lentus non deficit umor.   290
et quidam seros hiberni ad luminis ignes
pervigilat ferroque faces inspicat acuto ;
interea longum cantu solata laborem
arguto coniunx percurrit pectine telas,
aut dulcis musti Volcano decoquit umorem   295
et foliis undam trepidi despumat aëni.
at rubicunda Ceres medio succiditur aestu,
et medio tostas aestu terit area fruges.
nudus ara, sere nudus ; hiems ignava colono.
frigoribus parto agricolae plerumque fruuntur   300
mutuaque inter se laeti convivia curant.
invitat genialis hiems curasque resolvit,

   [277] Horcus *P.*   [282] invertere *P*[1].
   [283] deiecit *R.*   [284] vites *R.*
   [292] pervigilant *P.*
   [296] trepidi *P*[2]*γ, Servius :* trepidis *MR* (aenis): tepidi *P*[1].

loads his slow donkey's sides with oil or cheap fruits, and as he comes back from town brings with him an indented millstone or a mass of black pitch.

276 The Moon herself has ordained various days in various grades as lucky for work. Shun the fifth; then pale Orcus and the Furies were born: then in monstrous labour Earth bore Coeus, and Iapetus, and fierce Typhoeus, and the brethren [1] who were banded to break down Heaven. Thrice did they essay, forsooth, to pile Ossa on Pelion, and over Ossa to roll leafy Olympus; thrice, with his bolt, the Father dashed apart their up-piled mountains. The seventeenth is lucky for planting the vine, for yoking and breaking in oxen, and for adding the leashes to the warp. The ninth is a friend to the runaway, a foe to the thief.

287 Yea, and many things make better progress in the cool of night, or when at early sunrise the day-star bedews the earth. At night the light stubble is best shorn, at night the thirsty meadows; at night the softening moisture fails not. One I know spends wakeful hours by the late blaze of a winter-fire, and with sharp knife points torches; his wife the while solaces with song her long toil, runs the shrill shuttle through the web, or on the fire boils down the sweet juice of must, and skims with leaves the wave of the bubbling cauldron. But Ceres' golden grain is cut down in noonday heat, and in noonday heat the floor threshes the parched ears. Strip to plough, strip to sow; winter is the farmer's lazy time. In cold weather farmers chiefly enjoy their gains, and feast together in merry companies. Winter's cheer calls them, and loosens the weight of care—even as when laden

---

[1] i.e. the Giants, though what is here narrated is elsewhere (*Aen.* VI. 582) attributed to the two Aloidae.

ceu pressae cum iam portum tetigere carinae,
puppibus et laeti nautae imposuere coronas.
sed tamen et quernas glandes tum stringere tempus
et lauri bacas oleamque cruentaque myrta,   306
tum gruibus pedicas et retia ponere cervis
auritosque sequi lepores, tum figere dammas
stuppea torquentem Balearis verbera fundae,
cum nix alta iacet, glaciem cum flumina trudunt. 310
    Quid tempestates autumni et sidera dicam,
atque, ubi iam breviorque dies et mollior aestas,
quae vigilanda viris, vel cum ruit imbriferum ver,
spicea iam campis cum messis inhorruit et cum
frumenta in viridi stipula lactentia turgent?   315
saepe ego, cum flavis messorem induceret arvis
agricola et fragili iam stringeret hordea culmo,
omnia ventorum concurrere proelia vidi,
quae gravidam late segetem ab radicibus imis
sublimem expulsam eruerent; ita turbine nigro 320
ferret hiems culmumque levem stipulasque volantis.
saepe etiam immensum caelo venit agmen aquarum
et foedam glomerant tempestatem imbribus atris MR
collectae ex alto nubes; ruit arduus aether,
et pluvia ingenti sata laeta boumque labores   325
diluit; implentur fossae et cava flumina crescunt
cum sonitu fervetque fretis spirantibus aequor.
ipse pater media nimborum in nocte corusca
fulmina molitur dextra: quo maxuma motu
terra tremit; fugere ferae et mortalia corda   330
per gentes humilis stravit pavor: ille flagranti
aut Athon aut Rhodopen aut alta Ceraunia telo

[309] torquentes *R*.
[314] et cum] et iam *P*[1].
[315] latentia *M*[1]: iacentia *R*
[318] consurgere *R*.
[321] nigrantis *P*[1].
[327] spumantibus *R*.

keels have at last reached port, and the merry sailors
have crowned the poops with garlands. Still, then
is the time to strip the acorns and laurel-berries, the
olive and blood-red myrtle; the time to set snares
for cranes and nets for the stag, and to chase the
long-eared hares; the time to smite the does, as you
whirl the hempen thongs of a Balearic sling—when
the snow lies deep, when the rivers roll down the ice.

[311] Why need I tell of autumn's changes and
stars, and for what our workers must watch, as the day
now grows shorter and summer softer, or when spring
pours down in showers, as the bearded harvest now
bristles in the fields, and the corn on its green stem
swells with milk? Often, as the farmer was bringing
the reaper into his yellow fields and was now stripping
the brittle-stalked barley,[1] my own eyes have seen all
the winds clash in battle, tearing up the heavy crop
far and wide from its deepest roots and tossing it on
high; then with its black whirlwind the storm would
sweep off the light stalk and flying stubble. Often,
too, there appears in the sky a mighty column of
waters, and clouds mustered from on high roll up a
murky tempest of black showers: down falls the
lofty heaven, and with its deluge of rain washes
away the gladsome crops and the labours of oxen.
The dykes fill, the deep-channelled rivers swell and
roar, and the sea steams in its heaving friths. The
Father himself, in the midnight of storm-clouds,
wields his bolts with flashing hand. At that shock
shivers the mighty earth; far flee the beasts and
o'er all the world crouching terror lays low men's
hearts: he with blazing bolt dashes down Athos
or Rhodope or the Ceraunian peaks. The winds

---

[1] Page prefers "stripping the barley-ears from the brittle
(*i.e.* ripe) stalk."

deicit ; ingeminant Austri et densissimus imber,
nunc nemora ingenti vento, nunc litora plangunt.
hoc metuens caeli mensis et sidera serva,   335
frigida Saturni sese quo stella receptet,
quos ignis caelo Cyllenius erret in orbis.
in primis venerare deos, atque annua magnae
sacra refer Cereri laetis operatus in herbis
extremae sub casum hiemis, iam vere sereno.   340
tum pingues agni et tum mollissima vina,
tum somni dulces densaeque in montibus umbrae.
cuncta tibi Cererem pubes agrestis adoret :
cui tu lacte favos et miti dilue Baccho,
terque novas circum felix eat hostia fruges,   345
omnis quam chorus et socii comitentur ovantes,
et Cererem clamore vocent in tecta ; neque ante
falcem maturis quisquam supponat aristis,
quam Cereri torta redimitus tempora quercu
det motus incompositos et carmina dicat.   350
   Atquè haec ut certis possemus discere signis,
aestusque pluviasque et agentis frigora ventos,
ipse pater statuit, quid menstrua luna moneret,
quo signo caderent Austri, quid saepe videntes
agricolae propius stabuliş armenta tenerent.   355
continuo ventis surgentibus aut freta ponti
incipiunt agitata tumescere et aridus altis
montibus audiri fragor, aut resonantia longe
litora misceri et nemorum increbrescere murmur.
iam sibi tum curvis male temperat unda carinis,   360

334 plangit *R : Servius knows both.*
337 caeli *Rγ, Servius.*
339 orbis *M*[1].
340 casu *R.*
341 tunc . . . tunc *γ.*   agni pingues *c, Servius.*
351 possimus *M* (*late*).   dicere *R :* noscere *M*[2].
360 a curvis *R.*

redouble; more and more thickens the rain; now woods, now shores wail with the mighty blast.

335 In fear of this, mark the months and signs of heaven; whither Saturn's cold star withdraws itself and into what circles of the sky strays the Cyllenian fire.[1] Above all, worship the gods, and pay great Ceres her yearly rites, sacrificing on the glad sward, with the setting of winter's last days, when clear springtime is now come. Then are lambs fat and wine is most mellow; then sweet is sleep, and thick are the shadows on the hills. Then let all your country folk worship Ceres; for her wash the honeycomb with milk and soft wine, and three times let the luck-bringing victim pass round the young crops, while the whole choir of your comrades follow exulting, and loudly call Ceres into their homes; nor let any put his sickle to the ripe corn, ere for Ceres he crown his brows with oaken wreath, dance artless measures, and chant her hymns.

351 And that through unfailing signs we might learn these dangers—the heat, and the rain, and the cold-bringing winds—the Father himself decreed what warning the monthly moon should give, what should signal the fall of the wind, and what sight, oft seen, should prompt the farmer to keep his cattle nearer to their stalls. From the first, when the winds are rising, either the sea's straits begin to heave and swell, and on mountain-heights is heard a dry crash, or the shores ring a confused echo afar and the wood-land murmur waxes loud. Then, too, the wave scarce keeps itself from the curved keel, when the fleet gulls

---

[1] *i.e.* Mercury. Saturn and Mercury are representative of all the planets, Saturn being far away from the sun and Mercury near to it. Saturn when in Capricorn was supposed to bring rain; when in the Scorpion, hail.

cum medio celeres revolant ex aequore mergi
clamoremque ferunt ad litora, cumque marinae
in sicco ludunt fulicae, notasque paludes
deserit atque altam supra volat ardea nubem.
saepe etiam stellas vento impendente videbis   365
praecipites caelo labi, noctisque per umbram
flammarum longos a tergo albescere tractus ;
saepe levem paleam et frondes volitare caducas,
aut summa nantis in aqua colludere plumas.
at Boreae de parte trucis cum fulminat et cum   370
Eurique Zephyrique tonat domus, omnia plenis
rura natant fossis atque omnis navita ponto
umida vela legit.   numquam imprudentibus imber
obfuit : aut illum surgentem vallibus imis
aëriae fugere grues, aut bucula caelum   375
suspiciens patulis captavit naribus auras,
aut arguta lacus circumvolitavit hirundo
et veterem in limo ranae cecinere querellam.
saepius et tectis penetralibus extulit ova
angustum formica terens iter, et bibit ingens   380
arcus, et e pastu decedens agmine magno
corvorum increpuit densis exercitus alis.
iam variae pelagi volucres et quae Asia circum
dulcibus in stagnis rimantur prata Caystri ;
certatim largos umeris infundere rores,   385
nunc caput obiectare fretis, nunc currere in undas
et studio incassum videas gestire lavandi.
tum cornix plena pluviam vocat improba voce
et sola in sicca secum spatiatur harena.
ne nocturna quidem carpentes pensa puellae.   390
nescivere hiemem, testa cum ardente viderent
scintillare oleum et putris concrescere fungos.

[373] prudentibus M^1.
[383] varias *preferred by Servius.*   atque *M :* adque *R.*
[386] undam $M^2 R\gamma$.

GEORGICS BOOK I

fly back from mid-ocean, wafting their screams shore-
ward, and when the sea-coots sport on dry land, and
the heron quits its home in the marsh and soars aloft
above the clouds. Often, too, when wind is threaten-
ing, you will see stars shoot headlong from the sky,
and behind them long trails of flame, gleaming white
amid night's blackness; often light chaff and falling
leaves fly about and feathers dance as they float on
the water's top. But when it lightens from the
region of the grim North, and when the home of
the East and West winds thunders, then the ditches
overflow and all the fields are flooded, while on the
deep every mariner furls his dripping sails.

³⁷³ Never has rain brought ill to men unwarned.
Either, as it gathers, the skyey cranes flee before it
in the valleys' depths; or the heifer looks up to
heaven, and with open nostrils snuffs the breeze, or
the twittering swallow flits round the pools, and
in the mud the frogs croak their old-time plaint.
Often, too, the ant, wearing her narrow path, brings
out her eggs from her inmost cells and a great
rainbow drinks, and an army of rooks, quitting their
pasture in long array, clang with serried wings.
Again, there are the sea-birds manifold, and such
as, in Cayster's sweet pools, rummage round about
the Asian meadows. These you may see rivalling
each other in pouring the copious spray over their
shoulders, now dashing their heads in the waves,
now running into the waters, and aimlessly exulting
in the joy of the bath. Then the caitiff raven with
deep tones calls down the rain, and in solitary
state stalks along the dry sea-sand. Even at night,
maidens that spin their tasks have not failed to mark
a storm as they saw the oil sputter in the blazing
lamp, and a mouldy fungus gather on the wick.

VIRGIL

Nec minus ex imbri soles et aperta serena
prospicere et certis poteris cognoscere signis :
nam neque tum stellis acies obtunsa videtur   395
nec fratris radiis obnoxia surgere Luna,
tenuia nec lanae per caelum vellera ferri ;
non tepidum ad solem pinnas in litore pandunt
dilectae Thetidi alcyones, non ore solutos
immundi meminere sues iactare maniplos.   400
at nebulae magis ima petunt campoque recumbunt,
solis et occasum servans de culmine summo
nequiquam seros exercet noctua cantus.
apparet liquido sublimis in aëre Nisus
et pro purpureo poenas dat Scylla capillo :   405
quacumque illa levem fugiens secat aethera pinnis,
ecce inimicus, atrox, magno stridore per auras
insequitur Nisus ; qua se fert Nisus ad auras,
illa levem fugiens raptim secat aethera pinnis.
tum liquidas corvi presso ter gutture voces   410
aut quater ingeminant, et saepe cubilibus altis
nescio qua praeter solitum dulcedine laeti
inter se in foliis strepitant ; iuvat imbribus actis
progeniem parvam dulcisque revisere nidos ;
haud equidem credo, quia sit divinitus illis   415
ingenium aut rerum Fato prudentia maior ;
verum ubi tempestas et caeli mobilis umor
mutavere vias et Iuppiter uvidus Austris
denset erant quae rara modo, et quae densa relaxat,
vertuntur species animorum, et pectora motus   420
nunc alios, alios dum nubila ventus agebat,
concipiunt : hinc ille avium concentus in agris
et laetae pecudes et ovantes gutture corvi.

⁴⁰³ necquicquam *M*¹.   ⁴⁰⁴ aethere *R*.   ⁴¹⁸ umidus *R*γ.
      ⁴¹⁹ densat *M* (*late*).   ⁴²² hic *M*¹.

[393] Nor less after rain may you foresee bright
suns and cloudless skies, and know them by sure signs.
For then the stars' bright edge is seen undimmed,
and the moon rises under no debt to her brother's
rays,[1] and no thin fleecy clouds pass over the sky.
Not now do the halcyons, the pride of Thetis, spread
their wings on the shore to catch the warm sun, nor
do the uncleanly swine think of tossing straw bundles
to pieces with their snouts. But the mists are
prone to seek the valleys, and rest on the plain, and
the owl, as she watches the sunset from some high
peak, vainly plies her evening song. Nisus is seen
aloft in the clear sky, and Scylla suffers for the
crimson lock. Wherever she flees, cleaving the light
air with her wings, lo! savage and ruthless, with
loud whirr Nisus follows through the sky; where
Nisus mounts skyward, she flees in haste, cleaving
the light air with her wings. Then the rooks, with
narrowed throat, thrice or four times repeat their
soft cries, and oft in their high nests, joyous with some
strange, unwonted delight, chatter to each other
amid the leaves. Glad are they, the rains over, to
see once more their little brood and their sweet nests.
Not, methinks, that they have wisdom from on high,
or from Fate a larger foreknowledge of things to be;
but that when the weather and fitful vapours of the sky
have turned their course, and Jove, wet with the south
winds, thickens what just now was rare, and makes
rare what now was thick, the phases of their minds
change, and their breasts now conceive impulses, other
than they felt, when the wind was chasing the clouds.
Hence that chorus of the birds in the fields, the glad-
ness of the cattle, and the exulting cries of the rooks.

[1] "Apparently this means that the moon is very brilliant,
as though shining with her own and not with a borrowed
light" (Page).

Si vero solem ad rapidum lunasque sequentis
ordine respicies, numquam te crastina fallet   425
hora neque insidiis noctis capiere serenae.
luna revertentis cum primum colligit ignis,
si nigrum obscuro comprenderit aëra cornu,
maxumus agricolis pelagoque parabitur imber :
at si virgineum suffuderit ore ruborem,   430
ventus erit ; vento semper rubet aurea Phoebe.
sin ortu quarto (namque is certissimus auctor)
pura neque obtunsis per caelum cornibus ibit,
totus et ille dies et qui nascentur ab illo
exactum ad mensem pluvia ventisque carebunt,   435
votaque servati solvent in litore nautae
Glauco et Panopeae et Inoo Melicertae.
sol quoque et exoriens et cum se condet in undas
signa dabit ; solem certissima signa sequuntur,
et quae mane refert et quae surgentibus astris.   440
ille ubi nascentem maculis variaverit ortum
conditus in nubem medioque refugerit orbe,
suspecti tibi sint imbres ; namque urget ab alto
arboribusque satisque Notus pecorique sinister.
aut ubi sub lucem densa inter nubila sese   445
diversi rumpent radii, aut ubi pallida surget
Tithoni croceum linquens Aurora cubile,
heu ! male tum mitis defendet pampinus uvas :
tam multa in tectis crepitans salit horrida grando.
hoc etiam, emenso cum iam decedit Olympo,   450
profuerit meminisse magis ; nam saepe videmus
ipsius in voltu varios errare colores :
caeruleus pluviam denuntiat, igneus Euros ;
sin maculae incipient rutilo immiscerier igni,
omnia tum pariter vento nimbisque videbis   455

430 aut M^1.   **434** nascetur R.   **436** ad litora R.
439 sequuntur M : sequuntur R (*second* u *in erasure*).
446 rumpunt R. surgit R.   **450** decedet γbc.
454 incipiunt $M^1 R \gamma$.

⁴²⁴ But if you pay heed to the swift sun and the moons, as they follow in order, never will to-morrow's hour cheat you, nor will you be ensnared by a cloudless night. Soon as the moon gathers her returning fires, if she encloses a dark mist within dim horns, a heavy rain is awaiting farmers and seamen. But if over her face she spreads a maiden blush, there will be wind; as wind rises, golden Phoebe ever blushes. But if at her fourth rising—for that is our surest guide—she pass through the sky clear and with undimmed horns, then all that day, and the days born of it to the month's end, shall be free from rain and wind; and the sailors, safe in port, shall pay their vows on the shore to Glaucus, and to Panopea, and to Melicerta, Ino's son.

⁴³⁸ The sun, too, alike when rising and when sinking under the waves, will give tokens: tokens most sure attend the sun, both those he brings each dawn and those he shows as the stars arise. When, hidden in cloud, he has chequered with spots his early dawn, and is shrunk back in the centre of his disc,[1] beware of showers; for from the deep the South-wind is sweeping, foe to tree and crop and herd. Or when at dawn scattered shafts break out amid thick clouds, or when Aurora rises pale, as she leaves Tithonus' saffron couch, ah! poorly then will the vine-leaf guard the ripe grapes, so thick the bristling hail dances rattling on the roofs. This, too, when he has traversed the sky and now is setting, it will profit you more to bear in mind; for oft we see fitful hues flit over his face: a dark one threatens rain; a fiery, east winds; but if the spots begin to mingle with glowing fire, then shall you see all nature rioting with wind and storm-

1 *i.e.* when only the edge of the disc appears, the centre being covered by clouds—a phenomenon described by Aratus, whom Virgil closely follows in this passage.

fervere. non iiia quisquam me nocte per altum
ire neque ab terra moneat convellere funem.
at si, cum referetque diem condetque relatum,
lucidus orbis erit, frustra terrebere nimbis
et claro silvas cernes Aquilone moveri.   460
denique, quid vesper serus vehat, unde serenas
ventus agat nubes, quid cogitet umidus Auster,
sol tibi signa dabit. solem quis dicere falsum
audeat? ille etiam caecos instare tumultus
saepe monet fraudemque et operta tumescere bella.
ille etiam exstincto miseratus Caesare Romam,   466
cum caput obscura nitidum ferrugine texit
impiaque aeternam timuerunt saecula noctem.
tempore quamquam illo tellus quoque et aequora
        ponti,
obscenaeque canes importunaeque volucres   470
signa dabant. quotiens Cyclopum effervere in agros
vidimus undantem ruptis fornacibus Aetnam,
flammarumque globos liquefactaque volvere saxa!
armorum sonitum toto Germania caelo
audiit, insolitis tremuerunt motibus Alpes.   475
vox quoque per lucos volgo exaudita silentis
ingens, et simulacra modis pallentia miris
visa sub obscurum noctis, pecudesque locutae,
infandum! sistunt amnes terraeque dehiscunt,
et maestum inlacrimat templis ebur aeraque sudant.
proluit insano contorquens vertice silvas   481
fluviorum rex Eridanus camposque per omnis
cum stabulis armenta tulit. nec tempore eodem
tristibus aut extis fibrae apparere minaces
aut puteis manare cruor cessavit, et altae   485

---

457 moveat M^1.
461 ferat M^1R: verat M^2.
470 obsceni $R\gamma$.
473 montibus M^1R^2.

clouds alike. On such a night let none urge me to fare o'er the deep, or pluck my cable from the land. Yet if, both when he brings back the day, and when he closes the day he brought, his disc is bright, then vain will be your fear of storm-clouds, and you will see the woods sway in the clear north wind.

461 In short, the tale told by even-fall, the quarter whence the wind drives clear the clouds, the purpose of the rainy South—of all the Sun will give you signs. Who dare say the Sun is false? Nay, he oft warns us that dark uprisings threaten, that treachery and hidden wars are upswelling. Nay, he had pity for Rome, when, after Caesar sank from sight, he veiled his shining face in dusky gloom, and a godless age feared everlasting night.[1] Yet in that hour Earth also, and Ocean's plains, and ill-boding dogs and ominous birds, gave their tokens. How oft we saw Aetna flood the Cyclopes' fields, when streams poured from her rent furnaces, and she whirled balls of flame and molten rocks! Germany heard the clash of arms through all the sky; the Alps rocked with unwonted terrors. A voice, too, was heard of many amid the silence of solemn groves — an awful voice; and spectres, pale in wondrous wise, were seen at evening twilight; and beasts—O portent, terrible!— spake as men. Rivers halt, earth gapes wide, in temples the ivory weeps in sorrow, and bronzes sweat. Eridanus, king of rivers, washed away in the swirl of his mad eddy whole forests, and all across the plains swept cattle and stalls alike. Yea, in that same hour, threatening filaments ceased not to show themselves in ominous entrails, or blood to flow from

---

[1] Historians, as well as poets, assure us that the atmospheric conditions of the year 44 B.C. (the year of Caesar's assassination) were remarkable.

per noctem resonare lupis ululantibus urbes.
non alias caelo ceciderunt plura sereno
fulgura nec diri totiens arsere cometae.
ergo inter sese paribus concurrere telis
Romanas acies iterum videre Philippi;   490
nec fuit indignum superis, bis sanguine nostro
Emathiam et latos Haemi pinguescere campos.
scilicet et tempus veniet, cum finibus illis
agricola incurvo terram molitus aratro
exesa inveniet scabra robigine pila,   495
aut gravibus rastris galeas pulsabit inanis,
grandiaque effossis mirabitur ossa sepulcris.
di patrii, Indigetes, et Romule Vestaque mater,
quae Tuscum Tiberim et Romana Palatia servas,
hunc saltem everso iuvenem succurrere saeclo   500
ne prohibete! satis iam pridem sanguine nostro
Laomedonteae luimus periuria Troiae;
iam pridem nobis caeli te regia, Caesar,
invidet atque hominum queritur curare triumphos;
quippe ubi fas versum atque nefas: tot bella per
    orbem,   505
tam multae scelerum facies; non ullus aratro
dignus honos, squalent abductis arva colonis
et curvae rigidum falces conflantur in ensem.
hinc movet Euphrates, illinc Germania bellum;
vicinae ruptis inter se legibus urbes   510
arma ferunt; saevit toto Mars impius orbe:
ut cum carceribus sese effudere quadrigae,
addunt in spatia, et frustra retinacula tendens
fertur equis auriga neque audit currus habenas.

⁵¹³ addunt in spatia *M(late)*γ², *Servius:* addunt spatio
*M*¹: addunt in spatio γ¹: addunt spatia *R:* addunt se in
spatia c.

wells, or lofty cities to echo all the night with the
howl of wolves. Never from a cloudless sky fell
more lightnings; never so oft blazed fearful comets.
Therefore once more Philippi saw Roman armies clash
in the shock of brother [1] weapons, and the Powers
above thought it not unseemly that Emathia and the
broad plains of Haemus should twice batten on our
blood. Yea, and a time shall come when in those lands,
as the farmer toils at the soil with crooked plough,
he shall find javelins eaten up with rusty mould, or
with his heavy hoes shall strike on empty helms, and
marvel at the giant bones in the upturned graves.

[498] Gods of my country, Heroes of the land, thou
Romulus, and thou Vesta, our mother, that guardest
Tuscan Tiber and the Palatine of Rome, at least stay
not this young prince from aiding a world uptorn!
Enough has our life-blood long atoned for Lao-
medon's perjury at Troy; enough have Heaven's
courts long grudged thee, O Caesar, to us, murmur-
ing that thou payest heed to earthly triumphs! For
here are right and wrong inverted; so many wars
overrun the world, so many are the shapes of sin;
the plough meets not its honour due; our lands,
robbed of the tillers, lie waste, and the crooked
pruning-hooks are forged into stiff swords. Here
Euphrates, there Germany, awakes war; neighbour
cities break the leagues that bound them and draw
the sword; throughout the world rages the god of
unholy strife: even as when from the barriers the
chariots stream forth, round after round they speed,
and the driver, tugging vainly at the reins, is borne
along, and the car heeds not the curb!

---

[1] *i.e.* both armies were armed alike.

LIBER II

Hactenus arvorum cultus et sidera caeli :
nunc te, Bacche, canam, nec non silvestria tecum
virgulta et prolem tarde crescentis olivae.
huc, pater o Lenaee (tuis hic omnia plena
muneribus, tibi pampineo gravidus autumno   5
floret ager, spumat plenis vindemia labris),
huc, pater·o Lenaee, veni nudataque musto
tingue novo mecum dereptis crura cothurnis.

    Principio arboribus varia est natura creandis.
namque aliae nullis hominum cogentibus ipsae   10
sponte sua veniunt camposque et flumina late
curva tenent, ut molle siler lentaeque genistae,
populus et glauca canentia fronde salicta ;
pars autem posito surgunt de semine, ut altae
castaneae, nemorumque Iovi quae maxima frondet 15
aesculus, atque habitae Grais oracula quercus.
pullulat ab radice aliis densissima silva,
ut cerasis ulmisque ; etiam Parnasia laurus
parva sub ingenti matris se subicit umbra.
hos natura modos primum dedit, his genus omne 20
silvarum fruticumque viret nemorumque sacrorum.

    Sunt alii, quos ipse via sibi repperit usus.
hic plantas tenero abscindens de corpore matrum

---

  8 direptis *M*γ.   **19** subigit *M*.
  22 alie quos *M*[1] : aliae quas *M*[2] : alii quos *M* (*later*) *abc.*

BOOK II

Thus far the tillage of the fields and the stars of heaven: now thee, Bacchus, will I sing, and with thee the forest saplings, and the offspring of the slow-growing olive. Hither, O Lenaean sire! Here all is full of thy bounties; for thee blossoms the field teeming with the harvest of the vine, and the vintage foams in the brimming vats. Come hither, O Lenaean sire, strip off thy buskins and with me plunge thy naked legs in the new must.

⁹ Firstly, Nature has ways manifold for rearing trees. For some, under no man's constraint, spring up of their own free will, and far and wide claim the plains and winding rivers; such as the limber osier and lithe broom, the poplar, and the pale willow-beds with silvery leafage. But some spring from fallen seed, as tall chestnuts, and the broad-leaved tree,[1] mightiest of the woodland, that spreads its shade for Jove, and the oaks, deemed by the Greeks oracular. With others a dense undergrowth sprouts from the parent root, as with cherries and elms; the laurel of Parnassus, too, springs up, a tiny plant, beneath its mother's mighty shade. These are the modes Nature first ordained; these give verdure to every kind of forest-trees and shrubs and sacred groves.

²² Others there are which Experience has in her course discovered for herself. One man tears away

---

[1] The *aesculus* of Virgil is an oak, the *latifolia* variety of the *quercus robur*.

deposuit sulcis, hic stirpes obruit arvo
quadrifidasque sudes et acuto robore vallos;   **25**
silvarumque aliae pressos propaginis arcus
exspectant et viva sua plantaria terra;
nil radicis egent aliae summumque putator
haud dubitat terrae referens mandare cacumen.
quin et caudicibus sectis (mirabile dictu)   30
truditur e sicco radix oleagina ligno.
et saepe alterius ramos, impune videmus
vertere in alterius, mutatamque insita mala
ferre pirum et prunis lapidosa rubescere corna.

  Quare agite o proprios generatim discite cultus, 35
agricolae, fructusque feros mollite colendo,
neu segnes iaceant terrae.   iuvat Ismara Baccho
conserere atque olea magnum vestire Taburnum.
tuque ades inceptumque una decurre laborem,
o decus, o famae merito pars maxima nostrae,   40
Maecenas, pelagoque volans da vela patenti.
non ego cuncta meis amplecti versibus opto,
non mihi si linguae centum sint oraque centum,
ferrea vox.   ades et primi lege litoris oram;
in manibus terrae: non hic te carmine ficto   45
atque per ambages et longa exorsa tenebo.

  Sponte sua quae se tollunt in luminis oras,
infecunda quidem, sed laeta et fortia surgunt;
quippe solo natura subest. tamen haec quoque, si quis

[24] hinc M^1.   [38] oleam M^1.   [47] auras $M^2\gamma^2$.

---

  [1] Here, as in *decurre* (l. 39), and in l. 44, the poet invites
his patron to join him in a voyage on a broad sea, promis-
ing, however, that he will merely skirt the shore. Thus he

suckers from the mother's tender frame, and sets
them in furrows; another buries in the ground
stems, both as cross-cleft shafts and as sharp-pointed
stakes. Some trees await the arches of the bent
layer, and slips set while yet quick in their own soil;
others need no root, and the pruner fears not to take
the topmost spray and again entrust it to the earth.
Nay, when the trunks are cleft—how wondrous the
tale!—an olive root thrusts itself from the dry wood.
Often, too, we see one tree's branches turn harmless
into another's, the pear transformed bearing en-
grafted apples, and stony cornels blushing on the
plum.

[35] Up! therefore, ye husbandmen, learn the cul-
ture proper to each after its kind; your wild fruits
tame by tillage, and let not your soil lie idle. What
joy to plant all Ismarus with the vine, and clothe great
Taburnus with the olive! And draw thou near, O
Maecenas, and with me traverse the toilsome course
I have essayed, thou, my pride, to whom of right
belongs the chief share in my fame; yea, spread thy
sails to speed over an open sea.[1] Not mine the wish
to embrace all the theme within my verse, not though
I had a hundred tongues, a hundred mouths, and a
voice of iron! Draw nigh, and skirt the near shore-
line—the land is close at hand. Not here will I
detain thee with songs of fancy, amid rambling
paths and lengthy preludes.[2]

[47] Trees that of free will lift themselves into realms
of light spring up unfruitful, but rejoicing in their
strength, for within the soil is native force.[3] Yet even

indicates both the extent of the subject and his own modest
achievement in handling it.
  [2] *i.e.* " fable and wide digression and long prelude I
forego" (Kennedy).   [3] *Natura* here means "creative power."

VIRGIL

inserat aut scrobibus mandet mutata subactis, 50
exuerint silvestrem animum, cultuque frequenti
in quascumque voles artis haud tarda sequentur.
nec non et sterilis quae stirpibus exit ab imis,
hoc faciat, vacuos si sit digesta per agros:
nunc altae frondes et rami matris opacant 55
crescentique adimunt fetus uruntque ferentem.
iam quae seminibus iactis se sustulit arbos,
tarda venit, seris factura nepotibus umbram,
pomaque degenerant sucos oblita priores
et turpis avibus praedam fert uva racemos. 60
   Scilicet omnibus est labor impendendus et omnes
cogendae in sulcum ac multa mercede domandae.
sed truncis oleae melius, propagine vites
respondent, solido Paphiae de robore myrtus;
plantis et durae coryli nascuntur et ingens 65
fraxinus Herculeaeque arbos umbrosa coronae,
Chaoniique patris glandes; etiam ardua palma
nascitur et casus abies visura marinos.
inseritur vero et fetu nucis arbutus horrida,
et steriles platani malos gessere valentis; 70
castaneae fagus, ornusque incanuit albo
flore piri, glandemque sues fregere sub ulmis.
   Nec modus inserere atque oculos imponere simplex.
nam qua se medio trudunt de cortice gemmae
et tenuis rumpunt tunicas, augustus in ipso 75
fit nodo sinus; huc aliena ex arbore germen
includunt udoque docent inolescere libro.
aut rursum enodes trunci resecantur et alte
finditur in solidum cuneis via, deinde feraces
plantae immittuntur: nec longum tempus, et ingens

[54] faciet $M^2\gamma$.
[65] edurae *known to Servius and Berne Scholia.   So Sabb.*
[69] et nucis arbutus horrida fetu M(*late*): horrens *for* horrida *known to Servius.*
[71] fagus *Priscian:* fagos $M\gamma ab$, *Servius.   Both known to Berne Scholia.   Scaliger read* castaneas fagus.

120

these, if one graft them, or transplant and commit to well-worked trenches, will doff their wild spirit, and under constant tillage will readily follow any lessons you would have them learn. So, too, the sucker, which springs barren from the bottom of the stem, would do likewise, if set out amid open fields : as it is, the mother-tree's branches and deep leafage overshadow it, robbing it of fruit as it grows, and blasting it in the bearing. Again, the tree which rears itself from chance-dropped seeds rises slowly and will yield its shade to our children of later days ; its fruits, too, degenerate, forgetting the olden flavour, and the vine bears sorry clusters, for the birds to pillage.

[61] On all, be sure, must labour be spent ; all must be marshalled into trenches, and tamed with much trouble. But olives answer best from truncheons, vines from layers, Paphian myrtles from the solid stem. From suckers spring sturdy hazels, and the giant ash, the shady tree that crowned Hercules, and the acorns of the Chaonian sire. So, too, rises the lofty palm, and the fir that will see the perils of the deep. But the rough arbutus is grafted with a walnut shoot, and barren planes have oft borne hardy apple-boughs ; the beech has grown white with the chestnut's snowy bloom, the ash with the pear's ; and swine have crunched acorns beneath the elm.

[73] Nor is the mode of grafting and of budding the same. For where the buds push out from amid the bark, and burst their tender sheaths, a narrow slit is made just in the knot ; in this from an alien tree they insert a bud, and teach it to grow into the sappy bark. Or, again, knotless boles are cut open, and with wedges a path is cleft deep into the core ; then fruitful slips are let in, and in a little while, lo ! a mighty tree shoots up skyward with joyous boughs,

exiit ad caelum ramis felicibus arbos,   81
miraturque novas frondes et non sua poma.
   Praeterea genus haud unum nec fortibus ulmis
nec salici lotoque neque Idaeis cyparissis,
nec pingues unam in faciem nascuntur olivae,   85
orchades et radii et amara pausia baca,
pomaque et Alcinoi silvae, nec surculus idem
Crustumiis Syriisque piris gravibusque volemis.
non eadem arboribus pendet vindemia nostris,
quam Methymnaeo carpit de palmite Lesbos ;   90
sunt Thasiae vites, sunt et Mareotides albae,
pinguibus hae terris habiles, levioribus illae,   MV
et passo Psithia utilior tenuisque Lageos,
temptatura pedes olim vincturaque linguam,
purpureae preciaeque, et quo te carmine dicam   95
Rhaetica ? nec cellis ideo contende Falernis.
sunt et Aminneae vites, firmissima vina,
Tmolius adsurgit quibus et rex ipse Phanaeus ;
Argitisque minor, cui non certaverit ulla
aut tantum fluere aut totidem durare per annos. 100
non ego te, dis et mensis accepta secundis,
transierim, Rhodia, et tumidis, Bumaste, racemis.
sed neque quam multae species nec nomina quae sint,
est numerus : neque enim numero comprendere refert ;
quem qui scire velit, Libyci velit aequoris idem   105
discere quam multae Zephyro turbentur harenae,

   ⁸¹ exilit γ, *Nonius*.
   ⁸² miratasque *M*¹ : -tastque *M*² : -turque *M* (*late*) : mirata
estque γ, *Servius*.   ¹⁰⁶ dicere *MV*γ.

   1 Of these varieties of the olive, the first, ὀρχάδες, were oval-
shaped ; the *radii* resembled shuttles in form ; the pausian
was gathered unripe, while still bitter.
   2 This was a large pear, so called (it is said) from filling the
vola or hollow of the hand.
   3 The Psithian and Lagean wines are otherwise unknown.
   4 Perhaps in the sense " fine," " delicate." Servius explains

and marvels at its strange leafage and fruits not its own.

[83] Further, not single in kind are sturdy elms, or the willow, or the lotus, or the cypresses of Ida, nor do rich olives grow to one mould—the orchad and radius, and the pausian with its bitter berry.[1]   So, too, with apples and the gardens of Alcinous; nor are cuttings the same for Crustumian and Syrian pears, and the heavy volema.[2]   On our trees hangs not the same vintage as Lesbos gathers from Methymna's boughs: there are Thasian vines, there are the pale Mareotic—these suited for rich soils, those for lighter ones—the Psithian,[3] too, better for raisin-wine, and the thin [4] Lagean, sure some day to trouble the feet and tie the tongue; the Purple and the Precian [5] and thou, Rhaetic—how shall I sing thee?   Yet even so, vie not thou with Falernian vaults!   There are, too, Aminnean vines, soundest of wines, to which the Tmolian and the royal Phanaean itself pay homage ; and the lesser Argitis, which none may match, either in richness of stream or in lasting through many years. Nor would I pass by thee, vine of Rhodes, welcome to the gods and the banquet's second course, and thee, Bumastus,[6] with thy swelling clusters.   But for the many kinds, or the names they bear, there is no numbering—nor, indeed, is the numbering worth the pains.   He who would have knowledge of this would likewise be fain to learn how many grains of sand on the Libyan plain are stirred by the West-wind, or when the East falls in unwonted fury on

it as *penetrabilis, quae cito descendit ad venas;* and so Page, "subtle."

[5] According to Servius, *preciae = praecoquae*, being grapes that ripen early.

[6] The word is derived from μαστός, "breast," and the prefix βου-, indicating size.

aut ubi navigiis violentior incidit Eurus,
nosse quot Ionii veniant ad litora fluctus.

Nec vero terrae ferre omnes omnia possunt.
fluminibus salices crassisque paludibus alni   110
nascuntur, steriles saxosis montibus orni;
litora myrtetis laetissima; denique apertos
Bacchus amat colles, Aquilonem et frigora taxi.
aspice et extremis domitum cultoribus orbem
Eoasque domos Arabum pictosque Gelonos: 115
divisae arboribus patriae.   sola India nigrum
fert hebenum, solis est turea virga Sabaeis.
quid tibi odorato referam sudantia ligno   M
balsamaque et bacas semper frondentis acanthi?
quid nemora Aethiopum molli canentia lana,   120
velleraque ut foliis depectant tenuia Seres?
aut quos Oceano propior gerit India lucos,
extremi sinus orbis, ubi aëra vincere summum
arboris haud ullae iactu potuere sagittae?
et gens illa quidem sumptis non tarda pharetris. 125
Media fert tristis sucos tardumque saporem
felicis mali, quo non prasentius ullum,
pocula si quando saevae infecere novercae
[miscueruntque herbas et non innoxia verba,]
auxilium venit ac membris agit atra venena.   130
ipsa ingens arbos faciemque simillima lauro
(et, si non alium late iactaret odorem,
laurus erat); folia haud ullis labentia ventis;
flos ad prima tenax; animas et olentia Medi
ora fovent illo et senibus medicantur anhelis.   135

Sed neque Medorum silvae, ditissima terra
nec pulcher Ganges atque auro turbidus Hermus

¹⁰⁹ terra *M*¹.
¹²⁹ (= III. 283) *in margin M; retained by Janell and
Goelzer.*   ¹³⁶ regna *M*².   ¹³⁷ aura *M*¹.

---

¹ Not the herb of *Ecl.* III. 45, but the Egyptian acacia,
which yields a gum. Virgil seems to mistake the pods for
berries.   ² *molli lana, i.e.* cotton.

GEORGICS BOOK II

the ships, would know how many billows of the
Ionian sea roll shoreward.

109 Nor yet can all soils bear all fruits. In rivers
grow willows, in rank fens alders, on rocky hills
the barren ash. The shores rejoice most in myrtle-
groves. Lastly, Bacchus loves open hills, and the
yew-tree the cold of the North-wind. See, too,
earth's farthest bounds, conquered by tillage—the
Arabs' eastern homes, and the painted Gelonians:
trees have their allotted climes. India alone bears
black ebony; to the Sabaeans alone belongs the
frankincense bough. Why should I tell you of the
balsams that drip from the fragrant wood, or of
the pods of the ever-blooming acanthus? 1 Why tell
of the Aethiopian groves, all white with downy wool,2
or how the Seres comb from leaves their fine fleeces? 3
Or, nearer the Ocean, of the jungles which India
rears, that nook at the world's end where no arrows
can surmount the air at the tree-top? And yet not
slow is that race in handling the quiver. Media bears
the tart juices and lingering flavour of the health-
giving citron-tree, which, if cruel stepdames have
ever drugged the cups [mixing herbs and baleful
spells], comes as help most potent, and from the limbs
drives the deadly venom. The tree itself is large,
and in looks very like a bay ; and a bay it were, did
it not fling abroad another scent. In no winds fall
its leaves; its blossom clings most firmly ; with it
the Mede treats his mouth's noisome breath, and
cures the asthma of the old.

136 But neither Media's groves, land of wondrous
wealth, nor beauteous Ganges, nor Hermus, thick

3 In Virgil's time the Romans, knowing nothing of the
silkworm, supposed that the silk they imported from the
East grew on the leaves of trees.

125

laudibus Italiae certent, non Bactra neque Indi
totaque turiferis Panchaia pinguis harenis.　　　MP
haec loca non tauri spirantes naribus ignem　　　140
invertere satis immanis dentibus hydri
nec galeis densisque virum seges horruit hastis,
sed gravidae fruges et Bacchi Massicus umor
implevere ; tenent oleae armentaque laeta.
hinc bellator equus campo sese arduus infert,　　145
hinc albi, Clitumne, greges et maxima taurus
victima, saepe tuo perfusi flumine sacro,
Romanos ad templa deum duxere triumphos.
hic ver adsiduum atque alienis mensibus aestas,
bis gravidae pecudes, bis pomis utilis arbos.　　150
at rabidae tigres absunt et saeva leonum
semina, nec miseros fallunt aconita legentis,
nec rapit immensos orbis per humum neque tanto
squameus in spiram tractu se colligit anguis.
adde tot egregias urbes operumque laborem,　　155
tot congesta manu praeruptis oppida saxis
fluminaque antiquos subterlabentia muros.
an mare, quod supra, memorem, quodque adluit infra?
anne lacus tantos? te, Lari maxime, teque,
fluctibus et fremitu adsurgens Benace marino?　　160
an memorem portus Lucrinoque addita claustra
atque indignatum magnis stridoribus aequor,
Iulia qua ponto longe sonat unda refuso
Tyrrhenusque fretis immittitur aestus Avernis?
haec eadem argenti rivos aerisque metalla　　　165
ostendit venis atque auro plurima fluxit.

144 oleaeque *M* (*late*).

---

[1] *i.e.* Italy cannot boast of such mythical glories as Colchis,
where Jason yoked the fire-breathing oxen and sowed the
teeth of the Theban dragon.

126

with gold, may vie with Italy's glories—not Bactra,
nor India, nor all Panchaea, rich in incense-bearing
sand. This land no bulls,[1] with nostrils breathing
flame, ever ploughed for the sowing of the monstrous
dragon's teeth ; no human crop ever bristled with
helms and serried lances; but teeming fruits have
filled her and the Vine-god's Massic juice ; she is the
home of olives and of joyous herds. Hence comes
the war-horse, stepping proudly o'er the plain ; hence
thy snowy flocks, Clitumnus, and the bull, that
noblest victim, which, oft steeped in thy sacred
stream, have led to the shrines of the gods the
triumphs of Rome. Here is eternal spring, and
summer in months not her own ; twice the cattle
breed, twice the tree serves us with fruits. But
ravening tigers are far away, and the savage seed of
lions ; no aconite deludes hapless gatherers, nor does
the scaly serpent dart his huge rings over the ground,
or with his vast train wind himself into a coil. Think,
too, of all the noble cities, the achievement of man's
toil, all the towns his handiwork has piled high on
steepy crags, and the streams that glide beneath those
ancient walls. Shall I tell of the seas, washing the
land above and below ?[2] Or of our mighty lakes ? Of
thee, Larius, our greatest ; and thee, Benacus, with
the roaring, surging swell of the sea ? Shall I tell
of our havens, and the barrier thrown across the
Lucrine, and how Ocean roars aloud in wrath, where
the Julian waters echo afar as the sea is flung back,
and the Tyrrhenian tide pours into the channels of
Avernus ?[3] Yea, and this land has shown silver-
streams and copper-mines in her veins, and has flowed

[2] The *Mare superum* or Adriatic, and the *Mare inferum* or
Tyrrhenian.
[3] For explanation, see Index under " Lucrinus."

VIRGIL

haec genus acre virum, Marsos pubemque Sabellam
adsuetumque malo Ligurem Volscosque verutos
extulit, haec Decios, Marios magnosque Camillos,
Scipiadas duros bello et te, maxime Caesar,　　　170
qui nunc extremis Asiae iam victor in oris
imbellem avertis Romanis arcibus Indum.
salve, magna parens frugum, Saturnia tellus,
magna virum: tibi res antiquae laudis et artis
ingredior, sanctos ausus recludere fontis,　　　175
Ascraeumque cano Romana per oppida carmen.

　Nunc locus arvorum ingeniis, quae robora cuique,
quis color et quae sit rebus natura ferendis.
difficiles primum terrae collesque maligni,
tenuis ubi argilla et dumosis calculus arvis,　　　180
Palladia gaudent silva vivacis olivae.
indicio est tractu surgens oleaster eodem
plurimus et strati bacis silvestribus agri.
at quae pinguis humus dulcique uligine laeta,
quique frequens herbis et fertilis ubere campus　185
(qualem saepe cava montis convalle solemus
dispicere; huc summis liquuntur rupibus amnes
felicemque trahunt limum) quique editus Austro
et filicem curvis invisam pascit aratris:
hic tibi praevalidas olim multoque fluentis　　　190
sufficiet Baccho vitis, hic fertilis uvae,
hic laticis, qualem pateris libamus et auro,
inflavit cum pinguis ebur Tyrrhenus ad aras,
lancibus et pandis fumantia reddimus exta.

174 artem *P*.　　**178** qui *P*.　　**181** gaudet *M*.
187 despicere *MP*. hoc *P*[1].　　**194** patulis *M*[1].

1 After his victory at Actium (31 B.C.) Octavian went to
Alexandria and later passed in triumph through Palestine and
Syria. By *imbellem Indum* the poet refers generally to the
Eastern nations.
2 *pandus = patulus*, according to one explanation in Servius.

rich with gold. She has mothered a vigorous breed of
men, Marsians and the Sabine stock, the Ligurian,
inured to hardship, and the Volscian spearmen; yea,
the Decii, the Marii, the great Camilli, the Scipios,
hardy warriors, and thee, greatest of all, O Caesar, who,
already victorious in Asia's farthest bounds, now
drivest the craven Indian from our hills of Rome.[1]
Hail, land of Saturn, great mother of earth's fruits,
great mother of men! 'Tis for thee I essay the
theme of olden praise and art; for thee I dare to
unseal the sacred founts, and through Roman towns
to sing the song of Ascra.

[177] Now give we place to the genius of soils, the
strength of each, its hue, its native power for bear-
ing. First, then, churlish ground and unkindly hills,
where there is lean clay, and gravel in the thorny
fields, delight in Minerva's grove of the long-lived
olive. A token of this is the oleaster, springing up
freely in the same space, and the ground strewn
with its wild berries. But a rich soil, which rejoices
in sweet moisture, a level space thick with herbage
and prolific in nutriment (such as we may oft-times
descry in a mountain's hollow dell, for into it from
the rocky heights pour the streams, bearing with
them fattening mud), land which rises to the South
and feeds the fern, that plague of the crooked
plough—this land will some day yield you the
hardiest of vines, streaming with the rich flood of
Bacchus; this is fruitful in the grape, and in the
juice we offer from bowls of gold, what time by the
altars the sleek Tuscan has blown his ivory pipe,
and in broad[2] chargers we present the steaming
meat of sacrifice.

Others give "curved," "bent," *i.e.* under the weight of
the meat.

sin armenta magis studium vitulosque tueri,   195
aut ovium fetum aut urentis culta capellas,
saltus et saturi petito longinqua Tarenti,
et qualem infelix amisit Mantua campum,
pascentem niveos herboso flumine cycnos :
non liquidi gregibus fontes, non gramina derunt, 200
et quantum longis carpent armenta diebus,
exigua tantum gelidus ros nocte reponet.
nigra fere et presso pinguis sub vomere terra
et cui putre solum (namque hoc imitamur arando),
optima frumentis : non ullo ex aequore cernes   205
plura domum tardis decedere plaustra iuvencis :
aut unde iratus silvam devexit arator
et nemora evertit multos ignava per annos,
antiquasque domos avium cum stirpibus imis
eruit; illae altum nidis petiere relictis,   210
at rudis enituit impulso vomere campus.
nam ieiuna quidem clivosi glarea ruris
vix humilis apibus casias roremque ministrat,
et tofus scaber et nigris exesa chelydris
creta negant alios aeque serpentibus agros   215
dulcem ferre cibum et curvas praebere latebras. MPR
quae tenuem exhalat nebulam fumosque volucres
et bibit umorem et, cum volt, ex se ipsa remittit,
quaeque suo semper viridis se gramine vestit,
nec scabie et salsa laedit robigine ferrum,   220
illa tibi laetis intexet vitibus ulmos,
illa ferax oleo est, illam experiere colendo
et facilem pecori et patientem vomeris unci.
talem dives arat Capua et vicina Vesaevo
ora iugo et vacuis Clanius non aequus Acerris.   225

---

[196] fetus *Mγ, Priscian, Nonius.*   [202] reponit *M.*
[204] imitatur *M¹.*   [219] viridi *MSS.*   [220] aut *M².*
[221] intexit *P.*   [222] oleae *M.*

¹⁹⁵ But if you are more fain to keep herds and calves, or to breed sheep, or goats that blight the plants, then haste to the gladès and distant meads of rich Tarentum, or to such a plain as hapless Mantua lost, giving food to snowy swans with its grassy stream. There the flocks will lack nor limpid springs nor herbage, and all that the herds will crop in the long days the chilly dew will restore in one short night.

²⁰³ Land that is black, and rich beneath the share's pressure and with a crumbly soil—for such a soil we try to rival with our ploughing—is, in the main, best for corn ; from no other land will you see more wagons wending homeward behind slow bullocks; or land from which the angry ploughman has carried off the timber, levelling groves that have idled many a year, and up-tearing by their deepest roots the olden homes of the birds—these, lo! leave their nests and seek the sky, but forthwith the untried plain glistens under the driven ploughshare. For as to the hungry gravel of a hilly country, it scarce serves the bees with lowly spurge and rosemary ; and the rough tufa and the chalk that black water-snakes have eaten out betoken that no other lands give serpents food so sweet, or furnish such winding coverts. But if a soil exhales thin mists and curling vapours, if it drinks in moisture and throws it off again at will, if it always clothes itself in the verdure of its own grass, and harms not the steel with scurf and salt rust, that is the one to wreathe your elms in joyous vines, the one to be rich in oil of olive, the one you will find, as you till, to be indulgent to cattle and submissive to the crooked share. Such is the soil rich Capua ploughs, and the coast near the Vesuvian ridge, and Clanius, unkindly to forlorn Acerrae.

VIRGIL

Nunc quo quamque modo possis cognoscere dicam.
rara sit an supra morem si densa requires
(altera frumentis quoniam favet, altera Baccho,
densa magis Cereri, rarissima quaeque Lyaeo),
ante locum capies oculis, alteque iubebis   230
in solido puteum demitti, omnemque repones,
rursus humum et pedibus summas aequabis harenas.
si derunt, rarum pecorique et vitibus almis
aptius uber erit; sin in sua posse negabunt
ire loca et scrobibus superabit terra repletis,   235
spissus ager: glaebas cunctantis crassaque terga
exspecta et validis terram proscinde iuvencis.
salsa autem tellus et quae perhibetur amara,
(frugibus infelix ea, nec mansuescit arando
nec Baccho genus aut pomis sua nomina servat), 240
tale dabit specimen: tu spisso vimine qualos
colaque prelorum fumosis deripe tectis;
huc ager ille malus dulcesque a fontibus undae
ad plenum calcentur; aqua eluctabitur omnis
scilicet et grandes ibunt per vimina guttae;   245
at sapor indicium faciet manifestus, et ora
tristia temptantum sensu torquebit amaro.
pinguis item quae sit tellus, hoc denique pacto
discimus: haud umquam manibus iactata fatiscit,
sed picis in morem ad digitos lentescit habendo. 250
umida maiores herbas alit, ipsaque iusto
laetior.   a! nimium ne sit mihi fertilis illa,
nec se praevalidam primis ostendat aristis !
quae gravis est, ipso tacitam se pondere prodit,
quaeque levis.   promptum est oculis praediscere
    nigram,   255

    227 requiras *M²R*.
    247 amaro *MPRc, Macrobius:* amaror *M(late)bc²* (γ *wanting*), *Hyginus, Servius.   See Gellius,* I. 21.
    253 neu *M²*.

226 Now I will tell you how you may distinguish
each.   If you shall ask whether a soil be light or closer
than is the wont—for one is friendly to corn, the other
to the vine; the closer to Ceres, all the lightest to
Lyaeus—you must first look out a place and bid a
pit be sunk deep in the solid ground, then put all the
earth back again, and tread the earth level at the top.
If it fall short, this farm-land will be light, and better
suited for the herd and gracious vine; but if it shows
that it cannot return to its place, and if there is earth
to spare when the pit is filled, the soil is stiff: look
for reluctant clods and stiffness of ridge, and have
strong oxen break your ground.   As for salty land,
the kind called bitter (unfruitful it is for crops and
mellows not in ploughing; it preserves not for the
vine its lineage, or for apples their fame), it will
allow this test : pull down from the smoky roof your
close-woven wicker-baskets and wine-strainers : in
these let that sorry soil, mixed with fresh spring
water, be pressed in to the brim.   You will see all the
water trickle through and big drops pass between
the osiers; but the taste will tell its tale full
plainly, and with its bitter flavour will distort the
testers' soured mouths.   Again, richness of soil we
learn in this way only : never does it crumble when
worked in the hands, but like pitch grows sticky in
the fingers when held.   A moist soil rears taller grass
and is of itself unduly prolific.   Ah ! not mine be that
over-fruitful soil, and may it not show itself too strong
when the ears are young !   A heavy soil betrays itself
silently by its own weight ; so does a light one.   It
is easy for the eye to learn at once a black soil and

133

et quis cui color. at sceleratum exquirere frigus
difficile est : piceae tantum taxique nocentes
interdum aut hederae pandunt vestigia nigrae.

His animadversis terram multo ante memento
excoquere et magnos scrobibus concidere montis, 260
ante supinatas Aquiloni ostendere glaebas,
quam laetum infodias vitis genus.   optima putri
arva solo : id venti curant gelidaeque pruinae
et labefacta movens robustus iugera fossor.
at si quos haud ulla viros vigilantia fugit,   265
ante locum similem exquirunt, ubi prima paretur
arboribus seges et quo mox digesta feratur,
mutatam ignorent subito ne semina matrem.
quin etiam caeli regionem in cortice signant,
ut quo quaeque modo steterit, qua parte calores 270
austrinos tulerit, quae terga obverterit axi,
restituant : adeo in teneris consuescere multum est.
collibus an plano melius sit ponere vitem,
quaere prius. si pinguis agros metabere campi, MPRV ˙
densa sere ; in denso non segnior ubere Bacchus :
sin tumulis adclive solum collisque supinos,   276
indulge ordinibus ; nec setius omnis in unguem
arboribus positis secto via limite quadret.
ut saepe ingenti bello cum longa cohortis
explicuit legio et campo stetit agmen aperto,   280
derectaeque acies, ac late fluctuat omnis
aere renidenti tellus, necdum horrida miscent
proelia, sed dubius mediis Mars errat in armis :
omnia sint paribus numeris dimensa viarum ;

²⁵⁶ quis cuique *M*¹ : quisquis *M(late)P* : quis cui cive
color *R*.   ²⁶⁵ at *Pγ* : ad *R* : ac *M*.
²⁶⁷ ferantur *P*¹.   ²⁷⁴ campos *P* : agri . . . campos *γ*.

the hue of any kind. But to detect the villainous cold is hard; only pitch-pines or baleful yews and black ivy sometimes reveal its traces.

²⁵⁹ These points observed, remember first to bake the ground well, to cut up the huge knolls with trenches, and to expose the upturned clods to the North-wind, long ere you plant the vine's gladsome stock. Fields of crumbling soil are the best; to this the winds see, the chill frosts, and the stout delver, who loosens and stirs the acres. But men whose watchful care nothing escapes first seek out like plots—one where the crop may be nursed in infancy for its supporting trees, and one to which it may be moved anon when planted out, lest the nurslings should fail to recognize the mother suddenly changed. Nay, they print on the bark of the trees the quarter of the sky each faced, so as to restore the position in which they stood, the same side bearing the southern heat and the same back turned to the north pole; so strong is habit in tender years.

²⁷³ First inquire whether it be better to plant the vine on hills or on the plain. If it is rich level ground you lay out, plant close; in close-planted soil not less fertile is the wine god. But if it is a soil of rising mounds and sloping hills, give the ranks room; yet none the less, when the trees are set, let all the paths, with clear-cut line, square to a nicety.[1] As oft, in mighty warfare, when the legion deploys its companies in long array and the column halts on the open plain, when the lines are drawn out, and far and wide all the land ripples with the gleam of steel, not yet is the grim conflict joined, but the war-god wanders in doubt between the hosts: so let all your vineyard be meted out in even and uniform paths,

See Appendix, p. 582.

non animum modo uti pascat prospectus inanem, 285
sed quia non aliter viris dabit omnibus aequas
terra neque in vacuum poterunt se extendere rami.

Forsitan et scrobibus quae sint fastigia quaeras.
ausim vel tenui vitem committere sulco.
altior ac penitus terrae defigitur arbos, 290
aesculus in primis, quae quantum vertice ad auras
aetherias, tantum radice in Tartara tendit.
ergo non hiemes illam, non flabra neque imbres
convellunt; immota manet, multosque nepotes,
multa virum volvens durando saecula vincit. 295
tum fortis late ramos et bracchia tendens
huc illuc, media ipsa ingentem sustinet umbram.

Neve tibi ad solem vergant vineta cadentem,
neve inter vitis corylum sere, neve flagella   [MPR
summa pete aut summa defringe ex arbore plantas
(tantus amor terrae), neu ferro laede retunso 301
semina, neve oleae silvestris insere truncos.
nam saepe incautis pastoribus excidit ignis,
qui furtim pingui primum sub cortice tectus
robora comprendit, frondesque elapsus in altas 305
ingentem caelo sonitum dedit; inde secutus
per ramos victor perque alta cacumina regnat,
et totum involvit flammis nemus et ruit atram
ad caelum picea crassus caligine nubem,
praesertim si tempestas a vertice silvis 310
incubuit, glomeratque ferens incendia ventus.
hoc ubi, non a stirpe valent caesaeque reverti

---

287 se *omitted PR.*   **292** radicem *MP.*
294 per annos *Vγ.*
302 oleas *M, whence* olea *Wagner :* oleae *PR, Servius.*

---

1 *i.e.* with the fertile olive, because in case of fire the latter
would be destroyed, and the fresh growth would consist wholly
of the wild olive.   Others take *insere* as = *intersere* (*cf.* l. 299)
and suppose that Virgil forbids us to plant oleasters among

not merely that the view may feed an idle fancy, but because only thus will the earth give equal strength to all, and the boughs be able to reach forth into free air.

[288] Perchance you ask also what should be the trenches' depth. I should venture to entrust a vine even to a shallow furrow, but deeper and far within the earth is sunk the supporting tree, above all the great oak, which strikes its roots down towards the nether pit as far as it lifts its top to the airs of heaven. Hence no winter storms, no blasts or rains, uproot it; unmoved it abides, and many generations, many ages of men it outlives, letting them roll by while it endures. Stout limbs, too, and arms it stretches far, this side and that, itself in the centre upholding a mass of shade.

[298] Let not your vineyards slope towards the setting sun, nor plant the hazel among the vines, nor lop the highest sprays, nor pluck cuttings from the tree-top—so strong is their love of the earth—nor hurt young plants with a blunted knife, nor engraft wild trunks of olive.[1] For oft from thoughtless shepherds falls a spark, which, lurking at first unseen under the rich bark, fastens on the trunk, and, gliding to the leaves aloft, sends to heaven a mighty roar; then, running on, reigns supreme among all the boughs and high tree-tops, wrapping all the grove in fire, and belching skyward black clouds of thick pitchy darkness; most of all, if a tempest from above has swooped down upon the woods, and a favouring wind masses the flames. When this befalls, the trees are without virtue in their stock, and when cut down cannot revive or from the earth's depths resume their

vines as supports. This implies that the subject of *valent* (l. 312) is *vites*.

VIRGIL

possunt atque ima similes revirescere terra;
infelix superat foliis oleaster amaris.

  Nec tibi tam prudens quisquam persuadeat auctor
tellurem Borea rigidam spirante movere.   316
rura gelu tunc claudit hiems nec semine iacto
concretam patitur radicem adfigere terrae.
optima vinetis satio, cum vere rubente
candida venit avis longis invisa colubris,   320
prima vel autumni sub frigora, cum rapidus Sol
nondum hiemem contingit equis, iam praeterit aestas.
ver adeo frondi nemorum, ver utile silvis;
vere tument terrae et genitalia semina poscunt.
tum pater omnipotens fecundis imbribus Aether 325
coniugis in gremium laetae descendit et omnis
magnus alit magno commixtus corpore fetus.
avia tum resonant avibus virgulta canoris
et Venerem certis repetunt armenta diebus;
parturit almus ager Zephyrique tepentibus auris 330
laxant arva sinus; superat tener omnibus umor,
inque novos soles audent se gramina tuto
credere, nec metuit surgentis pampinus Austros
aut actum caelo magnis Aquilonibus imbrem,
sed trudit gemmas et frondes explicat omnis.   335
non alios prima crescentis origine mundi
inluxisse dies aliumve habuisse tenorem
crediderim: ver illud erat, ver magnus agebat
orbis et hibernis parcebant flatibus Euri,
cum primae lucem pecudes hausere, virumque   340
ferrea progenies duris caput extulit arvis,
immissaeque ferae silvis et sidera caelo.

---

316 moveri *PR.*   318 concretum *M.*
330 zephyrisque *M.*   trementibus *PRγ.*
332 gramine *P:* gramina *MRγ:* germina *Philargyrius.*
339 hiberni *M.*
341 terrea *M²*, *Philargyrius, Lactantius.*

138

olden bloom : the luckless oleaster with bitter leaves
alone survives.

[315] And let no counsellor seem so wise as to
persuade you to stir the stiff soil when the North-wind
blows. Then winter grips the land with frost, and
when the plant is set suffers it not to fasten its frozen
root in the earth. The best planting season for vines
is when in blushing spring the white bird,[1] the foe of
long snakes, is come, or close on autumn's first cold,
ere yet the fiery sun touches winter with his steeds,
and summer is now waning. Spring it is that aids
the woods and the forest leafage ; in spring the soil
swells and calls for life-giving seed. Then Heaven,
the Father almighty, comes down in fruitful showers
into the lap of his joyous spouse, and his might, with
her mighty frame commingling, nurtures all growths.
Then pathless copses ring with birds melodious, and in
their settled time the herds renew their loves. The
bountiful land brings forth, and beneath the West's
warm breezes the fields loosen their bosoms ; in all
things abounds soft moisture, and the grasses safely
dare to trust themselves to face the new suns;
the vine-tendrils fear not the rising of the South,
or a storm driven down the sky by mighty blasts of
the North, but thrust forth their buds and unfold all
their leaves. Even such days, I could suppose, shone
at the first dawn of the infant world ; even such was
the course they held. Springtime that was ; the
great world was keeping spring, and the East-winds
spared their wintry blasts, when the first cattle drank
in the light and man's iron race reared its head from
the hard fields, and wild beasts were let loose into
the forests and the stars into heaven. Nor could

---

[1] The white stork, *ciconia alba*.

nec res hunc tenerae possent perferre laborem,
si non tanta quies iret frigusque caloremque
inter et exciperet caeli indulgentia terras.   345
   Quod superest, quaecumque premes virgulta per
     agros,
sparge fimo pingui et multa memor occule terra,
aut lapidem bibulum aut squalentis infode conchas;
inter enim labentur aquae, tenuisque subibit
halitus atque animos tollent sata.   iamque reperti,
qui saxo super atque ingentis pondere testae   351
urgerent: hoc effusos munimen ad imbris,   MPRV
hoc, ubi hiulca siti findit Canis aestifer arva.
   Seminibus positis superest diducere terram
saepius ad capita et duros iactare bidentis,   355
aut presso exercere solum sub vomere et ipsa
flectere luctantis inter vineta iuvencos;
tum levis calamos et rasae hastilia virgae
fraxineasque aptare sudes furcasque valentis,
viribus eniti quarum et contemnere ventos   360
adsuescant summasque sequi tabulata per ulmos.
   Ac dum prima novis adolescit frondibus aetas,
parcendum teneris, et dum se laetus ad auras
palmes agit laxis per purum immissus habenis,
ipsa acie nondum falcis temptanda, sed uncis   365
carpendae manibus frondes interque legendae.
inde ubi iam validis amplexae stirpibus ulmos
exierint, tum stringe comas, tum bracchia tonde
(ante reformidant ferrum), tum denique dura
exerce imperia et ramos compesce fluentis.   370

---

[343] sufferre M^1.   [344] calorque P.   [351] ingenti M^1.
[353] scindit P. aestiper P.   [359] bicornis V.
[362] aestas P.
[365] acies M^2P: *both known to Servius and Berne Scholia.*
[367] viribus M (*late*).   [370] valentis R.

tender things endure this world's stress, did not such long repose come between the seasons' cold and heat, and did not heaven's gracious welcome await the earth.[1]

[346] Furthermore, whatever cuttings you plant in your fields, sprinkle them with rich dung, and forget not to cover them with deep soil; or bury with them porous stone or rough shells; for the water will glide between, the air's searching breath will steal in, and the plants sown will take heart. And, ere now, some have been known to overlay them with stones and jars of heavy weight, thus shielding them against pelting showers, and against the time when the sultry dog-star splits the fields that gape with thirst.

[354] When the sets are planted, it remains for you to break up the soil oft-times at the roots, and to swing the ponderous hoe, or to ply the soil under the share's pressure and turn your toiling bullocks even between your vineyard rows; then to shape smooth canes, shafts of peeled rods, ashen stakes and stout forks, by whose aid the vines may learn to mount, scorn the winds, and run from tier to tier amid the elm-tops.

[362] And when their early youth has fresh leaves budding, you must spare their weakness, and while the shoot, speeding through the void with loosened reins, pushes joyously skyward, you must not yet attack the plants themselves with the knife's edge, but with bent fingers pluck the leaves and pick them here and there. Later, when they have shot up and their stout stems have now clasped the elms, then strip their locks and clip their arms—ere that they shrink from the knife—then at last set up an iron sway and check the flowing branches.

[1] *i.e.* after the extremes of heat and cold. Heaven is compared to a nurse receiving a new-born child.

Texendae saepes etiam et pecus omne tenendum,
praecipue dum frons tenera imprudensque laborum ;
cui super indignas hiemes solemque potentem
silvestres uri adsidue capreaeque sequaces
inludunt, pascuntur oves avidaeque iuvencae.   375
frigora nec tantum cana concreta pruina
aut gravis incumbens scopulis arentibus aestas,
quantum illi nocuere greges durique venenum
dentis et admorso signata in stirpe cicatrix.
non aliam ob culpam Baccho caper omnibus aris MPR
caeditur et veteres ineunt proscaenia ludi,,   381
praemiaque ingeniis pagos et compita circum
Thesidae posuere, atque inter pocula laeti
mollibus in pratis unctos saluere per utres.
nec non Ausonii, Troia gens missa, coloni   385
versibus incomptis ludunt risuque soluto,
oraque corticibus sumunt horrenda cavatis,
et te, Bacche, vocant per carmina laeta, tibique
oscilla ex alta suspendunt mollia pinu.
hinc omnis largo pubescit vinea fetu,   390
complentur vallesque cavae saltusque profundi
et quocumque deus circum caput egit honestum.
ergo rite suum Baccho dicemus honorem
carminibus patriis lancesque et liba feremus,
et ductus cornu stabit sacer hircus ad aram,   395
pinguiaque in veribus torrebimus exta colurnis.
   Est etiam ille labor curandis vitibus alter,
cui numquam exhausti satis est : namque omne quot-
         annis
terque quaterque solum scindendum glaebaque versis

³⁷¹ tuendum *VR.*   ³⁷⁴ caprae *M.*
   ³⁷⁹ admorsum *P :* amorso *M¹ :* amorsu *M² :* admorsu *Rb¹ :*
admorso γ*b²c, Servius.*   ³⁸² ingentis *MPγ.*

---

   1 The *ludi* are *tragedies* (derived from τράγος, a goat), which
originated in the celebration of the vintage.

142

³⁷¹ You must also weave hedges, and keep out all cattle, chiefly while the leafage is tender and knows naught of trials, for besides unfeeling winters and the sun's tyranny, ever do wild buffaloes and pestering roes make sport of it; sheep and greedy heifers feed upon it. No cold, stiff with hoar frost, no summer heat, brooding heavily over parched crags, has done it such harm as the flocks and the venom of their sharp tooth, and the scar impressed on the deep-gnawed stem. For no other crime is it that a goat is slain to Bacchus at every altar, and the olden plays[1] enter on the stage; for this the sons of Theseus set up prizes for wit in their villages[2] and at the cross-ways, and gaily danced in the soft meadows on oiled goat-skins.[3] Even so Ausonia's swains,[4] a race sent from Troy, disport with rude verses and laughter unrestrained, and put on hideous masks of hollow cork, and call on thee, O Bacchus, in joyous songs, and to thee hang waving amulets from the tall pine. Hence every vineyard ripens in generous increase; fullness comes to hollow valleys and deep glades, and every spot towards which the god has turned his comely face. Duly, then, in our country's songs we will chant for Bacchus the praise he claims, bringing him cakes and dishes; the doomed he-goat, led by the horn, shall stand at the altar, and the rich flesh we will roast on spits of hazel.

³⁹⁷ There is, too, this other task of dressing the vines whereon never is enough pains spent; for thrice or four times each year must all your soil be split open,

² Virgil probably assumes that the word *comedy* comes from κώμη, a village. It really comes from κῶμος, a revel-band.
³ The rustics danced for a prize on the inflated skin of the sacrificial goat.
⁴ *i.e.* the Italians, whom Virgil, having, it would seem, already in view the myth upon which the *Aeneid* is founded, boldly calls Trojan colonists.

143

VIRGIL

aeternum frangenda bidentibus, omne levandum 400
fronde nemus.   redit agricolis labor actus in orbem,
atque in se sua per vestigia volvitur annus.
ac iam olim seras posuit cum vinea frondes,
frigidus et silvis Aquilo decussit honorem,
iam tum acer curas venientem extendit in annum
rusticus, et curvo Saturni dente relictam   406
persequitur vitem attondens fingitque putando.
primus humum fodito, primus devecta cremato
sarmenta et vallos primus sub tecta referto ;
postremus metito.   bis vitibus ingruit umbra,   410
bis segetem densis obducunt sentibus herbae ;
durus uterque labor : laudato ingentia rura,
exiguum colito.   nec non etiam aspera rusci
vimina per silvam et ripis fluvialis harundo
caeditur, incultique exercet cura salicti.   415
iam vinctae vites, iam falcem arbusta reponunt,
iam canit effectos extremus vinitor antes :
sollicitanda tamen tellus pulvisque movendus,
et iam maturis metuendus Iuppiter uvis.

Contra non ulla est oleis cultura, neque illae 420
procurvam exspectant falcem rastrosque tenacis,
cum semel haeserunt arvis aurasque tulerunt ;
ipsa satis tellus, cum dente recluditur unco,
sufficit umorem et gravidas, cum vomere, fruges.
hoc pinguem et placitam Paci nutritor olivam.   425

    [405] extendet *M.*   [406] agricola *R.*   [411] inducunt *P.*
    [413] asperetrusci *M*[1] : aspera rusti, *M*[2] : rusti *PR.*
    [417] effectus *M*(*late*).   [420] non nulla *Rγ, known to Servius.*
    [425] nutritur *MP.*
144

and the clods broken unceasingly with hoe reversed,
and all the grove lightened of its foliage. The
farmer's toil returns, moving in a circle, as the year
rolls back upon itself over its own footsteps. And
already, whenever the vineyard has shed her autumn
leafage, and the North-wind has shaken their glory
from the woods—already then the keen farmer ex-
tends his care to the coming year, and pursues the vine
he had left, lopping it with Saturn's crooked knife
and pruning it into shape. Be the first to dig the
ground, first to bear away and fire the prunings,
first to carry the poles under cover: be the last to
reap. Twice the shade thickens on the vines; twice
weeds cover the vineyard with thronging briars.
Heavy is either toil: "praise thou large estates, farm
a small one." [1] Further, rough shoots of broom must
be cut amid the woods, and river rushes on the banks,
and the care of the wild willow-bed keeps you at work.
Now the vines are bound, now the vineyard lays by
the pruning-knife, now the last vine-dresser sings of
his finished rows: still you have to worry the soil
and stir the dust, and fear Jove's rains for your now
ripened grapes.

[420] Olives, on the other hand, need no tending;
they look not for the crooked knife or gripping mat-
tock, when once they have laid hold of the fields and
braved the breeze. Earth of herself, when opened
with the hoe's curved fang, yields moisture enough
for the plants, and teeming fruits, when opened by
the plough. After this mode nurture the plump
olive, favoured of Peace.

---

[1] An old adage already used by Cato. A small farm
well tilled is more profitable than a large one poorly
tilled.

Poma quoque, ut primum truncos sensere valentis
et viris habuere suas, ad sidera raptim
vi propria nituntur opisque haud indiga nostrae.
nec minus interea fetu nemus omne gravescit,
sanguineisque inculta rubent aviaria bacis.   430
tondentur cytisi, taedas silva alta ministrat,
pascunturque ignes nocturni et lumina fundunt.
et dubitant homines serere atque impendere curam ?
quid maiora sequar ? salices humilesque genistae,
aut illae pecori frondem aut pastoribus umbram   435
sufficiunt saepemque satis et pabula melli.
et iuvat undantem buxo spectare Cytorum
Naryciaeque picis lucos, iuvat arva videre
non rastris, hominum non ulli obnoxia curae.
ipsae Caucasio steriles in vertice silvae,   440
quas animosi Euri adsidue franguntque feruntque,
dant alios aliae fetus, dant utile lignum
navigiis pinos, domibus cedrumque cupressosque ;
hinc radios trivere rotis, hinc tympana plaustris
agricolae, et pandas ratibus posuere carinas.   445
viminibus salices fecundae, frondibus ulmi,
at myrtus validis hastilibus et bona bello
cornus, Ituraeos taxi torquentur in arcus.
nec tiliae leves aut torno rasile buxum
non formam accipiunt ferroque cavantur acuto.   450
nec non et torrentem undam levis innatat alnus
missa Pado, nec non et apes examina condunt
corticibusque cavis vitiosaeque ilicis alvo.
quid memorandum aeque Baccheia dona tulerunt ?
Bacchus et ad culpam causas dedit ; ille furentis   455

---

[433] *omitted M.   cf. Aen.* VI. 806.   [435] umbras *Ry.*
[453] alveo *R.*

GEORGICS BOOK II

[426] Fruit-trees, too, so soon as they feel their stems firm, and come to their strength, swiftly push forth skyward with inborn force, needing no help from us. No less, meanwhile, does every wood grow heavy with fruit, and the birds' wild haunts blush with crimson berries. Cattle browse on the cytisus, the high wood yields pine-brands, the fires of night are fed and pour forth light. And can men be slow to plant and bestow care? Why need I pursue greater themes?[1] The willows and lowly broom—they either yield leafage for the sheep or shade for the shepherd, a fence for the crops and food for honey. And what joy it is to gaze on Cytorus waving with boxwood, and on groves of Narycian pitch! What joy to view fields that owe no debt to the harrow, none to the care of man! Even the barren woods on Caucasian peaks, which angry eastern gales ever toss and tear, yield products, each after its kind, yield useful timber, pines for ships, cedars and cypresses for houses. From these the farmers turn spokes for wheels, or drums[2] for their wains; from these they lay broad keels for boats. The willow's wealth is in its osiers, the elm's in its leaves, but the myrtle and the cornel, that weapon of war, abound in stout spear-shafts; yews are bent into Ituraean bows. So, too, smooth lindens and the box, polished by the lathe, take shape and are hollowed by the sharp steel. So, too, the light alder, sent down the Po, swims the raging wave; so, too, the bees hive their swarms in the hollow cork-trees, and in the heart of a rotting ilex. What boon of equal note have the gifts of Bacchus yielded? Bacchus has even given occasion of offence. It was he who quelled in death the maddened Centaurs,

---

[1] *i.e.* Why tell of larger trees, when even willows and broom are so useful?   [2] *i.e.* wheels of solid wood.

147

Centauros leto domuit, Rhoetumque Pholumque
et magno Hylaeum Lapithis cratere minantem.
  O fortunatos nimium, sua si bona norint,
agricolas! quibus ipsa, procul discordibus armis,
fundit humo facilem victum iustissima tellus.   460
si non ingentem foribus domus alta superbis
mane salutantum totis vomit aedibus undam,
nec varios inhiant pulchra testudine postis
inlusasque auro vestis Ephyreiaque aera,
alba neque Assyrio fucatur lana veneno,   465
nec casia liquidi corrumpitur usus olivi :
at secura quies et nescia fallere vita,
dives opum variarum, at latis otia fundis
(speluncae vivique lacus et frigida Tempe
mugitusque boum mollesque sub arbore somni)   470
non absunt ; illic saltus ac lustra ferarum,
et patiens operum exiguoque adsueta iuventus,
sacra deum sanctique patres : extrema per illos
Iustitia excedens terris vestigia fecit.
  Me vero primum dulces ante omnia Musae,   475
quarum sacra fero ingenti percussus amore,
accipiant caelique vias et sidera monstrent,
defectus solis varios lunaeque labores ;
unde tremor terris, qua vi maria alta tumescant
obicibus ruptis rursusque in se ipsa residant,   480
quid tantum Oceano properent se tinguere soles
hiberni, vel quae tardis mora noctibus obstet.
sin, has ne possim naturae accedere partis,
frigidus obstiterit circum praecordia sanguis,
rura mihi et rigui placeant in vallibus amnes,   485

    464 inciusas M^1PR, *Berne Scholia ; known to Servius.*
    467 vitam *PR.*
    469 et $M\gamma$: at $P\gamma^2$: ad *R.*
    476 perculsus $M^2\gamma^2$.

Rhoetus, and Pholus, and Hylaeus, menacing the Lapiths with mighty bowl.

⁴⁵⁸ O happy husbandmen! too happy, should they come to know their blessings! for whom, far from the clash of arms, most righteous [1] Earth, unbidden, pours forth from her soil an easy sustenance. What though no stately mansion with proud portals disgorges at dawn from all its halls a tide of visitors, though they never gaze at doors inlaid with lovely tortoise-shell or at raiment tricked with gold or at bronzes of Ephyra, though their white wool be not stained with Assyrian dye, or their clear oil's service spoiled by cassia? Yet theirs is repose without care, and a life that knows no fraud, but is rich in treasures manifold. Yea, the ease of broad domains, caverns, and living lakes, and cool vales, the lowing of the kine, and soft slumbers beneath the trees—all are theirs. They have woodland glades and the haunts of game; a youth hardened to toil and inured to scanty fare; worship of gods and reverence for age; among them, as she quitted the earth, Justice planted her latest steps.

⁴⁷⁵ But as for me—first above all, may the sweet Muses whose holy emblems, under the spell of a mighty love, I bear,[2] take me to themselves, and show me heaven's pathways, the stars, the sun's many lapses, the moon's many labours; whence come tremblings of the earth, the force to make deep seas swell and burst their barriers, then sink back upon themselves; why winter suns hasten so fast to dip in Ocean, or what delays clog the lingering nights. But if the chill blood about my heart bar me from reaching those realms of nature, let my delight be the country, and the running streams amid the dells—may I love the

---

[1] Because she pays her debts in fullest measure.
[2] *i.e.* the poet is a priest of the Muses.

flumina amem silvasque inglorius.   o ubi campi
Spercheosque et virginibus bacchata Lacaenis
Taygeta ! o qui me gelidis convallibus Haemi
sistat et ingenti ramorum protegat umbra !
felix, qui potuit rerum cognoscere causas,   490
atque metus omnis et inexorabile fatum
subiecit pedibus strepitumque Acherontis avari.
fortunatus et ille, deos qui novit agrestis,
Panaque Silvanumque senem Nymphasque sorores.
illum non populi fasces, non purpura regum   495
flexit et infidos agitans discordia fratres,
aut coniurato descendens Dacus ab Histro,
non res Romanae perituraque regna ; neque ille
aut doluit miserans inopem aut invidit habenti.
quos rami fructus, quos ipsa volentia rura   500
sponte tulere sua, carpsit, nec ferrea iura
insanumque forum aut populi tabularia vidit.
sollicitant alii remis freta caeca, ruuntque
in ferrum, penetrant aulas et limina regum ;
hic petit excidiis urbem miserosque penatis,   505
ut gemma bibat et Sarrano dormiat ostro ;
condit opes alius defossoque incubat auro ;
hic stupet attonitus rostris ; hunc plausus hiantem
per cuneos geminatus enim plebisque patrumque
corripuit ; gaudent perfusi sanguine fratrum,   510
exsilioque domos et dulcia limina mutant
atque alio patriam quaerunt sub sole iacentem.

150

waters and the woods, though fame be lost. O for those plains, and Spercheus, and Taygetus, where Spartan girls hold Bacchic rites! O for one to set me in the cool glens of Haemus, and shield me under the branches' mighty shade!

⁴⁹⁰ Blessed is he who has been able to win knowledge of the causes of things, and has cast beneath his feet all fear and unyielding Fate, and the howls of hungry Acheron! Happy, too, is he who knows the woodland gods, Pan and old Silvanus and the sister Nymphs! Him no honours the people give can move, no purple of kings, no strife rousing brother to break with brother, no Dacian swooping down from his leagued Danube, no power of Rome, no kingdoms doomed to fall : he knows naught of the pang of pity for the poor, or of envy of the rich. He plucks the fruits which his boughs, which his ready fields, of their own free will, have borne ; nor has he beheld the iron laws, the Forum's madness, or the public archives.¹ Others vex with oars seas unknown, dash upon the sword, or press into courts and the portals of kings. One wreaks ruin on a city and its hapless homes, that he may drink from a jewelled cup and sleep on Tyrian purple ; another hoards up wealth and broods over buried gold ; one is dazed and astounded by the Rostra ; another, open-mouthed, is carried away by the plaudits of princes and of people, rolling again and again along the benches.² Gleefully they steep themselves in their brothers' blood ; for exile they change their sweet homes and hearths, and seek a country that lies beneath an alien sun.

¹ Probably a reference to the Tabularium, or Hall of Records, standing across the west end of the *Forum Romanum*.

² *i.e.* of the theatres, where popular statesmen would be warmly applauded by all classes of citizens.

VIRGIL

agricola incurvo terram dimovit aratro :
hinc anni labor, hinc patriam parvosque nepotes
sustinet, hinc armenta boum meritosque iuvencos. 515
nec requies, quin aut pomis exuberet annus
aut fetu pecorum aut Cerealis mergite culmi,
proventuque oneret sulcos atque horrea vincat.
venit hiems : teritur Sicyonia baca trapetis,
glande sues laeti redeunt, dant arbuta silvae ;   520
et varios ponit fetus autumnus, et alte
mitis in apricis coquitur vindemia saxis.
interea dulces pendent circum oscula nati,
casta pudicitiam servat domus, ubera vaccae
lactea demittunt, pinguesque in gramine laeto   525
inter se adversis luctantur cornibus haedi.
ipse dies agitat festos fususque per herbam,
ignis ubi in medio et socii cratera coronant,
te libans, Lenaee, vocat pecorisque magistris
velocis iaculi certamina ponit in ulmo,   530
corporaque agresti nudant praedura palaestrae.
hanc olim veteres vitam coluere Sabini,
hanc Remus et frater, sic fortis Etruria crevit
scilicet et rerum facta est pulcherrima Roma,
septemque una sibi muro circumdedit arces.   MPRV
ante etiam sceptrum Dictaei regis et ante   536
impia quam caesis gens est epulata iuvencis,
aureus hanc vitam in terris Saturnus agebat ;
necdum etiam audierant inflari classica, necdum
impositos duris crepitare incudibus ensis.   540
    Sed nos immensum spatiis confecimus aequor,
et iam tempus equum fumantia solvere colla.

---

    513 molitus *M.*
    514 penates *M.*   518 aut *M1.*
    531 perdura *M1.* palaestra *PR, Servius, Berne Scholia.*
    532 vitam veteres *P.*
    542 spumantia *PR.*

152

GEORGICS BOOK II

[513] Meanwhile the husbandman has been cleaving the soil with crooked plough; hence comes his year's work, hence comes sustenance for his country and his little grandsons, hence for his herds of kine and faithful bullocks. No respite is there, but the season teems either with fruits, or with increase of the herds, or with the sheaves of Ceres' corn, loading the furrows with its yield and bursting the barns. Winter is come; Sicyon's berry is bruised in the mill, the swine come home gladdened with acorns, the forests yield arbutes, or autumn sheds its varied produce, and high on the sunny rocks basks the mellow vintage. Meanwhile his dear children hang upon his kisses; his unstained home guards its purity; the kine droop milk-laden udders, and on the glad sward, horn to horn, the fat kids wrestle. The master himself keeps holiday, and stretched on the grass, with a fire in the midst and his comrades wreathing the bowl, offers libation and calls on thee, O god of the Wine-press, and for the keepers of the flock sets up a mark on an elm for the contest of the winged javelin, or they bare their hardy limbs for the rustic wrestling-bout.

[532] Such a life the old Sabines once lived, such Remus and his brother. Thus, surely, Etruria waxed strong, thus Rome became of all things the fairest, and with a single city's wall enclosed her seven hills. Nay, before the Cretan king[1] held sceptre, and before a godless race banqueted on slaughtered bullocks, such was the life golden Saturn lived on earth, while yet none had heard the clarion blare, none the sword-blades ring, as they were laid on the stubborn anvil.

[541] But in our course we have traversed a mighty plain, and now it is time to unyoke the necks of our smoking steeds.

[1] Jupiter.

LIBER III

Te quoque, magna Pales, et te memorande
    canemus FMPRV
pastor ab Amphryso, vos, silvae amnesque Lycaei.
cetera quae vacuas tenuissent carmine mentes,
omnia iam volgata : quis aut Eurysthea durum
aut inlaudati nescit Busiridis aras ?   5
cui non dictus Hylas puer et Latonia Delos
Hippodameque umeroque Pelops insignis eburno,
acer equis ? temptanda via est, qua me quoque possim
tollere humo victorque virum volitare per ora.
primus ego in patriam mecum, modo vita supersit, 10
Aonio rediens deducam vertice Musas ;
primus Idumaeas referam tibi, Mantua, palmas
et viridi in campo templum de marmore ponam FMPR
propter aquam, tardis ingens ubi flexibus errat
Mincius et tenera praetexit harundine ripas.   15
in medio mihi Caesar erit templumque tenebit.
illi victor ego et Tyrio conspectus in ostro
centum quadriiugos agitabo ad flumina currus.
cuncta mihi, Alpheum linquens lucosque Molorchi,
cursibus et crudo decernet Graecia caestu.   20

    3 carmina $F^1MR\gamma$.   **5** arces M^1.   **8** possem P.
17 illic R.   **19** linquens] pubes P.
20 duro R. decernit FPR : decerniet M^1 : decertet M (*late*).
154

BOOK III

Thee, too, great Pales, we will sing, and thee, famed
shepherd of Amphrysus,[1] and you, ye woods and
streams of Lycaeus. Other themes, which else had
charmed with song some idle fancy, are now all trite.
Who knows not pitiless Eurystheus, or the altars
of detested Busiris? Who has not told of the boy
Hylas, of Latona's Delos, of Hippodame, and Pelops,
famed for ivory shoulder, and fearless with his steeds?
I must essay a path whereby I, too, may rise from
earth and fly victorious on the lips of men. I first,
if life but remain, will return to my country, bringing
the Muses with me in triumph from the Aonian
peak; first I will bring back to thee, Mantua, the
palms of Idumaea, and on the green plain will set up
a temple in marble beside the water, where great
Mincius wanders in slow windings and fringes his
banks with slender reeds.[2]

[16] In the midst I will have Caesar, and he
shall possess the shrine. In his honour I, a victor
resplendent in Tyrian purple, will drive a hundred
four-horse chariots beside the stream. For me, all
Greece, leaving Alpheus and the groves of Molorchus,
shall vie in races and with raw-hide gloves, and I,

---

[1] Apollo.
[2] Virgil's proposed poem is described allegorically as a
temple, in which Caesar is to be the deity.

VIRGIL

ipse caput tonsae foliis ornatus olivae
dona feram.   iam nunc sollemnis ducere pompas MPR
ad delubra iuvat caesosque videre iuvencos,
vel scaena ut versis discedat frontibus utque
purpurea intexti tollant aulaea Britanni.   25
in foribus pugnam ex auro solidoque elephanto
Gangaridum faciam victorisque arma Quirini,
atque hic undantem bello magnumque fluentem
Nilum ac navali surgentis aere columnas.
addam urbes Asiae domitas pulsumque Niphaten 30
fidentemque fuga Parthum versisque sagittis
et duo rapta manu diverso ex hoste tropaea
bisque triumphatas utroque ab litore gentes.
stabunt et Parii lapides, spirantia signa,
Assaraci proles demissaeque ab Iove gentis   35
nomina Trosque parens et Troiae Cynthius auctor.
Invidia infelix furias amnemque severum
Cocyti metuet tortosque Ixionis anguis
immanemque rotam et non exsuperabile saxum.
interea Dryadum silvas saltusque sequamur   40
intactos, tua, Maecenas, haud mollia iussa.
te sine nil altum mens incohat: en age, segnis
rumpe moras; vocat ingenti clamore Cithaeron
Taygetique canes domitrixque Epidaurus equorum,

25 tollent *P.*   28 huic *P*[1] : hic *P*[2].
29 navalis *P.*   33 metuens *P.*

[1] The stage "scaenae" either formed the background and,
when parted (*discedat*) in the centre, disclosed a new scene
within, or were triangular prisms, which revolved (*versis
frontibus*) on either side of the stage.   Both kinds, doubtless,
were often used at the same time.   The ancient curtain rose

156

with brows decked with shorn olive-leaves, will bring
gifts. Even now 'tis a joy to lead the solemn pro-
cession to the sanctuary, and view the slaughter of
the steers; or to watch how the scene retreats with
changing front, and how the inwoven Britons raise
the purple curtains.[1] On the doors I will fashion, in
gold and solid ivory, the battle of the Ganges' tribe,
and the arms of conquering Quirinus; there, too,
the Nile, surging with war and flowing full; and
columns soaring high with prows of bronze. I will
add Asia's vanquished cities, the routed Niphates, the
Parthian, whose trust is in flight and backward-shot
arrows, the two trophies torn perforce from far-
sundered foes and the nations on either shore that
yielded twofold triumphs.[2] Here, too, shall stand
Parian marbles, statues that breathe—the seed of
Assaracus, and the great names of the race sprung
from Jove, father Tros, and the Cynthian founder of
Troy. Loathly envy shall cower before the Furies
and the stern stream of Cocytus, Ixion's twisted
snakes and monstrous wheel, and the unconquerable
stone.[3]

[40] Meantime let us pursue the Dryads' woods and
virgin glades—no easy behest of thine, Maecenas.
Apart from thee, my mind essays no lofty theme;
arise then, break through slow delays! With mighty
clamour Cithaeron calls, and Taygetus' hounds and

instead of falling. The "inwoven Britons" are the figures
worked upon it.

[2] Upon the great temple-doors were to be sculptures in
relief showing Caesar's victories over foes in the far East
and the far West (of the Mediterranean). In the *pugnam
Gangaridum* Virgil refers to Antony's Oriental troops. The
rivers and mountains (*e.g.* the Niphates) of conquered people
were often represented in triumphal processions.

[3] *i.e.* of Sisyphus.

VIRGIL

et vox adsensu nemorum ingeminata remugit.   45
mox tamen ardentis accingar dicere pugnas
Caesaris et nomen fama tot ferre per annos,
Tithoni prima quot abest·ab origine Caesar.

    Seu quis Olympiacae miratus praemia palmae
pascit equos, seu quis fortis ad aratra iuvencos,   50
corpora praecipue matrum legat.   optima torvae
forma bovis, cui turpe caput, cui plurima cervix,
et crurum tenus a mento palearia pendent ;
tum longo nullus lateri modus ; omnia magna,
pes etiam ; et camuris hirtae sub cornibus aures. 55
nec mihi displiceat maculis insignis et albo,
aut iuga detrectans interdumque aspera cornu
et faciem tauro propior, quaeque ardua tota
et gradiens ima verrit vestigia cauda.
aetas Lucinam iustosque pati hymenaeos   60
desinit ante decem, post quattuor incipit annos ;
cetera nec feturae habilis nec fortis aratris.
interea, superat gregibus dum laeta iuventas,
solve mares ; mitte in Venerem pecuaria primus,
atque aliam ex alia generando suffice prolem.   65
optima quaeque dies miseris mortalibus aevi
prima fugit ; subeunt morbi tristisque senectus
et labor, et durae rapit inclementia mortis.
semper erunt, quarum mutari corpora malis :
semper enim refice ac, ne post amissa requiras,   70
anteveni et subolem armento sortire quotannis.

    Nec non et pecori est idem delectus equino.
tu modo, quos in spem statues submittere gentis,

---

48 quod *MPRγ* : quot *M* (*late*).
50 pascet *P*.
55 sub] cum *M*¹.
56 tibi *M*¹ : mihi *M*².
57 detractans *PR*.
63 iuventus *M*¹, *Priscian.*
65 ex aliis *P*.   69 mavis *M*.

Epidaurus, tamer of horses; and the cry, doubled by
the applauding groves, rings back. Yet anon I will
gird me to sing Caesar's fiery fights, and bear his
name in story through as many years as Caesar is
distant from the far-off birth of Tithonus.

⁴⁹ Whether a man aspires to the prize of Olympia's
palm and breeds horses, or rears bullocks, strong for
the plough, let his chief care be to choose the mould
of the dams. The best-formed cow is fierce-looking,
her head ugly, her neck thick, and her dewlaps
hanging down from chin to legs. Moreover, her
long flank has no limit; all points are large, even
the feet; and under the crooked horns are shaggy
ears. Nor should I dislike one marked with white
spots, or impatient of the yoke, at times fierce with
the horn, and more like a bull in face; tall through-
out, and as she steps sweeping her footprints
with the tail's tip. The age to bear motherhood
and lawful wedlock ends before the tenth year, and
begins after the fourth; the rest of their life is
neither fit for breeding nor strong for the plough.
Meantime, while lusty youth still abides in the
herds, let loose the males; be first to send your cattle
to mate, and supply stock after stock by breeding.
Life's fairest days are ever the first to flee for hap-
less mortals; on creep diseases, and sad age, and
suffering; and stern death's ruthlessness sweeps
away its prey.

⁶⁹ Ever will there be some kine whose mould you
would wish to change; ever, I pray, renew them, and,
lest too late you regret your losses, keep in advance,
and year by year choose new stock for the herd.

⁷² Likewise for your breed of horses is the same
choice needed. Only, upon those whom you mean
to rear for the hope of the race, be sure to spend

159

VIRGIL

praecipuum iam inde a teneris impende laborem.
continuo pecoris generosi pullus in arvis   75
altius ingreditur et mollia crura reponit;
primus et ire viam et fluvios temptare minacis
audet et ignoto sese committere ponti,
nec vanos horret strepitus.   illi ardua cervix
argutumque caput, brevis alvus obesaque terga,   80
luxuriatque toris animosum pectus.   honesti
spadices glaucique, color deterrimus albis
et gilvo.   tum, si qua sonum procul arma dedere,
stare loco nescit, micat auribus et tremit artus,
collectumque fremens volvit sub naribus ignem.   85
densa iuba, et dextro iactata recumbit in armo;
at duplex agitur per lumbos spina, cavatque
tellurem et solido graviter sonat ungula cornu.
talis Amyclaei domitus Pollucis habenis
Cyllarus et, quorum Grai meminere poetae,   90
Martis equi biiuges et magni currus Achilli;
talis et ipse iubam cervice effundit equina
coniugis adventu pernix Saturnus, et altum
Pelion hinnitu fugiens implevit acuto.
   Hunc quoque, ubi aut morbo gravis aut iam segnior
          annis   95
deficit, abde domo, nec turpi ignosce senectae.
frigidus in Venerem senior, frustraque laborem
ingratum trahit; et, si quando ad proelia ventum est,
ut quondam in stipulis magnus sine viribus ignis,
incassum furit.   ergo animos aevumque notabis 100
praecipue; hinc alias artis prolemque parentum,
et quis cuique dolor victo, quae gloria palmae.

77 minantis *P*.   78 ponto *M¹γ*.
85 primens *P:* praemens *R:* premens *γ, Seneca*.
88 quatit *R*.   96 defecit *M¹*.
99 in *lacking M¹γ*.   101 partis *P*.

160

special pains, even from their early youth. From the first, the foal of a noble breed steps higher in the fields and brings down his feet lightly. Boldly he leads the way, braves threatening rivers, entrusts himself to an untried bridge, and starts not at idle sounds. His neck is high, his head clean-cut, his belly short, his back plump, and his gallant chest is rich in muscles. Good colours are bay and grey; the worst, white and dun. Again, should he but hear afar the clash of arms, he cannot keep his place; he pricks up his ears, quivers in his limbs, and snorting rolls beneath his nostrils the gathered fire. His mane is thick and, as he tosses it, falls back on his right shoulder. A double ridge runs along his loins; his hoof scoops out the ground, and the solid horn gives it a deep ring. Such was Cyllarus, tamed by the reins of Amyclaean Pollux, and those whose fame Greek poets recount, the two steeds of Mars,[1] and the pair of the great Achilles.[2] Such, too, was Saturn himself, when at his wife's[3] coming he fled swiftly, flinging his horse's mane over his shoulders, and with shrill neigh filled the heights of Pelion.

[95] Yet even such a steed, when, worn with disease or sluggish through years, he begins to fail, shut up indoors and pity not his inglorious age. Cold is his passion when old, vainly he strives at a thankless toil, and whenever he comes to the fray his ardour is futile, as in the stubble a great fire rages at times without strength. Therefore note above all their spirit and years; then, other merits and the stock of their sires, the grief each shows at defeat or the pride in victory.

---

[1] See Homer, *Iliad*, XV. 119.

[2] Homer, *Iliad*, XVI. 148.

[3] *i.e.* Rhea or Ops, whom Saturn, when in love with Philyra (or Phillyra), tried to elude by changing himself into a horse.

VIRGIL

nonne vìdes, cum praecipiti certamine campum
corripuere, ruuntque effusi carcere currus,
cum spes arrectae iuvenum, exsultantiaque haurit 105
corda pavor pulsans? illi instant verbere torto
et proni dant lora, volat vi fervidus axis;
iamque humiles, iamque elati sublime videntur
aëra per vacuum ferri atque adsurgere in auras;
nec mora nec requies; at fulvae nimbus harenae 110
tollitur, umescunt spumis flatuque sequentum:
tantus amor laudum, tantae est victoria curae.
primus Erichthonius currus et quattuor ausus
iungere equos rapidusque rotis insistere victor.
frena Pelethronii Lapithae gyrosque dedere 115
impositi dorso, atque equitem docuere sub armis
insultare solo et gressus glomerare superbos.
aequus uterque labor, aeque iuvenemque magistri
exquirunt calidumque animis et cursibus acrem;
quamvis saepe fuga versos ille egerit hostis 120
et patriam Epirum referat fortisque Mycenas,
Neptunique ipsa deducat origine gentem.

His animadversis instant sub tempus et omnis
impendunt curas denso distendere pingui
quem legere ducem et pecori dixere maritum; 125
florentisque secant herbas fluviosque ministrant
farraque, ne blando nequeat superesse labori
invalidique patrum referant ieiunia nati.
ipsa autem macie tenuant armenta volentes,
atque ubi concubitus primos iam nota voluptas 130

---

[109] exsurgere *R*γ.   [114] rapidis *M* (*late*).
[122] gentem] nomen *R*.
[123] anima adversis *M*: animum adversis *P*.
[125] pecoris *P*. magistrum *P*.
[127] nequeant *P*: nequeans *M*^{1}.   [130] voluntas *P*.

---

[1] *i.e.* the task of breeding either racers or chargers.
[2] *i.e.* the old horse described in ll. 95 ff.

162

GEORGICS BOOK III

103 See you not, when in headlong contest the chariots have seized upon the plain, and stream in a torrent from the barrier, when the young drivers' hopes are high, and throbbing fear drains each bounding heart? On they press with circling lash, bending forward to slacken rein; fiercely flies the glowing wheel. Now sinking low, now raised aloft, they seem to be borne through empty air and to soar skyward. No rest, no stay is there; but a cloud of yellow sand mounts aloft, and they are wet with the foam and the breath of those in pursuit: so strong is their love of renown, so dear is triumph.

113 Erichthonius first dared to couple four steeds to the car, and to stand victorious over the flying wheels. The Thessalian Lapiths, mounting the horse's back, gave us the bit and circling course, and taught the horseman, in full armour, to gallop over the earth and round his proud paces. Equal is either task; [1] equally the trainers seek out a young steed, hot of spirit and keen in the race; though oft that other [2] have driven the foe in flight, and claim for birthplace Epirus or valiant Mycenae, and trace his line from Neptune's own ancestry. [3]

123 These points noted, they bestir themselves, as the time draws near, and take all heed to fill out with firm flesh him whom they have chosen as leader and assigned as lord of the herd. They cut him flowering grasses, and give fresh water and corn, that he may be more than equal to the seductive toil, and no feeble offspring may repeat the leanness of the sires. But the mares themselves they purposely make spare, and when now the familiar pleasure first prompts

[3] Referring probably to the contest between Neptune (Poseidon) and Minerva (Athena). See *Geor.* I. 12.

163

sollicitat, frondesque **negant** et fontibus arcent.
saepe etiam cursu quatiunt et sole fatigant,
cum graviter tunsis gemit area frugibus, et cum
surgentem ad Zephyrum paleae iactantur inanes.
hoc faciunt, nimio ne luxu obtunsior usus   135
sit genitali arvo et sulcos oblimet inertis,
sed rapiat sitiens Venerem interiusque recondat.

 Rursus cura patrum cadere et succedere matrum
incipit. exactis gravidae cum mensibus errant,
non illas gravibus quisquam iuga ducere plaustris, 140
non saltu superare viam sit passus et acri
carpere prata fuga fluviosque innare rapacis.
saltibus in vacuis pascunt et plena secundum
flumina, muscus ubi et viridissima gramine ripa,
speluncaeque tegant et saxea procubet umbra.   145
est lucos Silari circa ilicibusque virentem   FMPR
plurimus Alburnum volitans, cui nomen asilo
Romanum est, oestrum Grai vertere vocantes,
asper, acerba sonans, quo tota exterrita silvis
diffugiunt armenta, furit mugitibus aether   150
concussus silvaeque et sicci ripa Tanagri.
hoc quondam monstro horribilis exercuit iras
Inachiae Iuno pestem meditata iuvencae.
hunc quoque (nam mediis fervoribus acrior instat)
arcebis gravido pecori, armentaque pasces   155
sole recens orto aut noctem ducentibus astris.

  141 agri *Rγ*.   **143** pascant *M (late)*.
  144 gramina ripae *M*.
  145 protegit *M¹*, -at *then* -cubet *M²*. **150** fugit *Fγ*.
  155 pecorique *M (late)*: pecoris *P*. pascis *F*.

them to union, they withhold leafy fodder and
debar them from the springs. Oft, too, they rouse
them to the gallop and tire them in the sun, when
the floor groans heavily as the corn is threshed, and
the empty chaff is tossed to the freshening Zephyr.
This they do that by surfeit the usefulness of the
fruitful soil be not dulled, or the sluggish furrows
clogged, but that it may thirstily seize upon the seed,
and store it deep within.

[138] In turn, care for the sires begins to wane, and
that for the dams to take its place. When their months
are fulfilled and they roam heavy with young, then let
no one suffer them to draw the yokes of heavy wagons,
or leap across [1] the pathway, or scour the meadows in
swift flight, or stem the swirling current. They feed
them in open glades and by the side of brimming
rivers, where moss grows and the banks are greenest
with grass, where grottoes may shelter them and the
shadow of a rock be cast afar. Round the groves of
Silarus and the green holm-oaks of Alburnus swarms
a fly, whose Roman name is *asilus*, but the Greeks have
called it in their speech *oestrus*.[2] Fierce it is, and
sharp of note ; before it whole herds scatter in terror
through the woods : with their bellowings the air is
stunned and maddened, the groves, too, and the banks
of parched Tanager. With this monster Juno once
wreaked her awful wrath, when she devised a pest
for the heifer-maid of Inachus.[3] This, too—for in mid-
day heat more fierce is its attack—you will keep from
the pregnant herd, and will feed the flock when the
sun is new-risen, or the stars usher in the night.

---

[1] According to Servius, this often happened when they were
grazing, with their feet hobbled.

[2] *i.e.* the gadfly.

[3] *i.e.* Io, daughter of Inachus.

VIRGIL

Post partum cura in vitulos traducitur omnis;
continuoque notas et nomina gentis inurunt,
et quos aut pecori malint submittere habendo
aut aris servare sacros aut scindere terram   160
et campum horrentem fractis invertere glaebis.
cetera pascuntur viridis armenta per herbas.
tu quos ad studium atque usum formabis agrestem,
iam vitulos hortare viamque insiste domandi,
dum faciles animi iuvenum, dum mobilis aetas.   165
ac primum laxos tenui de vimine circlos
cervici subnecte; dehinc, ubi libera colla
servitio adsuerint, ipsis e torquibus aptos
iunge pares, et coge gradum conferre iuvencos;
atque illis iam saepe rotae ducantur inanes   170
per terram, et summo vestigia pulvere signent;
post valido nitens sub pondere faginus axis
instrepat, et iunctos temo trahat aereus orbis.
interea pubi indomitae non gramina tantum
nec vescas salicum frondes ulvamque palustrem,   175
sed frumenta manu carpes sata; nec tibi fetae
more patrum nivea implebunt mulctraria vaccae,
sed tota in dulcis consument ubera natos.

Sin ad bella magis studium turmasque ferocis,
aut Alphea rotis praelabi flumina Pisae   180
et Iovis in luco currus agitare volantis :   AFMPR
primus equi labor est animos atque arma videre
bellantum lituosque pati, tractuque gementem
ferre rotam et stabulo frenos audire sonantis;
tum magis atque magis blandis gaudere magistri 185

    [163] studia *FR*.   [166] circos *F¹P*.   [169] iuvencis *M¹*.
    [175] ulvam] ulvas *F*, silvam *R*.
    [176] consumant *M¹*   [182] equis *M¹*.

¹⁵⁷ After birth, all care passes to the calves, and at once they brand them with the mark and name of the stock, setting apart those they wish to rear for breeding, to keep sacred for the altar, to set to cleave the soil and turn up the field, rough with its broken clods. The rest of the kine graze in the green pastures; but such as you will shape for the farm's pursuits and service, do you school while yet calves, and enter on the path of training, while their youthful spirits are docile, while their age is still pliant. And, first, fasten about their shoulders loose circles of slender osier; then when their free necks are used to servitude, yoke the bullocks in pairs linked from the collars themselves,[1] and force them to step together. Then let them now draw empty carts oft-times over the land, and print their tracks on the surface of the dust. Later, let the beechen axle creak and strain under its heavy load and a brass-bound pole drag the coupled wheels. Meanwhile you will not feed their unbroken youth on grass alone or poor willow leaves and marshy sedge, but on young corn, plucked by hand; nor will your mother-cows fill the snowy pails, as in our fathers' days, but will spend all their udders' wealth on their dear offspring.

¹⁷⁹ But if your bent is more towards war and fierce squadrons, or to glide on wheels by Pisa's Alphean waters, and in Jupiter's grove[2] to drive the flying car, then the steed's first task is to view the arms of gallant warriors, to bear the trumpet-call, to endure the groaning of the dragged wheel, and to hear the jingle of bits in the stall; then more and more to delight in his trainer's caressing praise, and to love the

---

[1] No yoke is to be used, but the collars are to be tied together.

[2] *i.e.* the Altis, or wild-olive grove in which the Olympic racecourse by the Alpheus lay.

VIRGIL

laudibus et plausae sonitum cervicis amare.
atque haec iam primo depulsus ab ubere matris
audeat, inque vicem det mollibus ora capistris
invalidus etiamque tremens, etiam inscius aevi.
at tribus exactis ubi quarta accesserit aestas,   190
carpere mox gyrum incipiat gradibusque sonare
compositis, sinuetque alterna volumina crurum,
sitque laboranti similis; tum cursibus auras,
tum vocet, ac per aperta volans, ceu liber habenis,
aequora vix summa vestigia ponat harena: 195
qualis Hyperboreis Aquilo cum densus ab oris
incubuit, Scythiaeque hiemes atque arida differt
nubila; tum segetes altae campique natantes
lenibus horrescunt flabris, summaeque sonorem
dant silvae, longique urgent ad litora fluctus;   200
ille volat, simul arva fuga, simul aequora verrens.
hic vel ad Elei metas et maxima campi
sudabit spatia et spumas aget ore cruentas,
Belgica vel molli melius feret esseda collo.
tum demum crassa magnum farragine corpus   205
crescere iam domitis sinito: namque ante domandum
ingentis tollent animos, prensique negabunt
verbera lenta pati et duris parere lupatis.

Sed non ulla magis viris industria firmat,
quam Venerem et caeci stimulos avertere amoris,   210
sive boum sive est cui gratior usus equorum.
atque ideo tauros procul atque in sola relegant
pascua, post montem oppositum et trans flumina lata,
aut intus clausos satura ad praesepia servant.   214
carpit enim viris paulatim uritque videndo   AMPR
femina, nec nemorum patitur meminisse nec herbae

188 audiat $M^2R\gamma^3$.   189 iam iamque M (*late*).
190 occeperit F^1: acceperit M^2PR.   aetas F^2M, *Servius.*
194 provocet P..   202 hinc FM^2R.
203 agit FM^1P: aget M (*late*).   204 bellica M^1P.

168

sound of patting his neck. And this let him venture,
soon as he is weaned from his mother, and now and
again let him entrust his mouth to soft halters, while
still weak and trembling, still ignorant of life. But
when three summers are past and the fourth is come,
let him soon begin to run round the circuit,[1] to make
his steps ring evenly, to bend his legs in alternating
curves,[2] and be as one hard labouring : then, then let
him challenge the winds to a race, and, skimming over
the open plains, as though free from reins, let him
scarce plant his steps on the surface of the sand—as
when the gathered North-wind swoops down from
Hyperborean coasts, driving on Scythia's storms and
dry clouds, then the deep cornfields and the watery
plains quiver under the gentle gusts, the tree-tops
rustle, and long rollers press shoreward ; on flies the
wind, sweeping in his flight the fields and seas alike.
Such a horse will either sweat towards the Elean goal,
over the vast courses of the plain, and fling from his
mouth bloody foam, or will bear more nobly with
docile neck the Belgian car. Then at last, when the
colts are now broken, let their bodies wax plump with
coarse mash ; for ere the breaking they will raise their
mettle too high, and when caught will scorn to submit
to the pliant lash, or obey the cruel curb.

[209] But no care so strengthens their powers as
to keep from them desire and the stings of secret
passion, whether one's choice is to deal with cattle
or with horses. Therefore men banish the bull to
lonely pastures afar, beyond a mountain barrier and
across broad rivers, or keep him well mewed beside
full mangers. For the sight of the female slowly in-
flames and wastes his strength, nor, look you, does she,

---

[1] *i.e.* the ring or "circling course" (l. 115) for breaking
horses in.   [2] *cf.* 117, "round his proud paces."

dulcibus illa quidem inlecebris, et saepe superbos
cornibus inter se subigit decernere amantis.
pascitur in magna Sila formosa iuvenca :
illi alternantes multa vi proelia miscent   220
volneribus crebris, lavit ater corpora sanguis,   MPR
versaque in obnixos urgentur cornua vasto
cum gemitu ; reboant silvaeque et longus Olympus.
nec mos bellantis una stabulare, sed alter
victus abit longeque ignotis exsulat oris,   225
multa gemens ignominiam plagasque superbi
victoris, tum quos amisit inultus amores,
et stabula aspectans regnis excessit avitis.
ergo omni cura viris exercet et inter
dura iacet pernox instrato saxa cubili,   230
frondibus hirsutis et carice pastus acuta,
et temptat sese atque irasci in cornua discit
arboris obnixus trunco, ventosque lacessit
ictibus, et sparsa ad pugnam proludit harena.
post ubi collectum robur viresque refectae,   235
signa movet praecepsque oblitum fertur in hostem :
fluctus uti medio coepit cum albescere ponto,
longius ex altoque sinum trahit, utque volutus
ad terras immane sonat per saxa, neque ipso
monte minor procumbit ; at ima exaestuat unda   240
verticibus nigramque alte subiectat harenam.
  Omne adeo genus in terris hominumque ferarum-
      que,
et genus aequoreum, pecudes pictaeque volucres,

[219] silva $AM^1P\gamma$: *both known to Servius.*
[221] lavat M (*late*).
[223] resonant M. longus M^2, *Macrobius :* longius M^1: magnus
$PR\gamma$.
[230] pernox *Scholiast on Juvenal,* VIII. 10 : pernix *MSS.,
Servius, and Nonius, preferred by Philargyrius.*
[235] post] ast M. receptae R.   [236] oblicum M.
[237] ut in M. medio] primo M^2
[241] subvectat MR, *Berne Scholia.*
170

with her soft enchantments, suffer him to remember
woods or pastures ; nay, oft she drives her proud lovers
to settle their mutual contest with clash of horns. She
is grazing in Sila's great forest, a lovely heifer : the
bulls in alternate onset join battle with mighty force ;
many a wound they deal, black gore bathes their
frames, amid mighty bellowing the levelled horns are
driven against the butting foe ; the woods and the sky,
from end to end, re-echo. Nor is it the rivals' wont to
herd together, but the vanquished one departs, and
dwells an exile in unknown scenes afar. Much does
he bewail his shame, and the blows of his haughty
conqueror, and much the love he has lost unavenged
—then, with a wistful glance at his stall, he has
quitted his ancestral realm. Therefore with all heed
he trains his powers, and on an unstrewn couch
among flinty rocks, lies through the night, with
prickly leaves and pointed sedge for fare. Anon he
tests himself, and, learning to throw wrath into his
horns, charges a tree's trunk ; he lashes the winds with
blows, and paws the sand in prelude for the fray.
Soon, when his power is mustered and his strength
renewed, he advances the colours, and dashes head-
long on his unmindful foe : as, when a wave begins
to whiten in mid-sea, from the farther deep it arches
its curve, and, rolling shoreward, roars thundering
along the reefs, and, huge as a very mountain, falls
prone, while from below the water boils up in eddies,
and tosses black sand aloft.

242 Yea, every single race on earth, man and beast,
the tribes of the sea, cattle and birds brilliant of hue,

in furias ignemque ruunt : amor omnibus idem.
tempore non alio catulorum oblita leaena   245
saevior erravit campis, nec funera volgo
tam multa informes ursi stragemque dedere
per silvas ; tum saevus aper, tum pessima tigris ;
heu male tum Libyae solis erratur in agris.
nonne vides, ut tota tremor pertemptet equorum 250
corpora, si tantum notas odor attulit auras ?
ac neque eos iam frena virum neque verbera saeva,
non scopuli rupesque cavae atque obiecta retardant
flumina correptosque unda torquentia montis.
ipse ruit dentesque Sabellicus exacuit sus,   255
et pede prosubigit terram, fricat arbore costas,
atque hinc atque illinc umeros ad volnera durat.
quid iuvenis, magnum cui versat in ossibus ignem
durus amor ? nempe abruptis turbata procellis
nocte natat caeca serus freta ; quem super ingens 260
po ta tonat caeli, et scopulis inlisa reclamant
aequora ; nec miseri possunt revocare parentes,
nec moritura super crudeli funere virgo.
quid lynces Bacchi variae et genus acre luporum
atque canum ? quid quae imbelles dant proelia cervi ?
scilicet ante omnis furor est insignis equarum ;   266
et mentem Venus ipsa dedit, quo tempore Glauci
Potniades malis membra absumpsere quadrigae.
illas ducit amor trans Gargara transque sonantem
Ascanium ; superant montis et flumina tranant.   270
continuoque avidis ubi subdita flamma medullis

rush into fires of passion : all feel the same Love. At
no other season doth the lioness forget her cubs, or
prowl over the plains more fierce ; never doth the
shapeless bear spread death and havoc so widely
through the forest ; then savage is the boar, then
most fell the tigress. Ah ! it is ill faring then in
Libya's lonely fields ! See you not how a trembling
thrills through the steed's whole frame, if the scent
has but brought him the familiar breezes? No
longer now can the rider's rein or the cruel lash
stay his course, nor rocks and hollow cliffs, nay, nor
opposing rivers, that tear up mountains and hurl
them down the wave. On rushes the great Sabine
boar ; he whets his tusks, his foot paws the ground
in front, he rubs his sides against a tree, and on
either flank hardens his shoulders against wounds.
What of the youth, in whose marrow fierce Love
fans the mighty flame ? Lo ! in the turmoil of
bursting storms, late in the black night, he swims
the straits. Above him thunders Heaven's mighty
portal, and the billows, dashing on the cliffs, echo
the cry ; yet neither his hapless parents can call him
back, nor thought of the maid who in cruel fate
must die withal.[1] What of Bacchus' spotted lynxes,[2]
and the fierce tribe of wolves and dogs ? What of
the battles fought by peaceful stags ? But surely
the madness of mares surpasses all. Venus herself
inspired their frenzy, when the four Potnian steeds
tore with their jaws the limbs of Glaucus. Love
leads them over Gargarus and over the roaring
Ascanius ; they scale mountains, they swim rivers.
And, soon as the flame has stolen into their craving

[1] A reference to the famous story of Leander, who used to
swim the Hellespont to visit Hero, but was at last drowned.
[2] Lynxes and tigers drew the car of Bacchus from India.

(vere magis, quia vere calor redit ossibus), illae
ore omnes versae in Zephyrum stant rupibus altis
exceptantque levis auras, et saepe sine ullis
coniugiis vento gravidae (mirabile dictu) 275
saxa per et scopulos et depressas convallis
diffugiunt, non, Eure, tuos, neque solis ad ortus,
in Borean Caurumque, aut unde nigerrimus Auster
nascitur et pluvio contristat frigore caelum.
hic demum, hippomanes vero quod nomine dicunt 280
pastores, lentum destillat ab inguine virus,
hippomanes, quod saepe malae legere novercae
miscueruntque herbas et non innoxia verba.

   Sed fugit interea, fugit inreparabile tempus,
singula dum capti circumvectamur amore. FMPR
hoc satis armentis : superat pars altera curae, 286
lanigeros agitare greges hirtasque capellas.
hic labor, hinc laudem fortes sperate coloni.
nec sum animi dubius, verbis ea vincere magnum
quam sit et angustis hunc addere rebus honorem : 290
sed me Parnasi deserta per ardua dulcis
raptat amor ; iuvat ire iugis, qua nulla priorum
Castaliam molli devertitur orbita clivo.
nunc, veneranda Pales, magno nunc ore sonandum.

   Incipiens stabulis edico in mollibus herbam 295
carpere ovis, dum mox frondosa reducitur aestas,
et multa duram stipula filicumque maniplis
sternere subter humum, glacies ne frigida laedat

---

   273 in] ad M^2R.
   274 exceptant M^2R, *Servius, Philargyrius :* exspectant P :
expectant $M^1\gamma$.   **279** sidere R.
   286 superat est M^1.   **297** durum PR : dura F^1 : dura in F^2.

marrow (chiefly in spring, for in spring the heat
returns to their breasts), they all, with faces turned
to the Zephyrs, stand on a high cliff, and drink in
the gentle breezes.   Then oft, without any wedlock,
pregnant with the wind (a wondrous tale !) they flee
over rocks and crags and lowly dales, not towards thy
rising, East-wind, nor the Sun's, but to the North,
and the North-west, or thither where rises the
blackest South, saddening the sky with chilly
rain.[1] Then, and then only, does the slimy " horse-
madness," as shepherds rightly name it, drip slowly
from the groin—horse-madness, which cruel step-
dames oft gather, mixing herbs and baleful spells.

[284] But time meanwhile is flying, flying beyond
recall, while we, charmed with love of our theme,
linger around each detail ! Enough this for the
herds ; there remains the second part of my task,
to tend the fleecy flocks and shaggy goats. Here is
toil, hence hope for fame, ye sturdy yeomen ! And
well I know how hard it is to win with words a triumph
herein, and thus to crown with glory a lowly theme.
But sweet desire hurries me over the lonely steeps of
Parnassus ; joyous it is to roam o'er heights, where no
forerunner's track turns by a gentle slope down to
Castalia.[2] Now, worshipful Pales, now must we sing
in lofty strain.

[295] First I decree that the sheep crop the
herbage in soft pens, till leafy summer soon returns,
and that you strew the hard ground beneath them
with straw and handfuls of fern, lest the chill ice harm

----

[1] Aristotle, from whom this legend is taken, was speaking of
Crete, where the mares ran until stopped by the sea.   The
direction there would naturally be north or south.

[2] *i.e.* Virgil himself is the path-finder. In this metaphorical
way he claims originality.

VIRGIL

molle pecus scabiemque ferat turpisque podagras.
post hinc digressus iubeo frondentia capris   300
arbuta sufficere et fluvios praebere recentis,
et stabula a ventis hiberno opponere soli
ad medium conversa diem, cum frigidus olim
iam cadit extremoque inrorat Aquarius anno.
haec quoque non cura nobis leviore tuendae,   305
nec minor usus erit, quamvis Milesia magno
vellera mutentur Tyrios incocta rubores.
densior hinc suboles, hinc largi copia lactis;
quam magis exhausto spumaverit ubere mulctra,
laeta magis pressis manabunt flumina mammis.   310
nec minus interea barbas incanaque menta
Cinyphii tondent hirci saetasque comantis
usum in castrorum et miseris velamina nautis.
pascuntur vero silvas et summa Lycaei,
horrentisque rubos et amantis ardua dumos;   315
atque ipsae memores redeunt in tecta suosque
ducunt et gravido superant vix ubere limen.
ergo omni studio glaciem ventosque nivalis,
quo minor est illis curae mortalis egestas,
avertes, victumque feres et virgea laetus   320
pabula, nec tota claudes faenilia bruma.
at vero Zephyris cum laeta vocantibus aestas
in saltus utrumque gregem atque in pascua mittet,
Luciferi primo cum sidere frigida rura
carpamus, dum mane novum, dum gramina canent,
et ros in tenera pecori gratissimus herba.   326

305 haec . . . tuendae *FR, Servius:* haec . . . tuenda *M :*
hae . . . tuendae *Pγ.*
    307 colores *R.*   **308** hic largi *F.*
    309 quo *R.*
    310 flumina] ubera *PR, Nonius, known to Philargyrius.*
    312 hirqui *P.*
    316 inmemores *M.*
    323 mittes *FM²PRγ:* mittet *M¹.*
176

the tender flock, bringing scab and unsightly foot-rot.
Passing hence, I next bid you give the goats much
leafy arbutus, offering them fresh running water, and
placing the stalls away from the winds towards the
winter sun, to face the south, at the time when the
cold Water-bearer is now setting, sprinkling the
departing year.[1] These goats, too, we must guard
with no lighter care, and not less will be the profit,
albeit the fleeces of Miletus, steeped in Tyrian
purple, are bartered for a high price. From them is
a larger progeny, from them a plenteous store of milk ;
the more the milk-pail has foamed from the drained
udder, the more richly will flow the streams, when
again the teats are pressed. Nor less, meanwhile,
do herdsmen clip the beard on the hoary chin of the
Cinyphian goat, and shear his hairy bristles, for the
need of camps, and as coverings for hapless sailors.
Again, they feed in the woods and on the summits
of Lycaeus among the prickly briars and the hill-
loving brakes ; and of themselves they are mindful
to return home, leading their kids, and scarce able
to overtop the threshold with their teeming udders.
Therefore, the less they need man's care, the more
zealously should you screen them from frost and
snowy blasts, gladly bringing them their food and
provender of twigs, and closing not your hay lofts
throughout the winter.

[322] But when, at the Zephyrs' call, joyous Summer
sends both sheep and goats to the glades and pastures,
let us haste to the cool fields, as the morning-star
begins to rise, while the day is young, while the grass
is hoar, and the dew on the tender blade most sweet
to the cattle. Then, when heaven's fourth hour has

[1] Aquarius sets in February, and the old Roman year began
in March.

inde ubi quarta sitim caeli collegerit hora
et cantu querulae rumpent arbusta cicadae,
ad puteos aut alta greges ad stagna iubebo
currentem ilignis potare canalibus undam ;   330
aestibus at mediis umbrosam exquirere vallem,
sicubi magna Iovis antiquo robore quercus
ingentis tendat ramos, aut sicubi nigrum
ilicibus crebris sacra nemus accubet umbra ;
tum tenuis dare rursus aquas et pascere rursus   335
solis ad occasum, cum frigidus aëra vesper
temperat, et saltus reficit iam roscida luna
litoraque alcyonem resonant, acalanthida dumi.
    Quid tibi pastores Libyae, quid pascua versu
prosequar et raris habitata mapalia tectis ?   340
saepe diem noctemque et totum ex ordine mensem
pascitur itque pecus longa in deserta sine ullis
hospitiis : tantum campi iacet.   omnia secum
armentarius Afer agit, tectumque laremque
armaque Amyclaeumque canem Cressamque phare-
        tram ;   345
non secus ac patriis acer Romanus in armis
iniusto sub fasce viam cum carpit, et hosti
ante exspectatum positis stat in agmine castris. [MPR
    At non, qua Scythiae gentes Maeotiaque unda,
turbidus et torquens flaventis Hister harenas,   350
quaque redit medium Rhodope porrecta sub
        axem.   MPRV
illic clausa tenent stabulis armenta, neque ullae
aut herbae campo apparent aut arbore frondes ;
sed iacet aggeribus niveis informis et alto
terra gelu late septemque adsurgit in ulnas.   355
semper hiems, semper spirantes frigora Cauri.

    [329] iubeto $F^2MR\gamma$, *Nonius*.   [331] aut F^1P
    [347] invito *F*.   hostis *P* : hostem M^1.
    [348] agmina *P*.

brought thirst to all, and the plaintive cicalas rend the
thickets with song, I will bid the flocks at the side of
wells or deep pools drink of the water that runs in
oaken channels. But in midday heat let them seek
out a shady dell, where haply Jove's mighty oak with
its ancient trunk stretches out giant branches, or
where the grove, black with many holms, lies brooding
with hallowed shade. Then give them once more the
trickling stream, and once more feed them till sun-
set, when the cool evening-star allays the air, and the
moon, now dropping dew, gives strength to the glades,
when the shores ring with the halcyon, and the copses
with the finch.

[339] Why follow up for you in song the shepherds
of Libya, their pastures, and the settlements where
they dwell in scattered huts? Often, day and night,
and a whole month through, the flocks feed and roam
into the desert stretches, with no shelters; so vast a
plain lies outstretched. The African herdsman takes
with him his all—his house and home, his arms, his
Spartan dog and Cretan quiver [1]—even as the valiant
Roman, when, arrayèd in his country's arms, he hastes
on his march under a cruel load, and, ere the foe
awaits him, halts his column and pitches his camp.

[349] Far otherwise is it where dwell the tribes of
Scythia by the waters of Maeotis, where the turbid
Danube tosses his yellow sands, and where Rhodope
bends back, stretching up to the central pole. There
they keep the herds penned up in stalls, and no blade
is seen upon the plain, or leaf upon the tree; but far
and wide earth lies shapeless under mounds of snow
and piles of ice, rising seven cubits high. 'Tis ever
winter; ever North-west blasts, with icy breath.

[1] The epithets are merely ornamental, Spartan dogs and
Cretan archers being the most famous of their kind.

VIRGIL

tum Sol pallentis haud umquam discutit umbras,
nec cum invectus equis altum petit aethera, nec cum
praecipitem Oceani rubro lavit aequore currum.
concrescunt subitae currenti in flumine crustae,   360
undaque iam tergo ferratos sustinet orbis,
puppibus illa prius, patulis nunc hospita plaustris;
aeraque dissiliunt volgo, vestesque rigescunt
indutae, caeduntque securibus umida vina,
et totae solidam in glaciem vertere lacunae,   365
stiriaque impexis induruit horrida barbis.
interea toto non setius aëre ninguit :
intereunt pecudes, stant circumfusa pruinis
corpora magna boum, confertoque agmine cervi
torpent mole nova et summis vix cornibus exstant. 370
hos non immissis canibus, non cassibus ullis
puniceaeve agitant pavidos formidine pinnae,
sed frustra oppositum trudentis pectore montem
comminus obtruncant ferro, graviterque rudentis
caedunt, et magno laeti clamore reportant.   375
ipsi in defossis specubus secura sub alta
otia agunt terra, congestaque robora totasque
advolvere focis ulmos ignique dedere.
hic noctem ludo ducunt, et pocula laeti
fermento atque acidis imitantur vitea sorbis.   380
talis Hyperboreo septem subiecta trioni
gens effrena virum Rhipaeo tunditur Euro
et pecudum fulvis velatur corpora saetis.
   Si tibi lanitium curae, primum aspera silva
lappaeque tribolique absint; fuge pabula laeta,   385

[359] lavat *M (late)*.   [345] in solidam $R\gamma^1$.   [366] *omitted K.*
[369] confecto *VR.*   [377] totasque] totas *M(late)γ.*
[383] velantur *M.*

180

Then, too, never does the Sun scatter the pale mists,
either when, borne on his chariot, he climbs high
Heaven, or when he laves his headlong car in
Ocean's crimson plain. Sudden ice-crusts form on
the running stream, and anon the water bears on its
surface iron-bound wheels—giving welcome once to
ships, but now to broad wains ! Everywhere brass
splits, clothes freeze on the back, and with axes they
cleave the liquid wine ; whole lakes turn into a solid
mass, and the rough icicle hardens on the unkempt
beard. No less, meanwhile, does the snow fill the
sky ; the cattle perish, the oxen's great frames stand
sheathed in frost, the deer in crowded herd are numb
under the strange mass and above it scarce rise the
tips of their horns. These they hunt not by unloosing
hounds, or laying nets, or alarming with the terror of
the crimson feather,[1] but as their breasts vainly strain
against that mountain rampart men slay them, steel
in hand, cut them down bellowing piteously, and
bear them home with loud shouts of joy. Themselves,
in deep-dug caves, low in the earth, they live careless
and at ease, rolling to the hearths heaps of logs,
yea, whole elm-trees, and throwing them on the fire.
Here they spend the night in play, and with ale and
bitter service-juice [2] joyously mimic draughts of wine.
Such is the race of men lying under the Wain's seven
stars in the far north, a wild race, buffeted by the
Rhipaean East-wind, their bodies clothed in the
tawny furs of beasts.

[384] If wool be your care, first clear away the prickly
growth of burs and caltrops ; shun rich pastures, and

---

[1] A cord with scarlet feathers was stretched at the outlets
of a wood so as to drive the game back.

[2] Or "with barm and sour service-berries," *i.e.* by causing
fermentation in the juice of such berries, and so producing an
intoxicating drink (Page).

continuoque greges villis lege mollibus albos.
illum autem, quamvis aries sit candidus ipse,
nigra subest udo tantum cui lingua palato,
reice, ne maculis infuscet vellera pullis
nascentum, plenoque alium circumspice campo. 390
munere sic niveo lanae, si credere dignum est,
Pan deus Arcadiae captam te, Luna, fefellit,
in nemora alta vocans ; nec tu aspernata vocantem.

At cui lactis amor, cytisum lotosque frequentis
ipse manu salsasque ferat praesepibus herbas. 395
hinc et amant fluvios magis, et magis ubera tendunt
et salis occultum referunt in lacte saporem.
multi etiam excretos prohibent a matribus haedos,
primaque ferratis praefigunt ora capistris.
quod surgente die mulsere horisque diurnis, 400
nocte premunt ; quod iam tenebris et sole cadente,
sub lucem exportant calathis (adit oppida pastor) ; MPR
aut parco sale contingunt hiemique reponunt.

Nec tibi cura canum fuerit postrema, sed una
velocis Spartae catulos acremque Molossum 405
pasce sero pingui.   numquam custodibus illis
nocturnum stabulis furem incursusque luporum
aut impacatos a tergo horrebis Hiberos.
saepe etiam cursu timidos agitabis onagros,
et canibus leporem, canibus venabere dammas. 410
saepe volutabris pulsos silvestribus apros
latratu turbabis agens, montisque per altos
ingentem clamore premes ad retia cervum.

³⁹⁵ ipse *M*γ : ille *PR*.   ³⁹⁸ etiam *P :* iam *MR*γ. extremos *P.*
⁴⁰² exportant *MSS. :* exportans *Scaliger.*
⁴⁰⁸ indignatos *M*¹.   ⁴¹² terrebis *R.*

---

[1] *i.e.* Pan won Luna (Selene) by the gift of a fleece.   The
commoner form of the legend is that Pan beguiled her by
changing himself into a ram with a beautiful white fleece.
[2] The morning's milk is made into cheese at night ; the
evening's milk (probably in the form of cheese or curds) is

from the first choose flocks with white, soft fleeces. But the ram, however white be his fleece, if he have but a black tongue under his moist palate, cast out, lest with dusky spots he tarnish the coats of the new-born lambs; and look about for another in your teeming field. 'Twas with gift of such snowy wool, if we may trust the tale, that Pan, Arcadia's god, charmed and beguiled thee, O Moon, calling thee to the depths of the woods;[1] nor didst thou scorn his call.

394 But let him who longs for milk bring with his own hand lucerne and lotus in plenty and salted herbage to the stalls. Thus they love streams the more, and the more distend their udders, while their milk recalls a lurking savour of salt. Many bar the kids from the dams as soon as born, and from the first front their mouths with iron-bound muzzles. What milk they drew at sunrise or in the hours of day, they press at night; what they drew at night or sunset, they carry off in baskets at dawn, when a shepherd goes to town; or they sprinkle it with a pinch of salt, and store it for the winter.[2]

404 Nor let the care of dogs be last in your thoughts, but feed swift Spartan whelps and fierce Molossians alike on fattening whey. Never, with them on guard, need you fear for your stalls a midnight thief, or onslaught of wolves, or restless Spaniards[3] in your rear. Oft, too, you will course the shy wild ass, and with hounds will hunt the hare, with hounds the doe. Oft you will rout the boar from his forest lair, driving him forth with the baying pack, and o'er the high hills with loud cry will force a huge stag into the nets.

taken to town in plaited baskets; or, again, the milk, when made into cheese, is salted and stored up for future use,

[3] Here equivalent to " brigands " or " robbers."

VIRGIL

Disce et odoratam stabulis accendere cedrum,
galbaneoque agitare gravis nidore chelydros. 415
saepe sub immotis praesepibus aut mala tactu
vipera delituit caelumque exterrita fugit,
aut tecto adsuetus coluber succedere et umbrae
(pestis acerba boum) pecorique adspergere virus,
fovit humum. cape saxa manu, cape robora, pastor,
tollentemque minas et sibila colla tumentem 421
deice. iamque fuga timidum caput abdidit alte,
cum medii nexus extremaeque agmina caudae
solvuntur, tardosque trahit sinus ultimus orbis.
est etiam ille malus Calabris in saltibus anguis, 425
squamea convolvens sublato pectore terga
atque notis longam maculosus grandibus alvum,
qui, dum amnes ulli rumpuntur fontibus et dum
vere madent udo terrae ac pluvialibus Austris,
stagna colit, ripisque habitans hic piscibus atram 430
improbus ingluviem ranisque loquacibus explet;
postquam exusta palus, terraeque ardore dehiscunt,
exsilit in siccum, et flammantia lumina torquens
saevit agris asperque siti atque exterritus aestu.
ne mihi tum mollis sub divo carpere somnos 435
neu dorso nemoris libeat iacuisse per herbas,
cum positis novus exuviis nitidusque iuventa
volvitur, aut catulos tectis aut ova relinquens,
arduus ad solem, et linguis micat ore trisulcis.
  Morborum quoque te causas et signa docebo. 440
turpis ovis temptat scabies, ubi frigidus imber

415 galbaneos *M*. gravi *Nonius, Servius.*
422 namque *P*: cumque *M* (*late*).   423 agmine *R*.
426 corpore *P*.   427 aevom *P*.
429 ac] et *R*.   432 exhausta γ.
433 exilit *P*: extulit *M*: exiit γ.
434 exercitus *M* (*late*).
435 ne *PR, Quintilian*, IX. III 21: neo *M*γ. *So Sabb.*

[414] Learn, too, to burn in your stalls fragrant cedar and with fumes of Syrian gum to banish the noisome water-snakes. Oft under sheds uncleansed has lurked a viper, deadly to touch, and shrunk in terror from the light; or an adder, sore plague of the kine, that is wont to glide under the sheltering thatch and sprinkle venom on the cattle, has hugged the ground. Snatch up in thy hand, shepherd, snatch stones and staves, and as he rises in menace and swells his hissing neck, strike him down! Lo, now in flight he has buried deep his frightened head, while his mid coils and the end of his writhing tail are still untwining themselves, and the last curve slowly drags its folds. There is, too, that deadly serpent [1] in Calabria's glades, wreathing its scaly back, its breast erect, and its long belly mottled with large spots. So long as any streams gush from their founts, so long as earth is wet with spring's moisture and showery south winds, he haunts the pools, and, dwelling on the banks, there greedily fills his black maw with fish and croaking frogs. But when the fen is burnt up, and the soil gapes with heat, he springs forth to dry land and, rolling his blazing eyes, rages in the fields, fierce with thirst and frenzied with the heat. May I not then be fain to woo soft sleep beneath the open sky, or to lie outstretched in the grass on some wooded slope, when, his slough cast off, fresh and glistening in youth, he rolls along, leaving his young or eggs at home, towering towards the sun, and darting from his mouth a three-forked tongue!

[440] Diseases, too, their causes and tokens, I will teach you. Foul scab attacks sheep, when chilly rain and winter, bristling with hoar frost, have sunk deep

---

[1] *i.e.* the *chersydrus*, a water-snake.

altius ad vivum persedit et horrida cano
bruma gelu, vel cum tonsis inlotus adhaesit
sudor, et hirsuti secuerunt corpora vepres.
dulcibus idcirco fluviis pecus omne magistri   445
perfundunt, udisque aries in gurgite villis
mersatur, missusque secundo defluit amni ;
aut tonsum tristi contingunt corpus amurca,
et spumas miscent argenti vivaque sulpura
Idaeasque pices et pinguis unguine ceras   450
scillamque elleborosque gravis nigrumque bitumen.
non tamen ulla magis praesens fortuna laborum est,
quam si quis ferro potuit rescindere summum
ulceris os : alitur vitium vivitque tegendo,
dum medicas adhibere manus ad volnera pastor   455
abnegat, et meliora deos sedet omnia poscens.
quin etiam, ima dolor balantum lapsus ad ossa
cum furit atque artus depascitur arida febris,
profuit incensos aestus avertere et inter
ima ferire pedis salientem sanguine venam,   460
Bisaltae quo more solent acerque Gelonus,
cum fugit in Rhodopen atque in deserta Getarum,
et lac concretum cum sanguine potat equino.
quam procul aut molli succedere saepius umbrae
videris, aut summas carpentem ignavius herbas   465
extremamque sequi, aut medio procumbere campo
pascentem, et serae solam decedere nocti,
continuo culpam ferro compesce, prius quam
dira per incautum serpant contagia volgus.
non tam creber agens hiemem ruit aequore turbo,
quam multae pecudum pestes. nec singula morbi 471
corpora corripiunt, sed tota aestiva repente,

    [444] hirsutis *M*[1]*R*.
    [449] et sulpura viva *most MSS.* : vivaque sulpura *b*[2], *Macrobius, Servius, Berne Scholia.*   [456] aut *MR*γ[1]. omina *Mc*.
    [462] atque] aut *M*.   [465] aut] et *M*[1]. ignavius] segnius *R*.
    [466] concumbere *P*.   [469] serpunt *P*.   [470] aequora *R*γ[1].

into the quick, or when the sweat, unwashed, clings to the shorn flock, and prickly briars tear the flesh. Therefore the keepers bathe the whole flock in fresh streams; the ram is plunged in the pool with his dripping fleece, and let loose to float down the current. Or, after shearing, they smear the body with bitter oil-lees, blending silver-scum and native sulphur with pitch from Ida and richly oiled wax, squill, strong hellebore, and black bitumen. Yet no help for their ills is of more avail than when one has dared to cut open with steel the ulcer's head ; the mischief thrives and lives by concealment, while the shepherd refuses to lay healing hands on the wounds, and sits idle, praying the gods to better all. Nay more, when the pain runs to the very marrow of the bleating victims, there to rage, and when the parching fever preys on the limbs, it is well to turn aside the fiery heat, and within the hoof to lance a vein, throbbing with blood, even as the Bisaltae are wont to do, and the keen Gelonian, when he flees to Rhodope and the wilds of the Getae, and there drinks milk curdled with horses' blood. Should you see a sheep oft withdraw afar into soft shade, or listlessly nibble the top of the grass, lagging in the rear, or sink while grazing in the midst of the field and retire, late and lonely, before night's advance, straightway with the knife check the offence, ere the dread taint spreads through the unwary throng: Not so thick with driving gales sweeps a whirlwind from the sea, as scourges swarm among cattle. Not single victims do diseases seize, but a whole summer's fold in one stroke, the flock and

spemque gregemque simul cunctamque ab origine
    gentem.
tum sciat, aërias Alpis et Norica si quis
castella in tumulis et Iapydis arva Timavi   475
nunc quoque post tanto videat, desertaque regna
pastorum et longe saltus lateque vacantis.
   Hic quondam morbo caeli miseranda coorta est
tempestas totoque autumni incanduit aestu,
et genus omne neci pecudum dedit, omne ferarum,
corrupitque lacus, infecit pabula tabo.   481
nec via mortis erat simplex; sed ubi ignea venis
omnibus acta sitis miseros adduxerat artus,
rursus abundabat fluidus liquor omniaque in se
ossa minutatim morbo conlapsa trahebat.   485
saepe in honore deum medio stans hostia ad aram,
lanea dum nivea circumdatur infula vitta,
inter cunctantis cecidit moribunda ministros.
aut si quam ferro mactaverat ante sacerdos,
inde neque impositis ardent altaria fibris,   490
nec responsa potest consultus reddere vates,
ac vix supposliti tinguntur sanguine cultri
summaque ieiuna sanie infuscatur harena.
hinc laetis vituli volgo moriuntur in herbis
et dulcis animas plena ad praesepia reddunt;   495
hinc canibus blandis rabies venit, et quatit aegros
tussis anhela sues ac faucibus angit obesis.
labitur infelix studiorum atque immemor herbae
victor equus fontisque avertitur et pede terram
crebra ferit; demissae aures, incertus ibidem   500

[474] tunc *M, Servius*
[475] et] ut *P*. Iapydis *M, Probus, Servius:* Iapygis *PRγ,
Berne Scholia:* arva] ora *P :* arma *MR.*
[481] corripuitque *P.*
[483] attraxerat *P.*
[488] magistros *R.*

the hope of the flock, and the whole race, root and
branch. Of this may one be witness, should he see
—even now, so long after—the skyey Alps and the
forts on the Noric hills, and the fields of Illyrian
Timavus with the shepherds' realm desolate, and
their glades far and wide untenanted.

[478] On this land from the sickened sky there once
came a piteous season that glowed with autumn's
full heat. Every tribe of cattle, tame or wild, it
swept to death; it poisoned the lakes, it tainted the
pastures with venom. Not simple was the pathway
to death;[1] but when the fiery thirst had coursed
through all the veins and shrivelled the hapless
limbs, in its turn a watery humour welled up and
drew into itself all the bones, as piecemeal they
melted with disease. Oft in the midst of divine
rites, the victim, standing by the altar, even as the
woollen fillet's snowy band was passed round its brow,
fell in death's throes amid the tardy ministrants.
Or if, ere that, the priest had slain a victim with the
knife, yet the altars blazed not therewith, as the
entrails were laid on; the seer, when consulted, could
give no response; the knife beneath the throat is
scarce stained with blood, and only the surface sand is
darkened with the thin gore. Then on every side amid
gladsome herbage the young kine die or yield up
sweet life by their full folds. Then madness visits
fawning hounds; a racking cough shakes the sicken-
ing swine and chokes them with swollen throats.
The steed, once victor, sinks; failing in his efforts
and forgetful of the grass, he turns from the spring,
and oft-times paws the ground; his ears droop, on
them breaks out a fitful sweat—sweat that is cold as

---

[1] *i.e.* in the course of the disease opposite symptoms
succeeded each other.

VIRGIL

sudor et ille quidem morituris frigidus; aret
pellis et ad tactum tractanti dura resistit.
haec ante exitium primis dant signa diebus;
sin in processu coepit crudescere morbus,
tum vero ardentes oculi atque attractus ab alto   505
spiritus, interdum gemitu gravis, imaque longo
ilia singultu tendunt, it naribus ater
sanguis, et obsessas fauces premit aspera lingua.
profuit inserto latices infundere cornu
Lenaeos; ea visa salus morientibus una: 510
mox erat hoc ipsum exitio, furiisque refecti
ardebant, ipsique suos iam morte sub aegra
(di meliora piis erroremque hostibus illum!)
discissos nudis laniabant dentibus artus.

Ecce autem duro fumans sub vomere taurus   515
concidit et mixtum spumis vomit ore cruorem
extremosque ciet gemitus. it tristis arator,
maerentem abiungens fraterna morte iuvencum,
atque opere in medio defixa relinquit aratra.
non umbrae altorum nemorum, non mollia possunt 520
prata movere animum, non qui per saxa volutus
purior electro campum petit amnis; at ima
solvuntur latera, atque oculos stupor urget inertis
ad terramque fluit devexo pondere cervix.
quid labor aut benefacta iuvant? quid vomere terras
invertisse gravis? atqui non Massica Bacchi   526
munera, non illis epulae nocuere repostae:
frondibus et victu pascuntur simplicis herbae,
pocula sunt fontes liquidi atque exercita cursu
flumina, nec somnos abrumpit cura salubris.   530

Tempore non alio dicunt regionibus illis
quaesitas ad sacra boves Iunonis et uris

---

⁵⁰¹ morituri $M^1\gamma^1$.   ⁵⁰⁶ altaque M^1.   ⁵⁰⁹ insertos P.
⁵¹¹ exitio hoc ipsum P.   ⁵¹³ ardoremque R.
⁵¹⁷ it] et M^1P.   ⁵¹⁹ reliquit P, *Donatus, Servius.*
⁵³² aris P.

death, draws nigh; the skin is dry and, hard to the
touch, withstands the stroking hand. Such are the
signs they yield ere death in the first days; but as
in its course the sickness grows fierce, then the eyes
blaze, the breath is drawn deep—at times laden with
moans—their utmost flanks are strained with long-
drawn sobs, black blood gushes from the nostrils, and
the rough tongue chokes the blockaded throat. It
has availed to pour in wine-juice through a horn
inserted—this seemed the one hope for the dying.
Soon even this led to death; they burned with the
fury of fresh strength, and, though now in the weak-
ness of death (Heaven grant a happier lot to the
good, and such madness to our foes!), rent and
mangled their own limbs with bared teeth.

⁵¹⁵ But lo, the bull, smoking under the plough-
share's weight, falls; from his mouth he spurts blood,
mingled with foam, and heaves his dying groans.
Sadly goes the ploughman, unyokes the steer that
sorrows for his brother's death, and amid its half-
done task leaves the share rooted fast. No shades of
deep woods, no soft meadows can touch his heart, no
stream purer than amber, rolling over the rocks in its
course towards the plain; but his flanks are unstrung
throughout, numbness weighs upon his languid eyes,
and his neck sinks with drooping weight to earth.
Of what avail is his toil or his services? What avails
it, that he turned with the share the heavy clod?
And yet no Massic gifts of Bacchus, no feasts, oft
renewed, did harm to him and his. They feed on
leaves and simple grass; their cups are clear springs
and rivers racing in their course, and no care breaks
their healthful slumbers.

⁵³¹ Only at that time, they say, were kine in those
regions sought in vain for the rites of Juno, and

VIRGIL

imparibus ductos alta ad donaria currus.
ergo aegre rastris terram rimantur, et ipsis
unguibus infodiunt fruges, montisque per altos   535
contenta cervice trahunt stridentia plaustra.
non lupus insidias explorat ovilia circum
nec gregibus nocturnus obambulat; acrior illum
cura domat.   timidi dammae cervique fugaces
nunc interque canes et circum tecta vagantur.   540
iam maris immensi prolem et genus omne natantum
litore in extremo ceu naufraga corpora fluctus
proluit; insolitae fugiunt in flumina phocae.
interit et curvis frustra defensa latebris
vipera et attoniti squamis adstantibus hydri.   545
ipsis est aër avibus non aequus, et illae
praecipites alta vitam sub nube relinquunt
praeterea iam nec mutari pabula refert,
quaesitaeque nocent artes; cessere magistri,
Phillyrides Chiron Amythaoniusque Melampus.   550
saevit et in lucem Stygiis emissa tenebris
pallida Tisiphone Morbos agit ante Metumque
inque dies avidum surgens caput altius effert.
balatu pecorum et crebris mugitibus amnes
arentesque sonant ripae collesque supini.   555
iamque catervatim dat stragem atque aggerat
      ipsis
in stabulis turpi dilapsa cadavera tabo,
donec humo tegere ac foveis abscondere discunt.
nam neque erat coriis usus, nec viscera quisquam
aut undis abolere potest aut vincere flamma.   560
ne tondere quidem morbo inluvieque peresa

---

[535] altos] arduos *P.   So Sabb.*
[537] insidians *Rγ.*   [544] deprensa *P.*
[545] serpentibus *P.*
[548] nec iam mutari *R :* nec mutari iam *Macrobius.*
[549] cessare *M¹.*   [555] horrentes *R.*

chariots were drawn by ill-matched buffaloes to her
lofty treasure-house.[1] Therefore men painfully scratch
the earth with harrows, with their own nails bury the
seed, and over the high hills with straining necks
drag the creaking wains. The wolf tries not his
wiles around the sheepfold, nor prowls by night
about the flocks; a keener care tames him. Timorous
deer and shy stags now stray among the hounds and
about the houses. Yea, the brood of the great deep,
and all swimming things, like shipwrecked corpses,
are washed up by the waves on the verge of the
shore; in strange wise sea-calves flee to the rivers.
The viper, too, vainly defended in her winding lairs,
perishes, and the water-snake, his scales erect in
terror. The air is unkind even to the birds; headlong
they fall, leaving life beneath the clouds on high.
Further, even change of pasture avails no more; the
remedies sought work harm; masters in the art fail,
Chiron, son of Phillyra, and Melampus, Amythaon's
son. Ghastly Tisiphone rages, and, let forth into
light from Stygian gloom, drives before her Disease
and Dread, while day by day, uprising, she rears still
higher her greedy head. The rivers and thirsty
banks and sloping hills echo to the bleating of flocks
and incessant lowing of kine. And now in droves
she deals out death, and in the very stalls piles up
the bodies, rotting with putrid foulness, till men
learn to cover them in earth and bury them in pits.
For neither might the hides be used, nor could one
cleanse the flesh by water or master it by fire. They
could not even shear the fleeces, eaten up with sores

---

[1] At Argos the car of the priestess of Hera (Juno) was drawn
by white oxen. Virgil perhaps transfers this practice to the
Alpine district of Noricum and Timavus.

VIRGIL

vellera nec telas possunt attingere putris:
verum etiam invisos si quis temptarat amictus,
ardentes papulae atque immundus olentia sudor
membra sequebatur, nec longo deinde moranti   565
tempore contactos artus sacer ignis edebat.

[563] verum] quin *R.* temptaret *M*[1].
[566] contractos *P.*

and filth, nor touch the rotten web. Nay, if any man donned the loathsome garb, feverish blisters and foul sweat would run along his fetid limbs, and not long had he to wait ere the accursed fire was feeding on his stricken limbs.

LIBER IV

Protinus aërii mellis caelestia dona   MPR
exsequar.   hanc etiam, Maecenas, aspice partem.
admiranda tibi levium spectacula rerum
magnanimosque duces totiusque ordine gentis
mores et studia et populos et proelia dicam.   5
in tenui labor ; at tenuis non gloria, si quem
numina laeva sinunt auditque vocatus Apollo.
    Principio sedes apibus statioque petenda,
quo neque sit ventis aditus (nam pabula venti
ferre domum probibent) neque oves haedique petulci
floribus insultent, aut errans bucula campo   11
decutiat rorem et surgentis atterat herbas.
absint et picti squalentia terga lacerti
pinguibus a stabulis, meropesque aliaeque volucres
et manibus Procne pectus signata cruentis :   15
omnia nam late vastant ipsasque volantis
ore ferunt dulcem nidis immitibus escam.
at liquidi fontes et stagna virentia musco
adsint et tenuis fugiens per gramina rivus,
palmaque vestibulum aut ingens oleaster inumbret,
ut, cum prima novi ducent examina reges   21
vere suo, ludetque favis emissa iuventus,
vicina invitet decedere ripa calori,

    ^{11} campi *P.* ^{20} aut] atque *P.* ^{22} suo] muo (= novo?) *P.*

BOOK IV

Next will I discourse of Heaven's gift, the honey from the skies. On this part, too, of my task, Maecenas, look with favour. The wondrous pageant of a tiny world—chiefs great-hearted, a whole nation's character and tastes and tribes and battles—I will in due order unfold to thee. Slight is the field of toil; but not slight the glory, if adverse powers leave one free, and Apollo hearkens unto prayer.

[8] First seek a settled home for your bees, whither the winds may find no access—for the winds let them not carry home their food—where no ewes or sportive kids may trample the flowers, nor straying heifer brush off the dew from the mead and bruise the springing blade. Let the spangled lizard with his scaly back be also a stranger to the rich stalls, and the bee-eater and other birds, and Procne,[1] with breast marked by her blood-stained hands. For these spread havoc far and near, and, while the bees are on the wing, carry them off in their mouths, a sweet morsel for their cruel nestlings. But let clear springs be near, and moss-green pools, and a tiny brook stealing through the grass; and let a palm or huge wild olive shade the porch, so that, when the new kings lead forth the early swarms in the spring they love, and the youth revel in their freedom from the combs, a bank near by may tempt them to quit

---

[1] *i.e.* the swallow.

197

obviaque hospitiis teneat frondentibus arbos.
in medium, seu stabit iners seu profluet umor, 25
transversas salices et grandia conice saxa,
pontibus ut crebris possint consistere et alas
pandere ad aestivum solem, si forte morantis
sparserit aut praeceps Neptuno immerserit Eurus.
haec circum casiae virides et olentia late 30
serpulla et graviter spirantis copia thymbrae
floreat, inriguumque bibant violaria fontem.
ipsa autem, seu corticibus tibi suta cavatis
seu lento fuerint alvaria vimine texta,
angustos habeant aditus : nam frigore mella 35
cogit hiems, eademque calor liquefacta remittit.
utraque vis apibus pariter metuenda ; neque illae MP
nequiquam in tectis certatim tenuia cera
spiramenta linunt, fucoque et floribus oras
explent, collectumque haec ipsa ad munera gluten 40
et visco et Phrygiae servant pice lentius Idae.
saepe etiam effossis, si vera est fama, latebris
sub terra fovere larem, penitusque repertae
pumicibusque cavis exesaeque arboris antro.
tu tamen et levi rimosa cubilia limo 45
ungue fovens circum, et raras superinice frondes.
neu propius tectis taxum sine, neve rubentis
ure foco cancros, altae neu crede paludi,
aut ubi odor caeni gravis aut ubi concava pulsu
saxa sonant vocisque offensa resultat imago. 50
    Quod superest, ubi pulsam hiemem Sol aureus egit
sub terras caelumque aestiva luce reclusit,

    25 profluit *P*.   **43** fodiere *M*[1] : fodere *M*[2].
198

the heat, and a tree in their path may hold them in its sheltering leafage. In the midst of the water, whether it stand idle or flow onward, cast willows athwart and huge stones, that they may have many bridges whereon to halt and spread their wings to the summer sun, if haply the East-wind has sprinkled the loiterers or with swift gust has plunged them in the flood. All about let green cassia bloom, and wild thyme with fragrance far borne, and a wealth of strong-scented savory; and let violet-beds drink of the trickling spring.

³³ Then, let the hive itself, whether it be sewn of hollow bark, or woven of pliant osier, have its entrances narrow; for winter with its cold congeals the honey, while heat thaws and makes it run. Either trouble is alike to be feared for the bees; nor is it to no purpose that in their homes they smear the tiny crevices with wax, fill the chinks with paste from flowers, and keep a store of glue, gathered for this very purpose, more binding than lime or the pitch of Phrygian Ida. Oft, too, if report be true, they have made a snug home in tunnelled hiding-places underground, and are found deep in the hollows of pumice rock, or the cavern of a decayed tree. Yet do you keep them snug, smearing the chinks of their chambers with smooth clay, and flinging thereon a few leaves. And suffer no yew too near the hive, nor roast the reddening crab at your hearth; and trust not a deep marsh or a place where the smell of mud is strong, or where the hollow rocks ring when struck, and the echoed voice rebounds from the shock.

⁵¹ For the rest, when the golden Sun has driven winter in rout beneath the earth, and with summer light unlocked the sky, straightway they

illae continuo saltus silvasque peragrant
purpureosque metunt flores et flumina libant
summa leves. hinc nescio qua dulcedine laetae 55
progeniem nidosque fovent, hinc arte recentis
excudunt ceras et mella tenacia fingunt.
hinc ubi iam emissum caveis ad sidera caeli
nare per aestatem liquidam suspexeris agmen
obscuramque trahi vento mirabere nubem, 60
contemplator: aquas dulcis et frondea semper
tecta petunt. huc tu iussos adsperge sapores,
trita melisphylla et cerinthae ignobile gramen,
tinnitusque cie et Matris quate cymbala circum:
ipsae consident medicatis sedibus, ipsae 65
intima more suo sese in cunabula condent

    Sin autem ad pugnam exierint—nam saepe duobus
regibus incessit magno discordia motu;
continuoque animos volgi et trepidantia bello
corda licet longe praesciscere; namque morantis 70
Martius ille aeris rauci canor increpat et vox
auditur fractos sonitus imitata tubarum;
tum trepidae inter se coeunt pinnisque coruscant
spiculaque exacuunt rostris aptantque lacertos
et circa regem atque ipsa ad praetoria densae 75
miscentur magnisque vocant clamoribus hostem:
ergo ubi ver nactae sudum camposque patentis,
erumpunt portis: concurritur, aethere in alto
fit sonitus, magnum mixtae glomerantur in orbem
praecipitesque cadunt; non densior aëre grando, 80

---

[57] excludunt *P*.   [58] hic *P*.

---

[1] *i.e.* referring to the worship of Cybele, which was accompanied by the clash of cymbals.
[2] The sentence beginning *sin autem* . . . is never concluded, but the parenthesis beginning with *nam saepe* passes into a long description of the battle.

range through glades and groves, cull bright flowers, and lightly sip the stream's brink. Hence it is that, glad with some strange joy, they cherish nest and nestlings; hence they deftly mould fresh wax and fashion the gluey honey. Hence when you look up and see the host, just freed from the hive, floating towards the starry sky through the clear summer air—when you marvel at the dark cloud trailing down the wind—mark it well; they are ever in quest of sweet waters and leafy coverts. Here scatter the scents I prescribe—bruised balm, and the honeywort's lowly herb; raise a tinkling sound, and shake the Mighty Mother's cymbals round about.[1] Of themselves will they settle on the scented resting-places; of themselves, after their wont, will hide far within their cradling cells.

[67] But, if haply for battle they have gone forth [2]—for oft-times strife with terrible turmoil hath fallen on two kings; and straightway you may presage from afar the fury of the crowd, and how their hearts thrill with war; for the warlike ring of the hoarse clarion stirs the loiterers, and a sound is heard that is like unto broken trumpet-blasts. Then, all afire, they flock together: their wings flash, they whet their stings on their beaks[3] and make ready their arms. Round their king, and even by his royal tent, they swarm in throngs, and with loud cries challenge the foe. Therefore, when they have found a clear spring day and open field, they sally forth from the gates. There is a clash; in high air arises a din; they are mingled and massed in one great ball, then tumble headlong: no thicker is hail from the sky, not so dense

---

[3] Bees cannot do this, but perhaps the poet has in mind their custom of scraping the abdomen with their legs and then removing the dirt from their legs with their mandibles.

VIRGIL

nec de concussa tantum pluit ilice glandis.
ipsi per medias acies insignibus alis
ingentis animos angusto in pectore versant,
usque adeo obnixi non cedere, dum gravis aut hos
aut hos versa fuga victor dare terga subegit.   85
hi motus animorum atque haec certamina tanta
pulveris exigui iactu compressa quiescunt.
  Verum ubi ductores acie revocaveris ambo,
deterior qui visus, eum, ne prodigus obsit,
dede neci; melior vacua sine regnet in aula.   90
alter erit maculis auro squalentibus ardens.
nam duo sunt genera: hic melior, insignis et ore
et rutilis clarus squamis; ille horridus alter
desidia latamque trahens inglorius alvum.
ut binae regum facies, ita corpora plebis.   95
namque aliae turpes horrent, ceu pulvere ab alto
cum venit et sicco terram spuit ore viator   FMP
aridus; elucent aliae et fulgore coruscant
ardentes auro et paribus lita corpora guttis.
haec potior suboles, hinc caeli tempore certo   100
dulcia mella premes, nec tantum dulcia, quantum
et liquida et durum Bacchi domitura saporem.
  At cum incerta volant caeloque examina ludunt
contemnuntque favos et frigida tecta relinquunt,
instabilis animos ludo prohibebis inani.   105
nec magnus prohibere labor: tu regibus alas
eripe; non illis quisquam cunctantibus altum
ire iter aut castris audebit vellere signa.
invitent croceis halantes floribus horti
et custos furum atque avium cum falce saligna   110
Hellespontiaci servet tutela Priapi.

87 quiescent *P*.   88 ambos *P*.
          103 at] aut *P*.   105 in stabulis *M*[1].
          110 frugum *M*[1].

202

is the rain of acorns from the shaken oak. In the midst of the ranks the chiefs themselves, with resplendent wings, have mighty souls beating in tiny breasts, ever steadfast not to yield, until the victor's heavy hand has driven these or those to turn their backs in flight. These storms of passion, these conflicts so fierce, by the tossing of a little dust are quelled and laid to rest.

[88] But when you have called both captains back from the field, give up to death the meaner of look, that he prove no wasteful burden; let the nobler reign in the palace alone. The one will be aglow with rough spots of gold. For there are two sorts: one is better, noble of mien and bright with gleaming scales; the second squalid from sloth, and trailing ignobly a broad paunch. As twofold are the features of the kings, so are the bodies of the subjects. For some are ugly and unsightly, as when from out of deep dust comes the parched wayfarer, and spits the dirt from his dried mouth. Others gleam, and flash in splendour, their bodies all ablaze and flecked with equal drops of gold. This is the nobler breed; from this, in the sky's due season, you will strain sweet honey—yet not so sweet as clear, and fit to subdue the harsh flavour of wine.

[103] But when the swarms flit aimlessly and sport in the air, scorning their cells and leaving their hives chill, you must check their fickle spirit from such idle play. No hard task is it to check them. Do you tear from the monarchs their wings; while they tarry, no one will dare to go forth aloft, or pluck the standards from the camp. Let there be gardens fragrant with saffron flowers to invite them, and let the watchman against thieves and birds, guardian Priapus, lord of the Hellespont, protect them with his

ipse thymum tinosque ferens de montibus altis
tecta serat late circum, cui talia curae ;
ipse labore manum duro terat, ipse feracis
figat humo plantas et amicos inriget imbris.   115
- Atque equidem, extremo ni iam sub fine laborum
vela traham et terris festinem advertere proram,
forsitan et, pinguis hortos quae cura colendi
ornaret, canerem, biferique rosaria Paesti,
quoque modo potis gauderent intiba rivis   120
et virides apio ripae, tortusque per herbam
cresceret in ventrem cucumis ; nec sera comantem
narcissum aut flexi tacuissem vimen acanthi
pallentisque hederas et amantis litora myrtos.
namque sub Oebaliae memini me turribus arcis,   MP
qua niger umectat flaventia culta Galaesus,   126
Corycium vidisse senem, cui pauca relicti
iugera ruris erant, nec fertilis illa iuvencis
nec pecori opportuna seges nec commoda Baccho :
hic rarum tamen in dumis olus albaque circum   130
lilia verbenasque premens vescumque papaver
regum aequabat opes animis, seraque revertens
nocte domum dapibus mensas onerabat inemptis.
primus vere rosam atque autumno carpere poma,
et cum tristis hiems etiamnum frigore saxa   135
rumperet et glacie cursus frenaret aquarum,
ille comam mollis iam tondebat hyacinthi
aestatem increpitans seram Zephyrosque·morantis.

[112] tinos M^1P, *known to Philargyrius :* pinos FM^2.
[113] circum late *P.*   [120] rivis] fibris *Priscian.*
[124] -que *omitted F.*
[125] arcis *P :* altis FM^2, *Servius :* autis M^1.
[129] pecori] Cereri *Salmasius.*
[137] iam tum *P.* achanti *M* (*late, in margin*).

---

[1] Referring to the rude wooden figures of Priapus holding
a wooden sickle in the hand, which were set up in gardens to
protect them from thieves and birds.

willow-hook.[1] Let him, to whom such care falls, him-
self bring thyme and wild laurels [2] from high moun-
tains, and plant them widely round their homes; him-
self harden his hand with stern toil; himself plant in
the ground fruitful slips and sprinkle kindly showers.

[116] And in truth, were I not now hard on the
very close of my toils, furling my sails, and hastening
to turn my prow to land, perchance, too, I might
be singing what careful tillage decks rich gardens,
singing of the rose-beds of twice-blooming Paestum;
how the endive rejoices in the streams it drinks, and
the green banks in the parsley; and how the gourd,
winding along the ground, swells into its paunch.
Nor had I been silent on the late-blooming narcissus,
or the curling acanthus-stem, the pale ivy or the
shore-loving myrtle. For I call to mind how under
the towers of Oebalia's citadel,[3] where dark Galaesus
waters his yellow fields, I saw an old Corycian, who
had a few acres of unclaimed land, and this a soil
not rich enough for bullocks' ploughing, unfitted for
the flock, and unkindly to the vine. Yet, as he
planted herbs here and there among the bushes,
with white lilies about, and vervain, and slender
poppy, he matched in contentment the wealth of
kings, and, returning home in the late evening,
would load his board with unbought dainties. He
was first to pluck roses in spring and apples in
autumn; and when sullen winter was still bursting
rocks with the cold, and curbing running waters
with ice, he was already culling the soft hyacinth's
bloom, chiding laggard summer and the loitering

[2] The *tinus* is described by Philargyrius as a wild laurel with
dark blue berries. It is possibly the laurustinus of our gardens,
a great favourite with bees, but in no way related to the true
laurels.   [3] *i.c.* Tarentum, founded by Laconians.

ergo apibus fetis idem atque examine multo
primus abundare et spumantia cogere pressis   140
mella favis; illi tiliae atque uberrima tinus,
quotque in flore novo pomis se fertilis arbos
induerat, totidem autumno matura tenebat.
ille etiam seras in versum distulit ulmos
eduramque pirum et spinos iam pruna ferentis   145
iamque ministrantem platanum potantibus umbras.
verum haec ipse equidem spatiis exclusus iniquis
praetereo atque aliis post me memoranda relinquo.

Nunc age, naturas apibus quas Iuppiter ipse
addidit expediam, pro qua mercede canoros   150
Curetum sonitus crepitantiaque aera secutae
Dictaeo caeli regem pavere sub antro.
solae communis natos, consortia tecta   FMP
urbis habent, magnisque agitant sub legibus aevum,
et patriam solae et certos novere penatis,   155
venturaeque hiemis memores aestate laborem
experiuntur et in medium quaesita reponunt.
namque aliae victu invigilant et foedere pacto
exercentur agris; pars intra saepta domorum
narcissi lacrimam et lentum de cortice gluten   160
prima favis ponunt fundamina, deinde tenacis
suspendunt ceras; aliae spem gentis adultos
educunt fetus; aliae purissima mella
stipant et liquido distendunt nectare cellas;
sunt quibus ad portas cecidit custodia sorti,   165
inque vicem speculantur aquas et nubila caeli,
aut onera accipiunt venientum, aut agmine facto

---

¹³⁹ idemque P.
¹⁴¹ illic P.   tilia M.   tinus M¹: pinus M²P, *both known to
Philargyrius.*   ¹⁴⁶ post memoranda M P.   ¹⁵⁴ -que *omitted* P.

---

¹ Though editors commonly read *pinus*, Janell and Goelzer
have followed me in adopting *tinus*.   See Appendix, p. 583.
² *i.e.* he was able to transplant full-grown trees.
³ Saturn, knowing that one of his children was to depose

206

zephyrs. So he, too, was first to be enriched with
mother-bees and a plenteous swarm, the first to gather
frothing honey from the squeezed comb. Luxuriant
were his limes and wild laurels;[1] and all the fruits
his bounteous tree donned in its early bloom, full as
many it kept in the ripeness of autumn. He, too,
planted out in rows elms far-grown, pear-trees when
quite hard, thorns even now bearing plums, and the
plane already yielding to drinkers the service of its
shade.[2] But I, barred by these narrow bounds, pass
by this theme, and leave it for others after me to tell.

[149] Come now, the qualities which Jove himself
has given bees, I will unfold—even the reward, for
which they followed the tuneful sounds and clashing
bronzes of the Curetes, and fed the king of Heaven
within the cave of Dicte.[3] They alone have children
in common, hold the dwellings of their city jointly,
and pass their life under the majesty of law. They
alone know a fatherland and fixed home, and in
summer, mindful of the winter to come, spend toil-
some days and garner their gains into a common
store. For some watch over the gathering of food,
and under fixed covenant labour in the fields; some,
within the confines of their homes, lay down the
narcissus' tears and gluey gum from tree-bark as
the first foundation of the comb, then hang aloft
clinging wax; others lead out the full-grown young,
the nation's hope; others pack purest honey, and
swell the cells with liquid nectar. To some it has
fallen by lot to be sentries at the gates, and in
turn they watch the rains and clouds of heaven, or
take the loads of incomers, or in martial array drive

him, devoured them as they were born, but the infant Jupiter
was concealed by his mother in a cave of Mount Dicte, and the
Curetes drowned his cries by clashing their cymbals, while
the bees fed him with honey.

ignavum fucos pecus a praesepibus arcent.
fervet opus, redolentque thymo fragrantia mella.
ac veluti lentis Cyclopes fulmina massis   170
cum properant, alii taurinis follibus auras
accipiunt redduntque, alii stridentia tingunt
aera lacu; gemit impositis incudibus Aetna;
illi inter sese magna vi bracchia tollunt
in numerum, versantque tenaci forcipe ferrum: MP
non aliter, si parva licet componere magnis,   176
Cecropias innatus apes amor urget habendi
munere quamque suo.   grandaevis oppida curae
et munire favos et daedala fingere tecta.
at fessae multa referunt se nocte minores,   180
crura thymo plenae; pascuntur et arbuta passim   MPR
et glaucas salices casiamque crocumque rubentem
et pinguem tiliam et ferrugineos hyacinthos.
omnibus una quies operum, labor omnibus unus:
mane ruunt portis; nusquam mora; rursus easdem
Vesper ubi e pastu tandem decedere campis   186
admonuit, tum tecta petunt, tum corpora curant;
fit sonitus, mussantque oras et limina circum.
post ubi iam thalamis se composuere, siletur
in noctem, fessosque sopor suus occupat artus.   190
nec vero a stabulis pluvia impendente recedunt
longius, aut credunt caelo adventantibus Euris,
sed circum tutae sub moenibus urbis aquantur
excursusque brevis temptant, et saepe lapillos,
ut cumbae instabiles fluctu iactante saburram,   195
tollunt, his sese per inania nubila librant.

[170] lenti F^1: lente P.   [173] Aetna] antrum FP.
[185] numquam P.   [195] flatu P.

208

the drones, a lazy herd, from the folds. All aglow
is the work, and the fragrant honey is sweet with
thyme. And as, when the Cyclopes in haste forge
bolts from tough ore, some with ox-hide bellows
make the blasts come and go, others dip the hissing
brass in the lake, while Aetna groans under the
anvils laid upon her; they, with mighty force, now
one, now another, raise their arms in measured
cadence, and turn the iron with gripping tongs—
even so, if we may compare small things with great,
an inborn love of gain spurs on the Attic bees, each
after its own office. The aged have charge of the
towns, the building of the hives, the fashioning of
the cunningly wrought houses. But the young betake
them home in weariness, late at night, their thighs
freighted with thyme; far and wide they feed on
arbutus, on pale-green willows, on cassia and ruddy
crocus, on the rich linden, and the dusky hyacinth. All
have one season to rest from labour, all one season to
toil. At dawn they pour from the gates—no loiter-
ing; again, when the star of eve has warned them
to withdraw from their pasture in the fields, then
they seek their homes, then they refresh their
frames; a sound is heard, as they hum about the
entrances and on·the thresholds. Anon, when they
have laid them to rest in their chambers, silence
reigns into the night, and well-earned sleep seizes
their weary limbs. Nor yet, if rain impend, do they
stray far from their stalls, or trust the sky when
eastern gales are near, but round about, beneath the
shelter of their city walls, draw water, and essay
short flights; and often they raise tiny stones, as
unsteady barques take up ballast in a tossing sea,
and with these balance themselves amid the unsub-
stantial clouds.

VIRGIL

Illum adeo placuisse apibus mirabere morem,
quod neque concubitu indulgent, nec corpora segnes
in Venerem solvunt aut fetus nixibus edunt;
verum ipsae e foliis natos et suavibus herbis   200
ore legunt, ipsae regem parvosque Quirites
sufficiunt, aulasque et cerea regna refingunt.
saepe etiam duris errando in cotibus alas
attrivere, ultroque animam sub fasce dedere:
tantus amor florum et generandi gloria mellis.   205
ergo ipsas quamvis angusti terminus aevi
excipiat (neque enim plus septima ducitur aestas),
at genus immortale manet, multosque per annos
stat fortuna domus, et avi numerantur avorum.
praeterea regem non sic Aegyptus et ingens   210
Lydia nec populi Parthorum aut Medus Hydaspes
observant.   rege incolumi mens omnibus una est;
amisso rupere fidem, constructaque mella
diripuere ipsae et cratis solvere favorum.
ille operum custos, illum admirantur et omnes   215
circumstant fremitu denso stipantque frequentes,
et saepe attollunt umeris et corpora bello
obiectant pulchramque petunt per volnera mortem.

His quidam signis atque haec exempla secuti
esse apibus partem divinae mentis et haustus   220
aetherios dixere; deum namque ire per omnia,
terrasque tractusque maris caelumque profundum;
hinc pecudes, armenta, viros, genus omne ferarum,

---

200 e *omitted P.*   et γbc : e *MP :* sed *R.*
202 refigunt *M*γ : relingunt *P.*   211 aut] et *M*[1].
217 pectora *P.*   221 omnis *MSS. :* omnia *Peerlkamp.*
222 terrarum *M* (*late*).

[197] Yea, and you will marvel that this custom has found favour with bees, that they indulge not in conjugal embraces, nor idly unnerve their bodies in love, or bring forth young with travail, but of themselves[1] gather their children in their mouths from leaves and sweet herbs, of themselves provide a new monarch and tiny burghers, and remodel their palaces and waxen realms. Often, too, as they wander among rugged rocks they bruise their wings, and freely yield their lives under their load—so deep is their love of flowers and their glory in begetting honey. Therefore, though the limit of a narrow span awaits the bees themselves—for never stretches it beyond the seventh summer—yet the race abides immortal, for many a year stands firm the fortune of the house, and grandsires' grandsires are numbered on the roll.

[210] Moreover, neither Egypt nor mighty Lydia, nor the Parthian tribes, nor Median Hydaspes, show such homage to their king. While he is safe, all are of one mind; when he is lost, straightway they break their fealty, and themselves pull down the honey they have reared and tear up their trellised combs. He is the guardian of their toils; to him they do reverence; all stand round him in clamorous crowd, and attend him in throngs. Often they lift him on their shoulders, for him expose their bodies to battle, and seek amid wounds a glorious death.

[219] Led by such tokens and such instances, some have taught that the bees have received a share of the divine intelligence, and a draught of heavenly ether;[2] for God, they say, pervades all things, earth and sea's expanse and heaven's depth; from Him the flocks and

[1] *i.e.* without the male.
[2] The *aether*, according to ancient philosophers, was the lightest of the elements, and, rising above all the rest, surrounded the universe and fed the heavenly bodies.

211

VIRGIL

quemque sibi tenuis nascentem arcessere vitas ;
scilicet huc reddi deinde ac resoluta referri   225
omnia, nec morti esse locum, sed viva volare
sideris in numerum atque alto succedere caelo.

   Si quando sedem augustam servataque mella
thesauris relines, prius haustu sparsus aquarum
ora fove, fumosque manu praetende sequacis.   230
illis ira modum supra est, laesaeque venenum   236
morsibus inspirant, et spicula caeca relinquunt
adfixae venis, animasque in volnere ponunt.
bis gravidos cogunt fetus, duo tempora messis,   231
Taygete simul os terris ostendit honestum
Plias et Oceani spretos pede reppulit amnis,
aut eadem sidus fugiens ubi Piscis aquosi
tristior hibernas caelo descendit in undas.   235
sin duram metues hiemem parcesque futuro   239
contususosque animos et res miserabere fractas,   240
at suffire thymo cerasque recidere inanis
quis dubitet ? nam saepe favos ignotus adedit
stellio et lucifugis congesta cubilia blattis
immunisque sedens aliena ad pabula fucus ;
aut asper crabro imparibus se immiscuit armis,   245
aut dirum tiniae genus, aut invisa Minervae
laxos in foribus suspendit aranea cassis.

   227 succedere] se condere *R.*

   228 angustam *R.*

   229 thensauri *P :* thensauris *Rγ*[1] : thesauris *M, Servius.*
retines *P.*   astu *M*[1].

   230 ora *M*[2] : ore *M*[1]*PR, Servius, Philargyrius.*   fave *M*[1],
Philargyrius, known to Servius.   manu] sinu *P.*

   230.239 *The order of the lines as given in the MSS. is thus
departed from by Bentley, Ribbeck, and others.*

   231 flores *P.*   **238** vulnera *Rγ.*   **239** metuens *Rγ*[1].

   241 suffere *P :* sufferre *MR :* suffire *γ, Priscian.*

   242 iam *P.*   adhaesit *R.*

   244 pocula *M*[1].

herds, men and beasts of every sort draw, each at birth,
the slender stream of life ; yea, unto Him all beings
thereafter return, and, when unmade, are restored ;
no place is there for death, but, still quick, they fly
unto the ranks of the stars, and mount to the heavens
aloft.

²²⁸ Whenever you would break into the stately
dwelling and the honey hoarded in their treasure-
houses, first with a draught of water sprinkle and
rinse your mouth, and in your hand hold forth search-
ing smoke.¹ Their rage is beyond measure ; when
hurt, they breathe poison into their bites, and fasten-
ing on the veins leave there their unseen stings and
lay down their lives in the wound. Twice they
gather the teeming produce ; two seasons are there
for the harvest—first, so soon as Taygete the Pleiad ²
has shown her comely face to the earth, and spurned
with scornful foot the streams of Ocean, and when
that same star, fleeing before the sign of the watery
Fish, sinks sadly from heaven into the wintry waves.

²³⁹ But if you fear a rigorous winter, and would
be lenient with their future, and have pity for their
crushed spirits and broken fortunes—yet who would
hesitate to fumigate them with thyme, and cut
away the empty waxen cells? For oft the newt, un-
noticed, has nibbled at the combs, the light-shun-
ning beetles cram the chambers, and the unhelpful
drone seats him at another's board. Or the fierce
hornet has rushed upon their unequal forces, or the
moths appear, a pestilent race, or the spider, hateful
to Minerva, hangs in the doorway her loose-woven

---

¹ The Pleiades can first be seen in the eastern sky before
sunrise about June 15. They set shortly before sunrise early
in November. *Sidus Piscis* designates the winter season,
which is just coming on when they set.

quo magis exhaustae fuerint, hoc acrius omnes
incumbent generis lapsi sarcire ruinas
complebuntque foros et floribus horrea texent.   250
    Si vero, quoniam casus apibus quoque nostros
vita tulit, tristi languebunt corpora morbo—
quod iam non dubiis poteris cognoscere signis :
continuo est aegris alius color ; horrida voltum
deformat macies ; tum corpora luce carentum   255
exportant tectis et tristia funera ducunt ;
aut illae pedibus conexae ad limina pendent,
aut intus clausis cunctantur in aedibus omnes
ignavaeque fame et contracto frigore pigrae.
tum sonus auditur gravior, tractimque susurrant, 260
frigidus ut quondam silvis immurmurat Auster,
ut mare sollicitum stridit refluentibus undis,
aestuat ut clausis rapidus fornacibus ignis.
hic iam galbaneos suadebo incendere odores
mellaque harundineis inferre canalibus, ultro   265
hortantem et fessas ad pabula nota vocantem.
proderit et tunsum gallae admiscere saporem
arentisque rosas, aut igni pinguia multo
defruta vel psithia passos de vite racemos,
Cecropiumque thymum et grave olentia centaurea.
est etiam flos in pratis, cui nomen amello   271
fecere agricolae, facilis quaerentibus herba ;
namque uno ingentem tollit de caespite silvam,
aureus ipse, sed in foliis, quae plurima circum
funduntur, violae sublucet purpura nigrae ;   275
saepe deum nexis ornatae torquibus arae ;
asper in ore sapor ; tonsis in vallibus illum
pastores et curva legunt prope flumina Mellae.

[251] nostris *R.*   [259] ignava *PR.*
[260] tunc *P.*   [262] stridet *R.*
[264] hinc *M².*   [278] prope] per *P.*

214

nets.   The more their hoards are drained, the more
eagerly will they press on to repair the ruin of their
fallen race, filling up their cell-galleries and weaving
their granaries with flower-gum.

²⁵¹ But, since to bees as well hath life brought the
ills of man, if their bodies droop with a grievous disease
—and this you can at once discern by no uncertain
signs : straightway, as they sicken, their colour
changes, an unsightly leanness mars their looks ;
anon forth from their doors they bear the bodies of
those bereft of life, and lead the mournful funeral
train ; or else, linked foot to foot, there by the portal
they hang, or within locked doors they linger, all
spiritless with hunger and torpid with pinching cold.
Then is heard a duller sound, a long-drawn buzz, as
at times the chill South sighs in the woods, as the
fretted sea whistles with its ebbing surge, as seethes
in close-barred furnaces the devouring flame.   Then
would I have you burn forthwith fragrant gum,
and give them honey through pipes of reed, freely
heartening them, and calling the weary to their
familiar food.   It will be well, too, to blend the
flavour of pounded galls, and dried rose-leaves, or
must made rich over a strong fire, or dried clusters
from the Psithian vine, with Attic thyme and strong-
smelling centaury.   A flower, too, there is in the
meadows, which farmers have called *amellus,* a plant
easy for searchers to find, for from a single clump it
lifts a vast growth.   Golden is the disk, but in the
petals, streaming profusely round, there is a crimson
gleam amid the dark violet.   Often with its woven
garlands have the gods' altars been decked ; its
flavour is bitter in the mouth ; shepherds cull it in
meadows cropped by the flock, and by Mella's
winding streams.   This plant's roots you must boil in

huius odorato radices incoque Baccho
pabulaque in foribus plenis appone canistris.   280
    Sed si quem proles subito defecerit omnis,
nec genus unde novae stirpis revocetur habebit,
tempus et Arcadii memoranda inventa magistri
pandere, quoque modo caesis iam saepe iuvencis
insincerus apes tulerit cruor.   altius omnem   285
expediam prima repetens ab origine famam.
nam qua Pellaei gens fortunata Canopi
accolit effuso stagnantem flumine Nilum
et circum pictis vehitur sua rura phaselis,
quaque pharetratae vicinia Persidis urget   290
et diversa ruens septem discurrit in ora
et viridem Aegyptum nigra fecundat harena,
usque coloratis amnis devexus ab Indis,
omnis in hac certam regio iacit arte salutem.
    Exiguus primum atque ipsos contractus in usus 295
eligitur locus : hunc angustique imbrice tecti
parietibusque premunt artis, et quattuor addunt,
quattuor a ventis obliqua luce fenestras.
tum vitulus bima curvans iam cornua fronte
quaeritur : huic geminae nares et spiritus oris   300
multa reluctanti obstruitur, plagisque perempto
tunsa per integram solvuntur viscera pellem.
sic positum in clauso linquunt, et ramea costis
subiciunt fragmenta, thymum casiasque recentis.
hoc geritur Zephyris primum impellentibus undas, 305

[280] expone *R*.   [282] habebis *P*.
[290-293] *the order of* M*γ* : *P gives* 290, 292, 291, 293 :
R 290, 291, 293, 292.
[295] in *M¹P* : ad *M²Rγ*.   [301] opsuitur *M*.

---

[1] Probably the *amellus* is the *Aster atticus*, or purple Italian
starwort.
[2] Aristaeus (*cf.* I. 14).

fragrant wine, and set for food at their doors in full
baskets.[1]

[281] But if anyone's whole brood has suddenly
failed him, and he knows not how to restore the race in
a new line, then is it also time to reveal the famed
device of the Arcadian master,[2] and the mode whereby
oft, in the past, the putrid blood of slain bullocks has
engendered bees. From its fount I will unfold the
whole story, tracing it back from its first source. For
where the favoured people of Pellaean Canopus[3]
dwell by the outspread waters of the flooded
Nile, and sail about their fields in painted skiffs,
where the borderland of quivered Persia[4] presses
close, and where the river parts its rushing stream
into seven separate mouths, making green Egypt
rich with its black sands—the river that has swept
unbroken down from the swarthy Indians[5]—all the
country rests on this device its sure salvation.

[295] First is chosen a place, small and straitened
for this very purpose. This they confine with a
narrow roof of tiles and close walls, and towards
the four winds add four windows with slanting light.
Then a bullock is sought, one just arching his horns
on a brow of two summers' growth. Spite of all his
struggles, both his nostrils are stopped up, and the
breath of his mouth; then he is beaten to death,
and his flesh is pounded to a pulp through the
unbroken hide. As thus he lies, they leave him
in his prison, and strew beneath his sides broken
boughs, thyme, and fresh cassia. This is done when
the zephyrs begin to stir the waves, ere the meadows

[3] Egypt is here described according to its boundaries on the
west (Canopus), on the east (290), and on the south (293).
[4] Referring to the Parthian bowmen. "Parthian" and
"Persian" are almost equivalent in the Roman poets.
[5] *i.e.* the Ethiopians.

217

ante novis rubeant quam prata coloribus, ante
garrula quam tignis nidum suspendat hirundo.
interea teneris tepefactus in ossibus umor
aestuat, et visenda modis animalia miris,
trunca pedum primo, mox et stridentia pinnis,   310
miscentur, tenuemque magis magis aëra carpunt,
donec ut aestivis effusus nubibus imber
erupere, aut ut nervo pulsante sagittae,
prima leves ineunt si quando proelia Parthi.

    Quis deus hanc, Musae, quis nobis extudit artem?
unde nova ingressus hominum experientia cepit? 316
pastor Aristaeus fugiens Peneia Tempe,
amissis, ut fama, apibus morboque fameque,
tristis ad extremi sacrum caput astitit amnis,
multa querens, atque hac adfatus voce parentem: 320
"mater, Cyrene mater, quae gurgitis huius
ima tenes, quid me praeclara stirpe deorum
(si modo, quem perhibes, pater est Thymbraeus
      Apollo)
invisum fatis genuisti? aut quo tibi nostri
pulsus amor? quid me caelum sperare iubebas? 325
en etiam hunc ipsum vitae mortalis honorem,
quem mihi vix frugum et pecudum custod a sollers
omnia temptanti extuderat, te matre relinquo.
quin age et ipsa manu felicis erue silvas,
fer stabulis inimicum ignem atque interfice messis,
ure sata et validam in vitis molire bipennem,   331
tanta meae si te ceperunt taedia laudis."

      307 lignis *P.*
      311 magis ac magis $M^1R.$ captant *R.*
      313 erumpere M^1: eripuere *R.*
      319 sacrum] placidum *M.*
      322 a stirpe $R\gamma.$
      327 pecorum *PR*: pecudum $M\gamma^2$, *Nonius*
      331 validam] duramm $M^1.$

blush with their fresh hues, ere the chattering swallow hangs her nest from the rafters. Meantime the moisture, warming in the softened bones, ferments, and creatures of wondrous wise to view, footless at first, soon with buzzing wings as well, swarm together, and more and more essay the light air, until, like a shower pouring from summer clouds, they burst forth, or like arrows from the string's rebound, when the light-armed Parthians enter on the opening battle.[1]

[315] What god, ye Muses, forged for us this device? Whence did man's strange adventuring take its rise? Aristaeus the shepherd, quitting Tempe by the Peneus, when—so runs the tale—his bees were lost through sickness and hunger, sorrowfully stopped beside the sacred fount at the stream's head, and with many plaints called on his mother thus : " O mother, mother Cyrene, that dwellest in this flood's depths, why, from the gods' glorious line—if indeed, as thou sayest, Thymbraean Apollo is my father—didst thou give me birth, to be hated of the fates? Or whither is thy love for me banished? Why didst thou bid me hope for Heaven? Lo, even this very crown of my mortal life, which the skilful tending of crops and cattle had scarce wrought out for me for all my endeavour—though thou art my mother, I resign. Nay, come, and with thine own hand tear up my fruitful woods ; lay the hostile flame to my stalls, destroy my crops, burn my seedlings, and swing the stout axe against my vines, if such loathing for my honour hath seized thee."

[1] Here, according to Servius, there originally followed a eulogy on C. Cornelius Gallus, made prefect of Egypt by Octavian. On his disgrace and suicide in 26 B.C. the present beautiful episode was substituted by the poet.

VIRGIL

At mater sonitum thalamo sub fluminus alti
sensit.   eam circum Milesia vellera Nymphae
carpebant, hyali saturo fucata colore,   335
Drymoque Xanthoque Ligeaque Phyllodoceque,
caesariem effusae nitidam per candida colla,
[Nesaee Spioque Thaliaque Cymodoceque,]
Cydippeque et flava Lycorias, altera virgo,
altera tum primos Lucinae experta labores,   340
Clioque et Beroe soror, Oceanitides ambae,
ambae auro, pictis incinctae pellibus ambae,
atque Ephyre atque Opis et Asia Deiopea
et tandem positis velox Arethusa sagittis.
inter quas curam Clymene narrabat inanem   GMPR
Volcani Martisque dolos et dulcia furta,   346
aque Chao densos divom numerabat amores.
carmine quo captae dum fusis mollia pensa
devolvunt, iterum maternas impulit auris
luctus Aristaei, vitreisque sedilibus omnes   350
obstipuere ; sed ante alias Arethusa sorores
prospiciens summa flavum caput extulit unda,
et procul : " o gemitu non frustra exterrita tanto,
Cyrene soror, ipse tibi, tua maxima cura,
tristis Aristaeus Penei genitoris ad undam   355
stat lacrimans, et te crudelem nomine dicit."
huic percussa nova mentem formidine mater
"duc, age, duc ad nos ; fas illi limina divum
tangere" ait : simul alta iubet discedere late
flumina, qua iuvenis gressus inferret. at illum   360
curvata in montis faciem circumstetit unda,
accepitque sinu vasto misitque sub amnem.
iamque domum mirans genetricis et umida regna
speluncisque lacus clausos lucosque sonantis

    338 *omitted* $MPR\gamma^1$.   **339** Cydippe et $MP\gamma^2$.   **346** matris P.
    347 atque MR : adque G.   **348** fusis dum M : dum fusi G.
    350 amnes $M^1\gamma$.   **360** at] ad G.
    361 speciem M. circumstitit G : circumspicit P.

220

[333] But his mother heard the cry from her bower beneath the river's depths. About her the Nymphs were spinning fleeces of Miletus, dyed with rich glassy hue—Drymo and Xantho, Ligea and Phyllodoce, their shining tresses floating over snowy necks; Cydippe and golden-haired Lycorias—a maiden one, the other having but felt the first birth-throes; Clio and Beroe her sister, daughters of Ocean both, both arrayed in gold, and both in dappled hides;[1] Ephyre and Opis, and Asian Deiopea, and fleet Arethusa, her arrows laid aside at last. Among these Clymene was telling of Vulcan's baffled care, of the wiles and stolen joys of Mars, and from Chaos on was rehearsing the countless loves of the gods. And while, charmed by the strain, they unrolled the soft coils from their spindles, again the wail of Aristaeus smote upon his mother's ear, and all upon their crystal thrones were startled. Yet, first of all the sisters, Arethusa, looking forth, raised her golden head above the water's brim, and cried from afar: "O sister Cyrene, no idle alarm is thine at wailing so loud. 'Tis even he, thy chiefest care, thy Aristaeus, standing sadly and in tears by the wave of Father Peneus, and crying out on thee by name for cruelty."

[357] To her the mother, her soul smitten with strange dread, cries: "O bring him, bring him to us; lawful it is for him to tread the threshold divine." And withal, she bade the deep streams part asunder far, that so the youth might enter in. And lo, the wave, arched mountain-like, stood round about, and, welcoming him within the vast recess, ushered him beneath the stream. And now, marvelling at his mother's home, a realm of waters, at the lakes locked in caverns, and the echoing groves, he went on his

[1] *i.e.* arrayed as huntresses.

ibat, et ingenti motu stupefactus aquarum   365
omnia sub magna labentia flumina terra
spectabat diversa locis, Phasimque Lycumque
et caput, unde altus primum se erumpit Enipeus
unde pater Tiberinus et unde Aniena fluenta
saxosusque sonans Hypanis Mysusque Caïcus,   370
et gemina auratus taurino cornua voltu
Eridanus, quo non alius per pinguia culta
in mare purpureum violentior effluit amnis.
postquam est in thalami pendentia pumice tecta
perventum et nati fletus cognovit inanis   375
Cyrene, manibus liquidos dant ordine fontis
germanae, tonsisque ferunt mantelia villis ;
pars epulis onerant mensas et plena reponunt
pocula, Panchaeis adolescunt ignibus arae.
et mater " cape Maeonii carchesia Bacchi :   380
Oceano libemus " ait : simul ipsa precatur
Oceanumque patrem rerum Nymphasque sorores,
centum quae silvas, centum quae flumina servant.
ter liquido ardentem perfundit nectare Vestam,
ter flamma ad summum tecti subiecta reluxit.   385
omine quo firmans animum sic incipit ipsa :
    " Est in Carpathio Neptuni gurgite vates,
caeruleus Proteus, magnum qui piscibus aequor
et iuncto bipedum curru metitur equorum.
hic nunc Emathiae portus patriamque revisit   390
Pallenen ; hunc et Nymphae veneramur et ipse
grandaevus Nereus ; novit namque omnia vates,
quae sint, quae fuerint, quae mox ventura trahantur ;

[365] motus M^1.   [368] primus M.   rumpit $R\gamma^1$: rupit P.
[370] saxosum *Servius.*   [378] mensas] aras P.
[384] perfudit $M^2\gamma$.   [385] flammam M. tectis M. sublata M.
[393] trahentur M^1.

---

[1] The rivers are distinct below the earth, even as they are
above.

way, and, dazed by the mighty rush of waters, he gazed on all the rivers, as, each in his own place, they glide under the great earth [1]—Phasis and Lycus, the fount whence deep Enipeus first breaks forth, whence Father Tiber, whence the streams of Anio and rocky, roaring Hypanis, and Mysian Caicus, and Eridanus,[2] on whose bull's brow are twain gilded horns : no other stream of mightier force flows through the rich tilth to join the violet sea.

[374] Soon as he reached the bower with its hanging roof of stone, and Cyrene heard the tale of her son's idle tears, the sisters, in due order, pour on his hands clear spring-waters, and bring smooth-shorn napkins. Some load the board with the feast, and in turn set on the brimming cups ; the altars blaze up with Panchaean fires.[3] Then cried his mother : "Take the goblets of Maeonian wine ; [4] pour we a libation to Ocean !" And withal she prayed to Ocean, universal father, and the sister Nymphs, who guard a hundred forests and a hundred streams. Thrice with clear nectar she sprinkled the glowing hearth ; thrice the flame, shooting up to the roof-top, gleamed afresh. With this omen to cheer his heart, she thus herself began :

[387] "In Neptune's Carpathian flood there dwells a seer, Proteus, of sea-green hue, who traverses the mighty main in his car drawn by fishes and a team of two-footed steeds. Even now he revisits the havens of Thessaly and his native Pallene. To him we Nymphs do reverence, and aged Nereus himself; for the seer has knowledge of all things—what is, what hath been, what is in train ere long to happen—for so has it

---

[2] River-gods were usually represented with horns, perhaps because of the violence and roar of the water. The gilding may indicate fertility.   [3] cf. II. 139.

[4] i.e. Lydian, probably with reference to Mount Tmolus (cf. II. 98).

quippe ita Neptuno visum est, immania cuius
armenta et turpis pascit sub gurgite phocas.   395
hic tibi, nate, prius vinclis capiendus, ut omnem
expediat morbi causam eventusque secundet.
nam sine vi non ulla dabit praecepta, neque illum
orando flectes; vim duram et vincula capto
tende; doli circum haec demum frangentur inanes.
ipsa ego te, medios cum sol accenderit aestus,   401
cum sitiunt herbae et pecori iam gratior umbra est,
in secreta senis ducam, quo fessus ab undis
se recipit, facile ut somno adgrediare iacentem.
verum ubi correptum manibus vinclisque tenebis, 405
tum variae eludent species atque ora ferarum.
fiet enim subito sus horridus atraque tigris
squamosusque draco et fulva cervice leaena,
aut acrem flammae sonitum dabit atque ita vinclis
excidet, aut in aquas tenuis dilapsus abibit.   410
sed quanto ille magis formas se vertet in omnis
tam tu, nate, magis contende tenacia vincla,
donec talis erit mutato corpore, qualem
videris, incepto tegeret cum lumina somno."

   Haec ait et liquidum ambrosiae diffundit odorem,
quo totum nati corpus perduxit; at illi   416
dulcis compositis spiravit crinibus aura
atque habilis membris venit vigor. est specus ingens
exesi latere in montis, quo plurima vento
cogitur inque sinus scindit sese unda reductos,   MPR
deprensis olim statio tutissima nautis;   421
intus se vasti Proteus tegit obice saxi.

     400 franguntur *PR.*   406 ludent *R.*
     409 sonitum flammae *M.*   410 elabsus *G.*   habebit M^1.
     411 vertit *P.*
     412 tantu M^1P: tanto $M(late)R\gamma$, *Servius:* tantum b^1,
known to Servius: tam tu *Ribbeck.*
     415 defundit *G:* perfundit *P:* depromit *R.*
     416 perfudit *R.*

224

seemed good to Neptune, whose monstrous herds and
unsightly seals he pastures beneath the wave. Him,
my son, thou must first take in fetters, that he may
unfold to thee all the cause of the sickness, and bless
the issue. For without force he will give thee no
counsel, nor shalt thou bend him by prayer. With
stern force and fetters make fast the captive; thereon
alone his wiles will shatter themselves in vain. I
myself, when the sun has kindled his noonday heat,
when the grass is athirst, and the shade is now wel-
come to the flock, will guide thee to the aged one's
retreat, whither when weary he retires from the waves,
so that thou mayest assail him with ease as he lies
asleep. But when thou holdest him in the grasp of
hands and fetters, then will manifold forms baffle thee,
and figures of wild beasts. For of a sudden he will
become a bristly boar, a deadly tiger, a scaly serpent,
or a lioness with tawny neck; or he will give forth
the fierce roar of flame, and thus slip from his fetters,
or he will melt into fleeting water and be gone.
But the more he turn himself into all shapes, the
more, my son, strain thou his fetters, until after
his last changes of body he become such as thou
sawest when he closed his eyes at the beginning of
slumber."

[415] She spake, and shed abroad ambrosia's fragrant
stream, wherewith she steeped her son's whole
frame: and lo, a sweet effluence breathed from his
smoothened locks, and vigour and suppleness passed
into his limbs. There is a vast cavern, hollowed in a
mountain's side, whither many a wave is driven by
the wind, then parts into receding ripples [1]—at times
a haven most sure for storm-caught mariners. Within,
Proteus shelters himself with the barrier of a huge

---

[1] Or "and separates itself into the retiring bays."

hic iuvenem in latebris aversum a lumine Nympha
collocat, ipsa procul nebulis obscura resistit.
iam rapidus torrens sitientis Sirius Indos   425
ardebat caelo, et medium sol igneus orbem
hauserat; arebant herbae, et cava flumina siccis
faucibus ad limum radii tepefacta coquebant,
cum Proteus consueta petens e fluctibus antra
ibat: eum vasti circum gens umida ponti   430
exsultans rorem late dispergit amarum.
sternunt se somno diversae in litore phocae;
ipse velut stabuli custos in montibus olim,
Vesper ubi e pastu vitulos ad tecta reducit
auditisque lupos acuunt balatibus agni,   435
considit scopulo medius, numerumque recenset. MPRV
cuius Aristaeo quoniam est oblata facultas,
vix defessa senem passus componere membra
cum clamore ruit magno, manicisque iacentem
occupat. ille suae contra non immemor artis   440
omnia transformat sese in miracula rerum,
ignemque horribilemque feram fluviumque liquentem.
verum ubi nulla fugam reperit fallacia, victus
in sese redit atque hominis tandem ore locutus
"nam quis te, iuvenum confidentissime, nostras   445
iussit adire domos? quidve hinc petis?" inquit. at ille
"scis, Proteu, scis ipse; neque est te fallere quic-
          quam;
sed tu desine velle. deum praecepta secuti
venimus hinc lassis quaesitum oracula rebus."
tantum effatus. ad haec vates vi denique multa 450

---

[423] a *omitted R.*   [430] circum vasti *M.*
[431] discerpsit *P.*   [434] vespere *P.*
[436] consedit *M.*   [439] *omitted V.*
[443] pellacia *b¹, Berne Scholia, known to Philargyrius.*
[447] quicquam *MR, known to Servius:* quiquam *γ¹:* cuiquam
Pγ², Servius.   [449] lapeis *R.*

rock.   Here the Nymph stations the youth in
ambush, away from the light; she herself, veiled in
a mist, stands aloof. And now the Dog-star, fiercely
parching the thirsty Indians, was ablaze in heaven,
and the fiery Sun had consumed half his course; the
grass was withering and the hollow streams, in their
parched throats, were scorched and baked by the
rays down to the slime, when Proteus came from
the waves, in quest of his wonted grot. About
him the watery race of the vast deep gambolled,
scattering afar the briny spray. The seals lay them
down to sleep, here and there along the shore; he
himself—even as at times the warder of a sheep-
fold on the hills, when Vesper brings the steers
home from pasture, and the cry of bleating lambs
whets the wolf's hunger—sits down on a rock in
the midst and tells his tale. Soon as the chance
came to Aristaeus, he scarce suffered the aged one
to settle his weary limbs, ere he burst upon him with
a loud cry and surprised him in fetters as he lies.
On his part, the seer forgets not his craft, but
changes himself into all wondrous shapes—into
flame and hideous beast and flowing river. But
when no stratagem wins escape, vanquished he
returns to himself, and at last speaks with human
voice: "Why, who," he cried, "most presumptuous
of youths, bade thee invade our home? Or what
seekest thou hence?" But he: "Thou knowest,
Proteus; thou knowest of thyself, nor may one
deceive thee in aught, but do thou resign thy
wish to deceive. Following the counsel of Heaven,
we are come to seek hence an oracle for our
weary fortunes." So much he spoke. On this the
seer, yielding at last to mighty force, rolled on
him eyes ablaze with grey-green light, and, grimly

VIRGIL

ardentis oculos intorsit lumine glauco,
et graviter frendens sic fatis ora resolvit.

" Non te nullius exercent numinis irae :
magna luis commissa ; tibi has miserabilis Orpheus
haudquaquam ad meritum poenas, ni fata resistant,
suscitat et rapta graviter pro coniuge saevit.   456
illa quidem, dum te fugeret per flumina praeceps,
immanem ante pedes hydrum moritura puella
servantem ripas alta non vidit in herba.
at chorus aequalis Dryadum clamore supremos   460
implerunt montis ; flerunt Rhodopeiae arces
altaque Pangaea et Rhesi Mavortia tellus   MRV
atque Getae atque Hebrus et Actias Orithyia.
ipse cava solans aegrum testudine amorem
te, dulcis coniunx, te solo in litore secum,   MR
te veniente die, te decedente canebat.   466
Taenarias etiam fauces, alta ostia Ditis,
et caligantem nigra formidine lucum
ingressus, manisque adiit regemque tremendum
nesciaque humanis precibus mansuescere corda.   470
at cantu commotae Erebi de sedibus imis   FMR
umbrae ibant tenues simulacraque luce carentum,
quam multa in foliis avium se milia condunt,
Vesper ubi aut hibernus agit de montibus imber,
matres atque viri defunctaque corpora vita   475
magnanimum heroum, pueri innuptaeque puellae,
impositique rogis iuvenes ante ora parentum ;
quos circum limus niger et deformis harundo

⁴⁵⁴ lues *R, Servius, Philargyrius, Berne Scholia.*
⁴⁵⁵ ad *P :* ob *MR*γ, *Priscian, Servius.*   ⁴⁶⁰ supre.no *PR.*
⁴⁷² *After this verse* R *inserts the three lines, Aen.* VI. 311,
310, 312.   ⁴⁷³ foliis] silvis *M*γ.

gnashing his teeth, thus unlocked his lips to tell
the fates :

453 "There is a god whose anger pursues thee : a
heavy offence thou dost expiate. 'Tis Orpheus, un-
happy one, who evokes this vengeance against thee
—did not Fate interpose—far short of thy deserts,[1]
and wildly he rages for the loss of his bride. She,
in truth, hastening headlong along the river, if only
she might escape thee, saw not the monstrous serpent
that before her feet, doomed maiden, hugged the
banks amid the deep grass. But the band of her
Dryad comrades filled with their cries the mountain-
peaks ; the towers of Rhodope wept, and the Pangaean
heights, and the martial land[2] of Rhesus, the Getae
and Hebrus and Orithyia, child of Acte. But he,
solacing love's anguish with his hollow shell, sang of
thee, sweet wife—of thee, to himself on the lonely
shore ; of thee as day drew nigh, of thee as day
declined. Even the jaws of Taenarus, the lofty portals
of Dis, he entered, and the grove that is murky with
black terror, and came to the dead, and the king
of terrors, and the hearts that know not how to
soften at human prayers. Startled by the strain,
there came from the lowest realms of Erebus the
bodiless shadows and the phantoms of those bereft
of light, in multitude like the thousands of birds
that hide amid the leaves when the evening star
or a wintry shower drives them from the hills—
mothers and men, and bodies of high-souled heroes,
their life now done, boys and unwedded girls, and
sons placed on the pyre before their fathers' eyes.
But round them are the black ooze and unsightly

---

[1] If *ob meritum* is read, the meaning will be : "unhappy by
no means on account of his deserts," said of Orpheus.

[2] *i.e.* Thrace.

VIRGIL

Cocyti tardaque palus inamabilis unda
alligat et noviens Styx interfusa coercet.   480
quin ipsae stupuere domus atque intima Leti
Tartara caeruleosque implexae crinibus anguis
Eumenides, tenuitque inhians tria Cerberus ora,
atque Ixionii vento rota constitit orbis.
iamque pedem referens casus evaserat omnis,   485
redditaque Eurydice superas veniebat ad auras,
pone sequens (namque hanc dederat Proserpina
      legem),
cum subita incautum dementia cepit amantem,
ignoscenda quidem, scirent si ignoscere Manes :
restitit, Eurydicenque suam iam luce sub ipsa   490
immemor heu! victusque animi respexit.   ibi omnis
effusus labor atque immitis rupta tyranni
foedera, terque fragor stagnis auditus Avernis.
illa ' quis et me ' inquit ' miseram et te perdidit,
      Orpheu,
quis tantus furor ? en iterum crudelia retro   495
fata vocant conditque natantia lumina somnus.
iamque vale : feror ingenti circumdata nocte
invalidasque tibi tendens, heu! non tua, palmas.' ᴍʀ
dixit et ex oculis subito, ceu fumus in auras
commixtus tenuis, fugit diversa, neque illum   500
prensantem nequiquam umbras et multa volentem
dicere praeterea vidit ; nec portitor Orci
amplius obiectam passus transire paludem.
quid faceret ? quo se rapta bis coniuge ferret ?
quo fletu manis, quae numina voce moveret ?   505
illa quidem Stygia nabat iam frigida cumba.
septem illum totos perhibent ex ordine mensis

---

⁴⁸² caeruleis *M*¹.   impexae *M*², *Berne Scholia :* innexae *FR.*
⁴⁸⁸ subito *R.*   ⁴⁹³ stagni est *R.*   Averni *FR.*
⁵⁰⁰ fugit in diversa *M*².   ⁵⁰⁴ erepta *M*².
⁵⁰⁵ quo] quos *R :* quod *γ*¹.

reeds of Cocytus, the unlovely mere enchaining them
with its sluggish water, and Styx holding them fast
within his ninefold circles. Nay, the very halls of
Hell were spell-bound, and inmost Tartarus, and the
Furies with livid snakes entwined in their locks.
Cerberus held agape his triple mouths, and Ixion's
wheel was stayed by the still wind.

485 "And now as he retraced his steps he had
escaped every mischance, and the regained Eurydice
was nearing the upper world, following behind—for
that condition had Proserpine ordained—when a
sudden frenzy seized Orpheus, unwary in his love,
frenzy meet for pardon, did Hell know how to pardon !
He stopped, and on the very verge of light, unmindful,
alas! and vanquished in purpose, on Eurydice, now his
own, looked back ! In that moment all his toil was
spent, the ruthless tyrant's pact was broken, and
thrice a crash was heard amid the pools of Avernus.
She cried : 'What madness, Orpheus, what dreadful
madness hath ruined my unhappy self and thee ? Lo,
again the cruel Fates call me back and sleep veils my
swimming eyes. And now farewell ! I am swept off,
wrapped in uttermost night, and stretching out to
thee strengthless hands, thine, alas! no more.' She
spake, and straightway from his sight, like smoke
mingling with thin air, vanished afar, and, vainly
as he clutched at the shadows and yearned to say
much, never saw him more ; nor did the warden [1] of
Orcus suffer him again to pass that barrier of the
marsh. What could he do? Whither turn himself,
twice robbed of his wife ? With what tears move
Hell, with what prayers its powers ? She, alas ! even
now death-cold, was afloat in the Stygian barque.
Month in, month out, seven whole months, men say

[1] *i.e.* Charon.

rupe sub aëria deserti ad Strymonis undam
flevisse, et gelidis haec evolvisse sub antris,
mulcentem tigris et agentem carmine quercus; 510
qualis populea maerens philomela sub umbra
amissos queritur fetus, quos durus arator
observans nido implumis detraxit; at illa
flet noctem, ramoque sedens miserabile carmen
integrat, et maestis late loca questibus implet. 515
nulla Venus, non ulli animum flexere hymenaei.
solus Hyperboreas glacies Tanaimque nivalem
arvaque Rhipaeis numquam viduata pruinis
lustrabat, raptam Eurydicen atque inrita Ditis
dona querens; spretae Ciconum quo munere matres
inter sacra deum nocturnique orgia Bacchi 521
discerptum latos iuvenem sparsere per agros. FMRV
tum quoque marmorea caput a cervice revulsum
gurgite cum medio portans Oeagrius Hebrus
volveret, Eurydicen vox ipsa et frigida lingua, 525
a miseram Eurydicen! anima fugiente vocabat.
Eurydicen toto referebant flumine ripae.''
haec Proteus, et se iactu dedit aequor in altum,
quaque dedit, spumantem undam sub vertice torsit.
   At non Cyrene; namque ultro adfata timentem:
'' nate, licet tristis animo deponere curas. 531
haec omnis morbi causa, hinc miserabile Nymphae,
cum quibus illa choros lucis agitabat in altis,
exitium misere apibus. tu munera supplex [FGMRV
tende petens pacem, et facilis venerare Napaeas; 535

⁵⁰⁹ flesse sibi et *R.*   *So Sabb.*   astris *R:* antris *M*γ
⁵²⁴ medius *F.*   ⁵³¹ componere *M*¹.

beneath a skyey cliff by lonely Strymon's wave, he wept, and, deep in icy caverns, unfolded this his tale, charming the tigers, and making the oaks attend his strain; even as the nightingale, mourning beneath the poplar's shade, bewails the loss of her brood, that a churlish ploughman hath espied and torn unfledged from the nest: but she weeps all night long, and, perched on a spray, renews her piteous strain, filling the region round with sad laments. No love, no wedding-song could bend his soul. Alone he would roam the northern ice, the snowy Tanais, and the fields ever wedded to Rhipaean frosts, wailing Eurydice lost, and the gift of Dis annulled. But the Ciconian dames, scorned by such devotion, in the midst of their sacred rites and the midnight orgies of Bacchus, tore the youth limb from limb and strewed him broadcast over the fields. Even then, while Oeagrian[1] Hebrus swept and rolled in mid-current that head, plucked from its marble neck, the bare voice and death-cold tongue, with fleeting breath, called Eurydice—ah, hapless Eurydice! 'Eurydice' the banks re-echoed, all adown the stream."

[528] Thus Proteus, and at a bound plunged into the deep sea, and where he plunged, whirled the water into foam beneath the eddy. But not so Cyrene; for straightway she spake to the startled youth: "My son, thou mayest lay aside thy heart's sorrow and care. This is the whole cause of the sickness; hence it is that the Nymphs, with whom she was wont to tread the dance in the deep groves, sent this sore havoc on thy bees. Offer thou a suppliant's gifts, craving grace, and do homage to the gentle

---

[1] Oeagrus being the father of Orpheus, the epithet is equivalent to "paternal."

namque dabunt veniam votis, irasque remittent.
sed modus orandi qui sit prius ordine dicam.
quattuor eximios praestanti corpore tauros,
qui tibi nunc viridis depascunt summa Lycaei,
delige et intacta totidem cervice iuvencas.   540
quattuor his aras alta ad delubra dearum
constitue, et sacrum iugulis demitte cruorem
corporaque ipsa boum frondoso desere luco.
post ubi nona suos Aurora ostenderit ortus,
inferias Orphei Lethaea papavera mittes,   545
et nigram mactabis ovem, lucumque revises:
placatam Eurydicen vitula venerabere caesa."
    Haud mora: continuo matris praecepta facessit;
ad delubra venit, monstratas excitat aras,   GMRV
quattuor eximios praestanti corpore tauros   GMR
ducit et intacta totidem cervice iuvencas.   551
post ubi nona suos Aurora induxerat ortus,
inferias Orphei mittit, lucumque revisit.
hic vero subitum ac dictu mirabile monstrum
aspiciunt, liquefacta boum per viscera toto   555
stridere apes utero et ruptis effervere costis,
immensasque trahi nubes, iamque arbore summa
confluere et lentis uvam demittere ramis.

    Haec super arvorum cultu pecorumque canebam
et super arboribus, Caesar dum magnus ad altum 560

538 eximio *Rγ*.   praestantis *R*: prestantis *γ*.
540 intactis *RVγ*[1], *Berne Scholia.*
542 dimitte *Mγ*.
548 capessit *Mγ*, *Berne Scholia.*
550 eximio *Rγ*[1].   praestantis *R*[2]*γ*[2]
551 intactas *Rγ*[1]: intacto *M*[1].
553 dimittere *M*.
559 cultus *G*.

maidens of the woods; for they will grant pardon to
prayers, and relax their wrath. But first I will tell
thee in order the manner of thy supplication. Pick
out four choice bulls, of surpassing form, that now
graze among thy herds on the heights of green
Lycaeus, and as many heifers of unyoked neck. For
these set up four altars by the stately shrines of the
goddesses, and drain the sacrificial blood from their
throats, but leave the bodies of the steers within the
leafy grove. Anon, when the ninth[1] Dawn displays
her rising beams, thou shalt send unto Orpheus
funeral dues of Lethe's poppies, shalt slay a black
ewe and revisit the grove. Then to Eurydice, now
appeased, thou shalt do worship with the slaughter
of a calf."

[548] Tarrying not, he straightway does his mother's
bidding. He comes to the shrine, rears the altars
appointed, and leads thither four choice bulls, of
surpassing form, and as many heifers of unyoked
neck. Anon, when the ninth Dawn had ushered in
her rising beams, he sends unto Orpheus the funeral
dues, and revisits the grove. But here they espy
a portent, sudden and wondrous to tell—throughout
the paunch, amid the molten flesh of the oxen, bees
buzzing and swarming forth from the ruptured sides,
then trailing in vast crowds, till at last on a tree-top
they stream together, and hang in clusters from the
bending boughs.

[559] Thus[2] I sang of the care of fields, of cattle,
and of trees, while great Caesar thundered in war by

---

[1] A sacrifice to the dead was offered on the ninth day after
the funeral.
[2] Here follows an epilogue to the whole four books.

fulminat Euphraten bello victorque volentis
per populos dat iura viamque adfectat Olympo.
illo Vergilium me tempore dulcis alebat
Parthenope, studiis florentem ignobilis oti,
carmina qui lusi pastorum audaxque iuventa,   565
Tityre, te patulae cecini sub tegmine fagi.

[563] virgilium γc.
[565] audax] auxi *Berne Scholia*.

deep Euphrates [1] and gave a victor's laws unto willing nations, and essayed the path to Heaven. In those days I, Virgil, was nursed of sweet Parthenope, and rejoiced in the arts of inglorious ease—I who dallied with shepherds' songs, and, in youth's boldness, sang, Tityrus, of thee under thy spreading beech's covert. [2]

[1] After the battle of Actium, 31 B.C., Octavian made a triumphal progress through the East.

[2] See the opening line of the *Eclogues*.

THE AENEID

LIBER I

Arma virumque cano, Troiae qui primus ab oris MRV
Italiam fato profugus Laviniaque venit
litora—multum ille et terris iactatus et alto
vi superum, saevae memorem Iunonis ob iram,
multa quoque et bello passus, dum conderet urbem 5
inferretque deos Latio; genus unde Latinum
Albanique patres atque altae moenia Romae.
    Musa, mihi causas memora, quo numine laeso
quidve dolens regina deum tot volvere casus
insignem pietate virum, tot adire labores 10
impulerit.   tantaene animis caelestibus irae?

[*Ille ego, qui quondam gracili modulatus avena*   1a
carmen, et egressus silvis vicina coegi   1b
ut quamvis avido parerent arva colono,   1c
gratum opus agricolis ; at nunc horrentia Martis   1d]

1a-1d *only in* a, *on margin; recognized by Donatus* (Suetonius) *and Servius as written by Virgil, but withdrawn by Varius.*

2 Laviniaque *M¹V, known to Servius:* -que *omitted M²:* Lavinaque *Rγ: Servius approves of* Lavina.
7 alta *R.*

BOOK I

Arms I sing and the man who first from the coasts of Troy, exiled by fate, came to Italy and Lavinian shores; much buffeted on sea and land by violence from above, through cruel Juno's unforgiving wrath, and much enduring in war also, till he should build a city and bring his gods to Latium; whence came the Latin race, the lords of Alba,[2] and the walls of lofty Rome.[3]

[8] Tell me, O Muse, the cause; wherein thwarted in will or wherefore angered, did the Queen of heaven drive a man, of goodness so wondrous, to traverse so many perils, to face so many toils. Can resentment so fierce dwell in heavenly breasts?

[*I am he who once tuned my song on a slender reed, then, leaving the woodland, constrained the neighbouring fields to serve the husbandmen, however grasping—a work welcome to farmers: but now of Mars' bristling* [1]]

[1] These opening lines were probably written by Virgil in an experimental stage of composition, but rejected by his literary executors. In antiquity the words *Arma virumque* ("Arms and the man") were regularly regarded as the opening words of the epic. See Introduction, p. ix.

[2] Many of the great senatorial families of Rome, including the Julii, claimed descent from the families of Alba Longa.

[3] Reference is thus made to three stages of growth— Lavinium founded by Aeneas, Alba Longa by Ascanius, Rome by Romulus and Remus.

VIRGIL

    Urbs antiqua fuit (Tyrii tenuere coloni)
Karthago, Italiam contra Tiberinaque longe
ostia, dives opum studiisque asperrima belli;
quam Iuno fertur terris magis omnibus unam   **15**
posthabita coluisse Samo; hic illius arma,
hic currus fuit, hoc regnum dea gentibus esse,
si qua fata sinant, iam tum tenditque fovetque.
progeniem sed enim Troiano a sanguine duci
audierat, Tyrias olim quae verteret arces;   **20**
hinc populum late regem belloque superbum
venturum excidio Libyae: sic volvere Parcas.
id metuens veterisque memor Saturnia belli,
prima quod ad Troiam pro caris gesserat Argis
(necdum etiam causae irarum saevique dolores   **25**
exciderant animo; manet alta mente repostum
iudicium Paridis spretaeque iniuria formae,   MR
et genus invisum et rapti Ganymedis honores)—
his accensa super, iactatos aequore toto
Troas, reliquias Danaum atque immitis Achilli,   **30**
arcebat longe Latio; multosque per annos
errabant, acti fatis, maria omnia circum.
tantae molis erat Romanam condere gentem.

    Vix e conspectu Siculae telluris in altum
vela dabant laeti et spumas salis aere ruebant,   **35**
cum Iuno, aeternum servans sub pectore volnus,
haec secum: "mene incepto desistere victam
nec posse Italia Teucrorum avertere regem!

        ¹⁸ sinunt *M*¹.   ³⁰ Achillis *R.*

¹² There was an ancient city, the home of Tyrian settlers, Carthage, over against Italy and the Tiber's mouths afar, rich in wealth and stern in war's pursuits. This, 'tis said, Juno loved above all other lands, holding Samos itself less dear. Here was her armour, here her chariot; that here should be the capital of the nations, should the fates perchance allow it, was even then the goddess' aim and cherished hope. Yet in truth she had heard that a race was springing from Trojan blood, to overthrow some day the Tyrian towers; that from it a people, kings of broad realms and proud in war, should come forth for Libya's downfall: such was the course ordained of fate. The daughter of Saturn, fearful of this and mindful of the old war which erstwhile she had fought at Troy for her beloved Argos—not yet, too, had the cause of her wrath and her bitter sorrows faded from her mind: deep in her heart lie stored the judgment of Paris and her slighted beauty's wrong, her hatred of the race [1] and the honours paid to ravished Ganymede—inflamed hereby yet more, she tossed on the wide main the Trojan remnant, left by the Greeks and pitiless Achilles, and kept them far from Latium; and many a year they wandered, driven by the fates o'er all the seas. So vast was the struggle to found the race of Rome.

³⁴ Hardly out of sight of Sicilian land were they spreading their sails seaward, and merrily ploughing the foaming brine with brazen prow, when Juno, nursing an undying wound deep in her heart, thus to herself spake:

³⁷ " What! I resign my purpose, baffled, and fail to turn from Italy the Teucrian king! The fates, doubt-

---

[1] Hated, because sprung from Dardanus, son of Jupiter and Electra, Juno's rival.

VIRGIL

quippe vetor fatis.   Pallasne exurere classem
Argivum atque ipsos potuit submergere ponto   40
unius ob noxam et furias Aiacis Oilei ?
ipsa Iovis rapidum iaculata e nubibus ignem
disiecitque rates evertitque aequora ventis ;
illum exspirantem transfixo pectore flammas
turbine corripuit scopuloque infixit acuto ;   45
ast ego, quae divum incedo regina, Iovisque
et soror et coniunx, una cum gente tot annos
bella gero.   et quisquam numen Iunonis adorat
praeterea aut supplex aris imponet honorem ? ''

Talia flammato secum dea corde volutans   50
nimborum in patriam, loca feta furentibus Austris,
Aeoliam venit.   hic vasto rex Aeolus antro
luctantis ventos tempestatesque sonoras
imperio premit ac vinclis et carcere frenat.
illi indignantes magno cum murmure montis   55
circum claustra fremunt ; celsa sedet Aeolus arce
sceptra tenens, mollitque animos et temperat iras ;
ni faciat, maria ac terras caelumque profundum
quippe ferant rapidi secum verrantque per auras.
sed pater omnipotens speluncis abdidit atris,   60
hoc metuens, molemque et montis insuper altos
imposuit regemque dedit, qui foedere certo
et premere et laxas sciret dare iussus habenas.
ad quem tum Iuno supplex his vocibus usa est :

" Aeole, namque tibi divum pater atque hominum rex
et mulcere dedit fluctus et tollere vento,   66
gens inimica mihi Tyrrhenum navigat aequor,
Ilium in Italiam portans victosque Penatis :

   [41] Oili *M*.   [44] pectore] tempore *Probus*.
   [48] adoret *b²c²*, *Quintilian*, IX. 2, 10.
   [49] inponit *γ¹*, *b¹* : imponit *c.*

less, forbid me! Had Pallas power to burn up the Argive fleet and sink the sailors in the deep, because of one single man's guilt, and the frenzy of Ajax, son of Oileus? Her own hand hurled from the clouds Jove's swift flame, scattered their ships, and upheaved the sea in tempest; but him, as with pierced breast he breathed forth flame, she caught in a whirlwind and impaled on a spiky crag.[1] Yet I, who move as queen of gods, sister at once and wife of Jove, with one people am warring these many years. And will any still worship Juno's godhead or humbly lay sacrifice upon her altars?"

50 Thus inwardly brooding with heart inflamed, the goddess came to Aeolia, mother-land of storm-clouds, tracts teeming with furious blasts. Here in his vast cavern, Aeolus, their king, keeps under his sway and with prison bonds curbs the struggling winds and the roaring gales. They, to the mountain's mighty moans, chafe blustering around the barriers. In his lofty citadel sits Aeolus, sceptre in hand, taming their passions and soothing their rage; did he not so, they would surely bear off with them in wild flight seas and lands and the vault of heaven, sweeping them through space. But, fearful of this, the Father omnipotent hid them in gloomy caverns, and over them piled high mountain masses and gave them a king, who, under fixed covenant, should be skilled to tighten and loosen the reins at command. Him Juno now addressed thus in suppliant speech:

65 "Aeolus—for to thee hath the Father of gods and king of men given power to calm and uplift the waves with the wind—a people hateful to me sails the Tyrrhene sea, carrying into Italy Ilium's

[1] Minerva destroyed Ajax and his fleet because on the night of Troy's fall he had attacked Cassandra in her temple.

incute vim ventis submersasque obrue puppis,
aut age diversos et disice corpora ponto.   70
sunt mihi bis septem praestanti corpore Nymphae :
quarum quae forma pulcherrima, Deiopea,
conubio iungam stabili propriamque dicabo,
omnis ut tecum meritis pro talibus annos
exigat et pulchra faciat te prole parentem."   75

Aeolus haec contra : "tuus, o regina, quid optes,
explorare labor ; mihi iussa capessere fas est.
tu mihi quodcumque hoc regni, tu sceptra Iovemque
concilias, tu das epulis accumbere divum,
nimborumque facis tempestatumque potentem."   80

Haec ubi dicta, cavum conversa cuspide montem
impulit in latus ; ac venti, velut agmine facto,
qua data porta, ruunt et terras turbine perflant.
incubuere mari totumque a sedibus imis
una Eurusque Notusque ruunt creberque procellis 85
Africus et vastos volvunt ad litora fluctus ;
insequitur clamorque virum stridorque rudentum.
eripiunt subito nubes caelumque diemque
Teucrorum ex oculis ; ponto nox incubat atra.
intonuere poli, et crebris micat ignibus aether,   90
praesentemque viris intentant omnia mortem.
extemplo Aeneae solvuntur frigore membra ;
ingemit et duplicis tendens ad sidera palmas
talia voce refert : " O terque quaterque beati,
quis ante ora patrum Troiae sub moenibus altis   95
contigit oppetere !   O Danaum fortissime gentis

⁷⁰ et] aut *M*¹.   ⁸⁹ Teucrorumque *M*¹.

vanquished gods. Hurl fury into thy winds, sink and o'erwhelm the ships, or drive the men asunder and scatter their bodies o'er the deep. Twice seven nymphs have I of wondrous beauty, of whom Deiopea, fairest of form, I will link to thee in sure wedlock, making her thine for ever, that for such service of thine she may spend all her years with thee, and make thee father of fair offspring."

[76] Thus answered Aeolus: " Thy task, O queen, is to search out thy desire ; my duty is to do thy bidding. Of thy grace is all this my realm, of thy grace my sceptre and Jove's favour ; thou grantest me a couch at the feasts of the gods, and makest me lord of clouds and storms."

[81] So he spoke and, turning his spear, smote the hollow mount on its side ; when lo ! the winds, as if in armed array, rush forth where passage is given, and blow in storm-blasts across the world. They swoop down upon the sea, and from its lowest depths upheave it all—East and South winds together, and the South-wester, thick with tempests—and shoreward roll vast billows. Then come the cries of men and creaking of cables. In a moment clouds snatch sky and day from the Trojans' eyes ; black night broods over the deep. From pole to pole it thunders, the skies lighten with frequent flashes, all forebodes the sailors instant death. Straightway Aeneas' limbs weaken with chilling dread ; he groans and, stretching his two upturned hands to heaven, thus cries aloud : " O thrice and four times blest, whose lot it was to meet death before their fathers' eyes beneath the lofty walls of Troy ! O son of Tydeus,[1] bravest of the Danaan race, ah ! that I could not fall

---

[1] *i.e.* Diomedes, who had fought with Aeneas in single combat before Troy. *cf.* Homer, *Iliad*, v. 239 ff.

VIRGIL

Tydide! mene Iliacis occumbere campis
non potuisse tuaque animam hanc effundere dextra,
saevus ubi Aeacidae telo iacet Hector, ubi ingens
Sarpedon, ubi tot Simois correpta sub undis   100
scuta virum galeasque et fortia corpora volvit!''

   Talia iactanti stridens Aquilone procella
velum adversa ferit, fluctusque ad sidera tollit;
franguntur remi; tum prora avertit et undis
dat latus; insequitur cumulo praeruptus aquae mons.
hi summo in fluctu pendent; his unda dehiscens 106
terram inter fluctus aperit; furit aestus harenis.
tris Notus abreptas in saxa latentia torquet
(saxa vocant Itali, mediis quae in fluctibus, Aras,
dorsum immane mari summo), tris Eurus ab alto 110
in brevia et syrtis urget (miserabile visu)
inliditque vadis atque aggere cingit harenae.
unam, quae Lycios fidumque vehebat Oronten,
ipsius ante oculos ingens a vertice pontus
in puppim ferit; excutitur pronusque magister   115
volvitur in caput; ast illam ter fluctus ibidem
torquet agens circum et rapidus vorat aequore vertex.
apparent rari nantes in gurgite vasto,
arma virum tabulaeque et Troia gaza per undas.
iam validam Ilionei navem, iam fortis Achatae,   120
et qua vectus Abas, et qua grandaevus Aletes,
vicit hiems; laxis laterum compagibus omnes
accipiunt inimicum imbrem rimisque fatiscunt.

---

100 sub undas *also known to Servius.*
103 fluctum $M^1\gamma$.   **104** proram *M Rγ, Servius.*
109 mediisque *Mγ.*

on the Ilian plains and gasp out this life-blood at thy
hand! where, under the spear of Aeacides, fierce
Hector lies prostrate, where mighty Sarpedon;
where Simois seizes and sweeps beneath his waves
so many shields and helms and bodies of the
brave!"

[102] As he flings forth such words, a gust, shrieking
from the North, strikes full on his sail and lifts the
waves to heaven. The oars snap, then the prow
swings round and gives the broadside to the waves;
down in a heap comes a sheer mountain of water.
Some of the seamen hang upon the billow's crest;
to others the yawning sea shows ground beneath the
waves; the surges secthe with sand. Three ships
the South-wind catches and hurls on hidden rocks—
rocks the Italians call the Altars, rising amidst the
waves, a huge ridge topping the sea. Three the
East forces from the deep into shallows and sand-
banks,[1] a piteous sight, dashes on shoals and girds
with a mound of sand. One, which bore the Lycians
and loyal Orontes, before the eyes of Aeneas a mighty
toppling wave strikes astern. The helmsman is dashed
out and hurled head foremost, but the ship is thrice on
the same spot whirled round and round by the wave
and engulfed in the sea's devouring eddy. Here and
there are seen swimmers in the vast abyss, with
weapons of men, planks, and Trojan treasure amid
the waves. Now the stout ship of Ilioneus, now of
brave Achates, and that wherein Abas sailed and
that of aged Aletes, the storm has mastered; with
side-joints loosened, all let in the hostile flood and
gape at every seam.

[1] In *syrtis* there may be a reference to the famous Syrtes
(Gulfs of Cabes and Sidra), but these are considerably to the
east of Carthage.

Interea magno misceri murmure pontum
emissamque hiemem sensit Neptunus et imis   125
stagna refusa vadis, graviter commotus; et alto
prospiciens, summa placidum caput extulit unda.
disiectam Aeneae toto videt aequore classem,
fluctibus oppressos Troas caelique ruina.
nec latuere doli fratrem Iunonis et irae.   130
Eurum ad se Zephyrumque vocat, dehinc talia fatur:
    "Tantane vos generis tenuit fiducia vestri?
iam caelum terramque meo sine numine, venti,
miscere et tantas audetis tollere moles?
quos ego—! sed motos praestat componere fluctus:
post mihi non simili poena commissa luetis.   136
maturate fugam regique haec dicite vestro:
non illi imperium pelagi saevumque tridentem,
sed mihi sorte datum.   tenet ille immania saxa,
vestras, Eure, domos; illa se iactet in aula   140
Aeolus et clauso ventorum carcere regnet."
    Sic ait, et dicto citius tumida aequora placat
collectasque fugat nubes solemque reducit.
Cymothoe simul et Triton adnixus acuto
detrudunt navis scopulo; levat ipse tridenti   145
et vastas aperit syrtis et temperat aequor
atque rotis summas levibus perlabitur undas.
ac veluti magno in populo cum saepe coorta est
seditio, saevitque animis ignobile volgus,   149
iamque faces et saxa volant (furor arma ministrat),
tum pietate gravem ac meritis si forte virum quem
conspexere, silent arrectisque auribus adstant;

[129] ruinam $R^1\gamma^1$.

AENEID BOOK I

[124] Meanwhile Neptune saw the sea in a turmoil of wild uproar, the storm let loose and the still waters upheaved from their lowest depths. Greatly troubled was he, and gazing out over the deep he raised his serene[1] face above the water's surface. He sees Aeneas' fleet scattered over all the main, the Trojans o'erwhelmed by the waves and by the falling heavens, nor did Juno's wiles and wrath escape her brother. East-wind and West he calls before him, then speaks thus:

[132] " Hath pride in your birth such sway over you? Do ye now dare, O winds, without command of mine, to mingle earth and sky, and raise confusion thus? Whom I——! But better is it to calm the troubled waves: hereafter with no like penalty shall ye atone me your trespasses. Speed your flight and bear this word to your king: Not to him, but to me were given by lot the lordship of the sea and the dread trident. He holds the savage rocks, home of thee and thine, East-wind; in that hall let Aeolus lord it and rule within the barred prison of the winds."

[142] Thus he speaks, and swifter than his word he calms the swollen seas, puts to flight the gathered clouds, and brings back the sun. Cymothoë and Triton with common effort thrust the ships from the sharp rock; the god himself upheaves them with his trident, opens the vast quicksands, allays the flood, and on light wheels glides over the topmost waters. And as, when oft-times in a great nation tumult has risen, the base rabble rage angrily, and now brands and stones fly, madness lending arms; then, if haply they set eyes on a man honoured for noble character and service, they are silent and stand by with

---

[1] However angry, the god is outwardly serene.

ille regit dictis animos et pectora mulcet:
sic cunctus pelagi cecidit fragor, aequora postquam
prospiciens genitor caeloque invectus aperto   155
flectit equos curruque volans dat lora secundo.

　Defessi Aeneadae, quae proxima litora, cursu
contendunt petere, et Libyae vertuntur ad oras.
est in secessu longo locus: insula portum
efficit obiectu laterum, quibus omnis ab alto   160
frangitur inque sinus scindit sese unda reductos.
hinc atque hinc vastae rupes geminique minantur
in caelum scopuli, quorum sub vertice late
aequora tuta silent; tum silvis scaena coruscis
desuper, horrentique atrum nemus imminet umbra;
fronte sub adversa scopulis pendentibus antrum,   166
intus aquae dulces vivoque sedilia saxo,
Nympharum domus. hic fessas non vincula navis
ulla tenent, unco non alligat ancora morsu.
huc septem Aeneas collectis navibus omni   170
ex numero subit, ac magno telluris amore
egressi optata potiuntur Troes harena
et sale tabentis artus in litore ponunt.
ac primum silici scintillam excudit Achates
succepitque ignem foliis atque arida circum   175
nutrimenta dedit rapuitque in fomite flammam.
tum Cererem corruptam undis Cerealiaque arma
expediunt fessi rerum, frugesque receptas
et torrere parant flammis et frangere saxo.

---

　[1] The term *Aeneadae* is here used, in an extended sense, of the followers of Aeneas.
　[2] cf. *Georgics*, IV. 420, with note.
　[3] Virgil here describes the primitive process of making fire. First a spark is struck from flint. Secondly, the tinder is

attentive ears; he with speech sways their passion
and soothes their breasts : even so, all the roar of
ocean sank, soon as the Sire, looking forth upon the
waters and driving under a clear sky, guides his
steeds and, flying onward, gives reins to his willing
car.

¹⁵⁷ The wearied sons of Aeneas[1] strive to run for the
nearest shore and turn towards the coast of Libya.
There in a deep inlet lies a spot, where an island forms
a harbour with the barrier of its sides, on which every
wave from the main is broken, then parts into reced-
ing ripples.[2]   On either side loom heavenward huge
cliffs and twin peaks, beneath whose crest far and
wide is the stillness of sheltered water ; above, too,
is a background of shimmering woods with an over-
hanging grove, black with gloomy shade.   Under the
brow of the fronting cliff is a cave of hanging rocks ;
within are fresh waters and seats in the living stone,
a haunt of Nymphs.   Here no fetters imprison weary
ships, no anchor holds them fast with hooked bite.
Here, with seven ships mustered from all his fleet,
Aeneas takes shelter ; and, disembarking with earnest
longing for the land, the Trojans gain the welcome
beach and stretch their brine-drenched limbs upon
the shore.   At once Achates struck a spark from
flint, caught the fire in leaves, laid dry fuel about, and
waved the flame amid the tinder.[3]   Then, wearied
with their lot, they take out the corn of Ceres, spoiled
by the waves, with the tools of Ceres, and prepare
to parch the rescued grain in the fire and crush it
under the stone.

ignited (*succepit ignem foliis*).   Thirdly, the ignited fuel is
waved violently in the air until the smouldering fire bursts
into a flame.   Such is the practice of the North American
Indians.   The common rendering for *rapuit flammam*, " caught
the flame," leads to tautology.

VIRGIL

Aeneas scopu um interea conscendit et omnem 180
prospectum late pelago petit, Anthea si quem
iactatum vento videat Phrygiasque biremis,
aut Capyn, aut celsis in puppibus arma Caici.
navem in conspectu nullam, tris litore cervos
prospicit errantis; hos tota armenta sequuntur   FMR
a tergo et longum per vallis pascitur agmen.   186
constitit hic arcumque manu celerisque sagittas
corripuit, fidus quae tela gerebat Achates,
ductoresque ipsos primum, capita alta ferentis
cornibus arboreis, sternit, tum volgus et omnem 190
miscet agens telis nemora inter frondea turbam ;
nec prius absistit, quam septem ingentia victor
corpora fundat humi et numerum cum navibus
    aequet.
hinc portum petit et socios partitur in omnis.
vina bonus quae deinde cadis onerarat Acestes   195
litore Trinacrio dederatque abeuntibus heros
dividit, et dictis maerentia pectora mulcet :
    "O socii (neque enim ignari sumus ante
        malorum),
o passi graviora, dabit deus his quoque finem.
vos et Scyllaeam rabiem penitusque sonantis   200
accestis scopulos, vos et Cyclopia saxa
experti ; revocate animos maestumque timorem
mittite ; forsan et haec olim meminisse iuvabit.
per varios casus, per tot discrimina rerum
tendimus in Latium, sedes ubi fata quietas   205
ostendunt ; illic fas regna resurgere Troiae.
durate, et vosmet rebus servate secundis."
    Talia voce refert, curisque ingentibus aeger
spem voltu simulat, premit altum corde dolorem.

    [193] humo *FMR*γ, *Nonius :* humi c², *Servius*
    [200] vultus *F*¹.

AENEID BOOK I

¹⁸⁰ Meanwhile Aeneas climbs a peak and seeks a full view far and wide over the deep, if he may but see aught of storm-tossed Antheus and his Phrygian galleys, or of Capys or the arms of Caicus on the high stern. Ship in sight there is none; three stags he descries straying on the shore; whole herds follow these behind and in long line graze adown the valley. Thereon he stopped and seized in his hand his bow and swift arrows, the arms borne by loyal Achates; and first he lays low the leaders themselves, their heads held high with branching antlers, then routs the herd and all the common sort, driving them with his darts amid the leafy woods. Nor does he stay his hand till seven huge forms he stretches victoriously on the ground, equal in number to his ships. Then he seeks the harbour and divides them among all his company. Next he shares the wine, which good Acestes had stowed in jars on the Trinacrian shore, and hero-like had given at parting; and, speaking thus, calms their sorrowing hearts:

¹⁹⁸ "O comrades—for ere this we have not been ignorant of evils—O ye who have borne a heavier lot, to this, too, God will grant an end! Ye drew near to Scylla's fury and her deep-echoing crags; ye have known, too, the rocks of the Cyclopes; recall your courage and put away sad fear. Perchance even this distress it will some day be a joy to recall. Through divers mishaps, through so many perilous chances, we fare towards Latium, where the fates point out a home of rest. There 'tis granted to Troy's realm to rise again; endure, and keep yourselves for days of happiness."

²⁰⁸ So spake his tongue; while sick with weighty cares he feigns hope on his face, and deep in his heart stifles the anguish. The others make ready for

255

VIRGIL

illi se praedae accingunt dapibusque futuris; 210
tergora diripiunt costis et viscera nudant;
pars in frusta secant veribusque trementia figunt,
litore aëna locant alii flammasque ministrant.
tum victu rovocant viris, fusique per herbam
implentur veteris Bacchi pinguisque ferinae. 215
postquam exempta fames epulis mensaeque remotae,
amissos longo socios sermone requirunt,
spemque metumque inter dubii, seu vivere credant
sive extrema pati nec iam exaudire vocatos.
praecipue pius Aeneas nunc acris Oronti, 220
nunc Amyci casum gemit et crudelia secum
fata Lyci fortemque Gyan fortemque Cloanthum.
    Et iam finis erat, cum Iuppiter aethere summo
despiciens mare velivolum terrasque iacentis
litoraque et latos populos, sic vertice caeli 225
constitit et Libyae defixit lumina regnis.
atque illum talis iactantem pectore curas
tristior et lacrimis oculos suffusa nitentis
adloquitur Venus: "o qui res hominumque deumque
aeternis regis imperiis et fulmine terres, 230
quid meus Aeneas in te committere tantum,
quid Troes potuere, quibus tot funera passis
cunctus ob Italiam terrarum clauditur orbis?
certe hinc Romanos olim volventibus annis,
hinc fore ductores, revocato a sanguine Teucri, FMRV
qui mare, qui terras omnis dicione tenerent, 236
pollicitus. quae te, genitor, sententia vertit?
hoc equidem occasum Troiae tristisque ruinas
solabar, fatis contraria fata rependens;
nunc eadem fortuna viros tot casibus actos 240

      224 venivolum *F.*
      236 omni *MR*γ, *Servius.*

the spoil, the feast that is to be; they flay the hides
from the ribs and lay bare the flesh; some cut it into
pieces and impale it, still quivering, on spits; others set
cauldrons on the shore and feed them with fire. Then
with food they revive their strength, and stretched
along the grass take their fill of old wine and fat
venison. When hunger was banished by the feast and
the board was cleared, in long discourse they yearn
for their lost comrades, between hope and fear un-
certain whether to deem them still alive, or bearing
the final doom and hearing no more when called.
Chiefly does good Aeneas in silence mourn the loss
now of valiant Orontes, now of Amycus, the cruel
doom of Lycus, brave Gyas, and brave Cloanthus.

223 Now all was ended, when from the sky's summit
Jupiter looked forth upon the sail-winged sea and
outspread lands, the shores and peoples far and wide,
and, looking, paused on heaven's height and cast his
eyes on Libya's realm. And lo! as on such cares he
pondered in heart, Venus, saddened and her bright
eyes brimming with tears, spake to him:

229 "O thou that with eternal sway rulest the world
of men and gods, and dismayest with thy bolt, what
crime so great in thy eyes can my Aeneas have
wrought? what the Trojans? to whom, after many
disasters borne, the whole world is barred for Italy's
sake. Surely it was thy promise that from them some
time, as the years rolled on, the Romans were to arise;
from them, even from Teucer's restored line, should
come rulers, to hold the sea and all land beneath
their sway. What thought, father, has turned thee?
That promise, indeed, was my comfort for Troy's fall
and sad overthrow, when I weighed fate against the
fates opposed. Now, though tried by so many disasters,
the same fortune dogs them. What end of their toils,

insequitur.   quem das finem, rex magne, laborum?
Antenor potuit, mediis elapsus Achivis,
Illyricos penetrare sinus atque intima tutus
regna Liburnorum et fontem superare Timavi,
unde per ora novem vasto cum murmure montis 245
it mare proruptum et pelago premit arva sonanti.
hic tamen ille urbem Patavi sedesque locavit
Teucrorum et genti nomen dedit armaque fixit
Troia; nunc placida compostus pace quiescit:
nos, tua progenies, caeli quibus adnuis arcem,   250
navibus (infandum!) amissis unius ob iram
prodimur atque Italis longe disiungimur oris.
hic pietatis honos? sic nos in sceptra reponis?"
    Olli subridens hominum sator atque deorum
voltu, quo caelum tempestatesque serenat,   255
oscula libavit natae, dehinc talia fatur:
"parce metu, Cytherea; manent immota tuorum
fata tibi; cernes urbem et promissa Lavini
moenia, sublimemque feres ad sidera caeli   259
magnanimum Aenean; neque me sententia vertit.
hic tibi (fabor enim, quando haec te cura remor-
        det,   FMR
longius et volvens fatorum arcana movebo)
bellum ingens geret Italia populosque feroces
contundet moresque viris et moenia ponet,
tertia dum Latio regnantem viderit aestas;   265
ternaque transierint Rutulis hiberna subactis.
at puer Ascanius, cui nunc cognomen Iulo
additur (Ilus erat, dum res stetit Ilia regno),

²⁴⁶ praeruptum *F²M²V²γ¹, known to Servius.*

----

[1] The Timavus, which rises in the Julian Alps, after flowing
for eighteen miles underground, reappears in several springs
and then pursues a short but swift course to the Adriatic.
[2] The main subject of the second half of the *Aeneid.*

AENEID BOOK I

great king, dost thou grant? Antenor could escape
the Achaean host, thread safely the Illyrian gulfs and
inmost realms of the Liburnians, and pass the springs
of Timavus, whence through nine mouths, with a
mountain's mighty roar, it comes a bursting flood and
buries the fields under its sounding sea.[1] Yet here he
set Padua's town, a home for his Teucrians, gave a
name to the race, and hung up the arms of Troy;
now, settled in tranquil peace, he is at rest. But
we, thy offspring, to whom thou dost grant the
heights of heaven, have lost our ships—O shame
unutterable!—and, to appease one angry foe, are
betrayed and kept far from Italian shores. Is this
virtue's guerdon? Is it thus thou restorest us to
empire?"

[254] On her smiling, with that look wherewith he
clears sky and storms, the Father of men and gods
gently kissed his daughter's lips, and then spake
thus:

[257] "Spare thy fear, Lady of Cythera; thy children's
fates abide unmoved. Thou shalt see Lavinium's city
and its promised walls; and thou shalt raise on high
to the starry heaven great-souled Aeneas. No thought
has turned me. This thy son—for, since this care
gnaws at thy heart, I will speak and, further unroll-
ing the scroll of fate, will disclose its secrets—shall
wage a great war in Italy,[2] shall crush proud nations,
and for his people shall set up laws and city walls;
till the third summer has seen him reigning in Latium
and three winters have passed in camp since the
Rutulians were laid low.[3] But the lad Ascanius,
now surnamed Iulus—Ilus he was, while the Ilian
state stood firm in sovereignty—shall fulfil in empire

[3] *i.e.* after conquering the Rutulians Aeneas will spend
three winters in camp before founding Lavinium.

VIRGIL

triginta magnos volvendis mensibus orbis   MR
imperio explebit, regnumque ab sede Lavini   270
transferet, et longam multa vi muniet Albam.
hic iam ter centum totos regnabitur annos
gente sub Hectorea, donec regina sacerdos
Marte gravis geminam partu dabit Ilia prolem.
inde lupae fulvo nutricis tegmine laetus   275
Romulus excipiet gentem et Mavortia condet
moenia Romanosque suo de nomine dicet.   MPR
his ego nec metas rerum nec tempora pono ;
imperium sine fine dedi.   quin aspera Iuno,
quae mare nunc terrasque metu caelumque fatigat,
consilia in melius referet, mecumque fovebit   281
Romanos, rerum dominos, gentemque togatam.
sic placitum.   veniet lustris labentibus aetas,
cum domus Assaraci Phthiam clarasque Mycenas
servitio premet ac victis dominabitur Argis.   285
nascetur pulchra Troianus origine Caesar,
imperium Oceano, famam qui terminet astris,
Iulius, a magno demissum nomen Iulo.
hunc tu olim caelo, spoliis Orientis onustum,
accipies secura ; vocabitur hic quoque votis.   290
aspera tum positis mitescent saecula bellis ;
cana Fides et Vesta, Remo cum fratre Quirinus
iura dabunt ; dirae ferro et compagibus artis
claudentur Belli portae ; Furor impius intus
saeva sedens super arma et centum vinctus aënis   295
post tergum nodis fremet horridus ore cruento.''

[272] hinc *also known to Servius.*
[289] honestum *known to Servius.*

---

[1] Mars was the father of Romulus and Remus.
[2] *i.e.* the Trojan race, in their Roman descendants.
[3] Greece became a Roman province in 146 B.C.
[4] This is Augustus Caesar, as shown by ll. 289 and 294.

thirty great circles of rolling months, shall shift his throne from Lavinium's seat, and, great in power, shall build the walls of Alba Longa. Here then for thrice a hundred years unbroken shall the kingdom endure under Hector's race, until Ilia, a royal priestess, shall bear to Mars her twin offspring. Then Romulus, proud in the tawny hide of the she-wolf, his nurse, shall take up the line, and found the walls of Mars [1] and call the people Romans after his own name. For these I set neither bounds nor periods of empire; dominion without end have I bestowed. Nay, harsh Juno, who now in her fear troubles sea and earth and sky, shall change to better counsels and with me cherish the Romans, lords of the world, and the nation of the gown. Thus is it decreed. There shall come a day, as the sacred seasons glide past, when the house of Assaracus [2] shall bring into bondage Phthia and famed Mycenae, and hold lordship over vanquished Argos. [3] From this noble line shall be born the Trojan Caesar, who shall limit his empire with ocean, his glory with the stars, a Julius, [4] name descended from great Iulus! Him, in days to come, shalt thou, anxious no more, welcome to heaven, laden with Eastern spoils; he, too, shall be invoked in vows. Then shall wars cease and the rough ages soften; hoary Faith and Vesta, Quirinus with his brother Remus, [5] shall give laws. The gates of war, grim with iron and close-fitting bars, shall be closed; [6] within, impious Rage, sitting on savage arms, his hands fast bound behind with a hundred brazen knots, shall roar in the ghastliness of blood-stained lips."

[5] *i.e.* Romulus (Quirinus) will be at peace with Remus. Civil wars will cease.

[6] The reference is to the temple of Janus, which Augustus closed in 29 B.C., after it had remained open more than two centuries.

VIRGIL

Haec ait et Maia genitum demittit ab alto,
ut terrae utque novae pateant Karthaginis arces
hospitio Teucris, ne fati nescia Dido
finibus arceret.   volat ille per aëra magnum   300
remigio alarum ac Libyae citus adstitit oris.
et iam iussa facit, ponuntque ferocia Poeni
corda volente deo ; in primis regina quietum
accipit in Teucros animum mentemque benignam.

   At pius Aeneas, per noctem plurima volvens,   305
ut primum lux alma data est, exire locosque
explorare novos, quas vento accesserit oras,
qui teneant (nam inculta videt), hominesne feraene,
quaerere constituit sociisque exacta referre.
classem in convexo nemorum sub rupe cavata   310
arboribus clausam circum atque horrentibus umbris
occulit ; ipse uno graditur comitatus Achate,
bina manu lato crispans hastilia ferro.
cui mater media sese tulit obvia silva,
virginis os habitumque gerens et virginis arma,   315
Spartanae, vel qualis equos Threissa fatigat
Harpalyce volucremque fuga praevertitur Hebrum.
namque umeris de more habilem suspenderat arcum
venatrix dederatque comam diffundere ventis,
nuda genu nodoque sinus collecta fluentis.   320
ac prior " heus," inquit, " iuvenes, monstrate, mearum
vidistis si quam hic errantem forte sororum,
succinctam pharetra et maculosae tegmine lyncis,
aut spumantis apri cursum clamore prementem."

   Sic Venus, et Veneris contra sic filius orsus :   325

[297] dimittit *Pγ*.   [298] terra *P*[1].   [299] fatis *R*[1].
[317] Eurum *Rutgers.*
[323] faretram *R*[2], *known to Priscian.* tegmina *γ*[1]. lyncis
sometimes taken with cursum, *according to Priscian.*

[297] So speaking, he sends the son of Maia down from heaven, that the land and towers of new-built Carthage may open to greet the Teucrians, and Dido, ignorant of fate, might not bar them from her lands. Through the wide air he flies on the oarage of wings, and speedily alights on the Libyan coasts. At once he does his bidding, and, God willing it, the Phoenicians lay aside their savage thoughts; above all, the queen receives a gentle mind and gracious purpose towards the Teucrians.

[305] But good Aeneas, through the night revolving many a care, so soon as kindly light was given, determines to issue forth and explore the strange country; to learn to what coasts he has come with the wind, who dwells there, man or beast—for all he sees is waste—then bring back the tidings to his friends. The fleet he hides in over-arching groves beneath a hollow rock, closely encircled by trees and quivering shade; then, Achates alone attending, himself strides forth, grasping in hand two shafts, tipped with broad steel. Across his path, amid the forest, came his mother, with a maiden's face and mien, and a maiden's arms, whether one of Sparta or such a one as Thracian Harpalyce, when she out-tires horses and outstrips winged Hebrus in flight. For from her shoulders in huntress fashion she had slung the ready bow and had given her hair to the winds to scatter; her knee bare, and her flowing robes gathered in a knot. Before he speaks, "Ho!" she cries, "tell me, youths, if haply ye have seen a sister of mine here straying, girt with quiver and a dappled lynx's hide, or pressing with shouts on the track of a foaming boar."

[325] Thus Venus; and thus in answer Venus' son began:

"nulla tuarum audita mihi neque visa sororum,
o——quam te memorem, virgo? namque haud tibi voltus
mortalis, nec vox hominem sonat ; o dea certe !
an Phoebi soror ?   an Nympharum sanguinis una ?
sis felix nostrumque leves, quaecumque, laborem,   330
et quo sub caelo tandem, quibus orbis in oris
iactemur, doceas ; ignari hominumque locorumque
erramus, vento huc vastis et fluctibus acti ;
multa tibi ante aras nostra cadet hostia dextra."

   Tum Venus : " haud equidem tali me dignor
        honore ;   335
virginibus Tyriis mos est gestare pharetram
purpureoque alte suras vincire cothurno.
Punica regna vides, Tyrios et Agenoris urbem ;
sed fines Libyci, genus intractabile bello.
imperium Dido Tyria regit urbe profecta,   340
germanum fugiens.   longa est iniuria, longae
ambages ; sed summa sequar fastigia rerum.
huic coniunx Sychaeus erat, ditissimus agri
Phoenicum et magno miserae dilectus amore,
cui pater intactam dederat primisque iugarat   345
ominibus.   sed regna Tyri germanus habebat
Pygmalion, scelere ante alios immanior omnis.
quos inter medius venit furor.   ille Sychaeum
impius ante aras atque auri caecus amore
clam ferro incautum superat, securus amorum   350
germanae ; factumque diu celavit et aegram
multa malus simulans vana spe lusit amantem.
ipsa sed in somnis inhumati venit imago
coniugis ; ora modis attollens pallida miris

   ³³³ et vastis *M¹R*.   ³⁴³ auri *Huet*.   ³⁴⁸ medios *M, Servius*.

³²⁶ " None of thy sisters have I heard or seen—but by what name should I call thee, O maiden? for thy face is not mortal nor has thy voice a human ring; O goddess surely! sister of Phoebus, or one of the race of Nymphs? Be thou gracious, whoe'er thou art, and lighten this our burden. Inform us, pray, beneath what sky, on what coasts of the world, we are cast; knowing naught of country or of people, we wander hither driven by wind and huge billows. Many a victim shall fall for thee at our hand before thine altars."

³³⁵ Then said Venus: " Nay, I claim not such worship. Tyrian maids are wont to wear the quiver, and bind their ankles high with the purple buskin. 'Tis the Punic realm thou seest, a Tyrian people, and the city of Agenor; but the bordering country is Libyan, a race unconquerable in war. Dido wields the sceptre —Dido, who, fleeing from her brother, came from the city of Tyre. Long would be the tale of wrong, long its winding course—but the main heads of the story I will trace. Her husband was Sychaeus, richest of the Phoenicians in land, and fondly loved by unhappy Dido; to him her father had given the maiden, yoking her to him in the first bridal auspices. But the kingdom of Tyre was in the hands of her brother Pygmalion, monstrous in crime beyond all others. Between these two came frenzy. The king, impiously before the altars and blinded by lust of gold, strikes down Sychaeus by stealthy blow unawares, careless of his sister's love; and for long he hid the deed, and by many a pretence cunningly cheated the lovesick bride with empty hope. But in her sleep came the very ghost of her unburied husband; raising his face pale in wondrous wise, he laid bare the cruel altars and his breast pierced with

crudelis aras traiectaque pectora ferro   355
nudavit, caecumque domus scelus omne retexit.
tum celerare fugam patriaque excedere suadet
auxiliumque viae veteris tellure recludit
thesauros, ignotum argenti pondus et auri.
his commota fugam Dido sociosque parabat.   360
conveniunt, quibus aut odium crudele tyranni
aut metus acer erat; navis, quae forte paratae,
corripiunt onerantque auro; portantur avari
Pygmalionis opes pelago; dux femina facti.
devenere locos, ubi nunc ingentia cernis   365
moenia surgentemque novae Karthaginis arcem,
mercatique solum, facti de nomine Byrsam,
taurino quantum possent circumdare tergo.
sed vos qui tandem? quibus aut venistis ab oris?
quove tenetis iter?" quaerenti talibus ille   370
suspirans imoque trahens a pectore vocem:

   "O dea, si prima repetens ab origine pergam,
et vacet annalis nostrorum audire laborum,
ante diem clauso componet Vesper Olympo.
nos Troia antiqua, si vestras forte per auris   375
Troiae nomen iit, diversa per aequora vectos
forte sua Libycis tempestas appulit oris.
sum pius Aeneas, raptos qui ex hoste Penatis
classe veho mecum, fama super aethera notus.
Italiam quaero patriam et genus ab Iove summo. 380
bis denis Phrygium conscendi navibus aequor, GMPR

355 cernes *PRγ*: cernis *M*.
369 aut venistis *M²Pγ*: audvenistis *M¹*: advenistis *R*.
374 componat *P¹R*.   380 magno *R*. *So Sabb.*

266

steel, unveiling all the secret horror of the house.
Then he bids her speed flight and leave her country,
and to aid her journey brought to light from earth
old-time treasures, a mass of silver and gold known to
none. Moved hereby, Dido made ready her flight
and her company. Then assemble all who felt
towards the tyrant relentless hatred or keen fear;
ships, which by chance were ready, they seize, and
load with gold; the wealth of grasping Pygmalion
is borne overseas, the leader of the work a woman.
They came to the place where now thou seest the
huge walls and rising citadel of new Carthage, and
bought ground—Byrsa they called it therefrom—as
much as they could encompass with a bull's hide.[1]
But who, pray, are ye, or from what coasts come,
or whither hold ye your course?"

[370] As she questioned thus he, sighing and drawing
speech deep from his breast, replied:

"O goddess, should I, tracing back from the first
beginning, go on to tell, and thou have leisure to hear
the story of our woes, sooner would heaven close and
evening lay the day to rest. From ancient Troy, if
haply the name of Troy has passed through your
ears, sailing over distant seas, the storm at its own
caprice drove us to the Libyan coast. I am Aeneas
the good, who carry with me in my fleet my house-
hold gods, snatched from the foe; my fame is known
in the heavens above. Italy I seek, my country, and
a race sprung from Jove most high. With twice ten
ships I climbed the Phrygian sea, following the fates

[1] The legend ran that the Phoenician settlers bargained
with the Libyans for as much ground as could be covered by a
bull's hide. This was cut into very fine strips, which enclosed
a large tract of land. This myth probably arose from the fact
that the Phoenician *bosra*, "citadel," was confused with the
Greek βύρσα, "bull's-hide."

matre dea monstrante viam, data fata secutus;
vix septem convolsae undis Euroque supersunt.
ipse ignotus, egens, Libyae deserta peragro,
Europa atque Asia pulsus." nec plura querentem
passa Venus medio sic interfata dolore est :   386
 " Quisquis es, haud, credo, invisus caelestibus
  auras
vitalis carpis, Tyriam qui adveneris urbem.
perge modo atque hinc te reginae ad limina
 perfer.
namque tibi reduces socios classemque relatam   390
nuntio et in tutum versis Aquilonibus actam,
ni frustra augurium vani docuere parentes.
aspice bis senos laetantis agmine cycnos,
aetheria quos lapsa plaga Iovis ales aperto
turbabat caelo; nunc terras ordine longo   395
aut capere aut captas iam despectare videntur.
ut reduces illi ludunt stridentibus alis
et coetu cinxere polum cantusque dedere,
haud aliter puppesque tuae pubesque tuorum
aut portum tenet aut pleno subit ostia velo.   400
perge modo et, qua te ducit via, derige gressum."
 Dixit et avertens rosea cervice refulsit,
ambrosiaeque comae divinum vertice odorem
spiravere; pedes vestis defluxit ad imos,
et vera incessu patuit dea. ille ubi matrem   405
adgnovit, tali fugientem est voce secutus :
"quid natum totiens, crudelis tu quoque, falsis
ludis imaginibus? cur dextrae iungere dextram
non datur ac veras audire et reddere voces ?"
talibus incusat gressumque ad moenia tendit.   410
at Venus obscuro gradientis aëre saepsit

   396 aut captas *GMRγ²*: aut captus *P¹*: aut captos *P-γ¹.*
respectare *Pγ¹.*

declared, my goddess-mother pointing me the way;
scarcely do seven remain, shattered by waves and wind.
Myself unknown and destitute, I wander over the
Libyan wastes, driven from Europe and from Asia."

³⁸⁵ His further complaint Venus suffered not, but
in the midst of his lament broke in thus: "Whoever
thou art, not hateful, methinks, to the heavenly beings
dost thou draw the breath of life, seeing thou hast
reached the Tyrian city. Only go forward and be-
take thee hence to the queen's palace. For I bring
thee tidings of thy comrades restored and of thy
fleet recovered, driven to safe haven by shifting
winds—unless my parents falsely taught me augury
in vain. Lo! yonder twelve swans in exultant line,
which the bird of Jove, swooping from the skyey
expanse, was scattering in the open air; now in long
array they seem either to be settling in their places
or already to be gazing down on the places where
others have settled. As they, returning, sport with
rustling wings, and in company have circled the sky
and uttered their songs, with like joy thy ships and
the men of thy company hold the haven or under full
sail draw near to its mouth. Only go forward and,
where the path leads thee, turn thy steps!"

⁴⁰² She spake, and as she turned away, her roseate
neck flashed bright. From her head her ambrosial
tresses breathed celestial fragrance; down to her feet
fell her raiment, and in her step she was revealed, a
very goddess. He knew her as his mother, and as
she fled pursued her with these words: "Thou also
cruel! Why mockest thou thy son so often with
vain phantoms? Why am I not allowed to clasp
hand in hand and hear and utter words unfeigned?"
Thus he reproaches her and bends his steps towards
the city. But Venus shrouded them, as they went,

VIRGIL

et multo nebulae circum dea fudit amictu,
cernere ne quis eos neu quis contingere posset
molirive moram aut veniendi poscere causas.
ipsa Paphum sublimis abit sedesque revisit   **415**
laeta suas, ubi templum illi centumque Sabaeo
ture calent arae sertisque recentibus halant.

Corripuere viam interea, qua semita monstrat.
iamque ascendebant collem, qui plurimus urbi FMPR
imminet adversasque aspectat desuper arces.   420
miratur molem Aeneas, magalia quondam,
miratur portas strepitumque et strata viarum.
instant ardentes Tyrii, pars ducere muros
molirique arcem et manibus subvolvere saxa,
pars optare locum tecto et concludere sulco;   425
iura magistratusque legunt sanctumque senatum;
hic portus alii effodiunt, hic alta theatri
fundamenta locant alii, immanisque columnas
rupibus excidunt, scaenis decora alta futuris.
qualis apes aestate nova per florea rura   430
exercet sub sole labor, cum gentis adultos
educunt fetus, aut cum liquentia mella
stipant et dulci distendunt nectare cellas,
aut onera accipiunt venientum, aut augmine facto
ignavum fucos pecus a praesepibus arcent;   435
fervet opus redolentque thymo fragrantia mella.
"o fortunati, quorum iam moenia surgunt!"
Aeneas ait et fastigia suspicit urbis.
infert se saeptus nebula (mirabile dictu)
per medios miscetque viris neque cernitur ulli.   440

Lucus in urbe fuit media, laetissimus umbrae,
quo primum iactati undis et turbine Poeni

412 multum *G*.　　　　413 neu] ne *P¹*.　possit *GRγ*.
420 spectant *F¹*: adspectant *F²*.　　　425 aptare *R¹*.
427 alta] lata *F*. theatri *MP²γ²*, *Servius*: theatris *FP¹Rγ¹*.
428 locant] petunt *F¹*.　　433 dulcis *P¹*.
441 umbrae *F¹*, *Probus*: umbra *F²MPR*; *both known to Servius*.

270

with dusky air, and enveloped them, goddess as she was, in a thick mantle of cloud, that none might see or touch them, none delay or seek the cause of their coming. She herself through the sky goes her way to Paphos, and joyfully revisits her abode, where the temple and its hundred altars steam with Sabaean incense and are fragrant with garlands ever fresh.

[418] Meanwhile they have sped on the road where the pathway points. And now they were climbing the hill that looms large over the city and looks down on the confronting towers. Aeneas marvels at the massive buildings, mere huts once; marvels at the gates, the din and paved high-roads. Eagerly the Tyrians press on, some to build walls, to rear the citadel, and roll up stones by hand; some to choose the site for a dwelling and enclose it with a furrow. Laws and magistrates they ordain, and a holy senate. Here some are digging harbours, here others lay the deep foundations of their theatre and hew out of the cliffs vast columns, lofty adornments for the stage to be! Even as bees in early summer, amid flowery fields, ply their task in sunshine, when they lead forth the full-grown young of their race, or pack the fluid honey and strain their cells to bursting with sweet nectar, or receive the burdens of incomers, or in martial array drive from their folds the drones, a lazy herd; all aglow is the work and the fragrant honey is sweet with thyme. "Happy they whose walls already rise!" cries Aeneas, lifting his eyes towards the city-roofs. Veiled in a cloud, he enters—wondrous to tell—through their midst, and mingles with the people, seen by none!

[441] Amid the city was a grove, luxuriant in shade, the spot where first the Phoenicians, tossed by waves

effodere loco signum, quod regia Iuno
monstrarat, caput acris equi ; sic nam fore bello
egregiam et facilem victu per saecula gentem.   445
hic templum Iunoni ingens Sidonia Dido
condebat, donis opulentum et numine divae,
aerea cui gradibus surgebant limina nexaeque
aere trabes, foribus cardo stridebat aënis.
hoc primum in luco nova res oblata timorem   450
leniit, hic primum Aeneas sperare salutem
ausus et adflictis melius confidere rebus.
namque sub ingenti lustrat dum singula templo,
reginam opperiens, dum, quae fortuna sit urbi,
artificumque manus inter se operumque laborem   455
miratur, videt Iliacas ex ordine pugnas
bellaque iam fama totum volgata per orbem,
Atridas Priamumque et saevum ambobus Achillem.
constitit et lacrimans, "quis iam locus," inquit,
    "Achate,
quae regio in terris nostri non plena laboris ?   460
en Priamus !   sunt hic etiam sua praemia laudi,
sunt lacrimae rerum et mentem mortalia tangunt.
solve metus ; feret haec aliquam tibi fama salutem."
sic ait, atque animum pictura pascit inani
multa gemens, largoque umectat flumine voltum.   465
namque videbat, uti bellantes Pergama circum
hac fugerent Grai, premeret Troiana iuventus,

    [448] nixae b[1], *Probus, known to Servius:* -que *omitted* γ.
272

and whirlwind, dug up the token which queenly
Juno had pointed out, a head of the spirited horse;[1]
for thus was the race to be famous in war and rich
in substance through the ages. Here Sidonian Dido
was founding to Juno a mighty temple, rich in gifts
and the presence of the goddess. Brazen was its
threshold uprising on steps; bronze plates were its
lintel-beams, on doors of bronze creaked the hinges.
First in this grove did a strange sight appear to him
and allay his fears; here first did Aeneas dare to
hope for safety and put surer trust in his shattered
fortunes. For while beneath the mighty temple,
awaiting the queen, he scans each object, while he
marvels at the city's fortune, the handicraft of the
several artists and the work of their toil, he sees in
due order the battles of Ilium, the warfare now
known by fame throughout the world, the sons[2] of
Atreus, and Priam, and Achilles, fierce in his wrath
against both.[3]   He stopped and weeping cried :
"What land, Achates, what tract on earth is now not
full of our sorrow? Lo, Priam! Here, too, virtue
has its due rewards; here, too, there are tears for
misfortune and mortal sorrows touch the heart.[4]
Dismiss thy fears; this fame will bring thee some
salvation."

[464] So he speaks, and feasts his soul on the un-
substantial picture, sighing oft-times, and his face
wet with a flood of tears. For he saw how, as they
fought round Pergamus, here the Greeks were in
rout, the Trojan youth hard on their heels; there

---

[1] A horse's head was the symbol of Carthage and is com-
mon on Carthaginian coins.

[2] *i.e.* Agamemnon and Menelaus.

[3] *i.e.* the Atridae and Priam.

[4] The repetition of *sunt* implies that *hic etiam* should also
be repeated in sense.

hac Phryges, instaret curru cristatus Achilles.
nec procul hinc Rhesi niveis tentoria velis
adgnoscit lacrimans, primo quae prodita somno   470
Tydides multa vastabat caede cruentus,
ardentisque avertit equos in castra, prius quam
pabula gustassent Troiae Xanthumque bibissent.
parte alia fugiens amissis Troilus armis,
infelix puer atque impar congressus Achilli,   475
fertur equis curruque haeret resupinus inani,
lora tenens tamen; huic cervixque comaeque trahuntur
per terram et versa pulvis inscribitur hasta.
interea ad templum non aequae Palladis ibant
crinibus Iliades passis peplumque ferebant,   480
suppliciter tristes et tunsae pectora palmis;
diva solo fixos oculos aversa tenebat.
ter circum Iliacos raptaverat Hectora muros
exanimumque auro corpus vendebat Achilles.
tum vero ingentem gemitum dat pectore ab imo,   485
ut spolia, ut currus, utque ipsum corpus amici
tendentemque manus Priamum conspexit inermis.
se quoque principibus permixtum adgnovit Achivis,
Eoasque acies et nigri Memnonis arma.
ducit Amazonidum lunatis agmina peltis   490
Penthesilea furens mediisque in milibus ardet,
aurea subnectens exsertae cingula mammae,
bellatrix, audetque viris concurrere virgo.
   Haec dum Dardanio Aeneae miranda videntur,
dum stupet obtutuque haeret defixus in uno,   495
regina ad templum, forma pulcherrima Dido,

[469] nec *MRF²*: et *P¹*: haut *P²*: haud *γ*.
[488] adgnovit *MP:* agnovit *γb:* adgnoscit *F:* agnoscit *R*.
274

fled the Phrygians, plumed Achilles in his chariot pressing them close. Not far away he discerns with tears the snowy-canvassed tents of Rhesus, which, betrayed in their first sleep, the blood-stained son of Tydeus[1] laid waste with many a death, and turned the fiery steeds away to the camp, ere they should taste Trojan fodder or drink of Xanthus. Elsewhere Troilus, his arms flung away in flight—unhappy boy, and ill-matched in conflict with Achilles—is carried along by his horses and, fallen backward, clings to the empty car, yet clasping the reins; his neck and hair are dragged over the ground, and the dust is scored by his reversed spear. Meanwhile, to the temple of unfriendly Pallas the Trojan women passed along with streaming tresses,[2] and bore the robe, mourning in suppliant guise and beating breasts with hands: with averted face the goddess kept her eyes fast upon the ground. Thrice had Achilles dragged Hector round the walls of Troy and was selling the lifeless body for gold. Then indeed from the bottom of his heart he heaves a deep groan, as the spoils, as the chariot, as the very corpse of his friend met his gaze, and Priam outstretching weaponless hands. Himself, too, in close combat with the Achaean chiefs, he recognized, and the Eastern ranks, and swarthy Memnon's armour.[3] Penthesilea in fury leads the crescent-shielded ranks of the Amazons and rages amid her thousands; a golden belt binds her naked breast, while she, a warrior queen, dares battle, a maid clashing with men.

494 While these wondrous sights are seen by Dardan Aeneas, while in amazement he hangs rapt in one fixed gaze, the queen, Dido, moved towards the

---

[1] *i.e.* Diomedes.   [2] *cf.* Homer, *Iliad*, VI. 297 ff.
[3] Memnon was leader of the Ethiopians.

VIRGIL

incessit, magna iuvenum stipante caterva.
qualis in Eurotae ripis aut per iuga Cynthi
exercet Diana choros, quam mille secutae
hinc atque hinc glomerantur Oreades; illa phare-
    tram   500
fert umero gradiensque deas supereminet omnis;
Latonae tacitum pertemptant gaudia pectus:
talis erat Dido, talem se laeta ferebat
per medios, instans operi regnisque futuris.
tum foribus divae, media testudine templi,   505
saepta armis solioque alte subnixa resedit.
iura dabat legesque viris, operumque laborem
partibus aequabat iustis aut sorte trahebat:
cum subito Aeneas concursu accedere magno
Anthea Sergestumque videt fortemque Cloanthum
Teucrorumque alios, ater quos aequore turbo   511
dispulerat penitusque alias avexerat oras.
obstipuit simul ipse, simul percussus Achates
laetitiaque metuque; avidi coniungere dextras
ardebant, sed res animos incognita turbat.   515
dissimulant et nube cava speculantur amicti,
quae fortuna viris, classem quo litore linquant,
quid veniant; cunctis nam lecti navibus ibant
orantes veniam et templum clamore petebant.

Postquam introgressi et coram data copia fandi, 520
maximus Ilioneus placido sic pectore coepit:
" o regina, novam cui condere Iuppiter urbem   MPR
iustitiaque dedit gentis frenare superbas,
Troes te miseri, ventis maria omnia vecti,
oramus: prohibe infandos a navibus ignis,   525
parce pio generi et propius res aspice nostras.

⁵⁰¹ dea *M¹PR*.   ⁵¹² advexerat *M* (*late*): averterat *FP*
⁵¹³ perculsus *MP²*.
⁵¹⁸ cuncti *FMR, Servius.* lectis *P²R, known to Servius.*

temple, of surpassing beauty, with a vast company of youths thronging round her. Even as on Eurotas' banks or along the heights of Cynthus Diana guides her dancing bands, in whose train a thousand Oreads troop to right and left; she bears a quiver on her shoulder, and as she treads overtops all the goddesses; joys thrill Latona's silent breast—such was Dido, so moved she joyously through their midst, pressing on the work of her rising kingdom. Then at the door of the goddess, beneath the temple's central dome, girt with arms and high enthroned, she took her seat. Laws and ordinances she gave to her people; their tasks she adjusted in equal shares or assigned by lot; when suddenly Aeneas sees approaching, in the midst of a great crowd, Antheus and Sergestus and brave Cloanthus with others of the Trojans, whom the black storm had scattered on the sea and driven far away to other coasts. Amazed was he; amazed, too, was Achates, thrilled with joy and fear. They burned with eagerness to clasp hands, but the uncertain event confuses their hearts. They keep hidden, and, clothed in the enfolding cloud, look to see what is their comrades' fortune, on what shore they leave the fleet, and why they come; for from all the ships chosen men advanced, craving grace, and with loud cries made for the temple.

520 When they had entered, and freedom to speak before the queen was granted, the eldest, Ilioneus, with placid mien thus began: " O queen, to whom Jupiter hath given to found a new city, and to put the curb of justice on haughty tribes, we, unhappy Trojans, tempest-driven over every sea, make our prayer to thee: ward off the horror of flames from our ships; spare a pious race, and look more graciously on our fortunes. We have not come to spoil with the sword your

277

non nos aut ferro Libycos populare Penatis
venimus aut raptas ad litora vertere praedas;
non ea vis animo nec tanta superbia victis.
est locus, Hesperiam Grai cognomine dicunt,   530
terra antiqua, potens armis atque ubere glaebae;
Oenotri coluere viri, nunc fama minores
Italiam dixisse ducis de nomine gentem.
hic cursus fuit,
cum subito adsurgens fluctu nimbosus Orion   535
in vada caeca tulit penitusque procacibus Austris
perque undas superante salo, perque invia saxa
dispulit; huc pauci vestris adnavimus oris.
quod genus hoc hominum?' quaeve hunc tam barbara morem
permittit patria? hospitio prohibemur harenae; 540
bella cient primaque vetant consistere terra.
si genus humanum et mortalia temnitis arma,
at sperate deos memores fandi atque nefandi.
rex erat Aeneas nobis, quo iustior alter
nec pietate fuit, nec bello maior et armis.   545
quem si fata virum servant, si vescitur aura
aetheria neque adhuc crudelibus occubat umbris,
non metus, officio nec te certasse priorem
paeniteat. sunt et Siculis regionibus urbes
arvaque, Troianoque a sanguine clarus Acestes. 550
quassatam ventis liceat subducere classem
et silvis aptare trabes et stringere remos,
si datur Italiam sociis et rege recepto
tendere, ut Italiam laeti Latiumque petamus;
sin absumpta salus, et te, pater optime Teucrum, 555
pontus habet Libyae nec spes iam restat Iuli,
at freta Sicaniae saltem sedesque paratas,
unde huc advecti, regemque petamus Acesten."

             550 armaque $R\gamma$: arvaque M.

Libyan homes or to drive stolen booty to the shore.
No such violence is in our hearts, nor have the van-
quished such assurance. A place there is, by Greeks
named Hesperia, an ancient land, mighty in arms
and rich in soil. There dwelt Oenotrians; now the
rumour is that a younger race has called it from their
leader's name, Italy. Hither [1] lay our course, when,
rising with sudden swell, stormy Orion bore us on
hidden shoals and with fierce blasts scattered us afar
amid pathless rocks and waves of overwhelming
surge; hither to your shores have we few drifted.
What race of men is this? What land is so barbarous
as to allow this custom? We are debarred the
welcome of the beach; they stir up war and forbid
us to set foot on the border of their land. If ye
think light of human kinship and mortal arms, yet
look unto gods who will remember right and wrong.
Our king was Aeneas: none more righteous than he
in goodness, or greater in war and deeds of arms.
If fate still preserves that hero, if he feeds on the air
of heaven and lies not yet in the cruel shades, we
have no fear, nor wouldst thou repent of leading in
the rivalry of kindly service. In Sicilian regions, too,
are there cities and lands for tillage, and a prince of
Trojan blood, famed Acestes. Grant us to beach our
storm-battered fleet, to fashion planks in the forests
and trim oars, that if, with king and comrades found,
we may steer our course to Italy, Italy and Latium
we may gladly seek; but if our salvation is cut off, if
the Libyan gulf holds thee, good father of the Trojan
people, and no hope is left now in Iulus, that we at
least may seek the straits of Sicily, whence we came
hither, and the homes there ready, and Acestes for

[1] In l. 534 we encounter the first of fifty-five incomplete
verses in the *Aeneid.*

VIRGIL

talibus Ilioneus ; cuncti simul ore fremebant
Dardanidae.   560
　　Tum breviter Dido voltum demissa profatur :
" solvite corde metum, Teucri, secludite curas.
res dura et regni novitas me talia cogunt
moliri et late finis custode tueri.
quis genus Aeneadum, quis Troiae nesciat urbem 565
virtutesque virosque aut tanti incendia belli ?
non obtusa adeo gestamus pectora Poeni,
nec tam aversus equos Tyria Sol iungit ab urbe.
seu vos Hesperiam magnam Saturniaque arva
sive Erycis finis regemque optatis Acesten,   570
auxilio tutos dimittam opibusque iuvabo.
voltis et his mecum pariter considere regnis ?
urbem quam statuo vestra est ; subducite navis ;
Tros Tyriusque mihi nullo discrimine agetur.
atque utinam rex ipse Noto compulsus eodem   575
adforet Aeneas !　equidem per litora certos
dimittam et Libyae lustrare extrema iubebo,
si quibus eiectus silvis aut urbibus errat."
　　His animum arrecti dictis et fortis Achates
et pater Aeneas iamdudum erumpere nubem   580
ardebant.　prior Aenean compellat Achates :
" nate dea, quae nunc animo sententia surgit ?
omnia tuta vides, classem sociosque receptos.
unus abest, medio in fluctu quem vidimus ipsi
submersum ; dictis respondent cetera matris."   585

572 pariter mecum *P.*

280

our king." So spoke Ilioneus, and all the sons of Dardanus loudly shouted assent.

561 Then Dido, with downcast face, briefly speaks: "Free your hearts of fear, Teucrians; put away your cares. Stern necessity and the new estate of my kingdom force me to do such hard deeds and protect my frontiers far and wide with guards. Who could be ignorant of the race of Aeneas' people, who of Troy's town and her brave deeds and brave men, or of the fires of such a war? Not so dull are our Punic hearts, and not so far from this Tyrian city does the sun yoke his steeds.[1] Whether your choice be great Hesperia and the fields of Saturn,[2] or the lands of Eryx and Acestes for your king, I will send you hence guarded by an escort, and aid you with my wealth. Or is it your wish to settle with me on even terms within these realms? The city I build is yours; draw up your ships; Trojan and Tyrian I shall treat with no distinction. And would that your king were here, driven by the same wind —Aeneas himself! Nay, I will send trusty scouts along the coast and bid them traverse the ends of Libya, if haply he strays shipwrecked in forest or in town."

579 Stirred in spirit by these words, brave Achates and father Aeneas had long burned to break through the cloud. First Achates addresses Aeneas: "Goddess-born, what purpose now rises in thy heart? Thou seest all is safe, comrades and fleet restored. One[3] only is wanting, whom our own eyes saw engulfed amid the waves; all else agrees with thy mother's words."

[1] *i.e.* we do not live so far out of the world.
[2] Saturn lived in Italy in the Golden Age.
[3] *i.e.* Orontes.

vix ea fatus erat, cum circumfusa repente   FMPR
scindit se nubes et in aethera purgat apertum.
restitit Aeneas claraque in luce refulsit,
os umerosque deo similis ; namque ipsa decoram
caesariem nato genetrix lumenque iuventae   590
purpureum et laetos oculis adflarat honores ;
quale manus addunt ebori decus, aut ubi flavo
argentum Pariusve lapis circumdatur auro.
tum sic reginam adloquitur cunctisque repente
improvisus ait : " coram, quem quaeritis, adsum, 595
Troius Aeneas, Libycis ereptus ab undis.
o sola infandos Troiae miserata labores,
quae nos, reliquias Danaum, terraeque marisque
omnibus exhaustos iam casibus, omnium egenos,
urbe, domo socias, grates persolvere dignas   600
non opis est nostrae, Dido, nec quidquid ubique est
gentis Dardaniae, magnum quae sparsa per orbem.
di tibi, si qua pios respectant numina, si quid
usquam iustitia est, et mens sibi conscia recti,
praemia digna ferant. quae te tam laeta tulerunt 605
saecula ? qui tanti talem genuere parentes ?
in freta dum fluvii current, dum montibus umbrae
lustrabunt convexa, polus dum sidera pascet,
semper honos nomenque tuum laudesque manebunt,
quae me cumque vocant terrae." sic fatus, amicum
Ilionea petit dextra laevaque Serestum,   611
post alios, fortemque Gyan fortemque Cloanthum. MPR
    Obstipuit primo aspectu Sidonia Dido,
casu deinde viri tanto, et sic ore locuta est :
" quis te, nate dea, per tanta pericula casus   615
insequitur ? quae vis immanibus applicat oris ?

    590 numenque F^1. iuventa P.   **591** adflavit P^1.
    593 Pariusque P.   **599** exaustis F^1, *D. Servius.*
    604 iustitiae $BFM^2PR\gamma$.   **607** currunt B.
    608 convexa *was taken with* sidera *by some, according to
Servius.* poscet F: pascit M.

[586] Scarce had he said this, when the encircling cloud suddenly parts and clears into open heaven. Aeneas stood forth, gleaming in the clear light, godlike in face and shoulders; for his mother herself had shed upon her son the beauty of flowing locks, with youth's ruddy bloom, and on his eyes a joyous lustre; even as the beauty which the hand gives to ivory, or when silver or Parian marble is set in yellow gold. Then thus he addresses the queen, and, unforeseen by all, suddenly speaks:

[595] " I, whom ye seek, am here before you, Aeneas of Troy, snatched from the Libyan waves. O thou that alone hast pitied Troy's unutterable woes, thou that to us—the remnant left by the Greeks, now outworn by every mischance of land and sea, and destitute of all—givest a share in thy city and home, to pay thee fitting thanks, Dido, is not in our power, nor in theirs who anywhere survive of Trojan race, scattered over the wide world. May the gods, if any divine powers have regard for the good, if justice has any weight anywhere—may the gods and the consciousness of right bring thee worthy rewards! What happy ages bore thee? What glorious parents gave birth to so noble a child? While rivers run into the sea, while on the mountains shadows move over the slopes, while heaven feeds the stars, ever shall thy honour, thy name, and thy praises endure, whatever be the lands that summon me!" So saying, he grasps his dear Ilioneus with the right hand, and with the left Serestus; then others, brave Gyas and brave Cloanthus.

[613] Sidonian Dido was amazed, first at the sight of the hero, then at his strange misfortune, and thus her lips made utterance: "What fate pursues thee, goddess-born, amidst such perils? What violence

VIRGIL

tune ille Aeneas, quem Dardanio Anchisae
alma Venus Phrygii genuit Simoentis ad undam?
atque equidem Teucrum memini Sidona venire
finibus expulsum patriis, nova regna petentem   620
auxilio Beli ; genitor tum Belus opimam
vastabat Cyprum et victor dicione tenebat.
tempore iam ex illo casus mihi cognitus urbis
Troianae nomenque tuum regesque Pelasgi.
ipse hostis Teucros insigni laude ferebat   625
seque ortum antiqua Teucrorum ab stirpe volebat.
quare agite, o tectis, iuvenes, succedite nostris.
me quoque per multos similis fortuna labores
iactatam hac demum voluit consistere terra.
non ignara mali miseris succurrere disco.''   630
sic memorat; simul Aenean in regia ducit
tecta, simul divum templis indicit honorem.
nec minus interea sociis ad litora mittit
viginti tauros, magnorum horrentia centum
terga suum, pinguis centum cum matribus agnos, 635
munera laetitiamque dii.
at domus interior regali splendida luxu
instruitur, mediisque parant convivia tectis :
arte laboratae vestes ostroque superbo,
ingens argentum mensis, caelataque in auro   640
fortia facta patrum, series longissima rerum
per tot ducta viros antiqua ab origine gentis.
    Aeneas (neque enim patrius consistere mentem
passus amor) rapidum ad navis praemittit Achaten,
Ascanio ferat haec ipsumque ad moenia ducat ;   645

[620] patris P^1.   [625] insignis P^1, *Servius*.   [629] considere *P*. [635] dii *A. Gellius*, IX. xiv. 8: dei *MSS. Servius mentions* dei, dii, *and* die *as existing readings.*

284

drives thee to savage shores? Art thou that Aeneas,
whom gracious Venus bore to Dardanian Anchises by
the wave of Phrygian Simois? Yea, I myself re-
member well Teucer's coming to Sidon, when exiled
from his native land he sought a new kingdom by aid
of Belus; my father Belus was then wasting rich
Cyprus, and held it under his victorious sway. From
that time on the fall of the Trojan city has been
known to me; known, too, thine own name and the
Pelasgian kings. Even their foe often lauded the
Teucrians with highest praise and would have it that
he was sprung from the Teucrians' ancient stock.
Come therefore, sirs, and pass within our halls. Me,
too, has a like fortune driven through many toils,
and willed that at last I should find rest in this
land. Not ignorant of ill do I learn to befriend
the unhappy.''

[631] Thus she speaks, and at once leads Aeneas into
the royal house; at once proclaims a sacrifice at the
temples of the gods. Meanwhile not less careful is she
to send his comrades on the shore twenty bulls, a
hundred huge swine with bristling backs, a hundred
fatted lambs with their ewes, gifts for the day's
merriment.[1] But the palace within is laid out
with the splendour of princely pomp, and amid
the halls they prepare a banquet. Coverlets there
are, skilfully embroidered and of royal purple; on
the tables is massive silver plate, and in gold are
graven the doughty deeds of her sires, a long, long
course of exploits traced through many a hero from
the early dawn of the race.

[643] Aeneas—for a father's love did not suffer his
heart to rest—speedily sends Achates forward to the
ships to carry this news to Ascanius and lead him

---

[1] If *dei* of the MSS. is retained, it refers to Bacchus.

omnis in Ascanio cari stat cura parentis.
munera praeterea, Iliacis erepta ruinis,
ferre iubet, pallam signis auroque rigentem,
et circumtextum croceo velamen acantho,
ornatus Argivae Helenae, quos illa Mycenis,   650
Pergama cum peteret inconcessosque hymenaeos,
extulerat, matris Ledae mirabile donum;
praeterea sceptrum, Ilione quod gesserat olim,
maxima natarum Priami, colloque monile   **FMPR**
bacatum et duplicem gemmis auroque coronam. 655
haec celerans iter ad navis tendebat Achates.

    At Cytherea novas artis, nova pectore versat
consilia, ut faciem mutatus et ora Cupido
pro dulci Ascanio veniat, donisque furentem
incendat reginam atque ossibus implicet ignem: 660
quippe domum timet ambiguam Tyriosque bilinguis;
urit atrox Iuno et sub noctem cura recursat.
ergo his aligerum dictis adfatur Amorem:
" nate, meae vires, mea magna potentia, solus,
nate, patris summi qui tela Typhoëa temnis,   665
ad te confugio et supplex tua numina posco.
frater ut Aeneas pelago tuus omnia circum
litora iactetur odiis Iunonis acerbae,
nota tibi, et nostro doluisti saepe dolore.
hunc Phoenissa tenet Dido blandisque moratur   670
vocibus, et vereor, quo se Iunonia vertant
hospitia; haud tanto cessabit cardine rerum.
quocirca capere ante dolis et cingere flamma
reginam meditor, ne quo se numine mutet,

---

668 iacteturque $F^2MR\gamma$, *Servius.* acerbae: iniquae F^2MP^2R.
670 nunc F^1: hunc $F^2MR\gamma$; *P's reading lost.*
286

to the city; in Ascanius all his fond parental care is centred. Presents, too, snatched from the wreck of Ilium, he bids him bring, a mantle stiff with figures wrought in gold, and a veil fringed with yellow acanthus, once worn by Argive Helen when she sailed for Pergamos and her unlawful marriage—she had brought them from Mycenae, the wondrous gift of her mother Leda—the sceptre withal, which Ilione, Priam's eldest daughter, once had borne, a necklace, too, hung with pearls, and a coronet with double circlet of jewels and gold. Speeding these commands, Achates bent his way towards the ships.

657 But the Cytherean revolves in her breast new wiles, new schemes; how Cupid, changed in face and form, may come in the stead of sweet Ascanius, and by his gifts kindle the queen to madness and send the flame into her very marrow. In truth, she fears the uncertain house and double-tongued Tyrians; Juno's hate chafes her, and at nightfall her care rushes back. Therefore to winged Love she speaks these words:

664 "Son, who art alone my strength, my mighty power—O son, who scornest the mighty father's Typhoean[1] darts, to thee I flee and suppliant sue thy godhead. How thy brother Aeneas is tossed on the sea about all coasts by bitter Juno's hate is known to thee, and often hast thou grieved in our grief. Phoenician Dido now holds him, staying him with soft words, and I dread what may be the outcome of Juno's hospitality; at such a turning-point of fortune she will not be idle. Wherefore I purpose to outwit the queen with guile and encircle her with love's flame, that so no power may change her, but along with me she may be held

[1] So called because with them Jupiter slew the Titan Typhoeus.

sed magno Aeneae mecum teneatur amore.   675
qua facere id possis, nostram nunc accipe mentem.
regius accitu cari genitoris ad urbem
Sidoniam puer ire parat, mea maxima cura,
dona ferens pelago et flammis restantia Troiae.
hunc ego sopitum somno super alta Cythera   680
aut super Idalium sacrata sede recondam,   MPR
ne qua scire dolos mediusve occurrere possit.
tu faciem illius noctem non amplius unam
falle dolo, et notos pueri puer indue voltus,
ut, cum te gremio accipiet laetissima Dido   GMPR
regalis inter mensas laticemque Lyaeum,   686
cum dabit amplexus atque oscula dulcia figet,
occultum inspires ignem fallasque veneno.''
paret Amor dictis carae genetricis et alas
exuit et gressu gaudens incedit Iuli.   690
at Venus Ascanio placidam per membra quietem
inrigat, et fotum gremio dea tollit in altos
Idaliae lucos, ubi mollis amaracus illum
floribus et dulci adspirans complectitur umbra.

Iamque ibat dicto parens et dona Cupido   695
regia portabat Tyriis, duce laetus Achate.
cum venit, aulaeis iam se regina superbis
aurea composuit sponda mediamque locavit,
iam pater Aeneas et iam Troiana iuventus
conveniunt, stratoque super discumbitur ostro.   700
dant manibus famuli lymphas Cereremque canistris
expediunt tonsisque ferunt mantelia villis.
quinquaginta intus famulae, quibus ordine longo
cura penum struere et flammis adolere Penatis;
centum aliae totidemque pares aetate ministri,   705

⁶⁷⁶ quam γ : quo b.
⁷⁰¹ In M ll. 701–708 follow ll. 709–716. famulae MP.
⁷⁰³ longam Charisius, known to Gellius : longo MSS., Servius.

fast in strong love for Aeneas. How thou canst do this
take now my thought. The princely boy, my chiefest
care, at his dear father's bidding, makes ready to go to
the Sidonian city, bearing gifts that survive the sea
and the flames of Troy. Him will I lull to sleep, and
on the heights of Cythera or of Idalium will hide in
my sacred shrine, that in no wise he may learn my
wiles or come between to thwart them. Do thou, for
but a single night, feign by craft his form and, boy
as thou art, don the boy's familiar face, that so
when, in the fullness of her joy, amid the royal
feast and the flowing wine, Dido shall take thee to
her bosom, shall embrace thee and imprint sweet
kisses, thou mayest inbreathe a hidden fire and
beguile her with thy poison." Love obeys his dear
mother's words, lays by his wings, and walks joyously
with the step of Iülus. But Venus pours over the
limbs of Ascanius the dew of gentle repose and,
fondling him in her bosom, uplifts him with divine
power to Idalia's high groves, where soft marjoram
enwraps him in flowers and the breath of its sweet
shade.

695 And now, obedient to her word and rejoicing
in Achates as guide, Cupid went forth, carrying the
royal gifts for the Tyrians. As he enters, the queen
has already, amid royal hangings, laid herself on a
golden couch, and taken her place in their midst.
Now father Aeneas, now the Trojan youth gather,
and the guests recline on coverlets of purple.
Servants pour water on their hands, serve bread
from baskets, and bring smooth-shorn napkins.
There are fifty serving-maids within, whose task it
is to set out the feast in long array and honour the
hearth-gods with fire. A hundred more there are,
with as many pages of like age, to load the board

VIRGIL

qui dapibus mensas onerent et pocula ponant.
nec non et Tyrii per limina laeta frequentes
convenere, toris iussi discumbere pictis.
mirantur dona Aeneae, mirantur Iulum
flagrantisque dei voltus simulataque verba   710
pallamque et pictum croceo velamen acantho.
praecipue infelix, pesti devota futurae,
expleri mentem nequit ardescitque tuendo
Phoenissa, et pariter puero donisque movetur.
ille ubi complexu Aeneae colloque pependit   715
et magnum falsi implevit genitoris amorem,
reginam petit.   haec oculis, haec pectore toto
haeret et interdum gremio fovet, inscia Dido,
insidat quantus miserae deus.   at memor ille
matris Acidaliae paulatim abolere Sychaeum   720
incipit et vivo temptat pravertere amore
iam pridem resides animos desuetaque corda.
   Postquam   prima   quies   epulis   mensaeque   re-
         motae,   MPR
crateras magnos statuunt et vina coronant.
fit strepitus tectis vocemque per ampla volutant   725
atria ; dependent lychni laquearibus aureis
incensi et noctem flammis funalia vincunt.
hic regina gravem gemmis auroque poposcit
implevitque mero pateram, quam Belus et omnes
a Belo soliti ; tum facta silentia tectis.   730
" Iuppiter, hospitibus nam te dare iura loquuntur,
hunc laetum Tyriisque diem Troiaque profectis
esse velis, nostrosque huius meminisse minores.
adsit laetitiae Bacchus dator et bona Iuno ;
et vos, o, coetum, Tyrii, celebrate faventes."   735

---

706 onerant . . . ponunt *BGR.*
719 insideat *GR: both known to Servius:* insidiat γ1.
725 fit] it *b: both known to Servius:* id γ1.

290

with viands and set thereon the cups. Yea, the
Tyrians, too, are gathered in throngs throughout
the festal halls, summoned to recline on the embroi-
dered couches. They marvel at the gifts of Aeneas,
marvel at Iülus, at the god's glowing looks and well-
feigned words, at the robe and veil, embroidered with
saffron acanthus. Above all, the unhappy Phoenician,
doomed to impending ruin, cannot satiate her soul,
but takes fire as she gazes, thrilled alike by the boy
and by the gifts. He, when he has hung in embrace
on Aeneas' neck and satisfied the deluded father's
deep love, goes to the queen. She with her eyes,
with all her heart clings to him and anon fondles
him in her bosom, knowing not, poor Dido, how
great a god settles there to her sorrow. But he,
mindful of his Acidalian mother, little by little
begins to efface Sychaeus, and essays with a living
passion to surprise her long-slumbering soul and heart
unused to love.

[723] When first there came a lull in the feasting, and
the boards were cleared, they set down great bowls
and crown the wine. A din arises in the palace
and voices roll through the spacious halls; lighted
lamps hang down from the fretted roof of gold, and
flaming torches drive out the night. Then the queen
called for a cup, heavy with jewels and gold, and
filled it with wine—one that Belus and all of Belus'
line had been wont to use. Then through the hall
fell silence: "Jupiter—for they say that thou dost
appoint laws for host and guest—grant that this be
a day of joy for Tyrians and the voyagers from
Troy, and this our children may remember! May
Bacchus, giver of joy, be near, and bounteous Juno;
and do ye, O Tyrians, grace the gathering with
friendly spirit!" She spoke, and on the board

VIRGIL

dixit et in mensam laticum libavit honorem
primaque libato summo tenus attigit ore ;
tum Bitiae dedit increpitans ; ille impiger hausit
spumantem pateram et pleno se proluit auro ;
post alii proceres.   cithara crinitus Iopas   740
personat aurata, docuit quem maximus Atlas.
hic canit errantem lunam solisque labores,
unde hominum genus et pecudes, unde imber et ignes,
Arcturum pluviasque Hyadas geminosque Triones ;
quid tantum Oceano properent se tinguere soles 745
hiberni, vel quae tardis mora noctibus obstet.
ingeminant plausu Tyrii, Troesque sequuntur.
nec non et vario noctem sermone trahebat
infelix Dido longumque bibebat amorem,
multa super Priamo rogitans, super Hectore multa ;
nunc, quibus Aurorae venisset filius armis,   751
nunc, quales Diomedis equi, nunc, quantus Achilles.
" immo age et a prima dic, hospes, origine nobis
insidias " inquit " Danaum casusque tuorum
erroresque tuos ; nam te iam septima portat   755
omnibus errantem terris et fluctibus aestas."

741 quem] quae γ², *preferred by Servius.*

offered a libation of wine, and, after the libation, was first to touch the goblet with her lips; then with a challenge gave it to Bitias. He briskly drained the foaming cup, and drank deep in the brimming gold; then other lords drank. Long-haired Iopas, once taught by mighty Atlas, makes the hall ring with his golden lyre. He sings of the wandering moon and the sun's toils; whence sprang human kind and the brutes, whence rain and fire; of Arcturus, the rainy Hyades and the twin Bears; why wintry suns make such haste to dip themselves in Ocean, or what delay stays the slowly passing nights. With shout on shout the Tyrians applaud, and the Trojans follow. Yea, unhappy Dido, too, with varied talk prolonged the night and drank deep draughts of love, asking much of Priam, of Hector much; now of the armour wherein the son of Aurora came; now of the wondrous steeds of Diomedes; now of giant Achilles. "Nay, come," she cries, "and tell us, my guest, from the first beginning the treachery of the Greeks, thy comrades' misfortunes, and thine own wanderings; for it is now the seventh summer that bears thee a wanderer over every land and sea."

LIBER II

CONTICUERE omnes intentique ora tenebant.
inde toro pater Aeneas sic orsus ab alto:
  " Infandum, regina, iubes renovare dolorem,
Troianas ut opes et lamentabile regnum
eruerint Danai, quaeque ipse miserrima vidi   5
et quorum pars magna fui.   quis talia fando
Myrmidonum Dolopumve aut duri miles Ulixi
temperet a lacrimis?   et iam nox umida caelo
praecipitat suadentque cadentia sidera somnos.
sed si tantus amor casus cognoscere nostros   10
et breviter Troiae supremum audire laborem,
quamquam animus meminisse horret luctuque refugit,
incipiam.
            " Fracti bello fatisque repulsi
ductores Danaum, tot iam labentibus annis,
instar montis equum divina Palladis arte   15
aedificant sectaque intexunt abiete costas;
votum pro reditu simulant; ea fama vagatur.
huc delecta virum sortiti corpora furtim
includunt caeco lateri penitusque cavernas
ingentis uterumque armato milite complent.   20
  " Est in conspectu Tenedos, notissima fama
insula, dives opum, Priami dum regna manebant,
nunc tantum sinus et statio male fida carinis:

[18] dilecta *Pγ¹*.

BOOK II

ALL were hushed, and held their gaze bent upon him; then from his lofty couch father Aeneas thus began:

3 "Beyond all words, O queen, is the grief thou bidst me revive, how the Greeks overthrew Troy's wealth and woeful realm—the sights most piteous that I myself saw and whereof I was no small part. What Myrmidon or Dolopian, or soldier of stern Ulysses, could in telling such a tale refrain from tears? Now, too, dewy night is speeding from the sky [1] and the setting stars invite to sleep. Yet if thou hast such longing to learn our disasters, and in few words to hear of Troy's last agony, though my mind shudders to remember, and has recoiled in grief, I will begin.

13 "Broken in war and thrust back by the fates, the Danaan chiefs, now that so many years were gliding by, build by Pallas' divine art a horse of mountainous bulk, and interweave its ribs with planks of fir. They feign it as a votive offering; this rumour goes abroad. Here, within its dark sides, they stealthily enclose the choicest of their stalwart men and deep in the paunch fill the huge cavern with armed soldiery.

21 "There lies in sight Tenedos, an island well known to fame—rich in wealth while Priam's kingdom stood, now but a bay and unsafe anchorage for ships.

[1] i.e. into the ocean. The night is far spent. cf. II. 250.

huc se provecti deserto in litore condunt.
nos abiisse rati et vento petiisse Mycenas.   25
ergo omnis longo solvit se Teucria luctu.
panduntur portae; iuvat ire et Dorica castra
desertosque videre locos litusque relictum.
hic Dolopum manus, hic saevus tendebat Achilles,
classibus hic locus, hic acie certare solebant.   30
pars stupet innuptae donum exitiale Minervae
et molem mirantur equi; primusque Thymoetes
duci intra muros hortatur et arce locari,
sive dolo seu iam Troiae sic fata ferebant.
at Capys, et quorum melior sententia menti,   35
aut pelago Danaum insidias suspectaque dona
praecipitare iubent subiectisque urere flammis,
aut terebrare cavas uteri et temptare latebras.
scinditur incertum studia in contraria volgus.
   "Primus ibi ante omnis, magna comitante
        caterva,   40
Laocoon ardens summa decurrit ab arce
et procul: 'o miseri, quae tanta insania, cives?
creditis avectos hostis? aut ulla putatis
dona carere dolis Danaum?   sic notus Ulixes?
aut hoc inclusi ligno occultantur Achivi,   45
aut haec in nostros fabricata est machina muros,
inspectura domos venturaque desuper urbi,
aut aliquis latet error; equo ne credite, Teucri.
quidquid id est, timeo Danaos et dona ferentis.'
sic fatus validis ingentem viribus hastam   50
in latus inque feri curvam compagibus alvum
contorsit.   stetit illa tremens, uteroque recusso
insonuere cavae gemitumque dedere cavernae.

     [37] iubet *P²*, *Nonius.*   subiectisve *known to Servius.*
     [38] utero *P¹*.

Hither they sail and hide themselves on the barren
shore. We thought they had gone and before the
wind were bound for Mycenae. So all the Teucrian
land frees itself from her long sorrow. The gates
are opened; it is a joy to go and see the Doric camp,
the deserted stations and forsaken shore. Here the
Dolopian bands encamped, here cruel Achilles; here
lay the fleet; here they used to meet us in battle.
Some are amazed at maiden Minerva's gift of death,
and marvel at the massive horse: and first Thymoetes
urges that it be drawn within our walls and lodged
in the citadel, whether in treachery or that now the
doom of Troy was thus setting. But Capys, and they
whose minds were wiser in counsel, bid us either
hurl headlong into the sea this guile of the Greeks,
this distrusted gift, or fire it with flames heaped
beneath; or else pierce and probe the hollow hiding-
place of the womb. The wavering crowd is torn
into opposing factions.

  40 " Then, foremost of all and with a great throng
following, Laocoön in hot haste runs down from the
citadel's height, and cries from afar: ' Oh, wretched
citizens, what wild frenzy is this? Do ye believe the
foe has sailed away? or think ye any gifts of the Greeks
are free from treachery? Is it thus ye know Ulysses?
Either enclosed in this frame there lurk Achaeans, or
this has been built as an engine of war against our
walls, to spy into our homes and come down upon
the city from above; or some trickery lurks therein.
Trust not the horse, ye Trojans. Whatever it be, I
fear the Greeks, even when bringing gifts.' So saying,
with mighty force he hurled his great spear at the
beast's side and the arched frame of the belly. The
spear stood quivering and with the womb's rever-
beration the vaults rang hollow, sending forth a moan.

VIRGIL

et si fata deum, si mens non laeva fuisset,
impulerat ferro Argolicas foedare latebras, 55
Troiaque nunc staret, Priamique arx alta maneres.

"Ecce manus iuvenem interea post terga revinctum
pastores magno ad regem clamore trahebant
Dardanidae, qui se ignotum venientibus ultro, 59
hoc ipsum ut strueret Troiamque aperiret Achivis,
obtulerat, fidens animi atque in utrumque paratus,
seu versare dolos seu certae occumbere morti.
undique visendi studio Troiana iuventus
circumfusa ruit certantque inludere capto.
accipe nunc Danaum insidias et crimine ab uno 65
disce omnis.

namque ut conspectu in medio turbatus, inermis,
constitit atque oculis Phrygia agmina circumspexit,
'heu! quae nunc tellus,' inquit, 'quae me aequora
            possunt
accipere? aut quid iam misero mihi denique restat, 70
cui neque apud Danaos usquam locus, et super ipsi
Dardanidae infensi poenas cum sanguine poscunt?'
quo gemitu conversi animi, compressus et omnis MP
impetus. hortamur fari, quo sanguine cretus,
quidve ferat; memoret, quae sit fiducia capto. 75
ille haec, deposita tandem formidine, fatur.

" ' Cuncta equidem tibi, rex, fuerit quodcumque,
            fatebor
vera,' inquit : ' neque me Argolica de gente negabo :
hoc primum ; nec si miserum Fortuna Sinonem [MPV
finxit, vanum etiam mendacemque improba finget. 80
fando aliquod si forte tuas pervenit ad auris
Belidae nomen Palamedis et incluta fama
gloria, quem falsa sub proditione Pelasgi

⁵⁶ stares *PRγ*.   maneret *M* (*late*).   ⁵⁹ quis *preferred by*
Servius.   ⁶² certe *MP²γ*.   occurrere *P¹*.
⁶⁹ nunc] me *Quintilian*, IX. 2, 9.
⁷⁴ = III. 612 ; *omitted P : at foot of page, M* (*late*).
⁷⁷ fuerit quaecumque *P¹γ¹*.

And had the gods' decrees, had our mind not been perverse, he had driven us to befoul with steel the Argive den, and Troy would now be standing, and thou, lofty citadel of Priam, wouldst still abide!

⁵⁷ "Meanwhile, lo! some Dardan shepherds with loud shouts were haling to the king a youth whose hands were bound behind his back. To compass this very end and open Troy to the Achaeans, stranger though he was, he had of free will placed himself in the way of their coming, confident in spirit and ready for either event, whether to ply his crafty wiles or to meet certain death. From all sides, in eagerness to see, the Trojan youth run streaming in and vie in mocking the captive. Hear now the treachery of the Greeks and from one learn the wickedness of all. For as he stood amid the gazing crowd, dismayed, unarmed, and cast his eyes about the Phrygian bands, 'Alas!' he cried, 'what land now, what seas may receive me? or what fate at the last yet awaits my misery? No place at all have I among the Greeks, and the Trojans themselves, too, wildly clamour for vengeance and my life.' At that wail our mood was changed and all violence checked. We urge him to say from what blood he is sprung or what tidings he brings. 'Tell us,' we cry, 'on what thou reliest as prisoner.' He, when at length he has laid aside his fear, thus speaks:

⁷⁷ "'Surely, O king,' he says, 'whatever befalls, I will tell thee all truly, nor will I deny that I am of Argive birth. This first I own; nor, if Fortune has moulded Sinon for misery, will she also in her spite mould him as false and lying. If haply in speech there has reached your ears some rumour of Pala-medes, son of Belus, and the glory of his fame—whom under false evidence, by wicked witnessing,

insontem infando indicio, quia bella vetabat,
demisere neci, nunc cassum lumine lugent :   85
ille me comitem et consanguinitate propinquum
pauper in arma pater primis huc misit ab annis.
dum stabat regno incolumis regumque vigebat
conciliis, et nos aliquod nomenque decusque
gessimus.   invidia postquam pellacis Ulixi   90
(haud ignota loquor) superis concessit ab oris,
adflictus vitam in tenebris luctuque trahebam
et casum insontis mecum indignabar amici.
nec tacui demens et me, fors si qua tulisset,
si patrios umquam remeassem victor ad Argos,   95
promisi ultorem et verbis odia aspera movi.
hinc mihi prima mali labes, hinc semper Ulixes
criminibus terrere novis, hinc spargere voces
in volgum ambiguas et quaerere conscius arma.
nec requievit enim, donec Calchante ministro—   100
sed quid ego haec autem nequiquam ingrata revolvo ?
quidve moror ?   si omnis uno ordine habetis Achivos
idque audire sat est, iamdudum sumite poenas :
hoc Ithacus velit et magno mercentur Atridae.'

  " Tum vero ardemus scitari et quaerere causas, 105
ignari scelerum tantorum artisque Pelasgae.   ᴍᴘ
prosequitur pavitans et ficto pectore fatur :

  " ' Saepe fugam Danai Troia cupiere relicta
moliri et longo fessi discedere bello :
fecissentque utinam !   saepe illos aspera ponti   110
interclusit hiems et terruit Auster euntis ;
praecipue, cum iam hic trabibus contextus acernis

  ⁸⁸ regnu. . . . *P*¹.   ⁸⁹ consil(iis) *V*.   ⁹⁰ fallacis *PV* (?) γ.
  ¹⁰⁵ casus *P*¹.   ¹¹² iam cum *M*¹.
300

the Pelasgians sent down innocent to death, and
mourn him, now that he is bereft of light—in his
company, being of kindred blood, my father, poor as
he was, sent me hither to arms in my earliest years.
While he stood secure in princely power and strong
in the councils of the kings, we, too, bore some name
and renown. But when through the malice of subtle
Ulysses—not unknown is the tale—he passed from
this world above, I dragged on my ruined life in
darkness and grief, wrathful in my heart over the
fate of my innocent friend. Nor in my madness was
I silent, but, if any chance should offer, if I ever
returned in triumph to my native Argos, I vowed
myself his avenger and with my words awoke fierce
hate. Hence for me the first taint of ill; hence would
Ulysses ever affright me with new charges; hence
would he sow dark rumours in the crowd and, con-
scious of guilt,[1] seek his weapons. Nay, he rested
not until with Calchas as his tool—but why do
I vainly unroll this unwelcome tale? Or why
delay you? If ye hold all Achaeans in one rank,
and if it is enough to hear that, take your vengeance
at once; this the Ithacan would wish and the sons
of Atreus buy at a great price!'

105 "Then indeed we burn to inquire and ask
the causes, strangers as we were to wickedness so
great and to Pelasgian guile. Trembling he takes
up the tale and speaks with feigned feelings:

108 "'Often the Greeks longed to quit Troy,
compass a retreat, and depart, weary with the long
war; and oh that they had done so! Often a fierce
tempest of the deep cut them off and the gale scared
them from going. Above all, when yonder horse
now stood framed of maple-beams, storm clouds

[1] Some editors prefer to render "as a conspirator."

staret equus, toto sonuerunt aethere nimbi.
suspensi Eurypylum scitantem oracula Phoebi
mittimus, isque adytis haec tristia dicta reportat: 115
"sanguine placastis ventos et virgine caesa,
cum primum Iliacas, Danai, venistis ad oras:
sanguine quaerendi reditus animaque litandum
Argolica." volgi quae vox ut venit ad auris,
obstipuere animi, gelidusque per ima cucurrit 120
ossa tremor, cui fata parent, quem poscat Apollo.
hic Ithacus vatem magno Calchanta tumultu
protrahit in medios; quae sint ea numina divum,
flagitat. et mihi iam multi crudele canebant
artificis scelus et taciti ventura videbant. 125
bis quinos silet ille dies tectusque recusat
prodere voce sua quemquam aut opponere morti.
vix tandem, magnis Ithaci clamoribus actus,
composito rumpit vocem et me destinat arae.
adsensere omnes et, quae sibi quisque timebat, 130
unius in miseri exitium conversa tulere.

" 'Iamque dies infanda aderat, mihi sacra parari
et salsae fruges et circum tempora vittae.
eripui, fateor, leto me et vincula rupi
limosoque lacu per noctem obscurus in ulva 135
delitui, dum vela darent, si forte dedissent.
nec mihi iam patriam antiquam spes ulla videndi
nec dulcis natos exoptatumque parentem;
quos illi fors et poenas ob nostra reposcent
effugia et culpam hanc miserorum morte piabunt. 140
quod te per superos et conscia numina veri,
per si qua est quae restat adhuc mortalibus usquam

114 scitantem $P\gamma^1b^1$, *Servius:* scitantum M^1: scitatum
$M^2\gamma^2$, *Charisius, known to Servius.*
138 dulcis] duplicis P^1, *known to Servius.*
142 restet M^2, *Servius.* umquam M^1.

sounded throughout the sky. Perplexed, we send
Eurypylus to ask the oracle of Phoebus, and he
brings back from the shrine these gloomy words:
"With blood of a slain virgin ye appeased the winds,
when first, O Greeks, ye came to the Ilian coasts;
with blood must ye win your return and gain favour
by an Argive life." When this utterance came to
the ears of the crowd, their hearts were dazed, and
a cold shudder ran through their inmost marrow.
For whom is fate preparing this doom? Whom
does Apollo claim? On this the Ithacan with loud
clamour drags the seer Calchas into their midst and
demands what this is the gods will. And now
many foreboded for me the schemer's cruel crime
and silently saw what was to come. Twice five days
is the seer silent in his tent, refusing to denounce
any by his lips or to consign to death. But at length,
forced by the Ithacan's loud cries, even as agreed he
breaks into utterance and dooms me to the altar.
All approved; and what each feared for himself they
bore with patience, when turned, alas! to one man's
ruin.

132 "'And now the day of horror was at hand; for
me the rites were preparing, the salted meal, and the
fillets for my temples. I snatched myself, I confess,
from death; I burst my bonds, and lurked all night
in a muddy mere, hidden in the sedge, until they
should set sail, if haply they would. And now no
hope have I of seeing my dear old country, or my
sweet children and the father I long for. Of them
perchance they will demand due punishment for my
flight, and by their death, unhappy ones, expiate this
crime of mine. But I beseech thee, by the gods
above, by the powers that know the truth, by what-
ever faith may still be found unstained anywhere

intemerata fides, oro, miserere laborum
tantorum, miserere animi non digna ferentis.'   144

" His lacrimis vitam damus et miserescimus ultro.
ipse viro primus manicas atque arta levari
vincla iubet Priamus dictisque ita fatur amicis :

" ' Quisquis es, amissos hinc iam obliviscere Graios ;
noster eris. mihique haec edissere vera roganti : 149
quo molem hanc immanis equi statuere ? quis auctor ?
quidve petunt ? quae religio ? aut quae machina belli ? '
dixerat.   ille, dolis instructus et arte Pelasga,
sustulit exutas vinclis ad sidera palmas :
' vos, aeterni ignes, et non violabile vestrum
testor numen,' ait, ' vos arae ensesque nefandi,   155
quos fugi, vittaeque deum, quas hostia gessi :
fas mihi Graiorum sacrata resolvere iura,
fas odisse viros atque omnia ferre sub auras,   MPV
si qua tegunt ; teneor patriae nec legibus ullis.
tu modo promissis maneas servataque serves,   160
Troia, fidem, si vera feram, si magna rependam.

" ' Omnis spes Danaum et coepti fiducia belli
Palladis auxiliis semper stetit.   impius ex quo
Tydides sed enim scelerumque inventor Ulixes,
fatale adgressi sacrato avellere templo   165
Palladium, caesis summae custodibus arcis,
corripuere sacram effigiem manibusque cruentis
virgineas ausi divae contingere vittas :
ex illo fluere ac retro sublapsa referri
spes Danaum, fractae vires, aversa deae mens.   FMPV
304

among mortals, pity such distress; pity a soul that bears sorrow undeserved!'

¹⁴⁵ "To these tears we grant life and pity him besides. Priam himself first bids his fetters and tight bonds be removed, and thus speaks with words of kindness:

¹⁴⁸ "'Whoever thou art, from henceforth forget the Greeks thou hast lost; thou shalt be ours. And explain to me truly this that I ask. To what end have they set up this huge mass of a horse? Who is the contriver? or what is their aim? What religious offering is it? or what engine of war?' He ceased; the other, schooled in Pelasgian guile and craft, lifted to the stars his unfettered hands: 'Ye, O everlasting fires,' he cries, 'and your inviolable majesty, be ye my witness; ye, O altars, and accursed swords which I escaped, and chaplets of the gods, which I wore as victim! rightly may I break my solemn obligations to the Greeks, rightly hate them and bring all things to light if they hide aught; nor am I bound by any laws of country. Only do thou, O Troy, stand by thy promises and, preserved thyself, preserve thy faith, if my tidings prove true, if I shall make a large return!

¹⁶² "'All the hope of the Danaans and their confidence in beginning the war were ever stayed on the help of Pallas. But from the time that the ungodly son of Tydeus [1] and Ulysses, the contriver of crime, dared to tear the fateful Palladium from its hallowed shrine, slew the guards of the citadel-height, and, snatching up the sacred image, ventured with bloody hands to touch the fillets of the maiden goddess—from that time the hopes of the Danaans ebbed and, backward stealing, receded; their strength was broken and the heart of the goddess estranged.

[1] Diomedes.

VIRGIL

nec dubiis ea signa dedit Tritonia monstris. 171
vix positum castris simulacrum, arsere coruscae
luminibus flammae arrectis salsusque per artus
sudor iit, terque ipsa solo (mirabile dictu)
emicuit parmamque ferens hastamque trementem.
extemplo temptanda fuga canit aequora Calchas, 176
nec posse Argolicis exscindi Pergama telis,
omina ni repetant Argis numenque reducant,
quod pelago et curvis secum avexere carinis.
et nunc quod patrias vento petiere Mycenas, 180
arma deosque parant comites, pelagoque remenso
improvisi aderunt. ita digerit omina Calchas.
hanc pro Palladio moniti, pro numine laeso
effigiem statuere, nefas quae triste piaret. **FMP**
hanc tamen immensam Calchas attollere molem 185
roboribus textis caeloque educere iussit,
ne recipi portis aut duci in moenia posset,
neu populum antiqua sub religione tueri.
nam si vestra manus violasset dona Minervae, 189
tum magnum exitium (quod di prius omen in ipsum
convertant!) Priami imperio Phrygibusque futurum;
sin manibus vestris vestram ascendisset in urbem,
ultro Asiam magno Pelopea ad moenia bello
venturam, et nostros ea fata manere nepotes.'

" Talibus insidiis periurique arte Sinonis 195
credita res, captique dolis lacrimisque coactis,

[187] possit *FM. So Sabb.*   [196] coacti γ², *Nonius.*
306

AENEID BOOK II

And with no doubtful portents did Tritonia give
signs thereof. Scarcely was the image placed within
the camp, when from the upraised eyes there
blazed forth flickering flames, salt sweat coursed
over the limbs, and thrice, wonderful to relate, the
goddess herself flashed forth[1] from the ground with
shield and quivering spear. Straightway Calchas
prophesies that the seas must be essayed in flight, and
that Pergamus cannot be uptorn by Argive weapons,
unless they seek new omens at Argos, and escort
back the deity, whom they have taken away over-
seas in their curved ships. And now that before
the wind they are bound for their native Mycenae,
it is but to get them forces and attendant gods;
then, recrossing the sea, they will be here unlooked
for. So Calchas interprets the omens. This image,
at his warning, they have set up in atonement for
the Palladium, for the insulted deity, and to expiate
the woeful sacrilege. Yet Calchas bade them raise
this mass of interlaced timbers so huge, and so to
build it up to heaven, that it might find no entrance
at the gates, be drawn within the walls, or guard the
people under shelter of their ancient faith. For if
hand of yours should wrong Minerva's offering, then
utter destruction—may the gods turn rather on him-
self that augury!—would fall on Priam's empire and
the Phrygians; but if by your hands it climbed into
your city, Asia would even advance in mighty war
to the walls of Pelops,[2] and such would be the doom
awaiting our offspring!'

195 "Through such snares and craft of forsworn
Sinon the story won belief, and we were ensnared by

[1] The words indicate an apparition, which appears suddenly
like lightning.

i.e. the Trojans would advance against the cities of Greece.

quos neque Tydides nec Larissaeus Achilles,
non anni domuere decem, non mille carinae.

" Hic aliud maius miseris multoque tremendum MP
obicitur magis atque improvida pectora turbat.   200
Laocoon, ductus Neptuno sorte sacerdos,
sollemnis taurum ingentem mactabat ad aras.
ecce autem gemini a Tenedo tranquilla per alta
(horresco referens) immensis orbibus angues
incumbunt pelago pariterque ad litora tendunt: 205
pectora quorum inter fluctus arrecta iubaeque
sanguineae superant undas; pars cetera pontum
pone legit sinuatque immensa volumine terga.
fit sonitus spumante salo; iamque arva tenebant
ardentisque oculos suffecti sanguine et igni   210
sibila lambebant linguis vibrantibus ora.
diffugimus visu exsangues. illi agmine certo
Laocoonta petunt; et primum parva duorum
corpora natorum serpens amplexus uterque
implicat et miseros morsu depascitur artus;   215
post ipsum, auxilio subeuntem ac tela ferentem,
corripiunt spirisque ligant ingentibus: et iam
bis medium amplexi, bis collo squamea circum
terga dati, superant capite et cervicibus altis.
ille simul manibus tendit divellere nodos,   220
perfusus sanie vittas atroque veneno,
clamores simul horrendos ad sidera tollit,
qualis mugitus, fugit cum saucius aram
taurus et incertam excussit cervice securim.
at gemini lapsu delubra ad summa dracones   225
effugiunt saevaeque petunt Tritonidis arcem,
sub pedibusque deae clipeique sub orbe teguntur.

---

[201] Neptuni *Pγ.*
[216] diffugiunt *M.*

wiles and forced tears—we whom neither the son of
Tydeus nor Achilles of Larissa laid low, not ten years,
not a thousand ships!

¹⁹⁹ " Hereupon another portent, more fell and more
frightful by far, is thrust upon us, unhappy ones, and
confounds our unforeseeing souls. Laocoön, priest of
Neptune, as drawn by lot, was slaying a great bull at
the wonted altars ; and lo! from Tenedos, over the
peaceful depths—I shudder as I tell the tale—a pair of
serpents with endless coils are breasting the sea and
side by side making for the shore. Their bosoms
rise amid the surge, and their crests, blood-red, over-
top the waves ; the rest of them skims the main
behind and their huge backs curve in many a fold ;
we hear the sound sent from foaming seas. And now
they were gaining the fields and, with blazing eyes
suffused with blood and fire, were licking with quiver-
ing tongues their hissing mouths. Pale at the sight,
we scatter. They in unswerving course fare towards
Laocoön ; and first each serpent enfolds in its embrace
the youthful bodies of his two sons and with its fangs
feeds upon the hapless limbs. Then himself too, as
he comes to their aid, weapons in hand, they seize
and bind in mighty folds ; and now, twice encircling
his waist, twice winding their scaly backs around his
throat, they tower above with head and lofty necks.
He the while strains his hands to burst the knots, his
fillets steeped in gore and black venom ; the while he
lifts to heaven hideous cries, like the bellowings of
a wounded bull that has fled from the altar and
shaken from its neck the ill-aimed axe. But,
gliding away, the dragon pair escape to the lofty
shrines, and seek fierce Tritonia's citadel, there
to nestle under the goddess' feet and the circle of
her shield.

VIRGIL

"Tum vero tremefacta novus per pectora cunctis
insinuat pavor, et scelus expendisse merentem
Laocoonta ferunt, sacrum qui cuspide robur   230
laeserit et tergo sceleratam intorserit hastam.
ducendum ad sedes simulacrum orandaque divae
numina conclamant.
dividimus muros et moenia pandimus urbis.
accingunt omnes operi pedibusque rotarum   235
subiciunt lapsus et stuppea vincula collo
intendunt.   scandit fatalis machina muros,
feta armis.   pueri circum innuptaeque puellae
sacra canunt funemque manu contingere gaudent;
illa subit mediaeque minans inlabitur urbi.   240
o patria, o divum domus Ilium et incluta bello
moenia Dardanidum!   quater ipso in limine portae
substitit, atque utero sonitum quater arma dedere:
instamus tamen immemores caecique furore
et monstrum infelix sacrata sistimus arce.   245
tunc etiam fatis aperit Cassandra futuris
ora, dei iussu non umquam credita Teucris.
nos delubra deum miseri, quibus ultimus esset
ille dies, festa velamus fronde per urbem.

"Vertitur interea caelum et ruit Oceano nox,   250
involvens umbra magna terramque polumque
Myrmidonumque dolos; fusi per moenia Teucri
conticuere, sopor fessos complectitur artus.
et iam Argiva phalanx instructis navibus ibat   FMP
a Tenedo, tacitae per amica silentia lunae   255
litora nota petens, flammas cum regia puppis

magnam *Pγ*.

228 " Then indeed a strange terror steals through the shuddering hearts of all, and Laocoön, 'tis said, has rightly paid the penalty of crime, who with his lance profaned the sacred oak and hurled into its body the accursed spear. ' Draw the image to her house,' all cry, ' and supplicate her godhead.' We part the walls and lay bare the city's battlements. All gird themselves for the work ; under the feet they place gliding wheels, and about the neck stretch hempen bands. The fateful engine climbs our walls, big with arms. Around it boys and unwedded girls chant holy songs and delight to touch the cable with their hands. Up it moves, and glides threatening into the city's midst. O motherland ! O Ilium, home of gods, and ye Dardan battlements, famed in war ! Four times at the gates' very threshold it halted, and four times from its paunch the armour clashed ; yet we press on, heedless and blind with frenzy, and set the ill-omened monster on our hallowed citadel. Even then Cassandra opened her lips for the coming doom—lips at a god's command never believed by the Trojans. We, hapless ones, for whom that day was our last, wreathe the fanes of the gods with festal boughs throughout the city.

250 " Meanwhile the sky revolves and night rushes from the ocean, wrapping in its mighty shade earth and heaven and the wiles of the Myrmidons. Through the town the Teucrians lay stretched in silence ; sleep clasps their weary limbs.

254 " And now the Argive host, with marshalled ships, was moving from Tenedos, amid the friendly silence of the peaceful moon, seeking the well-known shores, when the royal galley had raised the beacon light[1]—and Sinon, shielded by the gods' malign doom,

[1] This was probably meant as a signal to Sinon. The *-que* (257) connects *laxat* with *ibat* (254).

extulerat, fatisque deum defensus iniquis
inclusos utero Danaos et pinea furtim
laxat claustra Sinon.   illos patefactus ad auras
reddit equus, laetique cavo se robore promunt   260
Thessandrus Sthenelusque duces et dirus Ulixes,
demissum lapsi per funem, Acamasque Thoasque
Pelidesque Neoptolemus primusque Machaon
et Menelaus et ipse doli fabricator Epeos.
invadunt urbem somno vinoque sepultam,   265
caeduntur vigiles, portisque patentibus omnis
accipiunt socios atque agmina conscia iungunt.

  " Tempus erat, quo prima quies mortalibus aegris
incipit et dono divum gratissima serpit.
in somnis, ecce, ante oculos maestissimus Hector   270
visus adesse mihi largosque effundere fletus,
raptatus bigis, ut quondam, aterque cruento
pulvere perque pedes traiectus lora tumentis.
ei mihi, qualis erat !   quantum mutatus ab illo
Hectore, qui redit exuvias indutus Achilli   275
vel Danaum Phrygios iaculatus puppibus ignis !
squalentem barbam et concretos sanguine crinis
volneraque illa gerens, quae circum plurima muros
accepit patrios.   ultro flens ipse videbar
compellare virum et maestas expromere voces :   280
' o lux Dardaniae, spes o fidissima Teucrum,
quae tantae tenuere morae ?   quibus Hector ab oris
exspectate venis ?   ut te post multa tuorum
funera, post varios hominumque urbisque labores
defessi aspicimus !   quae causa indigna serenos   285
foedavit voltus ?   aut cur haec volnera cerno ? '
ille nihil, nec me quaerentem vana moratur,
sed graviter gemitus imo de pectore ducens,   FMPV
' heu ! fuge, nate dea, teque his,' ait, ' eripe flammis.

  ²⁶¹ divus *F¹*, *Charisius:* dius *Macrobius:* durus *Berne
Scholia.*

332

stealthily sets free from the barriers of pine the
Danaans shut within the womb. The opened horse
restores them to the air, and there joyfully come
forth from the hollow wood Thessandrus and
Sthenelus the captains, and dread Ulysses, sliding
down the lowered rope; Acamas and Thoas and
Neoptolemus son of Peleus, the leader Machaon,
Menelaus, and Epeus himself, who devised the fraud.
They storm the city, buried in sleep and wine; slay
the watch, and at the open gates welcome their
comrades and unite confederate bands.

²⁶⁸ " It was the hour when for weary mortals their
first rest begins, and by grace of the gods steals over
them most sweet. In slumbers, lo! before my eyes
there seemed to stand Hector, most sorrowful and
shedding floods of tears; torn by the car, as once
of old, and black with gory dust, his swollen feet
pierced with thongs. Ah me! what aspect was his!
how changed from that Hector who returns after
donning the spoils of Achilles or hurling on Danaan
ships the Phrygian fires! with ragged beard, with
hair matted with blood, and bearing those many
wounds he gat around his native walls. Methought I
wept myself, hailing him first, and uttering words of
grief: 'O light of the Dardan land, O surest hope of
the Trojans, what long delay hath held thee? From
what shores, Hector, comest thou, the long looked
for? Oh, how gladly after the many deaths of thy
kin, after divers sorrows of people and city, our
weary eyes behold thee! What shameful cause hath
marred that unclouded face? or why see I these
wounds?' He replies naught, nor heeds my idle
questioning, but heavily drawing sighs from his
bosom's depths, 'Ah, flee, goddess-born,' he cries,
'and snatch thyself from these flames. The foe

313

hostis habet muros; ruit alto a culmine Troia.   290
sat patriae Priamoque datum : si Pergama dextra
defendi possent, etiam hac defensa fuissent.
sacra suosque tibi commendat Troia Penatis :
hos cape fatorum comites, his moenia quaere,
magna pererrato statues quae denique ponto.'   295
sic ait, et manibus vittas Vestamque potentem
aeternumque adytis effert penetralibus ignem.

" Diverso interea miscentur moenia luctu,
et magis atque magis, quamquam secreta parentis
Anchisae domus arboribusque obtecta recessit,   300
clarescunt sonitus armorumque ingruit horror.
excutior somno et summi fastigia tecti
ascensu supero atque arrectis auribus adsto :
in segetem veluti cum flamma furentibus Austris
incidit, aut rapidus montano flumine torrens   305
sternit agros, sternit sata laeta boumque labores
praecipitesque trahit silvas; stupet inscius alto
accipiens sonitum saxi de vertice pastor.
tum vero manifesta fides, Danaumque patescunt
insidiae.   iam Deiphobi dedit ampla ruinam   MPV
Volcano superante domus; iam proximus ardet   311
Ucalegon; Sigea igni freta lata relucent.
exoritur clamorque virum clangorque tubarum.
arma amens capio; nec sat rationis in armis,   MP
sed glomerare manum bello et concurrere in
          arcem   315
cum sociis ardent animi; furor iraque mentem
praecipitant, pulchrumque mori succurrit in armis.

" Ecce autem telis Panthus elapsus Achivum,
Panthus Othryades, arcis Phoebique sacerdos,

299 et] at *M*¹.
307 stupet] sedet *Quintilian*, VIII. VI. 10.
317 praecipitat *P*γ.

314

holds our walls; Troy falls from her lofty height. All claims are paid to king and country; if Troy's towers could be saved by strength of hand, by mine, too, had they been saved. Troy commits to thee her holy things and household gods; take them to share thy fortunes: seek for them the city—the mighty city which, when thou hast wandered over the deep thou shalt at last establish!' So he speaks and in his hands brings forth from the inner shrine the fillets, great Vesta, and the undying fire.

298 "On every side, meanwhile, the city is in a turmoil of anguish; and more and more, though my father Anchises' house lay far withdrawn and screened by trees, clearer grow the sounds and war's dread din sweeps on. I shake myself from sleep and, climbing to the roof's topmost height, stand with straining ears: even as, when fire falls on a corn-field while south winds are raging, or the rushing torrent from a mountain-stream lays low the fields, lays low the glad crops and labours of oxen and drags down forests headlong, spell-bound the be-wildered shepherd hears the roar from a rock's lofty peak. Then indeed the truth is clear and the guile of the Danaans grows manifest. Even now the spacious house of Deiphobus has fallen, as the fire-god towers above; even now his neighbour Ucalegon blazes; the broad Sigean straits reflect the flames. Then rise the cries of men and the blare of clarions. Frantic I seize arms; yet little purpose is there in arms, but my heart burns to muster a force for battle and hasten with my comrades to the citadel. Rage and wrath drive my soul headlong and I think how glorious it is to die in arms!

318 "But lo! Panthus, escaping from Achaean swords—Panthus, son of Othrys, priest of Phoebus

315

sacra manu victosque deos parvumque nepotem   320
ipse trahit cursuque amens ad limina tendit.
'quo res summa loco, Panthu? quam prendimus
    arcem?'
vix ea fatus eram, gemitu cum talia reddit:
' venit summa dies et ineluctabile tempus
Dardaniae. fuimus Troes, fuit Ilium et ingens   325
gloria Teucrorum; ferus omnia Iuppiter Argos
transtulit; incensa Danai dominantur in urbe.
arduus armatos mediis in moenibus adstans
fundit equus victorque Sinon incendia miscet
insultans. portis alii bipatentibus adsunt,   330
milia quot magnis umquam venere Mycenis;
obsedere alii telis angusta viarum
oppositis; stat ferri acies mucrone corusco
stricta, parata neci; vix primi proelia temptant
portarum vigiles et caeco Marte resistunt.'   335
talibus Othryadae dictis et numine divum
in flammas et in arma feror, quo tristis Erinys,
quo fremitus vocat et sublatus ad aethera clamor.
addunt se socios Ripheus et maximus armis
Epytus, oblati per lunam, Hypanisque Dymasque,   340
et lateri adglomerant nostro, iuvenisque Coroebus
Mygdonides: illis ad Troiam forte diebus
venerat, insano Cassandrae incensus amore,
et gener auxilium Priamo Phrygibusque ferebat,
infelix, qui non sponsae praecepta furentis   345
audierit!
quos ubi confertos audere in proelia vidi,
incipio super his: 'iuvenes, fortissima frustra
pectora, si vobis audentem extrema cupido
certa sequi, quae sit rebus fortuna videtis.   350
excessere omnes adytis arisque relictis

---

    321 cursum *also known to Servius.*
    333 oppositi $\gamma^2a^2bc^2$. *P's reading lost.*
    349 audendi $M\gamma^1a^1c$: auden- *P*: audentem γ^2a^2b, *preferred by Servius.*

on the citadel—in his own hand bearing the holy
things and vanquished gods, and dragging his little
grandchild, runs frantic to my doors. ' How fares the
state, Panthus ? What stronghold shall we seize ?'
Scarcely had I said the words, when with a groan he
answers thus: ' It is come—the last day and inevi-
table hour for Troy. We Trojans are not, Ilium is
not, and the great glory of the Teucrians; in wrath
Jupiter has taken all away to Argos ; our city is aflame,
and in it the Greeks are lords. The horse, standing
high in the city's midst, pours forth armed men, and
Sinon, victorious, insolently scatters flames ! Some
are at the wide-open gates, as many thousands
as ever came from mighty Mycenae ; others with
confronting weapons have barred the narrow ways ;
a standing line of steel, with flashing point un-
sheathed, is ready for the slaughter. Scarce do the
first guards of the gates essay battle, and resist in
blind warfare.'

[336] "By such words of Othrys' son and by divine
will I am driven amid flames and weapons, where the
fell Fury, where the roar and the shouts rising to
heaven call. Then, falling in with me in the moon-
light, comrades join me, and there gather to our side
Ripheus and Epytus, mighty in arms, Hypanis and
Dymas, with young Coroebus, son of Mygdon. In
those days, as it chanced, he had come to Troy, fired
with mad love for Cassandra, and as a son was bring-
ing aid to Priam and the Phrygians—luckless one,
not to have heeded the warning of his inspired
bride ! When I saw them in close ranks and eager for
battle, I thereon begin thus : *My men, hearts vainly
valiant, if your desire is fixed to follow me in my final
venture, ye see what is the fate of our cause. All the
gods on whom this empire was stayed have gone forth,

VIRGIL

di, quibus imperium hoc steterat; succurritis urbi
incensae: moriamur et in media arma ruamus.
una salus victis nullam sperare salutem.'
sic animis iuvenum furor additus. inde, lupi ceu 355
raptores atra in nebula, quos improba ventris
exegit caecos rabies catulique relicti
faucibus exspectant siccis, per tela, per hostis
vadimus haud dubiam in mortem mediaeque tenemus
urbis iter; nox atra cava circumvolat umbra.   360
quis cladem illius noctis, quis funera fando
explicet aut possit lacrimis aequare labores?
urbs antiqua ruit, multos dominata per annos;
plurima perque vias sternuntur inertia passim
corpora perque domos et religiosa deorum   365
limina. nec soli poenas dant sanguine Teucri:
quondam etiam victis redit in praecordia virtus
victoresque cadunt Danai. crudelis ubique
luctus, ubique pavor et plurima mortis imago.

"Primus se Danaum magna comitante caterva 370
Androgeos offert nobis, socia agmina credens
inscius, atque ultro verbis compellat amicis:
'festinate, viri! nam quae tam sera moratur
segnities? alii rapiunt incensa feruntque
Pergama; vos celsis nunc primum a navibus itis?'
dixit et extemplo (neque enim responsa dabantur 376
fida satis) sensit medios delapsus in hostis.
obstipuit retroque pedem cum voce repressit.
improvisum aspris veluti qui sentibus anguem
pressit humi nitens, trepidusque repente refugit 380
attollentem iras et caerula colla tumentem;
haud secus Androgeos visu tremefactus abibat.
318

leaving shrine and altar; the city ye aid is in flames. Let us die, and rush into the midst of arms. One safety the vanquished have, to hope for none!'

355 "Thus their young spirits were spurred to fury. Then, like ravening wolves in a black mist, when the belly's lawless rage has driven them blindly forth, and their whelps at home await them with thirsty jaws; through swords, through foes we pass to certain death, and hold our way to the city's heart; black night hovers around with sheltering shade. Who could unfold in speech that night's havoc? Who its carnage? or who could match our toils with tears? The ancient city falls, for many years a queen; in heaps lifeless corpses lie scattered amid the streets, amid the homes and hallowed portals of the gods. Nor do Teucrians alone pay penalty with their life-blood; at times valour returns to the hearts of the vanquished also and the Danaan victors fall. Everywhere is cruel grief, everywhere panic, and full many a shape of death!

370 "First, with a great throng of Greeks attending him, Androgeos meets us, in ignorance deeming us an allied band, and hails us forthwith in friendly words: 'Hasten, men; why, what sloth keeps you back so long? Others sack and ravage burning Pergamus; are ye but now coming from the tall ships?' He spoke, and at once—for no reply that he could well trust was offered—knew that he had fallen into the midst of foes. He was dazed, and drawing back checked foot and voice. As one who has crushed a serpent unseen amid the rough briars, when stepping firmly on the ground, and in sudden terror shrinks back as it rises in wrath and puffs out its purple neck; so Androgeos, affrighted at the sight, was drawing away. We

319

VIRGIL

inruimus densis et circumfundimur armis,
ignarosque loci passim et formidine captos
sternimus. adspirat primo Fortuna labori. 385
atque hic successu exsultans animisque Coroebus,
' o socii, qua prima' inquit ' fortuna salutis
monstrat iter, quaque ostendit se dextra, sequamur :
mutemus clipeos Danaumque insignia nobis
aptemus. dolus an virtus, quis in hoste requirat? 390
arma dabunt ipsi.'   sic fatus deinde comantem
Androgei galeam clipeique insigne decorum
induitur laterique Argivum accommodat ensem.
hoc Ripheus, hoc ipse Dymas omnisque iuventus
laeta facit ; spoliis se quisque recentibus armat. 395
vadimus immixti Danais haud numine nostro,
multaque per caecam congressi proelia noctem
conserimus, multos Danaum demittimus Orco.
diffugiunt alii ad navis et litora cursu
fida petunt, pars ingentem formidine turpi 400
scandunt rursus equum et nota conduntur in alvo.

   "Heu! nihil invitis fas quemquam fidere divis !
ecce trahebatur passis Priameia virgo
crinibus a templo Cassandra adytisque Minervae,
ad caelum tendens ardentia lumina frustra, 405
lumina, nam teneras arcebant vincula palmas.
non tulit hanc speciem furiata mente Coroebus
et sese medium iniecit periturus in agmen.
consequimur cuncti et densis incurrimus armis.
hic primum ex alto delubri culmine telis 410
nostrorum obruimur oriturque miserrima caedes
armorum facie et Graiarum errore iubarum.
tum Danai gemitu atque ereptae virginis ira

---

383 circumfudimus *P.*   **387** quae *Mγ¹a¹, known to Servius.*
392 Androgei *MSS., Servius :* Androgeo *known to gram-*
marians (*Aen.* VI. 20).   **396** immixtis *M¹.*
398 dimittimus *MPγ.*

320

charge and with serried arms stream around them;
in their ignorance of the ground and the surprise
of their panic we slay them on all sides.   Fortune
favours our first effort.   And here Coroebus, flushed
with success and courage, cries: 'Comrades, where
fortune first points out the road to safety and where
she shows herself auspicious, let us follow.   Change
we the shields and don the Danaan emblems;
whether deceit or valour, who would ask in warfare?
Our foes themselves shall give us weapons.'   So
saying, he then puts on the plumed helmet of
Androgeos, and the shield with its comely device, and
fits to his side the Argive sword.   So does Ripheus,
so Dymas too, and all the youth in delight; each
man arms himself in the new-won spoils.   We move
on, mingling with the Greeks, under gods not our
own, and in the blind night we clash in many a close
fight, and many a Greek send down to Orcus.   Some
scatter to the ships and make with speed for the
safe shores; some in base terror again climb the
huge horse and hide in the well-known womb.

402 "Alas! in naught may one trust the gods
against their will!   Lo! Priam's daughter, maiden
Cassandra, was being dragged with streaming hair
from the temple and shrine of Minerva, vainly uplift-
ing to heaven her blazing eyes—her eyes, for bonds
confined her tender hands!   Maddened in soul,
Coroebus brooked not this sight, but flung himself to
death into the midst of the band.   We all follow and
charge with serried arms.   Here first from the high
temple roof we are overwhelmed with the weapons
of our friends, and piteous slaughter arises from the
appearance of our arms and the confusion of our
Greek crests.   Then the Danaans, with a shout of
rage at the maiden's rescue, mustering from all sides,

undique collecti invadunt, acerrimus Aiax
et gemini Atridae Dolopumque exercitus omnis; 415
adversi rupto ceu quondam turbine venti
confligunt, Zephyrusque Notusque et laetus Eois
Eurus equis; stridunt silvae saevitque tridenti
spumeus atque imo Nereus ciet aequora fundo.
illi etiam, si quos obscura nocte per umbram   420
fudimus insidiis totaque agitavimus urbe,
apparent; primi clipeos mentitaque tela
adgnoscunt atque ora sono discordia signant.
ilicet obruimur numero; primusque Coroebus
Penelei dextra divae armipotentis ad aram   425
procumbit; cadit et Ripheus, iustissimus unus
qui fuit in Teucris et servantissimus aequi
(dis aliter visum); pereunt Hypanisque Dymasque
confixi a sociis; nec te tua plurima, Panthu,
labentem pietas nec Apollinis infula texit.   430
Iliaci cineres et flamma extrema meorum,
testor in occasu vestro nec tela nec ullas
vitavisse vices Danaum et, si fata fuissent,
ut caderem meruisse manu.   divellimur inde,
Iphitus et Pelias mecum, quorum Iphitus aevo   435
iam gravior, Pelias et volnere tardus Ulixi;
protinus ad sedes Priami clamore vocati.   FMP

    " Hic vero ingentem pugnam, ceu cetera nus-
        quam
bella forent, nulli tota morerentur in urbe,
sic Martem indomitum Danaosque ad tecta ruentis 440
cernimus obsessumque acta testudine limen.
haerent parietibus scalae, postisque sub ipsos
nituntur gradibus clipeosque ad tela sinistris

----

    [422] primi: *the erasure of a letter before* m *in* P *led Ribbeck
to read* Priami.
    [442] ac tela *F²MPγ, known to Servius and read by Mackail:*
ad tecta *F¹.*

fall upon us, Ajax most fiercely, the two sons of
Atreus, and the whole Dolopian host : even as at
times, when a hurricane bursts forth, diverse winds
clash, West and South and East, proud of his orient
steeds ; the forests groan and Nereus, steeped in
foam, storms with his trident, and stirs the seas from
their lowest depths. There appear, too, those whom
amid the shade of the dim night we had routed
by stratagem and driven throughout the town ; they
first recognize our shields and lying weapons, and
mark our speech as differing in tone. Straightway
we are overwhelmed with odds ; and first Coroebus
falls at the hand of Peneleus by the altar of the
warrior goddess ; Ripheus, too, falls, foremost in
justice among the Trojans, and most zealous for
the right—Heaven's will was otherwise ; Hypanis
and Dymas perish, pierced by friends ; nor could
all thy goodness, Panthus, nor Apollo's fillet shield
thee in thy fall ! O ashes of Ilium ! O funeral
flames of my kin ! I call you to witness that in
your doom I shunned not the Danaan weapons
nor their answering blows, and had the fates willed
my fall, I had earned it by my hand ! We are torn
from there, with me Iphitus and Pelias, Iphitus now
burdened with years, Pelias slow-footed, too, under a
wound from Ulysses. Straightway we are called by
the clamour to Priam's house.

⁴³⁸ " Here indeed is a mighty battle, as if the
rest of the fighting nowhere had place, as if none
were dying throughout the city ; so do we see the
god of war unbridled, Danaans rushing to the roof
and the threshold beset with an assaulting mantlet
of shields. Ladders hug the walls, under the very
door-posts men force a way on the rungs ; with left
hands they hold up protecting shields against the

protecti obiciunt, prensant fastigia dextris.
Dardanidae contra turris ac tecta domorum   445
culmina convellunt ; his se, quando ultima cernunt,
extrema iam in morte parant defendere telis ;
auratasque trabes, veterum decora illa parentum,
devolvunt : alii strictis mucronibus imas
obsedere fores ; has servant agmine denso.   450
instaurati animi regis succurrere tectis
auxilioque levare viros vimque addere victis.

"Limen erat caecaeque fores et pervius usus
tectorum inter se Priami postesque relicti
a tergo, infelix qua se, dum regna manebant,   455
saepius Andromache ferre incomitata solebat
ad soceros et avo puerum Astyanacta trahebat.
evado ad summi fastigia culminis, unde
tela manu miseri iactabant inrita Teucri.
turrim in praecipiti stantem summisque sub astra 460
eductam tectis, unde omnis Troia videri
et Danaum solitae naves et Achaica castra,
adgressi ferro circum, qua summa labantis
iuncturas tabulata dabant, convellimus altis
sedibus impulimusque ; ea lapsa repente ruinam 465
cum sonitu trahit et Danaum super agmina late
incidit.   ast alii subeunt, nec saxa nec ullum
telorum interea cessat genus.   [MP

"Vestibulum ante ipsum primoque in limine Pyrrhus
exsultat telis et luce coruscus aëna ;   MPV
qualis ubi in lucem coluber mala gramina pastus, 471
frigida sub terra tumidum quem bruma tegebat,
nunc positis novus exuviis nitidusque iuventa
lubrica convolvit sublato pectore terga,

⁴⁴⁵ tecta *F¹M, Priscian, Servius:* tɔta *P²:* tota *P¹γ, known
to Servius.*   ⁴⁴⁸ illa *F¹P:* alta *F²M, Priscian.*
⁴⁵⁰ asservant *P¹γ¹, known to Servius.*   ⁴⁶² Achaia *F.*
⁴⁶⁵ ea lapsa] elapsa *P¹.*   repente] ruente *P¹:* ruina *M¹.*
⁴⁷⁴ convolvens *V¹:* convolvent *V².*

darts, and with right they clutch the battlements.
The Trojans in turn tear down the towers and roof-
covering of the palace; with these as missiles—for
they see the end near—even at the point of death
they prepare to defend themselves; and roll down
gilded rafters, the splendours of their fathers of old.
Others with drawn swords have beset the doors
below, and guard them, closely massed. Our spirits
are quickened to succour the king's dwelling, to
relieve our men by our aid and bring fresh force to
the vanquished.

⁴⁵³ "There was an entrance with secret doors, a
passage running from hall to hall of Priam's palace,
a postern gate apart, by which, while the kingdom
yet stood, Andromache, poor soul! would oft-times
unattended pass to her husband's parents, and lead
the little Astyanax to his grandsire. I gain the
roof's topmost height, whence the hapless Teucrians
were hurling amain their useless missiles. A tower
stood on the sheer edge, rising skyward from the
roof-top, whence all Troy was wont to be seen, and
the Danaan ships and the Achaean camp. Assailing
this with iron round about, where the topmost stories
offered weak joints, we wrenched it from its lofty
place and thrust it forth. With sudden fall it trails a
thunderous ruin, and over the Danaan ranks crashes
far and wide. Yet more come up, nor meanwhile
do stones nor any kind of missiles cease.

⁴⁶⁹ "Just before the entrance-court and at the
very portal is Pyrrhus, proudly gleaming in the
sheen of brazen arms: even as when into the light
comes a snake, fed on poisonous herbs, whom cold
winter kept swollen underground, now, his slough
cast off, fresh and glistening in youth, with uplifted
breast he rolls his slippery length, towering towards

VIRGIL

arduus ad solem, et linguis micat ore trisulcis.   **475**
una ingens Periphas et equorum agitator Achillis,
armiger Automedon, una omnis Scyria pubes
succedunt tecto et flammas ad culmina iactant.
ipse inter primos correpta dura bipenni
limina perrumpit postisque a cardine vellit   **480**
aeratos; iamque excisa trabe firma cavavit
robora et ingentem lato dedit ore fenestram.
apparet domus intus et atria longa patescunt;
apparent Priami et veterum penetralia regum
armatosque vident stantis in limine primo.   **485**

"At domus interior gemitu miseroque tumultu
miscetur, penitusque cavae plangoribus aedes
femineis ululant; ferit aurea sidera clamor.
tum pavidae tectis matres ingentibus errant
amplexaeque tenent postis atque oscula figunt.   **490**
instat vi patria Pyrrhus : nec claustra nec ipsi
custodes sufferre valent; labat ariete crebro
ianua et emoti procumbunt cardine postes.
fit via vi ; rumpunt aditus primosque trucidant
immissi Danai et late loca milite complent.   **495**
non sic, aggeribus ruptis cum spumeus amnis
exiit oppositasque evicit gurgite moles,   MP
fertur in arva furens cumulo camposque per omnis
cum stabulis armenta trahit. vidi ipse furentem   499
caede Neoptolemum geminosque in limine Atridas,
vidi Hecubam centumque nurus Priamumque per aras
sanguine foedantem quos ipse sacraverat ignis.
quinquaginta illi thalami, spes tanta nepotum,

---

[503] spes tanta $M\gamma^2$, *Servius:* spes ampla P (pla *lacking*) γ^1.
326

the sun and darting from his mouth a three-forked
tongue! With him huge Periphas and Automedon
his armour-bearer, driver of Achilles' horses; with
him all the Scyrian youth close on the dwelling and
hurl flames to the roof. Pyrrhus himself among
the foremost grasps a battle-axe, bursts through the
stubborn gateway, and from their hinge tears the
brass-bound doors; and now, heaving out a panel, he
has breached the solid oak and made a huge wide-
mouthed gap. Open to view is the house within,
and the long halls are bared; open to view are the
inner chambers of Priam and the kings of old, and
armed men are seen standing at the very threshold.

486 "But within, amid shrieks and woeful uproar,
the house is in confusion, and at its heart the
vaulted halls ring with women's wails; the din strikes
the golden stars. Then through the vast dwelling
trembling matrons roam, clinging fast to the doors
and imprinting kisses thereon. On presses Pyrrhus
with his father's might; no bars, no warders even
can stay his course. The gate totters under the
ram's many blows and the doors, wrenched from
their sockets, fall forward. Force finds a way; the
Greeks, pouring in, burst a passage, slaughter the
foremost, and fill the wide space with soldiery. Not
with such fury, when a foaming river, bursting its
barriers, has overflowed and with its torrent over-
whelmed the resisting banks, does it rush furiously
upon the fields in a mass and over all the plains
sweep herds and folds. I myself saw on the threshold
Neoptolemus, mad with slaughter, and both the
sons of Atreus; I saw Hecuba and her hundred
daughters, and amid the altars Priam, polluting with
his blood the fires he himself had hallowed. The
famous fifty chambers, the rich promise of offspring,

barbarico postes auro spoliisque superbi
procubuere; tenent Danai, qua deficit ignis.   505
   " Forsitan et, Priami fuerint quae fata, requiras.
urbis uti captae casum convolsaque vidit
limina tectorum et medium in penetralibus hostem,
arma diu senior desueta trementibus aevo
circumdat nequiquam umeris et inutile ferrum   510
cingitur, ac densos fertur moriturus in hostis.
aedibus in mediis nudoque sub aetheris axe
ingens ara fuit iuxtaque veterrima laurus,
incumbens arae atque umbra complexa Penatis.
hic Hecuba et natae nequiquam altaria circum,   515
praecipites atra ceu tempestate columbae,
condensae et divum amplexae simulacra sedebant.
ipsum autem sumptis Priamum iuvenalibus armis
ut vidit, 'quae mens tam dira, miserrime coniunx,
impulit his cingi telis? aut quo ruis?' inquit.   520
'non tali auxilio nec defensoribus istis
tempus eget; non, si ipse meus nunc adforet Hector.
huc tandem concede; haec ara tuebitur omnis,
aut moriere simul.' sic ore effata recepit
ad sese et sacra longaevum in sede locavit.   525
   " Ecce autem elapsus Pyrrhi de caede Polites,
unus natorum Priami, per tela, per hostis,
porticibus longis fugit et vacua atria lustrat
saucius.   illum ardens infesto volnere Pyrrhus
insequitur, iam iamque manu tenet et premit hasta.
ut tandem ante oculos evasit et ora parentum,   531
concidit ac multo vitam cum sanguine fudit.

the doors proud with the spoils of barbaric gold, fall low; where the fire fails, the Greeks hold sway.

506 " Perchance, too, thou mayest inquire what was Priam's fate. When he saw the fall of the captured city, saw the doors of the house wrenched off, and the foe in the heart of his home, old as he is, he vainly throws his long-disused armour about his aged trembling shoulders, girds on his useless sword, and rushes to his death among his thronging foes.

512 " In the midst of the house and beneath the open arch of heaven was a huge altar, and hard by an ancient laurel, leaning against the altar and clasping the household gods in its shade. Here, round the shrines, vainly crouched Hecuba and her daughters, huddled together like doves swept before a black storm, and clasping the images of the gods. But when she saw even Priam harnessed in the armour of his youth, 'My poor, poor husband,' she cries, 'what thought so mad drove thee to gird on these weapons? or whither wouldst thou rush? Not such the aid nor these the defenders the hour craves, no, not though my own Hector were here himself! Draw hither, pray; this altar will guard us all, or thou wilt die with us!' Thus she spoke, then drew the aged man to her and placed him on the holy seat.

526 " But lo! escaping from the sword of Pyrrhus, through darts, through foes, Polites, one of Priam's sons, flees down the long colonnades and, wounded, traverses the empty courts. Pyrrhus presses hotly upon him eager to strike, and now, even now catches him and with spear plies him close. When at last he came before the eyes and faces of his parents, he fell, and poured out his life in a stream of blood. Hereupon Priam, though now in

hic Priamus, quamquam in media iam morte tenetur,
non tamen abstinuit nec voci iraeque pepercit:
'at tibi pro scelere' exclamat, 'pro talibus ausis 535
di, si qua est caelo pietas, quae talia curet,
persolvant grates dignas et praemia reddant
debita, qui nati coram me cernere letum
fecisti et patrios foedasti funere voltus.
at non ille, satum quo te mentiris, Achilles 540
talis in hoste fuit Priamo ; sed iura fidemque
supplicis erubuit corpusque exsangue sepulchro
reddidit Hectoreum meque in mea regna remisit.'
sic fatus senior, telumque imbelle sine ictu
coniecit, rauco quod protinus aere repulsum 545
et summo clipei nequiquam umbone pependit.
cui Pyrrhus: 'referes ergo haec et nuntius ibis
Pelidae genitori ; illi mea tristia facta
degeneremque Neoptolemum narrare memento ;
nunc morere.' hoc dicens altaria ad ipsa tre-
        mentem 550
traxit et in multo lapsantem sanguine nati,
implicuitque comam laeva, dextraque coruscum
extulit ac lateri capulo tenus abdidit ensem.
haec finis Priami fatorum ; hic exitus illum 554
sorte tulit, Troiam incensam et prolapsa videntem
Pergama, tot quondam populis terrisque superbum
regnatorem Asiae.   iacet ingens litore truncus,
avolsumque umeris caput et sine nomine corpus.

    "At me tum primum saevus circumstetit horror.
obstipui ; subiit cari genitoris imago, 560
ut regem aequaevum crudeli volnere vidi
vitam exhalantem ; subiit deserta Creusa
et direpta domus et parvi casus Iuli.
respicio et, quae sit me circum copia, lustro.

⁵⁵² coma *Pγ*.   laevam *P*.

death's closest grasp, yet held not back nor spared his voice and wrath: 'Nay, for thy crime, for deeds so heinous,' he cries, 'if in heaven there is any righteousness to mark such sins, may the gods pay thee fitting thanks and render thee due rewards, who hast made me look on my own son's murder, and defiled with death a father's face! Nay, not so with his foe Priam dealt that Achilles whose sonship thou falsely claimest, but he had respect for a suppliant's rights and trust; he gave back to the tomb Hector's bloodless corpse and sent me back to my realm.' So spake the old man and hurled his weak and harmless spear, which straight recoiled from the clanging brass and hung idly from the top of the shield's boss. To him Pyrrhus: 'Then thou shalt bear this news and go as messenger to my sire, Peleus' son; tell him, be sure, of my sorry deeds and his degenerate Neoptolemus! Now die!' So saying, to the very altar-stones he drew him, trembling and slipping in his son's streaming blood, and wound his left hand in his hair, while with the right he raised high the flashing sword and buried it to the hilt in his side. Such was the close of Priam's fortunes; such the doom that by fate befell him—to see Troy in flames and Pergamus laid·low, he once lord of so many tribes and lands, the monarch of Asia. He lies a huge trunk upon the shore, a head severed from the shoulders, a nameless corpse!

⁵⁵⁹ "Then first an awful horror encompassed me. I stood aghast, and there rose before me the form of my dear father, as I looked upon the king, of like age, gasping away his life under a cruel wound. There rose forlorn Creüsa, the pillaged house, and the fate of little Iülus. I look back and scan the force about me. All, outworn, have deserted me

deseruere omnes defessi et corpora saltu   565
ad terram misere aut ignibus aegra dedere.

Servius
in *Vita
Vergilii* " Iamque adeo super unus eram, cum limina Vestae
servantem et tacitam secreta in sede latentem
Tyndarida aspicio ; dant clara incendia lucem
erranti passimque oculos per cuncta ferenti.   570
illa sibi infestos eversa ob Pergama Teucros
et Danaum poenam et deserti coniugis iras
praemetuens, Troiae et patriae communis Erinys,
abdiderat sese atque aris invisa sedebat.
exarsere ignes animo ; subit ira cadentem   575
ulcisci patriam et sceleratas sumere poenas.
'scilicet haec Spartam incolumis patriasque Mycenas
aspiciet partoque ibit regina triumpho,
coniugiumque domumque patres natosque videbit,
Iliadum turba et Phrygiis comitata ministris ?   580
occiderit ferro Priamus ?   Troia arserit igni ?
Dardanium totiens sudarit sanguine litus ?
non ita.   namque etsi nullum memorabile nomen
feminea in poena est nec habet victoria laudem,
exstinxisse nefas tamen et sumpsisse merentis   585
laudabor poenas, animumque explesse iuvabit
ultricis flammae et cineres satiasse meorum.'
talia iactabam et furiata mente ferebar,
cum mihi se, non ante oculis tam clara, videndam MP
obtulit et pura per noctem in luce refulsit   590
alma parens, confessa deam qualisque videri

    ⁵⁶⁷⁻⁵⁸⁸ *eliminated by Varius and Tucca and omitted in all
the best MSS. (e.g. MPγabc), but preserved by Servius. Defended
by Fairclough in " Classical Philology,"* I. *pp.* 221–30.
    ⁵⁸⁴ nec habet] habet haec *MSS., Servius.*
    ⁵⁸⁷ flammae] famam *MSS.*

and flung their bodies to the ground or dropped helpless into the flames.

⁵⁶⁷ " And now,[1] now I alone was left, when I saw, close to Vesta's shrine and silently hiding in the sacred dwelling, the daughter of Tyndareus;[2] the bright fires give me light as I wander and cast my eyes, here and there, over the scene. She, fearing the Trojans' anger against her for the overthrow of Pergamus, the vengeance of the Greeks, and the wrath of her forsaken lord—she, common Fury of Troy and her motherland—had hidden herself and was crouching, hateful thing, by the altars. Fire blazed up in my heart; there comes an angry desire to avenge my falling country and exact the wages of her sin. ' Is she, forsooth, to look on Sparta and her native Mycenae unscathed, and go forth a queen in the triumph she has won? Is she to see husband and home, parents and children, attended by a throng of Ilian maids and Phrygian pages? Is Priam to have fallen by the sword? Troy to be burnt in flames? The Dardan shore to be so often soaked in blood? Not so! For though there is no glorious renown in a woman's punishment and such victory wins no honour, yet I shall have praise for blotting out the unholy thing and exacting a just recompense; and it will be joy to have filled full my soul with the fire of vengeance and to have sated the ashes of my kindred!'

⁵⁸⁸ " Such words I blurted out and in frenzied mind was rushing on, when my gracious mother, never before so brilliant to behold, came before my eyes, in pure radiance gleaming through the night, manifesting the goddess, in beauty and stature such as she is wont to appear to the lords of heaven. She

---

[1] See Introduction, p. ix.   [2] *i.e.* Helen.

caelicolis et quanta solet, dextraque prehensum
continuit roseoque haec insuper addidit ore :
' nate, quis indomitas tantus dolor excitat iras ?
quid furis ?   aut quonam nostri tibi cura recessit ?
non prius aspicies, ubi fessum aetate parentem   596
liqueris Anchisen, superet coniunxne Creusa,
Ascaniusque puer ?   quos omnis undique Graiae
circum errant acies et, ni mea cura resistat,
iam flammae tulerint inimicus et hauserit ensis.   600
non tibi Tyndaridis facies invisa Lacaenae
culpatusve Paris ; divum inclementia, divum,
has evertit opes sternitque a culmine Troiam.
aspice (namque omnem, quae nunc obducta tuenti
mortalis hebetat visus tibi et umida circum   605
caligat, nubem eripiam ; tu ne qua parentis
iussa time neu praeceptis parere recusa):
hic, ubi disiectas moles avolsaque saxis
saxa vides mixtoque undantem pulvere fumum,
Neptunus muros magnoque emota tridenti   610
fundamenta quatit totamque a sedibus urbem
eruit.   hic Iuno Scaeas saevissima portas
prima tenet sociumque furens a navibus agmen
ferro accincta vocat.
iam summas arces Tritonia, respice, Pallas   615
insedit, nimbo effulgens et Gorgone saeva.
ipse pater Danais animos virisque secundas
sufficit, ipse deos in Dardana suscitat arma.
eripe, nate, fugam finemque impone labori.
nusquam abero et tutum patrio te limine sistam.'   620
dixerat et spissis noctis se condidit umbris.
apparent dirae facies inimicaque Troiae
numina magna deum.   MPV

618 limbo *known to Servius:* nimbo MPγ, *preferred by*
Servius.
620 numquam *M*[1], *Servius* (on *Aen.* II. 801).

caught me by the hand and. stayed me, thus, too,
speaking with roseate lips : ' My son, what resent-
ment thus stirs ungovernable wrath ? Why this rage ?
or whither has thy care for me fled ? Wilt thou not
first see where thou hast left thy father, age-worn
Anchises, whether Creüsa thy wife and the boy
Ascanius still live ? All these the Greek lines com-
pass round on every side, and did not my love pre-
vent, ere this the flames had swept them off and the
hostile sword had drunk their blood. Know that it
is not the hated face of the Laconian woman, daughter
of Tyndareus ; it is not Paris that is to blame ; but
the gods, the relentless gods, overturn this wealth and
make Troy topple from her pinnacle. Behold—for all
the cloud, which now, drawn over thy sight, dulls thy
mortal vision and with dark pall enshrouds thee, I
will tear away; fear thou no commands of thy mother
nor refuse to obey her counsels—here, where thou
seest shattered piles and rocks torn from rocks, and
smoke eddying up mixed with dust, Neptune shakes
the walls and foundations that his mighty trident
hath upheaved, and uproots all the city from her
base. Here Juno, fiercest of all, is foremost to
hold the Scaean gates and, girt with steel, furiously
calls from the ships her allied band. Now on the
highest towers—turn and see—Tritonian Pallas is
planted, gleaming with storm-cloud and grim Gorgon.
The Sire himself gives the Greeks courage and
auspicious strength; he himself stirs up the gods
against the Dardan arms. Haste thy flight, my son,
and put an end to thy toil. Never will I leave thee,
but will set thee safely on thy father's threshold.'
She spoke, and vanished in the thick shades of
night. Dread shapes come to view—mighty powers
divine, warring against Troy.

VIRGIL

"Tum vero omne mihi visum considere in ignis
Ilium et ex imo verti Neptunia Troia ;   625
ac veluti summis antiquam in montibus ornum
cum ferro accisam crebrisque bipennibus instant
eruere agricolae certatim ; illa usque minatur
et tremefacta comam concusso vertice nutat,
volneribus donec paulatim evicta supremum 630
congemuit traxitque iugis avolsa ruinam,
descendo ac ducente deo flammam inter et hostis
expedior ; dant tela locum flammaeque recedunt.

"Atque ubi iam patriae perventum ad limina sedis
antiquasque domos, genitor, quem tollere in altos 635
optabam primum montis primumque petebam,
abnegat excisa vitam producere Troia
exsiliumque pati. 'vos o, quibus integer aevi
sanguis,' ait, 'solidaeque suo stant robore vires,
vos agitate fugam.   640
me si caelicolae voluissent ducere vitam,
has mihi servassent sedes. satis una superque
vidimus excidia et captae superavimus urbi.
sic o sic positum adfati discedite corpus.
ipse manu mortem inveniam: miserebitur hostis 645
exuviasque potet. facilis iactura sepulchri.
iam pridem invisus divis et inutilis annos
demoror, ex quo me divum pater atque hominum rex
fulminis adflavit ventis et contigit igni.'

[630] victa *V*. [632] deo *M²V²γ²*, *Macrobius, Donatus, Servius:* dea *M¹P²V¹γ*: de *P¹*. [644] *omitted,* *M¹*: *at foot of page,* *M².* [645] manum *Pγ¹a¹*: morte *P¹*, -em *P²*: manum morti *Klouček. So Sabb.*

[624] " Then, indeed, methought all Ilium sank in flames and Neptune's Troy was upturned from her base—even as when on mountain-tops woodmen emulously strain to overturn an ancient ash-tree, which has been hacked with many a blow of axe and iron; it ever threatens to fall, and nods with trembling leafage and rocking crest, till, little by little, overcome with wounds, it gives one loud last groan and, uptorn from the ridges, comes crashing down. I descend and, guided by a god, make my way amid fire and foes. Weapons give place and the flames retire.

[634] "And now, when I had reached the door of my father's house and the dear old home, my sire, whom it was my first longing to bear high into the hills, and whom first I sought, refused, since Troy was laid low, to prolong his days or suffer exile. 'Ye,' he cried, 'whose blood has the freshness of youth and whose strength stands sound in native vigour, do ye turn to flight. For me, had the lords of heaven willed that I should lengthen life's thread, they would have spared this my home. Enough and more is it that I have seen one destruction, and have survived one capture of the city.[1] To my body thus lying, yea thus, bid farewell and depart![2] With my own hand I shall find death; the foe will take pity and seek my spoils; light is the loss of burial. Hated of heaven and useless, I have long stayed the years, ever since the Father of gods and king of men breathed upon me with the winds of his bolt and touched me with his fire.'[3]

[1] Troy was once destroyed by Hercules, after Laomedon deceived him.

[2] *i.e.* treat me as a corpse laid out for burial.

[3] Anchises, it is said, was blasted by a lightning-bolt for boasting of the love of Venus.

VIRGIL

" Talia perstabat memorans fixusque manebat. 650
nos contra effusi lacrimis coniunxque Creusa
Ascaniusque omnisque domus, ne vertere secum
cuncta pater fatoque urgenti incumbere vellet.
abnegat inceptoque et sedibus haeret in isdem.
rursus in arma feror mortemque miserrimus opto. 655
nam quod consilium aut quae iam fortuna dabatur ?
' mene efferre pedem, genitor, te posse relicto
sperasti, tantumque nefas patrio excidit ore ?
si nihil ex tanta superis placet urbe relinqui,
et sedet hoc animo perituraeque addere Troiae   660
teque tuosque iuvat, patet isti ianua leto,
iamque aderit multo Priami de sanguine Pyrrhus,
gnatum ante ora patris, patrem qui obtruncat ad aras.
hoc erat, alma parens, quod me per tela, per ignis
eripis, ut mediis hostem in penetralibus utque   665
Ascanium patremque meum iuxtaque Creusam
alterum in alterius mactatos sanguine cernam ?
arma, viri, ferte arma ; vocat lux ultima victos.
reddite me Danais ; sinite instaurata revisam
proelia. numquam omnes hodie moriemur inulti.' 670

" Hinc ferro accingor rursus clipeoque sinistram
insertabam aptans meque extra tecta ferebam.
ecce autem complexa pedes in limine coniunx   FMPV
haerebat parvumque patri tendebat Iulum :
' si periturus abis, et nos rape in omnia tecum ;   675
sin aliquam expertus sumptis spem ponis in armis,
hanc primum tutare domum. cui parvus Iulus,
cui pater et coniunx quondam tua dicta relinquor ? '

[663] gnatum *M :* natum *PV.*   patremque *Mγ.*
[667] mactato *MPV.*   [671] cingor *P1.*   [678] relinquar *M1.*
338

650 " So he continued in his speech and remained unshaken. But we were dissolved in tears—my wife Creüsa, Ascanius, and all our household—pleading that our father bring not all to ruin along with him, nor add weight to our crushing doom. He refuses, and abides in his purpose and his place. Again I rush to arms, and in utter misery long for death, for what device or what chance was offered now? 'Didst thou think, my father, that I could go forth leaving thee? and did such a monstrous word fall from a father's lips? If the gods will that naught remain of our great city, if this purpose is firmly set in thy mind, if it be thy pleasure to cast thyself and thine into the wreck of Troy, for this death the gate is wide, and soon will come Pyrrhus, steeped in the blood of Priam—Pyrrhus who butchers the son before the father's eyes, the father at the altars. Was it for this, gracious mother, that thou savest me amid fire and sword, to see the foe in the heart of my home, and Ascanius, and my father, and Creüsa at their side, slaughtered in each other's blood? Arms, men, bring arms; the last light of life calls the vanquished. Give me back to the Greeks; let me seek again and renew the fight. Never this day shall we all die unavenged!'

671 " Therewith once more I gird me with the sword, pass my left arm into the shield, as I fit it on, and was hurrying forth from the house, when lo! my wife clung upon the threshold, clasping my feet and holding up little Iülus to his father. 'If thou goest to die, take us, too, with thee for any fate. But if, from past trial, thou dost place some hope in the armour thou hast donned, guard first this house. To whom is little Iülus, to whom is thy father, to whom am I, once called thine own wife, abandoned?'

VIRGIL

"Talia vociferans gemitu tectum omne replebat,
cum subitum dictuque oritur mirabile monstrum. 680
namque manus inter maestorumque ora parentum
ecce levis summo de vertice visus Iuli
fundere lumen apex, tactuque innoxia mollis
lambere flamma comas et circum tempora pasci.
nos pavidi trepidare metu crinemque flagrantem 685
excutere et sanctos restinguere fontibus ignis.
at pater Anchises oculos ad sidera laetus
extulit et caelo palmas cum voce tetendit:
'Iuppiter omnipotens, precibus si flecteris ullis,
aspice nos, hoc tantum, et, si pietate meremur, 690
da deinde augurium, pater, atque haec omina firma.'

"Vix ea fatus erat senior, subitoque fragore
intonuit laevum, et de caelo lapsa per umbras
stella facem ducens multa cum luce cucurrit.
illam, summa super labentem culmina tecti, 695
cernimus Idaea claram se condere silva
signantemque vias; tum longo limite sulcus
dat lucem, et late circum loca sulpure fumant.
hic vero victus genitor se tollit ad auras
adfaturque deos et sanctum sidus adorat. MPV
'iam iam nulla mora est; sequor et, qua ducitis,
  adsum. 701
di patrii, servate domum, servate nepotem.
vestrum hoc augurium, vestroque in numine Troia est.
cedo equidem nec, nate, tibi comes ire recuso.'
dixerat ille, et iam per moenia clarior ignis 705
auditur, propiusque aestus incendia volvunt.
'ergo age, care pater, cervici imponere nostrae;
ipse subibo umeris, nec me labor iste gravabit.
quo res cumque cadent, unum et commune periclum,

---

[380] subito $MPV\gamma^1$.　　　　　　[683] molli V.
[691] augurium *Probus, Servius:* auxilium MSS.
[699] tollere P.　ad auras] miras V.

679 "So crying, she filled all the house with moaning; when on a sudden arises a portent, wondrous to tell. For between the hands and faces of his sad parents, lo! from above the head of Iülus a light tongue of flame seemed to shed a gleam and, harmless in its touch, lick his soft locks and pasture round his temples. Trembling with alarm, we in haste shake out the blazing hair and quench with water the holy fires. But my father Anchises joyously raises his eyes to the skies and uplifts to heaven hands and voice : 'Almighty Jupiter, if by any prayers thou art moved, look upon us—this only do I ask—and if our goodness earn it, grant thereon a sign, O Father, and ratify this omen!'

692 "Scarcely had the aged man thus spoken, when with sudden crash it thundered on the left and a star shot from heaven, gliding through the shadows, and drawing a fiery trail amid a flood of light. We watch it glide over the palace-roof and bury in Ida's forest the splendour that marked its path ; then the long-drawn furrow shines, and far and wide all about reeks with sulphur. On this, indeed, my father was vanquished and, rising erect, salutes the gods, and worships the holy star. 'Now, now there is no delay ; I follow, and where ye lead, there am I ! Gods of my fathers'! save my house, save my grandson. Yours is this omen, and under your protection stands Troy. Yea, I yield, and refuse not, my son, to go in thy company.'

705 "He ceased, and now through the city more loudly is heard the blaze, and nearer the flames roll their fiery flood. 'Come then, dear father, mount upon my neck ; on my own shoulders I will stay thee, nor will such task o'erburden me. However things may fall, we both shall have one common

341

una salus ambobus erit.   mihi parvus Iulus   710
sit comes, et longe servet vestigia coniunx.
vos, famuli, quae dicam, animis advertite vestris.
est urbe egressis tumulus templumque vetustum
desertae Cereris, iuxtaque antiqua cupressus
religione patrum multos servata per annos ;   715
hanc ex diverso sedem veniemus in unam.
tu, genitor, cape sacra manu patriosque Penatis ;
me, bello e tanto digressum et caede recenti,
attrectare nefas, donec me flumine vivo
abluero.'   720
haec fatus latos umeros subiectaque colla
veste super fulvique insternor pelle leonis,
succedoque oneri ; dextrae se parvus Iulus
implicuit sequiturque patrem non passibus aequis ;
pone subit coniunx.   ferimur per opaca locorum, 725
et me, quem dudum non ulla iniecta movebant
tela neque adverso glomerati ex agmine Grai,   MP
nunc omnes terrent aurae, sonus excitat omnis
suspensum et pariter comitique onerique timentem.

     " Iamque propinquabam portis omnemque videbar
evasisse viam, subito cum creber ad auris   731
visus adesse pedum sonitus, genitorque per umbram
prospiciens, 'nate,' exclamat, 'fuge, nate ; propin-
     quant ;
ardentis clipeos atque aera micantia cerno.'
hic mihi nescio quod trepido male numen amicum
confusam eripuit mentem.   namque avia cursu   736
dum sequor et nota excedo regione viarum,
heu ! misero coniunx fatone erepta Creusa
substitit ?   erravitne via seu lassa resedit ?
incertum : nec post oculis est reddita nostris,   740
nec prius amissam respexi animumve reflexi,

     ⁷³⁹ lapsa *M :* rapta *P¹γ² :* lassa *P²γ¹.   Page's punctuation.*
Most editors place a comma after substitit *and another after*
resedit.   ⁷⁴¹ animumque *M.*
842

peril, one salvation. Let little Iülus come with me,
and let my wife follow our steps afar. Ye servants,
heed what I say. As one leaves the city, there is a
mound and ancient temple of forlorn Ceres, with an
old cypress hard by, saved for many years by the
reverence of our fathers. To this one goal from
divers parts we will wend. Father, do thou take in
thy hand the sacred things and our country's house-
hold gods; for me, fresh from such a conflict and
recent carnage, it were sin to handle them, until I
have washed me in a running stream.' So I spoke, and
over my broad shoulders and bowed neck I spread
the cover of a tawny lion's pelt and stoop to the
burden. Little Iülus clasps his hand in mine, and
follows his father with steps that match not his.
Behind comes my wife. We pass on amid the
shadows; and I, whom of late no shower of missiles
could move nor any Greeks thronging in opposing
mass, now am affrighted by every breeze and startled
by every sound, tremulous as I am and fearing alike
for my companion and my burden.

⁷³⁰ " And now I was nearing the gates, and thought
I had traversed all the way, when suddenly, crowding
on my ears, seemed to come a tramp of feet, and
peering through the gloom, my father cries: 'My
son, my son, flee; they draw near! I see their
glowing shields and glittering brass.' At this, in my
alarm, some unfriendly power bereft me of my dis-
tracted wits. For while I swiftly follow byways,
and leave the course of the streets I know, snatched
away, alas! by an unhappy fate, did my wife Creüsa
halt? or did she stray from the path or sink down
weary? I know not. Never again was she restored
to our eyes, nor did I look back for my lost one, or
cast a thought behind, until we came to the mound

quam tumulum antiquae Cereris sedemque sacratam
venimus.   hic demum collectis omnibus una
defuit, et comites natumque virumque fefellit.
quem non incusavi amens hominumque deorumque,
aut quid in eversa vidi crudelius urbe?   746
Ascanium Anchisenque patrem Teucrosque Penatis
commendo sociis et curva· valle recondo;
ipse urbem repeto et cingor fulgentibus armis.
stat casus renovare omnis omnemque reverti   750
per Troiam et rursus caput obiectare periclis.
principio muros obscuraque limina portae,
qua gressum extuleram, repeto et vestigia retro
observata sequor per noctem et lumine lustro.
horror ubique animo, simul ipsa silentia terrent. 755
inde domum, si forte pedem, si forte tulisset,
me refero. inruerant Danai et tectum omne tenebant.
ilicet ignis edax summa ad fastigia vento
volvitur; exsuperant flammae, furit aestus ad auras.
procedo et Priami sedes arcemque reviso.   760
et iam porticibus vacuis Iunonis asylo
custodes lecti Phoenix et dirus Ulixes
praedam adservabant.   huc undique Troia gaza
incensis erepta adytis, mensaeque deorum
crateresque auro solidi captivaque vestis·   765
congeritur.   pueri et pavidae longo ordine matres
stant circum.
ausus quin etiam voces iactare per umbram
implevi clamore vias, maestusque Creusam
nequiquam ingeminans iterumque iterumque vocavi.
quaerenti et tectis urbis sine fine furenti   771
infelix simulacrum atque ipsius umbra Creusae
visa mihi ante oculos et nota maior imago.
obstipui, steteruntque comae et vox faucibus haesit.

758 vento] tecti *M*¹.
771 ruenti *Pγ*¹: furenti *Mγ*² (*alliteration in its favour*).

and ancient Ceres' hallowed home. Here at last, when all were gathered, she alone was missing and failed the company, her child, and her husband. What man or god did I not reproach in my frenzy? or what crueller sight did I see in the overthrown city? Ascanius, my father Anchises, and the household gods of Troy I put in charge of my fellows and hid them in a winding vale. I myself seek again the city, and gird on my glittering arms. I am resolved to renew every risk, to retrace my way through all Troy and once more expose my life to every peril.

752 " First I seek again the walls and dark gateway whence my feet had issued; I mark and follow back my steps in the night, scanning them with close eye. Everywhere dread fills my heart; the very silence, too, dismays. Then homeward I turn, if haply— if haply she had made her way thither! The Danai had rushed in and filled all the house. At once the devouring fire rolls before the wind to the very roof; the flames tower above, the hot blast roars skyward. I pass on and see once more the citadel and Priam's home. And now in the empty courts of Juno's sanctuary Phoenix and dread Ulysses, chosen guards, watched the spoil. Here from all parts the treasures of Troy, torn from blazing shrines, tables of the gods, bowls of solid gold, and plundered raiment, are heaped up; boys and trembling matrons in long array stand round. Nay, I dared even to cast my cries upon the night; I filled the streets with shouts and in my misery, with vain iteration, called Creüsa again and yet again. In my quest, while madly and endlessly rushing among the dwellings of the city, there rose before my eyes the sad phantom and ghost of Creüsa herself, a form larger than her wont. I was appalled, my hair stood up, and the voice clave to my throat.

tum sic adfari et curas his demere dictis: 775
'quid tantum insano iuvat indulgere dolori,
o dulcis coniunx? non haec sine numine divum
eveniunt; nec te comitem hinc portare Creusam
fas aut ille sinit superi regnator Olympi.
longa tibi exsilia, et vastum maris aequor arandum;
et terram Hesperiam veniẹs, ubi Lydius arva 781
inter opima virum leni fluit agmine Thybris.
illic res laetae regnumque et regia coniunx
parta tibi. lacrimas dilectae pelle Creusae.
non ego Myrmidonum sedes Dolopumve superbas
aspiciam aut Grais servitum matribus ibo, 786
Dardanis et divae Veneris nurus;
sed me magna deum genetrix his detinet oris.
iamque vale et nati serva communis amorem.'
haec ubi dicta dedit, lacrimantem et multa volentem
dicere deseruit, tenuisque recessit in auras. 791
ter conatus ibi collo dare bracchia circum;
ter frustra comprensa manus effugit imago,
par levibus ventis volucrique simillima somno.
sic demum socios consumpta nocte reviso. 795
  "Atque hic ingentem comitum adfluxisse novorum
invenio admirans numerum, matresque virosque,
collectam exsilio pubem, miserabile volgus.
undique convenere, animis opibusque parati,
in quascumque velim pelago deducere terras. 800
iamque iugis summae surgebat Lucifer Idae
duçebatque diem, Danaique obsessa tenebant
limina portarum, nec spes opis ulla dabatur.
cessi et sublato montis genitore petivi.

---

[775] *Servius notes that this verse was often omitted.*
[778] te comitem hinc portare $\gamma^2 c^1$ (pr. tare M^1: asportare M (late)): te comitem hinc asportare $P\gamma^1 ac^2$, *Servius:* te hinc comitem asportare b (*in rasura*).
[782] laetae] Italae MP^2.
[804] montem $P\gamma$, *Servius: cf.* 636 *above.*

Then thus she spake to me and with these words took away my cares : ' Of what avail is it to yield thus to frantic grief, my sweet husband ? Not without the will of heaven does this befall ; that thou shouldst take Creüsa hence in thy company cannot be, nor does the mighty lord of high Olympus suffer it. Long exile is thy lot, a vast stretch of sea thou must plough ; and thou shalt come to the land Hesperia, where amid the rich fields of husbandmen the Lydian Tiber flows with gentle sweep. There in store for thee are happy days, kingship, and a royal wife. Banish tears for thy beloved Creüsa. I shall never look upon the proud homes of the Myrmidons or Dolopians, or go to be the slave of Greek matrons, I a Dardan woman and wife of the son of divine Venus ; but the mighty mother of the gods [1] holds me on these shores. And now farewell, and guard thy love for our common child.' When thus she had spoken, she left me weeping and fain to tell her much, and drew back into thin air. Thrice there I strove to throw my arms about her neck ; thrice the form, vainly clasped, fled from my hands, even as light winds, and most like a winged dream. Thus at last, when night is spent, I revisit my companions.

[796] " And here, astonished, I find that a vast number of new comrades has streamed in, mothers and men, a band gathered for exile, a piteous throng. From all sides they have come, with heart and fortune ready for any lands whereto I will lead them oversea. And now above Ida's topmost ridges the day-star was rising, ushering in the morn ; and the Danaans held the blockaded gates, nor was any hope of help offered. I gave way and, taking up my father, sought the mountains.

[1] *i.e.* Cybele.

LIBER III

"Postquam res Asiae Priamique evertere gentem   FMP
immeritam visum superis, ceciditque superbum
Ilium et omnis humo fumat Neptunia Troia,
diversa exsilia et desertas quaerere terras
auguriis agimur divum, classemque sub ipsa   5
Antandro et Phrygiae molimur montibus Idae,
incerti, quo fata ferant, ubi sistere detur,
contrahimusque viros.   vix prima inceperat aestas,
et pater Anchises dare fatis vela iubebat :
litora cum patriae lacrimans portusque relinquo   10
et campos, ubi Troia fuit.   feror exsul in altum
cum sociis natoque, Penatibus et magnis dis.

"Terra procul vastis colitur Mavortia campis
(Thraces arant), acri quondam regnata Lycurgo,
hospitium antiquum Troiae sociique Penates,   15
dum Fortuna fuit.   feror huc et litore curvo
moenia prima loco, fatis ingressus iniquis,
Aeneadasque meo nomen de nomine fingo.

"Sacra Dionaeae matri divisque ferebam
auspicibus coeptorum operum, superoque nitentem 20

⁷ ferunt *P*¹.

348

BOOK III

"After it pleased the gods above to overthrow the power of Asia and Priam's guiltless race, after proud Ilium fell, and all Neptune's Troy smokes from the ground, we are driven by heaven's auguries to seek distant scenes of exile in waste lands. Just under Antandros and the mountains of Phrygian Ida we build a fleet, uncertain whither the Fates lead or where it is granted us to settle; and there we muster our men. Scarcely had the beginning of summer come when my father Anchises bade us spread sails to Fate, and then with tears I quit my native shores and harbours, and the plains, where once was Troy. An exile, I fare forth upon the deep, with my comrades and son, and the great gods of the Penates.[1]

[13] "At a distance lies the war-god's land, of wide-spread plains, tilled by Thracians, and once ruled by fierce Lycurgus; friendly of old to Troy, with allied gods, as long as Fortune was ours. Hither I pass and on the winding shore found my first city, entering on the task with untoward fates, and from my own name fashion the name Aeneadae.

[19] "I was offering sacrifice to my mother, Dione's daughter, and the other gods, that they might bless

---

[1] Some suppose that two sets of gods are here mentioned, the Penates (household gods) and the great gods (Jupiter, Juno, &c.). Varro, however, identified them; cf. 148.

caelicolum regi mactabam in litore taurum.
forte fuit iuxta tumulus, quo cornea summo
virgulta et densis hastilibus horrida myrtus.
accessi, viridemque ab humo convellere silvam
conatus, ramis tegerem ut frondentibus aras,   25
horrendum et dictu video mirabile monstrum.
nam quae prima solo ruptis radicibus arbos
vellitur, huic atro liquuntur sanguine guttae
et terram tabo maculant.   mihi frigidus horror
membra quatit, gelidusque coit formidine sanguis.   30
rursus et alterius lentum convellere vimen
insequor et causas penitus temptare latentis;
ater et alterius sequitur de cortice sanguis.
multa movens animo Nymphas venerabar agrestis
Gradivumque patrem, Geticis qui praesidet arvis,   35
rite secundarent visus omenque levarent.
tertia sed postquam maiore hastilia nisu
adgredior genibusque adversae obluctor harenae
(eloquar, an sileam?), gemitus lacrimabilis imo
auditur tumulo, et vox reddita fertur ad auris: 40
'quid miserum, Aenea, laceras?   iam parce sepulto,
parce pias scelerare manus.   non me tibi Troia
externum tulit, aut cruor hic de stipite manat.
heu! fuge crudelis terras, fuge litus avarum.
nam Polydorus ego.   hic confixum ferrea texit   45
telorum seges et iaculis increvit acutis.'
tum vero ancipiti mentem formidine pressus
obstipui steteruntque comae et vox faucibus haesit.
"Hunc Polydorum auri quondam cum pondere
    magno
infelix Priamus furtim mandarat alendum   50
Threicio regi, cum iam diffideret armis

²³ alter *Fγ*.   ³⁹ eloquor *P²*. gemitum *P¹*.

the work begun, and to the high king of the lords of heaven was slaying a shining white bull upon the shore. By chance, hard by there was a mound, on whose top were cornel bushes and myrtles bristling with crowded spear-shafts. I drew near ; and essaying to tear up the green growth from the soil, that I might deck the altar with leafy boughs, I see an awful portent, wondrous to tell. For from the first tree, which is torn from the ground with broken roots, drops of black blood trickle and stain the earth with gore. A cold shudder shakes my limbs, and my chilled blood freezes with terror. Once more, from a second also I go on to pluck a tough shoot and probe deep the hidden cause ; from the bark of the second also follows black blood. Pondering much in heart, I prayed the woodland Nymphs, and father Gradivus, who rules over the Getic fields, duly to bless the vision and lighten the omen. But when with greater effort I assail the third shafts, and with my knees wrestle against the resisting sand—should I speak or be silent ?—a piteous groan is heard from the depth of the mound, and an answering voice comes to my ears. 'Woe is me! why, Aeneas, dost thou tear me? Spare me in the tomb at last; spare the pollution of thy pure hands! I, born of Troy, am no stranger to thee ; not from a lifeless stock oozes this blood. Ah ! flee the cruel land, flee the greedy shore ! For I am Polydorus. Here an iron harvest of spears covered my pierced body, and grew up into sharp javelins.' Then, indeed, with mind borne down with perplexing dread, I was appalled, my hair stood up, and the voice clave to my throat.

⁴⁹ "This Polydorus, with great weight of gold, luckless Priam had once sent in secret to be reared by the Thracian king, when he now mistrusted the

VIRGIL

Dardaniae cingique urbem obsidione videret.
ille, ut opes fractae Teucrum et Fortuna recessit,
res Agamemnonias victriciaque arma secutus
fas omne abrumpit; Polydorum obtruncat et auro MP
vi potitur.   quid non mortalia pectora cogis,   56
auri sacra fames!   postquam pavor ossa reliquit,
delectos populi ad proceres primumque parentem
monstra deum refero et, quae sit sententia, posco.
omnibus idem animus, scelerata excedere terra,   60
linqui pollutum hospitium et dare classibus Austros.
ergo instauramus Polydoro funus, et ingens
aggeritur tumulo tellus; stant Manibus arae,
caeruleis maestae vittis atraque cupresso,
et circum Iliades crinem de more solutae;   65
inferimus tepido spumantia cymbia lacte
sanguinis et sacri pateras, animamque sepulchro
condimus et magna supremum voce ciemus.
inde ubi prima fides pelago, placataque venti
dant maria et lenis crepitans vocat Auster in altum, 70
deducunt socii navis et litora complent.
provehimur portu, terraeque urbesque recedunt.

   " Sacra mari colitur medio gratissima tellus
Nereidum matri et Neptuno Aegaeo,
quam pius Arquitenens oras et litora circum   75
errantem Mycono e celsa Gyaroque revinxit,
immotamque coli dedit et contemnere ventos.
huc feror; haec fessos tuto placidissima portu
accipit.   egressi veneramur Apollinis urbem.   FMP

                    75 prius *known to Servius.*

arms of Dardania and saw the city girt with siege.
When the power of Troy was crushed and Fortune
withdrew, the Thracian, following Agamemnon's
cause and triumphant arms, severs every sacred tie,
slays Polydorus, and takes the gold perforce. To
what dost thou not drive the hearts of men, O
accursed hunger for gold! When fear had fled my
soul, I lay the divine portents before the chosen chiefs
of the people, my father first, and ask what is their
judgment. All are of one mind, to quit the guilty
land, to leave a place where hospitality is profaned,
and to give our fleet the winds. So for Polydorus
we solemnize fresh funeral rites, and earth is heaped
high upon the mound; altars are set up to the dead,
made mournful with sombre fillets and black cypress;
and about them stand Ilian women, with hair stream-
ing as custom ordains. We offer foaming bowls of
warm milk and cups of victims' blood, lay the spirit
at rest in the tomb, and with loud voice give the
last call.

⁶⁹ " Then, as soon as we can trust the main, and
the winds give us seas at peace, and the soft-
whispering South calls to the deep, my comrades
launch the ships and crowd the shores. We put out
from port, and lands and towns fade from view.

⁷³ " In mid-sea lies a holy land,[1] most dear to the
mother of the Nereids and Aegean Neptune, which,
as it wandered round coasts and shores, the grateful
archer-god bound fast to lofty Myconos and Gyaros,
suffering it to lie unmoved and slight the winds.
Hither I sail; and most peacefully the island wel-
comes our weary band in a safe haven. Landing,
we do homage to Apollo's town. King Anius—at

[1] Delos, birthplace of Apollo and Diana. Hence Apollo is
called *pius* or "grateful" in l. 75.

rex Anius, rex idem hominum Phoebique sacerdos, 80
vittis et sacra redimitus tempora lauro
occurrit, veterem Anchisen adgnoscit amicum;
iungimus hospitio dextras et tecta subimus.

   "Templa dei saxo venerabar structa vetusto:
'da propriam, Thymbraee, domum, da moenia
     fessis   85
et genus et mansuram urbem; serva altera Troiae
Pergama, reliquias Danaum atque immitis Achilli.
quem sequimur? quove ire iubes? ubi ponere
     sedes?
da, pater, augurium atque animis inlabere nostris.'

   "Vix ea fatus eram: tremere omnia visa repente, 90
liminaque laurusque dei, totusque moveri
mons circum et mugire adytis cortina reclusis.
summissi petimus terram, et vox fertur ad auris:
'Dardanidae duri, quae vos a stirpe parentum
prima tulit tellus, eadem vos ubere laeto   95
accipiet reduces.   antiquam exquirite matrem.
hic domus Aeneae cunctis dominabitur oris,
et nati natorum et qui nascentur ab illis.'
haec Phoebus; mixtoque ingens exorta tumultu
laetitia et cuncti, quae sint ea moenia, quaerunt, 100
quo Phoebus vocet errantis iubeatque reverti.
tum genitor, veterum volvens monumenta virorum,
'audite, o proceres,' ait, 'et spes discite vestras.
Creta Iovis magni medio iacet insula ponto,
mons Idaeus ubi et gentis cunabula nostrae.   105
centum urbes habitant magnas, uberrima regna;
maximus unde pater, si rite audita recordor,
Teucrus Rhoeteas primum est advectus ad oras
optavitque locum regno.   nondum Ilium et arces

---

      [82] accurrit M^2.   agnoscit M: adgnovit FP.
      [93] et *omitted* F^1P^1.   auras a^1: aureas P^1: aures $P^2\gamma a^2$.
      [108] ad] in FP.

once king of the people and priest of Phoebus—his brows bound with fillets and hallowed laurel, meets us, and in Anchises finds an old friend. We clasp hands in welcome, and pass beneath his roof.

84 "I was paying homage to the god's temple, built of ancient stone: 'Grant us, thou god of Thymbra, an enduring home; grant our weary band walls, and a race, and a city that shall abide; preserve Troy's second fortress, the remnant left by the Greeks and pitiless Achilles! Whom should we follow? or whither dost thou bid us go? Where fix our home? Grant, father, an omen, and inspire our hearts !'

90 "Scarcely had I thus spoken, when suddenly it seemed all things trembled, the doors and laurels of the god; the whole hill shook round about and the tripod moaned as the shrine was thrown open. Prostrate we fall to earth, and a voice comes to our ears: 'Ye long-suffering sons of Dardanus, the land which bare you first from your parent stock shall welcome you back to her fruitful bosom. Seek out your ancient mother. There the house of Aeneas shall lord it over all lands, even his children's children and their race that shall be born of them.' Thus Phoebus; and mighty joy arose, mingled with tumult; all ask, What walls are those? whither calls Phoebus the wanderers, bidding them return? Then my father, pondering the memorials of the men of old, cries: 'Hear, O princes, and learn your hopes. In mid-ocean lies Crete, the island of great Jove, where is Mount Ida, and the cradle of our race. There men dwell in a hundred great cities, a realm most fertile, whence our earliest ancestor Teucer, if I recall the tale aright, first sailed to the Rhoetean shores, and chose a site for his kingdom. Not yet

Pergameae steterant ; habitabant vallibus imis.   110
hinc Mater cultrix Cybelae Corybantiaque aera
Idaeumque nemus, hinc fida silentia sacris,
et iuncti currum dominae subiere leones.
ergo agite et, divum ducunt qua iussa, sequamur ;
placemus ventos et Gnosia regna petamus.   115
nec longo distant cursu ; modo Iuppiter adsit,
tertia lux classem Cretaeis sistet in oris.'
sic fatus meritos aris mactavit honores,
taurum Neptuno, taurum tibi, pulcher Apollo,
nigram Hiemi pecudem, Zephyris felicibus albam.   120
    " Fama volat pulsum regnis cessisse paternis
Idomenea ducem, desertaque litora Cretae,
hoste vacare domos sedesque adstare relictas.
linquimus Ortygiae portus pelagoque volamus,
bacchatamque iugis Naxon viridemque Donysam, 125
Olearon niveamque Paron sparsasque per aequor
Cycladas, et crebris legimus freta concita terris.
nauticus exoritur vario certamine clamor ;
hortantur socii, 'Cretam proavosque petamus.'
prosequitur surgens a puppi ventus euntis   130
et tandem antiquis Curetum adlabimur oris.
ergo avidus muros optatae molior urbis
Pergameamque voco, et laetam cognomine gentem
hortor amare focos arcemque attollere tectis.
iamque fere sicco subductae litore puppes ;   135
conubiis arvisque novis operata iuventus ;
iura domosque dabam : subito cum tabida membris,
corrupto caeli tractu, miserandaque venit

    [111] Cybele *FMP, known to Servius:* Cybeli *a²c², Servius:*
Cybelae *Heinsius.*
    [128] domos *M :* domum *FP.*
    [127] concita *most MSS. :* consita *some minor MSS.*
    [131] si tandem *M¹ :* et tandem *M².*

had Ilium and the towers of Pergamus been reared;
men dwelt in the low valleys.   Hence came the
Mother who haunts Cybele, the Corybantian cymbals
and the grove of Ida; hence came the faithful
silence of her mysteries, and yoked lions passed
under our lady's chariot.   Come then, and let us
follow where the gods' bidding leads, let us appease
the winds and seek the realm of Gnosus!   Nor is it
a long run thither; if only Jupiter be gracious, the
third dawn shall anchor our fleet on the Cretan coast.'
So he spake, and on the altars slew the sacrifices
due, a bull to Neptune, a bull to thee, fair Apollo,
a black sheep to the storm-god, a white to the
favouring Zephyrs.

   [121] " A rumour flies that Idomeneus, the chieftain,
has left his father's realm for exile, that the shores of
Crete are abandoned, her homes are void of foes, and
the deserted abodes stand ready for our coming.   We
leave the harbour of Ortygia and fly over the sea,
past Naxos with its Bacchic revels on the heights,
and green Donysa, Olearos, snow-white Paros, and
the sea-strewn Cyclades, and thread the straits that
foam round many a shore.   The sailors' shouts rise in
varied rivalry; the crews raise the cheer : ' On to
Crete and our forefathers ! '   A wind rising astern
attends us as we sail, and at last we glide up to the
ancient shores of the Curetes.   Eagerly, therefore, I
work on the walls of my chosen city, call it Pergamum,
and urge my people, who rejoice at the old name, to
love their hearths and build a citadel with lofty
roof.   And now the ships were just drawn up
on the dry beach; our youth were busy with
marriages and new tillage, and I was giving laws
and homes, when on a sudden, from a tainted quarter
of the sky, came a pestilence and season of death, to

arboribusque satisque lues et letifer annus.
linquebant dulcis animas aut aegra trahebant   140
corpora ; tum sterilis exurere Sirius agros ;
arebant herbae et victum seges aegra negabat.
rursus ad oraclum Ortygiae Phoebumque remenso
hortatur pater ire mari veniamque precari,
quam fessis finem rebus ferat, unde laborum   145
temptare auxilium iubeat, quo vertere cursus.
  " Nox erat et terris animalia somnus habebat ;
effigies sacrae divum Phrygiique Penates,
quos mecum a Troia mediisque ex ignibus urbis
extuleram, visi ante oculos adstare iacentis   150
in somnis, multo manifesti lumine, qua se
plena per insertas fundebat luna fenestras ;
tum sic adfari et curas his demere dictis :
' quod tibi delato Ortygiam dicturus Apollo est,
hic canit et tua nos en ultro ad limina mittit.   155
nos te Dardania incensa tuaque arma secuti,
nos tumidum sub te permensi classibus aequor,
idem venturos tollemus in astra nepotes
imperiumque urbi dabimus.   tu moenia magnis
magna para longumque fugae ne linque laborem. 160
mutandae sedes.   non haec tibi litora suasit
Delius aut Cretae iussit considere Apollo.
est locus, Hesperiam Grai cognomine dicunt,
terra antiqua, potens armis atque ubere glaebae ;
Oenotri coluere viri ; nunc fama minores   165
Italiam dixisse ducis de nomine gentem.
hae nobis propriae sedes, hinc Dardanus ortus
Iasiusque pater, genus a quo principe nostrum.

    142 negare *F¹*. *So Sabb.*
    146 temptari *M²* : temptaret *F¹*.   151 manifesto *Pγ*.
    153 *lacking in many copies, according to Servius.*
    157 permesi *M¹, recognized by Servius.*
    166 duxisse *F*.

358

the wasting of our bodies and the piteous ruin of trees and crops. Men gave up their sweet lives, or dragged enfeebled frames; Sirius, too, scorched the fields with drought; the grass withered, and the sickly crop denied her sustenance. My father urges us to remeasure the sea and go again to Phoebus and Ortygia's oracle, to pray for favour, and ask what end he grants to our weary lot; whence he bids us seek aid for our distress, whither bend our course.

[147] "It was night and on earth sleep held the living world. The sacred images of the gods, the Phrygian Penates, whom I had borne with me from Troy out of the midst of the burning city, seemed as I lay in slumber to stand before my eyes, clear in the flood of light, where the full moon streamed through the inset windows.. Then thus they spake to me and with these words dispelled my cares: 'What Apollo shall tell thee on reaching Ortygia, he here utters, and lo! he sends us unbidden to thy threshold. We followed thee and thine arms when Dardania was burned; under thee we traversed on ships the swelling sea; we, too, shall exalt to heaven thy sons that are to be, and give empire to their city. Do thou prepare mighty walls for the mighty, nor shrink from the long toil of flight. Thou must change thy home. Not these the shores the Delian Apollo counselled, not in Crete did he bid thee settle. A place[1] there is, by Greeks named Hesperia, an ancient land, mighty in arms and in richness of the soil. There dwelt Oenotrians; now the rumour is that a younger race has called it from their leader's name Italy. This is our abiding home; hence are Dardanus sprung and father Iasius, from whom first came our race. Come, arise, and with good cheer

[1] cf. Aen. I. 530 ff.

surge age et haec laetus longaevo dicta parenti
haud dubitanda refer, Corythum terrasque requirat
Ausonias; Dictaea negat tibi Iuppiter arva.'   171
talibus attonitus visis et voce deorum
(nec sopor illud erat, sed coram adgnoscere voltus
velatasque comas praesentiaque ora videbar;
tum gelidus toto manabat corpore sudor)   175
corripio e stratis corpus tendoque supinas
ad caelum cum voce manus et munera libo
intemerata focis.   perfecto laetus honore
Anchisen facio certum remque ordine pando.
adgnovit prolem ambiguam geminosque parentis, 180
seque novo veterum deceptum errore locorum.
tum memorat: 'nate, Iliacis exercite fatis,
sola mihi talis casus Cassandra canebat.
nunc repeto haec generi portendere debita nostro,
et saepe Hesperiam, saepe Itala regna vocare.   185
sed quis ad Hesperiae venturos litora Teucros
crederet?   aut quem tum vates Cassandra moveret?
cedamus Phoebo et moniti meliora sequamur.'
sic ait et cuncti dicto paremus ovantes.   189
hanc quoque deserimus sedem paucisque relictis [FGMP
vela damus vastumque cava trabe currimus aequor.
   "Postquam altum tenuere rates nec iam amplius
        ullae
apparent terrae, caelum undique et undique pontus,
tum mihi caeruleus supra caput adstitit imber,
noctem hiememque ferens, et inhorruit unda tenebris.
continuo venti volvunt mare magnaque surgunt   196
aequora; dispersi iactamur gurgite vasto.
involvere diem nimbi et nox umida caelum
abstulit; ingeminant abruptis nubibus ignes.
excutimur cursu et caecis erramus in undis.   200

----

174 videbam *M¹*.
199 abrupti *G*.

bear to thine aged parent these certain tidings, to seek Corythus and the lands of Ausonia. Jupiter denies thee the Dictaean fields.'

172 " Awed by such a vision and the voice of gods —nor was that a mere dream, but openly I seemed to know their looks, their filleted hair, and their living faces ; anon a cold sweat bedewed all my limbs—I snatch myself from my bed, raise my voice and up-turned hands to heaven, and offer pure gifts upon the hearth. This rite fulfilled, I gladly tell Anchises the tale and reveal all in order. He recognized the twofold stock and double parentage, and his own confusion through a novel error touching olden lands. Then he speaks : ' My son, much tried by Ilium's fate, Cassandra alone declared to me this fortune. Now I recall her foretelling this as due to our race, often naming Hesperia, often the Italian realm. But who was to believe that Teucrians should come to Hesperia's shores ? or whom would Cassandra's prophecies then sway ? Let us yield to Phoebus and at his warning pursue the better course.' So he says and we all obey his speech with joyfulness. This home, too, we quit and, leaving some behind, spread our sails and speed in hollow keels over the waste sea.

192 " After our ships gained the deep, and now no longer any land is seen, but sky on all sides and on all sides sea, then a murky rain-cloud loomed over-head, bringing night and tempest, while the wave shuddered darkling. Straightway the winds roll up the waters and great seas rise ; we are tossed hither and thither in the vast abyss. Storm-clouds en-wrapped the day, and a night of rain blotted out the sky : oft from the rent clouds dart lightning fires. We are hurled from our course and wander

361

VIRGIL

ipse diem noctemque negat discernere caelo
nec meminisse viae media Palinurus in unda.
tris adeo incertos caeca caligine soles
erramus pelago, totidem sine sidere noctes.
quarto terra die primum se attollere tandem   205
visa, aperire procul montis ac volvere fumum.
vela cadunt, remis insurgimus; haud mora, nautae
adnixi torquent spumas et caerula verrunt.   FMP
servatum ex undis Strophadum me litora primum 209
excipiunt. Strophades Graio stant nomine dictae FGMP
insulae Ionio in magno, quas dira Celaeno
Harpyiaeque colunt aliae, Phineia postquam
clausa domus mensasque metu liquere priores.
tristius haud illis monstrum, nec saevior ulla
pestis et ira deum Stygiis sese extulit undis.   215
virginei volucrum voltus, foedissima ventris
proluvies, uncaeque manus, et pallida semper   GMP
ora fame.
huc ubi delati portus intravimus, ecce
laeta boum passim campis armenta videmus   220
caprigenumque pecus nullo custode per herbas.
inruimus ferro et divos ipsumque vocamus
in partem praedamque Iovem: tum litore curvo
exstruimusque toros dapibusque epulamur opimis.
at subitae horrifico lapsu de montibus adsunt   225
Harpyiae et magnis quatiunt clangoribus alas,
diripiuntque dapes contactuque omnia foedant   MP
immundo; tum vox taetrum dira inter odorem.
rursum in secessu longo, sub rupe cavata
arboribus clausa circum atque horrentibus umbris, 230

---

[204] *According to Servius, these lines, coming after 204, were
bracketed or found in the margin:*

> hinc Pelopis gentis Maleaeque sonantia saxa
> circumstant, pariterque undae terraeque minantur,
> pulsamur salvis et circumsistimur undis

on the blind waves. Even Palinurus avows that he
knows not day from night in the sky nor remembers
the way amid the waters. For full three days,
shrouded in misty gloom, we wander on the deep, for
as many starless nights. On the fourth day at length
land first was seen to rise, disclosing mountains afar
and curling smoke. The sails drop down ; we bend
to the oars ; without delay the sailors lustily churn
the foam and sweep the blue waters.

209 " Saved from the waves, I am received first by
the shores of the Strophades—Strophades the Greek
name they bear—islands set in the great Ionian sea,
where dwell dread Celaeno and the other Harpies,
since Phineus' house was closed on them, and in
fear they left their former tables. No monster more
baneful than these, no fiercer plague or wrath of
the gods ever rose from the Stygian waves. Maiden
faces have these birds, foulest filth they drop, clawed
hands are theirs, and faces ever gaunt with hunger.

219 " When hither borne we entered the harbour,
lo ! we see goodly herds of cattle scattered over the
plains and flocks of goats untended on the grass.
We rush upon them with the sword, calling the
gods and Jove himself to share our spoil ; then on
the winding shore we build couches and banquet
on the rich dainties. But suddenly, with fearful
swoop from the mountains the Harpies are upon
us, and with loud clanging shake their wings,
plunder the feast, and with unclean touch mire every
dish ; then amid the foul stench comes a hideous
scream. Once more, in a deep recess under a
hollowed rock, closely encircled by trees and quiver-

---

209 prima M^1.   210 accipiunt M.
220 clausam $M^1P\gamma^1$; *perhaps the verse is interpolated from*
I. 311 : clausa $M^2\gamma^2$.

instruimus mensas arisque reponimus ignem;
rursum ex diverso caeli caecisque latebris
turba sonans praedam pedibus circumvolat uncis,
polluit ore dapes.   sociis tunc, arma capessant,
edico, et dira bellum cum gente gerendum.   235
haud secus ac iussi faciunt tectosque per herbam
disponunt ensis et scuta latentia condunt.
ergo ubi delapsae sonitum per curva dedere
litora, dat signum specula Misenus ab alta
aere cavo.   invadunt socii et nova proelia temptant,
obscenas pelagi ferro foedare volucris.   241
sed neque vim plumis ullam nec volnera tergo
accipiunt, celerique fuga sub sidera lapsae
semesam praedam et vestigia foeda relinquunt.
una in praecelsa consedit rupe Celaeno,   245
infelix vates, rumpitque hanc pectore vocem :
' bellum etiam pro caede boum stratisque iuvencis,
Laomedontiadae, bellumne inferre paratis
et patrio Harpyias insontis pellere regno?
accipite ergo animis atque haec mea figite dicta. 250
quae Phoebo pater omnipotens, mihi Phoebus Apollo
praedixit, vobis Furiarum ego maxima pando.
Italiam cursu petitis, ventisque vocatis
ibitis Italiam portusque intrare licebit ;
sed non ante datam cingetis moenibus urbem,   255
quam vos dira fames nostraeque iniuria caedis
ambesas subigat malis absumere mensas.'
dixit et in silvam pinnis ablata refugit.
at sociis subita gelidus formidine sanguis
deriguit ; cecidere animi, nec iam amplius armis, 260
sed votis precibusque iubent exposcere pacem,

[252] pendo P^1 : mando P^2.

ing shade, we spread the tables and renew the fire
on the altars; once more, from an opposite quarter
of the sky and from a hidden lair, the noisy crowd
with taloned feet hovers round the prey, tainting the
dishes with their lips. Then I bid my comrades
seize arms and declare war on the fell race. Even
as bidden they do, lay their swords in hiding in
the grass, and bury their shields out of sight. So
when, swooping down, the birds screamed along the
winding shore, Misenus on his hollow brass gave the
signal from his watch aloft. My comrades charge,
and essay a strange combat, to despoil with the sword
those filthy birds of ocean. Yet they feel no blows
on their feathers, nor wounds on their. backs, but,
soaring skyward with rapid flight, leave the half-
eaten prey and their foul traces. One only, Celaeno,
ill-boding seer, alights on a lofty rock, and breaks forth
with this cry : ' Is it even war, in return for slaugh-
tered kine and slain bullocks, is it war ye are ready to
bring upon us, ye sons of Laomedon, and would ye
drive the guiltless Harpies from their father's realm?
Take then to heart and fix there these words of
mine. What the Father omnipotent foretold to
Phoebus and Phoebus Apollo to me, I, eldest of the
Furies, reveal to you. Italy is the goal ye seek ;
wooing the winds, ye shall go to Italy and freely
enter her harbours ; but ye shall not gird with walls
your promised city until dread hunger and the wrong
of violence towards us force you to gnaw with your
teeth and devour your very tables !'

258 " She spake and, borne away on her wings,
fled back to the forest. But my comrades' blood
chilled and froze with sudden fear; their spirit fell,
and no longer with arms, but with vows and prayers
they now bid me sue for peace, whether these

365

sive deae seu sint dirae obscenaeque volucres.
et pater Anchises passis de litore palmis
numina magna vocat meritosque indicit honores :
' di, prohibete minas, di, talem avertite casum   265
et placidi servate pios !'   tum litore funem
deripere excussosque iubet laxare rudentis.
tendunt vela Noti; fugimus spumantibus undis,
qua cursum ventusque gubernatorque vocabat.
iam medio apparet fluctu nemorosa Zacynthos   270
Dulichiumque Sameque et Neritos ardua saxis.
effugimus scopulos Ithacae, Laertia regna,
et terram altricem saevi exsecramur Ulixi ;
mox ét Leucatae nimbosa cacumina montis
et formidatus nautis aperitur Apollo.   275
hunc petimus fessi et parvae succedimus urbi;
ancora de prora iacitur, stant litore puppes.

     " Ergo insperata tandem tellure potiti
lustramurque Iovi votisque incendimus aras
Actiaque Iliacis celebramus litora ludis.   280
exercent patrias oleo labente palaestras
nudati socii; iuvat evasisse tot urbes
Argolicas mediosque fugam tenuisse per hostis.
interea magnum sol circumvolvitur annum
et glacialis hiems Aquilonibus asperat undas :   285
aere cavo clipeum, magni gestamen Abantis,
postibus adversis figo et rem carmine signo :

AENEAS HAEC DE DANAIS VICTORIBUS ARMA.

linquere tum portus iubeo et considere transtris ;
certatim socii feriunt mare et aequora verrunt.   290

263 at M^1.   **266** placide $P\gamma$.
267 diripere M.   **268** fugimus] ferimur $P^2\gamma$.

be goddesses, or dread and ill-omened birds. And
father Anchises, with hands outstretched, from the
beach calls upon the mighty gods, and proclaims the
sacrifices due : ' Ye gods, stay their threats ! Gods,
turn such a hap away, and graciously save the guilt-
less ! ' Then he bids them tear the cable from the
shore, uncoil and loose the sheets. South winds
stretch the sails ; we flee over foaming waves, where
breeze and pilot called our course. Now amid the
waves appear wooded Zacynthus, Dulichium, and
Same, and Neritus with its steepy crags. We flee
past the rocks of Ithaca, Laërtes' realm, and curse
the land that nursed cruel Ulysses. Soon, too, Mount
Leucata's storm-capped peaks come in view, and
Apollo's shrine, dreaded by sailors. Hither we
wearily sail, and draw near the little town ; the
anchor is cast from the prow, the sterns rest upon
the beach.

278 " So having at last won land unhoped for,
we offer to Jove dues of cleansing, kindle the altars
with offerings, and throng the Actian shores in the
games of Ilium. My comrades strip and, sleek with
oil, engage in their native wrestling bouts, glad to
have slipped past so many Argive towns, and kept
on their flight through the midst of foes. Mean-
while the sun wheels round the mighty circuit of the
year, and icy winter ruffles the waters with northern
blasts. A shield of hollow brass, once borne by great
Abas, I fix on the entrance pillars and mark the event
with a verse :

These arms Aeneas from victorious Greeks.

Then I bid them quit the harbour and man the
benches ; with rival strokes my comrades lash the
sea and sweep the waters. Soon we lose from sight

VIRGIL

protinus aërias Phaeacum abscondimus arces,
litoraque Epiri legimus portuque subimus
Chaonio et celsam Buthroti accedimus urbem.

  " Hic incredibilis rerum fama occupat auris,
Priamiden Helenum Graias regnare per urbes,   295
coniugio Aeacidae Pyrrhi sceptrisque potitum,
et patrio Andromachen iterum cessisse marito.
obstipui, miroque incensum pectus amore
compellare virum et casus cognoscere tantos.
progredior portu, classis et litora linquens,   FMP
sollemnis cum forte dapes et tristia dona   301
ante urbem in luco falsi Simoentis ad undam
libabat cineri Andromache, Manisque vocabat
Hectoreum ad tumulum, viridi quem caespite inanem
et geminas, causam lacrimis, sacraverat aras.   305
ut me conspexit venientem et Troia circum
arma amens vidit, magnis exterrita monstris
deriguit visu in medio, calor ossa reliquit,
labitur et longo vix tandem tempore fatur:
' verane te facies, verus mihi nuntius adfers,   310
nate dea? vivisne? aut si lux alma recessit,
Hector ubi est?' dixit lacrimasque effudit et omnem
implevit clamore locum. vix pauca furenti
subicio et raris turbatus vocibus hisco:
' vivo equidem vitamque extrema per omnia duco;
ne dubita, nam vera vides.   316
heu! quis te casus deiectam coniuge tanto
excipit? aut quae digna satis fortuna revisit,
Hectoris Andromache? Pyrrhin conubia servas?'
deiecit voltum et demissa voce locuta est: 320

---

    [292] portus *M.*   [293] Chaonios *M*[2], *known to Servius.*
    [310] verum *M*[1].   [312] effundit *P. So Sabb.*
    [319] Andromachen *F*[2]*c*[1], *known to Servius, who directs us,
if we read the vocative, to construe it with what follows. So
Forbiger, Kennedy, Page, and Mackail. The accusative is read
by Conington and Goelzer.* Pyrrhi *F*[1]*P*[1].

the towering heights of the Phaeacians, skirt the shores of Epirus, enter the Chaonian harbour, and draw near Buthrotum's lofty city.

294 " Here the rumour of a tale beyond belief fills our ears, that Priam's son, Helenus, is reigning over Greek cities, having won the wife and kingdom of Pyrrhus, son of Aeacus, and that Andromache has again passed to a husband of her own race. I was amazed, and my heart burned with a wondrous desire to address him and learn of so strange a fortune. I advance from the harbour, leaving shore and fleet, just when, as it fell, Andromache, in a grove before the city, by the waters of a mimic Simois, was offering her yearly feast and gifts of mourning to the dust, and calling the ghost to Hector's tomb—the empty mound of green turf, that she had hallowed with altars twain, there to shed her tears. When she caught sight of me coming, and saw distractedly the arms of Troy around, awed by such marvels she stiffened even as she gazed, and the warmth forsook her limbs. She swoons, and at last after a long time speaks: ' Art thou a real form, a real messenger, coming to me, goddess-born? Art living? or if kindly light has fled, where is Hector?' She spake, and shedding a flood of tears filled all the place with her cries. To her frenzy scarce can I make a brief reply, and deeply moved gasp with broken words: ' I live indeed, and drag on my life through all extremes; doubt not, for the sight is real. Ah! what fate receives thee, fallen from such a husband? or what fortune worthy of thee, O Hector's Andromache, is thine again? Art thou still wedded to Pyrrhus?' She cast down her eyes, and with lowered voice spake:

'o felix una ante alias Priameia virgo,
hostilem ad tumulum Troiae sub moenibus altis
iussa mori, quae sortitus non pertulit ullos
nec victoris eri tetigit captiva cubile!
nos patria incensa diversa per aequora vectae   325
stirpis Achilleae fastus iuvenemque superbum,
servitio enixae, tulimus; qui deinde, secutus
Ledaeam Hermionen Lacedaemoniosque hymenaeos,
me famulo famulamque Heleno transmisit habendam.
ast illum ereptae magno inflammatus amore   330
coniugis et scelerum Furiis agitatus Orestes
excipit incautum patriasque obtruncat ad aras.
morte Neoptolemi regnorum reddita cessit
pars Heleno, qui Chaonios cognomine campos
Chaoniamque omnem Troiano a Chaone dixit,   335
Pergamaque Iliacamque iugis hanc addidit arcem.
sed tibi qui cursum venti, quae fata dedere?
aut quisnam ignarum nostris deus appulit oris?
quid puer Ascanius? superatne et vescitur aura,
quem tibi iam Troia . . .?   340
ecqua tamen puero est amissae cura parentis?
ecquid in antiquam virtutem animosque virilis   MP
et pater Aeneas et avunculus excitat Hector?'
talia fundebat lacrimans longosque ciebat
incassum fletus, cum sese a moenibus heros   345
Priamides multis Helenus comitantibus adfert,
adgnoscitque suos laetusque ad limina ducit
et multum lacrimas verba inter singula fundit.
procedo et parvam Troiam simulataque magnis
Pergama et arentem Xanthi cognomine rivum   350

---

[327] enixe a, *Donatus.*
[330] inflammatus $M\gamma^2a^2bc$: flammatus *the other MSS.*
[340] *Certain inferior MSS. complete the line in various ways.
Six of them add* peperit fumante Creusa.
[346] Helenus multis *P.*
[348] lacrimans $M^2P\gamma^1$, *known to Servius.*

[321] " 'O happy beyond all others, maiden daughter
of Priam, bidden to die at a foeman's tomb, beneath
Troy's lofty walls, who never bore the lot's award,
nor touched, as captive, a conquering master's bed !
We, our fatherland burnt, borne over distant seas,
have endured the pride of Achilles' son and his
youthful insolence, bearing children in slavery;
afterwards, seeking Leda's Hermione and Lacedae-
monian nuptials, he passed me over to Helenus'
keeping—a bondmaid and to a bondman. But him
Orestes, fired with strong desire for his stolen
bride, and goaded by the Furies of his crimes,
catches unawares and slays at his father's altar.
By the death of Neoptolemus a portion of the realm
passed as his due to Helenus, who called the plains
Chaonian and the whole land Chaonia from Chaon of
Troy, and placed on the heights a Pergamus, this
Ilian citadel. But to thee, what winds, what fates
gave a course? or what god has driven thee un-
knowing on our coasts? What of the boy Ascanius?
Lives he yet and feeds he on the air of heaven?
Whom now, lo, when Troy . . .[1] Has the lad none
the less some love for his lost mother? Do his
father Aeneas and his uncle Hector arouse him at
all to ancestral valour and to manly spirit?'

[344] " Such words she poured forth weeping, and
was idly awaking a long lament, when the hero
Helenus, Priam's son, draws near from the city with
a great company. He knows us for his kin, joy-
fully leads us to the gates, and freely pours forth
tears at every word. I advance, and recognize a
little Troy, with a copy of great Pergamus, and a
dry brook that takes its name from Xanthus, and

[1] This is the only incomplete line in Virgil where the sense
is also incomplete.

VIRGIL

adgnosco, Scaeaeque amplector limina portae.
nec non et Teucri socia simul urbe fruuntur.
illos porticibus rex accipiebat in amplis ;
aulaï medio libabant pocula Bacchi,
impositis auro dapibus, paterasque tenebant.   355

" Iamque dies alterque dies processit, et aurae
vela vocant tumidoque inflatur carbasus Austro :
his vatem adgredior dictis ac talia quaeso :
' Troiugena, interpres divum, qui numina Phoebi,
qui tripodas, Clarii laurus, qui sidera sentis   360
et volucrum linguas et praepetis omina pinnae,
fare age (namque omnem cursum mihi prospera dixit
religio, et cuncti suaserunt numine divi
Italiam petere et terras temptare repostas ;
sola novum dictuque nefas Harpyia Celaeno   365
prodigium canit et tristis denuntiat iras
obscenamque famem), quae prima pericula vito ?
quidve sequens tantos possim superare labores ? '
hic Helenus, caesis primum de more iuvencis,
exorat pacem divum vittasque resolvit   370
sacrati capitis meque ad tua limina, Phoebe,
ipse manu multo suspensum numine ducit,
atque haec deinde canit divino ex ore sacerdos :

" ' Nate dea, nam te maioribus ire per altum
auspiciis manifesta fides (sic fata deum rex   375
sortitur volvitque vices, is vertitur ordo),
pauca tibi e multis, quo tutior hospita lustres
aequora et Ausonio possis considere portu,
expediam dictis ; prohibent nam cetera Parcae
scire Helenum farique vetat Saturnia Iuno.   380

---

³⁵⁰ tripoda ac Clarii *Mackail.*
³⁵² omnis *Pγ*¹ : omnem, *M, Servius.   Mackail reads* omnis
cursu.   ³⁷² multo] voltu *P*¹.   suspensus *known to Servius.*
372

embrace the portals of a Scaean gate. No less, too, my Teucrians enjoy with me the friendly city. The king welcomed them amid broad cloisters; in the centre of the hall they poured libations of wine and held the bowls, while the feast was served on gold.

356 " And now day after day has passed; the breezes call to the sails, and the canvas fills with the swelling South. With these words I approach the seer, and thus make quest:

359 " ' O son of Troy, interpreter of the gods, who knowest the will of Phoebus, the tripods, the laurel of the Clarian, the stars, and tongues of birds and omens of the flying wing, come, tell me—for with fair words hath Heaven declared to me all my journey, and all the gods in their oracles have counselled me to make for Italy and explore lands remote; only Celaeno the Harpy prophesies a startling portent, horrible to tell of, and threatens baleful wrath and foul famine—what perils am I first to shun? or by what course may I surmount such suffering?'

369 " Then Helenus, first sacrificing steers in due form, craves the grace of heaven and unbinds the fillets of his hallowed brow; with his own hand he leads me to thy gates, O Phoebus, thrilled with thy full presence, and then with a priest's inspired lips thus prophesies:

374 " ' O Goddess-born! since there is clear proof that under higher auspices thou dost journey o'er the sea—for thus the king of the gods allots the destinies and rolls the wheel of change; and such is the circling course—a few things out of many I will unfold thee in speech, that so more safely thou mayest traverse the seas of thy sojourn, and find rest in Ausonia's haven; for the Fates forbid Helenus to know more and Saturnian Juno stays

373

principio Italiam, quam tu iam rere propinquam
vicinosque, ignare, paras invadere portus,
longa procul longis via dividit invia terris.
ante et Trinacria lentandus remus in unda
et salis Ausonii lustrandum navibus aequor   385
infernique lacus Aeaeaeque insula Circae,
quam tuta possis urbem componere terra.
signa tibi dicam, tu condita mente teneto.
cum tibi sollicito secreti ad fluminis undam
litoreis ingens inventa sub ilicibus sus   390
triginta capitum fetus enixa iacebit,
alba, solo recubans, albi circum ubera nati,
is locus urbis erit, requies ea certa laborum.
nec tu mensarum morsus horresce futuros;
fata viam invenient aderitque vocatus Apollo.   395
has autem terras Italique hanc litoris oram,
proxima quae nostri perfunditur aequoris aestu,
effuge; cuncta malis habitantur moenia Grais.
hic et Narycii posuerunt moenia Locri
et Sallentinos obsedit milite campos   400
Lyctius Idomeneus; hic illa ducis Meliboei
parva Philoctetae subnixa Petelia muro.
quin ubi transmissae steterint trans aequora classes
et positis aris iam vota in litore solves,
purpureo velare comas adopertus amictu,   405
ne qua inter sanctos ignis in honore deorum
hostilis facies occurrat et omina turbet.
hunc socii morem sacrorum, hunc ipse teneto;
hac casti maneant in religione nepotes.
ast ubi digressum Siculae te admoverit orae   410
ventus et angusti rarescent claustra Pelori,

his utterance. First of all, the Italy which now
thou deemest so near, and into whose neighbouring
ports, unwitting one! thou dost essay entrance, a
long trackless track with long land-reaches sunders
widely. First in the Trinacrian wave must thou
bend the oar, and traverse with thy ships the salt
Ausonian main, past the nether lakes and Aeaean
Circe's isle, ere thou mayest build thy city in a land
of safety. Tokens will I declare to thee; do thou
keep them stored in mind. When, in thy distress,
by the waters of a secluded stream, thou shalt find
a sow lying under the oaks on the shore, just de-
livered of a litter of thirty young, the mother
reclining on the ground white—white, too, the
young about her teats—there shall be the city's site,
there a sure rest from thy toils. And dread not the
gnawing of tables that awaits thee; the Fates will find
a way, and Apollo be present at thy call. But these
lands, and this nearest border of the Italian shore,
that is washed by the tide of our own sea, avoid; in
all the towns dwell evil Greeks! Here the Narycian
Locri have built a city, and Lyctian Idomeneus has
beset with soldiery the Sallentine plains; here is the
famous town of Philoctetes, the Meliboean captain
—tiny Petelia, strong within her wall. Moreover,
when thy ships have crossed the seas and anchored,
and when now thou raisest altars and payest vows on
the shore, veil thy hair with covering of purple
robe, that in the worship of the gods no hostile face
may intrude amid the holy fires and mar the omens.
This mode of sacrifice do thou keep, thou and thy
company; by this observance let thy children's
children in purity stand fast. But when, on part-
ing thence, the wind has borne thee to the Sicilian
coast, and the barriers of narrow Pelorus open

VIRGIL

laeva tibi tellus et longo laeva petantur
aequora circuitu ; dextrum fuge litus et undas.
haec loca vi quondam et vasta convolsa ruina
(tantum aevi longinqua valet mutare vetustas)   415
dissiluisse ferunt, cum protinus utraque tellus
una foret ; venit medio vi pontus et undis
Hesperium Siculo latus abscidit, arvaque et urbes
litore diductas angusto interluit aestu.
dextrum Scylla latus, laevum implacata Charybdis 420
obsidet, atque imo barathri ter gurgite vastos
sorbet in abruptum fluctus rursusque sub auras
erigit alternos, et sidera verberat unda.
at Scyllam caecis cohibet spelunca latebris
ora exsertantem et navis in saxa trahentem.   425
prima hominis facies et pulchro pectore virgo
pube tenus, postrema immani corpore pistrix,
delphinum caudas utero commissa luporum.
praestat Trinacrii metas lustrare Pachyni
cessantem, longos et circumflectere cursus,   430
quam semel informem vasto vidisse sub antro
Scyllam et caeruleis canibus resonantia saxa.
praeterea, si qua est Heleno prudentia, vati
si qua fides, animum si veris implet Apollo,
unum illud tibi, nate dea, proque omnibus unum 435
praedicam et repetens iterumque iterumque monebo:
Iunonis magnae primum prece numen adora,
Iunoni cane vota libens dominamque potentem
supplicibus supera donis : sic denique victor
Trinacria finis Italos mittere relicta.   440
huc ubi delatus Cumaeam acceseris urbem
divinosque lacus et Averna sonantia silvis,

419 deductas *M*.
        421 vasto *P*[1], *Servius, but* vastos *in note on* I. 117.
        433 *Punctuation before* vati *M*[2]*P*[2].
        440 mittere] misere *P*[1] : miscere *P*[2]γ[1].

376

out, make thou for the land on the left and the seas on the left, long though the circuit be; shun the shore and waters on the right. These lands, they say, of old broke asunder, torn by force of mighty upheaval—such vast change can length of time effect—when the two countries were one unbroken whole. The sea came in might between, cut off with its waters the Hesperian from the Sicilian coast, and with narrow tideway laves fields and cities on severed shores. Scylla guards the right side; Charybdis, insatiate, the left; and at the bottom of her seething chasm thrice she sucks the vast waves into the abyss, and again in turn casts them upwards, lashing the stars with spray. But Scylla a cavern confines in blind recesses, whence she thrusts forth her mouths and draws ships within her rocks. Above she is of human form, down to the waist a fair-bosomed maiden; below, she is a sea-dragon of monstrous frame, with dolphins' tails joined to a belly of wolves. Better is it to double the goal of Trinacrian Pachynus, and, lingering on thy way, fetch a long compass, than once get sight of misshapen Scylla in her vast cavern, and of the rocks that ring with her sea-green hounds. Moreover, if Helenus has any foresight, if the seer may claim any faith, if Apollo fills his soul with truth, this one thing, O Goddess-born, this one in lieu of all I will foretell, and again and again repeat the warning: mighty Juno's power honour thou first with prayer; to Juno joyfully chant vows, and win over the mighty mistress with suppliant gifts. So at last thou shalt leave Trinacria behind and be sped triumphantly to the bounds of Italy. And when, thither borne, thou drawest near to the town of Cumae, the haunted lakes, and Avernus with its rustling woods, thou

VIRGIL

insanam vatem aspicies, quae rupe sub ima
fata canit foliisque notas et nomina mandat.
quaecumque in foliis descripsit carmina virgo,   445
digerit in numerum atque antro seclusa relinquit.
illa manent immota locis neque ab ordine cedunt ;
verum eadem, verso tenuis cum cardine ventus
impulit et teneras turbavit ianua frondes,
numquam deinde cavo volitantia prendere saxo   450
nec revocare situs aut iungere carmina curat ;
inconsulti abeunt sedemque odere Sibyllae.
hic tibi ne qua morae fuerint dispendia tanti,
quamvis increpitent socii et vi cursus in altum
vela vocet possisque sinus implere secundos,   455
quin adeas vatem precibusque oracula poscas
ipsa canat vocemque volens atque ora resolvat.   GMP
illa tibi Italiae populos venturaque bella
et quo quemque modo fugiasque ferasque laborem,
expediet, cursusque dabit venerata secundos.   460
haec sunt, quae nostra liceat te voce moneri.
vade age et ingentem factis fer ad aethera Troiam.'

   "Quae postquam vates sic ore effatus amico est,
dona dehinc auro gravia sectoque elephanto
imperat ad navis ferri, stipatque carinis   465
ingens argentum Dodonaeosque lebetas,
loricam consertam hamis auroque trilicem,
et conum insignis galeae cristasque comantis,
arma Neoptolemi.   sunt et sua dona parenti.
addit equos additque duces ;   470
remigium supplet ; socios simul instruit armis.

⁴⁴⁹ teneras] terris *P*¹.   ⁴⁵⁵ vocent *M*²*P*²γ.
⁴⁶⁴ gravia ac secto *Schaper*.   *So Mackail.*
⁴⁶⁹ parentis *P*.

378

shalt look on an inspired prophetess, who deep in a rocky cave sings the Fates and entrusts to leaves signs and symbols. Whatever verses the maid has traced on leaves[1] she arranges in order and stores away in the cave. These remain unmoved in their places and quit not their rank; but when at the turn of the hinge a light breeze has stirred them, and the open door scattered the tender foliage, never does she thereafter care to catch them, as they flutter in the rocky cave, nor to recover their places, nor to unite the verses; uncounselled, men depart, and loathe the Sibyl's seat. Here let no loss in delay be of such account in thine eyes—though comrades chide, though the voyage urgently calls thy sails to the deep and thou mayest swell their folds with favouring gales—that thou visit not the prophetess and with prayers plead that she herself chant the oracles, and graciously open her lips in speech. The nations of Italy, the wars to come, the mode whereby thou art to flee or face each toil, she will unfold to thee; and, reverently besought, she will grant thee a prosperous voyage. This it is whereof by my voice thou mayest be warned. Now go thy way, and by thy deeds exalt Troy in greatness unto heaven!'

463 "When the seer had thus spoken with friendly lips, he next gives command that gifts of heavy gold and sawn ivory be brought to the ships, stows in the hulls massive silver and cauldrons of Dodona, a breastplate trebly woven with hooks of gold, and a brilliant pointed helm with crested plumes, the arms of Neoptolemus. My father, too, has gifts of his own; horses he brings, and guides he brings; he fills up our crews, and with arms, too, equips my comrades.

[1] The leaves and bark of trees were the earliest writing materials.

VIRGIL

" Interea classem velis aptare iubebat
Anchises, fieret vento mora ne qua ferenti.
quem Phoebi interpres multo compellat honore :
' coniugio, Anchisa, Veneris dignate superbo,   475
cura deum, bis Pergameis erepte ruinis,
ecce tibi Ausoniae tellus ; hanc arripe velis.
et tamen hanc pelago praeterlabare necesse est ;
Ausoniae pars illa procul, quam pandit Apollo.
vade,' ait, ' o felix nati pietate.   quid ultra   480
provehor et fando surgentis demoror Austros ? '
nec minus Andromache, digressu maesta supremo,
fert picturatas auri subtemine vestis
et Phrygiam Ascanio chlamydem, nec cedit honori,
textilibusque onerat donis ac talia fatur :   485
' accipe et haec, manuum tibi quae monumenta
            mearum
sint, puer, et longum Andromachae testentur amorem,
coniugis Hectoreae.   cape dona extrema tuorum,
o mihi sola mei super Astyanactis imago.
sic oculos, sic ille manus, sic ora ferebat ;   490
et nunc aequali tecum pubesceret aevo.'
hos ego digrediens lacrimis adfabar obortis :
' vivite felices, quibus est fortuna peracta
iam sua ; nos alia ex aliis in fata vocamur.
vobis parta quies ; nullum maris aequor arandum, 495
arva neque Ausoniae semper cedentia retro
quaerenda.   effigiem Xanthi Troiamque videtis,
quam vestrae fecere manus, melioribus, opto,
auspiciis, et quae fuerit minus obvia Grais.
si quando Thybrim vicinaque Thybridis arva   500
intraro gentique meae data moenia cernam,
cognatas urbes olim populosque propinquos,

    475 Anchisae $M^1P^2\gamma$: Anchise P^1.   476 erepta P.
    478 praeterlabere M^1 : praterlabre P^1.
    480 ait] age M^1.   483 subtegmine $GM^1\gamma^1$.

AENEID BOOK III

[472] " Meanwhile Anchises bade us fit the ships
with sails, that the favouring wind should meet no
delay. Him the interpreter of Phoebus with deep
respect accosts : ' Anchises, deemed worthy of lofty
wedlock with Venus, the gods' charge, twice rescued
from the fall of Pergamus, lo! before thee is the
land of Ausonia! Make sail and seize it! And yet
past this shore thou must needs drift upon the sea ;
far away is that part of Ausonia which Apollo reveals.
Fare forth,' he cries, ' blest in thy son's love. Why
go I on further, and with speech delay the rising
winds ? ' Andromache, too, sad at the last parting,
brings robes figured with inwoven gold, and for
Ascanius a Phrygian scarf, nor fails she in courtesy,
but loads him with gifts from the loom, and thus
speaks : ' Take these, too, my child, to be memorials
of my handiwork and witnesses of the abiding love
of Andromache, Hector's wife. Take these last gifts
of thy kin, O thou sole surviving image of my
Astyanax ! Such was he in eyes, in hands and face ;
even now would his youth be ripening in equal years
with thine ! '

[492] " My tears welled up as I spake to them my
parting words : ' Fare ye well, ye whose own destiny is
already achieved ; we are still summoned from fate
to fate. Your rest is won. No ocean plains need ye
plough, no ever-retreating Ausonian fields need ye
seek. A copy of Xanthus ye see and a Troy, which
your own hands have built under happier omens, I
pray, and more beyond the range of Greeks. If
ever I enter the Tiber and Tiber's neighbouring
fields and look on the city-walls granted to my race,
hereafter, of our sister cities and allied peoples, in

---

[484] honore $P\gamma^1a$, *known to Servius:* honori $GM\gamma^2bc$, *Servius.*
[499] fuerint $MP\gamma$, *known to Servius:* fueris G^1.

VIRGIL

Epiro, Hesperia, quibus idem Dardanus auctor
atque idem casus, unam faciemus utramque
Troiam animis ; maneat nostros ea cura nepotes.' 505
  " Provehimur pelago vicina Ceraunia iuxta,
unde iter Italiam cursusque brevissimüs undis.
sol ruit interea et montes umbrantur opaci.
sternimur optatae gremio telluris ad undam,
sortiti remos, passimque in litore sicco   510
corpora curamus ; fessos sopor inrigat artus.
necdum orbem medium Nox Horis acta subibat :
haud segnis strato surgit Palinurus et omnis
explorat ventos atque auribus aëra captat ;
sidera cuncta notat tacito labentia caelo,   515
Arcturum pluviasque Hyadas geminosque Triones,
armatumque auro circumspicit Oriona.
postquam cuncta videt caelo constare sereno,
dat clarum e puppi signum ; nos castra movemus
temptamusque viam et velorum pandimus alas.   520
iamque rubescebat stellis Aurora fugatis,
cum procul obscuros collis humilemque videmus
Italiam.   Italiam primus conclamat Achates,
Italiam laeto socii clamore salutant.
tum pater Anchises magnum cratera corona   525
induit implevitque mero divosque vocavit
stans celsa in puppi :
' di maris et terrae tempestatumque potentes,
ferte viam vento facilem et spirate secundi ! '   529
crebrescunt optatae aurae, portusque patescit   [MP
iam propior, templumque apparet in Arce Minervae.
vela legunt socii et proras ad litora torquent.

---

[503] Hesperiam *GMP*γ[1] : Hesperia γ[2], *Servius.*
[504] faciamus *G.*
[516] pluvias] pliadas γ[1], *Macrobius.*
[527] celsa] prima *G*γ (*in margin*): -ima *P*[1] : -elsa *P*[2].
[531] proprior *MP*γ.

Epirus, in Hesperia—who have the same Dardanus
for ancestor and the same disastrous story—of these
twain we shall make one Troy in spirit. May that
charge await our children's children!'[1]

506 " Along the sea we speed, by the near Ceraunian
cliffs,whence is the way to Italy and the shortest voyage
over the waves. Meanwhile the sun sets and the hills
lie dark in shade. Having allotted the oars, we fling
ourselves down near the water on the bosom of the
welcome land and refresh ourselves on the dry beach ;
sleep bedews our weary limbs. Nor yet was Night,
driven by the Hours, entering her mid course, when
Palinurus springs, alert, from his couch, tries all
the winds, and with eager ear catches the breeze ; he
marks all the stars gliding in the silent sky, Arcturus,
the rainy Hyades, and the twin Bears, and he scans
Orion, girt with golden armour. When he sees that
all is calm in a cloudless sky, he gives a loud signal
from the stern ; we break up camp, venture on our
way, and spread the wings of our sails. And now
the stars were put to rout and Dawn was blushing,
when far off we see dim hills and low-lying Italy.
' Italy !' first Achates shouts aloud ; Italy the crews
hail with joyful cry. Then father Anchises wreathed
a great bowl, filled it with wine, and standing on
the lofty stern called on the gods: ' Ye gods, lords
of the sea and earth and storms, waft us onward
with easy wind, and blow with favouring breath !'
The longed-for breezes freshen, a haven opens as we
now draw near, and a temple is seen on Minerva's
Height.[2] My comrades furl the sails and shoreward

[1] This probably refers to the founding of Nicopolis in
Epirus by Augustus.
[2] A reference to Castrum Minervae, near the Portus Veneris
in Calabria, the modern Castro.

383

portus ab Euroo fluctu curvatus in arcum;
obiectae salsa spumant aspargine cautes,
ipse latet; gemino demittunt bracchia muro   535
turriti scopuli, refugitque ab litore templum.
quattuor hic, primum omen, equos in gramine vidi,
tondentis campum late, candore nivali.
et pater Anchises: 'bellum, o terra hospita, portas;
bello armantur equi, bellum haec armenta minantur.
sed tamen idem olim curru succedere sueti   541
quadrupedes et frena iugo concordia ferre:
spes et pacis,' ait.   Tum numina sancta precamur
Palladis armisonae, quae prima accepit ovantis,
et capita ante aras Phrygio velamur amictu,   545
praeceptisque Heleni, dederat quae maxima, rite
Iunoni Argivae iussos adolemus honores.

   " Haud mora, continuo perfectis ordine votis
cornua velatarum obvertimus antemnarum
Graiugenumque domos suspectaque linquimus arva.
hinc sinus Herculei, si vera est fama, Tarenti   551
cernitur; attollit se diva Lacinia contra
Caulonisque arces et navifragum Scylaceum.
tum procul e fluctu Trinacria cernitur Aetna,
et gemitum ingentem pelagi pulsataque saxa   555
audimus longe fractasque ad litora voces,
exsultantque vada atque aestu miscentur harenae.
et pater Anchises: 'nimirum haec illa Charybdis;
hos Helenus scopulos, haec saxa horrenda canebat.
eripite, o socii, pariterque insurgite remis.'   560
haud minus ac iussi faciunt, primusque rudentem MPV
contorsit laevas proram Palinurus ad undas;
laevam cuncta cohors remis ventisque petivit.

   535 dimittunt *P*.   **545** capite *P*[1].   aram *P*γ.
   556 ab litore *M*[2], *so Mackail:* ab litora γ.
   558 haec γ[1]*c:* hic *MPb*[1].   **563** ventis remisque *M*[1].

turn the prows. There a harbour is bent bow-like by the eastern surge; its jutting reefs foam with the salt spray, itself lying hid; towering crags let down arms of twin walls, and the temple recedes from the shore. Here, for our first omen, four steeds I saw on the turf, grazing at large over the plain, as white as snow. Then father Anchises : ''Tis war thou bearest, O land of our reception ; for war are horses armed, war these herds portend. But yet,' he cries, 'those same steeds at times are wont to come under the car and beneath the yoke to bear the bit in concord ; there is hope also of peace !' Then we pray to the holy power of Pallas, queen of clashing arms, who first welcomed our cheers, before the altar veiled our heads in Phrygian robe, and, following the urgent charge which Helenus had given, duly offer to Argive Juno the burnt sacrifice prescribed.

548 " At once, soon as our vows are paid in full, we point windward the horns of our sail-clad yards, and leave the homes of the Greek-born race and the fields we distrust. Next is descried the bay of Tarentum, a town of Hercules, if the tale be true; while over against it rise the Lacinian goddess,[1] the towers of Caulon and shipwrecking Scylaceum. Then in the distance out of the waves appears Trinacrian Aetna, and from afar we hear the loud moaning of the main, the lashing of the rocks, and broken noises along the shore ; the shoals dash up and the sands mingle with the surge. Then father Anchises : 'Surely this is that Charybdis, these are the crags, these the dread rocks Helenus foretold. To the rescue, comrades, and rise together over the oars !' Even as bidden they do, and first Palinurus swung the groaning prow to the waves leftward ; leftward all our force plied

[1] There was a temple of Juno on the Lacinian promontory.

tollimur in caelum curvato gurgite et idem
subducta ad Manis imos desedimus unda ; 565
ter scopuli clamorem inter cava saxa dedere,
ter spumam elisam et rorantia vidimus astra.
interea fessos ventus cum sole reliquit,
ignarique viae Cyclopum adlabimur oris.

   " Portus ab accessu ventorum immotus et ingens 570
ipse, sed horrificis iuxta tonat Aetna ruinis,
interdumque atram prorumpit ad aethera nubem,
turbine fumantem piceo et candente favilla,
attollitque globos flammarum et sidera lambit ;
interdum scopulos avolsaque viscera montis 575
erigit eructans, liquefactaque saxa sub auras
cum gemitu glomerat, fundoque exaestuat imo.
fama est Enceladi semustum fulmine corpus
urgeri mole hac ingentemque insuper Aetnam
impositam ruptis flammam exspirare caminis, 580
et fessum quotiens mutet latus, intremere omnem
murmure Trinacriam et caelum subtexere fumo.
noctem illam tecti silvis immania monstra
perferimus nec, quae sonitum det causa, videmus,
nam neque erant astrorum ignes nec lucidus aethra
siderea polus, obscuro sed nubila caelo, 586
et lunam in nimbo nox intempesta tenebat. MP

   " Postera iamque dies primo surgebat Eoo
umentemque Aurora polo dimoverat umbram,
cum subito e silvis, macie confecta suprema, 590
ignoti nova forma viri miserandaque cultu
procedit supplexque manus ad litora tendit.
respicimus.   dira inluvies, immissaque barba,

   581 mutat $M^2P^2\gamma^1$, *known to Servius:* motat γ^2, *Servius:*
motet a^2b^2c.

with oars and wind. We mount up to heaven on
the arched billow and again, with the receding wave,
sink down to the depths of hell. Thrice amid the
rocky caverns the cliffs uttered a cry ; thrice we saw
the showered spray and the dripping stars. Mean-
while, at sundown the wind failed our weary band
and, in ignorance of the way, we drift up to the
Cyclopes' coast.

570 " There lies a harbour, safe from the winds'
approach and spacious in itself, but near at hand
Aetna thunders with terrifying crashes, and now
hurls forth to the sky a black cloud, smoking with
pitch-black eddy and glowing ashes, and uplifts balls
of flame and licks the stars—now violently vomits
forth rocks, the mountain's uptorn entrails, and whirls
molten stone skyward with a roar, and boils up from
its lowest depths. The story runs that Enceladus'
form, scathed by the thunderbolt, is weighed down
by that mass, and mighty Aetna, piled above, from
its burst furnaces breathes forth flame ; and ever as
he changes his weary side all Trinacria moans and
trembles, veiling the sky in smoke. All that night
we hide in the woods, enduring monstrous horrors,
and see not from what cause comes the sound. For
neither did the stars show their fires, nor was heaven
clear with stellar light, but mists darkened the sky
and the dead of night held fast the moon in cloud.

588 " And now the next day was rising with the
earliest morning star, and Dawn had scattered from
the sky the dewy shades, when on a sudden out of the
woods comes forth the strange shape of an unknown
man, outworn with uttermost hunger, and of piteous
guise, and towards the beach stretches suppliant
hands. We look back. Ghastly in his squalor, with
unshorn beard, and garb fastened with thorns, he was

consertum tegumen spinis ; at cetera Graius,
et quondam patriis ad Troiam missus in armis.   595
isque ubi Dardanios habitus et Troia vidit
arma procul, paulum aspectu conterritus haesit
continuitque gradum ; mox sese ad litora praeceps
cum fletu precibusque tulit : ' per sidera testor,
per superos atque hoc caeli spirabile lumen,   600
tollite me, Teucri ; quascumque abducite terras ;
hoc sat erit.   scio me Danais e classibus unum,
et bello Iliacos fateor petiisse Penatis.
pro quo, si sceleris tanta est iniuria nostri,
spargite me in fluctus vastoque immergite ponto : 605
si pereo, hominum manibus periisse iuvabit.'
dixerat et genua amplexus genibusque volutans
haerebat.   qui sit fari, quo sanguine cretus,
hortamur, quae deinde agitet fortuna, fateri.
ipse pater dextram Anchises, haud multa moratus, 610
dat iuveni atque animum praesenti pignore firmat.
ille haec, deposita tandem formidine, fatur :
' sum patria ex Ithaca, comes infelicis Ulixi,
nomine Achaemenides, Troiam genitore Adamasto
paupere (mansissetque utinam fortuna !) profectus.
hic me, dum trepidi crudelia limina linquunt,   616
immemores socii vasto Cyclopis in antro
deseruere.   domus sanie dapibusque cruentis,
intus opaca, ingens.   ipse arduus, altaque pulsat
sidera—di, talem terris avertite pestem !—   620
nec visu facilis nec dictu adfabilis ulli.
visceribus miserorum et sanguine vescitur atro.
vidi egomet, duo de numero cum corpora nostro
prensa manu magna medio resupinus in antro
frangeret ad saxum, sanieque aspersa natarent   625

    600 sperabile M^1.   numen M^1P^2: nomen P^1: lumen M^2P
(late).   601 adducite M^1.   621 effabilis P.
    625 adspersa M : aspersa P : exspersa *Servius*.

yet in all else a Greek, and had once been sent to Troy in his country's arms. When far off he saw the Dardan dress and the Trojan weapons, affrighted at the sight he stopped awhile and checked his steps; then rushed headlong to the shore with tears and prayers: ' By the stars I beseech you, by the gods above and this lightsome air we breathe, take me, O Trojans, carry me away to any lands whatever; that will be enough. I know that I am one from the Danaan ships, and own that I warred against the gods of Ilium. For that, if my guilt hath done so much wrong, fling me piecemeal over the waves or plunge me in the vast sea. If I die, it will be a boon to have died at the hands of men!' He ceased, and clung to our knees, clasping them and grovelling there. We urge him to tell what he is and of what blood born, then what fortune pursues him. My father Anchises himself, with little delay, gives the youth his hand and comforts his heart with the present pledge. At last he lays aside his fear and speaks thus:

613 " ' I come from the land of Ithaca, a companion of luckless Ulysses, Achaemenides by name, and, since my father Adamastus was poor—and would to heaven that fortune had so stayed!—I set out for Troy. Here my comrades, when hastily quitting the grim gateway, thoughtlessly left me in the Cyclops' vast cave. It is a house of gore and bloodstained feasts, dark and huge within. The master, gigantic, strikes the stars on high—ye gods, take such a pest away from earth!—in aspect forbidding, in speech to be accosted by none. He feeds on the flesh of wretched men and their dark blood. I myself saw when he seized in his huge hand two of our company and, lying back in the midst of the cave, crushed them on the rock, and the splashed courts swam with gore; I

VIRGIL

limina; vidi atro cum membra fluentia tabo
manderet et tepidi tremerent sub dentibus artus.
haud impune quidem; nec talia passus Ulixes
oblitusve sui est Ithacus discrimine tanto.
nam simul expletus dapibus vinoque sepultus   630
cervicem inflexam posuit, iacuitque per antrum
immensus, saniem eructans et frusta cruento
per somnum commixta mero, nos, magna precati
numina sortitique vices, una undique circum
fundimur et telo lumen terebramus acuto   635
ingens, quod torva solum sub fronte latebat,
Argolici clipei aut Phoebeae lampadis instar,
et tandem laeti sociorum ulciscimur umbras.
sed fugite, O miseri, fugite atque ab litore funem
rumpite.   640
nam qualis quantusque cavo Polyphemus in antro
lanigeras claudit pecudes atque ubera pressat,
centum alii curva haec habitant ad litora volgo
infandi Cyclopes et altis montibus errant.
tertia iam lunae se cornua lumine complent,   645
cum vitam in silvis inter deserta ferarum
lustra domosque traho vastosque ab rupe Cyclopas
prospicio sonitumque pedum vocemque tremesco.
victum infelicem, bacas lapidosaque corna,
dant rami, et volsis pascunt radicibus herbae.   650
omnia conlustrans hanc primum ad litora classem
prospexi venientem.   huic me, quaecumque fuisset,
addixi; satis est gentem effugisse nefandam.
vos animam hanc potius quocumque absumite leto.'
   "Vix ea fatus erat, summo cum monte videmus 655
ipsum inter pecudes vasta se mole moventem
pastorem Polyphemum et litora nota petentem,

[627] trepidi M^1P^2, *known to Servius.*
[629] oblitusque $P\gamma$.
[632] immensum P, *Servius.*

390

saw when he munched their limbs, all dripping
with black blood-clots, and the warm joints quivered
beneath his teeth. Yet not unpunished! Ulysses
brooked not this, nor in such a strait was he forgetful
of himself. For when, gorged with the feast and
drowned in wine, the monster rested his drooping
neck, and lay in endless length throughout the cave,
in his sleep vomiting gore and morsels mixed with
blood and wine, we prayed to the great gods, then,
with our parts allotted, pour round him on every side,
and with pointed weapon pierce the one huge eye, that
lay deep-set beneath his savage brow, like unto an
Argive shield or the lamp of Phoebus. And so at last
we gladly avenged our comrades' shades. But flee,
ye hapless ones, flee and cut your cables from the
shore! For in shape and size like Polyphemus, as
he pens his fleecy flocks in the rocky cave and drains
their udders, a hundred other monstrous Cyclopes
dwell all along these winding shores and roam the
high mountains. Thrice now do the moon's horns
fill with light since I began to drag out my life in
the woods among the lonely lairs and haunts of wild
beasts, viewing from a rock the huge Cyclopes and
trembling at their cries and tramping feet. A sorry
living, berries and stony cornels, the boughs supply;
and plants feed me with their uptorn roots. Scanning
all the view, at last I saw this fleet drawing to the
shore. To it, prove what it might, I surrendered
myself. 'Tis enough to have escaped the accursed
brood! Do ye rather, by any death whatever, take
away this life of mine!'

655 "Scarce had he spoken when on the mountain-
top we saw the giant himself, the shepherd Poly-
phemus, moving his mighty bulk among his flocks

---

634 nomina M^1.   635 tenebramus *known to Servius*.
652 conspexi $P\gamma^1$.   655 in monte $P^2\gamma^1$.

monstrum horrendum, informe, ingens, cui lumen
    ademptum.
trunca manu pinus regit et vestigia firmat;
lanigerae comitantur oves ; ea sola voluptas   FMP
solamenque mali.   661
postquam altos tetigit fluctus et ad aequora venit,
luminis effossi fluidum lavit inde cruorem,
dentibus infrendens gemitu, graditurque per aequor
iam medium, necdum fluctus latera ardua tinxit. 665
nos procul inde fugam trepidi celerare, recepto
supplice sic merito, tacitique incidere funem ;
verrimus et proni certantibus aequora remis.
sensit et ad sonitum vocis vestigia torsit.
verum ubi nulla datur dextra adfectare potestas 670
nec potis Ionios fluctus aequare sequendo,
clamorem immensum tollit, quo pontus et omnes
contremuere undae, penitusque exterrita tellus
Italiae curvisque immugiit Aetna cavernis.
at genus e silvis Cyclopum et montibus altis   675
excitum ruit ad portus et litora complent.
cernimus adstantis nequiquam lumine torvo
Aetnaeos fratres, caelo capita alta ferentis,
concilium horrendum : quales cum vertice celso
aëriae quercus aut coniferae cyparissi   680
constiterunt, silva alta Iovis lucusve Dianae.
praecipites metus acer agit quocumque rudentis
excutere et ventis intendere vela secundis.
contra iussa monent Heleni Scyllam atque Charybdim
inter, utramque viam leti discrimine parvo,   FMPR

    659 manum *M* (*late*), *Quintilian:* manu *M*[1], *Servius.*
    661 de collo fistula pendet *completes the verse* F(*late*)P*γab*[2]*c.*
    663 effuso *M*[1]: effusi *M*[2].   664 gemitum *P*[1].
    665 fluctu *M*[2]*P γ*[1], *Servius :* fluctur *F.*
    666 fuga *P*[1].   668 vertimus *MP :* verrimus *F.*
    670 dextram *FP*[2], *Servius.*   673 intremuere *FP.*
    682 ruentis *F*[1].
    684 monet *P*[1]: movent *Fγ*[1].   Scylla *FP*[1].   Charybdis *F.*

and seeking the well-known shore—a monster
awful, shapeless, huge, bereft of light. In his hand
a lopped pine guides and steadies his steps. His
fleecy sheep attend him—his sole joy they, sole
solace of his woe! Soon as he touched the deep
waves and reached the sea, with the water he washed
the oozing blood from his eye's socket, gnashing his
teeth and groaning, then strides through the open
sea; nor has the wave yet wetted his towering sides.
Anxiously we speed our flight far from there, taking
on board a suppliant so deserving, and silently cut
the cable; then, bending forward, sweep the seas
with emulous oars. He heard, and turned his steps
towards the sound of the splash. But when no power
is given him to lay hands on us, and he cannot match
in pursuit the Ionian waves, he raises a mighty roar,
whereat the sea and all its waves shuddered and the
land of Italy was affrighted far within, and Aetna
bellowed in its winding caverns. But the race of
the Cyclopes, roused from the woods and high
mountains, rush to the harbour and throng the
shores. We see them, standing impotent with glar-
ing eye, the Aetnean brothers, their heads towering
to the sky, a grim conclave: even as when on a moun-
tain-top lofty oaks or cone-clad cypresses stand in
mass, a high forest of Jove or grove of Diana. In
headlong speed, sharp fear drives us to fling out our
sheets for any course, and spread our sails to the
favouring winds. Yet the commands of Helenus
warn our crews not to hold on their course between
Scylla and Charybdis—either way but a hair's-breadth
removed from death.[1] We resolve to sail back again,

[1] Page prefers to render thus: "On the other hand stands in
warning the command of Helenus: ' *Between Scylla and Charyb-
dis the path on either hand is within a hair's-breadth of death, if ye
fail to hold your course.*'" The passage is faulty, and would prob-
ably have been altered by the poet on a revision of the work.

ni teneant cursus; certum est dare lintea retro. 686
ecce autem Boreas angusta ab sede Pelori
missus adest; vivo praetervehor ostia saxo
Pantagiae Megarosque sinus Thapsumque iacentem.
talia monstrabat relegens errata retrorsus   MPR
litora Achaemenides, comes infelicis Ulixi.   MPRV

"Sicanio praetenta sinu iacet insula contra
Plemyrium undosum; nomen dixere priores
Ortygiam.   Alpheum fama est huc Elidis amnem
occultas egisse vias subter mare, qui nunc   695
ore, Arethusa, tuo Siculis confunditur undis.
iussi numina magna loci veneramur et inde
exsupero praepingue solum stagnantis Helori.
hinc altas cautes proiectaque saxa Pachyni
radimus, et fatis numquam concessa moveri   700
apparet Camerina procul campique Geloi
immanisque Gela fluvii cognomine dicta.
arduus inde Acragas ostentat maxima longe
moenia, magnanimum quondam generator equorum;
teque datis linquo ventis, palmosa Selinus,   705
et vada dura lego saxis Lilybeia caecis.
hinc Drepani me portus et inlaetabilis ora
accipit.   hic pelagi tot tempestatibus actus
heu! genitorem, omnis curae casusque levamen,
amitto Anchisen; hic me, pater optime, fessum   710
deseris, heu! tantis nequiquam erepte periclis!
nec vates Helenus, cum multa horrenda moneret,
hos mihi praedixit luctus, non dira Celaeno.
hic labor extremus, longarum haec meta viarum;
hinc me digressum vestris deus appulit oris."   715

Sic pater Aeneas intentis omnibus unus
fata renarrabat divum cursusque docebat.   MPR
conticuit tandem factoque hic fine quievit.

686 ni *FMRγ²*: ne *P²γ¹*: nec *P¹*.
708 actis *PRγ, Servius:* act . . *V.*
717 cursu *P¹.*

when, lo! from the narrow fastness of Pelorus the north wind reaches us. Past the mouth of the Pantagias with its living rock I voyage—past the Megarian bay and low-lying Thapsus. Such were the coasts Achaemenides, comrade of the luckless Ulysses, pointed out, as he retraced his former wanderings.

692 "Stretched in front of a Sicanian bay lies an island, over against wave-beaten Plemyrium; men of old called it Ortygia. Hither, so runs the tale, Alpheus, river of Elis, forced a secret course beneath the sea, and now at thy fountain, Arethusa, mingles with the Sicilian waves. As bidden, we worship the great gods of the land, and thence I passed the wondrous rich soil of marshy Helorus. Next we skirt the high reefs and jutting rocks of Pachynus; and afar off Camerina—Fate forbade that she ever be disturbed —is seen with the Geloan plains, and Gela, named after its impetuous river. Then steep Acragas, once the breeder of noble steeds, shows in the distance her mighty walls; and, with the winds vouchsafed, I leave thee behind, palm-girt Selinus, and skirt the shoals of Lilybaeum, perilous with blind rocks. Next the harbour of Drepanum and its joyless shore receive me. Here I, who have been driven by so many ocean-storms, lose, alas! my father Anchises, solace of every care and chance; here, best of fathers, thou leavest me in my weariness, snatched, alas! from such mighty perils all for naught. Nor did the seer Helenus, though he warned me of many horrors, nor grim Celaeno foretell me this grief. This was my last trial, this the goal of my long voyaging; departing thence, the god drove me to your shores."

716 Thus father Aeneas, before an eager throng, alone recounted the dooms ordained of heaven, and taught the story of his wanderings. At last he ceased, and here, making an end, was still.

LIBER IV

At regina gravi iamdudum saucia cura   FGMPR
volnus alit venis et caeco carpitur igni.
multa viri virtus animo multusque recursat
gentis honos ; haerent infixi pectore voltus
verbaque, nec placidam membris dat cura quietem. 5
postera Phoebea lustrabat lampade terras
umentemque Aurora polo dimoverat umbram,
cum sic unanimam adloquitur male sana sororem :
" Anna soror, quae me suspensam insomnia terrent !
quis novus hic nostris successit sedibus hospes,   10
quem sese ore ferens, quam forti pectore et armis !
credo equidem, nec vana fides, genus esse deorum.
degeneres animos timor arguit.   heu ! quibus ille
iactatus fatis !   quae bella exhausta canebat !
si mihi non animo fixum immotumque sederet,   15
ne cui me vinclo vellem sociare iugali,
postquam primus amor deceptam morte fefellit ;
si non pertaesum thalami taedaeque fuisset,
huic uni forsan potui succumbere culpae.
Anna, fatebor enim, miseri post fata Sychaei   20
coniugis et sparsos fraterna caede Penatis
solus hic inflexit sensus animumque labantem

⁹ suspensa M^1.   terret *known to Servius*.
¹¹ quam] quem F^1.
¹⁸ fuissent $F^2MP^1\gamma^1$.

BOOK IV

But the queen, long since smitten with a grievous
love-pang, feeds the wound with her life-blood, and
is wasted with fire unseen. Oft to her heart rushes
back the chief's valour, oft his glorious stock ; his
looks and words cling fast within her bosom, and the
pang withholds calm rest from her limbs.

[6] The morrow's dawn was lighting the earth with
the lamp of Phoebus, and had scattered from the
sky the dewy shades, when, much distraught, she
thus speaks to her sister, sharer of her heart :
"Anna, my sister, what dreams thrill me with
fears ? Who is this stranger guest that hath en-
tered our home ? How noble his mien ! how brave
in heart and feats of arms ! I believe it well—nor
is assurance vain—that he is sprung from gods. 'Tis
fear that proves souls base-born. Alas ! by what
fates is he vexed ! What wars, long endured, did
he recount ! Were the purpose not planted in my
mind, fixed and immovable, to ally myself with
none in bond of wedlock, since my first love, turn-
ing traitor, cheated me by death ; were I not
utterly weary of the bridal bed and torch, to this
one weakness, perchance, I might have yielded !
Anna—for I will own it—since the death of my hap-
less lord Sychaeus, and the shattering of our home
by a brother's murder,[1] he alone has swayed my will
and overthrown my tottering soul. I recognize the

1 cf. *Aen.* i. 348 ff.

397

VIRGIL

impulit.　adgnosco veteris vestigia flammae.
sed mihi vel tellus optem prius ima dehiscat
vel pater omnipotens adigat me fulmine ad umbras,　25
pallentis umbras Erebi noctemque profundam,
ante, Pudor, quam te violo aut tua iura resolvo.
ille meos, primus qui me sibi iunxit, amores
abstulit ; ille habeat secum servetque sepulchro."
sic effata sinum lacrimis implevit obortis.　30
　　Anna refert : " O luce magis dilecta sorori,
solane perpetua maerens carpere iuventa,
nec dulcis natos Veneris nec praemia noris ?
id cinerem aut Manis credis curare sepultos ?
esto ; aegram nulli quondam flexere mariti,　35
non Libyae, non ante Tyro ; despectus Iarbas
ductoresque alii, quos Africa terra triumphis
dives alit ; placitone etiam pugnabis amori ?　FMPR
nec venit in mentem, quorum consederis arvis ?
hinc Gaetulae urbes, genus insuperabile bello,　40
et Numidae infreni cingunt et inhospita Syrtis ;
hinc deserta siti regio lateque furentes
Barcaei.　quid bella Tyro surgentia dicam
germanique minas ?
dis equidem auspicibus reor et Iunone secunda　45
hunc cursum Iliacas vento tenuisse carinas.
quam tu urbem, soror, hanc cernes, quae surgere
　　regna
coniugio tali !　Teucrum comitantibus armis,
Punica se quantis attollet gloria rebus !
tu modo posce deos veniam, sacrisque litatis　50
indulge hospitio causasque innecte morandi,
dum pelago desaevit hiems et aquosus Orion,
quassataeque rates, dum non tractabile caelum."

　　　　25 abigat *F.*
　　　　26 Erebo *FGP*1, *preferred by Servius :* Eribo *R.*
　　　　36 Libya *P*1.　　　　　　40 intractabile *R.*
　　　　51 hospitio et causas *F :* -que *omitted F.*

398

traces of the olden flame. But rather, I would pray, may earth yawn for me to its depths, or may the Almighty Father hurl me with his bolt to the shades—the pale shades and abysmal night of Erebus—before, O Shame, I violate thee or break thy laws! He, who first linked me to himself, has taken away my heart; may he keep it with him, and guard it in the grave!" So saying, she filled her bosom with upwelling tears.

³¹ Anna replies : " O dearer to thy sister than the light, wilt thou, lonely and sad, pine away all thy youth long, and know not sweet children or love's rewards? Thinkest thou that dust or buried shades give heed to that? Grant that heretofore no wooers moved thy sorrow, not in Libya, not ere then in Tyre ; that Iarbas was slighted, and other lords, whom the African land, rich in triumphs, rears ; wilt thou wrestle also with a love that pleases? And dost thou not call to mind in whose lands thou art settled? On this side Gaetulian cities, a race invincible in war, unbridled Numidians, and the unfriendly Syrtis hem thee in ; on that side lies a tract barren with drought, and Barcaeans, raging far and near. Why speak of the wars rising from Tyre, and thy brother's threats? With favouring gods, methinks indeed, and with Juno's aid, the Ilian ships have held their course hither with the wind. What a city thou wilt see rise here, my sister, what a realm, by reason of such wedlock! With Teucrian arms beside us, to what heights will Punic glory soar? Only do thou ask favour of the gods and, with sacrifice duly offered, be lavish with thy welcome, and weave pleas for delay, while at sea winter rages fiercely and Orion is stormy—while the ships are shattered, and the skies intractable!"

399

VIRGIL

His dictis incensum animum inflammavit amore
spemque dedit dubiae menti solvitque pudorem.   55
principio delubra adeunt pacemque per aras
exquirunt; mactant lectas de more bidentis
legiferae Cereri Phoeboque patrique Lyaeo,
Iunoni ante omnis, cui vincla iugalia curae;
ipsa tenens dextra pateram pulcherrima Dido   60
candentis vaccae media inter cornua fundit
aut ante ora deum pinguis spatiatur ad aras,
instauratque diem donis, pecudumque reclusis
pectoribus inhians spirantia consulit exta.
heu vatum ignarae mentes! quid vota furentem,   65
quid delubra iuvant? est mollis flamma medullas
interea et tacitum vivit sub pectore volnus.
uritur infelix Dido totaque vagatur
urbe furens, qualis coniecta cerva sagitta,
quam procul incautam nemora inter Cresia fixit   70
pastor agens telis liquitque volatile ferrum
nescius; illa fuga silvas saltusque peragrat
Dictaeos; haeret lateri letalis harundo.
nunc media Aenean secum per moenia ducit
Sidoniasque ostentat opes urbemque paratam;   75
incipit effari, mediaque in voce resistit;
nunc eadem labente die convivia quaerit,
Iliacosque iterum demens audire labores
exposcit pendetque iterum narrantis ab ore.
post ubi digressi, lumenque obscura vicissim   80
luna premit suadentque cadentia sidera somnos,
sola domo maeret vacua stratisque relictis
incubat. illum absens absentem auditque videtque,
aut gremio Ascanium, genitoris imagine capta,
detinet, infandum si fallere possit amorem.   85

⁵⁴ incensum] impenso *F*¹, *known to Servius:* penso *P*¹.
flammavit *FP*¹*R*.
⁵⁸ f(r)ugiferae *F*¹*Rγ*².   ⁸⁵ amantem *F:* imago *R.*

[54] With these words she fanned into flame the
queen's love-enkindled heart, put hope in her waver-
ing mind, and loosed the bonds of shame. First they
visit the shrines and sue for peace at every altar;
duly they slay chosen sheep to Ceres the law-giver,
to Phoebus and father Lyaeus, before all to Juno,
guardian of wedlock bonds. Dido herself, matchless
in beauty, with cup in hand, pours libation midway
between the horns of a white heifer, or in presence
of the gods moves slowly to the rich altars, and solem-
nizes the day with gifts, then, gazing into the opened
breasts of victims, consults the quivering entrails.
Ah, blind souls of seers! Of what avail are vows or
shrines to one wild with love? All the while the flame
devours her tender heart-strings, and deep in her
breast lives the silent wound. Unhappy Dido burns,
and through the city wanders in frenzy—even as a
hind, smitten by an arrow, which, all unwary, amid
the Cretan woods, a shepherd hunting with darts
has pierced from afar, leaving in her the winged
steel, unknowing: she in flight ranges the Dictaean
woods and glades, but fast to her side clings the
deadly shaft. Now through the city's midst she leads
with her Aeneas, and displays her Sidonian wealth
and the city built; she essays to speak and stops with
the word half-spoken. Now, as day wanes, she seeks
that same banquet, again madly craves to hear the
sorrows of Ilium and again hangs on the speaker's
lips. Then when all have gone their ways, and in
turn the dim moon sinks her light, and the setting
stars invite sleep, alone she mourns in the empty
hall, and falls on the couch he has left. Though
absent, each from each, she hears him, she sees him,
or, captivated by his father's look, she holds Ascanius
on her lap, if so she may beguile a passion beyond

non coeptae adsurgunt turres, non arma iuventus
exercet portusve aut propugnacula bello
tuta parant ; pendent opera interrupta minaeque
murorum ingentes aequataque machina caelo.

Quam simul ac tali persensit peste teneri   90
cara Iovis coniunx nec famam obstare furori,
talibus adgreditur Venerem Saturnia dictis :
" egregiam vero laudem et spolia ampla refertis
tuque puerque tuus ; magnum et memorabile numen,
una dolo divum si femina victa duorum est.   95
nec me adeo fallit veritam te moenia nostra
suspectas habuisse domos Karthaginis altae.
sed quis erit modus, aut quo nunc certamine tanto ?
quin potius pacem aeternam pactosque hymenaeos
exercemus ?   habes, tota quod mente petisti :   100
ardet amans Dido traxitque per ossa furorem.
communem hunc ergo populum paribusque regamus
auspiciis ; liceat Phrygio servire marito
dotalisque tuae Tyrios permittere dextrae."

Olli (sensit enim simulata mente locutam,   105
quo regnum Italiae Libycas averteret oras)
sic contra est ingressa Venus : "quis talia demens
abnuat aut tecum malit contendere bello,
si modo, quod memoras, factum fortuna sequatur ?
sed fatis incerta feror, si Iuppiter unam   110
esse velit Tyriis urbem Troiaque profectis
miscerive probet populos aut foedera iungi.
tu coniunx ; tibi fas animum temptare precando.
perge, sequar."   tum sic excepit regia Iuno :
" mecum erit iste labor. nunc qua ratione quod instat   115

91 furori] pudori *R.*
93-121 *a later hand in F.*
94 nomen *some inferior MSS. So Janell and Sabb.*
106 adverteret *known to Servius.*
112 foedere *known to Servius.*

402

all utterance. No longer rise the towers begun, no longer do the youth exercise in arms, or toil at havens or bulwarks for safety in war; the works are broken off and idle—huge threatening walls and the engine [1] uptowering to heaven.

[90] Soon as the loved wife of Jove saw that she was held in a passion so fatal, and that her good name was now no bar to her frenzy, the daughter of Saturn accosts Venus thus : " Splendid indeed is the praise and rich the spoils ye win, thou and thy boy ; mighty and glorious is the power divine, if one woman is subdued by the guile of two gods ! Nay, it escapes me not how, in fear of our city, thou hast held in suspicion the homes of high Carthage. But what shall be the end ? or how far goes all this contest now ? Why work we not rather an enduring peace and a plighted wedlock ? What thou didst seek with all thy heart thou hast ; Dido is on fire with love and has drawn the madness through her veins. Let us then rule this people jointly with equal sovereignty ; let her serve a Phrygian husband and yield her Tyrians to thy hand as dowry ! "

[105] To her—for she knew that with feigned purpose she had spoken, to turn the empire from Italy to Libya's coasts—Venus thus began in reply : " Who so mad as to refuse such terms, or choose rather to strive with thee in war, if only Fortune favour the fulfilment of thy word ? But the Fates send me adrift, uncertain whether Jupiter wills that there be one city for the Tyrians and the wanderers from Troy, or approves the blending of peoples and the league of union. Thou art his wife ; thou mayest probe his heart with entreaty. Go on ; I will follow ! "

[114] Then queenly Juno thus replied : " With me shall rest that task. Now in what way the present purpose

[1] Here, perhaps, it is a crane.

403

confieri possit, paucis, adverte, docebo.   FMR

venatum Aeneas unaque miserrima Dido

in nemus ire parant, ubi primos crastinus ortus

extulerit Titan radiisque retexerit orbem.

his ego nigrantem commixta grandine nimbum, 120

dum trepidant alae saltusque indagine cingunt,

desuper infundam et tonitru caelum omne ciebo. MR

diffugient comites et nocte tegentur opaca ;

speluncam Dido dux et Troianus eandem

devenient.   adero et, tua si mihi certa voluntas, 125

conubio iungam stabili propriamque dicabo ;

hic hymenaeus erit."   non adversata petenti

adnuit atque dolis risit Cytherea repertis.

   Oceanum interea surgens Aurora reliquit.

it portis iubare exorto delecta iuventus ;   130

retia rara, plagae, lato venabula ferro,

Massylique ruunt equites et odora canum vis.

reginam thalamo cunctantem ad limina primi

Poenorum exspectant, ostroque insignis et auro

stat sonipes ac frena ferox spumantia mandit. 135

tandem progreditur magna stipante caterva,

Sidoniam picto chlamydem circumdata limbo.

cui pharetra ex auro, crines nodantur in aurum,

aurea purpuream subnectit fibula vestem.

nec non et Phrygii comites et laetus Iulus   140

incedunt ; ipse ante alios pulcherrimus omnis

infert se socium Aeneas atque agmina iungit.

qualis ubi hibernam Lyciam Xanthique fluenta

deserit ac Delum maternam invisit Apollo   MRV

instauratque choros, mixtique altaria circum 145

Cretesque Dryopesque fremunt pictique Agathyrsi ;

ipse iugis Cynthi graditur mollique fluentem

---

[116] confieri] quod fieri $M^1\gamma^2$: quo fieri *F.*

[116] primus M^1R: primum M (*late*).

[126] = I. 73. *Rejected here by Mackail.*

[127] aversata *R, known to Servius.*   [129] relinquit $M^1.$

can be achieved, hearken and I will explain in brief. Aeneas and unhappy Dido plan to go a-hunting together in the forest, soon as to-morrow's sun shows his rising and with his rays unveils the world. On them, while the hunters run to and fro and gird the glades with nets, I will pour down from above a black rain mingled with hail, and wake the whole welkin with thunder. The company shall scatter and be veiled in gloom of night; to the same cave shall come Dido and the Trojan chief. I will be there and, if certain of thy goodwill, will link them in sure wedlock, sealing her for his own; this shall be their bridal!" Yielding to her suit, the Cytherean gave assent and smiled at the guile discovered.

129 Meanwhile Dawn rose and left the ocean. When sunlight has burst forth, there issues from the gates a chosen band of youth; with meshed nets, toils, broad-pointed hunting-spears, there stream forth Massylian horsemen and their strong, keen-scented hounds. As the queen lingers in her bower, the Punic princes await her at the doorway; her prancing steed stands brilliant in purple and gold, and fiercely champs the foaming bit. At last she comes forth, attended by a mighty throng, and clad in a Sidonian robe with embroidered border. Her quiver is of gold, her tresses are knotted into gold, golden is the buckle to clasp her purple cloak. With her pace a Phrygian train and joyous Iülus. Aeneas himself, goodly beyond all others, advances to join her and unites his band with hers. As when Apollo quits Lycia, his winter home, and the streams of Xanthus, to visit his mother's Delos, and renews the dance, while mingling about his altars Cretans and Dryopes and painted Agathyrsians raise their voices—he himself treads the Cynthian ridges,

fronde premit crinem fingens atque implicat auro,
tela sonant umeris : haud illo segnior ibat
Aeneas, tantum egregio decus enitet ore.   150
postquam altos ventum in montis atque invia lustra,
ecce ferae saxi deiectae vertice caprae
decurrere iugis ; alia de parte patentis
transmittunt cursu campos atque agmina cervi
pulverulenta fuga glomerant montisque relinquunt.
at puer Ascanius mediis in vallibus acri   156
gaudet equo iamque hos cursu, iam praeterit illos,
spumantemque dari pecora inter inertia votis
optat aprum aut fulvum descendere monte leonem.

Interea magno misceri murmure caelum   160
incipit ; insequitur commixta grandine nimbus,
et Tyrii comites passim et Troiana iuventus   MPRV
Dardaniusque nepos Veneris diversa per agros
tecta metu petiere ; ruunt de montibus amnes.
speluncam Dido dux et Troianus eandem   165
deveniunt.   prima et Tellus et pronuba Iuno
dant signum ; fulsere ignes et conscius Aether
conubiis, summoque ululauunt vertice Nymphae.
ille dies primus leti primusque malorum
causa fuit.   neque enim specie famave movetur 170
nec iam furtivum Dido meditatur amorem ;
coniugium vocat ; hoc praetexit nomine culpam.

Extemplo Libyae magnas it Fama per urbes,
Fama, malum qua non aliud velocius ullum.
mobilitate viget virisque adquirit eundo ;   175
parva metu primo, mox sese attollit in auras
ingrediturque solo et caput inter nubila condit.
illam Terra parens, ira inritata deorum,

168 conubii *P²RV*.
169 malorum] laborum *P¹*, *Philargyrius*.
174 quo *P¹Vγ²*, *Priscian*, *Servius*.

406

and with soft leafage shapes and binds his flowing
locks, braiding it with golden diadem; the shafts
rattle on his shoulders: so no less lightly than he
went Aeneas, such beauty shines forth from his noble
face! When they came to the mountain heights
and pathless lairs, lo! wild goats dislodged from the
rocky peaks ran down the ridges; in another part
stags scurry across the open moors and amid clouds
of dust mass their bands in flight, as they leave the
hills behind. But in the midst of the valleys the
young Ascanius glories in his fiery steed, galloping
past now these, now those, and prays that amid the
timorous herds a foaming boar may be granted
to his vows or a tawny lion come down from the
mountain.

160 Meanwhile in the sky begins the turmoil of a
wild uproar; rain follows, mingled with hail. The
scattered Tyrian train and the Trojan youth, with
the Dardan grandson of Venus, in their fear seek
shelter here and there over the fields; torrents
rush down from the heights. To the same cave
come Dido and the Trojan chief. Primal Earth and
nuptial Juno give the sign; fires flashed in Heaven,
the witness to their bridal, and on the mountain-top
screamed the Nymphs. That day was the first day
of death, that first the cause of woe. For no more
is Dido swayed by fair show or fair fame, no more does
she dream of a secret love: she calls it marriage and
with that name veils her sin!

173 Forthwith Rumour runs through Libya's great
cities—Rumour of all evils the most swift. Speed
lends her strength, and she wins vigour as she goes;
small at first through fear, soon she mounts up to
heaven, and walks the ground with head hidden in
the clouds. Her, 'tis said, Mother Earth, provoked

VIRGIL

extremam, ut perhibent, Coeo Enceladoque sororem
progenuit, pedibus celerem et pernicibus alis,   180
monstrum horrendum, ingens, cui, quot sunt corpore
    plumae,
tot vigiles oculi subter (mirabile dictu),
tot linguae, totidem ora sonant, tot subrigit auris.
nocte volat caeli medio terraeque per umbram,
stridens, nec dulci declinat lumina somno;   185
luce sedet custos aut summi culmine tecti,
turribus aut altis, et magnas territat urbes,
tam ficti pravique tenax quam nuntia veri.
haec tum multiplici populos sermone replebat
gaudens, et pariter facta atque infecta canebat: 190
venisse Aenean, Troiano sanguine cretum,
cui se pulchra viro dignetur iungere Dido;
nunc hiemem inter se luxu, quam longa, fovere
regnorum immemores turpique cupidine captos.
haec passim dea foeda virum diffundit in ora.   195
protinus ad regem cursus detorquet Iarban
incenditque animum dictis atque aggerat iras. MPR

Hic Hammone satus, rapta Garamantide Nympha,
templa Iovi centum latis immania regnis,
centum aras posuit vigilemque sacraverat ignem, 200
excubias divum aeternas; pecudumque cruore
pingue solum et variis florentia limina sertis.
isque amens animi et rumore accensus amaro
dicitur ante aras media inter numina divum
multa Iovem manibus supplex orasse supinis: 205
"Iuppiter omnipotens, cui nunc Maurusia pictis
gens epulata toris Lenaeum libat honorem,
aspicis haec? an te, genitor, cum fulmina torques,

179 extrema R^1.   187 magnas et M^1.
191 a sanguine R.
196 cursu P^2: cursum γ, *Nonius.*
204 numina] munera *known to Servius.*

408

to anger against the gods, brought forth last, as sister
to Coeus and Enceladus, swift of foot and fleet of
wing, a monster awful and huge, who for the many
feathers in her body has as many watchful eyes
below—wondrous to tell—as many tongues, as many·
sounding mouths, as many pricked-up ears. By night,
midway between heaven and earth, she flies through
the gloom, screeching, nor droops her eyes in sweet
sleep; by day she sits on guard on high roof-top or
lofty turrets, and affrights great cities, clinging to
the false and wrong, yet heralding truth. At this
time, exulting with manifold gossip, she filled the
nations and sang alike of fact and falsehood, how
Aeneas is come, one born of Trojan blood, to whom
in marriage fair Dido deigns to join herself; now
they spend the winter, all its length, in wanton ease
together, heedless of their realms and enthralled by
shameless passion. These tales the foul goddess
spreads here and there upon the lips of men.
Straightway to King Iarbas she bends her course,
and with her words fires his spirit and heaps high
his wrath.

198 He, son of Hammon by a ravished Garamantian
Nymph, set up to Jupiter in his broad realms a
hundred vast temples, a hundred altars, and had
hallowed the wakeful fire, the eternal sentry of the
gods. The ground was fat with the blood of beasts
and the portals bloomed with varied garlands.
Distraught in mind and fired with the bitter tale,
they say that before the altars and amid the divine
presences he oft besought Jove in prayer with up-
turned hands: "Almighty Jupiter, to whom now
the Moorish race, feasting on embroidered couches,
pour a Lenaean offering, beholdest thou these things?
Is it vainly, O father, that we shudder at thee, when

nequiquam horremus, caecique in nubibus ignes
terrificant animos et inania murmura miscent?   210
femina, quae nostris errans in finibus urbem
exiguam pretio posuit, cui litus arandum
cuique loci leges dedimus, conubia nostra
reppulit ac dominum Aenean in regna recepit.
et nunc ille Paris cum semiviro comitatu,   215
Maeonia mentum mitra crinemque madentem
subnixus, rapto potitur : nos munera templis   MP
quippe tuis ferimus famamque fovemus inanem."

   Talibus orantem dictis arasque tenentem
audiit Omnipotens, oculosque ad moenia torsit   220
regia et oblitos famae melioris amantis.
tum sic Mercurium adloquitur ac talia mandat :
"vade age, nate, voca Zephyros et labere pinnis
Dardaniumque ducem, Tyria Karthagine qui nunc
exspectat fatisque datas non respicit urbes,   225
adloquere et celeris defer mea dicta per auras.
non illum nobis genetrix pulcherrima talem
promisit Graiumque ideo bis vindicat armis ;
sed fore, qui gravidam imperiis belloque frementem
Italiam regeret, genus alto a sanguine Teucri   230
proderet, ac totum sub leges mitteret orbem.
si nulla accendit tantarum gloria rerum
nec super ipse sua molitur laude laborem,
Ascanione pater Romanas invidet arces?   FMP
quid struit?   aut qua spe inimica in gente moratur
nec prolem Ausoniam et Lavinia respicit arva?   236
naviget : haec summa est, hic nostri nuntius esto."

thou hurlest thy bolts? And do aimless fires amid
the clouds terrify our souls and stir murmurs void
of purpose? This woman who, straying in our
bounds, set up a tiny city at a price, to whom we
gave coast-land to plough and terms of tenure, hath
spurned my offers of marriage, and welcomed Aeneas
into her realm as lord. And now that Paris [1] with
his eunuch train, a Maeonian band propping his chin
and essenced locks, grasps the spoil; while we bring
offerings to thy temples, thine forsooth, and cherish
an idle story."

[219] As with such words he pleaded, clasping the
altars, the Almighty gave ear and turned his eyes
on the royal city and the lovers forgetful of their
nobler fame. Then thus to Mercury he speaks and
gives this charge: "Go forth, my son, call the
Zephyrs, glide on thy wings, and speak to the Dardan
chief, who now dallies in Tyrian Carthage and heeds
not the cities granted by the Fates; so carry down
my words through the swift winds. Not such as
this did his lovely mother promise him to us, nor for
this twice rescue him from Grecian arms; but he was
to rule over Italy, a land teeming with empire and
clamorous with war, to hand on a race from Teucer's
noble blood, and bring all the world beneath his laws.
If the glory of such a fortune fires him not and for
his own fame's sake he shoulders not the burden,
does he, the father, grudge Ascanius the towers of
Rome? What plans he? or in what hope tarries he
among a hostile people and regards not Ausonia's
race and the Lavinian fields? Let him set sail; this
is the sum; be this the message from me."

[1] Aeneas is like Paris in carrying off another's bride. By
"Maeonian" is meant Lydian, or rather Phrygian, because
Lydia bordered on Phrygia. The Phrygian cap had on either
side a band or ribbon, which could be tied under the chin.

Dixerat. ille patris magni parere parabat
imperio, et primum pedibus talaria nectit
aurea, quae sublimem alis sive aequora supra   240
seu terram rapido pariter cum flamine portant.
tum virgam capit ; hac animas ille evocat Orco
pallentis, alias sub Tartara tristia mittit,
dat somnos adimitque et lumina morte resignat.
illa fretus agit ventos et turbida tranat   245
nubila. iamque volans apicem et latera ardua cernit
Atlantis duri, caelum qui vertice fulcit,
Atlantis, cinctum adsidue cui nubibus atris
piniferum caput et vento pulsatur et imbri ;
nix umeros infusa tegit ; tum flumina mento   250
praecipitant senis, et glacie riget horrida barba.
hic primum paribus nitens Cyllenius alis
constitit ; hinc toto praeceps se corpore ad undas
misit avi similis, quae circum litora, circum
piscosos scopulos humilis volat aequora iuxta.   255
haud aliter terras inter caelumque volabat
litus harenosum ad Libyae, ventosque secabat
materno veniens ab avo Cyllenia proles.   MP
ut primum alatis tetigit magalia plantis,
Aenean fundantem arces ac tecta novantem   260
conspicit. atque illi stellatus iaspide fulva
ensis erat, Tyrioque ardebat murice laena
demissa ex umeris, dives quae munera Dido
fecerat, et tenui telas discreverat auro.
continuo invadit : " tu nunc Karthaginis altae   265
fundamenta locas pulchramque uxorius urbem

²⁴¹ portent *M*¹.   ²⁴³ mittit] ducit *P*¹.
²⁵⁷ ad *P*² : at *M*¹ : ꜱo *M* (*late*) : ꜱo *P*¹.

412

AENEID BOOK IV

238 He ceased. The god made ready to obey his mighty father's bidding, and first binds on his feet the golden shoes which carry him upborne on wings over seas or land, swift as the gale. Then he takes his wand;[1] with this he calls pale ghosts from Orcus and sends others down to gloomy Tartarus, gives or takes away sleep and unseals eyes in death;[2] on this relying, he drives the winds and skims the stormy clouds. And now in flight he descries the peak and steep sides of toiling Atlas, who props heaven on his peak—Atlas, whose pine-wreathed head is ever girt with black clouds, and beaten with wind and rain; fallen snow mantles his shoulders, while rivers plunge down the aged chin and his rough beard is stiff with ice.[3] Here, poised on even wings, the Cyllenian first halted; hence with his whole frame he sped sheer down to the waves like a bird, which round the shores, round the fish-haunted cliffs, flies low near to the waters. Even thus between earth and sky flew Cyllene's nursling to Libya's sandy shore, and cut the winds, coming from his mother's sire.

259 So soon as with winged feet he reached the huts, he sees Aeneas founding towers and building new houses. And lo! his sword was starred with yellow jasper, and a cloak hung from his shoulders ablaze with Tyrian purple—a gift that wealthy Dido had wrought, interweaving the web with thread of gold. At once he assails him : "Art thou now laying the foundations of lofty Carthage, and building up a fair city, a wife's minion? Alas! of thine own

---

[1] This is the *caduceus*, with which Mercury (Hermes) guided the dead. *cf.* Homer, *Od.* v. 47 ff.

[2] An allusion to the Roman custom of opening the eyes of the dead on the funeral pyre.

[3] Virgil describes Mount Atlas as it might have been represented, in the guise of a mountain-god, by the realistic art of his day.

exstruis? heu! regni rerumque oblite tuarum!
ipse deum tibi me claro demittit Olympo
regnator, caelum et terras qui numine torquet;
ipse haec ferre iubet celeris mandata per auras.   270
quid struis? aut qua spe Libycis teris otia terris?
si te nulla movet tantarum gloria rerum
nec super ipse tua moliris laude laborem,
Ascanium surgentem et spes heredis Iuli
respice, cui regnum Italiae Romanaque tellus   275
debentur." tali Cyllenius ore locutus
mortalis visus medio sermone reliquit
et procul in tenuem ex oculis evanuit auram.
   At vero Aeneas aspectu obmutuit amens,
arrectaeque horrore comae et vox faucibus haesit. 280
ardet abire fuga dulcisque relinquere terras,
attonitus tanto monitu imperioque deorum.
heu! quid agat? quo nunc reginam ambire furentem
audeat adfatu? quae prima exordia sumat?
atque animum nunc huc celerem, nunc dividit illuc 285
in partisque rapit varias perque omnia versat.   FMP
haec alternanti potior sententia visa est:
Mnesthea Sergestumque vocat fortemque Serestum,
classem aptent taciti sociosque ad litora cogant,
arma parent et, quae rebus sit causa novandis,   290
dissimulent; sese interea, quando optima Dido
nesciat et tantos rumpi non speret amores,
temptaturum aditus et, quae mollissima fandi
tempora, quis rebus dexter modus. ocius omnes
imperio laeti parent et iussa facessunt.   295
   At regina dolos (quis fallere possit amantem?)
praesensit motusque excepit prima futuros,

---

267 oblite] ignare *P*[1].   268 dimittit *P*.
269 et] ac *P*.   terram *P*.
273 *omitted in MP: given by* a[2]b[2]c, *and (in margin) by* γ.
276 debentur *M*[1]*P*[1], Servius:* debetur *M*[2]*P*[2]γ.
289 -que *omitted P*γ.   295 et] ac *M*[2].

kingdom and fortunes forgetful! Himself, the
sovereign of the gods, who sways heaven and earth
with his power, sends me down to thee from bright
Olympus. Himself he bids me bring this charge
through the swift breezes: What plannest thou?
or in what hope dost thou waste idle hours in Libyan
lands? If the glory of such a fortune stirs thee not,
and for thine own fame's sake thou shoulderest not
the burden, have regard for growing Ascanius and
the promise of Iülus thy heir, to whom the kingdom
of Italy and the Roman land are due." Such words
the Cyllenian spake, and while yet speaking left the
sight of men and far away from their eyes vanished
into thin air.

²⁷⁹ But in truth Aeneas, aghast at the sight, was
struck dumb; his hair stood up in terror and the
voice clave to his throat. He burns to flee away and
quit that pleasant land, awed by that warning and
divine commandment. Ah, what to do? With what
speech now dare he approach the frenzied queen?
What opening words choose first? And now hither,
now thither he swiftly throws his mind, casting it in
diverse ways, and turns to every shift. As he wavered,
this seemed the better counsel: he calls Mnestheus
and Sergestus and brave Serestus, bidding them
make ready the fleet in silence, gather the crews to
the shore, and order the armament, but hide the
cause of his altered plans. He meanwhile, since
gracious Dido knows naught, nor looks for the
breaking of so strong a love, will essay an approach
and seek the happiest season for speech, the plan
auspicious for his purpose. At once all gladly obey
his command and do his bidding.

²⁹⁶ But the queen—who may deceive a lover?—
divined his guile, and early caught news of the

omnia tuta timens.   eadem impia Fama furenti
detulit armari classem cursumque parari.
saevit inops animi totamque incensa per urbem   300
bacchatur, qualis commotis excita sacris
Thyias, ubi audito stimulant trieterica Baccho   AFMP
orgia nocturnusque vocat clamore Cithaeron.
tandem his Aenean compellat vocibus ultro :
   "Dissimulare etiam sperasti, perfide, tantum   305
posse nefas tacitusque mea decedere terra?   FMP
nec te noster amor nec te data dextera quondam
nec moritura tenet crudeli funere Dido?
quin etiam hiberno moliris sidere classem
et mediis properas Aquilonibus ire per altum,   310
crudelis?   quid?   si non arva aliena domosque   MP
ignotas peteres, et Troia antiqua maneret,
Troia per undosum peteretur classibus aequor?
mene fugis?   per ego has lacrimas dextramque tuam te
(quando aliud mihi iam miserae nihil ipsa reliqui),   315
per conubia nostra, per inceptos hymenaeos,
si bene quid de te merui, fuit aut tibi quicquam
dulce meum, miserere domus labentis et istam,
oro, si quis adhuc precibus locus, exue mentem.
te propter Libycae gentes Nomadumque tyranni   320
odere, infensi Tyrii; te propter eundem
exstinctus pudor et, qua sola sidera adibam,
fama prior.   cui me moribundam deseris, hospes,
hoc solum nomen quoniam de coniuge restat?
quid moror?   an mea Pygmalion dum moenia frater
destruat aut captam ducat Gaetulus Iarbas?   326

   [309] moliri *FP*.   [312] et] sed *P*[1].
   [323] morituram *Priscian.*

coming stir, fearful even when all was safe. The
same heartless Rumour brought her the maddening
news that they arm the fleet and make ready for
voyaging. Helpless in mind she rages, and all
aflame raves through the city, like some Thyiad
startled by the shaken emblems, what time, hearing
the Bacchic cry, the biennial revels fire her and at
night Cithaeron summons her with its din.[1] At
length, she thus accosts Aeneas first :

305 " False one ! didst thou hope also to cloak so
foul a crime, and to pass from my land in silence ?
Can neither our love keep thee, nor the pledge once
given, nor the doom of a cruel death for Dido ? Nay,
even in the winter season dost thou labour at thy
fleet, and in the midst of northern gales hasten to
pass overseas, heartless one ? What ! If thou wert not
in quest of alien lands and homes unknown, were
ancient Troy yet standing, would Troy be sought by
thy ships over stormy seas ? From me dost thou
flee ? By these tears and thy right hand, I pray
thee—since naught else, alas ! have I left myself—by
our marriage, by the wedlock begun, if ever I de-
served well of thee, or if aught of mine has been
sweet in thy sight, pity a falling house, and if yet
there be any room for prayers, put away this purpose
of thine. For thee the Libyan tribes and Numidian
chiefs hate me, the Tyrians are my foes ; for thee,
also, have I lost my honour and that former fame by
which alone I was winning a title to the stars. To
whom dost thou leave me, a dying woman, O guest—
since that alone is left from the name of husband ?
Why do I linger ? Is it till Pygmalion, my brother,
overthrow this city, or the Gaetulian Iarbas lead me

[1] Every other year a Bacchic festival was celebrated at
Thebes.

417

saltem si qua mihi de te suscepta fuisset
ante fugam suboles, si quis mihi parvulus aula
luderet Aeneas, qui te tamen ore referret,
non equidem omnino capta ac deserta viderer." 330
    Dixerat. ille Iovis monitis immota tenebat
lumina et obnixus curam sub corde premebat.
tandem pauca refert : " ego te, quae plurima fando
enumerare vales, numquam, regina, negabo
promeritam, nec me meminisse pigebit Elissae, 335
dum memor ipse mei, dum spiritus hos regit artus.
pro re pauca loquar. neque ego hanc abscondere furto
speravi (ne finge) fugam, nec coniugis umquam
praetendi taedas aut haec in foedera veni.
me si fata meis paterentur ducere vitam   340
auspiciis et sponte mea componere curas,
urbem Troianam primum dulcisque meorum
reliquias colerem, Priami tecta alta manerent,
et recidiva manu posuissem Pergama victis.
sed nunc Italiam magnam Gryneus Apollo,   345
Italiam Lyciae iussere capessere sortes ;
hic amor, haec patria est. si te Karthaginis arces
Phoenissam Libycaeque aspectus detinet urbis,
quae tandem Ausonia Teucros considere terra
invidia est ? et nos fas extera quaerere regna. 350
me patris Anchisae, quotiens umentibus umbris
nox operit terras, quotiens astra ignea surgunt,
admonet in somnis et turbida terret imago ;
me puer Ascanius capitisque iniuria cari,
quem regno Hesperiae fraudo et fatalibus arvis. 355

[348] detinet] demeret known to Servius.

AENEID BOOK IV

captive? At least, if ere thy flight a child had been
born to me by thee, if in my hall a tiny Aeneas were
playing, whose face, in spite of all, would bring back
thine, I should not think myself utterly vanquished
and forlorn."

³³¹ She ceased: he by Jove's command held his eyes
steadfast and with a struggle smothered the pain deep
within his heart. At last he briefly replies: " I will
never deny, O Queen, that thou hast deserved of me
the utmost thou canst set forth in speech, nor shall
my memory of Elissa be bitter, while I have memory
of myself, and while breath still sways these limbs.
For my course few words will I say. I did not hope
—think not that—to veil my flight in stealth. I
never held out the bridegroom's torch nor entered
such a compact. Did the Fates suffer me to shape
my life after my own pleasure and order my sorrows
at my own will, my first care should be the city of
Troy and the sweet relics of my kin. Priam's high
house would still abide and my own hand should have
set up a revived Pergamus for the vanquished. But
now of great Italy has Grynean Apollo bidden me lay
hold, of Italy the Lycian oracles.¹ There is my love,
there my country! If the towers of Carthage and
the sight of the Libyan city charm thee, a Phoenician,
why, pray, grudge the Trojans their settling on
Ausonian land? We, too, may well seek a foreign
realm. To me, oft as night with dewy shades veils
the earth, oft as the starry fires arise, in my dreams
my father Anchises' troubled ghost brings warning
and terror; to me comes the thought of young
Ascanius and the wrong done to one so dear, whom
I am cheating of an Hesperian kingdom and pre-
destined lands. Now, too, the messenger of the gods

¹ *i.e.* the oracles of Apollo; *cf.* 143 above.

419

nunc etiam interpres divum, Iove missus ab ipso
(testor utrumque caput), celeris mandata per auras
detulit; ipse deum manifesto in lumine vidi
intrantem muros vocemque his auribus hausi.
desine meque tuis incendere teque querellis.   360
Italiam non sponte sequor."
    Talia dicentem iamdudum aversa tuetur,
huc illuc volvens oculos, totumque pererrat
luminibus tacitis et sic accensa profatur:
" nec tibi diva parens, generis nec Dardanus auctor,
perfide, sed duris genuit te cautibus horrens   366
Caucasus, Hyrcanaeque admorunt ubera tigres.
nam quid dissimulo aut quae me ad maiora reservo?
num fletu ingemuit nostro?   num lumina flexit?
num lacrimas victus dedit aut miseratus amantem
        est?   370
quae quibus anteferam?   iam iam nec maxima Iuno
nec Saturnius haec oculis pater aspicit aequis.
nusquam tuta fides.   eiectum litore, egentem
excepi et regni demens in parte locavi;
amissam classem, socios a morte reduxi.   375
heu! furiis incensa feror: nunc augur Apollo,
nunc Lyciae sortes, nunc et Iove missus ab ipso
interpres divum fert horrida iussa per auras.
scilicet is superis labor est, ea cura quietos
sollicitat.   neque te teneo neque dicta refello: 380
i, sequere Italiam ventis, pete regna per undas.
spero equidem mediis, si quid pia numina possunt,
supplicia hausurum scopulis et nomine Dido
saepe vocaturum.   sequar atris ignibus absens

        [374] suscepi *Priscian.*   [378] iussa] dicta *M.*
420

sent from Jove himself—by thy head and mine, I swear—has borne his command down through the swift breezes; my own eyes saw the god in the clear light of day come within our walls and these ears drank in his words. Cease to fire thyself and me with thy complaints. Not of free will do I follow Italy!"

362 As thus he spake, all the while she gazes on him askance, turning her eyes to and fro, and with silent glances scans the whole man; then thus, inflamed, cries out:

365 "False one! no goddess was thy mother, nor was Dardanus founder of thy line, but rugged Caucasus on his flinty rocks begat thee, and Hyrcanian tigresses gave thee suck. For why hide my feelings? or for what greater wrongs do I hold me back? Did he sigh while I wept? Did he turn on me a glance? Did he yield and shed tears or pity her who loved him? What shall I say first? What next? Now, now neither mighty Juno nor the Saturnian sire looks on these things with righteous eyes! Nowhere is faith secure. A castaway on the shore, a beggar, I welcomed him and madly gave him a share in my throne; his lost fleet I rescued, his crews I saved from death. Alas! I am whirled on the fires of frenzy. Now prophetic Apollo, now the Lycian oracles, now the messenger of the gods, sent from Jove himself, brings through the air this dread command. Truly, this is work for gods, this is care to vex their peace! I keep thee not; I refute not thy words. Go, follow Italy down the winds; seek thy kingdom over the waves. Yet I trust, if the righteous gods can avail aught, that on the rocks midway thou wilt drain the cup of vengeance and often call on Dido's name. Though far away, I will chase thee

et, cum frigida mors anima seduxerit artus,   385
omnibus umbra locis adero.   dabis, improbe, poenas.
audiam et haec Manis veniet mihi fama sub imos."
his medium dictis sermonem abrumpit et auras
aegra fugit seque ex oculis avertit et aufert,
linquens multa metu cunctantem et multa parantem
dicere.   suscipiunt famulae conlapsaque membra 391
marmoreo referunt thalamo stratisque reponunt.

   At pius Aeneas, quamquam lenire dolentem
solando cupit et dictis avertere curas,
multa gemens magnoque animum labefactus amore,
iussa tamen divum exsequitur classemque revisit. 396
tum vero Teucri incumbunt et litore celsas
deducunt toto navis.   natat uncta carina,
frondentisque ferunt remos et robora silvis
infabricata fugae studio.   400
migrantis cernas totaque ex urbe ruentis.
ac veluti ingentem formicae farris acervum
cum populant hiemis memores tectoque reponunt;
it nigrum campis agmen, praedamque per herbas
convectant calle angusto; pars grandia trudunt   405
obnixae frumenta umeris, pars agmina cogunt
castigantque moras; opere omnis semita fervet.
quis tibi tum, Dido, cernenti talia sensus,
quosve dabas gemitus, cum litora fervere late
prospiceres arce ex summa, totumque videres   410
misceri ante oculos tantis clamoribus aequor!
improbe Amor, quid non mortalia pectora cogis
ire iterum in lacrimas, iterum temptare precando

[390] volentem *M* : parantem *P*.   [402] veluti *M* : velut *P*.
[407] operae *M*[1] : opere *M*[2]*P* : opera *Nonius*

with murky brands and, when chill death has severed
soul and body, everywhere my shade shall haunt
thee. Shameless one, thou shalt repay! I shall
hear, and the tale will reach me in the depths of
the world below!"

388 So saying, she breaks off her speech midway and
flees in anguish from the light, turning away, tearing
herself from his sight, and leaving him in fear and
much hesitance, though much he fain would say.
Her maids support her, carry her swooning form to
her marble bower, and lay her on her bed.

393 But good Aeneas, though longing to soothe
and assuage her grief and by his words turn aside her
sorrow, with many a sigh, his soul shaken by his
mighty love, yet fulfils Heaven's bidding and returns
to the fleet. Then, indeed, the Teucrians fall to and
all along the shore launch their tall ships. The keels,
well-pitched, are set afloat; the sailors, eager for
flight, bring from the woods leafy boughs for oars
and logs unhewn. One could see them moving away
and streaming forth from all the city. Even as
when ants, mindful of winter, plunder a huge heap
of corn and store it in their home; over the plain
moves a black column, and through the grass they
carry the spoil on a narrow track; some strain with
their shoulders and heave on the huge grains, some
close up the ranks and rebuke delay; all the path is
aglow with work. What feelings then were thine,
Dido, at such a sight! or what sighs didst thou utter,
viewing from the top of the fortress the beach aglow
far and near, and seeing before thy eyes the whole
main astir with loud cries! O tyrant Love, to what
dost thou not drive the hearts of men! Once more
she must needs break into tears, once more assail
him with prayer, and humbly bow down her pride to

VIRGIL

cogitur et supplex animos summittere amori,
ne quid inexpertum frustra moritura relinquat. 415
  " Anna, vides toto properari litore circum;
undique convenere; vocat iam carbasus auras,
puppibus et laeti nautae imposuere coronas.
hunc ego si potui tantum sperare dolorem,
et perferre, soror, potero. miserae hoc tamen unum
exsequere, Anna, mihi: solam nam perfidus ille 421
te colere, arcanos etiam tibi credere sensus;
sola viri mollis aditus et tempora noras.
i, soror, atque hostem supplex adfare superbum.
non ego cum Danais Troianam exscindere gentem
Aulide iuravi classemve ad Pergama misi, 426
nec patris Anchisae cineres Manisve revelli;
cur mea dicta negat duras demittere in auris?
quo ruit? extremum hoc miserae det munus amanti:
exspectet facilemque fugam ventosque ferentis. 430
non iam coniugium antiquum, quod prodidit, oro,
nec pulchro ut Latio careat regnumque relinquat;
tempus inane peto, requiem spatiumque furori,
dum mea me victam doceat fortuna dolere.
extremam hanc oro veniam (miserere sororis); 435
quam mihi cum dederit, cumulatam morte remittam."
  Talibus orabat, talisque miserrima fletus
fertque refertque soror. sed nullis ille movetur
fletibus, aut voces ullas tractabilis audit;
fata obstant, placidasque viri deus obstruit auris. 440
ac velut annoso validam cum robore quercum
Alpini Boreae nunc hinc nunc flatibus illinc

427 cinerem *M*: cineres *Pγ, Servius.*
   428 neget *M²P¹*: negat *M¹P²*. dimittere *Pγ.*
   434 dolore *M¹.*
   436 dederis *γ²abc, Servius:* cumulata *M, known to Servius:* dederis cumulatam *approved by Varius and Tucca, according to Servius.*

424

love, lest she leave aught untried and go to death in vain.

⁴¹⁶ "Anna, thou seest the bustle all along the shore; from all sides they have gathered; already the canvas courts the breeze, and the joyous sailors have crowned the sterns with garlands. If I have had strength to foresee this great sorrow, I shall also, sister, have strength to endure it. Yet this one service, Anna, do for me—for thee alone that traitor made his friend, to thee he confided even his secret thoughts, alone thou knowest the hour for easy access to him—go, sister, and humbly address our haughty foe. I never conspired with the Danaans at Aulis to root out the Trojan race; I never sent a fleet to Pergamus, nor uptore the ashes and spirit of his father Anchises.[1] Why refuses he to admit my words to his stubborn ears? Whither does he hasten? This, the last boon, let him grant his poor lover: let him await an easy flight and favouring winds. No more do I plead for the old marriage-tie which he forswore, nor that he give up fair Latium and resign his realm: for empty time I ask, for peace and reprieve for my frenzy, till fortune teach my vanquished soul to grieve. This last grace I crave—pity thy sister—and when he has granted it I will repay with full interest in my death."

⁴³⁷ Such was her prayer and such the tearful pleas the unhappy sister bears again and again. But by no tearful pleas is he moved, nor in yielding mood pays he heed to any words. Fate withstands and heaven seals his kindly, mortal ears. Even as when northern Alpine winds, blowing now hence, now thence, emulously strive to uproot an oak strong

1 There was a tradition that Diomedes stole the ashes of Anchises.

VIRGIL

eruere inter se certant; it stridor, et altae   **FMP**
consternunt terram concusso stipite frondes;
ipsa haeret scopulis et, quantum vertice ad auras 445
aetherias, tantum radice in Tartara tendit:
haud secus adsiduis hinc atque hinc vocibus heros
tunditur, et magno persentit pectore curas;
mens immota manet, lacrimae volvuntur inanes.

  Tum vero infelix fatis exterrita Dido   450
mortem orat; taedet caeli convexa tueri.
quo magis inceptum peragat lucemque relinquat,
vidit, turicremis cum dona imponeret aris,
(horrendum dictu!) latices nigrescere sacros
fusaque in obscenum se vertere vina cruorem.   455
hoc visum nulli, non ipsi effata sorori.
praeterea fuit in tectis de marmore templum
coniugis antiqui, miro quod honore colebat,
velleribus niveis et festa fronde revinctum;
hinc exaudiri voces et verba vocantis   460
visa viri, nox cum terras obscura teneret;
solaque culminibus ferali carmine bubo
saepe queri et longas in fletum ducere voces;
multaque praeterea vatum praedicta priorum
terribili monitu horrificant. agit ipse furentem 465
in somnis ferus Aeneas; semperque relinqui
sola sibi, semper longam incomitata videtur
ire viam et Tyrios deserta quaerere terra:
Eumenidum veluti demens videt agmina Pentheus,
et solem geminum et duplices se ostendere Thebas, 470
aut Agamemnonius scaenis agitatus Orestes
armatam facibus matrem et serpentibus atris
cum fugit, ultricesque sedent in limine Dirae.

⁴⁴³ alte *b, Servius.* ⁴⁴⁶ radicem *MP¹γ.*
⁴⁵⁶ sorori est *F.* ⁴⁶² seraque *Nonius.*
⁴⁶⁴ piorum *M, known to Servius:* priorum *other MSS.,
Priscian, Servius.* ⁴⁷³ divae *F¹Pγ¹.*

---

¹ In the *Bacchae* of Euripides Pentheus is driven mad by
426

with the strength of years, there comes a roar, the stem quivers and the high leafage thickly strews the ground, but the oak clings to the crag, and as far as it lifts its top to the airs of heaven, so far it strikes its roots down towards hell—even so with ceaseless appeals, from this side and from that, the hero is buffeted, and in his mighty heart feels the thrill of grief: steadfast stands his will ; the tears fall in vain.

⁴⁵⁰ Then, indeed, awed by her doom, luckless Dido prays for death ; she is weary of gazing on the arch of heaven. And to make her more surely fulfil her purpose and leave the light, she saw, as she laid her gifts on the altars ablaze with incense—fearful to tell !—the holy water darken and the outpoured wine change into loathsome gore. Of this sight she spoke to none—no, not to her sister. Moreover, there was in the palace a marble chapel to her former lord, which she cherished in wondrous honour, wreathing it with snowy fleeces and festal foliage. Thence she heard, it seemed, sounds and speech as of her husband calling, whenever darkling night held the world ; and alone on the house-tops with ill-boding song the owl would oft complain, drawing out its lingering notes into a wail; and likewise many a saying of the seers of old terrifies her with fearful boding. In her sleep fierce Aeneas himself hounds her in her frenzy ; and ever she seems to be left lonely, ever wending, companionless, an endless way, and seeking her Tyrians in a land forlorn—even as raving Pentheus sees the Furies' band, a double sun and two-fold Thebes rise to view ; or as when Agamemnon's son, Orestes, driven over the stage, flees from his mother, who is armed with brands and black serpents, while at the doorway crouch the avenging Fiends.[1]

Bacchus, and in the *Eumenides* of Aeschylus the ghost of Clytaemnestra stirs up the Furies against Orestes, her son.

VIRGIL

Ergo ubi concepit furias evicta dolore
decrevitque mori, tempus secum ipsa modumque 475
exigit, et maestam dictis adgressa sororem
consilium voltu tegit ac spem fronte serenat:
"inveni, germana, viam (gratare sorori),
quae mihi reddat eum vel eo me solvat amantem.
Oceani finem iuxta solemque cadentem 480
ultimus Aethiopum locus est, ubi maximus Atlas
axem umero torquet stellis ardentibus aptum:
hinc mihi Massylae gentis monstrata sacerdos,
Hesperidum templi custos, epulasque draconi
quae dabat et sacros servabat in arbore ramos, 485
spargens umida mella soporiferumque papaver.
haec se carminibus promittit solvere mentes
quas velit, ast aliis duras immittere curas;
sistere aquam fluviis et vertere sidera retro;
nocturnosque movet Manis; mugire videbis 490
sub pedibus terram et descendere montibus ornos.
testor, cara, deos et te, germana, tuumque
dulce caput, magicas invitam accingier artis.
tu secreta pyram tecto interiore sub auras
erige et arma viri, thalamo quae fixa reliquit 495
impius, exuviasque omnis lectumque iugalem,
quo perii, superimponas; abolere nefandi
cuncta viri monumenta iuvat, monstratque sacerdos."
haec effata silet; pallor simul occupat ora.
non tamen Anna novis praetexere funera sacris 500
germanam credit, nec tantos mente furores
concipit aut graviora timet quam morte Sychaei.
ergo iussa parat.

[476] et] ac *M*.　　　　　　　[481] attorquet *M¹*.
[486] *placed by Ribbeck after* 517 (*with* molam), *perhaps rightly*.
[490] movet] ciet *F²P²γ*.
[497] superinponant *FM¹, known to Servius*.
[498] iuvat *FM², Servius*: iubet *M¹P¹γ³*: ivat *F¹*: iubat *P²γ¹*.　　　[500] protexere *M¹*.

428

[474] So when, outworn with anguish, she caught the madness and resolved to die, in her own heart she determines the time and manner, and accosts her sorrowful sister, with mien that veils her plan and on her brow the calm of hope.

[478] "Sister mine, I have found a way—wish thy sister joy—to return him to me or release me from my love for him. Near Ocean's bound and the setting sun lies Aethiopia, farthest of lands, where mightiest Atlas on his shoulders turns the sphere, inset with gleaming stars. Thence a priestess of Massylian race has been shown me, warden of the fane of the Hesperides, who gave dainties to the dragon and guarded the sacred boughs on the tree, sprinkling dewy honey and slumberous poppies. With her spells she professes to set free the hearts of whom she wills, but on others to bring cruel love-pains; to stay the flow of rivers and turn back the stars; she awakes the ghosts of night; and thou shalt mark earth rumbling under thy feet and ash-trees coming down from mountains. I call heaven to witness and thee, dear sister mine, and thy dear life, that against my will I arm myself with magic arts! Do thou secretly raise up a pyre in the inner court under the sky, and heap up thereon the arms that heartless one left hanging in my bower, and all his attire and the bridal bed that was my undoing. I would fain destroy all memorials of the abhorred wretch, and the priestess so directs." Thus she speaks and is silent; pallor the while overspreads her face. Yet Anna thinks not that her sister veils her death under these strange rites; her mind dreams not of such frenzy nor fears she aught worse than when Sychaeus died. So she makes ready as bidden.

At regina, pyra penetrali in sede sub auras
erecta ingenti taedis atque ilice secta,   505
intenditque locum sertis et fronde coronat
funerea; super exuvias ensemque relictum
effigiemque toro locat, haud ignara futuri.
stant arae circum et crinis effusa sacerdos
ter centum tonat ore deos, Erebumque Chaosque 510
tergeminamque Hecaten, tria virginis ora Dianae.
sparserat et latices simulatos fontis Averni;
falcibus et messae ad lunam quaeruntur aënis
pubentes herbae nigri cum lacte veneni;
quaeritur et nascentis equi de fronte revolsus   515
et matri praereptus amor.
ipsa mola manibusque piis altaria iuxta,
unum exuta pedem vinclis, in veste recincta,
testatur moritura deos et conscia fati
sidera; tum, si quod non aequo foedere amantis 520
curae numen habet iustumque memorque, precatur.
    Nox erat, et placidum carpebant fessa soporem MP
corpora per terras, silvaeque et saeva quierant
aequora, cum medio volvuntur sidera lapsu,   524
cum tacet omnis ager, pecudes pictaeque volucres,
quaeque lacus late liquidos, quaeque aspera dumis
rura tenent, somno positae sub nocte silenti.
[lenibant curas et corda oblita laborum.]
at non infelix animi Phoenissa, neque umquam
solvitur in somnos, oculisve aut pectore noctem 530
accipit; ingeminant curae, rursusque resurgens
saevit amor, magnoque irarum fluctuat aestu.

    517 molam MPγ¹.
    528 omitted by P: added at foot of page, then deleted by late
hand, M.   529 neque P¹: naeque M¹: nec M², Servius.
430

AENEID BOOK IV

504 But the queen, when in her innermost dwelling [1]
the pyre rose heavenward, piled high with pine-
fagots and hewn ilex, hangs the place with garlands
and festoons it with funeral boughs.   On top, upon
the couch, she lays his vesture, the sword he left,
and his image, knowing well the end.   Round about
stand altars, while with streaming hair the priestess
calls in thunder tones on thrice a hundred gods,
Erebus and Chaos, and threefold Hecate, triple-faced
maiden Diana.   Waters, too, she had sprinkled,
feigned to be from the spring Avernus, and herbs
were sought, mown by moonlight with brazen
sickles, and juicy with milk of black venom; sought,
too, was the love-charm, torn from the brow of a colt
at birth ere the mother snatched it.   She herself,
with holy meal and holy hands, beside the altars,
one foot unsandalled and girdle loosened, calls on
the gods ere she die and on the stars, witnesses
of her doom; then she prays to whatever power,
righteous and mindful, watches over lovers unequally
allied.

522 It was night, and over the earth weary creatures
were tasting peaceful slumber; the woods and wild
seas had sunk to rest—the hour when stars roll
midway in their gliding course, when all the land
is still, and beasts and gay birds, both they that
far and near haunt the limpid lakes, and they
that dwell in fields of tangled brakes, are couched
in sleep beneath the silent night.   But not so
the soul-racked Phoenician queen; she never sinks
to sleep, nor draws the night into eyes or heart.
Her pangs redouble, and her love, swelling up,
surges afresh, as she heaves with a mighty tide of
passion.   Thus then she begins, and thus with her

---

[1] *cf.* 494, "in the inner court under the sky."

431

sic adeo insistit secumque ita corde volutat:
" en, quid ago ?   rursusne procos inrisa priores
experiar, Nomadumque petam conubia supplex,   535
quos ego sim totiens iam dedignata maritos ?
Iliacas igitur classis atque ultima Teucrum
iussa sequar ?   quiane auxilio iuvat ante levatos
et bene apud memores veteris stat gratia facti ?
quis me autem, fac velle, sinet ratibusve superbis 540
invisam accipiet ?   nescis, heu ! perdita, necdum
Laomedonteae sentis periuria gentis ?
quid tum ?   sola fuga nautas comitabor ovantis ?
an Tyriis omnique manu stipata meorum
inferar et, quos Sidonia vix urbe revelli,   545
rursus agam pelago et ventis dare vela iubebo ?
quin morere, ut merita es, ferroque averte dolorem.
tu lacrimis evicta meis, tu prima furentem
his, germana, malis oneras atque obicis hosti.
non licuit thalami expertem sine crimine vitam   550
degere, more ferae, talis nec tangere curas ;
non servata fides cineri promissa Sychaeo."
tantos illa suo rumpebat pectore questus.

    Aeneas celsa in puppi, iam certus eundi,
carpebat somnos, rebus iam rite paratis.   FMP
huic se forma dei voltu redeuntis eodem   556
obtulit in somnis rursusque ita visa monere est,
omnia Mercurio similis, vocemque coloremque
et crinis flavos et membra decora iuventa :
" nate dea, potes hoc sub casu ducere somnos,   560

    [540] sinat P^1.   [541] inrisam $M^2\gamma^2$.
    [552] Sychaei M: Sychaeies P^1: Sychaeo P^2, *Servius.*
    [559] iuventae $P\gamma$, *Servius:* iuventa FM.

heart alone revolves her thoughts: "Lo, what am
I to do? Shall I once more make trial of my old
wooers, only to be mocked, and shall I humbly sue
for marriage with Numidians, whom I have scorned
so often as husbands? Shall I then follow the Ilian
ships and the Trojan's uttermost commands? Is it
because they are grateful for aid once given, and
thankfulness for past kindness stands firm in mindful
hearts? But who—suppose that I do wish it—will
suffer me, or take one so hateful on those haughty
ships? Ah! lost one, dost thou not yet understand
nor perceive the treason of Laomedon's race? What
then? Shall I alone accompany the exultant sailors
in their flight? or, hedged with all my Tyrian band,
shall I pursue, and shall I again drive seaward, the
men whom I could scarce tear from the Sidonian
city, and bid them unfurl their sails to the winds?
Nay, die, as thou deservest, and with the steel end
thy sorrow. Won over by my tears, thou, my sister,
thou wert first to load my frenzied soul with these
ills, and drive me on the foe. Ah, that I could not
spend my life, apart from wedlock, a blameless life,
even as some wild creature, knowing not such cares!
The faith vowed to the ashes of Sychaeus I have not
kept!" Such were the wails that kept bursting
from her heart.

⁵⁵⁴ But now that all was duly ordered, and now
that he was resolved on going, Aeneas was snatch-
ing sleep on his vessel's high stern. In his sleep
there appeared to him a vision of the god, as he
came again with the same aspect, and once more
seemed to warn him thus, in all points like to
Mercury, in voice and hue, in golden hair and
the graceful limbs of youth : " Goddess-born, when
such hazard threatens, canst thou still slumber, and

VIRGIL

nec quae te circum stent deinde pericula cernis,
demens, nec Zephyros audis spirare secundos ?
illa dolos dirumque nefas in pectore versat,
certa mori, varioque irarum fluctuat aestu.
non fugis hinc praeceps, dum praecipitare potestas ?
iam mare turbari trabibus saevasque videbis   566
conlucere faces, iam fervere litora flammis,
si te his attigerit terris Aurora morantem.
heia age, rumpe moras !   varium et mutabile semper
femina."   sic fatus nocti se immiscuit atrae.   570

   Tum vero Aeneas subitis exterritus umbris
corripit e somno corpus sociosque fatigat :
" praecipites vigilate, viri, et considite transtris ;
solvite vela citi.   deus aethere missus ab alto
festinare fugam tortosque incidere funis   575
ecce iterum instimulat.   sequimur te, sancte deorum,
quisquis es, imperioque iterum paremus ovantes.
adsis o placidusque iuves et sidera caelo
dextra feras."   dixit vaginaque eripit ensem
fulmineum strictoque ferit retinacula ferro.   580
idem omnis simul ardor habet ; rapiuntque ruuntque ;
litora deseruere ; latet sub classibus aequor ;
adnixi torquent spumas et caerula verrunt.

   Et iam prima novo spargebat lumine terras   MP
Tithoni croceum linquens Aurora cubile.   585
regina, e speculis ut primum albescere lucem
vidit et aequatis classem procedere velis,
litoraque et vacuos sensit sine remige portus,
terque quaterque manu pectus percussa decorum
flaventisque abscissa comas, " pro Iuppiter ! ibit 590
hic," ait, " et nostris inluserit advena regnis ?

---

564 varios *FP :* (s)vario *M.* concitat *FP :* fluctuat *M.* aestu
FMab[1].
  565 hinc] in *F*[1]: hic *M*[1].   **576** stimulat *M, Servius.*
  586 primam *Pγ*[1].

seest thou not the perils that from henceforth hem thee in, madman! Hearest not the kindly breezes blowing? She, resolved on death, revolves in her heart fell craft and crime, and is tossed on the changing surge of passion. Wilt not flee hence in haste, while hasty flight is possible? Soon thou wilt see the waters swarming with ships, see fierce brands ablaze, and soon the shore flashing with flames, if the dawn find thee lingering in these lands. Up ho! break off delay! A fickle and changeful thing is woman ever." So he spake and melted into the black night.

[571] Then indeed Aeneas, scared by the sudden vision, tears himself from sleep and bestirs his comrades. "Make haste, my men, awake and man the benches! Unfurl the sails with speed! A god sent from high heaven, lo! again spurs us to hasten our flight and cut the twisted cables. We follow thee, holy among gods, whoe'er thou art, and again joyfully obey thy command. Oh, be with us, give thy gracious aid, and in the sky vouchsafe kindly stars!" He spoke, and from its sheath snatches his flashing sword and strikes the hawser with the drawn blade. The same zeal catches all at once; with hurry and scurry they have quitted the shore; the sea is hidden under their fleets; lustily they churn the foam and sweep the blue waters.

[584] And now early Dawn, leaving the saffron bed of Tithonus, was sprinkling her fresh rays upon the earth. Soon as the queen from her watch-tower saw the light whiten and the fleet move on with even sails, and knew the shores and harbours were void of oarsmen, thrice and four times she struck her comely breast with her hand, and tearing her golden hair, "O God," she cries, "shall he go? Shall the

non arma expedient totaque ex urbe sequentur,
deripientque rates alii navalibus? ite,
ferte citi flammas, date tela, impellite remos!
quid loquor? aut ubi sum? quae mentem insania
    mutat? 595
infelix Dido, nunc te facta impia tangunt?
tum decuit, cum sceptra dabas. en dextra fidesque,
quem secum patrios aiunt portare Penatis,
quem subiisse umeris confectum aetate parentem!
non potui abreptum divellere corpus et undis 600
spargere? non socios, non ipsum absumere ferro
Ascanium patriisque epulandum ponere mensis?
verum anceps pugnae fuerat fortuna. fuisset;
quem metui moritura? faces in castra tulissem
implessemque foros flammis natumque patremque 605
cum genere exstinxem, memet super ipsa dedissem.
Sol, qui terrarum flammis opera omnia lustras,
tuque harum interpres curarum et conscia Iuno,
nocturnisque Hecate triviis ululata per urbes
et Dirae ultrices et di morientis Elissae, 610
accipite haec, meritumque malis advertite numen
et nostras audite preces. si tangere portus
infandum caput ac terris adnare necesse est,
et sic fata Iovis poscunt, hic terminus haeret:
at bello audacis populi vexatus et armis, 615
finibus extorris, complexu avolsus Iuli,
auxilium imploret videatque indigna suorum
funera; nec, cum se sub leges pacis iniquae
tradiderit, regno aut optata luce fruatur.

593 diripient *MSS.:* de *Heinsius.*
597 tum *M :* tunc *Pγ, Priscian.*   **598** portasse *M.*
599 umeris *M²,* -as *M¹ :* umero *P¹.*

intruder have made of our realm a laughing-stock?
Will they not bring arms with speed, and pursue
from all the city, and some tear the ships from the
docks? Go, fetch fire in haste, serve weapons, ply
the oars! What do I say? or where am I? What
madness sways my brain? Unhappy Dido! now do
thy sinful deeds come home to thee! Then was the
fitting time, when thou didst offer the crown. Lo!
this is the pledge and faith of him who, they say,
carries about with him his country's home-gods! who
bore on his shoulders a father outworn with age!
Could I not have seized him, torn him limb from
limb and scattered him on the waves? Could I not
have slain his comrades with the sword—yea,
Ascanius himself, and served him in the feast at his
father's table? But the issue of battle had been
doubtful! Be it so; doomed to death, whom had I
to fear? I should have fired his camp, filled his
decks with flames, blotted out father and son with
the whole race, and flung myself on top of all. O Sun,
who with thy beams surveyest all the works of earth,
and thou, Juno, mediatress and witness of these my
sorrows, and Hecate, whose name is shrieked by night
at the cross-roads of cities, ye avenging Furies, and
ye gods of dying Elissa, hear ye this, and, as is meet,
let your power stoop to my ills, and hearken unto
my prayers! If that accursed wretch must needs
touch his haven and float to shore—if thus Jove's
doom demands, and there his goal stands fixed—yet
beset in war by the arms of a gallant race, driven
from his borders, and torn from Iülus' embrace, let
him sue for aid and see the cruel slaughter of his
friends! Then, when he hath yielded to the terms
of an unjust peace, may he not enjoy his kingdom
or the pleasant light, but let him fall before his

VIRGIL

sed cadat ante diem mediaque inhumatus harena. 620
haec precor, hanc vocem extremam cum sanguine fundo.
tum vos, o Tyrii, stirpem et genus omne futurum
exercete odiis, cinerique haec mittite nostro
munera.   nullus amor populis nec foedera sunto.
exoriare, aliquis nostris ex ossibus ultor,   625
qui face Dardanios ferroque sequare colonos,
nunc, olim, quocumque dabunt se tempore vires.
litora litoribus contraria, fluctibus undas
imprecor, arma armis; pugnent ipsique nepotesque."

Haec ait, et partis animum versabat in omnis, 630
invisam quaerens quam primum abrumpere lucem.
tum breviter Barcen nutricem adfata Sychaei,
namque suam patria antiqua cinis ater habebat:
" Annam, cara mihi nutrix, huc siste sororem;
dic corpus properet fluviali spargere lympha,   635
et pecudes secum et monstrata piacula ducat.
sic veniat, tuque ipsa pia tege tempora vitta.
sacra Iovi Stygio, quae rite incepta paravi,
perficere est animus finemque imponere curis
Dardaniique rogum capitis permittere flammae." 640
sic ait.   illa gradum studio celerabat anili.
at trepida et coeptis immanibus effera Dido,
sanguineam volvens aciem, maculisque trementis
interfusa genas, et pallida morte futura,
interiora domus inrumpit limina, et altos   645
conscendit furibunda rogos, ensemque recludit

---

[629] nepotesque] -que *omitted* $P^2\gamma$.
[632] Sychaei est *M*.   [640] flammis *M*.
[641] celerabat M^1, *Servius:* celebrabat M^2P, *known to Servius.*
inilem P^1: inili P^2: anilem γ^2.
[646] rogos *M :* gradus P^2: radus P^1.

438

time and lie unburied amid the sand! This is my prayer; this last utterance I pour out with my blood. Then do ye, O Tyrians, pursue with hate his whole stock and the race to come, and to my dust offer this tribute! Let no love nor league be between the nations. Arise from my ashes, unknown avenger! to chase with fire and sword the Dardan settlers, to-day, hereafter, whenever strength be given! May shore with shore clash, I pray, waters with waters, arms with arms; may they have war, they and their children's children!"[1]

[630] So she spoke, and on all sides turned her mind, seeking how with all speed to cut short the hateful life. Then briefly she spoke to Barce, nurse of Sychaeus, for the pyre's black ashes held her own in the olden land:

[634] "Dear nurse, fetch me Anna my sister hither. Bid her hasten to sprinkle her body with river-water, and bring with her the victims and offerings ordained for atonement. So let her come, and do thou, too, veil thy brows with a pure chaplet. I am minded to fulfil the rites of Stygian Jove that I have duly ordered and begun, to put an end to my woes, and give over to the flames the pyre of that Dardan wretch."

[641] So she spoke; the nurse hastened her steps with an old dame's zeal. But Dido, trembling and frenzied with her awful purpose, rolling her bloodshot eyes, her quivering cheeks flecked with burning spots, and pale at the coming of death, bursts into the inner courts of the house, mounts in madness the high pyre

[1] The curse involves a prophecy of the later fortunes of Aeneas, as told in the second half of the *Aeneid*, and of the Roman people, who in the course of time engaged in the famous Punic wars. The "unknown avenger" is Hannibal.

VIRGIL

Dardanium, non hos quaesitum munus in usus.
hic, postquam Iliacas vestis notumque cubile
conspexit, paulum lacrimis et mente morata
incubuitque toro dixitque novissima verba: 650
"dulces exuviae, dum fata deusque sinebat, FMP
accipite hanc animam meque his exsolvite curis.
vixi et, quem dederat cursum Fortuna, peregi,
et nunc magna mei sub terras ibit imago.
urbem praeclaram statui, mea moenia vidi, 655
ulta virum poenas inimico a fratre recepi,
felix, heu! nimium felix, si litora tantum
numquam Dardaniae tetigissent nostra carinae!"
dixit et os impressa toro, "moriemur inultae,
sed moriamur," ait. "sic, sic iuvat ire sub umbras.
hauriat hunc oculis ignem crudelis ab alto 661
Dardanus et secum nostrae ferat omina mortis."

Dixerat, atque illam media inter talia ferro
conlapsam aspiciunt comites, ensemque cruore
spumantem sparsasque manus. it clamor ad alta 665
atria; concussam bacchatur Fama per urbem.
lamentis gemituque et femineo ululatu
tecta fremunt, resonat magnis plangoribus aether,
non aliter, quam si immissis ruat hostibus omnis
Karthago aut antiqua Tyros, flammaeque furentes 670
culmina perque hominum volvantur perque deorum.
audiit exanimis, trepidoque exterrita cursu
unguibus ora soror foedans et pectora pugnis
per medios ruit ac morientem nomine clamat:
"hoc illud, germana, fuit? me fraude petebas? 675
hoc rogus iste mihi, hoc ignes araeque parabant?

651 sinebant *FF²*.
662 secum nostrae *M¹:* nostrae secum *other MSS.*
668 clangoribus *P.*
669 ruit *P¹.*
671 volvuntur *P¹γ².*

440

and unsheathes the Dardan sword, a gift besought
for no such end! Then, as she saw the Trojan garb
and the familiar bed, pausing awhile in tearful
thought, she threw herself on the couch and spoke
her latest words:

⁶⁵¹ "O relics once dear, while God and Fate
allowed! take my spirit, and release me from my
woes! I have lived, I have finished the course that
Fortune gave; and now in majesty my shade shall
pass beneath the earth. A noble city I have built;
my own walls I have seen; avenging my husband,
I have exacted punishment from my brother and
foe—happy, ah! too happy, had but the Dardan
keels never touched our shores!" She spoke, and
burying her face in the couch, "I shall die un-
avenged," she cries, "but let me die! Thus, thus
I go gladly into the dark! Let the cruel Dardan's
eyes drink in this fire from the deep, and carry with
him the omen of my death!"

⁶⁶³ She ceased; and even as she spoke her hand-
maids see her fallen on the sword, the blade reeking
with blood and her hands bespattered. A scream
rises to the lofty roof; Rumour riots through the
startled city. The palace rings with lamentation,
with sobbing and women's shrieks, and heaven echoes
with loud wails—even as though all Carthage or
ancient Tyre were falling before the inrushing foe,
and fierce flames were rolling on over the roofs of
men, over the roofs of gods. Swooning, her sister
heard, and in dismay rushed through the throng,
tearing her face with her nails, and beating her
breast with her fists, as she called on the dying
woman by name. "Was this thy purpose, sister?
Didst thou aim thy fraud at me? Was this for me
the meaning of thy pyre, this of thy altar and fires?

quid primum deserta querar ?   comitemne sororem
sprevisti moriens ?   eadem me ad fata vocasses;
idem ambas ferro dolor atque eadem hora tulisset.
his etiam struxi manibus patriosque vocavi   680
voce deos, sic te ut posita, crudelis, abessem?
exstinxti te meque, soror, populumque patresque
Sidonios urbemque tuam.   date volnera lymphis
abluam et, extremus si quis super halitus errat,
ore legam."   sic fata gradus evaserat altos,   685
semianimemque sinu germanam amplexa fovebat
cum gemitu atque atros siccabat veste cruores.
illa gravis oculos conata attollere rursus
deficit ; infixum stridit sub pectore volnus.   MP
ter sese attollens cubitoque adnixa levavit;   690
ter revoluta toro est oculisque errantibus alto
quaesivit caelo lucem ingemuitque reperta.

  Tum Iuno omnipotens, longum miserata dolorem
difficilisque obitus, Irim demisit Olympo,
quae luctantem animam nexosque resolveret artus.
nam quia nec fato, merita nec morte peribat,   696
sed misera ante diem subitoque accensa furore,
nondum illi flavum Proserpina vertice crinem
abstulerat Stygioque caput damnaverat Orco.
ergo Iris croceis per caelum roscida pinnis,   700

684 et *om. P.   So Sabb.*
690 attolllit *P*[1]: attolllens *P*[2].
692 repertam *M*[1].
698 necdum *P.*

442

Forlorn, what first shall I lament? In thy death didst thou scorn thy sister's company? Thou shouldst have called me to share thy doom; the same sword-pang, the same hour had taken us both! Did these hands indeed build the pyre, and did my voice call on our father's gods, in order that, when thou wert lying thus, I, the cruel one, should be far away? Thou hast destroyed thyself and me, O sister, the Sidonian senate and people, and thy city! Let me bathe her wounds with water, and catch with my lips whatever latest breath flutters over hers!" Thus speaking, she had climbed the high steps, and, throwing her arms round her dying sister, sobbed and clasped her to her bosom, stanching with her robe the dark streams of blood. She, essaying to lift her heavy eyes, swoons again, and the deep-set wound gurgles in her breast. Thrice rising, she struggled to lift herself upon her elbow; thrice she rolled back on the couch, and with wandering eyes sought the light in high heaven, and, as she found it, moaned.

693 Then almighty Juno, pitying her long pain and hard departure, sent Iris down from Olympus to release her struggling soul from the imprisoning limbs. For since neither in the course of fate did she perish, nor by a death she had earned,[1] but hapless before her day, and fired by sudden madness, not yet had Proserpine taken from her head the golden lock and consigned her to Stygian Orcus.[2] So Iris, all dewy on saffron wings, flits down through the sky,

[1] *i.e.* a violent death, such as one might incur in battle; not a self-inflicted death. *cf. Aen.* II. 434.

[2] Before sacrifice a few hairs were plucked from the fore-head of the victim, and as the dying were regarded as offerings to the nether gods, a similar custom was observed in their case.

VIRGIL

mille trahens varios adverso sole colores,
devolat et supra caput adstitit.   "hunc ego Diti
sacrum iussa fero teque isto corpore solvo " :
sic ait et dextra crinem secat; omnis et una
dilapsus calor atque in ventos vita recessit.   705

trailing athwart the sun a thousand shifting tints, and
halted above her head. " This offering, sacred to Dis,
I take as bidden, and from thy body set thee free " :
so she speaks, and with her hand shears the lock ;
and therewith all the warmth ebbed away, and the
life passed away into the winds.

LIBER V

Interea medium Aeneas iam classe tenebat   MP
certus iter fluctusque atros Aquilone secabat,
moenia respiciens, quae iam infelicis Elissae
conlucent flammis.   quae tantum accenderit ignem
causa latet; duri magno sed amore dolores   5
polluto notumque, furens quid femina possit,
triste per augurium Teucrorum pectora ducunt.

Ut pelagus tenuere rates nec iam amplius ulla
occurrit tellus, maria undique et undique caelum,
olli caeruleus supra caput adstitit imber,   10
noctem hiememque ferens, et inhorruit unda tenebris.
ipse gubernator puppi Palinurus ab alta :
"heu! quianam tanti cinxerunt aethera nimbi ?
quidve, pater Neptune, paras ?"   sic deinde locutus
colligere arma iubet validisque incumbere remis,   15
obliquatque sinus in ventum ac talia fatur :
"magnanime Aenea, non, si mihi Iuppiter auctor
spondeat, hoc sperem Italiam contingere caelo.
mutati transversa fremunt et vespere ab atro
consurgunt venti, atque in nubem cogitur aër.   20
nec nos obniti contra nec tendere tantum
sufficimus.   superat quoniam Fortuna, sequamur,
quoque vocat, vertamus iter.   nec litora longe

---

⁶ posset *M*.   ¹⁹ atro] alto *M*².   ²³ vacat *M*¹.

446

BOOK V

Meanwhile Aeneas with his fleet was now holding steadfastly his mid-sea course, and cleaving the waves that darkened under the north wind, looking back on the city walls which now gleam with unhappy Elissa's funeral flames. What cause kindled so great a flame is unknown; but the cruel pangs when deep love is profaned, and knowledge of what a woman can do in frenzy, lead the hearts of the Trojans amid sad forebodings.

8 When the ships gained the deep and no longer any land is in sight, but sea on all sides and on all sides sky, then overhead loomed a black rain-cloud, bringing night and tempest, and the wave shuddered darkling. Even the helmsman Palinurus cries from the high stern : " Alas ! why have such clouds girt the heaven ? What wilt thou, Father Neptune ? " So he cries, and straightway bids them gather in the tackling and bend to their stout oars, then turns the sails aslant the wind and thus speaks :

17 " Noble Aeneas, not though Jupiter should warrant his word, could I hope to reach Italy with such a sky. The winds have shifted and roar athwart our course, gathering from the black west ; the air thickens into cloud and we cannot resist or stem the gale. Since Fortune is victor, let us follow and turn our course whither she calls. Nor far distant, methinks, are the faithful shores of thy brother

fida reor fraterna Erycis portusque Sicanos,
si modo rite memor servata remetior astra."   **25**
tum pius Aeneas : "equidem sic poscere ventos
iamdudum et frustra cerno te tendere contra.
flecte viam velis.   an sit mihi gratior ulla,
quove magis fessas optem demittere navis,
quam quae Dardanium tellus mihi servat Acesten **30**
et patris Anchisae gremio complectitur ossa?"
haec ubi dicta, petunt portus, et vela secundi
intendunt Zephyri; fertur cita gurgite classis,
et tandem laeti notae advertuntur harenae.
   At procul ex celso miratus vertice montis   **35**
adventum sociasque rates occurrit Acestes,
horridus in iaculis et pelle Libystidis ursae,   MPR
Troia Criniso conceptum flumine mater
quem genuit.   veterum non immemor ille parentum
gratatur reduces et gaza laetus agresti   **40**
excipit, ac fessos opibus solatur amicis.
   Postera cum primo stellas Oriente fugarat
clara dies, socios in coetum litore ab omni
advocat Aeneas tumulique ex aggere fatur:
"Dardanidae magni, genus alto a sanguine divum, **45**
annuus exactis completur mensibus orbis,
ex quo reliquias divinique ossa parentis
condidimus terra maestasque sacravimus aras.
iamque dies, nisi fallor, adest, quem semper
     acerbum,
semper honoratum (sic di voluistis) habebo.   **50**
hunc ego Gaetulis agerem si Syrtibus exsul,
Argolicove mari deprensus et urbe Mycenae,
annua vota tamen sollemnisque ordine pompas

    29 demittere *c:* dimittere *other MSS., Priscian.*
    35 *Both* excelso *and* ex celso *known to Servius.*
    52 urbe] arce *P¹.* Mycenis *R; so Sabb.*

Eryx and the Sicilian ports, if only my memory prove true as I retrace the stars I watched before."

[26] Then good Aeneas: "Even I have long seen that the winds will so have it, and that in vain thou headest against them. Change the course of our sailing. Could any land be more welcome to me, any whereto I would sooner steer my weary ships, than that which holds my Dardan friend Acestes, and enfolds in her embrace my father Anchises' ashes?" This said, they make for harbour, and favouring Zephyrs fill their sails; the fleet runs swiftly on the flood, and at last they gladly turn to the familiar shore.

[35] But afar off, on a high hill-top, Acestes marvels at the coming of friendly ships and hastens towards them, bristling with weapons and a Libyan she-bear's skin—Acestes, born of a Trojan mother to the river-god Crinisus. Not unmindful of his old lineage, he bids them joy on their return, gladly welcomes them with rustic wealth, and comforts their weariness with friendly cheer.

[42] When on the morrow at early dawn bright day had put the stars to rout, Aeneas calls his comrades from all the shore together and from a mounded hill speaks:

[45] "Great sons of Dardanus, born of heaven's high race, with the passing of the months the circling year draws to an end since we laid in earth the dust, all that was left, of my divine father, and hallowed the altars of grief. And now, if I err not, the day is at hand which I shall keep (such, O gods, was your will) ever as a day of grief, ever as of honour. Were I spending it in exile in the Gaetulian Syrtes, or caught on the Argolic sea or in Mycenae's town, yet would I perform the yearly vow with rites of solemn ordinance

VIRGIL

exsequerer strueremque suis altaria donis.
nunc ultro ad cineres ipsius et ossa parentis   **55**
(haud equidem sine mente, reor, sine numine divum)
adsumus et portus delati intramus amicos.
ergo agite et laetum cuncti celebremus honorem ;
poscamus ventos, atque haec me sacra quotannis
urbe velit posita templis sibi ferre dicatis.   **60**
bina boum vobis Troia generatus Acestes
dat numero capita in navis ; adhibete Penatis
et patrios epulis et quos colit hospes Acestes.
praeterea, si nona diem mortalibus almum
Aurora extulerit radiisque retexerit orbem,   **65**
prima citae Teucris ponam certamina classis ;
quique pedum cursu valet, et qui viribus audax
aut iaculo incedit melior levibusque sagittis,
seu crudo fidit pugnam committere caestu,
cuncti adsint meritaeque exspectent praemia palmae.
ore favete omnes et cingite tempora ramis."   **71**
   Sic fatus velat materna tempora myrto.
hoc Helymus facit, hoc aevi maturus Acestes,   MPRV
hoc puer Ascanius, sequitur quos cetera pubes.
ille e concilio multis cum milibus ibat   **75**
ad tumulum, magna medius comitante caterva.
hic duo rite mero libans carchesia Baccho
fundit humi, duo lacte novo, duo sanguine sacro,
purpureosque iacit flores ac talia fatur :
" salve, sancte parens, iterum ; salvete, recepti   **80**
nequiquam cineres animaeque umbraeque paternae.
non licuit finis Italos fataliaque arva ˙
nec tecum Ausonium, quicumque est, quaerere
    Thybrim."
dixerat haec, adytis cum lubricus anguis ab imis
septem ingens gyros, septena volumina traxit,   **85**

[68] levibusve *R*.

and pile the altars with due gifts. But now, lo! by my
sire's own dust and bones we stand—not, methinks,
without the purpose and will of heaven—and wafted
hither enter a friendly haven. Come then, one and
all, and let us solemnize the sacrifice with joy; let us
pray for winds and may he grant that year by year
when my city is founded I may offer these rites in
temples consecrated to him! Two head of oxen
Acestes, of Trojan birth, gives you for every ship;
summon to the feast both your own hearth-gods and
those whom our host Acestes worships. Moreover,
should the ninth Dawn lift her kindly light for mortals
and with her rays lay bare the world, I will ordain
contests for the Trojans: first of the swift ships; then
whoever excels in the foot-race, and who, bold in his
strength, steps forward superior with the javelin and
light shafts, or who dares to join battle with gloves
of raw hide—let all appear and look for the palm, the
prize of victory. Be silent all, and wreathe your
brows with leaves."

[72] So speaking, he crowns his brows with his
mother's myrtle. Thus does Helymus, thus Acestes,
ripe of years, thus the boy Ascanius, the rest of the
youth following. Then from the assembly to the
mound he passed, amid many thousands, the centre
of the great attending throng. Here in due libation
he pours on the ground two goblets of unmixed wine,
two of fresh milk, two of the blood of victims, and
showering bright blossoms, thus he cries: " Hail, holy
father, once again; hail, ye ashes, rescued though in
vain, and thou, soul and shade of my sire! Not with
thee was I suffered to seek the destined bounds and
fields of Italy, nor Ausonian Tiber, whate'er it be."
So had he spoken, when from the foot of the shrine
a slippery serpent trailed seven huge coils, fold upon

amplexus placide tumulum lapsusque per aras,
caeruleae cui terga notae maculosus et auro
squamam incendebat fulgor, ceu nubibus arcus
mille iacit varios adverso sole colores.
obstipuit visu Aeneas.   ille agmine longo   90
tandem inter pateras et levia pocula serpens
libavitque dapes, rursusque innoxius imo
successit tumulo, et depasta altaria liquit.
hoc magis inceptos genitori instaurat honores,
incertus, geniumne loci famulumne parentis   95
esse putet ; caedit binas de more bidentis
totque sues, totidem nigrantis terga iuvencos ;
vinaque fundebat pateris animamque vocabat
Anchisae magni Manisque Acheronte remissos.   MPR
nec non et socii, quae cuique est copia, laeti   100
dona ferunt ; onerant aras mactantque iuvencos ;
ordine aëna locant alii fusique per herbam
subiciunt veribus prunas et viscera torrent.

Exspectata dies aderat, nonamque serena
Auroram Phaethontis equi iam luce vehebant,   105
famaque finitimos et clari nomen Acestae
excierat ; laeto complebant litora coetu,
visuri Aeneadas, pars et certare parati.
munera principio ante oculos circoque locantur FMPR
in medio, sacri tripodes viridesque coronae   110
et palmae, pretium victoribus, armaque et ostro
perfusae vestes, argenti aurique talenta ;
et tuba commissos medio canit aggere ludos.

Prima pares ineunt gravibus certamina remis
quattuor ex omni delectae classe carinae.   115

⁸⁹ iacit] trahit $R\gamma^2$.
⁹³ linquit M^1.
⁹⁶ caedit binas M : caeditque binas R : caedit quinas $PV\gamma$
¹⁰⁷ complebant M : complerant PR.
¹¹² talentum MP : talenta FR, *Servius*.

fold seven times, peacefully circling the mound and
gliding among the altars; his back chequered with
blue spots, and his scales ablaze with the sheen of
dappled gold, even as in the clouds the rainbow
darts a thousand shifting tints athwart the sun.
Aeneas was awestruck at the sight.   At last, crawl-
ing with long train amid the bowls and polished
cups, the serpent tasted the viands, and again, all
harmless, crept beneath the tomb, leaving the altars
where he fed.   More eagerly, therefore, does he
renew his father's interrupted rites, knowing not
whether to deem it the genius of the place or the
attendant spirit of his sire.   Two sheep he slays,
as is meet, two swine, and as many dark-backed
heifers, while he poured wine from bowls and called
great Anchises' shade and the ghost released from
Acheron.   Moreover, his comrades, as each has store,
gladly bring gifts, heap the altars and slay the
steers; others in turn set the cauldrons and, stretched
along the grass, put live coals under the spits and
roast the flesh.

    104 The looked-for day had come, and now the
steeds of Phaëthon ushered in the ninth Dawn with
cloudless light.   The name and fame of noble
Acestes had stirred the countryside; in merry
groups the people thronged the shore, some to
see the sons of Aeneas, and some ready to contend.
First of all the prizes are laid out to view in the
midst of the course — sacred tripods, green gar-
lands and palms, the victors' prize; armour and
purple-dyed garments, with talents of silver and
gold.   Then from a central mound the trumpet
proclaims the opening of the games.

    114 For the first contest enter four well-matched
ships of heavy oars, picked from all the fleet.

VIRGIL

velocem Mnestheus agit acri remige Pristim,
mox Italus Mnestheus, genus a quo nomine Memmi,
ingentemque Gyas ingenti mole Chimaeram,
urbis opus, triplici pubes quam Dardana versu
impellunt, terno consurgunt ordine remi ;   120
Sergestusque, domus tenet a quo Sergia nomen,
Centauro invehitur magna, Scyllaque Cloanthus
caerulea, genus unde tibi, Romane Cluenti.

Est procul in pelago saxum spumantia contra
litora, quod tumidis submersum tunditur olim   125
fluctibus, hiberni condunt ubi sidera Cori ;
tranquillo silet immotaque attollitur unda
campus et apricis statio gratissima mergis.
hic viridem Aeneas frondenti ex ilice metam
constituit signum nautis pater, unde reverti   130
scirent et longos ubi circumflectere cursus.
tum loca sorte legunt, ipsique in puppibus auro
ductores longe effulgent óstroque decori ;
cetera populea·velatur fronde iuventus
nudatosque umeros oleo perfusa nitescit.   135
considunt transtris, intehtaque bracchia remis ;
intenti exspectant signum, exsultantiaque haurit
corda pavor pulsans laudumque arrecta cupido.
inde ubi clara dedit sonitum tuba, finibus omnes,
haud mora, prosiluere suis ; ferit aethera clamor 140
nauticus, adductis spumant freta versa lacertis.
infindunt pariter sulcos, totumque dehiscit
convolsum remis rostrisque tridentibus aequor.
non tam praecipites biiugo certamine campum
corripuere ruuntque effusi carcere currus ;   145

[133] longe] auro *Priscian.*

454

Mnestheus with his eager crew drives the swift
Sea-dragon, soon to be Mnestheus of Italy, from
whose name comes the Memmian line; Gyas the
huge Chimaera of huge bulk, a city afloat, urged by
the Dardan youth in triple tier, with oars rising in
threefold rank. Sergestus, from whom the Sergian
house has its name, rides in the great Centaur; and
in the sea-blue Scylla Cloanthus, whence comes thy
family, Cluentius of Rome! [1]

[124] Far out at sea, over against the foaming shores
lies a rock which at times the swollen waves beat
and o'erwhelm, when stormy North-westers hide the
stars; in time of calm it is voiceless, and rises from
the placid wave a level surface, and a welcome haunt
for sun-loving gulls. Here as a mark father Aeneas
set up a green goal of leafy ilex, for the sailors to know
whence to return and where to double round the long
course. Then they choose places by lot, and on the
sterns the captains themselves shine forth afar in
glory of gold and purple; the rest of the crews
are crowned with poplar wreaths, and their naked
shoulders glisten, moist with oil. They man the
thwarts, their arms strained to the oars; straining,
they await the signal, while throbbing fear and eager
passion for glory drain each bounding heart. Then,
when the clear trumpet sounded, all at once shot forth
from their starting-places; the mariners' shouts strike
the heavens; as arms are drawn back the waters are
turned into foam. They cleave the furrows abreast,
and all the sea gapes open, uptorn by the oars and
triple-pointed beaks. Not such the headlong speed
when in the two-horse chariot race the cars seize the
plain and dart forth from their stalls! Not so wildly

---

[1] In Virgil's day certain Roman families, three of whom
are named in this passage, claimed a Trojan origin.

nec sic immissis aurigae undantia lora
concussere iugis pronique in verbera pendent.
tum plausu fremituque virum studiisque faventum
consonat omne nemus, vocemque inclusa volutant
litora, pulsati colles clamore resultant.   150

    Effugit ante alios primisque elabitur undis
turbam inter fremitumque Gyas ; quem deinde
    Cloanthus
consequitur, melior remis, sed pondere pinus
tarda tenet.   post hos aequo discrimine Pristis
Centaurusque locum tendunt superare priorem ;   155
et nunc Pristis habet, nunc victam praeterit ingens
Centaurus, nunc una ambae iunctisque feruntur
frontibus et longa sulcant vada salsa carina.   [MPR
iamque propinquabant scopulo metamque tenebant,
cum princeps medioque Gyas in gurgite victor   160
rectorem navis compellat voce Menoeten :
"quo tantum mihi dexter abis ? huc dirige gressum ;
litus ama et laeva stringat sine palmula cautes ;
altum alii teneant."   dixit sed caeca Menoetes
saxa timens proram pelagi detorquet ad undas.   165
"quo diversus abis ?" iterum "pete saxa, Menoete !"
cum clamore Gyas revocabat, et ecce Cloanthum
respicit instantem tergo et propiora tenentem.
ille inter navemque Gyae scopulosque sonantis
radit iter laevum interior subitoque priorem   170
praeterit et metis tenet aequora tuta relictis.
tum vero exarsit iuveni dolor ossibus ingens,
nec lacrimis caruere genae, segnemque Menoeten,
oblitus decorisque sui sociumque salutis,
in mare praecipitem puppi deturbat ab alta ;   175
ipse gubernaclo rector subit, ipse magister,
hortaturque viros clavumque ad litora torquet.

      154 aequo] aliquo *F*[1].   158 carinae *F*[1].
      162 derige *PR.* gressum] cursum *M*[2], *Seneca.*
      163 laevas *Rγ*[2].

over their dashing steeds do the charioteers shake
the waving reins, bending forward to the lash!
Then with applause and shouts of men, and zealous
cries of partisans, the whole woodland rings; the
sheltered beach rolls up the sound, and the hills,
smitten, echo back the din.

151 Gyas flies in front of the rest and glides fore-
most on the waves amid confusion and uproar; next
Cloanthus follows close, better manned but held
back by his pine's slow bulk. After them, at equal
distance, the Dragon and Centaur strive to win the
lead; and now the Dragon has it, now the huge
Centaur wins past her, now both move together with
even prows, and plough the salt waters with long
keel. And now they neared the rock and were close
to the turn, when Gyas, still first, and leader in the
half-course, loudly hails his ship's pilot, Menoetes:
"Whither, man, so far off to the right? This way
steer her course; hug the shore, and let the oar-
blade graze the rocks on the left; let others keep to
the deep!" He spoke; but Menoetes, fearing blind
rocks, wrenches the prow aside towards the open
sea. "Whither so far off the course? Make for the
rocks, Menoetes!" again shouted Gyas to call him
back; when lo! he sees Cloanthus hard behind and
keeping the nearer course. Between Gyas' ship
and the roaring rocks he grazes his way nearer in on
the left, suddenly passes his leader, and leaving the
goal behind gains safe water. Then indeed anger
burned deep in the young man's frame; tears sprang
to his cheeks, and heedless alike of his own pride
and his crew's safety, he heaves timid Menoetes from
the high stern sheer into the sea; himself steersman
and captain, he steps to the helm, cheers on his
men, and turns the rudder shoreward. But Menoetes,

VIRGIL

at gravis, ut fundo vix tandem redditus imo est,
iam senior madidaque fluens in veste Menoetes
summa petit scopuli siccaque in rupe resedit.   180
illum et labentem Teucri et risere natantem
et salsos rident revomentem pectore fluctus.

Hic laeta extremis spes est accensa duobus,
Sergesto Mnestheique, Gyan superare morantem.
Sergestus capit ante locum scopuloque propinquat, 185
nec tota tamen ille prior praeeunte carina;
parte prior; partem rostro premit aemula Pristis.
at media socios incedens nave per ipsos
hortatur Mnestheus: "nunc, nunc insurgite remis,
Hectorei socii, Troiae quos sorte suprema   190
delegi comites; nunc illas promite viris,
nunc animos, quibus in Gaetulis Syrtibus usi
Ionioque mari Maleaeque sequacibus undis.
non iam prima peto Mnestheus neque vincere certo;
quamquam o—sed superent, quibus hoc, Neptune,
      dedisti—   195
extremos pudeat rediisse; hoc vincite, cives,
et prohibete nefas." olli certamine summo
procumbunt; vastis tremit ictibus aerea puppis,
subtrahiturque solum; tum creber anhelitus artus
aridaque ora quatit, sudor fluit undique rivis.   200
attulit ipse viris optatum casus honorem.
namque furens animi dum proram ad saxa suburget
interior spatioque subit Sergestus iniquo,
infelix saxis in procurrentibus haesit.
concussae cautes, et acuto in murice remi   205
obnixi crepuere, inlisaque prora pependit.
consurgunt nautae et magno clamore morantur
ferratasque trudes et acuta cuspide contos
expediunt fractosque legunt in gurgite remos.

---

[187] partem M: partim PR.   [198] aurea M^1P^1.
[202] animo $P\gamma^1$.   prora M.   [208] sudes M.

when scarce at last he rose heavily from the sea
bottom, old as he was and dripping in his drenched
clothes, makes for the top of the crag and sat him
down on the dry rock. The Teucrians laughed as he
fell and swam, and they laugh as he spews the salt
waters from his chest.

[183] Here a joyful hope was kindled in the two
behind, Sergestus and Mnestheus, to pass the laggard
Gyas. Sergestus takes the lead and nears the rock;
yet is he ahead not by a whole boat's length, but in
part alone; the rival Dragon overlaps with her prow.
Then, pacing amidships among his crew, Mnestheus
cheers them on: " Now, now, rise to the oars, com-
rades of Hector, ye whom in Troy's last hour I chose
as my followers; now put forth that strength, that
courage, which ye showed in Gaetulian quicksands,
on the Ionian sea, and amid Malea's racing waves!
No more do I, Mnestheus, seek the first place, no
more strive to win; yet oh !—but let those conquer to
whom thou, Neptune, hast granted it—it were a
shame to return last ! Win but this, my countrymen,
and ward off disgrace ! " Straining to the utmost,
his men bend forward; with their mighty strokes
the brazen poop quivers, and the ocean-floor flies from
under them. Then rapid panting shakes their limbs
and parched mouths; while sweat streams down all
their limbs. Mere chance brought them the glory
craved. For while Sergestus, mad at heart, drives
his prow inward towards the rocks and enters on the
perilous course, he stuck, alas ! on a jutting reef.
The cliffs were jarred, on the sharp flint the oars
struck and snapped; the bow hung where it crashed.
Up spring the sailors and, clamouring loudly at the
delay, get out iron-shod pikes and sharp-pointed
poles, or pick up in the flood their broken oars. But

VIRGIL

At laetus Mnestheus successuque acrior ipso   210
agmine remorum celeri ventisque vocatis
prona petit maria et pelago decurrit aperto.
qualis spelunca subito commota columba,
cui domus et dulces latebroso in pumice nidi,
fertur in arva volans plausumque exterrita pinnis 215
dat tecto ingentem, mox aëre lapsa quieto
radit iter liquidum celeris neque commovet alas:
sic Mnestheus, sic ipsa fuga secat ultima Pristis
aequora, sic illam fert impetus ipse volantem.
et primum in scopulo luctantem deserit alto   220
Sergestum brevibusque vadis frustraque vocantem
auxilia et fractis discentem currere remis.
inde Gyan ipsamque ingenti mole Chimaeram
consequitur; cedit, quoniam spoliata magistro est.
Solus iamque ipso superest in fine Cloanthus; 225
quem petit et summis adnixus viribus urget.
tum vero ingeminat clamor, cunctique sequentem
instigant studiis, resonatque fragoribus aether.
hi proprium decus et partum indignantur honorem
ni teneant, vitamque volunt pro laude pacisci :   230
hos successus alit ; possunt, quia posse videntur.
et fors aequatis cepissent praemia rostris,
ni palmas ponto tendens utrasque Cloanthus
fudissetque preces divosque in vota vocasset.
"di, quibus imperium est pelagi, quorum aequora curro,
vobis laetus ego hoc candentem in litore taurum 236
constituam ante aras voti reus, extaque salsos
porriciam in fluctus et vina liquentia fundam."
dixit, eumque imis sub fluctibus audiit omnis

210 et *M*[1].   212 pelago] caelo *Quintilian.*   220 in *om. M.*
226 enixus *Pγ.*   226 -que *omitted Pγ.*   clamoribus *Pγ.*
245 pelagi est *M²Rc.*   aequore *PRγ.*
238 porriciam *M (late):* porriciam *Macrobius, known to
Servius :* proiciam *M¹PR, known to Servius.*   et] ac *Pγb.*

460

Mnestheus, cheered and enlivened by his very success,
with swift play of oars and a prayer to the winds,
seeks the sloping waters and glides down the open
sea. Even as, if startled suddenly from her cave, a
dove whose home and sweet nestlings are in the
rocky coverts, wings her flight to the fields and,
frightened from her home, flaps loudly with her
wings; soon, gliding in the peaceful air, she skims
her liquid way and stirs not her swift pinions—so
Mnestheus, so the Dragon of herself, cleaves in flight
the final stretch, so her mere speed carries her on
her winged course! And first he leaves Sergestus
behind, struggling on the high rock and in shallow
waters, making vain appeals for help and learning to
race with broken oars. Then he overhauls Gyas,
even the Chimaera with her huge bulk; she gives
way, robbed of her helmsman.

²²⁵ And now, hard on the very goal, Cloanthus
alone is left. For him he makes, striving with all his
might and pressing hard. Then indeed the shouts
redouble, all together with cheers hearten the
pursuer, the sky echoes to their din. These think
it shame not to keep the honour that is theirs, the
glory they have won, and would barter life for fame:
those success heartens; strong are they, for strong
they deem themselves. And perchance, the prows
now brought abreast, they had taken the prize,
had not Cloanthus, stretching both hands seawards,
poured forth prayers, and called the gods to hear his
vows. "Ye gods, whose kingdom is the deep, over
whose waters I run, gladly, in discharge of my vow,
will I on this shore set before your altars a snow-
white bull, and fling entrails into the salt flood
and pour liquid wine!" He spake, and under
the deep waves the whole band of Nereids and of

VIRGIL

Nereidum Phorcique chorus Panopeaque virgo,　240
et pater ipse manu magna Portunus euntem　　MPRV
impulit : illa Noto citius volucrique sagitta
ad terram fugit et portu se condidit alto.

Tum satus Anchisa, cunctis ex more vocatis,
victorem magna praeconis voce Cloanthum　　245
declarat viridique advelat tempora lauro,
muneraque in navis ternos optare iuvencos
vinaque et argenti magnum dat ferre talentum.
ipsis praecipuos ductoribus addit honores :
victori chlamydem auratam, quam plurima circum 250
purpura Maeandro duplici Meliboea cucurrit,
intextusque puer frondosa regius Ida
velocis iaculo cervos cursuque fatigat,
acer, anhelanti similis ; quem praepes ab Ida
sublimem pedibus rapuit Iovis armiger uncis ;　255
longaevi palmas nequiquam ad sidera tendunt
custodes, saevitque canum latratus in auras.
at qui deinde locum tenuit virtute secundum,
levibus huic hamis consertam auroque trilicem
loricam, quam Demoleo detraxerat ipse　　260
victor apud rapidum Simoenta sub Ilio alto,
donat habere viro, decus et tutamen in armis.
vix illam famuli Phegeus Sagarisque ferebant
multiplicem, conixi umeris ; indutus at olim
Demoleos cursu palantis Troas agebat.　　265
tertia dona facit geminos ex aere lebetas
cymbiaque argento perfecta atque aspera signis.
　Iamque adeo donati omnes opibusque superbi
puniceis ibant evincti tempora taenis,
cum saevo e scopulo multa vix arte revolsus,　270

Neptunus γ^1.

Phorcus, and the virgin Panopea, heard him, and
the sire Portunus with his own great hand drave
him on his way. Swifter than wind or winged arrow
the ship speeds landward, and found shelter in the
deep harbour.

²⁴⁴ Then the son of Anchises, duly summoning all,
by loud cry of herald proclaims Cloanthus victor,
and with green bay wreathes his brows; next, as
gifts for each ship, bids him choose and take away
three bullocks, wine, and a large talent of silver. For
the captains themselves he adds special honours; to
the winner, a cloak wrought with gold, about which
ran deep Meliboean purple in double waving line;
inwoven thereon the royal boy,[1] with javelin and
speedy foot, on leafy Ida tires fleet stags, eager, and
like to one who pants; him Jove's swift armour-
bearer[2] has caught up aloft from Ida in his talons;
his aged guardians in vain stretch their hands to the
stars, and the savage barking of dogs rises skyward.
But to him, who next by merit won the second place,
a coat of mail, linked with polished hooks of triple
gold, once torn by his own hand from Demoleos,
when he worsted him by swift Simois under lofty
Ilium, he gives to keep—a glory and defence in
battle. Scarce could the servants, Phegeus and
Sagaris, bear its folds with straining shoulders;
yet, clad in this, Demoleos of yore drove full speed
the scattered Trojans. The third prize he makes
a pair of brazen cauldrons, and bowls wrought in
silver and rough with reliefs.

²⁶⁸ And now all had their gifts and, proud of their
wealth, were going their way, their brows bound with
purple fillets, when—hardly, by dint of much skill,

[1] Ganymede.
[2] So called because he carries the thunderbolt.

463

amissis remis atque ordine debilis uno,
inrisam sine honore ratem Sergestus agebat.
qualis saepe viae deprensus in aggere serpens,
aerea quem obliquum rota transiit aut gravis ictu
seminecem liquit saxo lacerumque viator ;   275
nequiquam longos fugiens dat corpore tortus,
parte ferox ardensque oculis et sibila colla
arduus attollens ; pars volnere clauda retentat
nixantem nodis seque in sua membra plicantem :
tali remigio navis se tarda movebat ;   280
vela facit tamen et plenis subit ostia velis.
Sergestum Aeneas promisso munere donat,
servatam ob navem laetus sociosque reductos.
olli serva datur, operum haud ignara Minervae,
Cressa genus, Pholoe, geminique sub ubere nati. 285
    Hoc pius Aeneas misso certamine tendit
gramineum in campum, quem collibus undique curvis
cingebant silvae, mediaque in valle theatri
circus erat ; quo se multis cum milibus heros
consessu medium tulit exstructoque resedit.   290
hic, qui forte velint rapido contendere cursu,
invitat pretiis animos, et praemia ponit.
undique conveniunt Teucri mixtique Sicani,   MPR
Nisus et Euryalus primi,
Euryalus forma insignis viridique iuventa,   295
Nisus amore pio pueri ; quos deinde secutus
regius egregia Priami de stirpe Diores ;
hunc Salius simul et Patron, quorum alter Acarnan,
alter ab Arcadio Tegeaeae sanguine gentis ;
tum duo Trinacrii iuvenes, Helymus Panopesque, 300

    278 vulnera $P\gamma^1$.   cauda M^1P^2V.
    279 nixantem $M^1P\gamma^1$: nitentem M^2: nexantem $M(late)RV\gamma^2$,
Priscian.   **280** ferebat $P\gamma$.
    281 plenis . . . velis M : velis . . . plenis *other MSS.*
    285 ubera $MPR\gamma$.

cleared from the cruel rock, oars lost, and one tier crippled, Sergestus, amid jeers, brought in his inglorious barque. Even as oft a serpent, caught upon the highway, which a brazen wheel has crossed aslant, or with blow of a heavy stone a wayfarer has crushed and left half-dead, vainly tries to escape and trails its long coils; part defiant, his eyes ablaze and his hissing neck raised aloft; part, maimed by the wound, holding him back, as he struggles on with his coils and twines himself upon his own limbs—with such oarage, the ship moved slowly on, yet hoists sail and under full sail makes the harbour's mouth. Aeneas presents Sergestus with his promised reward, glad that the ship is saved and the crew brought back. A slave-woman is given him, not unskilled in Minerva's tasks, Pholoë of Cretan stock, with twin-boys at her breast.

²⁸⁶ This contest sped, good Aeneas moves to a grassy plain, girt all about with winding hills, well-wooded, where, at the heart of the valley, ran the circuit of a theatre. To this, with many thousands, the hero betook himself into the midst of the company and sat him down on a raised seat. Here, if haply any would vie in speed of foot, he lures them with hope of rewards and sets up prizes. From all sides flock Trojans and Sicilians, mingled, Nisus and Euryalus foremost—Euryalus famed for beauty and flower of youth, Nisus for tender love for the boy. Next followed princely Diores, of Priam's noble race; then Salius and Patron together, whereof one was an Acarnanian, the other of Arcadian blood, a Tegean born; then two Sicilian youths, Helymus and Panopes, inured to the forests

---

²⁹⁰ consensu *M¹*.   ²⁹⁵ insigni *Pγ¹*.
²⁹⁶ quem *Pγ¹*.   ²⁹⁹ Arcadia *Pγ*. Tegeae de *M²P²γ*.

adsueti silvis, comites senioris Acestae ;
multi praeterea, quos fama obscura recondit.
Aeneas quibus in mediis sic deinde locutus :
" accipite haec animis laetasque advertite mentes.
nemo ex hoc numero mihi non donatus abibit.   305
Gnosia bina dabo levato lucida ferro
spicula caelatamque argento ferre bipennem ;
omnibus hic erit unus honos.   tres praemia primi
accipient flavaque caput nectentur oliva.
primus equum phaleris insignem victor habeto ;   310
alter Amazoniam pharetram plenamque sagittis
Threiciis, lato quam circum amplectitur auro
balteus et tereti subnectit fibula gemma ;
tertius Argolica hac galea contentus abito."
    Haec ubi dicta, locum capiunt signoque repente 315
corripiunt spatia audito limenque relinquunt,
effusi nimbo similes ; simul ultima signant.
primus abit longeque ante omnia corpora Nisus
emicat, et ventis et fulminis ocior alis ;
proximus huic, longo sed proximus intervallo,   320
insequitur Salius ; spatio post deinde relicto
tertius Euryalus ;
Euryalumque Helymus sequitur ; que deinde sub ipso
ecce volat calcemque terit iam calce Diores,
incumbens umero ; spatia et si plura supersint,   325
transeat elapsus prior ambiguumve relinquat.
iamque fere spatio extremo fessique sub ipsam
finem adventabant, levi cum sanguine Nisus
labitur infelix, caesis ut forte iuvencis
fusus humum viridisque super madefecerat herbas. 330
hic iuvenis iam victor ovans vestigia presso
haud tenuit titubata solo, sed pronus in ipso
concidit immundoque fimo sacroque cruore,

³⁰⁹ flava] fulva *known to Servius*.
³¹⁰ primum *M*¹.   equam *M*¹.   ³¹² circumplectitur *M*.
³²³ quo] quod *MR :* quem *P*¹.   ³²⁶ -ve *Heinsius, Bentley :*
-que *MSS. See Appendix*.   ³²⁷ ipsum *M*¹.
466

and attendants on old Acestes; with many besides,
whose fame is hid in darkness. Then in their midst
Aeneas thus spoke: " Take these words to heart and
pay cheerful heed. None of this number shall leave
without a gift from me. To each will I give two
Gnosian arrows, gleaming with polished steel, and
an axe chased with silver to bear away; all alike shall
have this same reward. The three first shall receive
prizes, and have pale-green olive crown their heads.
Let the first take as winner a horse gay with trap-
pings; the second an Amazonian quiver, filled with
Thracian arrows, girt about with a broad belt
of gold and clasped by a buckle with polished
gem; with this Argive helmet let the third depart
content."

    315 This said, they take their place, and suddenly,
the signal heard, dash over the course, and leave
the barrier, streaming forth like a storm-cloud, their
eyes fixed the while upon the goal. Away goes
Nisus first, and far in front of all darts forth, swifter
than the winds or than winged thunderbolt. Next
to him, but next by a long distance, follows Salius;
then, some space between them left, Euryalus third;
and, after Euryalus, Helymus; then, close upon him,
lo! Diores flies, now grazing foot with foot and
pressing on his shoulder! And did more of the
course remain, he would shoot past him to the fore or
leave the issue in doubt! And now, with course well-
nigh covered, panting they neared the very goal,
when Nisus, luckless one, falls in some slippery
blood, which, haply spilt where steers were slain,
had soaked the ground and greensward. Here,
even in the joy of triumph, the youth could not hold
his tottering steps on the ground he trod, but fell
prone, right in the filthy slime and blood of sacrifice.

non tamen Euryali, non ille oblitus amorum :
nam sese opposuit Salio per lubrica surgens,   335
ille autem spissa iacuit revolutus harena.
emicat Euryalus et munere victor amici
prima tenet plausuque volat fremituque secundo.
post Helymus subit, et, nunc tertia palma, Diores.

   Hic totum caveae consessum ingentis et ora   340
prima patrum magnis Salius clamoribus implet,
ereptumque dolo reddi sibi poscit honorem.
tutatur favor Euryalum lacrimaeque decorae,
gratior et pulchro veniens in corpore virtus.
adiuvat et magna proclamat voce Diores,   345
qui subiit palmae frustraque ad praemia venit
ultima, si primi Salio reddantur honores.
tum pater Aeneas, " vestra," inquit, " munera vobis
certa manent, pueri, et palmam movet ordine nemo ;
me liceat casus miserari insontis amici."   350
sic fatus tergum Gaetuli immane leonis
dat Salio, villis onerosum atque unguibus aureis.
hic Nisus, " si tanta," inquit, " sunt praemia victis,
et te lapsorum miseret, quae munera Niso
digna dabis, primam merui qui laude coronam,   355
ni me, quae Salium, fortuna inimica tulisset ? "
et simul his dictis faciem ostentabat et udo
turpia membra fimo.   risit pater optimus olli
et clipeum efferri iussit, Didymaonis artis,
Neptuni sacro Danais de poste refixum ;   360
hoc iuvenem egregium praestanti munere donat.

    [337] amico M^1.   [340] consensum $M^1R\gamma^1$.
    [347] reddantur $M^1R\gamma^1$: redduntur M^2: reddentur P.
    [350] miserari P^1R.   [354] munera] praemia M.
    [359] artem $PR\gamma$.

Yet not of Euryalus, not of his love was he forgetful;
for as he rose amid the sodden ground he threw
himself in the way of Salius, who, rolling over, fell
prostrate on the clotted sand. Euryalus darts by and,
winning by grace of his friend, takes first place, and
flies on amid favouring applause and cheers. Behind
come Helymus, and Diores, now third prize.

340 Hereupon Salius fills with loud clamour the
whole concourse of the great theatre and the gazing
elders in front, claiming that the prize wrested from
him by fraud be given back. Goodwill befriends
Euryalus, and his seemly tears and worth, that shows
more winsome in a fair form. Diores backs him, making
loud protest; he has reached the palm, but in vain won
the last prize, if the highest honours be restored to
Salius. Then said father Aeneas: "Your rewards
remain assured to you, my lads, and no one alters the
prizes' order; be it mine to pity the mischance of a
hapless friend!" So saying, he gives to Salius the huge
hide of a Gaetulian lion, heavy with shaggy hair and
gilded claws. Then said Nisus: "If such be the prize
for defeat, and thou hast pity for the fallen, what fit
reward wilt thou give Nisus? The first crown I had
earned by merit, had not Fortune's malice fallen
on me, as on Salius." And with the words he
displayed his face and limbs foul with wet filth.
The gracious father smiled on him and bade a
shield be brought out, the handiwork of Didymaon,
once taken down by Greeks from Neptune's hallowed
doorway.[1] This he bestows on the noble youth, a
lordly prize.

[1] Aeneas had apparently captured this shield from a
Greek hero who, on setting out for Troy, had taken it
down from the temple where it had been placed as a dedicated
object.

Post ubi confecti cursus et dona peregit:
"nunc, si cui virtus animusque in pectore praesens,
adsit et evinctis attollat bracchia palmis."
sic ait, et geminum pugnae proponit honorem,   365
victori velatum auro vittisque iuvencum,
ensem atque insignem galeam solacia victo.
nec mora; continuo vastis cum viribus effert
ora Dares magnoque virum se murmure tollit,
solus qui Paridem solitus contendere contra,   370
idemque ad tumulum, quo maximus occubat Hector,
victorem Buten, immani corpore qui se
Bebrycia veniens Amyci de gente ferebat,
perculit et fulva moribundum extendit harena.
talis prima Dares caput altum in proelia tollit,   375
ostenditque umeros latos alternaque iactat
bracchia protendens et verberat ictibus auras.
quaeritur huic alius; nec quisquam ex agmine tanto
audet adire virum manibusque inducere caestus.
ergo alacris cunctosque putans excedere palma   380
Aeneae stetit ante pedes, nec plura moratus
tum laeva taurum cornu tenet atque ita fatur:
"nate dea, si nemo audet se credere pugnae,
quae finis standi? quo me decet usque teneri?
ducere dona iube."   cuncti simul ore fremebant   385
Dardanidae reddique viro promissa iubebant.
    Hic gravis Entellum dictis castigat Acestes,
proximus ut viridante toro consederat herbae:
"Entelle, heroum quondam fortissime frustra,
tantane tam patiens nullo certamine tolli   390
dona sines? ubi nunc nobis deus ille magister,
nequiquam memoratus Eryx? ubi fama per omnem
Trinacriam et spolia illa tuis pendentia tectis?"

    364 vinctis $P\gamma^1$.   374 pertulit M^1: percutit R.
    382 laevo $P\gamma^1$.   387 his *Nonius*.
    388 herba R.

362 Then, when the races were ended and the gifts assigned, " Now," he cries, "whoso hath valour in his breast and a stout heart, let him come and lift up his arms with hidebound hands." So he speaks, and sets forth a double prize for the fray ; for the victor, a steer deckèd with gold and fillets ; a sword and noble helmet to console the vanquished. Forthwith, without pause, Dares shows himself in all his huge strength, rising amid a mighty murmuring of the throng—Dares, who alone was wont to face Paris : 'twas he who, by the mound, where great Hector lies, smote the champion Butes, offspring of Amycus' Bebrycian race, as he strode forward in his huge bulk, and stretched him dying on the yellow sand. Such was Dares, who at once raises his head high for the fray, displays his broad shoulders, stretches his arms, spars right and left, and lashes the air with blows. For him a match is sought ; but none from all that throng durst face him or draw the gloves on to his hands. So, exultant and thinking all resign the prize, he stood before Aeneas' feet ; then, tarrying no longer, grasps the bull's horn in his left hand, speaking thus : " Goddess-born, if no man dare trust himself to the fray, what end shall there be to my standing ? How long is it fitting to keep me waiting ? Bid me lead off thy gift !" Therewith all the Dardans shouted applause, and bade the promised prize be duly given him.

387 At this Acestes sternly chides Entellus, as he sat next him on the green couch of grass : " Entellus, once bravest of heroes, though in vain, wilt thou so tamely let gifts so great be carried off without a struggle ? Where now, pray, is that divine teacher, Eryx, idly famed ? Where thy renown over all Sicily, and those spoils hanging in thy house ?" Thereon

471

ille sub haec : " non laudis amor nec gloria cessit
pulsa metu ; sed enim gelidus tardante senecta   395
sanguis hebet, frigentque effetae in corpore vires.
si mihi, quae quondam fuerat quaque improbus iste
exsultat fidens, si nunc foret illa iuventas,
haud equidem pretio inductus pulchroque iuvenco
venissem, nec dona moror."   sic deinde locutus   400
in medium geminos immani pondere caestus
proiecit, quibus acer Eryx in proelia suetus
ferre manum duroque intendere bracchia tergo.
obstipuere animi ; tantorum ingentia septem
terga boum plumbo insuto ferroque rigebant.   405
ante omnis stupet ipse Dares longeque recusat,
magnanimusque Anchisiades et pondus et ipsa
huc illuc vinclorum immensa volumina versat.
tum senior talis referebat pectore voces :
"quid, si quis caestus ipsius et Herculis arma   410
vidisset tristemque hoc ipso in litore pugnam ?
haec germanus Eryx quondam tuus arma gerebat ;
(sanguine cernis adhuc sparsoque infecta cerebro)
his magnum Alciden contra stetit ; his ego suetus,
dum melior viris sanguis dabat, aemula necdum   415
temporibus geminis canebat sparsa senectus.
sed si nostra Dares haec Troius arma recusat,
idque pio sedet Aeneae, probat auctor Acestes,
aequemus pugnas.   Erycis tibi terga remitto
(solve metus), et tu Troianos exue caestus."   420
haec fatus duplicem ex umeris reiecit amictum,
et magnos membrorum artus, magna ossa lacertosque
exuit atque ingens media consistit harena.
    Tum satus Anchisa caestus pater extulit aequos
et paribus palmas amborum innexuit armis.   425

398 iuventus $P\gamma^1$.   **421** deiecit P^1.
422 -que *omitted* P^2.   **423** extulit *Macrobius*.
425 intexuit M^1.

he : " 'Tis not that love of fame is gone, or pride, routed by fear ; but my blood is chilled and dulled by sluggish age, and my strength of body is numb and lifeless. Had I that which once I had, that in which yonder braggart boldly exults—had I now that youth, then not from lure of prize or goodly steer had I come forward, nor care I for gifts ! " So he spoke and thereon threw into the ring a pair of gloves of giant weight, wherewith valiant Eryx was wont to enter contests, binding his arms with the tough hide. Amazed were the hearts of all, so vast were the seven huge ox-hides, all stiff with insewn lead and iron. Above all Dares himself is dazed and, shrinking back, declines the contest ; while Anchises' noble son turns this way and that the thongs' huge and ponderous folds. Then the old man spoke thus from his breast : " What if any had seen the gloves and arms of Hercules himself, and the fatal feud on this very shore ? These arms thy brother Eryx once wore ; thou seest them yet stained with blood and spattered brains. With these he faced great Alcides ; with these was I wont to fight, while sounder blood gave me strength, nor yet had envious age sprinkled my temples with snow. But if the Trojan Dares declines these our arms, and this is resolved on by good Aeneas and approved by my patron Acestes, let us make the battle even. At thy wish I waive the gauntlets of Eryx ; dismiss thy fears ; and do thou doff thy Trojan gloves ! " So speaking, from his shoulders he threw back his twofold cloak, stripped his great joints and limbs, his great bones and thews, and stood a giant in the arena's midst.

[424] Then, with a father's care, the seed of Anchises brought out gloves of like weight and with equal **weapons** bound the hands of both. Straightway

VIRGIL

constitit in digitos extemplo arrectus uterque
bracchiaque ad superas interritus extulit auras.
abduxere retro longe capita ardua ab ictu
immiscentque manus manibus pugnamque lacessunt,
ille pedum melior motu fretusque iuventa,   430
hic membris et mole valens ; sed tarda trementi
genua labant, vastos quatit aeger anhelitus artus.
multa viri nequiquam inter se volnera iactant,
multa cavo lateri ingeminant et pectora vastos
dant sonitus, erratque auris et tempora circum   435
crebra manus, duro crepitant sub volnere malae.
stat gravis Entellus nisuque immotus eodem,
corpore tela modo atque oculis vigilantibus exit.
ille, velut celsam oppugnat qui molibus urbem
aut montana sedet circum castella sub armis,   440
nunc hos, nunc illos aditus omnemque pererrat
arte locum et variis adsultibus inritus urget.
ostendit dextram insurgens Entellus et alte
extulit; ille ictum venientem a vertice velox
praevidit celerique elapsus corpore cessit;   445
Entellus viris in ventum effudit et ultro
ipse gravis graviterque ad terram pondere vasto
concidit, ut quondam cava concidit aut Ery-
    mantho   MPRV
aut Ida in magna radicibus eruta pinus.
consurgunt studiis Teucri et Trinacria pubes;   450
it clamor caelo, primusque accurrit Acestes
aequaevumque ab humo miserans attollit amicum.
at non tardatus casu neque territus heros
acrior ad pugnam redit ac vim suscitat ira.
tum pudor incendit viris et conscia virtus,   455
praecipitemque Daren ardens agit aequore toto,
nunc dextra ingeminans ictus,, nunc ille sinistra.

428 sonitum Pγ¹.   446 effundit P¹.   449 radicitus Rγ¹.
451 -que om. M¹. So Sabb. ; add. M (late).
457 ille] deinde M.

474

each took his stand, poised on tiptoe, and, undaunted, lifted his arms high in air. Raising their heads high and drawing them far back from blows, they spar, hand with hand, and provoke the fray, the one nimbler of foot and confident in his youth, the other mighty in massive limbs; yet his slow knees totter and tremble and a painful gasping shakes his huge frame. Many hard blows they launch at each other idly, many they rain on hollow flank, while their chests ring loudly; hands play oft about ears and brows, and cheeks rattle under the hard strokes. Solidly stands Entellus, motionless, unmoved, with selfsame poise, shunning blows with body and watchful eyes alone. The other, like one who assails with siege-works some high city or besets a mountain stronghold in arms, tries this entrance and now that, skilfully ranges over all the ground, and presses with varied but vain assaults. Then Entellus, rising, put forth his right, lifted high; the other speedily foresaw the down-coming blow and, slipping aside with nimble body, foiled it. Entellus spent his strength on air, yea, and in his huge bulk this mighty man fell in his might to earth, as at times falls on Erymanthus or mighty Ida a hollow pine, uptorn by the roots! Eagerly the Teucrians and men of Sicily rise up; a shout mounts to heaven, and first Acestes runs forward, and in pity raises his aged friend from the ground. But neither downcast nor dismayed by the fall, the hero returns keener to the fray, and rouses violence with wrath. Shame, too, and conscious valour kindle his strength, and in fury he drives Dares headlong over the whole arena, redoubling his blows, now with the right hand, and now, lo! with the left. No stint, no stay is there—

nec mora, nec requies; quam multa grandine nimbi
culminibus crepitant, sic densis ictibus heros
creber utraque manu pulsat versatque Dareta.　　460
　　Tum pater Aeneas procedere longius iras
et saevire animis Entellum haud passus acerbis,
sed finem imposuit pugnae fessumque Dareta
eripuit, mulcens dictis, ac talia fatur:
"infelix, quae tanta animum dementia cepit?　　465
non viris alias conversaque numina sentis?
cede deo." dixitque et proelia voce diremit.
ast illum fidi aequales, genua aegra trahentem
iactantemque utroque caput crassumque cruorem
ore eiectantem mixtosque in sanguine dentes,　　470
ducunt ad navis; galeamque ensemque vocati
accipiunt, palmam Entello taurumque relinquunt.
hic victor, superans animis tauroque superbus,
"nate dea vosque haec," inquit, "cognoscite, Teucri,
et mihi quae fuerint iuvenali in corpore vires,　　475
et qua servetis revocatum a morte Dareta."
dixit et adversi contra stetit ora iuvenci,
qui donum adstabat pugnae, durosque reducta
libravit dextra media inter cornua caestus,
arduus, effractoque inlisit in ossa cerebro:　　480
sternitur exanimisque tremens procumbit humi bos.
ille super talis effundit pectore voces:
"hanc tibi, Eryx, meliorem animam pro morte Daretis
persolvo; hic victor caestus artemque repono."
　　Protinus Aeneas celeri certare sagitta　　485
invitat qui forte velint et praemia ponit
ingentique manu malum de nave Seresti

---

[470] ore eiectantem $P\gamma^1$: ore iectantem M: ore iactan
tem R: ore reiectantem γ^2. mixtoque M^1.
[473] animo V.　　[477] aversi $P\gamma$.　　[480] in *omitted* R.
[484] reponit R, *Servius*: repon- V^2.
[486] ponit MRV, *Nonius*: dicit $P\gamma$.

thick as the hail when storm-clouds rattle on the
roof, so thick are the blows from either hand as the
hero oft beats and batters Dares.

⁴⁶¹ Then father Aeneas suffered not their fury to
go farther, nor Entellus to rage in bitterness of soul,
but set an end to the fray and rescued the sore-spent
Dares, speaking thus in soothing words : " Unhappy
man ! How could such frenzy seize thy mind ? Seest
thou not the strength is another's and the gods are
changed ? Yield to heaven ! " He spoke, and with
his voice broke off the fight. But Dares his loyal
mates lead to the ships, his feeble knees trailing, his
head swaying from side to side, while he spat from
his mouth clotted gore and teeth mingled with the
blood. At summons, they receive the helmet and the
sword ; the palm and the bull they leave to Entellus.
Thereat the victor, triumphant in spirit and glory-
ing in the bull, cries: " O Goddess-born and ye,
O Trojans, learn what strength I had in my youthful
frame, and from what a death ye recall and rescue
Dares." He spoke, and set himself in face of the
confronting steer as it stood by, the prize of battle ;
then drew back his right hand and, at full height,
swung the hard gauntlet just between the horns,
and broke into the skull, scattering the brains. Out-
stretched and lifeless, the bull falls quivering on
the ground. Above it he pours forth from his breast
these words: " This better life I offer thee, Eryx,
due for death of Dares; here victorious I lay down
the gauntlet and my art ! "

⁴⁸⁵ Straightway Aeneas invites all, who may so
wish, to contend with swift arrows, and sets forth the
prizes. With a large throng ¹ he raises the mast from

---

¹ So taken by Servius, who explains the phrase by *magna
multitudine*. Editors commonly render, " with his own mighty
hand," as if Aeneas were an Homeric hero.

erigit et volucrem traiecto in fune columbam,
quo tendant ferrum, malo suspendit ab alto.
convenere viri deiectamque aerea sortem   490
accepit galea; et primus clamore secundo
Hyrtacidae ante omnis exit locus Hippocoontis.
quem modo navali Mnestheus certamine victor
consequitur, viridi Mnestheus evinctus oliva.
tertius Eurytion, tuus, o clarissime, frater,   495
Pandare, qui quondam, iussus confundere foedus,
in medios telum torsisti primus Achivos.
extremus galeaque ima subsedit Acestes,
ausus et ipse manu iuvenum temptare laborem.

Tum validis flexos incurvant viribus arcus   MPR
pro se quisque viri et depromunt tela pharetris,   501
primaque per caelum nervo stridente sagitta
Hyrtacidae iuvenis volucris diverberat auras,
et venit adversique infigitur arbore mali.
intremuit malus, timuitque exterrita pinnis   505
ales, et ingenti sonuerunt omnia plausu.
post acer Mnestheus adducto constitit arcu,
alta petens, pariterque oculos telumque tetendit.
ast ipsam miserandus avem contingere ferro
non valuit; nodos et vincula linea rupit,   510
quis innexa pedem malo pendebat ab alto;
illa Notos atque atra volans in nubila fugit.
tum rapidus, iamdudum arcu contenta parato
tela tenens, fratrem Eurytion in vota vocavit,
iam vacuo laetam caelo speculatus, et alis   515
plaudentem nigra figit sub nube columbam.
decidit exanimis vitamque reliquit in astris
aetheriis fixamque refert delapsa sagittam.
amissa solus palma superabat Acestes;

⁴⁹¹ primum *RV*.   ⁴⁹⁹ manum *V*. labore *V*.   ⁵⁰³ volucri(s)
iuvenis *Pγ*¹.   ⁵⁰⁵ micuit *Slater*.   ⁵¹² atra *MRγ*²: alta *P*.
⁵¹⁶ figit nigra *P*¹*γ*.   ⁵¹⁸ aeriis *MR*: aetheriis *P*.

Serestus' ship, and from the high pole, on a cord
passed across her, suspends a fluttering dove as mark
for their shafts. The rivals gather, and a brazen
helmet received the lots thrown in. First before all,
amid warm cheers, comes forth the turn of Hippo-
coon, son of Hyrtacus; on him follows Mnestheus,
but now victor in the ship-race—Mnestheus, wreathed
in green olive. Third is Eurytion, thy brother, O
famous Pandarus, who of old, when bidden to con-
found the treaty, didst first hurl a shaft amid the
Achaeans. Last, and in the helmet's depths, lay
Acestes, even he daring to lay hand to the task of
youth.

⁵⁰⁰ Then with might and main they bend their
bows into a curve, each for himself, and draw shafts
from quivers. And first through the sky, from the
twanging string, the dart of the son of Hyrtacus
cleft the fleet breezes, reached its mark, and struck
full in the wood of the mast. The mast quivered,
the bird fluttered her wings in terror, and the whole
place rang with loud applause. Next valiant Mnes-
theus took his stand with bow bent, aiming aloft,
and eyes and shaft levelled alike; yet could
not, alas! hit the bird herself with the bolt, but
severed the knots and hempen bands tying her
foot, as from the high mast she hung: off
to the south winds and black clouds she sped
in flight. Then quickly Eurytion, who had long
held his bow ready and dart drawn, called upon
his brother to hear his vow, marked the dove, now
exulting in the free sky, and pierced her as she
flapped her wings under a dark cloud. Down she
fell dead, left her life amid the stars of heaven,
and, falling, brought down the arrow that pierced
her. Acestes alone was left, the prize now lost; yet

qui tamen aërias telum contorsit in auras,   520
ostentans artemque pater arcumque sonantem.
hic oculis subitum obicitur magnoque futurum
augurio monstrum ; docuit post exitus ingens
seraque terrifici cecinerunt omina vates.
namque volans liquidis in nubibus arsit harundo 525
signavitque viam flammis tenuisque recessit
consumpta in ventos, caelo ceu saepe refixa
transcurrunt crinemque volantia sidera ducunt.
attonitis haesere animis, superosque precati
Trinacrii Teucrique viri.; nec maximus omen   530
abnuit Aeneas, sed laetum amplexus Acesten
muneribus cumulat magnis ac talia fatur :
" sume, pater : nam te voluit rex magnus Olympi
talibus auspiciis exsortem ducere honores.
ipsius Anchisae longaevi hoc munus habebis,   535
cratera impressum signis, quem Thracius olim
Anchisae genitori in magno munere Cisseus
ferre sui dederat monumentum et pignus amoris."
sic fatus cingit viridanti tempora lauro
et primum ante omnis victorem appel.it Acesten. 540
nec bonus Eurytion praelato invidit honori,
quamvis solus avem caelo deiecit ab alto.
proximus ingreditur donis, qui vincula rupit ;
extremus, volucri qui fixit harundine malum.
    At pater Aeneas nondum certamine misso   545
custodem ad sese comitemque impubis Iuli
Epytiden vocat et fidam sic fatur ad aurem :
" vade age et Ascanio, si iam puerile paratum

520 contorsit $M^2P\gamma$: contendit M^1R, *Nonius*.
522 subito *most MSS.*: subitum *minor MSS.*
534 honores M^1PR: honorem $M^2\gamma^2$.
541 honore P^1.   **545** paratus P^1.

480

upward into the air he aimed his bolt, displaying his
olden skill and the ringing of his bow. On this a
sudden portent meets their eyes, destined to prove
of lofty presage; this in after time the mighty
issue showed, and in late days terrifying seers pro-
claimed the omen.[1] For, flying amid the airy clouds,
the reed caught fire, marked its path with flames, then
vanished away into thin air; as often, shooting stars,
unloosed from heaven, speed across the sky, their
tresses streaming in their wake. In amazement the
Trinacrians and Trojans stood rooted, praying to the
powers above. Nor did great Aeneas reject the
omen, but, embracing glad Acestes, loaded him with
noble gifts, and spoke thus: "Take them, father,
for the great king of Olympus hath willed by these
tokens that thou shouldst receive honours out of due
course. This gift thou shalt have, once the aged
Anchises' own, a bowl graven with figures, that in
days gone by Cisseus of Thrace gave my sire Anchises,
memorial of himself and pledge of love." So speak-
ing, he binds his brows with green laurel and hails
Acestes victor, first above them all; nor did good
Eurytion grudge the prize preferred, though he
alone brought down the bird from high heaven.
Next for the reward comes he who cut the cord; last
is he who with fleet reed pierced the mast.

545 But father Aeneas, ere yet the match was sped,
calls to him Epytides, guardian and companion of
young Iülus, and thus speaks into his faithful ear:
"Away," he cries, "go tell Ascanius, if he has with
him his boyish band in readiness, and has marshalled

---

[1] Some great event of later days is referred to here, perhaps
the Punic Wars, in which Sicily played so great a part. When
the event occurred seers explained it as a fulfilment of the
portent here described.

agmen habet secum cursusque instruxit equorum,
ducat avo turmas et sese ostendat in armis,   550
dic," ait.   ipse omnem longo decedere circo
infusum populum et campos iubet esse patentis.
incedunt pueri pariterque ante ora parentum
frenatis lucent in equis, quos omnis euntis
Trinacriae mirata fremit Troiaeque iuventus.   555
omnibus in morem tonsa coma pressa corona ;
cornea bina ferunt praefixa hastilia ferro,
pars levis umero pharetras ; it pectore summo
flexilis obtorti per collum circulus auri.
tres equitum numero turmae ternique vagantur   560
ductores ; pueri bis seni quemque secuti
agmine partito fulgent paribusque magistris.
una acies iuvenum, ducit quam parvus ovantem
nomen avi referens Priamus, tua clara, Polite,
progenies, auctura Italos ; quem Thracius albis   565
portat equus bicolor maculis, vestigia primi
alba pedis frontemque ostentans arduus albam.
alter Atys, genus unde Atii duxere Latini,
parvus Atys pueroque puer dilectus Iulo.
extremus formaque ante omnis pulcher Iulus   570
Sidonio est invectus equo, quem candida Dido
esse sui dederat monumentum et pignus amoris.
cetera Trinacriis pubes senioris Acestae
fertur equis.

    551 discedere *P :* discendere γ^1.
    558 it M^2, *Servius :* et $M^1 R \gamma^1$: iet P^1 : id γ^2.
    564 cara P^1.   **570** formam M^1.
    573 Trinacriis *minor MSS. :* Trinacrii *R, Servius :* Trina-
criae $M P^2$: Trinacrie P^1.

AENEID BOOK V

the manoeuvres of his horses, to lead forth his troops
in his grandsire's honour and show himself in arms."
He himself bids all the streaming throng quit the
long course and leave the field clear. On come
the boys, and in even array glitter before their
fathers' eyes on bridled steeds; as they pass by,
the men of Trinacria and Troy murmur in admira-
tion. All have their hair duly crowned with a
trimmed garland; each carries two cornel spear-
shafts tipped with iron; some have polished quivers
on their shoulders; high on the breast around the
neck passes a pliant circlet of twisted gold.[1] Three
in number are the troops of horse, and three the
riding captains; the boys, two groups of six following
each, look gay with parted troop and like com-
manders.[2] One line of youths in triumphal joy is led
by a little Priam, renewing his grandsire's name—
thy noble seed, Polites, and destined to swell the
Italian race! Him a Thracian horse bears, dappled
with spots of white, showing white pasterns as it steps
and a white, high-towering brow. The second is
Atys, from whom the Latin Atii have drawn their
line—little Atys, a boy beloved of the boy Iülus.
Last, and in beauty excelling all, Iülus rode on a
Sidonian horse, that fairest Dido had given as memo-
rial of herself and pledge of her love. The rest of
the youth ride on the Sicilian steeds of old Acestes.

[1] The golden *torques*, a military decoration, was worn low
down on the neck.
[2] Thirty-six boys were divided into three companies
(*turmae*), which were commanded alike (*paribus magistris*),
each having a captain (*terni ductores*). The *ductores* and the
magistri are the same; *cf.* 176 with 133. (The trainers,
however, are also called *magistri* in 669, and of these Epytides
was the chief.) Each company, again, was subdivided into
two groups (*chori*) of six each.

483

excipiunt plausu pavidos gaudentque tuentes   575
Dardanidae veterumque adgnoscunt ora parentum.
postquam omnem laeti consessum oculosque suorum
lustravere in equis, signum clamore paratis
Epytides longe dedit insonuitque flagello.
olli discurrere pares atque agmina terni   580
diductis solvere choris rursusque vocati
convertere vias infestaque tela tulere.
inde alios ineunt cursus aliosque recursus
adversi spatiis, alternosque orbibus orbis
impediunt, pugnaeque cient simulacra sub armis; 585
et nunc terga fuga nudant, nunc spicula vertunt
infensi, facta pariter nunc pace feruntur.
ut quondam Creta fertur Labyrinthus in alta
parietibus textum caecis iter ancipitemque
mille viis habuisse dolum, qua signa sequendi   590
falleret indeprensus et inremeabilis error:
haud alio Teucrum nati vestigia cursu
impediunt texuntque fugas et proelia ludo,
delphinum similes, qui per maria umida nando
Carpathium Libycumque secant luduntque per undas.
hunc morem cursus atque haec certamina primus 596
Ascanius, Longam muris cum cingeret Albam,
rettulit et Priscos docuit celebrare Latinos,
quo puer ipse modo, secum quo Troia pubes ;
Albani docuere suos ; hinc maxima porro   600
accepit Roma et patrium servavit honorem ;

577 cossensum M^1: concessum $P\gamma^1$.
581 deductis MR.   584 adversis $P\gamma$.   alternisque R.
591 frangeret $PR\gamma$, *Servius*: falleret M.
592 alioter R^1: aliter R^2.   nati Teucrum $P\gamma$.
595 luduntque per undas $M(late)R$: *omitted* $M^1P\gamma^1$.

---

[1] After riding in double column down the centre, the boys
wheeled, half to the right and half to the left, and galloped
to the sides of the arena ; then, at the word of command,
given by Epytides, they turned right about face, and the two

⁵⁷⁵ The Dardanians greet the bashful boys with cheers and rejoice as they gaze, seeing in them the features of their sires of old. When the lads had ridden gaily round the whole circuit of their gazing kinsfolk, Epytides shouted from afar the looked-for signal and cracked his whip. They galloped apart in equal ranks, and the three companies, parting their bands, broke up the columns; then recalled, they wheeled about and charged with levelled lances.[1] Next they enter on other marches and other counter-marches in opposing groups, interweaving circle with alternate circle, and waking an armed mimicry of battle. And now they bare their backs in flight, now turn their spears in charge, now make peace and ride on side by side. As of old in high Crete 'tis said the Labyrinth held a path woven with blind walls, and a bewildering work of craft with a thousand ways, where the tokens of the course were confused by the indiscoverable and irretrace-able maze : even in such a course do the Trojan children entangle their steps, weaving in sport their flight and conflict, like dolphins that, swim-ming through the wet main, cleave the Carpathian or Libyan seas and play amid the waves. This manner of horsemanship, these contests Ascanius first revived when he girt Alba Longa with walls, and taught the Early Latins, even as he himself solemnized them in boyhood, and with him the Trojan youth. The Albans taught their children ; from them in turn mighty Rome received them and kept as an ancestral observance ; and to-day the

sides (eighteen each) charged each other. Meanwhile the three captains probably act as pivot points or mark the centre of the field, where the charging half-companies re-form in marching column.

Troiaque nunc pueri, Troianum dicitur agmen.
hac celebrata tenus sancto certamina patri.

   Hic primum Fortuna fidem mutata novavit.
dum variis tumulo referunt sollemnia ludis,   605
Irim de caelo misit Saturnia Iuno
Iliacam ad classem ventosque adspirat eunti,
multa movens necdum antiquum saturata dolorem.
illa viam celerans per mille coloribus arcum
nulli visa cito decurrit tramite virgo.   610
conspicit ingentem concursum et litora lustrat
desertosque videt portus classemque relictam.
at procul in sola secretae Troades acta
amissum Anchisen flebant cunctaeque profundum
pontum aspectabant flentes.   "heu! tot vada fessis
et tantum superesse maris!"   vox omnibus una. 616
urbem orant; taedet pelagi perferre laborem.
ergo inter medias sese haud ignara nocendi
conicit et faciemque deae vestemque reponit;
fit Beroe, Tmarii coniunx longaeva Dorycli,   620
cui genus et quondam nomen natique fuissent,
ac sic Dardanidum mediam se matribus infert:
"o miserae, quas non manus," inquit, "Achaica
    bello
traxerit ad letum patriae sub moenibus! o gens
infelix, cui te exitio Fortuna reservat?   625
septima post Troiae excidium iam vertitur aestas,
cum freta, cum terras omnis, tot inhospita saxa
sideraque emensae ferimur, dum per mare magnum

       [604] hinc *PR.*   [609] çelebrans *M*[1].
       [611] consessum *M*[1].

boys are called Troy and the troop Trojan.[1] Thus far were solemnized the sports in honour of the holy sire.

604 Here first Fortune changed and broke her faith. While at the tomb with various games they pay the due rites, Juno, daughter of Saturn, sends Iris down from heaven to the Ilian fleet, and breathes fair winds to waft her on, pondering many a thought and with her ancient grudge still unsated. She, speeding her way along her thousand-hued rainbow, runs swiftly down her path, a maiden seen of none. She views the vast throng, scans the shore, and sees the harbour forsaken and the fleet abandoned. But far apart on the lonely shore the Trojan women wept for Anchises' loss, and all, as they wept, gazed on the fathomless flood. "Ah, for weary folk what waves remain, what wastes of sea!" Such is the one cry of all. 'Tis a city they crave; weary are they of bearing the ocean-toil. So into their midst, well versed in working ill, Iris flings herself, and lays aside the face and robe of a goddess. She becomes Beroë, aged wife of Tmarian Doryclus, who had once had family, fame, and children, and in such form joins the throng of Dardan mothers. "Ah, wretched we," she cries, "whom Achaean hands dragged not to death in war beneath our native walls! Ah, hapless race, for what destruction does Fortune reserve thee? The seventh summer is now on the wane since Troy's overthrow and we measure in our course all seas and lands, with many rocks and stars inhospitable, while o'er the great

---

[1] The brilliant equestrian sports, known as *ludus Troiae*, were introduced by Sulla, and fully developed by Augustus. Virgil, in compliment to the Emperor, connects them with Aeneas and Ascanius.

Italiam sequimur fugientem et volvimur undis.
hic Erycis fines fraterni atque hospes Acestes ;   630
quis prohibet muros iacere et dare civibus urbem ?
o patria et rapti nequiquam ex hoste Penates,
nullane iam Troiae dicentur moenia ?   nusquam
Hectoreos amnis, Xanthum et Simoenta, videbo ?
quin agite et mecum infaustas exurite puppis.   635
nam mihi Cassandrae per somnum vatis imago
ardentis dare visa faces : ' hic quaerite Troiam,
hic domus est,' inquit ' vobis.'   iam tempus agi
         res,
nec tantis mora prodigiis.   en quattuor arae
Neptuno ; deus ipse faces animumque ministrat." 640
   Haec memorans prima infensum vi corripit
         ignem
sublataque procul dextra conixa coruscat
et iacit.   arrectae mentes stupefactaque corda
Iliadum.   hic una e multis, quae maxima natu,
Pyrgo, tot Priami natorum regia nutrix :   645
" non Beroe vobis, non haec Rhoeteia, matres,
est Dorycli coniunx ; divini signa decoris
ardentisque notate oculos, qui spiritus illi,
qui voltus vocisque sonus vel gressus eunti.
ipsa egomet dudum Beroen digressa reliqui   650
aegram, indignantem, tali quod sola careret
munere nec meritos Anchisae inferret honores."
haec effata.
at matres primo ancipites oculisque malignis
ambiguae spectare rates miserum inter amorem   655
praesentis terrae fatisque vocantia regna,
cum dea se paribus per caelum sustulit alis
ingentemque fuga secuit sub nubibus arcum.
tum vero attonitae monstris actaeque furore
conclamant rapiuntque focis penetralibus ignem ; 660

deep we chase a fleeing Italy and toss upon the waves. Here are the lands of our brother Eryx, and here is our host Acestes. Who forbids us to cast up walls and give our citizens a city? O fatherland, O household gods, in vain rescued from the foe, shall no town hereafter be called Troy's? Shall I nowhere see a Xanthus and a Simois, the rivers of Hector? Nay, come! and burn with me these accursed ships. For in my sleep the phantom of Cassandra, the soothsayer, seemed to give me blazing brands: 'Here seek Troy,' she said; 'here is your home.' Now 'tis time that deeds be done; such portents brook no delay. Lo, four altars to Neptune! The god himself lends the brands and the resolve."

641 Thus speaking, she first strongly seized the deadly flame, and raising her hand aloft, with full force brandished it and threw. Startled are the minds of the Trojan dames, their wits bewildered. Hereon one from out their throng, and she the eldest, Pyrgo, royal nurse for Priam's many sons: "This, look you, mothers, is not Beroë; this is not the Rhoeteian wife of Doryclus. Mark the signs of divine beauty and the flashing eyes; what fire she has, what lineaments, the sound of her voice, or her step as she moves. I myself but even now left Beroë behind, sick, and fretting that she alone had no part in such a rite, nor could pay to Anchises the offerings due!" So she spake. But at first the matrons were gazing on the ships doubtfully and with jealous eyes, wavering between an unhappy yearning for the land now reached and the realm that called them with the voice of fate, when the goddess on poised wings rose through the sky, cleaving in flight the mighty bow beneath the clouds. Then, indeed, amazed at the marvels and driven by frenzy, they cry aloud,

pars spoliant aras, frondem ac virgulta facesque
coniciunt.   furit immissis Volcanus habenis
transtra per et remos et pictas abiete puppis.

Nuntius Anchisae ad tumulum cuneosque theatri
incensas perfert navis Eumelus, et ipsi   665
respiciunt atram in nimbo volitare favillam.
primus et Ascanius, cursus ut laetus equestris
ducebat, sic acer equo turbata petivit
castra, nec exanimes possunt retinere magistri.
" quis furor iste novus? quo nunc, quo tenditis,"
     inquit,   670
" heu ! miserae cives? non hostem inimicaque
     castra
Argivum, vestras spes uritis.   en ego vester
Ascanius !"   galeam ante pedes proiecit inanem,
qua ludo indutus belli simulacra ciebat.
accelerat simul Aeneas, simul agmina Teucrum. 675
ast illae diversa metu per litora passim
diffugiunt silvasque et sicubi concava furtim
saxa petunt ; piget incepti lucisque, suosque
mutatae adgnoscunt, excussaque pectore Iuno est.

Sed non idcirco flammae atque incendia viris   680
indomitas posuere ; udo sub robore vivit
stuppa vomens tardum fumum, lentusque carinas
est vapor, et toto descendit corpore pestis,
nec vires heroum infusaque flumina prosunt.
tum pius Aeneas umeris abscindere vestem   685
auxilioque vocare deos et tendere palmas :
" Iuppiter omnipotens, si nondum exosus ad
     unum
Troianos, si quid pietas antiqua labores
respicit humanos, da flammam evadere classi

⁶⁸⁰ flamma M^2P^1, *Donatus:* flammam $M^1P^2\gamma^1$: flammae
$M(late)R\gamma^2$.
⁶⁸⁵ abscindere P: abscidere R: excindere M.
490

and some snatch fire from the hearths within; others strip the altars, and throw on leaves and twigs and brands. With free rein Vulcan riots amid thwarts and oars and hulls of painted pine.

⁶⁶⁴ To the tomb of Anchises and the seats of the theatre Eumelus bears tidings of the burning ships, and looking back, their own eyes see the black ash floating in a smoky cloud. And first Ascanius, as gaily he led the galloping troops, spurred his horse to the bewildered camp, nor can the breathless trainers hold him back. "What strange madness this?" he cries. "Whither now, whither are ye bound, ah! my wretched countrywomen? 'Tis not the foe, not the hostile Argive camp ye burn, but your own hopes. Lo! I am your own Ascanius!" And before his feet he flung the empty helmet wherewith he was arrayed as he awoke in sport the mimicry of battle. Thither hastens Aeneas, too; thither, too, the Trojan bands. But the women scatter in dismay over the shores here and there, and make stealthily for the woods and the hollow rocks they anywhere can find. They loathe the deed and the light of day; with changed thoughts they know their kin, and Juno is shaken from their hearts.

⁶⁸⁰ But not for that did the burning flames lay aside their unquelled fury; under the wet oak the tow is alive, slowly belching smoke; the smouldering heat devours the keels, a plague sinking through the whole frame, nor can the heroes' strength, nor the floods they pour, avail. Then good Aeneas rent the garment from his shoulders, and called the gods to his aid, lifting up his hands: "Almighty Jupiter, if thou dost not yet utterly abhor the Trojans to their last man, if thy loving-kindness of old hath any regard for human sorrows, grant to the fleet to

nunc, pater, et tenuis Teucrum res eripe leto;   690
vel tu, quod superest, infesto fulmine morti,
si mereor, demitte tuaque hic obrue dextra."
vix haec ediderat, cum effusis imbribus atra
tempestas sine more furit tonitruque tremescunt
ardua terrarum et campi ; ruit aethere toto   695
turbidus imber aqua densisque nigerrimus Austris,
implenturque super puppes, semusta madescunt
robora, restinctus donec vapor omnis et omnes,
quattuor amissis, servatae a peste carinae.

At pater Aeneas, casu concussus acerbo,   700
nunc huc ingentis, nunc illuc pectore curas
mutabat versans, Siculisne resideret arvis,
oblitus fatorum, Italasne capesseret oras.
tum senior Nautes, unum Tritonia Pallas
quem docuit multaque insignem reddidit arte,   705
(haec responsa dabat, vel quae portenderet ira
magna deum vel quae fatorum posceret ordo),
isque his Aenean solatus vocibus infit :
" nate dea, quo fata trahunt retrahuntque sequamur;
quidquid erit, superanda omnis fortuna ferendo est.
est tibi Dardanius divinae stirpis Acestes;   711
hunc cape consiliis socium et coniunge volentem,
huic trade, amissis superant qui navibus et quos
pertaesum magni incepti rerumque tuarum est ;
longaevosque senes ac fessas aequore matres   715
et quidquid tecum invalidum metuensque pericli est
delige, et his habeant terris sine moenia fessi ;
urbem appellabunt permisso nomine Acestam."

escape the flame even now, O Father, and snatch
from doom the slender fortunes of the Trojans! Or
if I deserve it, do thou with levelled thunderbolt send
down to death the little that remains, and here over-
whelm us with thy hand." Scarce had he uttered
this when with streaming showers a black tempest
rages unrestrained; with thunder tremble hills
and plains; from the whole sky down rushes a
fierce storm of rain, pitch-black with laden south
winds. The ships are filled to overflowing, the
half-burnt timbers are soaked, till all the heat is
quenched, and all the hulls save four are rescued
from the plague.

700 But father Aeneas, stunned by the bitter blow,
now this way, now that, within his heart shifted
mighty cares, pondering whether, forgetful of fate,
he should settle in Sicilian fields, or aim to reach
Italian coasts. Then aged Nautes, whom, above all,
Tritonian Pallas taught, and with deep lore made
famous—she it was who gave him answers, telling
either what the mighty wrath of the gods portended,
or what the course of fate demanded—he with these
words essays to comfort Aeneas: "Goddess-born,
whither the Fates,in their ebb and flow, draw us, let us
follow; whatever befall, all fortune is to be o'ercome
by bearing. Thou hast Trojan Acestes, of divine
stock; him take to share thy counsels, a willing
partner; to him entrust those who, their ships thus
lost, are left over, and those who have grown aweary
of thy great emprise and of thy fortunes. Choose out
the old men full of years and sea-worn matrons, and
all of thy company who are weak and fearful of peril,
and grant that the wearied find their city in this
land. This town, so thou allow the name, they shall
call Acesta."

Talibus incensus dictis senioris amici
tum vero in curas animo diducitur omnis.　　　720
et Nox atra polum bigis subvecta tenebat :
visa dehinc caelo facies delapsa parentis
Anchisae subito talis effundere voces :
" nate, mihi vita quondam, dum vita manebat,
care magis, nate, Iliacis exercite fatis,　　　725
imperio Iovis huc venio, qui classibus ignem
depulit, et caelo tandem miseratus ab alto est.
consiliis pare, quae nunc pulcherrima Nautes
dat senior ; lectos iuvenes, fortissima corda,
defer in Italiam.　gens dura atque aspera cultu　730
debellanda tibi Latio est.　Ditis tamen ante
infernas accede domos et Averna per alta
congressus pete, nate, meos.　non me impia namque
Tartara habent, tristes umbrae, sed amoena piorum
concilia Elysiumque colo.　huc casta Sibylla　735
nigrarum multo pecudum te sanguine ducet.
tum genus omne tuum et quae dentur moenia disces.
iamque vale ; torquet medios Nox umida cursus,
et me saevus equis Oriens adflavit anhelis."
dixerat et tenuis fugit ceu fumus in auras.　　　740
Aeneas, " quo deinde ruis?　quo proripis ?" inquit,
" quem fugis? aut quis te nostris complexibus arcet ?"
haec memorans cinerem et sopitos suscitat ignis,
Pergameumque Larem et canae penetralia Vestae
farre pio et plena supplex veneratur acerra.　　　745
　　Extemplo socios primumque accersit Acesten
et Iovis imperium et cari praecepta parentis
edocet et quae nunc animo sententia constet.

[719] accensus *R*.　　　　　　　　　　[720] animum γ^2, *Servius*.
[722] facies caelo *Rγ*.　　　　　　　[731] est Latio *P*.
[734] tristesve *M* (*late*) : tristesque *c*².
[740] in] ad *P :* in ad γ^1.　　　　　　[744] arcessit *P*.

719 Then, indeed, kindled by such words of his aged friend, he is torn asunder in soul amid all his cares. And now, borne upwards in her chariot, black Night held the sky, when there seemed to glide down from heaven the likeness of his father Anchises and suddenly to utter thus his words:

724 " O son, dearer to me than life, in days when life was mine ; O son, much tried by Ilium's fate ! I come hither by Jove's command, who drove the fire from thy fleet, and at last has had pity from high heaven. Obey the fair advice that aged Nautes now gives; chosen youths, the bravest hearts, lead thou to Italy. A people hard and rugged in nurture must thou subdue in Latium. Yet first draw nigh the nether halls of Dis, and through the depths of Avernus seek, my son, a meeting with me. For impious Tartarus, with its gloomy shades, holds me not, but I dwell in Elysium amid the sweet assemblies of the blest. Hither, with much blood of black sheep, the pure Sibyl will lead thee ; and then shalt thou learn of all thy race, and what city is given thee. And now farewell ; dewy Night wheels her midway course, and the cruel East has breathed on me with panting steeds." He spake, and passed like smoke into thin air. " Whither art thou rushing now?" cries Aeneas. " Whither hurriest thou ? Whom fleest thou, or who bars thee from our embraces?" So speaking, he rouses the embers of the slumbering fires, and with holy meal and full censer humbly worships the Lar of Troy and the shrine of hoary Vesta.

746 Straightway he summons his comrades—Acestes first—and instructs them of Jove's command, the counsel of his dear father, and the resolve now settled in his soul. Not long is their debate ; nor

haud mora consiliis, nec iussa recusat Acestes.
transcribunt urbi matres populumque volentem   750
deponunt, animos nil magnae laudis egentis.
ipsi transtra novant flammisque ambesa reponunt
robora navigiis, aptant remosque rudentisque,
exigui numero, sed bello vivida virtus.
interea Aeneas urbem designat aratro   755
sortiturque domos; hoc Ilium et haec loca Troiam
esse iubet.   gaudet regno Troianus Acestes
indicitque forum et patribus dat iura vocatis.
tum vicina astris Erycino in vertice sedes
fundatur Veneri Idaliae, tumuloque sacerdos   760
ac lucus late sacer additur Anchiseo.

  Iamque dies epulata novem gens omnis, et aris
factus honos; placidi straverunt aequora venti,
creber et adspirans rursus vocat Auster in altum.
exoritur procurva ingens per litora fletus;   765
complexi inter se noctemque diemque morantur.
ipsae iam matres, ipsi, quibus aspera quondam
visa maris facies et non tolerabile nomen,
ire volunt omnemque fugae perferre laborem.
quos bonus Aeneas dictis solatur amicis   770
et consanguineo lacrimans commendat Acestae.
tris Eryci vitulos et Tempestatibus agnam
caedere deinde iubet solvique ex ordine funem.
ipse, caput tonsae foliis evinctus olivae,
stans procul in prora pateram tenet extaque salsos 775
porricit in fluctus ac vina liquentia fundit.
prosequitur surgens a puppi ventus euntis;
certatim socii feriunt mare et aequora verrunt.

      [751] egestes M^1.   [761] additus $P\gamma^1$.   *So Sabb.*
      [767] ipsi] ipsae *Nonius.*
      [768] nomen M^1: numen M^2P, *Servius* (*Aen.* VI. 560):
caelum *R.*
      [772] agnos *M.*

does Acestes refuse his bidding. They enrol the
matrons for the town, and set on shore the folk who
wish it so—souls with no craving for high renown.
They themselves renew the thwarts, and replace the
fire-charred timbers of the ships, and fit up oars and
rigging—scant of number, but a brave band alive for
war. Meanwhile Aeneas marks out the city with a
plough and allots homes; this he bids be Ilium and
these lands Troy. Trojan Acestes delights in his
kingdom, proclaims a court, and gives laws to the
assembled senate. Then, on the crest of Eryx, a
shrine, nigh to the stars, is founded to Venus of
Idalia, and to Anchises' tomb is assigned a priest
with breadth of hallowed grove.

[762] And now for nine days all the folk have
feasted and offerings been paid at the altars; gentle
winds have lulled the seas, and the South, breath-
ing oft upon them, calls again to sea. Along the
winding shore arises a mighty wail; embracing one
another, they linger a night and a day. Now the
very mothers, the very men to whom once the face of
the sea seemed cruel and its name intolerable, are
fain to go out and bear all toil of exile. These good
Aeneas comforts with kindly words, and commends
with tears to his kinsman Acestes. Then he bids
slay three steers to Eryx and a lamb to the
Tempests, and duly loose the moorings. He him-
self, with temples bound in leaves of trimmed olive,
standing apart on the prow, holds the cup, flings the
entrails into the salt flood, and pours the liquid wine.
A wind, rising astern, attends them on their way,
and with rival strokes his comrades lash the sea and
sweep the waters.

---

[776] proicit *most MSS.* : proiecit *c* : porricit *Heinsius. cf.* 238.
[778] *precedes* 777 *P.*

At Venus interea Neptunum exercita curis
adloquitur talisque effundit pectore questus: 780
"Iunonis gravis ira nec exsaturabile pectus
cogunt me, Neptune, preces descendere in omnis
quam nec longa dies, pietas nec mitigat ulla,
nec Iovis imperio fatisque infracta quiescit. FMPR
non media de gente Phrygum exedisse nefandis 785
urbem odiis satis est nec poenam traxe per omnem
reliquias Troiae; cineres atque ossa peremptae
insequitur. causas tanti sciat illa furoris.
ipse mihi nuper Libycis tu testis in undis
quam molem subito excierit; maria omnia caelo 790
miscuit, Aeoliis nequiquam freta procellis,
in regnis hoc ausa tuis.
per scelus ecce etiam Troianis matribus actis
exussit foede puppis et classe subegit
amissa socios ignotae linquere terrae. 795
quod superest, oro, liceat dare tuta per undas
vela tibi, liceat Laurentem attingere Thybrim,
si concessa peto, si dant ea moenia Parcae."
tum Saturnius haec domitor maris edidit alti:
"fas omne est, Cytherea, meis te fidere regnis, 800
unde genus ducis. merui quoque; saepe furores
compressi et rabiem tantam caelique marisque.
nec minor in terris (Xanthum Simoentaque testor)
Aeneae mihi cura tui. cum Troia Achilles
exanimata sequens impingeret agmina muris, 805
milia multa daret leto, gemerentque repleti
amnes nec reperire viam atque evolvere posset
in mare se Xanthus, Pelidae tunc ego forti

783 in] ad *Servius.*   784 fatisve *F*γ.   785 excedisse *F.*
786 traxe *P²b²*: traxere *F¹P¹*: traxisse *F²M¹*γ¹. omnis *P¹*.
787 *punctuation as indicated by MPR.*
794 excussit *M¹P¹*γ¹.
795 ignota *MP²R.* relinquere *P²*γ. terra *MP²*.
805 inmitteret *F¹*.   807 atque] neque *P.*

498

779 But Venus meanwhile, distressed with cares, speaks thus to Neptune, and from her heart pours out her plaint: "Juno's fell wrath and implacable heart constrain me, O Neptune, to stoop to every prayer. Her no lapse of time, nor any goodness softens, nor doth she rest, still unbent by Fate and Jove's command. 'Tis not enough that from the midst of the Phrygian race she in her fell hate has devoured their city and dragged through utmost vengeance the remnants of Troy; the very ashes and dust of the slaughtered race she still pursues. The causes of such madness be it hers to know. Thyself art my witness what sudden turmoil she raised of late in the Libyan waters; all the seas she mingled with the sky, in vain relying on the storms of Aeolus; and this she dared in thy realm. Lo! too, wickedly driving on the Trojan matrons, she hath foully burnt their ships, and forced them— their fleet lost—to abandon their comrades to an unknown shore. Grant, I pray, that the remnant may give their sails safely to thee across the waters; grant them to gain Laurentine Tiber; if I ask what is right, if those walls are granted by the Fates."

799 Then Saturn's son, lord of the deep sea, spake thus: "Every right hast thou, O Cytherean, to put trust in this, my realm, whence thou drawest birth. This, too, I have earned; often have I checked the fury and mighty rage of sea and sky. Nor less on land—I call Xanthus and Simois to witness—has been my care for thy Aeneas. When Achilles in his pursuit hurled the Trojan bands in panic on their walls, and sent many thousands to death, when the choked rivers groaned, and Xanthus could not find his way or roll out to sea—then 'twas I who, in a

VIRGIL

congressum Aenean nec dis nec viribus aequis
nube cava rapui, cuperem cum vertere ab imo   810
structa meis manibus periurae moenia Troiae.
nunc quoque mens eadem perstat mihi; pelle
    timorem.
tutus, quos optas, portus accedet Averni.
unus erit tantum, amissum quem gurgite quaeres;
unum pro multis dabitur caput."
his ubi laeta deae permulsit pectora dictis,   816
iungit equos auro Genitor spumantiaque addit
frena feris manibusque omnis effundit habenas.
caeruleo per summa levis volat aequora curru;
subsidunt undae tumidumque sub axe tonanti   820
sternitur aequor aquis; fugiunt vasto aethere nimbi.
tum variae comitum facies, immania cete,
et senior Glauci chorus Inousque Palaemon
Tritonesque citi Phorcique exercitus omnis;
laeva tenet Thetis et Melite Panopeaque virgo,   825
Nesaee Spioque Thaliaque Cymodoceque.

   Hic patris Aeneae suspensam blanda vicissim
gaudia pertemptant mentem; iubet ocius omnis
attolli malos, intendi bracchia velis.
una omnes fecere pedem pariterque sinistros,   830
nunc dextros solvere sinus; una ardua torquent
cornua detorquentque; ferunt sua flamina classem.
princeps ante omnis densum Palinurus agebat
agmen; ad hunc alii cursum contendere iussi.
iamque fere mediam caeli Nox umida metam   835
contigerat; placida laxabant membra quiete
sub remis fusi per dura sedilia nautae:

810 eripui F^2.   811 periturae $F^1 M^1$.
812 timorem F (?) M: timores $PR\gamma$.   814 missum M^1.
821 equis $M^1 b^1$. fugiuntque ex aethere M^2.
825 tenent P: tent R.
829 velis] remis MR.
837 sedilia] silentia P^1.

hollow cloud, caught Aeneas, as he confronted the brave son of Peleus and neither the gods nor his strength were in his favour, even though I was eager to uproot from their base the walls of perjured Troy that my own hands had built. Now, too, my purpose stands the same; away with fear. In safety, as thou prayest, shall he reach the haven of Avernus. One only shall there be whom, lost in the flood, thou shalt seek in vain; one life shall be given for many.''

[816] When with these words he had soothed to gladness the goddess' heart, the Sire yokes his wild steeds with gold, fastens their foaming bits, and lets all the reins stream freely in his hand; then over the water's surface lightly he flies in azure car. The waves sink to rest, beneath the thundering axle the sea of swollen waters is smoothed, and the storm-clouds vanish from the wide sky. Then come the diverse forms of his train—monstrous whales, the aged company of Glaucus, with Ino's son, Palaemon, the swift Tritons, and the whole host of Phorcus. Thetis and Melite keep the left, and maiden Panopea, Nesaea and Spio, Thalia and Cymodoce.

[827] On this in their turn soothing joys thrill father Aeneas' anxious heart. He bids all the masts be raised with speed and the yards spread with sails. Together all set the sheets, and all at once, now to the left and now to the right, they let out the canvas; together they turn to and fro the yard-arms aloft; favouring breezes bear on the fleet. First before all, leading the close column, was Palinurus; by him the rest are bidden to shape their course.

[835] And now dewy Night had just reached its mid-goal in heaven; the sailors, stretched on their hard benches under the oars, relaxed their limbs in quiet

cum levis aetheriis delapsus Somnus ab astris
aëra dimovit tenebrosum et dispulit umbras,
te, Palinure, petens, tibi somnia tristia portans 840
insonti ; puppique deus consedit in alta,
Phorbanti similis, funditque has ore loquelas :
" Iaside Palinure, ferunt ipsa aequora classem,
aequatae spirant aurae, datur hora quieti.
pone caput fessosque oculos furare labori. 845
ipse ego paulisper pro te tua munera inibo."
cui vix attollens Palinurus lumina fatur :
" mene salis placidi voltum fluctusque quietos
ignorare iubes ? mene huic confidere monstro ?
Aenean credam quid enim fallacibus auris, 850
et caeli totiens deceptus fraude sereni ? "
talia dicta dabat clavumque adfixus et haerens
nusquam amittebat oculosque sub astra tenebat.
ecce deus ramum Lethaeo rore madentem
vique soporatum Stygia super utraque quassat 855
tempora, cunctantique natantia lumina solvit.
vix primos inopina quies laxaverat artus,
et super incumbens cum puppis parte revolsa
cumque gubernaclo liquidas proiecit in undas
praecipitem ac socios nequiquam saepe vocantem ;
ipse volans tenuis se sustulit ales ad auras. 861
currit iter tutum non setius aequore classis
promissisque patris Neptuni interrita fertur.
iamque adeo scopulos Sirenum advecta subibat,
difficilis quondam multorumque ossibus albos, 865
(tum rauca adsiduo longe sale saxa sonabant),
cum pater amisso fluitantem errare magistro

843 ipsa aequora] sua flamina *M*1.
850 fallacius *Donatus.* austris *P*1γ.
851 caelo *P*1γ1. sereno γ1c1.
852 dictabat *P.*
860 saepe] voce *M.* 861 ad] in *Pγ*

rest; when Sleep, sliding lightly down from the stars of heaven, parted the dusky air and cleft the gloom, seeking thee, O Palinurus, and bringing thee baleful dreams, guiltless one! There on the high stern sat the god, in semblance of Phorbas, and poured these words from his lips: " Palinurus, son of Iasus, the seas of themselves bear on the fleet; steadily breathe the breezes; the hour is given to rest. Lay down thy head and steal thy weary eyes from toil. I myself for a space will take thy duty in thy stead." To him, scarce lifting his eyes, speaks Palinurus: " Me dost thou bid shut my eyes to the sea's calm face and peaceful waves? Me put faith in this monster? And Aeneas—why, indeed, am I to trust him to the treacherous breezes, I whom a clear sky has so often deceived?" Such words he said and, clinging fast to the tiller, never let loose his hold, and kept his eyes upturned to the stars. But lo! the god, shaking over his temples a bough dripping with Lethe's dew and steeped in the drowsy might of Styx, despite his efforts relaxes his swimming eyes. Hardly had a sudden slumber begun to unbend his limbs when, leaning above, Sleep flung him headlong into the clear waters, tearing away, as he fell, the helm and part of the stern, and calling oft-times vainly on his comrades. The god himself winged his way in flight to the thin air above. None the less the fleet speeds safely on its course over the sea and, trusting in Father Neptune's promise, glides on unafraid. And now, onward borne, it was nearing the cliffs of the Sirens, perilous of old and white with the bones of many men—at this time with the ceaseless surf the rocks afar were booming hoarsely—when the sire found that his ship was

503

VIRGIL

sensit et ipse ratem nocturnis rexit in undis,
multa gemens casuque animum concussus amici :
" o nimium caelo et pelago confise sereno,   870
nudus in ignota, Palinure, iacebis harena."

[871] *According to Servius and Probus, it is due to Varius and
Tucca that the book closes with this verse, Virgil himself having
added here ll. 1 and 2 of Book VI.*

drifting aimlessly, her pilot lost, and himself steered her amid the waves of night, oft sighing and stunned at heart by his friend's mischance. "Ah, too trustful in the calm of sky and sea, naked shalt thou lie, Palinurus, on an unknown strand!"

LIBER VI

Sɪc fatur lacrimans classique immittit habenas,   ᴍᴘʀ
et tandem Euboicis Cumarum adlabitur oris.
obvertunt pelago proras, tum dente tenaci
ancora fundabat navis, et litora curvae
praetexunt puppes.   iuvenum manus emicat ardens 5
litus in Hesperium; quaerit pars semina flammae
abstrusa in venis silicis, pars densa ferarum
tecta rapit silvas, inventaque flumina monstrat.
at pius Aeneas arces, quibus altus Apollo
praesidet, horrendaeque procul secreta Sibyllae,   10
antrum immane, petit, magnam cui mentem ani-
        mumque
Delius inspirat vates aperitque futura.
iam subeunt Triviae lucos atque aurea tecta.
    Daedalus, ut fama est, fugiens Minoia regna,
praepetibus pinnis ausus se credere caelo,   15
insuetum per iter gelidas enavit ad Arctos
Chalcidicaque levis tandem super adstitit arce.
redditus his primum terris tibi, Phoebe, sacravit
remigium alarum posuitque immania templa.
in foribus letum Androgeo; tum pendere poenas 20
Cecropidae iussi, miserum! septena quotannis
corpora natorum; stat ductis sortibus urna.

    [17] arcaem M^1 : arca R : arce M^2P.
    [20] Androgeo bc, *Priscian, Servius, &c.* : Androgei $MPR\gamma$.

506

BOOK VI

Thus he cries weeping, and gives his fleet the reins, and at last glides up to the shores of Euboean Cumae. They turn the prows seaward, then with the grip of anchors' teeth made fast the ships, and the round keels fringe the beach.   In hot haste the youthful band leaps forth on the Hesperian shore; some seek the seeds of flame hidden in veins of flint, some pillage the woods,[1] the thick coverts of game, and point to new found streams.   But good Aeneas seeks the heights, where Apollo sits enthroned,[2] and a vast cavern hard by, hidden haunt of the dread Sibyl, into whom the Delian seer breathes a mighty mind and soul, revealing the future.   Now they pass under the grove of Trivia and the roof of gold.

[14] Daedalus, 'tis said, when fleeing from Minos' realm, dared on swift wings to trust himself to the sky; on his unwonted way he floated forth towards the cold North, and at last stood lightly poised above the Chalcidian hill.   Here first restored to earth, he dedicated to thee, O Phoebus, the oarage of his wings and built a vast temple.   On the doors is the death of Androgeos; then the children of Cecrops, bidden, alas! to pay as yearly tribute seven living sons; there stands the urn, the lots now drawn.

---

[1] *i.e.* for firewood.   Virgil here dignifies commonplace themes, the gathering of fuel and the procuring of water.

[2] Cumae was on high ground, capped by two summits, on one of which was the temple of Apollo.

contra elata mari respondet Gnosia tellus :
hic crudelis'amor tauri suppostaque furto
Pasiphae mixtumque genus prolesque biformis   25
Minotaurus inest, Veneris monumenta nefandae; FMPR
hic labor ille domus et inextricabilis error ;
magnum reginae sed enim miseratus amorem
Daedalus ipse dolos tecti ambagesque resolvit,
caeca regens filo vestigia.   tu quoque magnam   30
partem opere in tanto, sineret dolor, Icare, haberes;
bis conatus erat casus effingere in auro,
bis patriae cecidere manus.   quin protinus omnia
perlegerent oculis, ni iam praemissus Achates
adforet atque una Phoebi Triviaeque sacerdos,   35
Deiphobe Glauci, fatur quae talia regi :
"non hoc ista sibi tempus spectacula poscit :
nunc grege de intacto septem mactare iuvencos
praestiterit, totidem lectas de more bidentis."
talibus adfata Aenean (nec sacra morantur   40
iussa viri) Teucros vocat alta in templa sacerdos.

   Excisum Euboicae latus ingens rupis in antrum,
quo lati ducunt aditus centum, ostia centum,
unde ruunt totidem voces, responsa Sibyllae.
ventum erat ad limen, cum virgo, "poscere fata · 45
tempus" ait : "deus, ecce, deus!"   cui talia fanti
ante fores subito non voltus, non color unus,
non comptae mansere comae, sed pectus anhelum,
et rabie fera corda tument, maiorque videri
nec mortale sonans, adflata est numine quando   50

---

²³ Cnosia *P.*   ³³ omne *Rb :* omnem *c.*
³⁷ poscunt *M¹R, known to Servius.*   ³⁹ de] ex *F.*

Opposite, rising from the sea, the Gnosian land
faces this; here is the cruel love of the bull, Pasiphaë
craftily mated, and the mongrel breed of the Mino-
taur, a twiformed offspring, record of monstrous
love; there that house of toil, a maze inextricable;
but lo! Daedalus, pitying the princess' great love,
himself unwound the deceptive tangle of the palace,
guiding blind feet with the thread. Thou, too, O
Icarus, wouldst have large share in such a work, did
grief permit : twice had he essayed to fashion thy fall
in gold; twice sank the father's hands. Ay, and all
the tale throughout would their eyes have scanned,
but now came Achates from his errand, and with
him the priestess of Phoebus and Trivia, Deïphobe,
daughter of Glaucus, who thus bespeaks the king:
"Not sights like these does this hour demand!
Now it were better to sacrifice seven bullocks from
the unbroken herd, and as many ewes fitly chosen."
Having thus addressed Aeneas—and not slow are they
to do her sacred bidding—the priestess calls the
Teucrians into the lofty fane.

⁴² The huge side of the Euboean rock is hewn into
a cavern, whither lead a hundred wide mouths, a
hundred gateways, whence rush as many voices, the
answers of the Sibyl.[1] They had come to the thresh-
old, when the maiden cries: "'Tis time to ask the
oracles; the god, lo! the god!" As thus she spake
before the doors, suddenly nor countenance nor colour
was the same, nor stayed her tresses braided; but
her bosom heaves, her heart swells with wild frenzy,
and she is taller to behold, nor has her voice a
mortal ring, since now she feels the nearer breath of

[1] The volcanic hills of Cumae are pierced by many grottos.
One of these, the *antrum* of the Sibyl, could be approached
through the temple.

VIRGIL

iam propiore dei. " cessas in vota precesque,   MPR
Tros," ait, " Aenea?   cessas?   neque enim ante
    dehiscent
attonitae magna ora domus."   et talia fata
conticuit.   gelidus Teucris per dura cucurrit
ossa tremor, funditque preces rex pectore ab imo : 55
" Phoebe, gravis Troiae semper miserate labores,
Dardana qui Paridis direxti tela manusque
corpus in Aeacidae, magnas obeuntia terras
tot maria intravi duce te penitusque repostas
Massylum gentis praetentaque Syrtibus arva ;   60
iam tandem Italiae fugientis prendimus oras ;
hac Troiana tenus fuerit fortuna secuta.
vos quoque Pergameae iam fas est parcere genti,
dique deaeque omnes, quibus obstitit Ilium et ingens
gloria Dardaniae.   tuque, o sanctissima vates,   65
praescia venturi, da (non indebita posco
regna meis fatis) Latio considere Teucros
errantisque deos agitataque numina Troiae.
tum Phoebo et Triviae solido de marmore templum
instituam festosque dies de nomine Phoebi.   70
te quoque magna manent regnis penetralia nostris.
hic ego namque tuas sortis arcanaque fata
dicta meae genti ponam, lectosque sacrabo,
alma, viros.   foliis tantum ne carmina manda,
ne turbata volent rapidis ludibria ventis ;   75
ipsa canas oro."   finem dedit ore loquendi.

        [67] consistere *R*.   [69] templa *Pγ*.
        [70] constituam *R.*

510

deity. "Art thou slow to vow and to pray?" she cries. "Art slow, Trojan Aeneas? For till then the mighty mouths of the awestruck house will not gape open." So she spake and was mute. A chill shudder ran through the Teucrians' sturdy frames, and their king pours forth prayers from inmost heart :

56 "O Phoebus, who hast ever pitied the heavy woes of Troy, who didst guide the Dardan shaft and hand of Paris against the body of Aeacus' son, under thy guidance did I enter so many seas, skirting mighty lands, the far remote Massylian tribes, and the fields the Syrtes fringe; now at last we grasp the shores of fleeing Italy; thus far only may Troy's fortune have followed us! Ye, too, may now fitly spare the race of Pergamus, ye gods and goddesses all, to whom Troy and Dardania's great glory were an offence. And thou, most holy prophetess, who foreknowest the future, grant—I ask no realm unpledged by my fate—that the Teucrians may rest in Latium, with the wandering gods and storm-tossed powers of Troy. Then to Phoebus and Trivia will I set up a temple of solid marble, and festal days in Phoebus' name.[1] Thee also a stately shrine awaits in our realm;[2] for here will I place thy oracles and mystic utterances, told to my people, and ordain chosen men, O gracious one. Only trust not thy verses to leaves, lest they fly in disorder, the sport of rushing winds; chant them thyself, I pray." His lips ceased speaking.

[1] A reference both to the temple of Apollo, dedicated on the Palatine 28 B.C., and to the Apollo games, instituted in 212 B.C.

[2] Referring to the secret place for the Sibylline books, which were deposited under the statue of Apollo in the temple on the Palatine.

VIRGIL

At Phoebi nondum patiens, immanis in antro
bacchatur vates, magnum si pectore possit
excussisse deum ; tanto magis ille fatigat
os rabidum, fera corda domans, fingitque premendo. 80
ostia iamque domus patuere ingentia centum
sponte sua vatisque ferunt responsa per auras :
" o tandem magnis pelagi defuncte periclis
(sed terrae graviora manent), in regna Lavini
Dardanidae venient (mitte hanc de pectore curam);
sed non et venisse volent. bella, horrida bella   86
et Thybrim multo spumantem sanguine cerno.
non Simois tibi nec Xanthus nec Dorica castra
defuerint ; alius Latio iam partus Achilles,
natus et ipse dea ; nec Teucris addita Iuno   90
usquam aberit, cum tu supplex in rebus egenis
quas gentis Italum aut quas non oraveris urbes !
causa mali tanti coniunx iterum hospita Teucris
externique iterum thalami.
tu ne cede malis, sed contra audentior ito,   95
quam tua te Fortuna sinet.   via prima salutis,
quod minime reris, Graia pandetur ab urbe."
  Talibus ex adyto dictis Cumaea Sibylla
horrendas canit ambages antroque remugit,
obscuris vera involvens ; ea frena furenti   100
concutit et stimulos sub pectore vertit Apollo.

  78 posset *R.*
  84 terra *R. known to Servius.* Latini *known to Servius.*
  96 quam *MSS., Servius :* qua *Seneca (Ep.* LXXXII. 18).

  [1] The Simois and Xanthus of Troyland will have their
counterparts in the Numicius and Tiber of Latium.
  [2] *i.e.* Turnus.
  [3] Lavinia, wooed by Turnus, but wedded to Aeneas, will
be the second Helen.
  [4] A Stoic maxim. The brave man may rise superior to
fortune, however adverse. The reading *qua* ("with bolder

512

[77] But the prophetess, not yet brooking the sway
of Phoebus, storms wildly in the cavern, if so she may
shake the mighty god from off her breast; so much
the more he tires her raving mouth, tames her wild
heart, and moulds her by constraint. And now the
hundred mighty mouths of the house have opened of
their own will, and bring through the air the seer's
reply:

[83] "O thou that at last hast fulfilled the great perils
of the sea—yet by land more grievous woes await
thee—into the realm of Lavinium the sons of Dar-
danus shall come—relieve thy heart of this care—
yet they shall not also joy in their coming. Wars,
grim wars I see, and Tiber foaming with streams of
blood. A Simois thou shalt not lack, nor a Xanthus,[1]
nor a Doric camp. Even now another Achilles[2] is
raised up in Latium, he, too, goddess-born; nor shall
Juno anywhere fail to dog the Trojans, whilst thou,
a suppliant in thy need, what races, what cities of
Italy shalt thou not implore! The cause of all this
Trojan woe is again an alien bride, again a foreign
marriage![3] Yield not thou to ills, but go forth to face
them more boldly than thy Fortune shall allow thee![4]
Thy path of safety shall first, little as thou deemest it,
be opened from a Grecian city."[5]

[98] In such words the Cumaean Sibyl chants from
the shrine her dread enigmas and echoes from the
cavern, wrapping truth in darkness—so does Apollo
shake the reins as she rages, and ply the spur
beneath her breast. Soon as the frenzy ceased

heart advance to meet it, by such road as thy Destiny shall
allow thee") is apparently a corruption in Seneca, who inter-
prets the passage as if he read *quam*.

[5] viz. Pallanteum, city of Evander, on the site of the later
Rome.

ut primum cessit furor et rabida ora quierunt,
incipit Aeneas heros : " non ulla laborum,
o virgo, nova mi facies inopinave surgit ;
omnia praecepi atque animo mecum ante peregi.' 105
unum oro : quando hic inferni ianua regis
dicitur et tenebrosa palus Acheronte refuso,
ire ad conspectum cari genitoris et ora
contingat ; doceas iter et sacra ostia pandas.
illum ego per flammas et mille sequentia tela   110
eripui his umeris medioque ex hoste recepi ;
ille meum comitatus iter maria omnia mecum
atque omnis pelagique minas caelique ferebat,
invalidus, viris ultra sortemque senectae.
quin, ut te supplex peterem et tua limina adirem, 115
idem orans mandata dabat.   gnatique patrisque,
alma, precor, miserere ; potes namque omnia, nec te
nequiquam lucis Hecate praefecit Avernis.
si potuit Manis accersere coniugis Orpheus
Threicia fretus cithara fidibusque canoris ;   120
si fratrem Pollux alterna morte redemit
itque reditque viam totiens—quid Thesea magnum,
quid memorem Alciden?—et mi genus ab Iove summo."

   Talibus orabat dictis arasque tenebat,
cum sic orsa loqui vates : "sate sanguine divum, 125
Tros Anchisiade, facilis descensus Averno :
noctes atque dies patet atri ianua Ditis ;
sed revocare gradum superasque evadere ad auras,
hoc opus, hic labor est.   pauci, quos aequus amavit
Iuppiter aut ardens evexit ad aethera virtus,   130
dis geniti potuere.   tenent media omnia silvae,

---

[100] contingam $PR\gamma^1$.   [113] caelique minas pelagique M.
[115] et *omitted* $P^1R\gamma^2b$.   [116] nati $R\gamma^2$.   [119] arcersere P.
[122] *Servius preferred to punctuate after* Thesea.
[126] Averno M^1P^1: Averni $P^2R\gamma$: *Servius knows both*:
Averno est M^2.

and the raving lips were hushed, Aeneas the hero begins: "For me no form of toils arises, O maiden, strange or unlooked for; all this ere now have I forecast and inly traversed in thought. One thing I pray: since here is the famed gate of the nether king, and the gloomy marsh from Acheron's overflow, be it granted me to pass into my dear father's sight and presence; teach thou the way and open the hallowed portals! Him, amid flames and a thousand pursuing spears, I rescued on these shoulders, and brought safe from the enemy's midst. He, the partner of my way, endured with me all the seas and all the menace of ocean and sky, weak as he was, beyond the strength and portion of age. Nay, he, too, prayed and charged me humbly to seek thee and draw near to thy threshold. Pity both son and sire, I beseech thee, gracious one; for thou art all-powerful, and not in vain hath Hecate made thee mistress in the groves of Avernus. If Orpheus availed to summon his wife's shade, strong in his Thracian lyre and tuneful strings; if Pollux, dying in turn, ransomed his brother and so often comes and goes his way—why speak of great Theseus, why of Alcides?—I, too, have descent from Jove most high!" [1]

[124] In such words he prayed and clasped the altar, when thus the prophetess began to speak: "Sprung from blood of gods, son of Trojan Anchises, easy is the descent to Avernus: night and day the door of gloomy Dis stands open; but to recall thy steps and pass out to the upper air, this is the task, this the toil! Some few, whom kindly Jupiter has loved, or shining worth uplifted to heaven, sons of the gods, have availed. In all the mid-space lie woods, and Cocytus

[1] Through his mother Venus, a daughter of Jupiter.

VIRGIL

Cocytusque sinu labens circumvenit atro.
quod si tantus amor menti, si tanta cupido est
bis Stygios innare lacus, bis nigra videre
Tartara, et insano iuvat indulgere labori,   135
accipe quae peragenda prius. latet arbore opaca
aureus et foliis et lento vimine ramus,
Iunoni infernae dictus sacer; hunc tegit omnis
lucus et obscuris claudunt convallibus umbrae.
sed non ante datur telluris operta subire,   140
auricomos quam qui decerpserit arbore fetus.
hoc sibi pulchra suum ferri Proserpina munus
instituit; primo avolso non deficit alter
aureus, et simili frondescit virga metallo.
ergo alte vestiga oculis et rite repertum   145
carpe manu; namque ipse volens facilisque sequetur,
si te fata vocant; aliter non viribus ullis
vincere nec duro poteris convellere ferro.
praeterea iacet exanimum tibi corpus amici
(heu! nescis) totamque incestat funere classem, 150
dum consulta petis nostroque in limine pendes.
sedibus hunc refer ante suis et conde sepulchro.
duc nigras pecudes; ea prima piacula sunto.
sic demum lucos Stygis et regna invia vivis,
aspicies." dixit pressoque obmutuit ore.   155
  Aeneas maesto defixus lumina voltu
ingreditur, linquens antrum, caecosque volutat
eventus animo secum. cui fidus Achates
it comes et paribus curis vestigia figit.
multa inter sese vario sermone serebant,   160
quem socium exanimem vates, quod corpus humandum
diceret. atque illi Misenum in litore sicco,

133 est *omitted* M^2P.
144 similis M.
151 pendens R.
156 deflexus P^1
141 quis $PR\gamma$.
147 non] nec R.
154 Stygiis $M^1R\gamma^1$: Stygios $P^2\gamma^2$.
161 exanimum $PR\gamma$.

516

girds it, gliding with murky folds. But if such love is in thy heart—if such a yearning, twice to swim the Stygian lake, twice to see black Tartarus—and if thou art pleased to give rein to the mad endeavour, hear what must first be done. There lurks in a shady tree a bough, golden in leaf and pliant stem, held consecrate to nether Juno ; [1] this all the grove hides, and shadows veil in the dim valleys. But 'tis not given to pass beneath earth's hidden places, save to him who hath plucked from the tree the golden-tressed fruitage. This hath beautiful Proserpine ordained to be borne to her as her own gift. When the first is torn away, a second fails not, golden too, and the spray bears leaf of the selfsame ore. Search then with eyes aloft and, when found, duly pluck it with thy hand ; for of itself will it follow thee, freely and with ease, if Fate be calling thee ; else with no force wilt thou avail to win it or rend it with hard steel. Moreover, there lies the dead body of thy friend—ah ! thou knowest not !—and defiles all the fleet with death, whilst thou seekest counsel and hoverest on our threshold. Him bear first to his own place and hide him in the tomb. Lead black cattle ; be these thy first peace-offerings. Only so shalt thou survey the Stygian groves and realms the living may not tread.'' She spake, and with closed lips was silent.

[156] With sad countenance and downcast eyes Aeneas wends his way, quitting the cavern, and ponders in his mind the dark issues. At his side goes loyal Achates, and plants his steps under a like load of care. Much varied discourse were they weaving, each with each—of what dead comrade spoke the soothsayer, of what body for burial ? And lo ! as they came, they see on the dry beach Misenus, cut

[1] *i.e.* Proserpine.

VIRGIL

ut venere, vident indigna morte peremptum,
Misenum Aeoliden, quo non praestantior alter
aere ciere viros Martemque accendere cantu.   165
Hectoris hic magni fuerat comes, Hectora circum
et lituo pugnas insignis obibat et hasta.
postquam illum vita victor spoliavit Achilles,
Dardanio Aeneae sese fortissimus heros
addiderat socium, non inferiora secutus.   170
sed tum, forte cava dum personat aequora concha,
demens, et cantu vocat in certamina divos,
aemulus exceptum Triton, si credere dignum est,
inter saxa virum spumosa immerserat unda.
ergo omnes magno circum clamore fremebant,   175
praecipue pius Aeneas. tum iussa Sibyllae,
haud mora, festinant flentes aramque sepulchri
congerere arboribus caeloque educere certant.
itur in antiquam silvam, stabula alta ferarum ;
procumbunt piceae, sonat icta securibus ilex   180
fraxineaeque trabes cuneis et fissile robur
scinditur, advolvunt ingentis montibus ornos.
    Nec non Aeneas opera inter talia primus
hortatur socios paribusque accingitur armis.
atque haec ipse suo tristi cum corde volutat,   185
aspectans silvam immensam, et sic forte precatur :
" si nunc se nobis ille aureus arbore ramus
ostendat nemore in tanto ! quando omnia vere
heu nimium de te vates, Misene, locuta est."
vix ea fatus erat, geminae cum forte columbae   190
ipsa sub ora viri caelo venere volantes
et viridi sedere solo. tum maximus heros
maternas adgnovit avis laetusque precatur :
" este duces o, si qua via est, cursumque per auras
derigite in lucos, ubi pinguem dives opacat   195

177 sepulchro *P.*   186 forte] voce *R.*
193 agnoscit *R :* adgnoscit *P.*   195 dirigite *M.*

518

off by untimely death—Misenus, son of Aeolus, sur-
passed by none in stirring men with his bugle's blare,
and in kindling with his clang the god of war.   He
had been great Hector's comrade, at Hector's side he
braved the fray, glorious for clarion and spear alike ;
but when Achilles, victorious, stripped his chief of
life, the valiant hero came into the fellowship of
Dardan Aeneas, following no meaner standard.   Yet
on that day, while haply he makes the seas ring
with his hollow shell, madman ! and with his blare
calls the gods to contest, jealous Triton—if the tale
can win belief—caught and plunged him in the
foaming waves amid the rocks.   So, with loud lament,
all were mourning round him, good Aeneas foremost.
Then weeping, they quickly carry out the Sibyl's
commands, and toil in piling trees for the altar of
his tomb and in rearing it to the sky.   They pass
into the forest primeval, the deep lairs of beasts ;
down drop the pitchy pines, and the ilex rings to
the stroke of the axe ; ashen logs and splintering oak
are cleft with wedges, and from the mountains they
roll in huge rowans.

[183] No less Aeneas, first amid such toils, cheers
his comrades and girds on like weapons.   And alone
he ponders with his own sad heart, gazing on the
boundless forest, and, as it chanced, thus prays : " O if
now that golden bough would show itself to us on the
tree in the deep wood ! For all things truly—ah ! too
truly—spake the seer of thee, Misenus."   Scarce had
he so said when under his very eyes twin doves, as it
chanced, came flying from the sky and lit on the green
grass.   Then the great hero knew them for his mothers'
birds, and prays with joy : " O be my guides, if any
way there be, and through the air steer a course into
the grove, where the rich bough overshades the

VIRGIL

ramus humum.   tuque o, dubiis ne defice rebus,
diva parens." sic effatus vestigia pressit,
observans, quae signa ferant, quo tendere pergant.
pascentes illae tantum prodire volando,
quantum acie possent oculi servare sequentum.   200
inde ubi venere ad fauces grave olentis Averni,
tollunt se celeres liquidumque per aëra lapsae
sedibus optatis gemina super arbore sidunt,
discolor unde auri per ramos aura refulsit.
quale solet silvis brumali frigore viscum   205
fronde virere nova, quod non sua seminat arbos,
et croceo fetu teretis circumdare truncos :
talis erat species auri frondentis opaca
ilice, sic leni crepitabat brattea vento.
corripit Aeneas extemplo avidusque refringit   210
cunctantem, et vatis portat sub tecta Sibyllae.
    Nec minus interea Misenum in litore Teucri
flebant, et cineri ingrato suprema ferebant.
principio pinguem taedis et robore secto
ingentem struxere pyram, cui frondibus atris   215
intexunt latera, et feralis ante cupressos
constituunt, decorantque super fulgentibus armis.
pars calidos latices et aëna undantia flammis
expediunt, corpusque lavant frigentis et ungunt. FMPR
fit gemitus. tum membra toro defleta reponunt 220
purpureasque super vestis, velamina nota,
coniciunt. pars ingenti subiere feretro,
triste ministerium, et subiectam more parentum
aversi tenuere facem. congesta cremantur
turea dona, dapes, fuso crateres olivo.   225

200 acies *M*¹.   sequentur *P*².
203 geminae *R*.
214 faces *P*¹γ¹.
225 dapes] ferunt *P*¹ : fervent *P*² : dape ferunt γ.

fruitful ground! And thou, O goddess-mother, fail not my dark hour!" So speaking, he checked his steps, marking what signs they bring, whither they direct their course. They, as they fed, advanced in flight just so far as a pursuer's eyes could keep them within ken; then, when they came to the jaws of noisome Avernus, they swiftly rise and, dropping through the buxom air, settle on the site longed for, the twofold tree, whence, with diverse hue, shone out amid the branches the gleam of gold. As in winter's cold, amid the woods, the mistletoe, sown of an alien tree, is wont to bloom with strange leafage, and with yellow fruit embrace the shapely stems: such was the vision of the leafy gold on the shadowy ilex, so rustled the foil in the gentle breeze. Forthwith Aeneas plucks it and greedily breaks off the clinging bough, and carries it beneath the roof of the prophetic Sibyl.

[212] No less meanwhile on the beach the Teucrians were weeping for Misenus and paying the last dues to the thankless dust. And first they raise a huge pyre, rich with pitchy pine and oaken logs. Its sides they entwine with sombre foliage, set in front funereal cypresses, and adorn it above with gleaming arms.[1] Some heat water, setting cauldrons a-bubbling on the flames, and wash and anoint the cold body. Loud is the wailing; then, their weeping done, they lay his limbs upon the couch, and over them cast purple robes, the familiar dress. Some shouldered the heavy bier—sad ministry! and in ancestral fashion, with averted eyes, held the torch below. The gifts are piled up in the blaze—frankincense, flesh, viands, and bowls of flowing oil. After the ashes fell in and

---

[1] Probably the arms of his comrades. His own arms are mentioned in 233 below.

VIRGIL

postquam conlapsi cineres et flamma quievit,
reliquias vino et bibulam lavere favillam,
ossaque lecta cado texit Corynaeus aëno.
idem ter socios pura circumtulit unda,
spargens rore levi et ramo felicis olivae,   230
lustravitque viros, dixitque novissima verba.
at pius Aeneas ingenti mole sepulchrum
imponit, suaque arma viro remumque tubamque,
monte sub aërio, qui nunc Misenus ab illo
dicitur, aeternumque tenet per saecula nomen.   235
  His actis propere exsequitur praecepta Sibyllae.
spelunca alta fuit vastoque immanis hiatu,
scrupea, tuta lacu nigro nemorumque tenebris,
quam super haud ullae poterant impune volantes
tendere iter pinnis : talis sese halitus atris   240
faucibus effundens super ad convexa ferebat
[unde locum Grai dixerunt nomine Aornon].   R
quattuor hic primum nigrantis terga iuvencos FMPR
constituit, frontique invergit vina sacerdos,
et summas carpens media inter cornua saetas 245
ignibus imponit sacris, libamina prima,
voce vocans Hecaten caeloque Ereboque potentem.
supponunt alii cultros tepidumque cruorem
succipiunt pateris.   ipse atri velleris agnam
Aeneas matri Eumenidum magnaeque sorori 250
ense ferit sterilemque tibi, Proserpina, vaccam.
tum Stygio regi nocturnas incohat aras
et solida imponit taurorum viscera flammis,
pingue super oleum fundens ardentibus extis.
ecce autem primi sub lumina solis et ortus 255

231 viros] domos P^1R.   241 supera $FM^2P^2\gamma$.
242 *omitted FM^1P: added on margin of M by late hand, then deleted: placed before 241 in γ.* Avernum R: aornum γ.
249 succipiunt FP, *Servius:* suscipiunt $MR\gamma^1$.
254 superque *best MSS.:* super *late MSS.*　infundens M.
255 limina FM: lumina $PR\gamma$.

522

the flame died away, they washed with wine the remnant of thirsty dust, and Corynaeus, gathering the bones, hid them in a brazen urn. He, too, with pure water thrice encircled his comrades and cleansed them, sprinkling light dew from a fruitful olive-bough, and spake the words of farewell. But good Aeneas heaps over him a massive tomb, with the soldier's own arms, his oar and trumpet, beneath a lofty mount, which now from him is called Misenus, and keeps from age to age an ever-living name.

²³⁶ This done, he fulfils with haste the Sibyl's behest. A deep cave there was, yawning wide and vast, shingly, and sheltered by dark lake and woodland gloom, over which no flying creatures could safely wing their way; such a vapour from those black jaws poured into the over-arching heaven [whence the Greeks spoke of Avernus, the Birdless Place]. Here first the priestess set in line four dark-backed heifers, and pours wine upon their brows; then, plucking the topmost bristles from between the horns, lays them on the sacred fire for first offering, calling aloud on Hecate, supreme both in Heaven and in Hell. Others set knives to the throat and catch the warm blood in bowls. Aeneas himself slays with the sword a black-fleeced lamb to the mother [1] of the Eumenides and her great sister, and to thee, O Proserpine, a barren heifer. Then for the Stygian king [2] he inaugurates an altar by night, and lays upon the flames whole carcasses of bulls, pouring fat oil over the blazing entrails. But lo! hard upon the dawning light of the early sun the ground

[1] Night, who, with her sister Terra, was a daughter of Chaos.
[2] Pluto.

VIRGIL

sub pedibus mugire solum et iuga coepta moveri
silvarum, visaeque canes ululare per umbram
adventante dea. "procul o, procul este, profani,"
conclamat vates, "totoque absistite luco;
tuque invade viam vaginaque eripe ferrum :   260
nunc animis opus, Aenea, nunc pectore firmo."
tantum effata furens antro se immisit aperto;
ille ducem haud timidis vadentem passibus aequat.

　　Di, quibus imperium est animarum, umbraeque
　　　silentes
et Chaos et Phlegethon, loca nocte tacentia late, 265
sit mihi fas audita loqui ; sit numine vestro
pandere res alta terra et caligine mersas.

　　Ibant obscuri sola sub nocte per umbram
perque domos Ditis vacuas et inania regna,
quale per incertam lunam sub luce maligna   270
est iter in silvis, ubi caelum condidit umbra
Iuppiter, et rebus nox abstulit atra colorem.
vestibulum ante ipsum primisque in faucibus
　　　Orci   MPR
Luctus et ultrices posuere cubilia Curae,
pallentesque habitant Morbi tristisque Senectus 275
et Metus et malesuada Fames ac turpis Egestas,
terribiles visu formae, Letumque Labosque;
tum consanguineus Leti Sopor et mala mentis
Gaudia, mortiferumque adverso in limine Bellum
ferreique Eumenidum thalami et Discordia demens,
vipereum crinem vittis innexa cruentis.   281

---

²⁵⁷ altas *M*¹.
²⁷⁰ incertum *F*¹ : inceptam *bc*², *Servius, who knows* incertam.
²⁷³ primis in *P*.　　　　　　　　　　　²⁸¹ innixa *R*.

---

¹ Hecate, who comes to open the way.
² The realm of Pluto is conceived as being approached
through an entrance court, at the far side of which is the
threshold (*limen*, 279), with the doors (*fores*, 286), admitting

524

rumbled underfoot, the wooded ridges began to quiver, and through the gloom dogs seemed to howl as the goddess[1] drew nigh. "Away! away! unhallowed ones!" shrieks the seer, "withdraw from all the grove! And do thou rush on the road and unsheathe thy sword! Now, Aeneas, thou needest thy courage, now thy stout heart!" So much she said, and plunged madly into the opened cave; he, with fearless steps, keeps pace with his advancing guide.

264 Ye gods, who hold the domain of spirits! ye voiceless shades! Thou, Chaos, and thou, Phlegethon, ye broad, silent tracts of night! Suffer me to tell what I have heard; suffer me of your grace to unfold secrets buried in the depths and darkness of the earth!

268 On they went dimly, beneath the lonely night amid the gloom, through the empty halls of Dis and his phantom realm, even as under the grudging light of an inconstant moon lies a path in the forest, when Jupiter has buried the sky in shade, and black Night has stolen from the world her hues. Just before the entrance,[2] even within the very jaws of Hell, Grief and avenging Cares have made their bed; there pale Diseases dwell, and sad Age, and Fear, and ill-counselling Famine, and loathly Want, shapes terrible to view; and Death and Distress; next, Death's own brother Sleep, and the soul's Guilty Joys, and, on the threshold opposite, the death-bearer War, and the Furies' iron cells, and savage Strife, her snaky locks entwined with bloody fillets.

to the interior. Once within the *fores*, Aeneas finds a vast domain, divided into several parts. He first follows a path leading to Acheron.

VIRGIL

In medio ramos annosaque bracchia pandit
ulmus opaca, ingens, quam sedem Somnia volgo
vana tenere ferunt, foliisque sub omnibus haerent.
multaque praeterea variarum monstra ferarum,   285
Centauri in foribus stabulant Scyllaeque biformes
et centumgeminus Briareus ac belua Lernae,
horrendum stridens, flammisque armata Chimaera,
Gorgones Harpyiaeque et forma tricorporis umbrae.
corripit hic subita trepidus formidine ferrum   290
Aeneas, strictamque aciem venientibus offert;
et, ni docta comes tenuis sine corpore vitas
admoneat volitare cava sub imagine formae,
inruat et frustra ferro diverberet umbras.
    Hinc via, Tartarei quae fert Acherontis ad undas.
turbidus hic caeno vastaque voragine gurges   296
aestuat, atque omnem Cocyto eructat harenam.
portitor has horrendus aquas et flumina servat
terribili squalore Charon, cui plurima mento
canities inculta iacet, stant lumina flamma,   300
sordidus ex umeris nodo dependet amictus.
ipse ratem conto subigit velisque ministrat
et ferruginea subvectat corpora cumba,
iam senior, sed cruda deo viridisque senectus.
huc omnis turba ad ripas effusa ruebat,   305
matres atque viri, defunctaque corpora vita
magnanimum heroum, pueri innuptaeque puellae
impositique rogis iuvenes ante ora parentum :
quam multa in silvis autumni frigore primo

---

³⁰⁰ flamma M^2P^1, *Servius on* I. 646 : flammae $M^1P^2R\gamma$.

---

¹ *i.e.* Geryon, a giant with three bodies, slain by Hercules.
² The *portitor* (from *portus*) is properly the harbour-master,
who watches over the port (cf. *flumina servat*) and collects the
portoria, or port-tolls. But this official must occasionally
526

282 In the midst an elm, shadowy and vast, spreads her boughs and aged arms, the home which, men say, false Dreams hold in throngs, clinging under every leaf. And many monstrous forms besides of various beasts are stalled at the doors, Centaurs and double-shaped Scyllas, and the hundredfold Briareus, and the beast of Lerna, hissing horribly, and the Chimaera armed with flame, Gorgons and Harpies, and the shape of the three-bodied shade.[1] Here on a sudden, in trembling terror, Aeneas grasps his sword, and turns the naked edge against their coming; and did not his wise companion warn him that these were but faint, bodiless lives, flitting under a hollow semblance of form, he had rushed upon them and vainly cleft shadows with the steel.

295 Hence a road leads to the waters of Tartarean Acheron. Here, thick with mire and of fathomless flood, a whirlpool seethes and belches into Cocytus all its sand. A grim warden[2] guards these waters and streams, terrible in his squalor—Charon, on whose chin lies a mass of unkempt, hoary hair; his eyes are staring orbs of flame; his squalid garb hangs by a knot from his shoulders. Unaided, he poles the boat, tends the sails, and in his murky craft convoys the dead—now aged, but a god's old age is hardy and green. Hither rushed all the throng, streaming to the banks; mothers and men and bodies of high-souled heroes, their life now done, boys and unwedded girls, and sons placed on the pyre before their fathers' eyes; thick as the leaves of the forest that at autumn's first frost dropping fall, and thick as the

have acted as a ferryman, as Charon certainly does, and the idea that he was primarily a ferryman was probably furthered by the resemblance of the word to *portare*. After Virgil the original meaning faded away.

lapsa cadunt folia, aut ad terram gurgite ab alto   310
quam multae glomerantur aves, ubi frigidus annus
trans pontum fugat et terris immittit apricis.
stabant orantes primi transmittere cursum
tendebantque manus ripae ulterioris amore.
navita sed tristis nunc hos nunc accipit illos,   315
ast alios longe submotos arcet harena.
Aeneas miratus enim motusque tumultu
"dic," ait, "o virgo, quid volt concursus ad amnem?
quidve petunt animae? vel quo discrimine ripas
hae linquunt, illae remis vada livida verrunt?"   320
olli sic breviter fata est longaeva sacerdos:
"Anchisa generate, deum certissima proles,
Cocyti stagna alta vides Stygiamque paludem,
di cuius iurare timent et fallere numen.   324
haec omnis, quam cernis, inops inhumataque turba est;
portitor ille Charon; hi, quos vehit unda, sepulti;
nec ripas datur horrendas et rauca fluenta
transportare prius quam sedibus ossa quierunt.
centum errant annos volitantque haec litora circum;
tum demum admissi stagna exoptata revisunt."   330
constitit Anchisa satus et vestigia pressit,
multa putans sortemque animi miseratus iniquam.
cernit ibi maestos et mortis honore carentis
Leucaspim et Lyciae ductorem classis Oronten,
quos simul ab Troia ventosa per aequora vectos   335
obruit Auster, aqua involvens navemque virosque.
  Ecce gubernator sese Palinurus agebat,
qui Libyco nuper cursu, dum sidera servat,
exciderat puppi mediis effusus in undis.
hunc ubi vix multa maestum cognovit in umbra,   340

---

310 vertunt P.   **319** haec] hi P^1.
332 animo PR: animi M^1 (*with final* i *erased* M^2).
334 Orontem $MR\gamma$: Oronten P.
335 ab P^1: a $MP^2R\gamma$.
336 viru P^1: virum P^2: viros P (*late*).

birds that from the seething deep flock shoreward,
when the chill of the year drives them overseas and
sends them into sunny lands. They stood, pleading
to be the first ferried across, and stretched out hands in
yearning for the farther shore. But the surly boat-
man takes now these, now those, while others he
thrusts apart, back from the brink. Then aroused
and amazed by the disorder, Aeneas cries : " Tell me,
O maiden, what means the crowding to the river ?
What seek the spirits ? or by what rule do these
leave the banks, and those sweep the lurid stream
with oars ? " To him thus briefly spake the aged
priestess : " Anchises' son, true offspring of gods,
thou seest the deep pools of Cocytus and the Stygian
marsh, by whose power the gods fear to swear falsely.
All this crowd thou seest is helpless and graveless ;
yonder warden is Charon; those whom the flood
carries are the buried. Nor may he bear them o'er
the dreadful banks and hoarse-voiced waters ere
their bones have found a resting-place. A hundred
years they roam and flit about these shores; then
only are they admitted and revisit the longed-for
pools."

[331] Anchises' son paused and stayed his steps,
pondering much, and pitying in soul their cruel lot.
There he espies, doleful and reft of death's honour,
Leucaspis and Orontes, captain of the Lycian fleet,
whom, while voyaging together from Troy over windy
waters, the South overwhelmed, engulfing alike ship
and sailors.

[337] Lo ! there passed the helmsman, Palinurus, who
of late, on the Libyan voyage, while he marked the
stars, had fallen from the stern, flung forth in the
midst of the waves. Him, when at last amid the deep
gloom he knew the sorrowful form, he first accosts

sic prior adloquitur : " quis te, Palinure, deorum
eripuit nobis medioque sub aequore mersit?
dic age.   namque mihi, fallax haud ante repertus,
hoc uno responso animum delusit Apollo,
qui fore te ponto incolumem finisque canebat   345
venturum Ausonios.   en haec promissa fides est?"
ille autem : " neque te Phoebi cortina fefellit,
dux Anchisiade, nec me deus aequore mersit.
namque gubernaclum multa vi forte revolsum,
cui datus haerebam custos cursusque regebam,   350
praecipitans traxi mecum.   maria aspera iuro
non ullum pro me tantum cepisse timorem,
quam tua ne, spoliata armis, excussa magistro,
deficeret tantis navis surgentibus undis.
tris Notus hibernas immensa per aequora noctes 355
vexit me violentus aqua; vix lumine quarto
prospexi Italiam summa sublimis ab unda.
paulatim adnabam terrae; iam tuta tenebam,
ni gens crudelis madida cum veste gravatum,
prensantemque uncis manibus capita aspera montis,
ferro invasisset praedamque ignara putasset.   361
nunc me fluctus habet versantque in litore venti.
quod te per caeli iucundum lumen et auras,
per genitorem oro, per spes surgentis Iuli,
eripe me his, invicte, malis : aut tu mihi terram 365
inice (namque potes) portusque require Velinos ;
aut tu, si qua via est, si quam tibi diva creatrix
ostendit (neque enim, credo, sine numine divum
flumina tanta paras Stygiamque innare paludem),
da dextram misero et tecum me tolle per undas, 370
sedibus ut saltem placidis in morte quiescam."

[349] vi forte] vix arte *P*.
[350] gerebam *P*γ[1].
[352] illum *M*[1]: nullum γ.
[355] *punctuation after* adnabam *M*[2]*P*[2], *preferred by Servius.*

530

thus: "What god, Palinurus, tore thee from us and plunged beneath the open ocean? O tell me! for Apollo, never before found false, with this one answer tricked my soul, for he foretold that thou wouldst escape the sea and reach Ausonian shores. Lo! is it thus his promise holds?" But he: "Neither did tripod of Phoebus fail thee, my captain, Anchises' son, nor did a god plunge me in the deep. For by chance the helm to which, as my charge, I clung, steering our course, was violently torn from me, and I, dropping headlong, dragged it with me. By the rough seas I swear that not for myself felt I such fear as for thy ship, lest, stripped of its gear and reft of its helmsman, it might fail amid such surging waves. Three stormy nights over the measureless seas the South drove me wildly on the water; scarce on the fourth dawn, aloft on the crest of a wave, I sighted Italy. Little by little I swam shoreward, and even now was grasping at safety, but as, weighted by dripping garb, I caught with bent fingers at the rugged cliff-peaks, the barbarous folk assailed me with the sword, in ignorance deeming me a prize. Now the wave holds me, and the winds toss me on the beach. Oh, by heaven's sweet light and air, I beseech thee, by thy father, by the rising hope of Iülus, snatch me from these woes, unconquered one! Either do thou, for thou canst, cast earth on me [1] and seek again the haven of Velia; or if there be a way, if thy goddess-mother shows thee one—for not without divine favour, I ween, dost thou essay to stem these great streams and the Stygian mere—give thy hand to one so unhappy, and take me with thee across the waves, that at least in death I may find a quiet resting-place!"

[1] The sprinkling of three handfuls of earth upon a dead body was regarded as a burial.

talia fatus erat, coepit cum talia vates :
" unde haec, o Palinure, tibi tam dira cupido ?
tu Stygias inhumatus aquas amnæmque severum
Eumenidum aspicies ripamve iniussus adibis ?   375
desine fata deum flecti sperare precando.
sed cape dicta memor, duri solacia casus :
nam tua finitimi, longe lateque per urbes
prodigiis acti caelestibus, ossa piabunt
et statuent tumulum et tumulo sollemnia mittent, 380
aeternumque locus Palinuri nomen habebit."
his dictis curae emotae, pulsusque parumper
corde dolor tristi ; gaudet cognomine terrae.

    Ergo iter inceptum peragunt fluvioque propinquant.
navita quos iam inde ut Stygia prospexit ab unda 385
per tacitum nemus ire pedemque advertere ripae,
sic prior adgreditur dictis atque increpat ultro :
" quisquis es, armatus qui nostra ad flumina tendis,
fare age, quid venias, iam istinc, et comprime gressum.
umbrarum hic locus est, Somni Noctisque soporae ;
corpora viva nefas Stygia vectare carina.   391
nec vero Alciden me sum laetatus euntem
accepisse lacu nec Thesea Pirithoumque,   FMPR
dis quamquam geniti atque invicti viribus essent.
Tartareum ille manu custodem in vincla petivit, 395
ipsius a solio regis, traxitque trementem ;
hi dominam Ditis thalamo deducere adorti."
quae contra breviter fata est Amphrysia vates :

³⁷⁵ abibis *preferred by Servius*.   ³⁸³ terra *Servius*.
³⁸⁵ conspexit *M*.   ³⁸⁷ adloquitur *R*.
³⁸⁸ tendes *Pγ*¹.   ³⁹⁰ est] et *R*.

532

³⁷² So had he spoken, and the soothsayer thus
began : " Whence, O Palinurus, this wild longing of
thine ? Shalt thou, unburied, view the Stygian waters
and the Furies' stern river,¹ and unbidden draw near
the bank ? Cease to dream that heaven's decrees may
be turned aside by prayer. But hear and remember
my words, to solace thy hard lot; for the neighbour-
ing people, in their cities far and wide, shall be driven
by celestial portents to appease thy dust, and shall
stablish a tomb, and to the tomb pay solemn offer-
ings; and for ever the place shall bear the name of
Palinurus." ² By these words his cares are banished,
and grief is driven for a space from his gloomy heart;
he rejoices in the land bearing his name.

³⁸⁴ So they pursue the journey begun, and draw
near to the river. But when, even from the Stygian
wave, the boatman saw them passing through the
silent wood and turning their feet towards the bank,
he first, unhailed, accosts and rebukes them : " Whoso
thou art that comest to our river in arms, O tell me,
even from there, why thou comest, and check thy
step. This is the land of Shadows, of Sleep and
drowsy Night ; living bodies I may not carry in the
Stygian boat. And in truth it brought me no joy
that I took Alcides in his journey o'er the lake, or
Theseus and Pirithoüs, though sons of gods and
invincible in valour. The one by force sought to drag
into chains, even from the monarch's throne, the
warder of Tartarus, and tore him off trembling ; these
essayed to carry off our queen from the chamber
of Dis." Thereto the Amphrysian ³ soothsayer spake

¹ *i.e.* the Cocytus.
² The reference is to Capo Palinuro.
³ The Sibyl is so called because she is a servant of
Apollo, the "shepherd of Amphrysus" (*Georg.* III. 2).

" nullae hic insidiae tales (absiste moveri),
nec vim tela ferunt ; licet ingens ianitor antro   400
aeternum latrans exsanguis terreat umbras ;
casta licet patrui servet Proserpina limen.
Troius Aeneas, pietate insignis et armis,
ad genitorem imas Erebi descendit ad umbras.
si te nulla movet tantae pietatis imago,   405
at ramum hunc " (aperit ramum, qui veste latebat)
" adgnoscas." tumida ex ira .tum corda residunt.
nec plura his.   ille admirans venerabile donum
fatalis virgae, longo post tempore visum,
caeruleam advertit puppim ripaeque propinquat. 410
inde alias animas, quae per iuga longa sedebant,
deturbat laxatque foros ; simul accipit alveo
ingentem Aeneam.   gemuit sub pondere cumba
sutilis et multam accepit rimosa paludem.
tandem trans fluvium incolumis vatemque virumque
informi limo glaucaque exponit in ulva.   416
   Cerberus haec ingens latratu regna trifauci
personat, adverso recubans immanis in antro.
cui vates, horrere videns iam colla colubris,
melle soporatam et medicatis frugibus offam   420
obicit. ille fame rabida tria guttura pandens
corripit obiectam, atque immania terga resolvit
fusus humi totoque ingens extenditur antro.
occupat Aeneas aditum custode sepulto   MPR
evaditque celer ripam inremeabilis undae.   425
   Continuo auditae voces vagitus et ingens
infantumque animae flentes, in limine primo
quos dulcis vitae exsortis et ab ubere raptos

                    [428] vita $P^2\gamma^1$.
534

briefly : " No such trickery is here ; be not troubled ; our weapons offer no force ; the huge doorkeeper may from his cave with endless howl affright the bloodless shades ; Proserpine may in purity keep within her uncle's threshold. Trojan Aeneas, famous for piety and arms, descends to his father, to the lowest shades of Erebus. If the picture of such piety moves thee in no wise, yet know this bough ! "—and she shows the bough, hidden in her robe. Thereon, after his anger, his swelling breast subsides. No more is said ; but he, marvelling at the dread gift, the fateful wand so long unseen, turns his blue barge and nears the shore. Then other souls that sat on the long thwarts he routs out, and clears the gangways ; the while he takes aboard giant Aeneas. The seamy craft groaned under the weight, and through its chinks took in a marshy flood. At last, across the water, he lands seer and soldier unharmed on the ugly mire and grey sedge.

⁴¹⁷ These realms huge Cerberus makes ring with his triple-throated baying, his monstrous bulk crouching in a cavern opposite. To him, seeing the snakes now bristling on his necks, the seer flung a morsel drowsy with honey and drugged meal. He, opening his triple throat in ravenous hunger, catches it when thrown and, with monstrous frame relaxed, sinks to earth and stretches his bulk over all the den. The warder buried in sleep, Aeneas wins the entrance, and swiftly leaves the bank of that stream whence none return.

⁴²⁶ At once are heard voices and wailing sore—the souls of infants weeping, whom, on the very threshold of the sweet life they shared not, torn from the breast, the black day swept off and plunged in bitter

abstulit atra dies et funere mersit acerbo.
hos iuxta falso damnati crimine mortis.   430
nec vero hae sine sorte datae, sine iudice, sedes:
quaesitor Minos urnam movet; ille silentum
conciliumque vocat, vitasque et crimina discit.
proxima deinde tenent maesti loca, qui sibi letum
insontes peperere manu lucemque perosi   435
proiecere animas. quam vellent aethere in alto
nunc et pauperiem et duros perferre labores!
fas obstat tristisque palus inamabilis undae
alligat et noviens Styx interfusa coercet.

    Nec procul hinc partem fusi monstrantur in omnem
Lugentes Campi; sic illos nomine dicunt.   441
hic, quos durus amor crudeli tabe peredit,
secreti celant calles et myrtea circum
silva tegit; curae non ipsa in morte relinquunt.
his Phaedram Procrimque locis maestamque Eriphylen,
crudelis nati monstrantem volnera, cernit,   446
Euadnenque et Pasiphaën; his Laodamia
it comes et iuvenis quondam, nunc femina, Caeneus
rursus et in veterem fato revoluta figuram.
inter quas Phoenissa recens a volnere Dido   450
errabat silva in magna. quam Troius heros
ut primum iuxta stetit adgnovitque per umbras
obscuram, qualem primo qui surgere mense
aut videt aut vidisse putat per nubila lunam,
demisit lacrimas dulcique adfatus amore est: 455
"infelix Dido, verus mihi nuntius ergo
venerat exstinctam, ferroque extrema secutam?
funeris heu! tibi causa fui? per sidera iuro,

---

[433] consilium $P\gamma^1$.   [436] quas M (*late*).
[438] fata obstant $M^2\gamma^2$, *Augustinus, Servius.*   tristi *Servius.*
unda $M^2R^2\gamma^1$, *Servius.*   [442] peremit M^1.
[449] revocata R.   [452] umbra M^1 : umbram $M^2\gamma^1$.
[455] dimisit M.

536

death.[1] Near them were those on false charge con-
demned to die. Yet not without lot, not without
a judge, are these places given: Minos, presiding,
shakes the urn; 'tis he calls a court of the silent, and
learns men's lives and misdeeds. The region there-
after is held by those sad souls who in innocence
wrought their own death and, loathing the light, flung
away their lives. How gladly now, in the air above,
would they bear both want and harsh distress! Fate
withstands; the unlovely mere with its dreary water
enchains them and Styx imprisons with his ninefold
circles.

440 Not far from here, outspread on every side, are
shown the Mourning Fields; such is the name they
bear. Here those whom stern Love has consumed
with cruel wasting are hidden in walks withdrawn,
embowered in a myrtle grove; even in death the
pangs leave them not. In this region he sees
Phaedra and Procris, and sad Eriphyle, pointing to
the wounds her cruel son had dealt, and Evadne and
Pasiphaë. With them goes Laodamia, and Caeneus,
once a youth, now a woman, and again turned back
by Fate into her form of old. Among them, with
wound still fresh, Phoenician Dido was wandering in
the great forest, and soon as the Trojan hero stood
nigh and knew her, a dim form amid the shadows
—even as, in the early month, one sees or fancies he
has seen the moon rise amid the clouds—he shed
tears, and spoke to her in tender love: "Unhappy
Dido! then was the tale brought me true, that thou
wert no more, and hadst sought thy doom with the
sword? Was I, alas! the cause of death to thee?

[1] As Henry says, infants are placed in the very entrance of
Hades, because they had died at the entrance of life. Their
place is one neither of punishment nor of joy.

per superos, et si qua fides tellure sub ima est,
invitus, regina, tuo de litore cessi.   460
sed me iussa deum, quae nunc has ire per umbras,
per loca senta situ cogunt noctemque profundam,
imperiis egere suis; nec credere quivi
hunc tantum tibi me discessu ferre dolorem.
siste gradum teque aspectu ne subtrahe nostro.   465
quem fugis? extremum fato, quod te adloquor, hoc
    est."
talibus Aeneas ardentem et torva tuentem
lenibat dictis animum lacrimasque ciebat.
illa solo fixos oculos aversa tenebat
nec magis incepto voltum sermone movetur,   470
quam si dura silex aut stet Marpesia cautes.
tandem corripuit sese atque inimica refugit
in nemus umbriferum, coniunx ubi pristinus illi
respondet curis aequatque Sychaeus amorem.
nec minus Aeneas, casu concussus iniquo,   475
prosequitur lacrimis longe et miseratur euntem.
   Inde datum molitur iter.   iamque arva tenebant
ultima, quae bello clari secreta frequentant.
hic illi occurrit Tydeus, hic inclutus armis
Parthenopaeus et Adrasti pallentis imago.   480
hic multum fleti ad superos belloque caduci
Dardanidae, quos ille omnis longo ordine cernens
ingemuit, Glaucumque Medontaque Thersilochumque,
tris Antenoridas, Cererique sacrum Polyboeten,
Idaeumque etiam currus, etiam arma tenentem. 485
circumstant animae dextra laevaque frequentes.
nec vidisse semel satis est; iuvat usque morari

    [474] respondit *R.*   [475] percussus *R.*
    [476] lacrimas M^1: lacrimans M^2.
    [477] tenebat *P.*   [481] hi *M.*
    [484] Polyboten P^1.
    [486] frementes *P. So Sabb.*

By the stars I swear, by the world above, and whatever is sacred in the grave below, unwillingly, O queen, I parted from thy shores. But the gods' decrees, which now constrain me to pass through these shades, through lands squalid and forsaken, and through abysmal night, drove me with their behests; nor could I deem my going thence would bring on thee distress so deep. Stay thy step and withdraw not from our view. Whom fleest thou? The last word Fate suffers me to say to thee is this!"

⁴⁶⁷ With such speech amid springing tears Aeneas would soothe the wrath of the fiery, fierce-eyed queen. She, turning away, kept her looks fixed on the ground and no more changes her countenance as he essays to speak than if she were set in hard flint or Marpesian rock. At length she flung herself away and, still his foe, fled back to the shady grove, where Sychaeus, her lord of former days, responds to her sorrows and gives her love for love. Yet none the less, dazed by her unjust doom, Aeneas attends her with tears afar and pities her as she goes.

⁴⁷⁷ Thence he toils along the way that offered itself. And now they gained the farthest fields,[1] where the renowned in war dwell apart. Here Tydeus meets him; here Parthenopaeus, famed in arms, and the pale shade of Adrastus; here, much wept on earth above and fallen in war, the Dardan chiefs; whom as he beheld, all in long array, he moaned—Glaucus and Medon and Thersilochus, the three sons of Antenor, and Polyboetes, priest of Ceres, and Idaeus, still keeping his car, still his arms. Round about, on right and left, stand the souls in throngs. To have seen him once is not enough; they delight to linger on, to pace

---

[1] i.e. of the neutral region, neither Elysium nor Tartarus.

VIRGIL

et conferre gradum et veniendi discere causas.
at Danaum proceres Agamemnoniaeque phalanges,
ut videre virum fulgentiaque arma per umbras,   490
ingenti trepidare metu : pars vertere terga,   FMPR
ceu quondam petiere rates ; pars tollere vocem
exiguam, inceptus clamor frustratur hiantis.

Atque hic Priamiden laniatum corpore toto
Deiphobum vidit, lacerum crudeliter ora,   495
ora manusque ambas, populataque tempora raptis
auribus et truncas inhonesto volnere naris.
vix adeo adgnovit pavitantem ac dira tegentem
supplicia, et notis compellat vocibus ultro :
" Deiphobe armipotens, genus alto a sanguine
        Teucri,   500
quis tam crudelis optavit sumere poenas ?
cui tantum de te licuit ?   mihi fama suprema
nocte tulit fessum vasta te caede Pelasgum
procubuisse super confusae stragis acervum.
tunc egomet tumulum Rhoeteo litore inanem   505
constitui et magna Manis ter voce vocavi.
nomen et arma locum servant ; te, amice, nequivi
conspicere et patria decedens ponere terra."
ad quae Priamides : " nihil o tibi, amice, relictum ;
omnia Deiphobo solvisti et funeris umbris.   510
sed me fata mea et scelus exitiale Lacaenae
his mersere malis ; illa haec monumenta reliquit.
namque ut supremam falsa inter gaudia noctem
egerimus, nosti ; et nimium meminisse necesse est.
cum fatalis equus saltu super ardua venit   515

    488 poscere *R.*
    495 vidit *Servius :* vidit et *M¹* : videt *FM²PRγ* : videt et
Heinsius.
    498 ac *MP :* et *FRγ.*   **500** a omitted *F¹.*
    505 in litore *MP²*, *Servius.*
    509 atquae *M¹P :* atque hic *M²γ¹* : atque haec *c.*

AENEID BOOK VI

beside him, and to learn the causes of his coming. But
the Danaan princes and Agamemnon's battalions, soon
as they saw the man and his arms flashing amid the
gloom, trembled with mighty fear; some turn to flee,
as of old they sought the ships; some raise a shout—
faintly; the cry essayed mocks their gaping mouths.[1]

494 And here he saw Deiphobus, son of Priam, his
whole frame mangled, his face cruelly torn—his face
and either hand—his ears wrenched from despoiled
brows, and his nostrils lopped by a shameful wound.
Scarce, indeed, did he know the quivering form that
would hide its awful punishment; then, with familiar
accents, unhailed, he accosts him:

500 "Deiphobus, strong in battle, thou scion of
Teucer's high lineage, who chose to wreak a penalty
so cruel? Who had power so to deal with thee?
Rumour told me that on that last night, weary with
endless slaughter of Pelasgians, thou hadst sunk upon
a heap of mingled carnage. Then I myself set up an
empty tomb upon the Rhoetean shore, and with loud
cry called thrice upon thy spirit. Thy name and arms
guard the place; thee, my friend, I could not see, nor
lay, as I departed, in thy native land."

509 To this the son of Priam: "Naught, my friend,
hast thou left undone; all dues hast thou paid Dei-
phobus and the dead man's shade. But me my own
fate and the Laconian woman's[2] death-dealing crime
o'erwhelmed in these woes. Lo! 'twas she left
these memorials! For how we spent that last night
amid deluding joys, thou knowest; and all too well
must thou remember! When the fateful horse leapt
over the heights of Troy, and brought armed infantry

---

[1] Being unsubstantial shades, they can raise but a faint
echo of their former voices.
[2] He disdains to name Helen.

541

Pergama et armatum peditem gravis attulit alvo,
illa, chorum simulans, euhantis orgia circum
ducebat Phrygias; flammam media ipsa tenebat
ingentem et summa Danaos ex arce vocabat.
tum me, confectum curis somnoque gravatum,   520
infelix habuit thalamus, pressitque iacentem
dulcis et alta quies placidaeque simillima morti.
egregia interea coniunx arma omnia tectis
emovet, et fidum capiti subduxerat ensem ;
intra tecta vocat Menelaum et limina pandit,   525
scilicet id magnum sperans fore munus amanti,
et famam exstingui veterum sic posse malorum.
quid moror? inrumpunt thalamo, comes additur
        una
hortator scelerum Aeolides. di, talia Grais
instaurate, pio si poenas ore reposco.   530
sed te qui vivum casus, age fare vicissim,
attulerint. pelagine venis erroribus actus
an monitu divum? an quae te fortuna fatigat,
ut tristis sine sole domos, loca turbida, adires ?"

  Hac vice sermonum roseis Aurora quadrigis   535
iam medium aetherio cursu traiecerat axem;
et fors omne datum traherent per talia tempus,
sed comes admonuit breviterque adfata Sibylla est :
"nox ruit, Aenea ; nos flendo ducimus horas.
hic locus est, partis ubi se via findit in ambas :   540
dextera quae Ditis magni sub moenia tendit,
hac iter Elysium nobis ; at laeva malorum

516 alveo *MR*.   520 coris *a*¹: choreis *Schrader*.
524 emovet *F*¹*Rγ*: etmovet *P*¹: amovet *F*²*MP*².
526 thalamos *R*.   additus *PR*.
532 attulerit *M*¹.   530 fando *Reinach*

AENEID BOOK VI

to weight its womb, she feigned a solemn dance and
round the city led the Phrygian wives, shrieking in
their Bacchic rites; she herself in the midst held a
mighty torch and called the Danaans from the castle-
height. Care-worn and sunk in slumber, I was then
fast in our ill-starred bridal chamber, sleep weighing
upon me as I lay—sweet and deep, very image of
death's peace. Meanwhile, this peerless wife takes
every weapon from the house—even from under my
head she had withdrawn my trusty sword; into
the house she calls Menelaus and flings wide the
door, hoping, I doubt not, that her lover would find
herein a great boon, and so the fame of old misdeeds
might be blotted out. Why linger? They burst
into my chamber; with them comes their fellow-
counsellor of sin, the son of Aeolus.[1] Ye gods, with
like penalties requite the Greeks, if with pious lips I
pray for vengeance!   But come, tell in turn what
chance hath brought thee here, alive.   Comest thou
driven in thy ocean-wanderings, or at Heaven's
command?   Or what doom wearies thee, that thou
shouldst visit these sad, sunless dwellings, this land
of disorder?"

[535] In such interchange of talk, Dawn, with roseate
car, had now crossed mid-heaven in her skyey course,
and perchance in such wise they would have spent
all the allotted time, but the Sibyl beside him gave
warning with brief words: "Night is coming, Aeneas;
we waste the hours in weeping.   Here is the place,
where the road parts in twain:[2] there to the right, as
it runs under the walls of great Dis, is our way to
Elysium, but the left wreaks the punishment of the

---

[1] Ulysses was son of Laertes, but gossip made him the son
of Sisyphus, whose father was Aeolus.
[2] Thus far the way has led through neutral ground.

exercet poenas, et ad impia Tartara mittit."
Deiphobus contra : " ne saevi, magna sacerdos ;
discedam, explebo numerum reddarque tenebris. 545
i decus, i, nostrum ; melioribus utere fatis."
tantum effatus, et in verbo vestigia torsit.

Respicit Aeneas subito et sub rupe sinistra
moenia lata videt, triplici circumdata muro,
quae rapidus flammis ambit torrentibus amnis, 550
Tartareus Phlegethon, torquetque sonantia saxa.
porta adversa, ingens, solidoque adamante columnae,
vis ut nulla virum, non ipsi exscindere bello
caelicolae valeant ; stat ferrea turris ad auras,
Tisiphoneque sedens, palla succincta cruenta, 555
vestibulum exsomnis servat noctesque diesque.
hinc exaudiri gemitus, et saeva sonare
verbera, tum stridor ferri tractaeque catenae.
constitit Aeneas strepituque exterritus haesit. 559
"quae scelerum facies ? o virgo, effare : quibusve MPR
urgentur poenis ?   quis tantus clangor ad auras ? "
tum vates sic orsa loqui : "·dux inclute Teucrum,
nulli fas casto sceleratum insistere limen ;
sed me cum lucis Hecate praefecit Avernis,
ipsa deum poenas docuit perque omnia duxit. 565
Gnosius haec Rhadamanthus habet durissima regna
castigatque auditque dolos subigitque fateri,
quae quis apud superos, furto laetatus inani,
distulit in seram commissa piacula mortem.
continuo sontis ultrix accincta flagello 570
Tisiphone quatit insultans, torvosque sinistra

547 torsit] pressit *MR*γ (*in margin*).
553 bello] ferro *M*.
556 insomnis *R*.
559 strepitumque *FP¹R*, *Servius*. hausit *F²P¹*γ, *Servius*.
561 qui *P¹R*. plangor *MP¹R*: clangor *P²*γ, *Servius.*, auris *P*.
562 tunc *P*. sic] hinc *PR*.   **571** turtos *P¹*.

544

wicked, and sends them on to pitiless Tartarus."
Thereto Deiphobus : " Be not wroth, great priestess ;
I will go my way ; I will fill up the tale [1] and get me
back to the darkness. Go thou, our glory, go ; enjoy
a happier fate ! " Thus much he said and, as he spoke,
turned his steps.

[548] Suddenly Aeneas looks back, and under a cliff
on the left sees a broad castle, girt with triple wall
and encircled with a rushing flood of torrent flames—
Tartarean Phlegethon, that rolls along thundering
rocks. In front stands the huge gate, and pillars of
solid adamant, that no might of man, nay, not even
the sons of heaven, may uproot in war ; there stands
the iron tower, soaring high, and Tisiphone, sitting
girt with bloody pall, keeps sleepless watch o'er the
portal night and day. Therefrom are heard groans
and the sound of the savage lash ; withal, the clank
of iron and dragging of chains. Aeneas stopped,
rooted to the spot in terror of the din. " What
forms of crime are these ? Say, O maiden ! With
what penalties are they scourged ? What cry so loud
uprises ? " Then the seer thus began to speak :
" Famed chieftain of the Teucrians, no pure soul may
tread the accursed threshold ; but when Hecate set
me over the groves of Avernus, she taught me the
gods' penalties and guided me through all. Gnosian
Rhadamanthus holds here his iron sway ; he chastises,
and hears the tale of guilt, exacting confession of
crimes, whenever in the world above any man,
rejoicing in vain deceit, has put off atonement until
death's late hour. Straightway avenging Tisiphone,
girt with the lash, leaps on the guilty to scourge them,

---

[1] A metaphorical expression. The ghosts are flocks, which
Hades, as shepherd, counts. Deiphobus will return to the
fold, filling up the place he had left vacant.

intentans anguis vocat agmina saeva sororum.
tum demum horrisono stridentes cardine sacrae
panduntur portae.   cernis, custodia qualis
vestibulo sedeat, facies quae limina servet?   575
quinquaginta atris immanis hiatibus Hydra
saevior intus habet sedem.   tum Tartarus ipse
bis patet in praeceps tantum tenditque sub umbras,
quantus ad aetherium caeli suspectus Olympum.
hic genus antiquum Terrae, Titania pubes,   580
fulmine deiecti fundo volvuntur in imo.
hic et Aloidas geminos immania vidi
corpora, qui manibus magnum rescindere caelum
adgressi superisque Iovem detrudere regnis.
vidi et crudelis dantem Salmonea poenas,   585
dum flammas Iovis et sonitus imitatur Olympi.
quattuor hic invectus equis et lampada quassans
per Graium populos mediaeque per Elidis urbem
ibat ovans, divumque sibi poscebat honorem,   FMPR
demens, qui nimbos et non imitabile fulmen   590
aere et cornipedum pulsu simularet equorum.
at pater omnipotens densa inter nubila telum
contorsit, non ille faces nec fumea taedis
lumina, praecipitemque immani turbine adegit.
nec non et Tityon, Terrae omniparentis alumnum,
cernere erat, per tota novem cui iugera corpus   596
porrigitur, rostroque immanis voltur obunco
immortale iecur tondens fecundaque poenis
viscera, rimaturque epulis, habitatque sub alto
pectore, nec fibris requies datur ulla renatis.   600
quid memorem Lapithas, Ixiona Pirithoumque,

573 proles *R*.   **586** flammam *P*.
591 cursu *F*(*late*)*M²Rγ²*.   simularat *F*(*late*).
595 omnipotentis *F¹M¹*, *Nonius*.
597 abunco *FRc:* adunco *Pγ*.

---

¹ Tisiphone.
². To dwellers below, this region of light, our world, would

and with left hand brandishing her grim snakes, calls
on her savage sister band. Then at last, grating on
harsh, jarring hinge, the infernal gates open. Seest
thou what sentry[1] sits in the doorway? what shape
guards the threshold? The monstrous Hydra, still
fiercer, with her fifty black gaping throats, dwells
within. Then Tartarus itself yawns sheer down,
stretching into the gloom twice as far as is yon sky's
upward view[2] to heavenly Olympus. Here the ancient
sons of Earth, the Titan's brood, hurled down by the
thunderbolt, writhe in the lowest abyss. Here, too, I
saw the twin sons of Aloeus, giant in stature, whose
hands essayed to tear down high Heaven and thrust
down Jove from his realm above. Salmoneus, too, I
saw, who paid a cruel penalty while aping Jove's fires
and the thunders of Olympus. He, borne by four
horses and brandishing a torch, rode triumphant
through the Greek peoples and his city in the heart
of Elis, claiming as his own the homage of deity.
Madman! to mimic the storm-clouds and inimitable
thunder with brass and the tramp of horn-footed
horses! But the Father Almighty amid thick clouds
launched his bolt—no firebrands he, nor pitch-pines'
smoky glare—and drave him headlong with furious
whirlwind. Likewise one might see Tityos, nursling
of Earth, the universal mother. Over nine full acres
his body is stretched, and a monstrous vulture with
crooked beak gnaws at his deathless liver and vitals
fruitful for anguish; deep within the breast he lodges
and gropˌs for his feast; nor is any respite given to the
filaments that grow anew. Why tell of the Lapithae,
Ixion and Pirithoüs, over whom hangs a black crag

be a sort of *caelum*, a sky; *cf.* 719 and 896 below. More
commonly, *caeli suspectus* is taken as "man's skyward gaze,"
which makes *ad aetherium Olympum* redundant. Some editors
connect *caeli* with *Olympum*.

quos super atra silex iam iam lapsura cadentique
imminet adsimilis ?   lucent genialibus altis
aurea fulcra toris, epulaeque ante ora paratae
regifico luxu ; Furiarum maxima iuxta   605
accubat et manibus prohibet contingere mensas,
exsurgitque facem attollens atque intonat ore.
hic quibus invisi fratres, dum vita manebat,
pulsatusve parens, et fraus innexa clienti,
aut qui divitiis soli incubuere repertis   610
nec partem posuere suis (quae maxima turba est),
quique ob adulterium caesi, quique arma secuti
impia nec veriti dominorum fallere dextras,
inclusi poenam exspectant. ne quaere doceri,
quam poenam, aut quae forma viros fortunave mersit.
saxum ingens volvunt alii, radiisque rotarum   616
districti pendent ; sedet aeternumque sedebit
infelix Theseus ; Phlegyasque miserrimus omnis
admonet et magna testatur voce per umbras :
' discite iustitiam moniti et non temnere divos.' 620
vendidit hic auro patriam dominumque potentem
imposuit ; fixit leges pretio atque refixit ;
hic thalamum invasit natae vetitosque hymenaeos
ausi omnes immane nefas ausoque potiti.
non mihi si linguae centum sint oraque centum,   625
ferrea vox, omnis scelerum comprendere formas,
omnia poenarum percurrere nomina possim."
    Haec ubi dicta dedit Phoebi longaeva sacerdos,
" sed iam age, carpe viam et susceptum perfice munus;

    602 quos $F^2MP\gamma$, *Probus*, *Macrobius:* quod F^1 : quo R.
-que *omitted* $R\gamma$.   604 paternae R.   607 increpat $P\gamma^1$.
    617 districti F^1 : de- $F^2MP^2R\gamma$: -te P^1.   629 et iam M.
548

that now, yea now, would seem to slip and fall? [1]
High festal couches gleam with frames [2] of gold, and
before their eyes is spread a banquet in royal splen-
dour. Yet, reclining hard by, the eldest Fury stays
their hands from touch of the table, springing forth
with uplifted torch and thunderous cries.

[608] "Here were they who in lifetime hated their
brethren, or smote a sire, and entangled a client in
wrong; or who brooded in solitude over wealth they
had won, nor set aside a portion for their kin—the
largest number this; who were slain for adultery; or
who followed unholy warfare,[3] and feared not to break
faith with their lords—all these, immured, await their
doom. Seek not to learn that doom, or what form
of crime, or fate, o'erwhelmed them! Some roll a
huge stone, or hang outstretched on spokes of
wheels; hapless Theseus sits and evermore shall sit,
and Phlegyas, most unblest, gives warning to all and
with loud voice bears witness amid the gloom: *Be
warned; learn ye to be just and not to slight the gods!*
This one sold his country for gold, and fastened on her
a tyrant lord; he made and unmade laws for a bribe.
This forced his daughter's bed and a marriage for-
bidden. All dared a monstrous sin, and what they
dared attained. Nay, had I a hundred tongues, a
hundred mouths, and voice of iron, I could not sum
up all the forms of crime, or rehearse all the tale of
torments."

[628] So spake the aged priestess of Phoebus; then
adds: "But come now, take thy way and fulfil the
task in hand. Let us hasten. I descry the ramparts

---

[1] The punishment here assigned to Ixion and Pirithoüs is
usually referred to Tantalus.
[2] The *fulcra* correspond to the heads of our modern sofas.
[3] *i.e.* those engaged in warfare against their own country.

acceleremus," ait. " Cyclopum educta caminis 630
moenia conspicio atque adverso fornice portas,
haec ubi nos praecepta iubent deponere dona."
dixerat, et pariter gressi per opaca viarum
corripiunt spatium medium foribusque propinquant.
occupat Aeneas aditum corpusque recenti 635
spargit aqua ramumque adverso in limine figit.

His demum exactis, perfecto munere divae,
devenere locos laetos et amoena virecta
Fortunatorum Nemorum sedesque beatas.
largior hic campos aether et lumine vestit 640
purpureo, solemque suum, sua sidera norunt.
pars in gramineis exercent membra palaestris,
contendunt ludo et fulva luctantur harena ;
pars pedibus plaudunt choreas et carmina dicunt.
nec non Threïcius longa cum veste sacerdos 645
obloquitur numeris septem discrimina vocum,
iamque eadem digitis, iam pectine pulsat eburno.
hic genus antiquum Teucri, pulcherrima proles,
magnanimi heroes, nati melioribus annis,
Ilusque Assaracusque et Troiae Dardanus auctor. 650
arma procul currusque virum miratur inanis ;
stant terra defixae hastae, passimque soluti
per campum pascuntur equi ; quae gratia currum
armorumque fuit vivis, quae cura nitentis
pascere equos, eadem sequitur tellure repostos. 655
conspicit ecce alios dextra laevaque per herbam
vescentis laetumque choro paeana canentis
inter odoratum lauri nemus, unde superne
plurimus Eridani per silvam volvitur amnis.

630 ducta *FPRγ¹*.
640 campus *F¹Rγ²* : campis *P¹*.
651 mirantur *F Mγ²*. 652 terrae *F*.

reared by Cyclopean forges and the gates with fronting arch, where they bid us lay the appointed gifts." She ended, and advancing side by side along the dusky way, they haste over the mid-space and draw nigh the doors. Aeneas wins the entrance, sprinkles his body with fresh water, and plants the bough full on the threshold.

[637] This at length performed and the task of the goddess fulfilled, they came to a land of joy, the green pleasaunces and happy seats of the Blissful Groves. Here an ampler ether clothes the meads with roseate light, and they know their own sun, and stars of their own. Some disport their limbs on the grassy wrestling-ground, vie in sports, and grapple on the yellow sand; some trip it in the dance and chant songs. There, too, the long-robed Thracian priest [1] matches their measures with the seven clear notes,[2] striking them now with his fingers, now with his ivory quill. Here is Teucer's olden line, family most fair, high-souled heroes born in happier years—Ilus and Assaracus and Dardanus, Troy's founder. From afar he marvels at their phantom arms and chariots. Their lances stand fixed in the ground, and their steeds, unyoked, browse freely over the plain. The selfsame pride in chariot and arms that was theirs in life, the selfsame care in keeping sleek steeds, attends them when hidden beneath the earth. Lo! others he sees, to right and left, feasting on the sward, and chanting in chorus a joyous paean within a fragrant laurel grove, whence, in the world above, the full flood of the Eridanus rolls amid the forest.[3]

[1] *i.e.* Orpheus, a priest of Apollo.
[2] These are the notes of the scale, corresponding to the lyre's seven strings.
[3] The Eridanus, or Po, has an underground course of about two miles near its source, and so was said to spring from the lower world.

hic manus ob patriam pugnando volnera passi,   660
quique sacerdotes casti, dum vita manebat,
quique pii vates et Phoebo digna locuti,
inventas aut qui vitam excoluere per artis,
quique sui memores aliquos fecere merendo :
omnibus his nivea cinguntur tempora vitta.   665
quos circumfusos sic est adfata Sibylla,
Musaeum ante omnis ; medium nam plurima turba
hunc habet atque umeris exstantem suspicit altis :
"dicite, felices animae, tuque, optime vates,
quae regio Anchisen, quis habet locus ?   illius ergo
venimus et magnos Erebi tranavimus amnis."   671
atque huic responsum paucis ita reddidit heros :
"nulli certa domus ; lucis habitamus opacis
riparumque toros et prata recentia rivis
incolimus.   sed vos, si fert ita corde voluntas,   675
hoc superate iugum, et facili iam tramite sistam."
dixit et ante tulit gressum camposque nitentis
desuper ostentat ; dehinc summa cacumina linquunt.
   At pater Anchises penitus convalle virenti
inclusas animas superumque ad lumen ituras   680
lustrabat studio recolens, omnemque suorum
forte recensebat numerum carosque nepotes
fataque fortunasque virum moresque manusque.
isque ubi tendentem adversum per gramina vidit
Aenean, alacris palmas utrasque tetendit,   685
effusaeque genis lacrimae et vox excidit ore :
" venisti tandem, tuaque exspectata parenti

        [661] maneret *Nonius*.   [664] alios *F²*
        [685] alacris] lacrimans *P¹*.

552

⁶⁶⁰ Here is the band of those who suffered wounds, fighting for fatherland; those who in lifetime were ·priests and pure, good bards, whose songs were meet for Phoebus; or they who ennobled life by truths[1] discovered and they who by service have won remembrance among men—the brows of all bound with snowy fillet. These, as they streamed round, the Sibyl thus addressed, Musaeus before all; for he is centre of the vast throng that gazes up to him, as with shoulders high he towers aloft: " Say, happy souls, and thou best of bards, what land, what place holds Anchises? For his sake are we come, and have sailed across the great rivers of Erebus."

⁶⁷² And to her the hero thus made brief reply: "Fixed home hath none. We dwell in shady groves, and live on cushioned river-banks and in meadows fresh with streams. But ye, if the wish in your heart so inclines, surmount this ridge, and soon I will set you on an easy path." He spake and stepped on before, and from above points out the shining fields. Then they leave the mountain-tops.

⁶⁷⁹ But, deep in a green vale, father Anchises was surveying with earnest thought the imprisoned souls that were to pass to the light above, and, as it chanced, was telling the full tale of his people and beloved children, their fates and fortunes, their works and ways. And he, as he saw Aeneas coming towards him over the sward, eagerly stretched forth both hands, while tears streamed from his eyes and a cry fell from his lips: " Art thou come at last, and hath the love thy father looked for vanquished the

---

[1] The word *artis* here does not refer merely, or even mainly, to material inventions. It applies rather to the principles of philosophy, including natural science, as understood by the ancients; *cf.* Servius: *significat philosophos, qui aliquid excogitaverunt, unde vita coleretur.*

vicit iter durum pietas? datur ora tueri,   FGMPR
nate, tua et notas audire et reddere voces ?
sic equidem ducebam animo rebarque futurum,   690
tempora dinumerans, nec me mea cura fefellit.
quas ego te terras et quanta per aequora vectum
accipio ! quantis iactatum, nate, periclis !
quam metui, ne quid Libyae tibi regna nocerent ! "
ille autem : " tua me, genitor, tua tristis imago   695
saepius occurrens haec limina tendere adegit ;
stant sale Tyrrheno classes.   da iungere dextram,
da, genitor, teque amplexu ne subtrahe nostro."
sic memorans largo fletu simul ora rigabat.
ter conatus ibi collo dare bracchia circum,   700
ter frustra comprensa manus effugit imago,
par levibus ventis volucrique simillima somno.
   Interea videt Aeneas in valle reducta
seclusum nemus et virgulta sonantia silvae   704
Lethaeumque, domos placidas qui praenatat, amnem.
hunc circum innumerae gentes populique volabant ;
ac veluti in pratis ubi apes aestate serena
floribus insidunt variis et candida circum
lilia funduntur, strepit omnis murmure campus.
horrescit visu subito causasque requirit   710
inscius Aeneas, quae sint ea flumina porro,
quive viri tanto complerint agmine ripas.
tum pater Anchises : "animae, quibus altera fato
corpora debentur, Lethaei ad fluminis undam
securos latices et longa oblivia potant.   715
has equidem memorare tibi atque ostendere coram,
iampridem hanc prolem cupio enumerare meorum,
quo magis Italia mecum laetere reperta."

[702] *omitted P.*
[704] reclusum *R.*   silvis *FM²γ(in margin).*
[707] velut *PR.*
[718] Italiam . . . repertam *F¹R.*

toilsome way? Is it given me to see thy face, my
son, and hear and utter familiar tones? Even so I
mused and deemed the hour would come, counting
the days thereto, nor has my yearning failed me.
O'er what lands, what wide seas hast thou journeyed
to my welcome! What dangers have tossed thee,
O my son! How I feared the realm of Libya might
work thee harm!"

695 But he: "Thy shade, father, thy sad shade,
meeting me so oft, drove me to seek these portals.
My ships ride the Tuscan sea. Grant me to clasp
thy hand, grant me, O father, and withdraw thee
not from my embrace!"

699 So he spoke, his face wet with flooding tears.
Thrice there he strove to throw his arms about his neck;
thrice the form, vainly clasped, fled from his hands,
even as light winds, and most like a winged dream.

703 Meanwhile, in a retired vale, Aeneas sees a se-
questered grove and rustling forest thickets, and the
river of Lethe drifting past those peaceful homes.
About it hovered peoples and tribes unnumbered;
even as when, in the meadows, in cloudless summer-
time, bees light on many-hued blossoms and stream
round lustrous lilies and all the fields murmur with
the humming. Aeneas is thrilled by the sudden
sight and, knowing not, asks the cause—what is
that river yonder, and who are the men thronging
the banks in such a host? Then father Anchises:
"Spirits they are, to whom second bodies are owed
by Fate, and at the water of Lethe's stream they
drink the soothing draught and long forgetfulness.
These in truth I have long yearned to tell and show
thee to thy face, yea, to count this, my children's
seed, that so thou mayest rejoice with me the more
at finding Italy."

VIRGIL

"o pater, anne aliquas ad caelum hinc ire putandum
    est
sublimis animas iterumque ad tarda reverti   720
corpora? quae lucis miseris tam dira cupido?"
"dicam equidem nec te suspensum, nate, tenebo,"
suscipit Anchises atque ordine singula pandit.

   "Principio caelum ac terras camposque liquentis
lucentemque globum lunae Titaniaque astra   FMPR
spiritus intus alit, totamque infusa per artus   726
mens agitat molem et magno se corpore miscet.
inde hominum pecudumque genus, vitaeque volantum,
et quae marmoreo fert monstra sub aequore pontus.
igneus est ollis vigor et caelestis origo   730
seminibus, quantum non noxia corpora tardant
terrenique hebetant artus moribundaque membra.
hinc metuunt cupiuntque, dolent gaudentque, neque
    auras
dispiciunt clausae tenebris et carcere caeco.
quin et supremo cum lumine vita reliquit,   735
non tamen omne malum miseris nec funditus omnes
corporeae excedunt pestes, penitusque necesse est
multa diu concreta modis inolescere miris.
ergo exercentur poenis veterumque malorum
supplicia expendunt: aliae panduntur inanes   740
suspensae ad ventos, aliis sub gurgite vasto
infectum eluitur scelus aut exuritur igni;

[719] est *omitted in* FG^1.   [721] cupido est F^1.
[723] suspicit $F^2MP\gamma^1$.   [724] terram F^1PR.
[725] lucentem] ingentem M^1.   luna F^1.
[731] corpora noxia $P\gamma^1$.   [733] hic M^1.
[734] despiciunt *most MSS.:* di- γ^1: respiciunt $a^2b^2c^2$, *Servius.*
[735] relinquit F^1.   [742] aut] adque F.

556

[719] " But, father, must we think that any souls pass aloft from here to yon sky,[1] and return a second time to sluggish bodies? What means, alas! this their mad longing for the light?" "I will surely tell thee, my son, nor hold thee in doubt," replies Anchises, and reveals each truth in order.

[724] " First, the heaven and earth, and the watery plains, the shining orb of the moon and Titan's star,[2] a spirit within sustains, and mind, pervading its members, sways the whole mass and mingles with its mighty frame. Thence[3] the race of man and beast, the life of winged things, and the strange shapes ocean bears beneath his glassy floor. Fiery is the vigour and divine the source of those life-seeds, so far as harmful bodies clog them not, nor earthly limbs and mortal frames dull them. Hence[4] their fears and desires, their griefs and joys; nor discern they the light, pent up in the gloom of their dark dungeon. Nay, when at their last day life is fled, still not all the evil, alas! not all the plagues of the body quit them utterly ; and it must needs be that many a taint, long linked in growth, should in wondrous wise become deeply ingrained. Therefore are they schooled with penalties, and for olden sins pay punishment: some are hung stretched out to the empty winds ; from some the stain of guilt is washed away under swirling floods or burned out in fire. Each of us

---

[1] For *caelum* see note on 579 above.
[2] *i.e.* the sun, called Titan in IV. 119.
[3] *i.e.* from this mind or spirit, the *anima mundi*, which is of the nature of fire, and is the source of all life.
[4] The meaning is that human emotions are due to this union with the body, which disturbs the normal tranquillity of the soul.

quisque suos patimur Manis. exinde per amplum
mittimur Elysium, et pauci laeta arva tenemus,
donec longa dies, perfecto temporis orbe   745
concretam exemit labem, purumque relinquit
aetherium sensum atque aurai simplicis ignem.
has omnis, ubi mille rotam volvere per annos,
Lethaeum ad fluvium deus evocat agmine magno,
scilicet immemores supera ut convexa revisant,   750
rursus et incipiant in corpora velle reverti."

  Dixerat Anchises, natumque unaque Sibyllam
conventus trahit in medios turbamque sonantem
et tumulum capit, unde omnis longo ordine posset
adversos legere et venientum discere voltus.   755

  "Nunc age, Dardaniam prolem quae deinde
    sequatur   MPR
gloria, qui maneant Itala de gente nepotes,
inlustris animas nostrumque in nomen ituras
expediam dictis et te tua fata docebo.
ille, vides, pura iuvenis qui nititur hasta,   760
proxima sorte tenet lucis loca, primus ad auras
aetherias Italo commixtus sanguine surget,
Silvius, Albanum nomen, tua postuma proles,
quem tibi longaevo serum Lavinia coniunx
educet silvis regem regumque parentem,   765
unde genus Longa nostrum dominabitur Alba.
proxima ille Procas, Troianae gloria gentis,

  746 tabem R. reliquit F²PRγ.
  747 aurae FMPR: aurai γ²c, Servius.
  750 super ut M¹: supera aut F¹: superaut M²R: super-
ane P¹.   754 possit Fγ.   762 surgit M.
  765 educit M¹.   766 nostrum Longa M¹.

---

  1 The attendant spirit, *genius*, or, as here, his *Manes*, accompanies a man through life, and into the other world, where the taint of guilt is purged away. Possibly the spirit is itself the agent of punishment. For Plato's account see the *Phaedo*, ch. lvii. But the precise meaning of this statement in Virgil is uncertain.

suffers his own spirit;[1] then through wide Elysium
are we sent, a few of us to abide in the joyous fields;[2]
till lapse of days, when time's cycle is complete,
takes out the inbred taint and leaves unsoiled the
ethereal sense and pure flame of spirit. All these,
when they have rolled time's wheel through a
thousand years, the god summons in vast throng
to the river of Lethe, in sooth that, reft of memory,
they may revisit the vault above and conceive desire
to return again to the body."

[752] Anchises ceased, and drew his son and, with
him, the Sibyl into the midst of the concourse and
murmuring throng, then chose a mound whence, face
to face, he might scan all the long array, and note
their countenances as they came.

[756] " Come now, what glory shall hereafter attend
the Dardan line, what children of Italian stock[3] await
thee, souls illustrious and heirs of our name—this
will I set forth, and teach thee thy destiny. Yonder
youth thou seest, who leans on headless spear,[4] holds
by lot a place nearest the light, and first shall rise
into the air of heaven, mingling with Italian blood—
Silvius of Alban name, thy last-born child, whom
late in thy old age thy wife Lavinia shall bring forth
in the woodland, a king and father of kings; from
him shall our race have sway in Long Alba. He
next is Procas, glory of the Trojan race; and Capys

---

[2] All the souls, of whom Anchises has been speaking in
739 ff., are sent to Elysium, but there a separation takes place.
A few (Anchises being one of these) remain for ever there,
regaining in time their original purity; but most of the souls
must drink of the water of oblivion and then return to new
bodies (*cf.* 713-715).
[3] *i.e.* the descendants of Aeneas and his Italian wife,
Lavinia.
[4] In early days this was given as a prize to a young warrior
after winning his first success.

et Capys et Numitor et, qui te nomine reddet,
Silvius Aeneas, pariter pietate vel armis
egregius, si umquam regnandam acceperit Albam. 770
qui iuvenes ! quantas ostentant, aspice, viris,
atque umbrata gerunt civili tempora quercu !
hi tibi Nomentum et Gabios urbemque Fidenam,
hi Collatinas imponent montibus arces,
Pometios Castrumque Inui Bolamque Coramque. 775
haec tum nomina erunt, nunc sunt sine nomine terrae.

    "Quin et avo comitem sese Mavortius addet
Romulus, Assaraci quem sanguinis Ilia mater
educet.   viden, ut geminae stant vertice cristae
et pater ipse suo superum iam signat honore ?   780
en huius, nate, auspiciis illa incluta Roma
imperium terris, animos aequabit Olympo,
septemque una sibi muro circumdabit arces,
felix prole virum : qualis Berecyntia mater
invehitur curru Phrygias turrita per urbes,   785
laeta deum partu, centum complexa nepotes,
omnis caelicolas, omnis supera alta tenentis.
huc geminas nunc flecte acies, hanc aspice gentem
Romanosque tuos.   hic Caesar et omnis Iuli
progenies, magnum caeli ventura sub axem.   790
hic vir, hic est, tibi quem promitti saepius audis,
Augustus Caesar, Divi genus, aurea condet
saecula qui rursus Latio regnata per arva

> [776] terrae] gentes M^1.
> [787] super alta M^1PR : superata γ^1.
> [793] arva] annos R.

---

[1] He is said to have been kept out of his kingdom for half
a century.
[2] The garland of the "civic oak" was given to one who
saved the life of a citizen in battle.
[3] Referring to the double-plumed helmet worn by Mars.
[4] *i.e.* for earth.   [5] *cf. Geor.* II. 535.

and Numitor, and he who shall renew thy name,
Silvius Aeneas, like thee peerless in piety or in arms,
if ever he win the Alban throne.[1] What youths!
What mighty strength, lo! they display, and bear
brows shaded with the civic oak![2] These, I tell thee,
shall rear Nomentum and Gabii and Fidenae's city;
these shall crown hills with Collatia's turrets, with
Pometii, and the Fort of Inuus, with Bola and Cora.
These shall then be names that now are nameless
lands.

[777] " Nay more, a child of Mars shall join his grand-
sire, even Romulus, whom his mother Ilia shall bear of
the blood of Assaracus. Seest thou how the twin plumes
stand upon his crest,[3] and how his father himself by
his own token even now marks him for the world
above?[4] Lo! under his auspices, my son, that glorious
Rome shall bound her empire by earth, her pride by
heaven, and with a single city's wall shall enclose her
seven hills,[5] blest in her brood of men : even as the
Berecyntian Mother,[6] turret-crowned, rides in her car
through the Phrygian cities, glad in her offspring of
gods, and clasping a hundred of her children's children,
all denizens of heaven, all tenants of the heights above.
Hither now turn thy two eyes: behold this people,
thine own Romans. Here is Caesar, and all Iülus'
seed, destined to pass beneath the sky's mighty vault.[7]
This, this is he, whom thou so oft hearest promised
to thee, Augustus Caesar, son of a god,[8] who shall
again set up the Golden Age amid the fields where

[6] Cybele, the *Magna Mater* of the gods, appears in works of
art wearing a mural crown, *i.e.* one representing walls and
battlements, she having first taught men to fortify cities.

[7] *i.e.* destined to appear on earth, in the world above. See
780, with note.

[8] *i.e.* son of Julius Caesar, who was deified after death.
Augustus was his adopted son.

VIRGIL

Saturno quondam, super et Garamantas et Indos
proferet imperium (iacet extra sidera tellus,   795
extra anni solisque vias, ubi caelifer Atlas
axem umero torquet stellis ardentibus aptum):
huius in adventum iam nunc et Caspia regna
responsis horrent divum et Maeotia tellus,
et septemgemini turbant trepida ostia Nili.   800
nec vero Alcides tantum telluris obivit,
fixerit aeripedem cervam licet, aut Erymanthi
pacarit nemora, et Lernam tremefecerit arcu;
nec qui pampineis victor iuga flectit habenis
Liber, agens celso Nysae de vertice tigris.   805
et dubitamus adhuc virtutem extendere factis,
aut metus Ausonia prohibet consistere terra?

  "Quis procul ille autem ramis insignis olivae
sacra ferens?   nosco crinis incanaque menta
regis Romani, primam qui legibus urbem   810
fundabit, Curibus parvis et paupere terra
missus in imperium magnum.   cui deinde subibit
otia qui rumpet patriae residesque movebit
Tullus in arma viros et iam desueta triumphis
agmina.   quem iuxta sequitur iactantior Ancus, 815
nunc quoque iam nimium gaudens popularibus
              auris.
vis et Tarquinios reges, animamque superbam
ultoris Bruti fascisque videre receptos?
consulis imperium hic primus saevasque securis

  803 pacaret *M¹R:* placarit *b²c.*
  806 virtutem . . . factis *Mγ², Servius:* virtute . . . vires
PRc: virtutem . . . vires *γ¹.*
  809 noscon *R.   So Sabb.*   819 primum *M.*

562

Saturn once reigned, and shall spread his empire
past Garamant and Indian, to a land that lies beyond
the stars, beyond the paths of the year and the sun,[1]
where heaven-bearing Atlas turns on his shoulders
the sphere, inset with gleaming stars.[2]   Against his
coming even now the Caspian realms and Maeotian
land shudder at Heaven's oracles, and the mouths of
sevenfold Nile are in tumult of terror.   Nor, in truth,
did Alcides range o'er such space of earth, though he
pierced the brazen-footed deer,[3] or brought peace to
the woods of Erymanthus, and made Lerna tremble
at his bow ; nor he who guides his car with vine-leaf
reins, triumphant Liber, driving his tigers down
from Nysa's lofty crest.   And do we still hesitate to
enlarge our prowess by deeds, or does fear forbid our
settling on Ausonian land ?

    [808] " But who is he apart, crowned with olive-sprays,
and bearing the sacrifice ? I know the locks and hoary
chin of that king of Rome, who, called from the poor
land of lowly Cures to sovereign might, shall base the
infant city on his laws.[4]   To him shall then succeed
Tullus, who shall break his country's peace, and rouse
to arms a slothful folk and ranks long unused to
triumphs.   Hard on him follows over-boastful Ancus,
even now rejoicing overmuch in the people's breath.
Wilt thou see, too, the Tarquin kings, and the
proud soul of avenging Brutus, and the fasces
regained ?   He shall be first to win a consul's

---

    [1] The phrase " beyond the stars " means " beyond the signs
of the zodiac," *i.e.*, as further explained, beyond the path
followed by the sun in his annual course. To this path in the
heavens corresponds a great tract of earth, beyond which the
Roman empire shall extend.   [2] *cf.* IV. 482.
    [3] The reference is to the fourth labour of Hercules, his
capture of the wonderful Arcadian deer.
    [4] This is Numa, second king of Rome.

accipiet, natosque pater nova bella moventis   820
ad poenam pulchra pro libertate vocabit,
infelix, utcumque ferent ea facta minores:
vincet amor patriae laudumque immensa cupido.

   " Quin Decios Drusosque procul saevumque securi
aspice Torquatum et referentem signa Camillum. 825
illae autem, paribus quas fulgere cernis in armis,
concordes animae nunc et dum nocte premuntur,
heu ! quantum inter se bellum, si lumina vitae
attigerint, quantas acies stragemque ciebunt,
aggeribus socer Alpinis atque arce Monoeci   830
descendens, gener adversis instructus Eois !
ne, pueri, ne tanta animis adsuescite bella,
neu patriae validas in viscera vertite viris ;
tuque prior, tu parce, genus qui ducis Olympo ;
proice tela manu, sanguis meus!   835

   " Ille triumphata Capitolia ad alta Corintho
victor aget currum, caesis insignis Achivis ;
eruet ille Argos Agamemnoniasque Mycenas
ipsumque Aeaciden, genus armipotentis Achilli,
ultus avos Troiae, templa et temerata Minervae. 840
quis te, magne Cato, tacitum aut te, Cosse, relinquat ?
quis Gracchi genus aut geminos, duo fulmina belli,
Scipiadas, cladem Libyae, parvoque potentem

---

[824] Druscs] Brutos R.   [827] prementur P[1]R.   [839] Achiilei P.

---

   [1] The father put his sons to death for plotting to restore the Tarquins.
   [2] The reference is to Caesar and Pompey, who married Julia, Caesar's daughter. Caesar passed from Gaul into Italy ; Pompey's troops came largely from Greece and Asia Minor.

power and cruel axes, and when his sons stir up
new war, the father, for fair freedom's sake, shall
call them to their doom—unhappy he, howe'er
posterity extol that deed! Yet love of country
shall prevail, and boundless passion for renown.[1]

824 " Nay, see apart the Decii and Drusi, and Tor-
quatus of the cruel axe, and Camillus bringing home
the standards. But they whom thou seest gleaming
in equal arms, souls harmonious now, while wrapped
in night, alas! if they but reach the light of life,
what mutual war, what battles and carnage shall they
arouse! the father coming down from Alpine ramparts,
and the fortress of Monoecus, his daughter's spouse
arrayed against him with the armies of the East.[2]
O my sons, make not a home within your hearts for
such warfare, nor upon your country's very vitals turn
her vigour and valour! And do thou first forbear, thou
who drawest thy race from heaven; cast from thy
hand the sword, thou blood of mine!

836 " Yonder is one [3] who, triumphant over Corinth,
shall drive a victor's car to the lofty Capitol, famed
for the Achaeans he has slain. Yon other [4] shall
uproot Argos and Agamemnon's Mycenae, yea and
even one born of Aeacus, seed of Achilles the
strong in battle, taking vengeance for his Trojan
sires and Minerva's outraged temple. Who would
leave thee in silence, great Cato, or thee, Cossus?
Who the Gracchan race, or the pair of Scipio's line,
two thunderbolts of war, the bane of Libya? or thee,

---

[3] Mummius, who destroyed Corinth, 146 B.C.
[4] L. Aemilius Paulus defeated Perseus, the last king of
Macedon, at Pydna, 168 B.C. Perseus claimed to be de-
scended from Achilles, the grandson of Aeacus. Argos and
Mycenae, ancient seats of Greek power, represent Greece as a
whole.

Fabricium vel te sulco, Serrane, serentem?
quo fessum rapitis, Fabii? tu Maximus ille es, 845
unus qui nobis cunctando restituis rem.
excudent alii spirantia mollius aera,
(credo equidem), vivos ducent de marmore voltus;
orabunt causas melius, caelique meatus
describent radio et surgentia sidera dicent: 850
tu regere imperio populos, Romane, memento
(hae tibi erunt artes) pacique imponere morem,
parcere subiectis et debellare superbos."

   Sic pater Anchises, atque haec mirantibus addit:
"aspice, ut insignis spoliis Marcellus opimis 855
ingreditur victorque viros supereminet omnis.
hic rem Romanam, magno turbante tumultu,
sistet eques, sternet Poenos Gallumque rebellem, ғмрʀ
tertiaque arma patri suspendet capta Quirino."

   Atque hic Aeneas (una namque ira videbat 860
egregium forma iuvenem et fulgentibus armis,
sed frons laeta parum et deiecto lumina voltu):
" quis, pater, ille, virum qui sic comitatur euntem?

---

⁸⁴⁵ tun *P*¹. *See Appendix.*   ⁸⁴⁶ restitues *R*.
⁸⁴⁸ cedo *P*¹γ².
⁸⁵² haec *P*¹. pacis *Servius; see note* 2 (*below*) *and* Proceedings
of the American Philological Association, *vol.* 38, *p. xxxviii.*

---

   ¹ This verse (846) is a close reproduction of one in the
Annals of Ennius, referring to Q. Fabius Maximus, the opponent
of Hannibal, who by his tactics earned the surname of
Cunctator.
   ² The poet has in mind the beneficent rule of Augustus,
who brought peace to the world, and then to that peaceful
world gave the blessings of law and order. With the common

Fabricius, poor, yet a prince? or thee, Serranus,
sowing the seed in thy furrow? Whither do ye
hurry my weary steps, O Fabii? Thou art he, the
mightiest, who singly, by delaying, restorest our
state.[1] Others, I doubt not, shall beat out the
breathing bronze with softer lines; shall from marble
draw forth the features of life; shall plead their causes
better; with the rod shall trace the paths of heaven
and tell the rising of the stars: remember thou, O
Roman, to rule the nations with thy sway—these
shall be thine arts—to crown Peace with Law,[2] to spare
the humbled, and to tame in war the proud!"

[854] Thus father Anchises, and, as they marvel,
pursues: "Lo! how Marcellus advances, glorious in
his splendid spoils,[3] and towers triumphant over all!
The Roman realm, when upheaved in utter confusion,
he, a knight,[4] shall support: he shall strike down
Carthaginian and insurgent Gaul, and a third time
hang up the captured arms to father Quirinus!"

[860] And hereon Aeneas, for he saw coming with
him a youth [5] of wondrous beauty and brilliant in his
arms—but his face was sad and his eyes downcast:
"Who, father, is he who thus attends him on his

reading *pacis* (for which there is slight authority) the meaning
is "to impose (on the conquered) the law of peace."

[3] The *spolia opima* were the spoils taken "when the general
slew the general of the enemy." M. Claudius Marcellus won
them at Clastidium in 222 B.C., when he slew the chief of
the Insubrian Gauls. His only predecessors in this feat were
Romulus and Cossus (841).

[4] The battle of Clastidium was mainly a cavalry engagement.
It was also under Marcellus that the Romans won their first
victory over Hannibal at Nola.

[5] This is the young Marcellus, son of the Emperor's sister
Octavia. He was adopted by Augustus and chosen as his
successor, but died in 23 B.C., in his twentieth year, universally
lamented.

filius, anne aliquis magna de stirpe nepotum?
qui strepitus circa comitum! quantum instar in
    ipso!   865
sed nox atra caput tristi circumvolat umbra."
tum pater Anchises lacrimis ingressus obortis:
"o gnate, ingentem luctum ne quaere tuorum.
ostendent terris hunc tantum fata, nec ultra
esse sinent. nimium vobis Romana propago   870
visa potens, superi, propria haec si dona fuissent.
quantos ille virum magnam Mavortis ad urbem [MPR
campus aget gemitus! vel quae, Tiberine, videbis
funera, cum tumulum praeterlabere recentem!
nec puer Iliaca quisquam de gente Latinos   875
in tantum spe tollet avos, nec Romula quondam
ullo se tantum tellus iactabit alumno.
heu pietas, heu prisca fides, invictaque bello
dextera! non illi se quisquam impune tulisset   FMPR
obvius armato, seu cum pedes iret in hostem,   880
seu spumantis equi foderet calcaribus armos.
heu! miserande puer, si qua fata aspera rumpas,
tu Marcellus eris! manibus date lilia plenis,
purpureos spargam flores animamque nepotis
his saltem accumulem donis et fungar inani   885

865 quis $F^2MR\gamma^2$.
885 inanis F^1M^1.

---

[1] *i.e.* the *Campus Martius*, in which the Mausoleum of
Augustus was built in 27 B.C.

[2] Marcellus, while yet a boy, will reflect glory on his Latin
ancestors; *spe* means the promise shown by the youth, the

way? A son, or one of the mighty stock of his children's children? What whispers in the encircling crowd! What noble presence in himself! But black night hovers about his head with its mournful shade."

[867] Then father Anchises with upwelling tears began: "O my son, ask not of the vast sorrow of thy people. Him the fates shall but show to earth, nor longer suffer him to stay. Too mighty, O gods, ye deemed the Roman stock would be, were these gifts lasting. What wailing of men shall that famous Field [1] waft to Mavors' mighty city! What funeral-state, O Tiber, shalt thou see, as thou glidest past the new-built tomb! No youth of Ilian stock shall exalt so greatly with his promise his Latin forefathers,[2] nor shall the land of Romulus ever take such pride in any of her sons. Alas for goodness! alas for old-world honour, and the hand invincible in war! Against him in arms would none have advanced unscathed, whether on foot he met the foe, or dug his spurs into the flanks of his foaming horse. Ah! child of pity, if haply thou couldst burst the harsh bonds of fate, thou shalt be Marcellus![3] Give me lilies with full hand; let me scatter purple flowers; let me heap o'er my offspring's shade at least these gifts and fulfil an unavailing service."

promise of what he is likely to become. Some render, "shall raise so high in hope."

[3] To "burst the harsh bonds of fate" means to escape the early death to which he is doomed. The conditional sentence is mixed in form, because Anchises expresses a wish as well as a condition, for even as he utters the thought he realizes its hopelessness. Page (after Wagner) treats *si qua fata aspera rumpas* as an exclamation, and makes *tu Marcellus eris* an independent sentence. The same view, though not the traditional one, is accepted by Goelzer and Mackail.

munere." sic tota passim regione vagantur
aëris in campis latis atque omnia lustrant.
quae postquam Anchises natum per singula duxit
incenditque animum famae venientis amore,
exin bella viro memorat quae deinde gerenda,   890
Laurentisque docet populos urbemque Latini,
et quo quemque modo fugiatque feratque laborem.

Sunt geminae Somni portae; quarum altera fertur
cornea, qua veris facilis datur exitus umbris,
altera candenti perfecta nitens elephanto,   895
sed falsa ad caelum mittunt insomnia Manes.
his ubi tum natum Anchises unaque Sibyllam
prosequitur dictis portaque emittit eburna;
ille viam secat ad navis sociosque revisit;
tum se ad Caietae recto fert litore portum.   900
ancora de prora iacitur; stant litore puppes.

[889] venientis] melioris *M.*
[897] his ubi] hibi *P*[1]: his ibi *FP*[2]*R.*
[900] limite *π (Codex Pragensis). So Bentley, Heine, Henry Mackail.*
[901] = III. 277.

[886] Thus, through the whole region, they freely range, in the broad, misty plains, surveying all. And when Anchises had led his son over every scene, and fired his soul with love of fame that was to be, he tells him then of the wars he must thereafter wage, and instructs him of the Laurentine peoples and the city of Latinus, and how he is to flee or face each toil.

[893] Two gates of Sleep there are, whereof the one is said to be of horn, and thereby an easy outlet is given to true shades; the other gleaming with the sheen of polished ivory, but false are the dreams sent by the spirits to the world above. There then with these words Anchises attends both his son and the Sibyl, and dismisses them by the ivory gate. Aeneas speeds his way to the ships and revisits his comrades; then straight along the shore sails for Caieta's haven. The anchor is cast from the prow; the sterns rest upon the beach.

APPENDIX

P. xii. Specimen pages of the most important Virgilian MSS., in facsimile, may be seen in Émile Chatelain, *Paléographie des classiques Latins*, Hachette, Paris: Première Partie, 1884–92; Deuxième Partie, 1894–1900. Handsome facsimile reproductions have been published as follows:

In the series of *Codices e Vaticanis Selecti*—

> Vol. I. Fragmenta et picturae Vergiliani codicis Vaticani 3225 (= F). Rome, Danesi, 1899. Reprinted 1930.
>
> Vol. II. Picturae, ornamenta, complura scripturae specimina codicis Vaticani 3867 (= R). *Ibid.* 1902. To be reprinted.
>
> Vol. XIV. Vergilius Palatinus (= P). Éditions Historiques. Paris, 1929.
>
> Vol. XV. Codicis Vergiliani, qui Augusteus appellatur, Reliquiae (= A). Torino, 1926.

A facsimile of the famous Petrarch Virgil (Francisci Petrarcae Vergilianus Codex) was published in Milan, 1930. The beautiful and famous Codex Mediceus (= M) was published in facsimile in Rome, April 21, 1931.[1]

For B, see Sabbadini's edition, Vol. I, p. 20, also

[1] A printed reproduction of M, prepared by P. F. Foggini and published in Florence in 1741, is very faulty and has led to many errors in our editions. A collation of M, made by Dr. Max Hoffmann, was published in Leipzig, 1889 and (II Teil) 1901. In an article on " The Value of the Medicean Codex of Vergil " in the *Bulletin of the John Rylands Library*,

APPENDIX

E. A. Lowe, in the *Classical Review*, XXXVI (1922), p. 154.

For the poet's biography we may consult Nettleship's *Ancient Lives of Vergil* (Oxford, 1880); Ernst Diehl's *Die Vitae Vergilianae* (Bonn, 1911), and J. Brummer's *Vitae Vergilianae* (Leipzig, 1912).

Other works on Virgil are: J. S. Tunison's *Master Virgil* (Cincinnati, 1890); J. W. Mackail's *Virgil and his Meaning to the World of To-day* (Boston, 1922); H. W. Prescott's *The Development of Virgil's Art* (Chicago, 1927); Wili's *Vergil* (Munich, 1930); E. K. Rand's *The Magical Art of Virgil* (Harvard University Press, Cambridge, Mass., 1931); and Bernhard Rehm's *Das geographische Bild des alten Italien in Vergils Aeneis* (Leipzig, 1932).

Additional essays on Virgil are the following: R. S. Conway's *New Studies of a Great Inheritance* (London, 1921) and *Harvard Lectures on the Vergilian Age* (Cambridge, Mass., 1928); H. R. Fairclough's "Virgil's Knowledge of Greek" in *Classical Philology*, XXV (1930), 37–46; three papers on "The Tradition of Virgil" (Princeton University Press, 1930); eight papers in the "Special Vergil Number" of the *Classical Journal*, XXVI (Oct. 1930); the *Virgilio* Supplement to *L'Illustrazione Italiana* (No. 49, Dec. 7, 1930); J. W. Mackail's *Virgil*, the 1930 "annual lecture on a Master Mind" (Proceedings of the British Academy, Vol. XVII, London, 1931); J. W. Duff's *The Magic of Virgil* (Newcastle upon

---

Manchester, XV (1931), 336 ff., Professor R. S. Conway, agreeing in general with Hoffmann, refers the MS. "to a period, and not at all a late period, in the second century." Surely this is much too early. E. A. Lowe, like most palaeographers, assigns it to the fifth century (*Classical Quarterly*, XIX (1925), 197 ff.).

APPENDIX

Tyne, 1931); N. W. De Witt's "Vergil and Epicureanism" in the *Classical Weekly*, XXV (1932), 89–96.

The beautiful metrical art of Virgil deserves careful study. A fresh impetus was given to this by Eduard Norden, when he published his impressive edition of *Aeneid* VI (Leipzig, 1903), and some of his principles have been applied to other books of the epic in my school-edition of *Aeneid* I–VI (Sanborn & Co., Boston; latest reprint, 1930). A noteworthy paper on Virgil's artistic and varied handling of the fourth foot of the hexameter, by W. F. J. Knight, is published in the *Classical Quarterly*, XXV (1931), 184–94.

THE ECLOGUES

RECENT books bearing on the *Eclogues* include the following: J. S. Phillimore, *Pastoral and Allegory* (Oxford, 1925); Jean Hubaux, *Le Réalisme dans les Bucoliques de Virgile* (Université de Liége, Fasc. XXXVII, 1927); Bruno Nardi, *La Giovinezza di Virgilio* (Mantua, 1927); translated by Belle Palmer Rand as *The Youth of Virgil* (Harvard University Press, 1930); Léon Hermann, *Les Masques et les Visages dans les Bucoliques de Virgile* (Bruxelles, 1930).

I

Hermann (*op. cit.*) has a theory that throughout the *Eclogues* the same name denotes the same person wherever it occurs, and that the same person is never denoted by more than one name. Thus Menalcas represents Virgil himself not only in *Ecl.* IX, but also in *Ecl.* III. For the same reason Tityrus in *Ecl.* I is not Virgil. He may be Q. Caecilius

575

APPENDIX

Epirota, once a slave of Atticus, whom he served as literary amanuensis. This fairly plausible theory has won the approval of Professor R. S. Conway (*Classical Review*, XLV (1931), 30 f.).

65. Many editors accept *rapidum cretae* as " chalk-rolling " and suppose that *Oaxes* is another form of *Oxus*, name of a river in Scythia. Though Servius is quoted as in favour of this interpretation, yet, in his note on *Ecl.* II, 24, he shows that he was familiar with the view that *Cretae* here means the island of Crete. There is a geographical difficulty, whichever way we read the line, but with *rapidum cretae* there is a grammatical one as well. Besides, it is known that Augustus gave land in Crete to Roman colonists who were forced to leave Capua.

69. Servius took *aristas* as equivalent to *messes*, but " after some harvests " sounds flat in view of the preceding *longo post tempore*.

II

Jean Hubaux (*op. cit.*) shows that in this eclogue Virgil made use, not only of Theocritus, but also of Meleager of Gadara.

III

60. Whether *Musae* is a vocative plural or a genitive singular is a question which puzzled even Servius. Greek parallels for either rendering may be cited, but the most convincing is the opening of Idyl XVII of Theocritus,

Ἐκ Διὸς ἀρχώμεσθα καὶ ἐς Δία λήγετε, Μοῖσαι.

IV

A great deal of literature has been written upon this famous poem. Special mention may be made

APPENDIX

of *Virgil's Messianic Eclogue*, three studies by Mayor, Fowler and Conway (Murray, London, 1907); *Virgil and Isaiah*, by T. F. Royds (Blackwell, Oxford, 1918); *Die Geburt des Kindes*, by Ed. Norden (Leipzig, 1924); and *Virgile et le Mystère de la IVᵉ Eglogue* (Paris, 1930), by Carcopino. In this last work the author sets forth the Pythagorean element in the poem. A notable article is W. A. Heidel's " Vergil's Messianic Expectations " in the *American Journal of Philology*, XLV (1924), pp. 205–37, largely a reply to Norden, who " fathers upon Egypt the entire tradition regarding the Αἰών and the divine child."

R. G. Austin, in " Virgil and the Sybil " (*Classical Quarterly*, XXI (1927), pp. 100 ff.), seeks to prove that in this poem Virgil made the Sibylline Oracles themselves his model both in style and material.

As to the identity of the wonder child of the poem, the question will probably never be settled. For centuries, since Constantine and Augustine, Christian writers have regarded the eclogue as a prophecy of the coming of the Messiah. At the other extreme, Norden argues that the child is merely a sort of personification, or incarnation, of the new golden age itself.

If the poems written by Pollio were preserved, we should probably hold the key to the riddle. In his *Pastoral and Allegory*, J. S. Phillimore thinks that Virgil is poking fun at Pollio's orientalism and supposedly Jewish connection. In an interesting paper in the *Classical Review*, XLII (1928), 123 ff., Ernest I. Robson, after remarking that the Fourth Eclogue seems to have attracted very little attention during the first two centuries after its publication, sets forth a theory that the poem is only a playful

577

birthday ode, written in humorous vein, when
" Pollio's wife is expecting a child." It is to be
remembered that years afterwards C. Asinius Gallus,
a son of Pollio, claimed that he was the child men-
tioned.

Others, of course, have associated the child with
the marriage of Octavian and Scribonia, but their
child proved to be a girl, the infamous Julia. A
curious theory, however, is propounded by. H. J.
Rose, viz. that Virgil meant to honour Octavian
in the poem, but wrote in such an enigmatical
fashion that a reader might take it as " a pretty
compliment to the master of the eastern world,"
i.e. Antony (*Classical Quarterly*, XVIII (1924),
113–18). But the height of absurd speculation is
reached by M. Jeanmaire, who in *Le Messianisme de
Virgile* (Paris, 1930) solemnly assures us that the
infant expected was to be the offspring of Antony
and Cleopatra!

18. *munuscula :* according to Robson (*loc. cit.*)
the ivy is to wreathe the poet's brow, the foxglove
to defend him from critics (cf. *Ecl.* VII, 27), and
the acanthus to decorate the wine-cup (hence
ridenti). The wine-cup itself is furnished by *colocasia*,
for the Egyptian bean bore κιβώρια, and a κιβώριον
is a kind of drinking-cup.

26. Carcopino, who (*ibid.* p. 27, note 2) adopts
parentum here, fails to note that the *parentis* of
" certain scholiasts " is also the original reading of
Codex Gudianus, which is almost as weighty an
authority as the *Romanus*. Unfortunately, the
Palatinus, with which the *Gudianus* so often agrees,
is here lacking. The Berne MSS., *b* and *c*, also
give *parentis*.

49. *incrementum :* many regard this word as

merely a synonym for *suboles*, or as meaning " son."
So Tenney Frank, who cites inscriptions (*Classical Philology*, XI, 1916, 334 ff.), and W. H. D. Rouse (*ibid*. XII, 1927, 308).

62. Sabbadini very wisely adheres to the MSS.,
and Servius, instead of following Quintilian, who
(IX, 3, 8) gives *qui non risere parentes*, a reading
which involves two marked improbabilities : (1)
qui (plural) . . . *hunc*, and (2) *ridere* with the accusa-
tive in the sense of *smiling at*. Both of these irregu-
larities might pass muster in comedy, but are quite
unparalleled in Virgil. Sabbadini supposes that
Quintilian mistook the dative form *qui* (also written
quoi) for the nominative. Such a form is given
(*e.g.*) by P in *Georgic* II, 204, and by V in *Aen*. X,
565.

Many scholars, finding the general meaning
implied in Quintilian's citation very plausible, viz.
" such infants as have not smiled on their parents,
receive no divine favours," adopt *qui* as a nominative
plural, though relative to the singular *hunc*, and
accept the arbitrary conjecture *parenti* in place of
parentes. Among these is Carcopino, who (p. 2,
note 1) thinks it is no longer necessary to discuss
the readings on the ground that the text of the
poems is now " solidement établi " !

But the very plausibility of the meaning according
to Quintilian's reading makes us suspicious, for,
if that reading was ever the authoritative one, how
are we to account for the unanimity of the MSS.
against it, especially in view of the oft-quoted line
from Catullus, *dulce rideat ad patrem* ? Servius sup-
ports the MSS., and Wagner gives the meaning
intended : *Incipe ergo tuo risu parentes ad mutuam
arrisionem provocare*.

APPENDIX

It is quite probable that Quintilian is here quoting from memory, as he certainly does elsewhere. Editors do not adopt his *agrestem* (for *silvestrem*) in *Ecl.* I, 2, or *praecipiam* (for *praedicam*) in *Aen.* III, 436, or *caelo* (for *pelago*) in *Aen.* V, 212.

V

In the *Classical Quarterly*, XVI (1922), 57, D. L. Drew has a paper on " Virgil's Fifth Eclogue: A Defence of the Julius Caesar-Daphnis Theory." But Hermann (*op. cit.*) identifies Daphnis with the poet Catullus.

VI

74. We must suppose that Virgil confuses the monstrous Scylla of Homer with Scylla, daughter of Nisus, king of Megara. A. Waltz, however, accepts the reading of *Codex Pragensis*, which gives this verse thus :

Quid loquar aut Scyllam Nisi, aut quam fama secuta est.

Servius, whose text had only one *aut*, suggests that this may be repeated before *quam*.

VII

25. The original reading of M is *nascente*, which would go with *hedera* " sprouting ivy." Professor Conway strangely approves of this reading, but *vati futuro* (28) is surely in favour of an accusative here, whether *crescentem* or *nascentem*, and the former participle looks like a gloss upon the latter.

48. *laeto in palmite:* there is about equal MS. authority for *laeto* and *lento* here, and both epithets are used of the vine; cf. *Ecl.* III, 38 and *Georg.* II,

APPENDIX

262. The personal feeling implied by *laetus*, which is a favourite word with Virgil, gives it support.

VIII

41. On *ut vidi, ut perii,* Servius comments thus: *Unum'ut' est temporis, aliud quantitatis.* The Greek of the Theocritus original is ὡς—ὡς, " as (when) -how!" I have discussed these expressions in the *Classical Review*, XIV (1900), pp. 394 f.

IX

35. The site of the poet's farm has lately been discussed by two well-known scholars. Professor R. S. Conway, in his *Harvard Lectures on the Vergilian Age*, Ch. II, seeks to prove that the farm was not far from Calvisano and Carpenodolo, nearer Brescia than Mantua. Professor E. K. Rand favours the traditional site at Pietole, only two miles southeast of Mantua (see *In Quest of Virgil's Birthplace,* Harvard University Press, 1930). The discussion is continued in the *Classical Quarterly* (April 1931, and Jan. 1932).

THE GEORGICS

Some useful books bearing upon the *Georgics* are T. F. Royds' *The Beasts, Birds and Bees of Virgil* (Blackwell, Oxford, 1914); W. E. Heitland's *Agricola* (Cambridge University Press, 1921); R. Billiard's *L'Agriculture dans l'Antiquité d'après les Georgiques de Virgile* (De Boccard, Paris, 1928); and P. d'Hérouville's *À la campagne avec Virgile* (Paris, 1930).

APPENDIX

Book I

218. Hirtzel and Sabbadini prefer the reading *averso . . . astro*, "with averted star," *i.e.* the Dog himself, who beats a retreat. But this involves redundancy of expression.

406–9. Repeated in *Ciris*, 538–41.

Book II

A good work of reference in connection with Book II is Sargeaunt's *The Trees, Shrubs, and Plants of Virgil* (Blackwell, Oxford, 1920).

247. Gellius tells us that *amaror* was the reading given in a copy that had once belonged to Virgil's own household. All the major MSS., however, give *amaro*, for the final 'r' in M's *amaror* is a late addition.

278. In the *Classical Review*, XLII (1928), p. 59, F. H. Sandbach argues that *via* and *limes* are to be carefully distinguished in this line. The *viae* are paths, the *limites* the broad ways which divided a field into sections. He would therefore render the passage: "let every path, when the trees are cut, make an exact right angle with the main way which is cut by it."

341. Most editors read *terrea*, obviously an easy corruption of *ferrea*. The human race is *ferrea*, because, as Servius says, it was *procreata ex lapidibus ad laborem.* Cf. *Geor.* I, 62 f.

514. *nepotes.* Ribbeck and Janell follow M, which has *penates*, apparently from *Aen.* VIII, 543.

Book III

10–39. D. L. Drew shows how closely in both thought and expression this passage is paralleled by *Aen.* VIII, 675–728 (*Classical Quarterly*, XVIII (1924), 195 ff.).

APPENDIX

56. Sabbadini incorrectly gives 'sibi M².' It is *mihi*. Goelzer is also wrong in giving ' tibi M²'. It is *mihi*, the original reading being *tibi*.

144. P reads *gramine*, not *gramina*, as Sabbadini has it. But M has *gramina ripae*, with *ripa* M².

430. Sabbadini is in error in giving *sibi*, not *hic*, as the reading of M. Ribbeck, however, conjectured *sibi*.

456. *omnia.* M has *omina*, which may be correct. It is adopted by Janell and Goelzer, though the latter wrongly assigns *omnia* to M.

BOOK IV

Another work worth consulting in connection with this book is *Bee-keeping in Antiquity*, by H. Malcolm Fraser (University of London Press, 1931).

112 and 141. The *tinus* of Virgil is the *viburnum tinus*, commonly known as the laurustinus or laurestine. It is very abundant in Italy and especially in mountainous Corsica, where it forms large forests and grows to a height of ten to twenty feet. In other countries it is often cultivated in shrubberies and hedges, and wherever it is grown it is much frequented by bees. Bevan, in *The Honey Bee* (Philadelphia, 1843), includes it (p. 25) among " the earliest resources of the bee " in the spring of the year.

As to *de montibus altis*, the *montes* are not high mountains like the Apennines, but rather hills. It is in the hill country, rather than in the plains, that the bee-keeper will find the early-blooming laurestine, as well as the frequent wild thyme. Some of the hills of Rome were called *montes*, and as for the conventional epithet *alti*, which is found

583

coupled with *montes* fourteen times in Virgil, its vagueness may be illustrated by *Geor.* III, 535, where men who till the ground had to draw the wagons themselves *montis per altos*, because the cattle had died from the plague. Sargeaunt's account of the *tinus* (*op. cit.*, p. 128) is not altogether correct.

It is commonly said that the pine (on the assumption that *pinus* is the correct reading) would furnish pollen as food, and propolis as glue for bees. But in a country like Italy, where the best kinds of pollen are available and abundant, no bee-keeper would take the trouble to plant pines for the sake of their pollen, and as for propolis, it is really a nuisance. " Our principal trouble," says Root, in *The A B C of Bee Culture* (1908), p. 233, " has been to get rid of the surplus propolis, and I should much rather hear of some invention to keep it out of the way than to add more." For a full discussion of the question, see *Classical Philology*, X (1915), 405 ff. That the view I there advocate is correct is conceded by T. F. Royds in the *Journal of Roman Studies*, XX (1930), p. 96.

464 ff. This episode of Orpheus and Eurydice, as is well known, is a substitute for an earlier passage which dealt with Egypt and its first governor under Rome, Virgil's dear friend Gallus, who, being suspected of disloyalty to Augustus, took his own life. Professor J. Wight Duff agrees with me in what I have elsewhere written (*Love of Nature among the Greeks and Romans*,[1] p. 215), that the marvellous pathos of the story we now read may reflect the poet's grief over the sad and untimely end of Gallus. Gladly would Virgil have brought his

[1] 1930: George G. Harrap & Co., London; Longmans, Green & Co., New York.

APPENDIX

friend back from the grave, but even Orpheus could not

> " quite set free
> His half regain'd Eurydice."

Professor Duff also thinks that my " parallel from Milton to the *fragor* of line 493 is excellently appropriate."

THE AENEID

In these notes, frequent mention will be made of Professor J. W. Mackail's recently published edition of the *Aeneid* (Oxford, Clarendon Press, 1930) which offers interesting solutions of many old problems.

Book I

2. Though naturally translated with *profugus*, the word *fato* belongs to *venit* as well.

8. *quo numine laeso.* The *numen* is the divine will, the divinity of the *regina deum*. In *Aeneid* II, 183 *pro numine laeso* is rendered " for the insult to deity," and here Mackail gives, " for what attaint on her divinity."

198. This verse is a close rendering of *Odyssey* XII, 208,

ὦ φίλοι, οὐ γάρ πώ τι κακῶν ἀδαήμονές εἰμεν.

With *ante* = πω, every element in the original is reproduced in the Latin equivalent. I cannot therefore accept " the quasi-adjectival " use of *ante* with *malorum*, " former ills," first suggested by Servius and therefore adopted by many editors. Such usage is to be expected only when the substantive has a strong verbal or adjectival force. Thus in *populum late regem* (*Aen.* I, 21), *regem* = *regnantem*.

585

APPENDIX

Most of the adverbs cited by Mackail in his note on *Aen.* I, 13 as quasi-adjectival are more easily explained as pure adverbs.

224. *despiciens.* So all the MSS. Lachmann introduced *dispiciens*, on the ground that *despicere* is never used literally, but see *Classical Review*, XLV (1931), p. 142.

251. Mackail construes *infandum* as an adverb with *amissis*, " woefully lost," and compares *miserum* in *Aen.* VI, 21, but in his note on the latter passage he takes *miserum* as " the shortened form of *miserorum.*" Servius gives both possibilities for *infandum.*

380. Dardanus, son of Jupiter and Electra and founder of Troy, was said to have come from Italy. But in view of *Aen.* VI, 123, *et mi genus ab Iove summo,* Mackail punctuates with a semicolon after *patriam,* supplies *est* with *genus* and makes Aeneas claim that his own descent is *ab Iove summo.* In this case *et* is an obstacle and should make way for the *est* conjectured by Kvičala.

400. To take *portum tenet,* with Mackail, as " makes for harbour " is quite possible. In this case, however, the phrase becomes almost synonymous with the following one, and implies that *capere* (396) must mean, not " to settle in," but " to choose " (= *capere oculis*), a less likely rendering. Moreover, *tenere* more commonly means " holds," " has possession of," as in *tenet saxa* (*Aen.* I, 139), *ima tenes* (*Geor.* IV, 322), *portas tenet* (*Aen.* II, 613), *prima tenet* (*Aen.* V, 338), *laeva tenet* (*Aen.* V, 825), *tenet loca* (*Aen.* VI, 761), etc. In *Aen.* VIII, 653, *Capitolia tenebat,* which certainly means " held the Capitol," is followed, four lines later, by *arcem tenebant,* which *may* mean " were making for the citadel," but more

APPENDIX

probably " were laying hold of the citadel." The Gauls *per dumos aderant*, " were near amid the thickets," but Livy tells us that one was already on the top when the alarm was sounded.

550. *arvaque.* Since P is defective here, there is really better MS. authority for *arva* than for *arma.* Cf. *arva et urbes* in *Aen.* VII, 45.

Book II

54. Mackail follows Conington in taking *si fata* (*fuissent*) as independent of *non laeva*, " had fate so willed."

263. The epithet *primus* surely means rank of some sort. In Homer (*Il.* XI, 505) Machaon is a ποιμὴν λαῶν. Mackail finds no difficulty in supposing that the man mentioned seventh was the *first* to come out of the horse.

333. P is not " illegible " here, as Goelzer and Mackail suppose. The first half of the page has been destroyed.

349. Sabbadini has no right to claim *audendi* as the reading of P. Only AVDEN survives, the rest of the word being lost because the acid of the ink has here worn a hole in the parchment. As a matter of fact there is room for three letters.

412. Mackail takes *facie* as a genitive with *errore.* It is, of course, logically parallel to *iubarum*, but such liberty of expression is allowable in poetry.

567–88. The authenticity of this passage is upheld by Gerloff, in *Vindiciae Vergilianae*, Jena, 1911.

691. *augurium.* This word, rather than *auxilium*, is adopted by Ribbeck, Ladewig, Hirtzel, and Sabbadini. It was evidently read by Servius, whose note is : *non enim unum augurium vidisse sufficit, nisi*

APPENDIX

confirmatur ex simili. The change from *augurium* to *auxilium* would be the easier corruption.

727. Janell gives *exagmine* as one word. So too Mackail (after Housman). It is assumed to be the archaic form of *examine*.

778. *nec te comitem hinc portare Creusam.* The original reading of M was either *pretare* or *protare*, with *asportare* a late correction. As P, with *asportare*, has the order *comitem hinc*, not *hinc comitem* (which *asportare* necessitates), it is probable that the original reading was that given in the text.

Book III

In connection with Book III as a whole, one may profitably consult M. M. Crump, *The Growth of the Aeneid* (Blackwell, Oxford, 1920) and C. Saunders in *Classical Quarterly*, XIX (1925), 85–91.

192. There is a good article on " Virgil's Seamanship " in *Classical Weekly*, XV (1922), 201 ff., by M. P. Peaks.

247. *pro caede boum* is ironical. " Is it in payment for the slaughter of cattle that you make war ? " But Mackail takes the phrase to mean " to secure the oxen you have slain."

293. The Italian Archaeological Mission to Albania under Professor Ugolini has made very interesting and important discoveries at Butrinto, the site of ancient Buthrotum. See *Art and Archaeology*, XXX (1930), 151–55, and XXXI (1931), 961–67.

362. Servius apparently read *omnem cursum* and *prosp. a religio*, but explains the phrases as meaning *omnis religio dixit prosperum cursum.* Mackail conjectures *cursu* and, with *omnis*, renders the whole

APPENDIX

by " all sacred sanction announced to me prosperity on my course." It is simpler to regard *prospera* as a transferred epithet.

398. On the early Greek settlements in southern Italy, see Saunders' *Vergil's Primitive Italy*, Ch. I.

484. The dative *honori* is a more difficult reading than *honore*, and therefore, presumably, the original. Servius, while recording the fact that Scaurus read *honore*, explains *honori non cedere* as meaning *parem esse meritis accipientis*.

493. Following La Cerda, Mackail punctuates after *vivite*. The sense then is : " Farewell. Lucky are they whose own destiny is already achieved." This avoids the difficulty of applying *sua* to the second person, and may well be correct.

503. We accept *Hesperia* on the evidence of Servius, but all the major MSS. (including P) give *Hesperiam*, which would be in apposition to *populos*, " Hesperia allied to Epirus."

707. The epithet *inlaetabilis* is explained by 709 ff. The coast itself is far from unattractive, and, with Mt. Eryx towering above it, is really quite picturesque.

Book IV

A full commentary on Book IV is given by Corso Buscaroli in his *Virgilio : il Libro di Didone*, Milano, 1932.

276. Note that *debentur*, not *debetur*, is the original reading in both M and P.

323. Both here and in II, 678 *cui* is surely masculine rather than neuter as Mackail would take it. No clear case of the pronoun *cui* as a neuter form occurs in Virgil.

357. It is probably best to take *utrumque caput*

APPENDIX

as "mine and thine." Ovid's imitation is *tuum nostrumque caput* (*Heroid.* III, 107), and the first of three possible explanations offered by Servius is *meum et tuum*. The other two are: *aut Iovis et Mercurii ; aut meum et Ascanii*. Mackail would refer the phrase to Anchises and Ascanius. The Daniel-Servius suggests Aeneas and Ascanius.

Book V

In connection with the games described in this book, Professor Drew's *The Allegory of the Aeneid* (Blackwell, Oxford, 1927) is worthy of perusal.

44. As Mackail reminds us, the *tumulus* is probably the mound over the tomb of Anchises.

326. *ambiguumve relinquat.* Janell, Sabbadini and Mackail reject *-ve* and return to the *-que* of the MSS. This may be right, but Mackail's rendering is not convincing: " would slip forward past him, and leave him, now in a doubtful position, behind." If this had been the poet's general meaning, he would surely have omitted *ambiguum* altogether. But even with *-que* we might keep the usual rendering. It often happens in a race that the leader, when overtaken and passed, recovers himself sufficiently to make the result a tie. But some early scribe may have inserted a ' q ' before ' ve ' by mistake, for the corresponding verse in Homer (*Il.* XXIII, 382) has the disjunctive :

καί νυ κεν ἢ παρέλασσ', ἢ ἀμφήριστον ἔθηκεν.

488. *volucrem.* Holding that *volucrem columbam* should mean " the flying pigeon," Mackail conjectures and adopts *volucre*, to be taken with the distant *ferrum*, " winged shaft." This is not very plausible.

APPENDIX

505. Because *timuit exterrita* seems "hopelessly feeble," Mackail adopts Professor Slater's clever conjecture of *micuit* in place of *timuit*. But why, in a capital MS., should MIC be "all but indistinguishable" from TIM-?

518. *aeriis*. Rightly preferred by Janell and Mackail to the more learned *aetheriis*.

522. Janell and Mackail may be right in returning to *subito* of the MSS., but we thus get an awkward phrasing, since *subito* and *obicitur* cannot be taken together, as would naturally be expected.

524. Drew (p. 44) supposes that the burning arrow of Acestes symbolizes the *Caesaris astrum* of *Ecl.* IX, 47—a bold but interesting conjecture.

591. *frangeret*. As compared with the rival reading *falleret*, the word *frangeret* not only has the weight of authority, but presents the more striking and specific picture.

Book VI

2. For an account of early Cumae, see *Vergil's Primitive Italy*, by Saunders (pp. 13 ff.); *Greek Cities in Italy and Sicily*, by David Randall-MacIver (Oxford: Clarendon Press, 1931), Ch. I.

14. For illustrations of the temple of Apollo and the Grotto of the Sibyl, as laid bare by recent excavations, see "Virgilio," the beautiful supplement to N. 49 of *L'Illustrazione Italiana*, Dec. 7, 1930.

95 f. Placing a full-stop after *ito*, Mackail takes *quam* as a relative pronoun, anticipating *via*. But this makes it difficult to provide an infinitive for *te*. With the adverb *quam* this is easy enough (*ire* from *ito*).

APPENDIX

203. Conington, Goelzer and Mackail adopt *ʒeminae*, the reading of R, in preference to *gemina*, as read by M and P, as well as by Donatus and Priscian. The plural is probably a reminiscence of l. 190, and *gemina* is explained by Virgil himself in l. 204.

289. At this point the Daniel-Servius cites the following hexameters descriptive of the Gorgon, which he says were removed from the poet's manuscript by his editors. Mackail is of the opinion that Virgil composed them first, and later substituted for them the single line, 289. There are given thus:

> Gorgonis in medio portentum immane Medusae,
> viperiae circum ora comae, cui sibila torquent
> infamesque rigent oculi, mentoque sub imo
> serpentum extremis nodantur vincula caudis.

468. *animum.* Jortin's conjecture of *animam* has won the approval of Deuticke and Mackail. But as *animae* (*anima* being properly the breath of life, the physical life), though the regular word for souls apart from the body, can yet be used freely of living souls (cf. *animae qualis neque candidiores terra tulit,* Hor. *Sat.* I, v, 41); so *animi* (*animus* being properly the rational or spiritual life) can surely be used of the souls of the dead. Dido is now *nihil praeter animum* (Cic. *Tusc.* I, 20, 47), an *animus vacans corpore* (*ib.* I, 22, 50). The weaker *animam* could hardly have carried with it the very bold personification involved in *ardentem et torva tuentem* (*animum*), " the burning and fierce-eyed soul," as Mackail himself so well translates it. Probably the Greek θυμός may have influenced Virgil here.

585 ff. There seems to be no good reason for departing from the traditional text. Salmoneus

APPENDIX

was punished in the midst of his folly. Several editors, however, place a full-stop after *poenas*. In that case, 587 should precede 586, as *hic* (587) should be at or near the head of the new sentence. Such is the order given by Goelzer.

601 ff. The QUOSUPER of the Romanus illustrates a common error in MSS., where a single consonant often does duty for two of the same kind (*quos super*). But certain editors, puzzled by the absence of any mention of Tantalus, read *quo super* and either add *et* at the end of 601, or suppose that after 601 a line has been lost which furnished *Tantalus* in some case and form as an antecedent to *quo*. Goelzer, following Havet and Cartault, resorts to transposition, placing 616–20 after 601, and referring *quo* (602) to Phlegyas. All these changes are unnecessary.

739–51. This difficult passage is discussed by E. A. Hahn in *Classical Weekly*, XX (1927), 215 ff.

845. *tu*. The original reading of P, *tun*, is adopted by Ribbeck, Janell, and Sabbadini, and may be correct.

852. Norden, Mackail, and Sabbadini all recognize the superior authority and significance of *paci* as compared with *pacis*. Norden translates *paci imponere morem* by " dem Frieden gib Gesittung und Gesetze," and Mackail paraphrases thus : " to make peace into a fixed tradition, or more largely to build up character upon peace."

893 ff. Virgil's gates of sleep correspond to Homer's gates of dreams (*Odyssey*, XIX, 562 ff.). It was a popular idea that false dreams came before, and true dreams after, midnight. Cf. Horace, *Sat.* I, x, 33 :

post mediam noctem visus, cum somnia vera.

See *Classical Review*, XIV (1900), 153 ff.

THE LOEB CLASSICAL LIBRARY

VOLUMES ALREADY PUBLISHED

Latin Authors

AMMIANUS MARCELLINUS. Translated by J. C. Rolfe. 3 Vols.

APULEIUS: THE GOLDEN ASS (METAMORPHOSES). W. Adling-
ton (1566). Revised by S. Gaselee.

ST. AUGUSTINE: CITY OF GOD. 7 Vols. Vol. I. G. E.
McCracken. Vols. II and VII. W. M. Green. Vol. III.
D. Wiesen. Vol. IV. P. Levine. Vol. V. E. M. Sanford
and W. M. Green. Vol. VI. W. C. Greene.

ST. AUGUSTINE, CONFESSIONS OF. W. Watts (1631). 2 Vols.

ST. AUGUSTINE, SELECT LETTERS. J. H. Baxter.

AUSONIUS. H. G. Evelyn White. 2 Vols.

BEDE. J. E. King. 2 Vols.

BOETHIUS: TRACTS and DE CONSOLATIONE PHILOSOPHIAE.
Rev. H. F. Stewart and E. K. Rand. Revised by S. J. Tester.

CAESAR: ALEXANDRIAN, AFRICAN and SPANISH WARS. A. G.
Way.

CAESAR: CIVIL WARS. A. G. Peskett.

CAESAR: GALLIC WAR. H. J. Edwards.

CATO: DE RE RUSTICA. VARRO: DE RE RUSTICA. H. B. Ash
and W. D. Hooper.

CATULLUS. F. W. Cornish. TIBULLUS. J. B. Postgate.
PERVIGILIUM VENERIS. J. W. Mackail.

CELSUS: DE MEDICINA. W. G. Spencer. 3 Vols.

CICERO: BRUTUS and ORATOR. G. L. Hendrickson and H. M.
Hubbell.

[CICERO]: AD HERENNIUM. H. Caplan.

CICERO: DE ORATORE, etc. 2 Vols. Vol. I. DE ORATORE,
Books I and II. E. W. Sutton and H. Rackham. Vol. II.
DE ORATORE, Book III. DE FATO; PARADOXA STOICORUM;
DE PARTITIONE ORATORIA. H. Rackham.

CICERO: DE FINIBUS. H. Rackham.

CICERO: DE INVENTIONE, etc. H. M. Hubbell.

CICERO: DE NATURA DEORUM and ACADEMICA. H. Rackham.

CICERO: DE OFFICIIS. Walter Miller.

CICERO: DE REPUBLICA and DE LEGIBUS. Clinton W. Keyes.

1

CICERO: DE SENECTUTE, DE AMICITIA, DE DIVINATIONE.
W. A. Falconer.
CICERO: IN CATILINAM, PRO FLACCO, PRO MURENA, PRO SULLA.
New version by C. Macdonald.
CICERO: LETTERS TO ATTICUS. E. O. Winstedt. 3 Vols.
CICERO: LETTERS TO HIS FRIENDS. W. Glynn Williams,
M. Cary, M. Henderson. 4 Vols.
CICERO: PHILIPPICS. W. C. A. Ker.
CICERO: PRO ARCHIA, POST REDITUM, DE DOMO, DE HARUS-
PICUM RESPONSIS, PRO PLANCIO. N. H. Watts.
CICERO: PRO CAECINA, PRO LEGE MANILIA, PRO CLUENTIO,
PRO RABIRIO. H. Grose Hodge.
CICERO: PRO CAELIO, DE PROVINCIIS CONSULARIBUS, PRO
BALBO. R. Gardner.
CICERO: PRO MILONE, IN PISONEM, PRO SCAURO, PRO FONTEIO,
PRO RABIRIO POSTUMO, PRO MARCELLO, PRO LIGARIO, PRO
REGE DEIOTARO. N. H. Watts.
CICERO: PRO QUINCTIO, PRO ROSCIO AMERINO, PRO ROSCIO
COMOEDO, CONTRA RULLUM. J. H. Freese.
CICERO: PRO SESTIO, IN VATINIUM. R. Gardner.
CICERO: TUSCULAN DISPUTATIONS. J. E. King.
CICERO: VERRINE ORATIONS. L. H. G. Greenwood. 2 Vols.
CLAUDIAN. M. Platnauer. 2 Vols.
COLUMELLA: DE RE RUSTICA. DE ARBORIBUS. H. B. Ash,
E. S. Forster and E. Heffner. 3 Vols.
CURTIUS, Q.: HISTORY OF ALEXANDER. J. C. Rolfe. 2 Vols.
FLORUS. E. S. Forster.
FRONTINUS: STRATAGEMS and AQUEDUCTS. C. E. Bennett and
M. B. McElwain.
FRONTO: CORRESPONDENCE. C. R. Haines. 2 Vols.
GELLIUS. J. C. Rolfe. 3 Vols.
HORACE: ODES and EPODES. C. E. Bennett.
HORACE: SATIRES, EPISTLES, ARS POETICA. H. R. Fairclough.
JEROME: SELECTED LETTERS. F. A. Wright.
JUVENAL and PERSIUS. G. G. Ramsay.
LIVY. B. O. Foster, F. G. Moore, Evan T. Sage, and A. C.
Schlesinger and R. M. Geer (General Index). 14 Vols.
LUCAN. J. D. Duff.
LUCRETIUS. W. H. D. Rouse. Revised by M. F. Smith.
MANILIUS. G. P. Goold.
MARTIAL. W. C. A. Ker. 2 Vols. Revised by E. H. Warm-
ington.
MINOR LATIN POETS: from PUBLILIUS SYRUS to RUTILIUS
NAMATIANUS, including GRATTIUS, CALPURNIUS SICULUS,
NEMESIANUS, AVIANUS and others, with " Aetna " and the
" Phoenix." J. Wight Duff and Arnold M. Duff. 2 Vols.

2

MINUCIUS FELIX. Cf. TERTULLIAN.
NEPOS CORNELIUS. J. C. Rolfe.
OVID: THE ART OF LOVE and OTHER POEMS. J. H. Mosley. Revised by G. P. Goold.
OVID: FASTI. Sir James G. Frazer
OVID: HEROIDES and AMORES. Grant Showerman. Revised by G. P. Goold
OVID: METAMORPHOSES. F. J. Miller. 2 Vols. Revised by G. P. Goold.
OVID: TRISTIA and EX PONTO. A. L. Wheeler.
PERSIUS. Cf. JUVENAL.
PERVIGILIUM VENERIS. Cf. CATULLUS.
PETRONIUS. M. Heseltine. SENECA: APOCOLOCYNTOSIS. W. H. D. Rouse. Revised by E. H. Warmington.
PHAEDRUS and BABRIUS (Greek). B. E. Perry.
PLAUTUS. Paul Nixon. 5 Vols.
PLINY: LETTERS, PANEGYRICUS. Betty Radice. 2 Vols.
PLINY: NATURAL HISTORY. 10 Vols. Vols. I–V and IX. H. Rackham. VI.–VIII. W. H. S. Jones. X. D. E. Eichholz.
PROPERTIUS. H. E. Butler.
PRUDENTIUS. H. J. Thomson. 2 Vols.
QUINTILIAN. H. E. Butler. 4 Vols.
REMAINS OF OLD LATIN. E. H. Warmington. 4 Vols. Vol. I. (ENNIUS AND CAECILIUS) Vol. II. (LIVIUS, NAEVIUS PACUVIUS, ACCIUS) Vol. III. (LUCILIUS and LAWS OF XII TABLES) Vol. IV. (ARCHAIC INSCRIPTIONS)
RES GESTAE DIVI AUGUSTI. Cf. VELLEIUS PATERCULUS.
SALLUST. J. C. Rolfe.
SCRIPTORES HISTORIAE AUGUSTAE. D. Magie. 3 Vols.
SENECA, THE ELDER: CONTROVERSIAE, SUASORIAE. M. Winterbottom. 2 Vols.
SENECA: APOCOLOCYNTOSIS. Cf. PETRONIUS.
SENECA: EPISTULAE MORALES. R. M. Gummere. 3 Vols.
SENECA: MORAL ESSAYS. J. W. Basore. 3 Vols.
SENECA: TRAGEDIES. F. J. Miller. 2 Vols.
SENECA: NATURALES QUAESTIONES. T. H. Corcoran. 2 Vols.
SIDONIUS: POEMS and LETTERS. W. B. Anderson. 2 Vols.
SILIUS ITALICUS. J. D. Duff. 2 Vols.
STATIUS. J. H. Mozley. 2 Vols.
SUETONIUS. J. C. Rolfe. 2 Vols.
TACITUS: DIALOGUS. Sir Wm. Peterson. AGRICOLA and GERMANIA. Maurice Hutton. Revised by M. Winterbottom, R. M. Ogilvie, E. H. Warmington.
TACITUS: HISTORIES and ANNALS. C. H. Moore and J. Jackson. 4 Vols.

TERENCE.   John Sargeaunt.   2 Vols.
TERTULLIAN: APOLOGIA and DE SPECTACULIS.   T. R. Glover.
    MINUCIUS FELIX.   G. H. Rendall.
TIBULLUS.   Cf. CATULLUS.
VALERIUS FLACCUS.   J. H. Mozley.
VARRO: DE LINGUA LATINA.   R. G. Kent.   2 Vols.
VELLEIUS PATERCULUS and RES GESTAE DIVI AUGUSTI.   F. W.
    Shipley.
VIRGIL.   H. R. Fairclough.   2 Vols.
VITRUVIUS: DE ARCHITECTURA.   F. Granger.   2 Vols.

Greek Authors

ACHILLES TATIUS.   S. Gaselee.
AELIAN: ON THE NATURE OF ANIMALS.   A. F. Scholfield.   3
    Vols.
AENEAS TACTICUS. ASCLEPIODOTUS and ONASANDER.   The
    Illinois Greek Club.
AESCHINES.   C. D. Adams.
AESCHYLUS.   H. Weir Smyth.   2 Vols.
ALCIPHRON, AELIAN, PHILOSTRATUS: LETTERS.   A. R. Benner
    and F. H. Fobes.
ANDOCIDES, ANTIPHON.   Cf. MINOR ATTIC ORATORS.
APOLLODORUS.   Sir James G. Frazer.   2 Vols.
APOLLONIUS RHODIUS.   R. C. Seaton.
APOSTOLIC FATHERS.   Kirsopp Lake.   2 Vols.
APPIAN: ROMAN HISTORY.   Horace White.   4 Vols.
ARATUS.   Cf. CALLIMACHUS.
ARISTIDES: ORATIONS.   C. A. Behr.   Vol. I.
ARISTOPHANES.   Benjamin Bickley Rogers.   3 Vols.   Verse
    trans.
ARISTOTLE: ART OF RHETORIC.   J. H. Freese.
ARISTOTLE: ATHENIAN CONSTITUTION, EUDEMIAN ETHICS,
    VICES AND VIRTUES.   H. Rackham.
ARISTOTLE: GENERATION OF ANIMALS.   A. L. Peck.
ARISTOTLE: HISTORIA ANIMALIUM.   A. L. Peck.   Vols. I.–II.
ARISTOTLE: METAPHYSICS.   H. Tredennick.   2 Vols.
ARISTOTLE: METEOROLOGICA.   H. D. P. Lee.
ARISTOTLE: MINOR WORKS.   W. S. Hett.   On Colours, On
    Things Heard, On Physiognomies, On Plants, On Marvellous
    Things Heard, Mechanical Problems, On Indivisible Lines,
    On Situations and Names of Winds, On Melissus, Xenophanes,
    and Gorgias.
ARISTOTLE: NICOMACHEAN ETHICS.   H. Rackham.

ARISTOTLE: OECONOMICA and MAGNA MORALIA. G. C. Armstrong (with METAPHYSICS, Vol. II).

ARISTOTLE: ON THE HEAVENS. W. K. C. Guthrie.

ARISTOTLE: ON THE SOUL, PARVA NATURALIA, ON BREATH. W. S. Hett.

ARISTOTLE: CATEGORIES, ON INTERPRETATION, PRIOR ANALYTICS. H. P. Cooke and H. Tredennick.

ARISTOTLE: POSTERIOR ANALYTICS, TOPICS. H. Tredennick and E. S. Forster.

ARISTOTLE: ON SOPHISTICAL REFUTATIONS.
On Coming to be and Passing Away, On the Cosmos. E. S. Forster and D. J. Furley.

ARISTOTLE: PARTS OF ANIMALS. A. L. Peck; MOTION AND PROGRESSION OF ANIMALS. E. S. Forster.

ARISTOTLE: PHYSICS. Rev. P. Wicksteed and F. M. Cornford. 2 Vols.

ARISTOTLE: POETICS and LONGINUS. W. Hamilton Fyfe; DEMETRIUS ON STYLE. W. Rhys Roberts.

ARISTOTLE: POLITICS. H. Rackham.

ARISTOTLE: PROBLEMS. W. S. Hett. 2 Vols.

ARISTOTLE: RHETORICA AD ALEXANDRUM (with PROBLEMS. Vol. II). H. Rackham.

ARRIAN: HISTORY OF ALEXANDER and INDICA. Rev. E. Iliffe Robson. 2 Vols. New version P. Brunt.

ATHENAEUS: DEIPNOSOPHISTAE. C. B. Gulick. 7 Vols.

BABRIUS AND PHAEDRUS (Latin). B. E. Perry.

ST. BASIL: LETTERS. R. J. Deferrari. 4 Vols.

CALLIMACHUS: FRAGMENTS. C. A. Trypanis. MUSAEUS: HERO AND LEANDER. T. Gelzer and C. Whitman.

CALLIMACHUS, Hymns and Epigrams, and LYCOPHRON. A. W. Mair; ARATUS. G. R. Mair.

CLEMENT OF ALEXANDRIA. Rev. G. W. Butterworth.

COLLUTHUS. Cf. OPPIAN.

DAPHNIS AND CHLOE. Thornley's Translation revised by J. M. Edmonds: and PARTHENIUS. S. Gaselee.

DEMOSTHENES I.: OLYNTHIACS, PHILIPPICS and MINOR ORATIONS I.–XVII. AND XX. J. H. Vince.

DEMOSTHENES II.: DE CORONA and DE FALSA LEGATIONE. C. A. Vince and J. H. Vince.

DEMOSTHENES III.: MEIDIAS, ANDROTION, ARISTOCRATES, TIMOCRATES and ARISTOGEITON I. and II. J. H. Vince.

DEMOSTHENES IV.–VI: PRIVATE ORATIONS and IN NEAERAM. A. T. Murray.

DEMOSTHENES VII: FUNERAL SPEECH, EROTIC ESSAY, EXORDIA and LETTERS. N. W. and N. J. DeWitt.

DIO CASSIUS: ROMAN HISTORY. E. Cary. 9 Vols.

Dio Chrysostom. J. W. Cohoon and H. Lamar Crosby. 5 Vols.

Diodorus Siculus. 12 Vols. Vols. I.–VI. C. H. Oldfather. Vol. VII. C. L. Sherman. Vol. VIII. C. B. Welles. Vols. IX. and X. R. M. Geer. Vol. XI. F. Walton. Vol. XII. F. Walton. General Index. R. M. Geer.

Diogenes Laertius. R. D. Hicks. 2 Vols. New Introduction by H. S. Long.

Dionysius of Halicarnassus: Roman Antiquities. Spelman's translation revised by E. Cary. 7 Vols.

Dionysius of Halicarnassus: Critical Essays. S. Usher. 2 Vols. Vol. I.

Epictetus. W. A. Oldfather. 2 Vols.

Euripides. A. S. Way. 4 Vols. Verse trans.

Eusebius: Ecclesiastical History. Kirsopp Lake and J. E. L. Oulton. 2 Vols.

Galen: On the Natural Faculties. A. J. Brock.

Greek Anthology. W. R. Paton. 5 Vols.

Greek Bucolic Poets (Theocritus, Bion, Moschus). J. M. Edmonds.

Greek Elegy and Iambus with the Anacreontea. J. M. Edmonds. 2 Vols.

Greek Lyric. D. A. Campbell. 4 Vols. Vol. I.

Greek Mathematical Works. Ivor Thomas. 2 Vols.

Herodes. Cf. Theophrastus: Characters.

Herodian. C. R. Whittaker. 2 Vols.

Herodotus. A. D. Godley. 4 Vols.

Hesiod and The Homeric Hymns. H. G. Evelyn White.

Hippocrates and the Fragments of Heracleitus. W. H. S. Jones and E. T. Withington. 4 Vols.

Homer: Iliad. A. T. Murray. 2 Vols.

Homer: Odyssey. A. T. Murray. 2 Vols.

Isaeus. E. W. Forster.

Isocrates. George Norlin and LaRue Van Hook. 3 Vols.

[St. John Damascene]: Barlaam and Ioasaph. Rev. G. R. Woodward, Harold Mattingly and D. M. Lang.

Josephus. 10 Vols. Vols. I.–IV. H. Thackeray. Vol. V. H. Thackeray and R. Marcus. Vols. VI.–VII. R. Marcus. Vol. VIII. R. Marcus and Allen Wikgren. Vols. IX.–X. L. H. Feldman.

Julian. Wilmer Cave Wright. 3 Vols.

Libanius. A. F. Norman. 3 Vols. Vols. I.–II.

Lucian. 8 Vols. Vols. I.–V. A. M. Harmon. Vol. VI. K. Kilburn. Vols. VII.–VIII. M. D. Macleod.

Lycophron. Cf. Callimachus.

6

LYRA GRAECA, J. M. Edmonds. 2 Vols.

LYSIAS. W. R. M. Lamb.

MANETHO. W. G. Waddell.

MARCUS AURELIUS. C. R. Haines.

MENANDER. W. G. Arnott. 3 Vols. Vol. I.

MINOR ATTIC ORATORS (ANTIPHON, ANDOCIDES, LYCURGUS, DEMADES, DINARCHUS, HYPERIDES). K. J. Maidment and J. O. Burtt. 2 Vols.

MUSAEUS: HERO AND LEANDER. Cf. CALLIMACHUS.

NONNOS: DIONYSIACA. W. H. D. Rouse. 3 Vols.

OPPIAN, COLLUTHUS, TRYPHIODORUS. A. W. Mair.

PAPYRI. NON-LITERARY SELECTIONS. A. S. Hunt and C. C. Edgar. 2 Vols. LITERARY SELECTIONS (Poetry). D. L. Page.

PARTHENIUS. Cf. DAPHNIS and CHLOE.

PAUSANIAS: DESCRIPTION OF GREECE. W. H. S. Jones. 4 Vols. and Companion Vol. arranged by R. E. Wycherley.

PHILO. 10 Vols. Vols. I.–V. F. H. Colson and Rev. G. H. Whitaker. Vols. VI.–IX. F. H. Colson. Vol. X. F. H. Colson and the Rev. J. W. Earp.

PHILO: two supplementary Vols. (*Translation only.*) Ralph Marcus.

PHILOSTRATUS: THE LIFE OF APOLLONIUS OF TYANA. F. C. Conybeare. 2 Vols.

PHILOSTRATUS: IMAGINES; CALLISTRATUS: DESCRIPTIONS. A. Fairbanks.

PHILOSTRATUS and EUNAPIUS: LIVES OF THE SOPHISTS. Wilmer Cave Wright.

PINDAR. Sir J. E. Sandys.

PLATO: CHARMIDES, ALCIBIADES, HIPPARCHUS, THE LOVERS, THEAGES, MINOS and EPINOMIS. W. R. M. Lamb.

PLATO: CRATYLUS, PARMENIDES, GREATER HIPPIAS, LESSER HIPPIAS. H. N. Fowler.

PLATO: EUTHYPHRO, APOLOGY, CRITO, PHAEDO, PHAEDRUS, H. N. Fowler.

PLATO: LACHES, PROTAGORAS, MENO, EUTHYDEMUS. W. R. M. Lamb.

PLATO: LAWS. Rev. R. G. Bury. 2 Vols.

PLATO: LYSIS, SYMPOSIUM, GORGIAS. W. R. M. Lamb.

PLATO: Republic. Paul Shorey. 2 Vols.

PLATO: STATESMAN, PHILEBUS. H. N. Fowler; ION. W. R. M. Lamb.

PLATO: THEAETETUS and SOPHIST. H. N. Fowler.

PLATO: TIMAEUS, CRITIAS, CLITOPHO, MENEXENUS, EPISTULAE. Rev. R. G. Bury.

PLOTINUS: A. H. Armstrong. 7 Vols. Vols. I.–V.

PLUTARCH: MORALIA. 16 Vols. Vols I.–V. F. C. Babbitt. Vol. VI. W. C. Helmbold. Vols. VII. and XIV. P. H. De Lacy and B. Einarson. Vol. VIII. P. A. Clement and H. B. Hoffleit. Vol. IX. E. L. Minar, Jr., F. H. Sandbach, W. C. Helmbold. Vol. X. H. N. Fowler. Vol. XI. L. Pearson and F. H. Sandbach. Vol. XII. H. Cherniss and W. C. Helmbold. Vol. XIII 1–2. H. Cherniss. Vol. XV. F. H. Sandbach.

PLUTARCH: THE PARALLEL LIVES. B. Perrin. 11 Vols.

POLYBIUS. W. R. Paton. 6 Vols.

PROCOPIUS. H. B. Dewing. 7 Vols.

PTOLEMY: TETRABIBLOS. F. E. Robbins.

QUINTUS SMYRNAEUS. A. S. Way. Verse trans.

SEXTUS EMPIRICUS. Rev. R. G. Bury. 4 Vols.

SOPHOCLES. F. Storr. 2 Vols. Verse trans.

STRABO: GEOGRAPHY. Horace L. Jones. 8 Vols.

THEOCRITUS. Cf. GREEK BUCOLIC POETS.

THEOPHRASTUS: CHARACTERS. J. M. Edmonds. HERODES, etc. A. D. Knox.

THEOPHRASTUS: ENQUIRY INTO PLANTS. Sir Arthur Hort, Bart. 2 Vols.

THEOPHRASTUS: DE CAUSIS PLANTARUM. G. K. K. Link and B. Einarson. 3 Vols. Vol. I.

THUCYDIDES. C. F. Smith. 4 Vols.

TRYPHIODORUS. Cf. OPPIAN.

XENOPHON: CYROPAEDIA. Walter Miller. 2 Vols.

XENOPHON: HELLENICA. C. L. Brownson. 2 Vols.

XENOPHON: ANABASIS. C. L. Brownson.

XENOPHON: MEMORABILIA AND OECONOMICUS. E. C. Marchant. SYMPOSIUM AND APOLOGY. O. J. Todd.

XENOPHON: SCRIPTA MINORA. E. C. Marchant. CONSTITUTION OF THE ATHENIANS. G. W. Bowersock.